Heartaches by the Number

CLAYTN-RIV STACKS
31012000480770
781.6 CANTWELL, DAVID
Friskics-Warren, Bill.
Heartaches by the number
: 3/03

D1121368

Heartaches by the Number

Country Music's 500 Greatest Singles

Bill Friskics-Warren
and David Cantwell

CLAYTON COUNTY LIBRARY
RIVERDALE BRANCH
420 VALLEY HILL ROAD
RIVERDALE, GA 30274

Vanderbilt University Press

Country Music Foundation Press

For Doris,
and for Kate
and Marshall.

© 2003 Bill Friskics-Warren and David Cantwell
All rights reserved
First Edition 2003

Published by Vanderbilt University Press and the
Country Music Foundation Press

This book is printed on acid-free paper.
Manufactured in the United States of America
Design by Dariel Mayer

Library of Congress Cataloging-in-Publication Data

Cantwell, David.
Heartaches by the number : country music's 500 greatest
singles / David Cantwell and Bill Friskics-Warren. — 1st ed.
       p. cm.
       Includes bibliographical references (p.   ) and index.
       ISBN 0-8265-1423-5 (cloth : alk. paper)
       ISBN 0-8265-1424-3 (pbk. : alk. paper)
       1. Country music—History and criticism.
I. Friskics-Warren, Bill.   II. Title.
ML3524.C326 2002
781.642'09—dc21

                                      2002013662

Contents

Acknowledgments
Thanks a Lot

Heartaches by the Number is our end of a conversation with many of the writers who've inspired us. When people asked us to describe the book we were writing, our pat response was: "Do you know Dave Marsh's *The Heart of Rock and Soul: The 1,001 Greatest Singles Ever Made*? Ours is a country answer to that book." Without Marsh's model, this book wouldn't exist.

As someone pointed out to us halfway through our writing, *Heartaches* is also something of a singles version of John Morthland's album-oriented, and regrettably out-of-print, *The Best of Country Music*. Furthermore, without the groundbreaking career of country historian Bill Malone, we—and quite a few others—wouldn't be writing about country music today. The work of Charles Wolfe, Ronnie Pugh, John Rumble, Colin Escott, Rich Kienzle, Mary Bufwack and Robert K. Oermann, Daniel Cooper, Peter Guralnick, Stanley Booth, Robert Palmer, Ellen Willis, and Greil Marcus had an enormous influence on us. So have the comments and perspectives of our colleagues on Postcard 2, an e-mail discussion group dedicated to the discussion of all things "country," in the broadest sense of the word.

Others contributed more directly to the book. Craig Werner read and improved virtually every entry. Cheryl Cline, Mike Warren, Don Yates, Ronnie Pugh, Peter Cooper, Ron Wynn, Jim Ridley, Gary Wilson, Mike Ireland, and Leo Rauh nominated dozens, and in some cases hundreds, of singles for us to consider, many of which actually made the final cut. Jon Weisberger, Roy Kasten, and Barry Mazor always answered our questions quickly and definitively, no matter how often we pestered them. Dawn Oberg and Lauren Bufferd of the Country Music Foundation graciously ran down discographical and session information for us. Lauren and Becky Miley located records in the Foundation's collection. Photo curator Denny Adcock scanned hundreds of label images. Doris Saltkill suggested revisions for any number of entries and solved every computer crisis we faced. Paul Kingsbury was more than just insightful and assiduous; his early and sustained support for the book was a gift. We also thank Betsy Phillips, Polly Rembert, Erin McVay, and Dariel Mayer of Vanderbilt University Press for their enthusiasm, dedication, and guidance.

Finally, we'd like to thank several of our editors, notably Grant Alden and Peter Blackstock of *No Depression*, Jonathan Marx at the *Nashville Scene*, and Michael McCall at *Country Music*, for their patience with our at times extended absence from the pages of their publications, as well as for giving us the space to work out some of our ideas. Chris Dickinson, former editor of *The Journal of Country Music*, also permitted us to do the latter. Her commitment to this book won't be forgotten.

David would like to thank his parents, Dave and Judy Cantwell, for introducing him to the music of Hank Snow and Kitty Wells, Bing Crosby and Elvis Presley.

Bill wishes to thank his parents, Ann and Bill Friskics, for teaching him how to listen; Dave Hallquist, for helping him keep his ears open; and, most of all, his brother Scott, for listening with him.

Introduction
Don't Fence Me In

Now I've got heartaches by the number, troubles by the score
Everyday you love me less, each day I love you more
Yes, I've got heartaches by the number, a love that I can't win
But the day that I stop counting is the day my world will end

That's the chorus to "Heartaches by the Number," a prime example of songwriter Harlan Howard's knack, through catchy melodies and clever wordplay, for counting off the myriad ways that love hurts. It's a really great song.

The record's even better. Ray Price's 1959 hit tallies heartaches that Howard's melody and words only suggest. Price strains for dignity but quivers nearly every syllable of the way; Tommy Jackson's fiddle unleashes two short, sharp sobs at the kickoff; Jimmy Day's pedal steel cries, too, tossing off every tear that Ray's holding back. All the while that driving rhythm makes clear that this record's for swinging your baby 'round the dance floor, heartaches be damned. Howard's song is great, classic even, but if you haven't heard Price's recording, you haven't heard the half of it.

* * *

This is a book about listening. It's not an encyclopedia. It's not a history. It isn't a series of biographies or a collection of record reviews or merely a list of favorites, though it contains elements of each of these. Rather, *Heartaches by the Number* is an argument for a sensibility, a way of hearing. It's comprised of critical essays that each can stand alone but that, when read in sequence, comment upon each other and tell a larger story—one that we hope challenges some of the prevailing assumptions about what country music is and what it can mean. At its core, *Heartaches* is about dialogues: conversations between singers and songs, between singers and musicians and producers, between audiences, between the past, present, and future, between records and listeners, and, perhaps most of all, between the records themselves.

This approach to writing about music isn't very common,

particularly when it comes to country music. In fact, our primary motivation for writing *Heartaches* was our frustration with the limited ways that country gets talked about. You can find plenty of country music publications that discuss sales figures and concert grosses, or ballyhoo the latest signings by the record execs on Nashville's Music Row, or describe the sound of the music, or function as thumbs-up-or-down consumer guides. All of them serve their purposes. But rarely does anyone write about what would seem to be the point of listening to the music in the first place—how it feels to hear a great record or why you might decide it's great to begin with, let alone how it speaks to, or even defines, its historical and cultural moment. In country music, the records that have done this, almost always, have been singles.

Heartaches includes only records that were released as singles, whether they first appeared as 78s, 45s, cassettes, or CDs, and whether or not they were commercially successful. Singles, after all, have inspired the most visceral, passionate reactions among most fans of country music. In the beginning, *everything* was "singles." People produced and consumed country recordings one at a time, and for the most part, that's still true today. Albums, whether they sell well or not, are usually what get covered by the music press, and certainly they're what the industry wants us to buy. Albums are how record companies make their money. In fact, by the close of the twentieth century, it had become common for a recording to be marketed to radio as a "single" without ever being released in that format. Even so, singles are still a mainstream country album's primary attraction. In the worst cases, this amounts to releases that consist of nothing more than "hits plus filler," but even on the best albums, it's normally the singles that stand out and that motivate us to buy albums to begin with.

Indeed, it's singles (and not live performances as is sometimes claimed) that define country music for most listeners. Country fans, like fans of any genre, are most often exposed to the music via their radios and through their record, tape, or CD players, not live shows. And, though live performances were heard widely on radio during the twenties, thirties, forties, and fifties, this has generally been as true of dance hall regulars as it is of those who never venture out to clubs at all. We sing along with singles in the car, our hands flying to crank up the volume every time a recording we love comes on the radio; or we punch out the preset the instant a single we can't stand returns to the drive-time mix. A great record can get our hearts racing or calm us down, trigger memories or spur dancing; it can know our minds or change them altogether.

That's what *Heartaches* is about: great *records*. They may also be great songs, but that's not as important to us. You can take a lousy-to-good song and, by virtue of a strong vocal performance, arrangement, and production, turn it into a great record. The opposite doesn't work. A lousy vocal, a ho-hum arrangement, and aimless production will add up to a bad record *every time*, no matter how great the song is. It's how the words of a song are sung and how they track through the melody, as well as how the music that surrounds them informs, or even transforms, the lyrics that creates meaning (and in instrumentals, the music alone creates the meaning). It typically has been through specific recorded performances that songs have resonated, both within their cultural moment and down through the years. All of which takes place through the give-and-take among singers, writers, producers, musicians, and arrangers working together in the studio, as well as the audiences who listen at home, in their cars, or online wherever they may be.

Records are, almost always, the result of compromise and calculation. Not in the pejorative senses of those words but in a spirit of cooperation and deliberation that's the very essence of the record-making process. One consequence of our commitment to records, as opposed to songs, is that many of our picks will be more "produced" than what normally gets tagged as great country music. This is more than just a matter of taste, of preferring records that are more fussed over to glorified demos or live recordings (which actually accounts for how records were made for at least the first couple of decades of country music history). As much as anything, our commitment to records means engaging singles on their own terms. It means listening— not just hearing but listening—to what those "unwanted" violins, for instance, are doing on a country record, no matter how much we expect, or think we prefer, the sound of sawing twin fiddles to the lush coloration of a thirteen-piece string section.

This doesn't mean every single will reveal itself as great if we only attend to it closely enough. But this openness helps counter one-sided and often received notions of what makes great music in the first place, particularly the illusory, or at least incomplete,

faith in authenticity over artifice, rawness over polish, obscurity over popularity, spontaneity over premeditation. Neither does this mean that more production or tweaking in the studio necessarily makes for better records. Hardly. Nevertheless, we believe that being willing to hear singles on their own terms instead of through preexisting filters ("Everyone knows country records aren't supposed to sound like *this*!") lets us reclaim some important and amazing music that might otherwise be dismissed out of hand.

Just as significantly, a singles approach enables us to embrace a broader range of human emotion. Although some who write about the music might have us believe otherwise, country isn't just about lost highways, whiskey rivers, and slippin' around. It's also about satisfied minds, seeing the light, and taking it on home to your sweetheart. More than just tears in your beer, feeling like you were born to lose, and trying to drown the working-man or -woman blues, country is about kicking up your heels, finding courage enough to make it through the night, and laughing to keep from crying. For every record about the virtues of the old homestead, there's one about starting over in a strange city; for every hit that spells d-i-v-o-r-c-e, there's another struggling with what it means to stand by your man or woman.

Many great country records don't lend themselves to such polarities at all because the feelings they express are too complex, even conflicted, to be reduced to a single emotion. The proverbial dark and sunny sides of which the Carter Family sang aren't separate. The best sad records in country music, for example, are often not just sad, and the happiest are rarely merely happy. Much more often than their rock counterparts do, country records tend to speak to adults—to people who have done a bit of living, people for whom songs about young love are more nostalgia than reality, people who are raising children, mourning faded dreams, hungering for relationships that offer both romance and commitment. Counting off the aches and skipped beats of any human heart, the best country music is as varied, rich, and complex as the lives of the people who love it.

Maybe that's one of the reasons why fans so fiercely debate what qualifies as country music and what doesn't. As much as any form of popular music, country tends its fences. The genre is constantly building and shoring them up, mending and diverting them, and there are always those fans quick to declare this new record or that new sound too far afield, "not country." Even so, those criticisms have rarely, if ever, stopped most country fans from eventually warming to those "not country" styles, whether in the form of Jimmie Rodgers recording with Louis Armstrong, a Tin Pan Alley ballad from Gene Autry, the dappled variations producer Owen Bradley worked on the Nashville Sound, or the down-home equivalents of Motown and Philly Soul that auteur Billy Sherrill crafted in the countrypolitan era.

As with any living, breathing musical form—which is to say any musical form that's changing enough to remain vital—a definition of country music is tough to corral, in any precise sense, without strangling the life right out of it. Fences stake out boundaries, but they're also maddeningly porous in even the most stable periods. We're not interested in defining country music so much as in engaging the tradition, in tracing country's shifting fence lines to understand where the music, in all its manifestations, has been and where it's going. This isn't to say that the music doesn't have certain defining features, such as its rural, southern, working-class roots, or a penchant for certain stringed instruments or harmony patterns. Or that we think everything is or can be construed as country. More than anything else, it's the tradition the people making records perceive themselves working out of, or the roots or influences they acknowledge, or just the affinities they display, that make their records country. That's why, when push comes to shove, we'd rather err on the side of inclusion, if only to recognize the fact that country acts were hopping fences, not to mention letting "outsiders" crawl under and over them, well before the Carter Family drove down from the Clinch Mountains in 1927.

This is country music's dirty little secret. Virtually all of its commercially successful performers—even those heralded today as "traditional" or "hardcore"—were constantly absorbing so-called outside influences. We can't really have a serious discussion about country music without facing this fact. Whether we're talking about 78s by Charlie Poole, the Carter Family, Patsy Montana, Bill Monroe, Milton Brown, Rose Maddox, and Hank Williams, or 45s by Ray Price, Kitty Wells, Johnny Cash, Buck Owens, George Jones, Tammy Wynette, and the Kendalls, or CDs by Alan Jackson and Lee Ann Womack, we're talking about singles that have been influenced, profoundly, by almost every conceivable form of pop music, many of them associated with African American performers. In practice, if not always in philosophy, country's most significant and popular performers were championing a "no fences" approach to tradition before Garth Brooks was born. In *Heartaches*, we walk the fence lines, keeping an eye out for breaks in the rows where external influences have crept into the country fold. Now and then, we

even trail after the music as it's moved into the pastures of pop, where country-influenced singers like Bing Crosby, Elvis Presley, and Ray Charles have also sung the praises of "no fences"—literally, in the case of Crosby's "Don't Fence Me In." One of our book's guiding principles is that this perennial fence hopping is not merely a chapter in the country story, or a tangent, or a threat to the main gist of the tale. It is the tale.

*   *   *

We both grew up in homes where our parents usually had the radio tuned to the local AM country station. But we only began to understand country music as part of our story, not just that of our parents, at about the same time that we began to fall head over heels in love with pop singles generally. For both of us, that love affair began during what we've come to call "the crossover years," the period from roughly 1967 to 1973 when we both experienced our musical awakening—that is, when we started paying close attention to the radio, as well as buying, playing, and obsessing over our favorite 45s. It is our immense good fortune to have come of age to such an amazing soundtrack of Top Forty singles. It's during the crossover years that Aretha Franklin, Marvin Gaye, and the Rolling Stones cut the records widely regarded as their best. The crossover years also include Elvis's successful return to Memphis, the last days of the Beatles, and what amounts to the entire recording careers of Jimi Hendrix, Sly & the Family Stone, and Creedence Clearwater Revival, as well as the emergence of Al Green and the glory days of Philly soul. And that just scratches the surface.

An explosion of classic country singles was occurring during these years, too, a development that was doubly obvious to us. That's because during that time, the country and pop stations we tuned in—WLS and WJJD in Chicago; WDAF and WHB in Kansas City, Missouri—played some of the *same records*. Records by the rock, pop, and soul acts listed above often segued into hits by, among others, Conway Twitty, Charlie Rich, Merle Haggard, Tammy Wynette, Lynn Anderson, Ray Price, Johnny Cash, Glen Campbell, Jeannie C. Riley, Bobbie Gentry, Jerry Reed, Donna Fargo, Sammi Smith, and Charley Pride. And this is to say nothing of reverse crossover acts such as Bobby Goldsboro, John Denver, Anne Murray, and Olivia Newton-John, all of whom scored major county hits. Hardly a fair trade—country radio had no business waiting another ten years to play CCR—but a trade nonetheless, one that underlined the mutual value of fence hopping.

This exchange was one of the period's defining, most thrilling characteristics. During the crossover years, many popular recording acts and their audiences, country or otherwise, seemed to accept a "no fences" approach to making music as a given. The result was a climate in which rock records could twang and soul records could rock—and where country music began to rock with a new, deep down soul, at once altering and maintaining its unique identity. The 45s we collected made it clear to us that when boundaries were crossed, it could be a wonderful thing. We certainly couldn't have articulated this back in junior high, but it was a lesson we were learning by heart.

It'll come as no surprise to those keeping track, then, that our list of country's 500 greatest singles contains loads of records from our beloved crossover years. A lot more, no doubt, than would be included in lists by writers who came of age during what's considered the Golden Age of honky-tonk (when Hank and Lefty walked the earth together) or during the Hot New Country boom of Shania and Garth. We embrace our perspective. Our crossover lens does more than cast a spotlight on some great (and critically overlooked) records; it lets us reexamine basic assumptions about what makes a country record great in the first place.

Placing Sammi Smith's "Help Me Make It through the Night" at #1, for instance, helped us launch many of the arguments we wanted to weave throughout the 499 entries that follow it. A 1971 country hit that crossed over and became a major pop hit, "Help Me Make It through the Night" was the product of intense and extensive collaboration. The single also spoke to its moment; its frank themes tapped the era's zeitgeist and addressed many of its pressing issues. Musically and thematically, its impact has reverberated through the years, not least because it captures such tangled adult emotions. "Help Me Make It through the Night" was also an unmistakably country record that was willing to open its arms to—and be touched by—pop and soul.

In other words, the crossover years generally, and "Help Me Make It through the Night" specifically, offered us a touchstone for understanding where country music was headed and for reflecting on its past. After all, those fertile crossover periods during which fence jumpers reign have been scattered throughout country music's commercial history: the genre's first recorded decade, when country was busy incorporating jazz and blues; that period right after World War II, when pop singers began to record country songs and when pop-inflected country records occasionally became national hits; those whirlwind years when first

rockabilly and then the Nashville Sound exploded on country and pop radio; and off and on right up to the turn of the present century.

* * *

Will there still be something called country music at the end of the twenty-first century? We hope so. We know it'll only happen, though, if the music continues to change. Some people get the wrong idea about tradition in country music. They think the way to preserve the music they love is to protect it from noncountry impurities; the better to ensure it remains the same. But that approach couldn't be more wrong. If country music hadn't been changing all along, it would've ceased to be relevant generations ago, and then there'd be no country story to tell—there'd be nothing for Jimmie Rodgers to be the father of. As one-time Rodgers acolyte and eventual country crooner Tommy Duncan liked to sing, "Time Changes Everything." Everything, that is, except what it buries.

The country tradition isn't about the way things have stayed the same—it's about how they've changed, *yet remained connected*. As shown by the careers of country Hall of Famers Bill Monroe and Buck Owens, Elvis Presley and Dolly Parton—really, you can pick any major figure you like—jumping the fence is not the same as leaving home for good. Perceiving yourself as a link in a chain of tradition doesn't mean you're chained to it. Traditions persist only as long as their orthodoxies are enlivened by innovation, and fence jumpers have been the life's blood of the country tradition all along. It might even be more accurate to say that the fence jumpers *are* the tradition.

This isn't to suggest that many country musicians, or the country music industry as a whole, haven't regularly resisted innovation, clung to outdated formulas and hierarchies, stuck a collective head in the sand to ignore the issues of the moment (the issue of race, in particular), or opted for a sound or style simply because that was the way it was done before. Country music has seen its share of stagnation and shortsightedness. The *Urban Cowboy* period of the early 1980s is perhaps the most obvious example. Nashville record execs, eager to put country's hayseed image behind them, mortgaged the music's rural sounds and birthright for a chance to run with the rock and disco crowds in New York and Los Angeles. Granted, *Urban Cowboy* employed a crossover approach to making music. Yet in contrast to the "no fences" aesthetic we defend, the records it produced, as well as those by contemporaries such as Kenny Rogers and Dave & Sugar, crossed over by divorcing themselves from country's past rather than by engaging that past in new and innovative ways. Not unrelated, they also often made music devoid of the complex stories and impassioned sentiments that we associate with the best country music made before or since.

The music seems to be going through a similarly uninspired period at the turn of the twenty-first century. Just turn on the radio and proceed to your local Hot New Country station. Chances are, apart from records by Lee Ann Womack, Alan Jackson, the Dixie Chicks, and a handful of others, you'll hear emotionally simplistic ditties that are scarcely discernible from—and indeed, that segue imperceptibly into—the frothy jingles sponsored by the station's advertisers. Shut out of the mix are many of even the most commercially successful recordings, such as the bluegrass and old-time *O Brother, Where Art Thou?* soundtrack, a #1 country album for two months in 2001, as well as so-called heritage acts—even those like George Jones and Dolly Parton who continue to make great, contemporary-sounding records. All have fallen victim to the shrinking playlists, increasingly fragmented audiences, and sweeping consolidation that plague the radio industry as a whole.

Low points like these are an important part of country's ongoing story—a portion of the tale upon which writers in both popular and academic circles have focused time and again, and doubtless will continue to rehash well into the future. We want to tell a different part of the story. In *Heartaches by the Number,* we

play the changes; we listen to and attempt to get inside the records that have signaled those shifts in order to get at what and how they mean. Country music has reinvented itself as southerners moved from rural and agrarian lives to urban and industrial ones; the music has evolved from a series of regional styles to a national genre; it has progressed from folk music to commercial entertainment; the tradition has incorporated emerging technologies and modernist impulses; and, perhaps most importantly, it has survived *as* a tradition, as opposed to something that's merely traditional and not long for this world?

That tradition may yet survive. There will be those who pitch fits that the country music of the future ain't like the country music of the past, which will be true enough as an observation but ridiculous as a value judgment. To give the curmudgeons their due, their prodding will help ensure that the music stays connected to its past even as it changes. Mostly though, such complaints will miss the point. They always have. Can the circle be unbroken? Of course it can. Given how country got to where it is today, it's likely there will still be a home waiting for country music after its second seventy-five or eighty years. Getting there, though, depends on listening to the old records, on drinking deeply of their wisdom before hopping the fence—and being transformed yet again—on our way back home.

—*Bill Friskics-Warren*
and David Cantwell

How to Use the Book
20/20 Vision (and Walkin' 'Round Blind?)

Lists of great records (or albums or movies or what have you) drive some people crazy. Understandably, too, since many lists appear to be little more than a diverting but ultimately useless roll call of the compilers' favorites or, worse, a presumptuous presentation of the right answers. As if there could ever be but one correct reply to the question: "What are the greatest country singles?" Queries like that demand responses as varied, complex, and rich as human experience itself; they demand multiple answers.

Heartaches by the Number is our answer. We know it would be possible to come up with an equally valid and compelling list of country's greatest singles that didn't include many of the titles we've chosen, though it's hard to imagine one without "I'm So Lonesome I Could Cry," "I Fall to Pieces," or "He Stopped Loving Her Today." For that matter, *we* could have proposed a somewhat different 500 records and still written more or less the same book. We weren't, after all, trying to establish a new country canon so much as rethink the old one.

That said, we believe our list is representative and then some. We stand by our 500 as individual records; as exemplars of the sensibility, musical aesthetic, and emotional range set forth in the preceding essay ("Don't Fence Me In"); and as ties that bind country's as-yet-unbroken circle. Most of all, we want the singles we've selected—and what we say about them—to stimulate debate, just as they have at the kitchen table, in the local bar, and over the back fence for generations. The more spirited that debate, the better. We're eager to engage fellow fans in animated discussion about what singles you believe we've heedlessly omitted and what record makers you think we've been unfair to.

At the same time, we hope the debate moves beyond such concerns. As authors, we believe that simply praising or bemoaning our selections ("How could you leave out my favorite?") or quibbling over placement ("Number 423 actually should've been number 279!") is to misread our book.

Indeed, "It's a book, not a list"—Dave Marsh's admonition in *The Heart of Rock and Soul*—was the credo we adopted through-

out the writing of *Heartaches by the Number*. So while there's no doubt something inherently subjective about the task we've undertaken here, the results are far from arbitrary. The choices we've made aren't necessarily the country singles we believe are the "best" (that would've made for a very different book—*two* very different books, in fact), though of course we're convinced that every record included here is emotionally powerful, musically compelling, or both. Rather, the 500 singles we've chosen also had to help us make the points we wanted to make—and they had to be ones about which we had something interesting, entertaining, or provocative to say.

If we determined we had nothing much worthwhile to add to the conversation about a single, then that record didn't make the cut, no matter how good it was. Elvis Presley's "Are You Lonesome Tonight" and Trisha Yearwood's "Wrong Side of Memphis," for example, were both on our short list for a long time. By the end, though, we accepted that writers Daniel Wolff and James Hunter, respectively, had already expressed all we might've said, and then some. Consequently, those singles were bumped down to "Once More with Feeling: An Alternate 100." That supplemental list gathers, for the curious, our runners-up, but, just as importantly, it presents an alternate, compressed version of the arguments made throughout the book.

Our desire to make *Heartaches* a coherent and enjoyable read also influenced the way we ordered the entries. Connections between singles usually mattered more to us than any claim of one record's superiority to another. So, while the singles we'd nominate as the greatest of the great tend to be toward the front of the book, generally speaking, and those of lesser greatness are placed in the back half, such concerns were always secondary to the links between the entries themselves, that is, to the way one entry or record seemed to speak directly to, or nod in the direction of, another. Sometimes these connections add up over several entries to suggest a thematic or historical narrative, or they riff on a similar style or subject matter—the Nashville Sound, say, or the reasons lovers cheat. Other times the links are more fanciful than literal. Always, though, it was our "No Fences" ethos set forth in the preceding section, the version of the country story we have to tell, that drove our decisions. Indeed, it's fairer to say that the 500 entries here aren't so much ranked as they are ordered.

There's also no denying that many important country musicians may appear to be underrepresented or overlooked altogether. Omissions of certain figures were almost always deliberate, as were the number of repeat appearances. We selected more records by Dolly Parton than Reba McEntire for a reason. But just because you don't see your favorite Hank Williams single doesn't mean we don't think it's great too. Hank made dozens of timeless records, no doubt, but including all of them in this not-nearly-so-big-as-it-looks list wouldn't have told you anything you didn't already know, plus it wouldn't have left as much room for records by other deserving figures. We hope that the number of records we've included by each artist, as well as how we've ordered them, and the combination of which titles we've included, present a clear enough picture of the life and music of the performer in question. But if we could draw that portrait in just one or two entries—as we did for Connie Smith—it's by no means to say Smith only made two great records, not by a long shot.

Similarly, what appears, at first glance, to be a slight may not be one. Willie Nelson and Glen Campbell, for example, each have four entries, but we're not suggesting they've played equal roles in country history. We suspect Nelson would fare much better in a book about country's greatest albums or songwriters, projects where Campbell would likely be shut out altogether. In the world of singles, however, we feel comfortable noting that Campbell has created at least as many indelible singles as Nelson. At any rate, number crunchers would do well to note that Nelson actually shows up in eight entries—four times as a recording act and four as the songwriter for someone else's record—a proportion we think pretty accurately summarizes his contributions even as it reemphasizes that records are typically the products of collaboration.

We're aware our singles focus leaves out some great country music. There's no latter-day bluegrass here, for example, despite our admiration for, say, J. D. Crowe & the New South's "The Old Homeplace." There aren't as many country rockers here as might be expected given our "Don't Fence Me In" banner, and there are very few cosmic cowboys and three-named Texas singer-songwriters. There are also next to no folk-revival troubadours,

and there's not much that would fall under even the biggest-tent definition of what's termed alternative country: We especially mourn the absence of the Bottle Rockets' "Kerosene," Iris DeMent's "No Time to Cry," and Mike Ireland & Holler's "House of Secrets"—and those are just the ones from Missouri. In earlier eras, many of these recordings would've become singles as a matter of course. But released as they were during the ascendancy of FM radio—when artists typically have been relegated to either the mainstream single or album categories, and when shrinking playlists dictated that only recordings with big money behind them received consideration—they were strictly album tracks and therefore outside of our project.

Then again, it's not as if the country story that albums recount hasn't already been told. Indeed, it's today's critical and commercial bias toward albums that, in large part, has marginalized and obscured so much of country music's history. Albums have their unique strengths—they'll beat singles almost every time at spinning far-flung narratives and developing complex themes. But you just can't make much sense of country music history from a strictly album perspective. After all, Mr. and Mrs. Stoneman and the original Carter Family, Jimmie Rodgers and Hank Williams, never even made albums.

Plus, great singles are more emblematic of their historical and cultural moments, and are better at crystallizing intense emotional experiences—joy, devotion, loss, playfulness, jealousy, and so on—than albums. Much of this is due to the "limitations" of the single's two-to-four-minute format. But it's also because, when heard by thousands if not millions of listeners, singles offer people a shared language—and the potential for a wider public conversation. They're also a hell of a lot of fun to sing and dance to.

We want to advocate for this singles perspective in a way that's dialogical rather than divisive and that makes clear why we think it's important to do so in the first place. We hope that *Heartaches* champions the country tradition and that it exhibits a range of emotion as vibrant, complex, and full as that of the music itself. And, as much as anything, that it models a way of listening.

A few other comments:

- The year supplied in the headnote of each entry denotes the year of release of the record.
- The peak chart positions listed in entry headnotes are courtesy of Joel Whitburn's indispensable compilations of the *Billboard* charts: *Top Country Singles 1944–1997*, *Top Pop Singles 1955–1996*, and *Top R&B Singles 1942–1995*. The

designation "Pre-chart" in the headnote for records released prior to 1944 denotes only that no reliable means of monitoring country airplay existed before that time.

- Several headnotes include multiple release numbers for the same record. All of these were issued by the American Record Corporation (ARC) from 1929 to 1938. ARC regularly released records on two or more labels simultaneously. Each of these releases contained identical song couplings.

- Sources of the session information listed in headnotes include RCA and American Federation of Musicians session logs, credits listed in reissue and original recordings, as well as various published and unpublished discographies at the Country Music Hall of Fame and Museum. Some factual information contained in the body of the entries came from interviews we conducted, but most came from secondary sources, everything from liner notes to the books and newspaper and magazine articles listed in the bibliography. Also included in the bibliography are volumes that influenced our thinking, whether they have any explicit relationship to country music or not. For better or worse, the interpretations of the records themselves are solely our responsibility.

- The data listed in the headnotes was the most complete we could find. In some cases, such as those in which senior record executives received sole credit as producers when it was generally acknowledged that the label's Artist & Repertoire representative (A&R rep) also functioned in that capacity—for example, when Owen Bradley collaborated with his boss Paul Cohen at Decca during the early-to-mid-1950s—we went with the official producer credit rather than any anecdotal evidence that may have indicated otherwise. Similarly, official credits rarely suggest the role of the studio musicians, particularly frequent session leaders such as Grady Martin and Harold Bradley, who in many cases fulfilled the duties (arranging, hiring musicians, identifying material) that today are often considered the role of a producer.

- The letters "bfw" or "dc" at the end of each entry are, of course, the initials of the authors. All of the essays here are, in important respects, collaborations, as was the selection process itself, but we hope that by identifying the primary author of each entry we have further embodied the spirit of dialogue—between records and between ourselves—that lies at the core of *Heartaches by the Number*.

We welcome any corrections, clarifications, or other information that might enrich any future editions of the book.

Country Music's 500 Greatest Singles

1

Help Me Make It through the Night, Sammi Smith
Produced by Jim Malloy; Written by Kris Kristofferson
Mega 0015   1970   #1 country (3 weeks); #8 pop

"Help Me Make It through the Night" begins like the releasing of a breath—Junior Huskey's bass, Jerry Carrigan's cymbal, Chip Young's guitar, all playing one warm note that will return like a pulse. As Young picks out a delicate, urgent acoustic riff and Huskey's bass sounds the bottom, a string section enters. The cellos play a low, earthy obbligato that serves as a kind of motif or hook throughout the song while the violins merely offer one long, high note that, suspended above, suggests some greater longing. It's amazing that such an assembly of people and sounds can so readily convey intimacy and silence. And that's to say nothing of Sammi Smith's startlingly vulnerable vocals that follow.

"Help Me Make It through the Night" would be a monumental record if it did nothing more than plumb the crushing effects of loneliness on the human spirit. Yet it was also a watershed event in the history of Nashville and country music. After years of reacting against the rock & roll of Elvis Presley and the Beatles—the raison d'être of the Nashville Sound—Music City was at last producing records that reckoned with virtually all that had gone on in pop music since Elvis recorded "Don't Be Cruel" in 1956. None was better than "Help Me Make It through the Night." The dynamic country soul of the recording—thanks, for starters, to producer Jim Malloy and arranger Bill Walker—revealed the influences of a generation of Nashville music makers who had grown up listening not only to country music but also to rock & roll, jazz, pop, R&B, and even classical music. A crossover smash, "Help Me Make It through the Night" signaled country's belated arrival in the rock and soul era.

Also telling were the lyrics of Kris Kristofferson, a hippie Rhodes scholar with a yen for Bob Dylan and the Beat Poets. Kristofferson takes the period's political and cultural impulses—impulses endemic to, among others, the civil rights, women's, and counterculture movements—and boils them down to their emotional essence: the desire for community, freedom, and love, and the suffering that results when those needs go unmet. When unpacked by a great singer and a great arrangement,

Kristofferson's plea for deliverance reveals an existential weight. Nashville's answer to "Gimme Shelter," the record echoed not just the alienation of the moment but the fundamental human drive for intimacy and connection.

"Help Me Make It through the Night" had been recorded several times before Smith's version appeared. Bill Nash first cut the song in 1969, and Ray Price included an inexplicably jaunty take of the ballad on his *For the Good Times* LP. All of these versions had been made by men because Kristofferson had written from his male viewpoint. "Take the ribbon from your hair" was an opening line that in the wrong hands could have come off more than a little creepy. Smith altered the lyric to reflect a woman's point of view; her edit, "Take the ribbon from *my* hair," was simple yet significant. It not only switched the gender of the singer, it transformed the relationship of the song's protagonist to her lover. Now, instead of a man attempting to seduce a woman by urging her to undress while he watches, it's the woman who's doing the seducing. One reason the single was eventually so shocking to some—Bible thumper Albert Outler decried it as an example of "defiant hedonism"—was that, at a moment when the women's movement was only just starting to make its way into mainstream consciousness, Sammi was advocating for a woman's right to initiate sex. And to enjoy it.

But what's most remarkable here is the way that—thanks to Smith's revision, her performance, and the music surrounding it—the single is only superficially about sex at all. Kristofferson's sensual imagery—a woman's hair tumbling upon the bare skin of the lover who then lies at her side—sets us up for a seduction. Instead it embraces a deeper feeling, the fear that one cannot make it alone.

Kristofferson has said that he found the title for his song in a Frank Sinatra interview he'd read, where the singer talked about using a bottle or a lover to get through the night. Smith is using the latter but not in any tawdry sense. This is what Ralph Ellison meant when he wrote of "the mysteriousness of the blues" and "their capacity to make the details of sex convey meanings which touch upon the metaphysical." Listening to "Help Me Make It through the Night," we don't know what, exactly, has led the singer to her dark night of the soul; we only know that the darkness is about to overcome her.

"Take the ribbon from my hair," Sammi sings in a husky, soul-on-ice drawl as the music that opens the record pauses around her. Then Young and Huskey come back in as Carrigan, now on wood block, keeps time. Smith calls to her lover, and the strings respond with increasingly more elaborate variations on their opening motif. Her longing increasing with every line, Smith rides the groove, asking her lover first merely to lay down by her side, then to stay with her till morning, and finally pleading with him just to help her make it through the night. It's too personal a thing to have to say out loud, but when she does, Sammi's voice vibrates with the common need to know that we are not alone because others recognize our pain, and are moved by it.

At the bridge, Smith raises her voice in despair. She doesn't care about right or wrong or figuring out what it all means or what consequences tomorrow may bring; she needs only to know, this very moment, that she's not alone. The strings raise their voices too, but now, driving through a fierce counter melody, they are off on their own and no longer a comfort. The tension between the singer and the strings builds—a chasm deepened by Carrigan, who has now forsaken wood block for drumhead—and there is no resolution, only conflict. There's no narrative climax, just an emotional one: " . . . tonight I need a friend." Then Carrigan offers his version of the motif, and it drums the song to a halt.

The singer fears that she may not be able to make it through this crisis; all that sustains her is the absolute conviction that making it through the night will be worth it. She starts again. Smith has found her composure once more, but if anything she seems more trapped in this awful moment than ever—yesterday and tomorrow don't exist for her anymore. Then she gives up on words altogether and begins to hum. David Briggs enters on piano for the first time, breathing out as she breathes in, finishing her lines. "It's sad to be alone," she sings. "I don't want to be alone." The lack of background singers, ubiquitous on Nashville recording sessions at the time, only underscores Sammi's predicament. Behind her, the strings play their old parts, but their notes tremble now, and, here and there, Carrigan's bass drum punches up the rhythm like he's trying to keep the whole fragile

thing from collapsing around them. There's something uncomfortably naked about it all. With her body and her wordless voice, Sammi is begging for help, risking rejection and everything else. Yet, as the record ends, we know she has discovered, in the wisdom of rhythm and the grace of melody, a way to communicate the essential human dignity of her plea.

"Help Me Make It through the Night" was the Country Music Association's Single of the Year in 1971. In its grooves, song and singer, its arranger, musicians and producer, all comes together to create something more powerful than either the sum of its parts, or its antecedents in the Nashville Sound, might have predicted. It is more than just a great song put over by a great singer; it is a great record.—dc/bfw

2

Lost Highway, Hank Williams with His Drifting Cowboys
Produced by Fred Rose; Written by Leon Payne
MGM 10506   1949   #12 country

This is the record that best embodies Hank Williams's myth, especially among acolytes who see his death in the back of a Cadillac as country's answer to the romantic fantasy of living fast, dying young, and leaving a beautiful corpse.

Hank surely wasn't thinking about his own myth when he first heard Leon Payne's cautionary tale about the wages of sin; there wasn't any Hank Williams myth to consider yet. Still, he must have sensed that the song's cry of spiritual and moral alienation prefigured his destiny. "I'm a rollin' stone, all alone and lost / For a life of sin, I've paid the cost / When I pass by, all the people say / Just another guy, on the lost highway." The fateful resolve with which Williams renders these lines—echoed by the ghostly groans of Don Davis's steel guitar—makes "Lost Highway" one of the eeriest records ever made. But what's unsettling here isn't so much that Hank sees himself as bound for hell as that he sounds like he's *already* there, which in a very real sense he was.

Born poor and sickly to a mother whose idea of love was to dominate him, Williams never felt at home in this world. "Alone and forsaken," he sang on the record of the same name, "forsaken, forgotten, without any love." This isn't to say, as some would have it, that Hank was unrelentingly dark; far from it. He was by many accounts warmhearted and full of the dickens. But given the gaping hole in his heart, it's no wonder he became a rolling stone, no wonder he sought to dull his pain with whatever was beyond the horizon: the next bottle, the next woman, the next gig. Trouble was, no amount of running could put enough distance between Hank and his tortured soul.

In an alternate universe, he might have turned to the church; he'd glimpsed the light of grace, even sang about it on occasion. Too often, though, it was as if Hank didn't believe himself worthy of love or forgiveness, much less of redemption. Trapped in what was for him hell on earth, his only escape lay in self-destruction. Williams's story isn't tragically hip, as some would have it; it's just plain tragic. He couldn't, for the life of him, see another way out. Witness the despair in his voice when he cries, "And now I'm lost, too late to pray," before urging others not to follow him on his spiraling descent. It's as if Hank knows it would have been too late for him to pray even if he could have gotten down on his knees the day he was born.—bfw

3

Crazy, Patsy Cline
Produced by Owen Bradley; Written by Willie Nelson
Decca 31317   1961   #2 country; #9 pop

Pick any piece of the arrangement you like; then trace it through to the end. Floyd Cramer's nightclub piano; the sultry pulse of Buddy Harman's brushwork; the Jordanaires' billowing do-do-doo's; Harold Bradley's six-string electric bass doubling Bob Moore's stand-up for a clicking tic-tac effect that turns each bass note into a tiny explosion; Patsy Cline herself expressing the misery and confusion in Willie Nelson's lyric by making her voice break and sob. Every element of "Crazy" is essential to the whole, yet each is an endlessly compelling hook in its own right. Every element is calculated for effect, yet nothing in the effect feels calculated—there's just a woman in pain, and somehow, suddenly, wherever

we are, we hear her voice again and are swept up with the pain she's feeling right now. Forty years later, "Crazy" unexpectedly comes on the radio or jukebox and conversations just stop.

And that clears the space for one of the most amazing emotional turns in all of country music. Roiling in exquisite torment, Cline slips in that sexy, moaned "Ohhhh," and then, just as . . . wait, hold on a minute. Is that a *smile* playing across her face? Does she actually *enjoy* feeling this bad? Misery has never sounded so inviting. Must be why it's called "Crazy."—dc

4

Can the Circle Be Unbroken (Bye and Bye), The Carter Family
Produced by Art Satherley; Written by A. P. Carter
Banner 33465, Melotone M13452, Oriole 0909, Perfect 13155, Romeo 5484, Conqueror 8529   1935   Pre-chart

In the summer of 1998, Welsh-born painter, punk rocker, and all-purpose anarchist Jon Langford came to Nashville to host an exhibition of his artwork called "The Death of Country Music." The two-week show ran at a gallery just three blocks off Music Row, the epicenter of the country music industry. Part of it consisted of art-damaged portraits of Nashville legends—everyone from Johnny Cash to Tammy Wynette—inspired by the smoke- and graffiti-defiled photos that adorn the walls of Tootsie's Orchid Lounge, the famous Nashville watering hole located across the alley from the Ryman Auditorium (the one-time home of the Grand Ole Opry). The rest of the exhibit revolved around a dozen or so tombstones, each of them a 135-pound slab of chiseled pink granite mourning the passing of country music. A stone bearing the words "bury your dead high on bar room walls" depicted a death's-head staring out blankly above a cowboy holding a guitar etched with the word "neglect." Another titled "Country Music" portrayed Hank Williams as the third-century martyr Saint Sebastian. Engraved alongside the image of the singer, his protruding ribcage riddled with arrows, was an epitaph that read: "The bones of country music / Lie there in their casket / Beneath the towers of Nashville / In a deep black pool of neglect."

Langford's point, as hard-hitting as it was heavy-handed, was that country had forsaken its roots in favor of the "suburban rock music with a cowboy hat on" of Garth Brooks and his peers.

Langford's show gave voice to one side of an enduring polemic, a debate that's raged since the dawn of country music. During the late twenties, for example, some feared that the blatantly commercial sounds of hot, new stringband musicians like Gid Tanner's Skillet Lickers and Uncle Dave Macon signaled the death of the traditional folk ballad. Similar concerns resurfaced a decade or so later when the antics of Roy Acuff and his fellow singing stars started supplanting the then-respectable hoedown bands on the Opry. Then there was the threat the amplified twang of drinking- and cheating-obsessed honky-tonk posed to Acuff's beloved mountain music and, after that, the hellfire of Jerry Lee and Elvis that had so many teenagers (and their parents) all shook up. When the Nashville Sound came along, some viewed the move uptown as tantamount to auctioning off country's birthright to the highest bidder. From the discofied jive of *Urban Cowboy* to the "Hot New Country" of Garth and Shania, it's always been more or less the same story. No matter how durable or elastic country has proven itself to be, something new invariably comes along that has dour pundits prophesying the end of the music as they know it.

Through the years, the Carter Family's recording of the funereal hymn "Can the Circle Be Unbroken" has come to symbolize the key aspects of this conversation. Outwardly, the record conveys a mix of hope and doubt (the title is, after all, a question) about the persistence of the human community beyond the grave. Yet it also speaks, figuratively, to each successive generation's anxiety over whether the links they forge in country music's chain will extend the tradition or bring it to an end. "Lord I told the undertaker, 'Undertaker, please drive slow / For this body you are hauling / Lord I hate to see her go,' " Sara Carter intones, her voice much deeper than it was when she, her husband A. P., and cousin Maybelle first came down from the Clinch Mountains nearly a decade earlier. Sara's grieving her dead mother, but the body in that horse-drawn wagon now serves as a metaphor for the Carters and their peers. The circle they ponder on the chorus represents the larger country tradition, just as the trio's faith in "a better home a-waiting" testifies to their belief that the tradition will endure if its adherents build on the past to create something new, a future of their own making.

From Mother Maybelle's innovative thumb-brush picking to the way A. P. updated the old mountain ballads he unearthed, this dialectical impulse is evident throughout the Carter Family's recordings. It's also there in much of the best music that followed in their wake—music born of artists' understanding of themselves as links in a larger chain that depends on the forging of new ties that at once refer to and expand the tradition. This isn't to say that all new links are of equal value—that, for example, the "country lite" of *Urban Cowboy* strengthened these bonds as much as the rough-cut honky-tonk of Rex Griffin and Hank Williams. Nevertheless, embracing this dialectical sensibility holds out the best hope for keeping country's circle intact, a hope embodied explicitly on the Nitty Gritty Dirt Band's 1972 LP *Will the Circle Be Unbroken*. On that album, the Dirt Band gathered several generations of pickers and singers—a cloud of witnesses that included Roy Acuff, Earl Scruggs, and the venerable Mother Maybelle herself—to reaffirm their belief in the ongoing vitality of a tradition shared, among others, by hippies and old-timers alike.—bfw

5

Don't Be Cruel, Elvis Presley
Produced by Steve Sholes;
Written by Otis Blackwell
RCA Victor 47–6604   1956
#1 country (10 weeks); #1 R&B (6 weeks); #1 pop (11 weeks)

Tell me if you've heard this one. With Elvis Presley and the other rockabillies invading its turf, the country music industry created the sweeter, more pop-influenced Nashville Sound in a three-pronged attack to broaden its pop audience, to secure its more mature country audience, and to beat back the young heathens. That is, the Nashville Sound was a reaction to Elvis. This tale has been repeated as gospel for four decades now, but it doesn't tell the whole truth. Though he should certainly be credited for forcing the repositioning that the country music industry underwent in the late fifties, Elvis wasn't just a catalyst for the stylistic creations of other people. Fact is, Elvis was one of the Nashville Sound's chief architects, as important to the style's development as any other single figure—perhaps most important.

Although it refers to a means of production (not to mention an era and a mystique) as much as to an actual sound, and though it was created over many years rather than in one epiphanic flash, the Nashville Sound is generally dated from 1957 or 1958. Country historian Rich Kienzle says that "Gone," a Ferlin Husky hit recorded in November 1956, "may well have pointed the way to the Nashville Sound." Writer Colin Escott identifies Jim Reeves's "Four Walls"—produced in February 1957 by Chet Atkins—as the "first 'Nashville Sound' record." And Atkins himself, the RCA-based producer and guitarist most often credited with being the Sound's primary artistic creator, pointed to his production of Don Gibson's "Oh Lonesome Me" late that same year.

The country boy from Memphis beat them all. Elvis's initial RCA recordings had been attempts to recreate the slap-back sound Sam Phillips pioneered at Sun Studios. By the time Elvis entered a New York studio on July 2, 1956, though, he was already charting new paths. First he put down "Hound Dog," as explosive a rock & roll cut as has ever been recorded (albeit one that took him in a direction he would rarely pursue again). Next he turned to "Don't Be Cruel." The result included all of the defining characteristics of the Nashville Sound. The spare instrumentation and restrained playing that left lots of open spaces; the at-ease yet crisply defined production with just a touch of echo; the singer's voice (and the bass) way out front in the mix; the backing bop-bop-bop vocals by the Jordanaires; the "head" arrangements devised on the spot by the musicians; and, of course, no fiddle and no pedal steel. Just as importantly, "Don't Be Cruel" had the unmistakably warm, relaxed *feel* of the Nashville Sound. It was all there, and the result was a new kind of rock & roll, a new kind of pop, and the beginnings of what would be a new kind of country music.

RCA A&R director Steve Sholes was behind the glass for all these sessions. But what was different about the recording process for "Hound Dog" / "Don't Be Cruel" was that, for the first time, Elvis was the one in charge. He made the final song selections, choosing "Don't Be Cruel" right there in the studio from the acetate demos provided by publishing house Hill and Range. He worked out the basic arrangement on the piano. He had Scotty Moore all but lay out on guitar and told drummer D. J. Fontana to slow the tempo. He sang, and he insisted they keep at it until they got it right. The result, twenty-eight takes later, was a record that sounds perfectly effortless.

A two-sided single with "Hound Dog," "Don't Be Cruel" topped the country charts for over two months, heralding the arrival of

what would soon be called the Nashville Sound. Elvis didn't create that sound all by his lonesome any more than he invented rock & roll by himself. Certainly, Atkins (who had been behind the board on some of Elvis's earlier RCA sessions and played guitar on his first), pianist Floyd Cramer (who had backed Presley at the *Louisiana Hayride,* played on Elvis's very first RCA date, and later became an Elvis studio fixture), Don Robertson (who created the slip-note piano style Cramer made famous and wrote many of Presley's most country early sixties offerings), guitarist Hank Garland (who would become another Elvis studio staple), and the Jordanaires (who would quickly became synonymous with both the Nashville Sound and Elvis Presley) all played significant roles. So did producers Owen Bradley, Ken Nelson, and Don Law, and any number of other musicians and engineers. But Elvis was the key. Listening closely to Presley's 1956 RCA sessions makes it clear that what Chet Atkins and the rest were about to do was not to take country music pop, but to countrify "Don't Be Cruel."—dc

6

Crazy Arms, Ray Price
Produced by Don Law;
Written by Charles Seals and Ralph Mooney
Columbia 21510   1956   #1 country (20 weeks)

The year is 1956. Hepcats from Memphis have hot-wired hillbilly music to R&B and staged a coup against the country music industry. Or at least that's how it must have seemed to the Nashville brass when Elvis Presley or Carl Perkins occupied the top spot on the country charts for all but a few weeks during the first half of the year. Superstars like Eddy Arnold and Red Foley took the hardest knocks, all but vanishing from the hit parade for the rest of the decade. Others such as Webb Pierce and Hank Thompson tried to figure out what the new teenbeat was all about, releasing rockabilly-influenced records of their own ("Teenage Boogie," "Rockin' in the Congo") with predictably mixed results.

Ray Price, by contrast, pretty much ignored the threat posed by pompadoured insurgents like Perkins and Presley. Price had

just begun to hit his stride with his own brand of honky-tonk after having spent his early career imitating his old roommate, Hank Williams; he wasn't about to jump on anyone else's bandwagon now. Yet when he and the Cherokee Cowboys went into the studio in March of 1956 to cut "Crazy Arms," they did more than just hold their own. They created a sound, later dubbed the "Ray Price beat," that became an enduring part of the American musical vernacular, as durable in its way as the "hambone" rhythms of Bo Diddley or the one-chord funk vamps of James Brown and the JBs.

"We were having trouble getting a good clean bass sound," Price recalled of the session. "So instead of going with the standard 2/4 beat, I said, 'Let's try a 4/4 bass and a shuffle rhythm.' And it cut—it cut clean through." Indeed, Buddy Killen's surging bassline—which Price suggested be played on both electric *and* acoustic bass, making it *doubly* rocking—cut a swath wide enough for honky-tonk to rocket straight into the modern era. Spurred on by Tommy Jackson's blazing fiddle and Jimmy Day's sobbing steel—and joined near the end of the record by Floyd Cramer's pealing barroom piano—Price and company transformed the gutbucket country shuffle of the postwar era into a pop-wise rhythm that kicked as hard as big-beat rock & roll. Hard enough, in fact, to knock Perkins's "Blue Suede Shoes" off the top of the country charts.

For awhile, the success of "Crazy Arms"—the single spent forty-five weeks on the country charts, including twenty at #1—allayed Nashville's fears that rock & roll would supplant honky-tonk in the hearts of young record buyers. Not even Price, though, could fend off Elvis for long—"I Want You, I Need You, I Love You," a creamy pop ballad, eventually replaced "Crazy Arms" at #1. It was poetic justice. After all, the pulsing bassline Price urged Killen to play here was lifted right off one of the Presley hits that had been barnstorming the country charts earlier that year. Never again would country or rock & roll singers think twice about looking to each other for inspiration.—bfw

how strong a songwriter Jones was in his first half decade or so of recording and how it was, in fact, the very twists and turns of his own songs that allowed him to refine his unique ballad style. Jones's songs in these early years are rarely what you'd call clever, they don't recount involved stories, and they aren't given to poetry like Hank Williams's "The silence of a falling star lights up a purple sky." Instead, Jones's best solo compositions use the syntax of actual speech to home in on hearts and minds in the process of breaking.

In "The Window Up Above," Jones's lyrics describe a man confronting a wife whom he dearly loves but who has been unfaithful. He knows this for a fact because the night before he was "watching from the window up above" while she embraced her lover in the front yard. "You must  have thought that I was sleeping," George tells her, and when he adds, "and I wish that I had been," it is almost too painful to bear. But only almost. Jones's deftness with melody, his ability to phrase within it and, in this case, even to create it, trebles the impact of his words and makes it hard for us to turn away. One moment his voice is matter of fact, understated even, and the next he's stretching out a word until you think he'll choke on it.

Still, a great vocalist singing a great song doesn't always result in a great record. So "The Window Up Above" is elucidated by Nashville Sound studio touches—echo on Jones's voice, a slip-note piano solo, a vocal chorus for heightened drama—as well as by pedal-steel fills that slide through the otherwise spare honky-tonk setting like a tear down a cheek. It's the way Jones's blue and memorable melody, his plainspoken lyrics, and his legendary voice all coalesce within this sympathetic arrangement that makes it into a masterpiece.—dc

7

The Window Up Above, George Jones
Produced by Harold "Pappy" Dailey; Written by George Jones
Mercury 71700   1960   #2 country

To call George Jones the greatest country singer of all time has become something of a cliché over the past few decades, but that doesn't mean it isn't true. What no one talks about, though, is just

8

Coat of Many Colors, Dolly Parton
Produced by Bob Ferguson; Written by Dolly Parton
RCA Victor 0538   1971   #4 country

"Coat of Many Colors" builds to a declaration—"One is only poor only if they choose to be"—that upon first listen seems more than a little naïve. After all, the choices Dolly Parton had in whether or not she would grow up poor in the East Tennessee hills numbered exactly zero. But then, that's not what she's saying. In the very next line, she concedes that "we had no money," so she's clearly not denying her poverty. Rather, she's claiming that her poverty need not define her. "One is *only* poor only if they choose to be," she sings, a meaning that would have been obscured if Parton had deleted either one of those seemingly redundant "only"s.

Not that "Coat of Many Colors" doesn't indulge in a bit of nostalgia. Skillfully weaving her autobiography into the biblical tale of Joseph, Parton recalls how her mother once made her a coat from tiny, rainbow-colored rags and how the kids at school laughed and mocked her. It's a painfully honest song, yet even so it leaves a lot out. Most notably, it omits the anger and humiliation Parton felt as her friends, who couldn't have come from homes much better off than hers, pointed and laughed at her mangy coat. They yanked off its buttons and very nearly ripped it from her back (a terrifying possibility, she once told an interviewer, since she wasn't wearing so much as a t-shirt beneath) before they locked her in the school's closet. The song never confronts such levels of shame and cruelty. Instead, Parton presents herself as merely perplexed and a little sad that her friends can't see how special this coat is and how special she is to be wearing it.

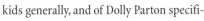

Which is just fine since "Coat of Many Colors" is not a documentary or even a memory, but a story she's telling herself. How the adult Parton presents this childhood story says a lot about the survival tactics of poor kids generally, and of Dolly Parton specifically. It might, for example, explain Parton's flamboyant stage dress through the years. More substantially, it tells how a poor kid from the Blue Ridge Mountains has to make sense of life if she has ambitions, as we know Dolly Parton most certainly did, to get out of those mountains one day and conquer the world.

I refuse, Parton insists as she wanders back through the years, to believe a story about myself in which poor is all I am. I am poor, but I will be more than that—I *am* more than that. Despite your contempt, the things I love are worth loving. And since my mother slaved over this amazing coat "just for me," I must be worth loving too.—dc

9

Rank Stranger, The Stanley Brothers & the Clinch Mountain Boys
No producer credited; Written by Albert E. Brumley
Starday 506   1960   Did not chart

Records as evocative as "Rank Stranger" cry out for multiple interpretations. The song's narrative is as straightforward as it is sketchy—and as harrowing. After years of being away from their mountain home, Carter Stanley and his kid brother Ralph return to find, to their horror, that everything has changed; they recognize neither the faces they see nor their surroundings. Other than their unsettling encounter with a stranger in the final verse, we can only guess what's happened, or what their fate might be.

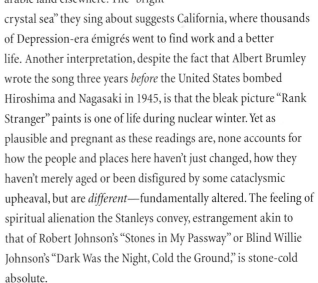

One theory, and it makes sense given the strip-mining that had been ravaging the Stanleys' beloved Clinch Mountains for decades, is that the hills have been scarred beyond recognition and that the brothers' friends and kin have moved away in search of arable land elsewhere. The "bright crystal sea" they sing about suggests California, where thousands of Depression-era émigrés went to find work and a better life. Another interpretation, despite the fact that Albert Brumley wrote the song three years *before* the United States bombed Hiroshima and Nagasaki in 1945, is that the bleak picture "Rank Stranger" paints is one of life during nuclear winter. Yet as plausible and pregnant as these readings are, none accounts for how the people and places here haven't just changed, how they haven't merely aged or been disfigured by some cataclysmic upheaval, but are *different*—fundamentally altered. The feeling of spiritual alienation the Stanleys convey, estrangement akin to that of Robert Johnson's "Stones in My Passway" or Blind Willie Johnson's "Dark Was the Night, Cold the Ground," is stone-cold absolute.

Another possibility is that the dystopia depicted in "Rank Stranger" isn't so much a physical place (although it's certainly that) as a moral condition. Heard this way, the record picks up where the Monroe Brothers' 1936 recording of "What Would You Give in Exchange?" left off nearly a quarter-century before. From their waltz-time rhythms and guitar- and mandolin-based arrangements, to the way that Ralph's moaning behind Carter on the verses recalls Bill Monroe's ghostly "echoes" on "What Would You Give," the parallels between the two records are striking. That's to say nothing of the thematic continuity between them; just as the Monroes' cautionary tale exhorts rural folk who go off to the big city to cleave to the ties that bind, the Stanleys' sequel shows what happens when those bonds unravel.

"Everybody I met seemed to be a rank stranger," Ralph pines in a piercing, unearthly tenor to open the chorus. Then Carter picks up the vocal, as Curley Lambert's mandolin keens inconsolably in the background. "No mother or dad, not a friend could I see / They knew not my name and I knew not their faces / I found they were all rank strangers to me," he mourns, after which a nameless man informs them that their loved ones have gone on to their homes in glory. The stranger trusts he'll also reach that beautiful place by and by, but whether the Stanleys will join him there isn't clear. Adrift in some infernal limbo, Ralph's aggrieved wailing floats, untethered, on the chorus, making it plain that, for now, the brothers are stuck in a living hell.—bfw

10

Born to Lose, Ted Daffan's Texans
Produced by Art Satherley;
Written by Frankie Brown [Ted Daffan]
OKeh 6706   1942   Pre-chart

Songwriter, steel player, and bandleader Ted Daffan contributed several classic songs to the country music repertoire—"Worried Mind," "No Letter Today," and "Truck Driver's Blues"—but "Born to Lose" is his masterpiece. Rarely have lyric, melody, and arrangement come together to create a recording of such spiritual desolation. Cuts like this made Daffan a favorite of the folks who crowded the dance halls of California and the Southwest during World War II. Also, as critic John Morthland has noted, "for the millions of displaced working people forced to stay in cities like Detroit and Chicago in order to keep jobs, ['Born to Lose'] was received as a metaphor for modern life in general."

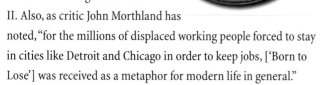

Embrace such a metaphor too tightly, and you have a recipe for misery; internalize it as your one true fate, and it's a death

sentence. No doubt that's why Woody Guthrie once declared, "I hate a song that makes you think you are just born to lose. Bound to lose." Still, that's how Daffan's character here feels—lines such as "I've lived my life in vain," "There's no use to dream of happiness," and "My every hope is gone, it's so hard to face an empty dawn" scream that the guy should probably be on suicide watch.

Don't give up on him just yet, though. Beaten down by a series of defeats, and facing the loss of his girl, the man wrestles, desperately, with one of life's hardest truths—our dreams and loves will always be, by definition, the very things that cause us the most pain. That this man may yet find a way to keep on dreaming and loving is here in the way Texans singer/fiddler Leon Seago is still bothering to croon so sweetly. It's in the way that Freddy Courtney's accordion and Daffan's own steel respond to every grim thought with music that sounds more empathetic than defeated; and it's in the way the swinging Texans' rhythm section lets us know the guy still likes to go out with his friends and dance. This may not be hope exactly, but it's on the way.—dc

11

Stand by Your Man, Tammy Wynette
Produced by Billy Sherrill;
Written by Billy Sherrill and Tammy Wynette
Epic 10398   1968   #1 country (3 weeks); #19 pop

"Stand by Your Man" could well be the most controversial record in the history of country music. It certainly caused a stir when it came out during the late sixties, a time when the women's movement was gaining strength and both the Roe v. Wade decision and the battle over the Equal Rights Amendment loomed on the horizon. Feminists decried the record as a prescription for female slavery while the religious right hailed it as a recipe for becoming "the total woman"—that is, a woman totally subordinate to her husband.

These reactions were inevitable given the record's anthemic power, as well as the era's social and political climate. Doubtless both responses delighted producer and co-writer Billy Sherrill, who had an ax to grind with "women's libbers" long before he scribbled down the song's title on a scrap of paper in 1967. Nevertheless, the uproar caused by the single puzzled co-writer Wynette, for whom "Stand" wasn't so much a call for submission as an expression of a romantic ideal. For Tammy, commitment to making love work was what love was all about; it superseded virtually any personal shortcoming.

Which isn't to suggest that "Stand by Your Man" advocates that women stay in abusive relationships. Witness the song's final chorus; amid a crescendo of voices, steel, and guitar, Tammy stretches out the penultimate line with palpable hurt, wailing, "Keep giving all the love you *can*." She isn't telling her long-suffering sisters to take whatever their men dish out, but rather encouraging them to give whatever love they can find it within themselves to give.

Within reason. Tammy herself knew when enough was enough. By the time this record topped the charts she had already escaped two bad marriages. The same would be true of her impending union with George Jones. Writing about that relationship years later in her autobiography, she observed, "There's no love in the world that can't be killed if you beat it to death long enough." Those words evince uncharacteristic realism for an idealist like Wynette, but they also underline that "Stand By Your Man" presents a standard to live by, not one worth dying for.

Jerry Kennedy's opening guitar figure sets a pregnant, yet intimate and conversational tone from the outset. The bruised, undulating notes he plays as the record begins conjure images of Tammy gulping hard before confessing to her sisters that, "Sometimes it's hard to be a woman," the lump in her throat going absolutely nowhere. Then there's the pivotal phrase, "If you love him, you'll forgive him," which—judging by the catch in her voice and the way Pete Drake's steel rains down tears with her—isn't so much an injunction for her peers to follow as a statement of love's painful reality.

In other words, whatever Tammy envisioned, "Stand" isn't the invitation for women to become doormats that its detractors have made it out to be. Relationships not built on mutuality and respect ultimately become oppressive. Tammy isn't preaching dependency; she isn't urging the beleaguered housewife in Loretta Lynn's "One's on the Way," for example, to exult in her indentured servitude. More than anything she's reaching out to women who, for better and for worse, share her vision of commitment, women who know the cost of loving, and perhaps of loving too much.—bfw

12

It Wasn't God Who Made Honky Tonk Angels,
Kitty Wells
Produced by Paul Cohen; Written by J. D. Miller
Decca 9–28232   1952   #1 country (6 weeks); #27 pop

13

The Wild Side of Life,
Hank Thompson & His Brazos Valley Boys
Produced by Ken Nelson; Written by A. A. Carter and W. Warren
Capitol   F1942   1952   #1 country (15 weeks)

Kitty Wells didn't think much of "It Wasn't God Who Made Honky Tonk Angels" when her husband Johnnie Wright first played her a demo of the song in 1952; at the time, she wasn't too keen on recording anything. The eight sides she'd done for RCA in 1949 and 1950 had stiffed, and her husband's career was the one really taking off; as half of the duo Johnnie & Jack, he had a runaway hit with the rumba-flavored "Poison Love." By then a mother of three, Wells was ready to trade her microphone for a pair of apron strings. The only reason she says she cut "Honky Tonk Angels" was to collect the $125 union scale the session would bring. She certainly didn't think the record would fare any better than the poorly promoted sides she'd made for Chet Atkins and Steve Sholes at RCA. "I wasn't expecting it to make a hit," Wells admitted. "I just thought it was another song. It was just the women getting back at the men."

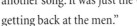

"Honky Tonk Angels," a rejoinder to Hank Thompson's "The Wild Side of Life," turned out to be a whole lot more than just the women getting back at the men. Written by fabled Louisiana record man Jay Miller, the song gave voice to the feelings of countless women living in postwar America. When thousands of GIs marched off to war a decade earlier, women picked up the slack—and wore the slacks—entering the work force and gaining a measure of social and financial independence. But when the men came home, they tried to turn back the clock, expecting women to resume their roles as homebodies. Those who refused became scapegoats, their morals called into question by their newfound freedom.

#1 on the country charts for fifteen weeks during the spring and summer of 1952, "The Wild Side of Life" played directly into this male insecurity. The ballad cast Thompson in the role of the jilted lover, crying in his beer as he wondered, twin fiddles quivering along with his doleful wail, if some women might just be wild and independent by nature. It's not hard to see why the era's men, who felt threatened with so many women in the work force and the divorce rate on the rise, might have identified with the singer and applied the song's premise to *all* women. So imagine their consternation when Wells's mournful whine pierced the airwaves that summer with the straightforward retort "It's a shame that all the blame is on us women." Or when, on the chorus, with Shot Jackson's steel guitar bawling away in the background, Wells charged, "Too many times married men think they're still single / That has caused many a good girl to go wrong."

In the hands of one of Wells's saucier contemporaries—a barroom belter such as Texas Ruby or Rose Maddox, for example—the song doubtless would have seemed like an endorsement of loose living and sunk like a stone. But there's nothing brazen about Wells's performance here. She's empathizing with fallen women, not condoning the wild life, and that's a big reason why the record spent six weeks at the top of the country charts. Wells's matronly persona made the song even less threatening—the thirty-two-year-old housewife wore the gingham associated with the prewar Carter Family instead of the spangly new western wear favored by her fifties counterparts. Even listeners who'd only *heard* Wells could tell from her stolid delivery, a dignified style that again harked back to the Carter Family—in this case, to Sara's keening alto—that she wasn't singing about her own exploits.

Something else that made "Honky Tonk Angels" palatable to the public was its familiar, antediluvian tune, a melody drawn from the Carter Family's "I'm Thinking Tonight of My Blue Eyes" (as were "The Wild Side of Life" and Roy Acuff's "Great Speckle Bird"). Practically anyone could hum along with "Angels" the first time they heard it. So while Wells's words gave men their comeuppance, musically the song had a nostalgic air. Recalling a time when gender roles, and most other things, were more clearly defined, this comforting old-time ditty softened the blow of what was then a fairly radical lyric.

Wells gave little thought to these sorts of musicological and sociological considerations when "Honky Tonk Angels" was making its way up the charts. From her perspective, the single's success just meant she was going back to work outside the home, and therein lies yet another reason "Angels" was such a pivotal record. More than just tapping the malaise felt by many of the era's women, Wells's breakthrough hit helped open the doors of Nashville's recording studios to dozens, perhaps hundreds, of female singers. (Despite the fact that Patsy Montana's "I Wanna Be a Cowboy's Sweetheart" was rumored to have moved a million units back in 1935, postwar country execs didn't think women could sell records—that is, until "Honky Tonk Angels" reportedly sold 800,000 copies.) Soon Nashville record labels were signing women without giving the pen time to cool. RCA snatched up Charline Arthur, the Davis Sisters, and Betty Cody; MGM grabbed Rita Faye and Audrey Williams; King Records recruited Ann Jones and Bonnie Lou. Even Decca, Wells's label, got in on the act, landing Goldie Hill, "The Golden Hillbilly."

None of these women, though, could hold a candle to Wells, who by the mid-fifties had been dubbed the Queen of Country Music by publishing mogul Fred Rose. With the fistfuls of best-selling singles she racked up during this period, including "Release Me," "Making Believe," and "Heartbreak USA," Wells deserved the title. She took home top female vocalist honors in the country trade magazines every year from 1952 to 1965—a feat that today would be comparable to Faith Hill or Shania Twain winning female vocalist of the year awards from both the Country Music Association and the Academy of Country Music for fourteen straight years. By 1967, when Wells's unprecedented string of hits ended, she had placed thirty-five singles in the country Top Ten and a total of sixty-three on the charts. In the process, she not only became country's first female superstar of the postwar era, but she also emerged as a vocal prototype for subsequent generations of country women, from Hazel Dickens and Loretta Lynn to Dolly Parton and Iris DeMent.

None of which detracts from the quality of "The Wild Side of Life." A showcase for Thompson's liquid baritone and the Brazos Valley Boys' trademark blend of honky-tonk and western swing, it remains one of the greatest country singles ever made. Although perhaps not quite as dramatically as it did for Wells, it also marked a turning point in the careers of Thompson and producer Ken Nelson, becoming the first #1 single for both men. Thompson went on to chart sixty-nine more singles over the next thirty-one years and, as of the year 2001, was still playing about 100 dates annually. Nelson became a giant among A&R reps, signing the likes of Faron Young, Wanda Jackson, and Wynn Stewart to Capitol Records, and lending his hands-off production style to the greatest recordings of Buck Owens and Merle Haggard.

Oh, and just to set the record straight: unlike the dolt he played in "The Wild Side of Life," Thompson was a champion of honky-tonk angels, among other things urging Nelson, in 1952, to sign Jean Shepard, arguably the purist female honky-tonker of all time.—bfw

14

Carolyn, Merle Haggard & the Strangers
Produced by Ken Nelson; Written by Tommy Collins
Capitol 3222   1971   #1 country; #58 pop

It's hard to believe anyone could still believe that good string arrangements and good country music don't mix. But if you should chance upon someone still arguing this nonsense, all you need offer in rebuttal is a single word: "Carolyn."

At first Merle Haggard feared that "Carolyn," written by Bakersfield legend Leonard "Tommy Collins" Sipes, might be a little too pop for his style. But when his old friend asked him to give it a shot, Haggard couldn't refuse. Good thing, too, because the single that Haggard and his Strangers created in collaboration with producer Ken Nelson and string arranger Larry Muhoberac is as riveting as any record you're ever likely to hear. The strings that kick things off are low, 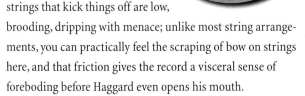 brooding, dripping with menace; unlike most string arrangements, you can practically feel the scraping of bow on strings here, and that friction gives the record a visceral sense of foreboding before Haggard even opens his mouth.

When he does, he's playing a man who is recounting to his wife a story he's just heard. Some man has skipped work and wandered, lonely, to another city, where he's tempted by women whose "warm lips like a honeycomb dripped with honey." "Something about the smell of strange perfume made him feel warm, and not alone," he's telling her about this other man, but he sure sings it like someone who still has the fragrance fresh in his nostrils. Behind him, bass and piano thump, drums keep almost martial time, and an acoustic guitar throws off bitter licks. All the while those angular strings hover. They're holding themselves in line, just barely.

Then they, and he, stop pretending. In an instant, the song flashes into a dramatic crescendo (this must be what Haggard heard as pop), and those strings are free to soar. They set Haggard free too, and he delivers his thinly veiled threat in a rush—if you don't appreciate me more, don't be surprised by what I do. "Carolyn, a man will do that, always, when he's treated bad at home," he tells her, and the scratchy strings and the soaring ones battle all the way to the fade.

Whoa. The only thing that could be more perfectly menacing than those strings would be the ones that should've backed his wife on a sequel, when she tells her husband to take his "story" and stick it up his game-playin' ass.—dc

15

How Much More Can She Stand, Conway Twitty
Produced by Owen Bradley;
Written by Harry Compton
Decca 32801   1971   #1 country (1 week); #105 pop

In the 1968 hit "Stand by Your Man," Tammy Wynette commiserated with her female listeners, noting the likelihood that at some point in a relationship "You'll have bad times, and he'll have good times / doing things you don't understand." Three years later, Conway Twitty's "How Much More Can She Stand" illustrated the point with a worst-case scenario. Twitty's protagonist cheats on his wife, repeatedly, and though he is clearly wracked with guilt, he shows no sign of  ever being true. Instead, he rationalizes his deceptions (he lies to his wife to protect her), denies responsibility (the devil makes him do it), and retreats into little-boy helplessness ("I did wrong again last night, now I just want to go back home"). Mirroring his conflict, the music plods through the verses; Twitty's half-hearted attempts to "love only her, play with the kids and watch TV" are reflected in John Hughey's deflated pedal steel and the repetitive fills of pianist Larry Butler. At each chorus, though, the band lurches into dramatic, soulful crescendos, where the nagging thwack of Tommy Markham's drum agitates Twitty to ever-greater fits of anxiety. "My reasons for cheating, they're as good as lies can be," he admits to himself in a rare moment of clarity. But he knows he's still going to lie and cheat, even now when he "can see it in her eyes" that she's on to him. What's most pathetic is how easily he believes he can't change. What's most cruel is how that assessment dumps all the hard decisions on his wife.

Tammy's advice had been "If you love him, you'll forgive him." Of course, that's a mighty significant condition—Twitty's record dramatizes just how ominously that "if" can hang over a relationship as troubled as the one here. If he continues to lie and cheat this way, you can bet he'll kill whatever love and forgiveness his wife has left to give. "How much more can she stand and still stand by me," Twitty wonders, but he knows. Twitty's ravaged voice, coupled with Joe E. Lewis's taunting high tenor, prophesies that the end is coming, any day now.—dc

16

After the Fire Is Gone, Conway Twitty & Loretta Lynn
Produced by Owen Bradley; Written by L. E. White
Decca 32776   1971   #1 country (2 weeks); #56 pop

Nothing is as chilling as being stuck in a loveless marriage, and few cheating songs convey a craving for that vanished warmth better than Conway and Loretta's "After the Fire Is Gone." "Love is where you find it / When you find no love at home," they sing, their voices locked in a ravaged wail on the first half of the phrase; when Loretta takes the second-half solo, hers positively throbs with desperation.

Not that he had to tell us, what with John Hughey's steel slurring away in the background, but Conway seconds that emotion. Sitting at home emptying a bottle, trying in vain to generate a little heat, he finally gives in and picks up the phone. He's just got to see her. They both know it's wrong to cheat, but as Loretta moans, "Your lips are warm and tender / Your arms hold me just right / Sweet words of love you remember / That the one at home forgot."

Harold Bradley's walking bass line says the rest—Conway and Loretta are going to keep on stepping out, if only to keep defrosting their cold, aching hearts.—bfw

17

Right or Wrong, Milton Brown & His Brownies
Produced by Dave Kapp;
Written by Arthur L. Sizemore, Haven Gillespie, and Paul Biese
Decca 5342   1936   Pre-chart

"Milton Brown and myself started this thing."

—Bob Wills

Well, yes, but really no. Wills and Brown both were members of the Light Crust Doughboys, a popular Texas dance band and proto-western swing outfit, and both went on from there to form orchestras that became the twin pillars of the genre. Yet it was Brown, a former cigar salesman, and not Wills, who truly set western swing's pendulum in motion.

The first to leave the Doughboys (over a financial dispute with the band's emcee W. Lee O'Daniel), Brown was also the first to assemble an ensemble organized around the core elements of what soon would become known as western swing. Virtually all of those components are writ large in "Right or Wrong," one of the true classics of the idiom. There are the record's burning jazz rhythms, cadences much closer to those of Louis Armstrong's Hot Fives and Sevens, or those of Joe Venuti and Eddie Lang, than those of any hillbilly stringband. There are the twin fiddles of Cecil Brower and Cliff Bruner playing—no, singing—in harmony with each other. There's the stride piano of Fred "Papa" Calhoun and the brassy, amped-up steel of fretmaster Bob Dunn. Galvanized by their leader's affable, Bing Crosby–inspired crooning, "Right or Wrong" (a song Brown learned from Emmett Miller's recording) finds the Brownies grabbing country dance music by the scruff of the neck and whipping it—literally, in the case of bass fiddle player Wanna Coffman—into an art form on a par with jazz. Which is just how young lions like Charlie Christian and Charlie Parker heard it, as music they could plug into the changes they would soon ring at Birdland and the Savoy.

Today, "Right or Wrong" might be associated more with Wills and his Playboys (as are the likes of "Corinne, Corinna" and "Sittin' on Top of the World,"), but Brown and company were the ones who introduced the song to the western swing canon. That said, there's no mistaking the music of the two bandleaders.

Whereas Wills augmented his sound with horns and drums and included fiddle breakdowns and other forms of hillbilly music in his repertoire, Brown favored a more traditional stringband lineup and a more uptown mix of Tin Pan Alley favorites, blues, and jazz. He stuck with that approach until his untimely death at age thirty-two, due to complications from injuries suffered in an auto wreck in 1936. Had Brown survived the accident, it would have been interesting to see if he would have followed Wills's lead, going head-to-head with his rival the way West Coast bandleader Spade Cooley later would. As it was, during his lifetime Brown's unit was arguably the more popular of the two, and easily the more prolific, recording some 100 sides for Bluebird and Decca in less than three years. Despite Wills's willingness to "share" the honor with him, Brown was without a doubt the first to play western swing.—bfw

18

Time Changes Everything,
Bob Wills & His Texas Playboys
Produced by Art Satherley and Don Law;
Written by Tommy Duncan
OKeh 05753   1940   Pre-chart

Tommy Duncan's singing is frequently termed bluesy, but that description mostly points out the obvious—in the years leading up to World War II, pop and country music had already begun to absorb elements of the blues. If you're looking for what's distinctive about his sound, you need to mix in several other elements. Duncan began his career, as did so

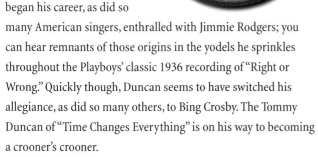

many American singers, enthralled with Jimmie Rodgers; you can hear remnants of those origins in the yodels he sprinkles throughout the Playboys' classic 1936 recording of "Right or Wrong." Quickly though, Duncan seems to have switched his allegiance, as did so many others, to Bing Crosby. The Tommy Duncan of "Time Changes Everything" is on his way to becoming a crooner's crooner.

This style of singing, particularly when compared to the blues, is often knocked as pretty and precise yet emotionless, lacking any real complexity. Duncan's vocals here stand such prejudices

on their heads. As he informs his ex that the heart she broke has healed at last, and extracts a lesson from this unexpected turn of events, his singing is both unadorned and all about its subtle adornments. His high, rich baritone toys gently with meter, adds vibrato on key words, stretches out others. Throughout, Duncan is tangibly holding himself in check, and the result is to heighten the intensity of what he says and what he's unable to admit. We can sense in his restraint just how much he has invested in this new philosophy—no life is static, he asserts, and he offers his newfound willingness to suspect such a lesson as proof. Yet in the bluesier spots, where his croon slips almost imperceptibly out of his grasp, we can sense that not as much time has passed as he wants to believe.

Time changes everything? Undoubtedly. But then how do we explain that sixty years later, Tommy Duncan is still as expressive a singer as American music has produced?—dc

19

I Don't Hurt Anymore, Hank Snow
Produced by Steve Sholes;
Written by Don Robertson and Jack Rollins
RCA Victor 47-5698   1954   #1 country (20 weeks)

If Lefty Frizzell, George Jones, or some other hardcore honky-tonker had recorded "I Don't Hurt Anymore," they likely would have played the song for what it has to say about self-deception. "I say I don't hurt anymore," their versions would have hinted, "but my voice reveals I still hurt very, very much." Hank Snow's "I Don't Hurt Anymore," a country chart topper for five months in

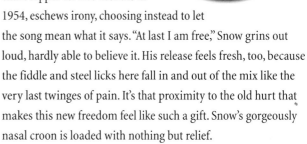

1954, eschews irony, choosing instead to let the song mean what it says. "At last I am free," Snow grins out loud, hardly able to believe it. His release feels fresh, too, because the fiddle and steel licks here fall in and out of the mix like the very last twinges of pain. It's that proximity to the old hurt that makes this new freedom feel like such a gift. Snow's gorgeously nasal croon is loaded with nothing but relief.

In some critical circles, where despair is prized more than joy, such a straightforward approach would probably be dismissed as insipid, or worse, naïve. For those of us who've had our hearts broken and lived to tell about it—who know what it feels like to say "I wanted to die," and then to know the darkness has lifted—well, for us, "I Don't Hurt Anymore" sounds a lot like a miracle. Or at least a fresh start.—dc

20

I Love You So Much, It Hurts, Floyd Tillman
Produced by Art Satherley; Written by Floyd Tillman
Columbia 20430   1948   #5 country

No country record tapped the zeitgeist of the American people during World War II more than Floyd Tillman's 1944 hit, "Each Night at Nine." The song depicts a solitary GI in his barracks just before "Taps," dreaming of his wife and kids some 2,000 miles away. Yet as much of an impact as "Each Night at Nine" had on the public, it wasn't until the 1948 release of "I Love You So Much, It Hurts" that Tillman, who served as a radio operator during the fighting, expressed his deepest feelings about the experience. "After the war, I was so happy to have my freedom that I wrote 'I Love You So Much, It Hurts,' " he told interviewer Patsi Bale Cox. "The song is really about love and freedom."

As Tillman points out, "I Love You So Much, It Hurts" is indeed a love song, and one with legs, as subsequent versions of the tune by Red Foley, Perry Como, Vic Damone, and Andy Williams attest. But the eerie mix of heartache and rapture in Floyd's bluesy baritone when he sings, "I'm so afraid to go to bed at night, afraid of losing you," suggests that more than just romance is at stake. The bittersweet lilt of the twin fiddles that open the record confirm as much. Commingled with Tillman's tears of joy over having come through the war is his grief for all the lives that were lost, and with that sorrow, the realization that freedom—the freedom to live and the freedom to love—is fragile and not for a second to be taken for granted.—bfw

21

Folsom Prison Blues, Johnny Cash
& the Tennessee Two
Produced by Sam Phillips; Written by Johnny Cash
Sun 232   1956   #4 country

One of the great prison songs, and one that's about two different, though related, prisons. The first, and most infamous, is the one in which Cash is doing time for shooting a man in Reno, "just to watch him die." The second, and ultimately more oppressive, prison is the confinement of class, particularly the feelings of alienation that attend it. It isn't so much the murder he committed that tortures Johnny as how those rich folks smoking cigars in that fancy dining car "keep a-movin' "; as the inexorable "boom-chicka" beat of the Tennessee Two attests, that train doesn't stop for poor sods like Cash, a sharecropper's son. It's the unfairness of it all, and especially the way those fat cats ride on the backs of people like him, that sticks in Johnny's craw. Even more than the stone walls and steel bars that hold him, it's that injustice that makes him hang his head and cry.

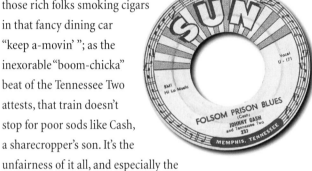

Then again, that corrosive snarl of his sounds like it could be just enough to send that locomotive barreling straight to hell.—bfw

22

Mama Tried, Merle Haggard & the Strangers
Produced by Ken Nelson; Written by Merle Haggard
Capitol 2219   1968   #1 country (4 weeks)

23

The Fugitive, Merle Haggard & the Strangers
Produced by Ken Nelson;
Written by Liz Anderson and Casey Anderson
Capitol 5803   1966   #1 country (1 week)

Country music has seen its share of rebels over the years—from rough and rowdy Jimmie Rodgers and rollin' stone Hank Williams to the immutable Man in Black and those media-christened outlaws "Waylon and Willie and the boys." But among the music's bona fide icons, only Merle Haggard comes close to embodying the archetypal outlaw-hero who actually lives outside the law yet manages to achieve a certain nobility. Hag's rap sheet (burglary, petty theft, etc.) hardly qualifies him for "social bandit" status à la Pretty Boy Floyd or Railroad Bill, both Robin Hood–style desperadoes who broke the law in service of some higher ideal. Yet between his unflinching public struggle to cope with the stigma of his imprisonment and his career-long, almost quixotic indifference to prevailing norms and expectations, Merle is the nearest thing to an outlaw-hero that country music has known.

Much of what makes Haggard's persona so compelling is the mix of candor and self-awareness that suffuses his records. "I turned twenty-one in prison doin' life without parole / No one could steer me right but mama tried," he confesses, referring to the three years of hard time (out of a possible fifteen) he did in San Quentin during the late fifties. Not only does Merle accept responsibility for what he's done, he evinces plenty of empathy for his God-fearing, widowed mama as well. His band is right there with him; the bluesy jabs traded by guitarists James Burton and Roy Nichols echo Merle's regret over his actions just as Red Simpson's tender fingerpicking rings with pathos for Merle's mother.

Unlike "Mama Tried," Merle didn't write "The Fugitive," but he could have. "I raised a lot of cane back in my younger days / While mama used to pray my crops would fail," he begins, his sober phrasing all but free of its usual Lefty-inspired curlicues and slides. "Now I'm a hunted fugitive with just two ways / Outrun the law or spend my life in jail." Hag didn't spend any time on the lam before he got locked up (he and his buddies were too drunk to run after they tried to knock off that Bakersfield roadhouse), but as he sang a few months after "The Fugitive" hit #1, he knew what it felt like to be a "Branded Man." And not just as an ex-con, but as a loner who followed his own, often maddeningly inscrutable, moral and emotional compass. From perennial Nashville outsider ("My Own Kind of Hat") to hippie-hectoring pot smoker ("Okie from Muskogee") to proponent of tolerance ("Irma Jackson") to jingoistic sloganeer ("The Fightin' Side of Me"), Merle has found that down every road there's always one more run-in.

"I'd like to settle down but they won't let me," he complains to the restless cadences of the Strangers rhythm section, and doubtless he's felt that way his entire life. At the same time, he knows it's not in his makeup to take the line of least resistance, and it's that self-awareness that makes him so heroic in the first place. Over the years everything from poverty and prison to creditors and critics has made him feel like a fugitive, but the one thing Merle's almost never run from is himself.—bfw

24

Someday, Steve Earle

Produced by Emory Gordy Jr. and Tony Brown;
Written by Steve Earle
MCA 52920   1986   #28 country

"Someday" is for anyone who has ever felt suffocated by the place where they grew up. "There ain't a lot that you can do in this town," Steve Earle observes in a drawl that might as well be a snarl. "You drive down to the lake and then you turn back around." The specifics of that weekend-night ritual differ depending on where you grew up—if you're from a rural county seat, you might've looped between the square and the local drive-in; if you grew up in a working-class suburb, you may have cruised up and down the main drag—but that restless pull to beat the boredom and, what's more, to test your own limits instead of accepting the ones you've been handed, is pretty much the same no matter where you're from.

Earle grew up outside San Antonio, where he was raised on a west Texas tradition of twang that included such luminaries as Lefty Frizzell, Roy Orbison, and Buddy Holly. At eighteen, he took off for good—first to Houston, where he discovered Dylan-influenced singer-songwriters like Townes Van Zandt and Jerry Jeff Walker, then to Nashville. There he landed a gig as Guy Clark's bassist, wrote songs for a publishing company, cut a few neo-rockabilly sides, and recorded an unreleased album for Epic, all before signing with MCA.

Working closely with guitarist Richard Bennett and producers Tony Brown and Emory Gordy Jr., Earle finally scored a Top Ten hit in 1986, with the country-rockin' "Guitar Town," a record that was his journey from Texas to Nashville, writ large. An immediate critic's darling, Earle was included among a group of country acts then being hailed as "New Traditionalists." The description was certainly apt. Earle was, and remains, traditional in the most vital (which is to say, least static) sense of that word. His work clearly draws thematic, musical and spiritual inspiration from the past. But his version of country music suggests a possible future for the genre, as well—a future that transforms that past to serve the thematic, musical, and spiritual needs of our present.

That impulse for a tomorrow of your own creation is what "Someday" is all about. It captures what a dream deferred feels like as well as any record ever made—and, worse, it knows what it feels like never even to have had the chance to discover what your dreams might be in the first place. "You go to school and you learn to read and write / So you can walk into the county bank and sign away your life," Earle sighs with disgust before declaring "I know there's a better way." As stabs of electric guitar battle with Paul Franklin's pedal steel, an acoustic guitar keeps a hard time. When the drums thunder in at the chorus, you wouldn't be at all surprised if Earle's next line was swiped straight from Bruce Springsteen: "This town's a death trap . . . baby, we were born to run."

Run where, though? This isn't New Jersey. Out here where Earle pumps gas and counts out-of-state plates, there's no Manhattan beckoning just across the river, not even an Atlantic City down the shore. There's just a highway disappearing into someday, a '67 Chevy, and a gnawing in your gut.—dc

25

Life's Little Ups and Downs, Charlie Rich
Produced by Billy Sherrill; Written by Margaret Ann Rich
Epic 5-10492   1969   #41 country

A working marriage meets the world of work, and lives to tell about it.

"I don't know how to tell her that I didn't get that raise in pay today," Charlie Rich begins, but you know that once his wife hears the weariness in his voice and sees his slumped shoulders and

teary eyes, he won't have to tell her anything. He's beating himself up because that dress his wife wanted, the celebration they'd planned, the new house—all their hopes and dreams—will have to be put on hold one more time . . . because of him. Rich knew this sort of guilt and frustration only too well. By the time Billy Sherrill signed him to Epic in 1967, he'd been flirting with stardom and striking out for nearly a decade—his two middling pop hits, "Lonely Weekends" and "Mohair Sam," teased him with a success that always eluded him. That disappointment contributed to a familiar litany of problems: a family that endured a constant state of financial anxiety, an on-again-off-again battle with the bottle, and a marriage that had seen more than its share of hard times.

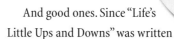

And good ones. Since "Life's Little Ups and Downs" was written by his wife, Margaret Ann, Charlie Rich would have understood the song as a promise that she'd always love him, even if his career never took off. At the same time, though, the song let Margaret Ann blow her own horn. "She wears a gold ring on her finger, and I'm so glad that it's mine," the song concludes. By putting those words in her husband's mouth, she reminded Charlie of all she'd done for him and how grateful he should feel for his supportive and longsuffering wife. After all, she was the one who'd taken his demos to Sun and kicked off his career in the first place.

Yet Margaret Ann was motivated to write "Life's Little Ups and Downs" out of a sense of *her* failure, not her husband's. Seeking some modicum of financial stability for a household that included three children, she approached Shelby Singleton in 1969 in search of a publishing deal. He praised her songs but declined to offer her a contract. Her work was just a little too uptown he said, "too flowery," for any mass-market appeal. When she went home to tell Charlie about the rejection—just as he'd come home empty-handed, so many times before—she wrote a song that told the story of their lives together.

The song works because the basic outline of the Riches' story is so familiar. "Life has its little ups and downs, like ponies on a merry-go-round," Margaret Ann wrote, and even on paper her simile effectively nails the inevitability of life's highs and lows, not to mention the way a market economy can keep smacking you down right back where you started, love and hard work be damned.

Charlie's recording only heightens these issues. Sherrill's spare, bluesy production throbs like a headache that isn't going away anytime soon. In Rich's voice you can hear all the ambition and disappointment, all the love and obligation and guilt, of a real marriage—and it doesn't matter whether you know the details of the Riches' relationship or not. "She wears a gold ring on her finger and I'm so glad its mine," Charlie repeats at the end, and he sounds both desperate and fortified, up and down, all at once.

Within a few years, of course, Rich would have success beyond his wildest dreams, and Margaret Ann and Charlie would face a whole new set of problems, not to mention many of the old ones. In the meantime, "Life's Little Ups and Downs" was one more chart dud, albeit a particularly poignant one for the Riches considering the song's theme of a love that perseveres in the face of persistent economic strain. Indeed, when Charlie Rich died in 1995, "Life's Little Ups and Downs" was widely hailed as his finest moment. And songwriter Margaret Ann Rich was still his wife.—dc

26

The Last Letter, Rex Griffin
Produced by Dave Kapp; Written by Rex Griffin
Decca 5383   1937   Pre-chart

"The Last Letter" has been recorded to devastating effect through the years by any number of singers (Jack Greene and Connie Smith cut particularly powerful versions), but Rex Griffin's original continues to set the standard.

Plaintive and spare, Griffin's record defines emotional isolation. There's no real chorus to the song, and in his version there's no backing band either. It's just Griffin alone and forsaken, singing as if he's given up hope that anyone might hear. His guitar 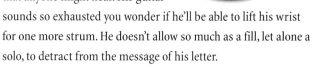 sounds so exhausted you wonder if he'll be able to lift his wrist for one more strum. He doesn't allow so much as a fill, let alone a solo, to detract from the message of his letter.

That letter has mostly been interpreted as a suicide note,

which is just the way he wants his lost love to take it. The singer is, it appears, an old man who must face his impending death alone, now that his younger lover has run off with a younger man. It's painfully obvious why she's gone; he can't satisfy her anymore, neither materially nor sexually—twin failings that blur into one: "I cannot offer you clothes that your young body craves."

By the time she reads his words, he writes, he'll be dead and gone. But the rest of his note makes it clear he hopes that's not true. He asks his lover questions ("What have I done that has made you so different and cold?"), encourages her return ("But if you say that you long to forever be mine, think of the heartaches, the tears and the sorrows you'll save"), and seeks her pity even as he lashes out ("Will you be happy when you are withered and old?")—all tactics designed to get her to come running before it's too late. Not before he kills himself, but before he dies of old age and a broken heart. Before he can whisper goodbye.—dc

27

Farewell Party, Gene Watson
Produced by Russ Reeder; Written by Lawton Williams
Capitol 4680   1979   #5 country

George Strait, John Anderson, and Ricky Skaggs get most of the credit for ushering in the neotraditionalist revival that saved country music from the mechanical bull of *Urban Cowboy*. As even a cursory glance at the charts from the early eighties attests, they deserve it. But that take on history also masks the fact that hard-core singers like Moe Bandy, Vern Gosdin, and John Conlee were already fighting the good fight back when the 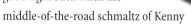 middle-of-the-road schmaltz of Kenny Rogers, Ronnie Milsap, and Dave & Sugar was ruling the country airwaves in the late seventies.

Gene Watson is another neotraditionalist torchbearer whose records provided throbbing testimony to the verities of sawdust-and-steel honky-tonk during those lean years. In "Farewell Party," his wrenching signature song, Watson plays a lovelorn man who's about to take his own life. "When the last breath of life is gone from my body, and my lips are as cold as the sea / When my friends gather 'round for my farewell party, won't you pretend you love me," he gulps in a tearful quaver. Kenny Malone's skittish cymbal and snare, Pig Robbins's tinkling piano, and Harold Bradley's teardrop guitar tread lightly around Watson as he utters this final, unattainable wish, his anguish aggravated by the realization that his wife will be only too glad to see him go.

What makes this weeper go down so smoothly—a crucial consideration for a honky-tonker angling for a spot on the slick playlists of late-seventies country radio—is Watson's bell-like tenor. It's an instrument as honeyed and pure as Glen Campbell's, but one that replaces the Hollywood cool of the Rhinestone Cowboy with a controlled desperation worthy of master balladeers Jack Greene and Conway Twitty, as well as Elvis Presley and the Statesmen's Jake Hess before them. Watson controls his voice until the last chorus, where, with Lloyd Green's steel blubbering away behind him and the heavenly harmonies of the Nashville Edition calling him home, he again imagines how happy his wife will be at his funeral. Wailing the final three words "when I'm gone" with the agony of someone who knows he'll never awaken from his dark night of the soul, Watson gets off a parting shot that, he hopes, will ring in her ears for all eternity.—bfw

28

Country Blues, Dock Boggs
No producer credited; Written by Dock Boggs
Brunswick 131   1927   Pre-chart

Critic Greil Marcus would have us believe that every Appalachian ballad recorded before the Second World War is a vestige of some mythical realm he calls the "old, weird America." Old, yes. Primitive, maybe. But much of the hillbilly music from that period 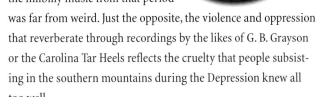 was far from weird. Just the opposite, the violence and oppression that reverberate through recordings by the likes of G. B. Grayson or the Carolina Tar Heels reflects the cruelty that people subsisting in the southern mountains during the Depression knew all too well.

Still, applied to singer–banjo player Dock Boggs's 1920s recordings, Marcus's construct is spot-on. Boggs's music *was* weird, his grinding voice the whir of a drill boring through bone, his finger-picked banjo owing more to the brooding blows of a Delta blues guitarist than to the good-time clawhammer banjoists of the day. Unvarnished even by prewar standards, Boggs's records, paradoxically, sound strangely modern compared to those of his peers.

Boggs's worldview, as Marcus has observed, was also ahead of its time. Like Hank Williams, he was a modernist, someone who took little solace in the institutions (family, church, etc.) that saw most of his neighbors through hard times. Boggs's music, which was as harsh and unyielding as the terrain that surrounded his Clinch Mountain home, cried out that all one could expect between the cradle and the grave was struggle in a world that offered neither encouragement nor the remotest hope of transcendence.

As stiff a draught of hillbilly existentialism as any ever recorded, "Country Blues" features only Boggs's banjo and vocals. He learned the song as "Hustling Gamblers," a variant of "Darling Cory" or "Little Maggie," from a rounder named Homer Crawford, but by the time Boggs had finished with it, adding verses and turning it into the story of *his* life, there was no mistaking to whom it belonged.

The action shifts abruptly between scenes of drinking, betrayal, and woe, including scrapes with fickle friends and a faithless lover, until Boggs ends up in jail, where whiskey weakens his body and images of pretty women addle his mind. Finally, with his banjo racing ahead of him just as it has throughout his inexorable descent, he arrives at the site of his own grave. "Go dig a hole in the meadow, good people / Go dig a hole in the ground / Come around all you good people / And see this poor rounder go down," he exhorts the town folk. Narrating one's own burial scene has been done before, and since. What's truly weird in Boggs's version is the way his unflinching banjo and raw, nasal whine present the spiritual abandonment that preceded his interment as an incontrovertible fact of life. Seventy-five years later, his resolve remains as eerie as it is astounding, the unflagging voice of a man who knows all along that he'll never get out of this world alive.—bfw

29

I'll Never Get Out of This World Alive,
Hank Williams with His Drifting Cowboys
Produced by Fred Rose; Written by Hank Williams and Fred Rose
MGM 11366   1953   #1 country (1 week)

In the years since Hank Williams's death, "I'll Never Get Out of This World Alive" has acquired a morbid notoriety, as if Hank were predicting his own impending demise. Eerily, the song was in the Top Ten the very week he died, and from there it climbed to #1.

But while the grim reputation is understandable, it obscures the fact that "I'll Never Get Out of This World Alive" is a comedy number, a novelty song about those times we've all experienced when nothing seems to go right. Its punch line title is swiped straight from W. C. Fields. Its "I've had a lot of luck and it's all been bad" anticipates that hilariously self-pitying *Hee Haw* set piece, "If it weren't for bad luck, I'd have no luck at all (Gloom, despair and agony on me)." And when Hank sings "If I jumped into the river, I'd probably drown," it's not because he's wishing for his own death (as he is in "Long, Gone Lonesome Blues") but simply because the lousy way things are going, it would just figure. The song's best lines—especially the bit about Hank's shoes being so holey he could tell you if a dime's heads or tails just by stepping on it—are prime examples of down-on-your-luck country humor. Jerry Rivers and Don Helms, on fiddle and steel guitar, respectively, provide the laugh track.

Still, there's no denying this humor leans heavily to the grim side. Turns out that, as a prediction, "I'll never get out of this world alive" is dead-on accurate. And not just for Hank Williams.—dc

30

Back in the Saddle Again, Gene Autry
Produced by Art Satherley;
Written by Gene Autry and Ray Whitley
OKeh 05080, Columbia 37010, Vocalion 05080,
Conqueror 9341   1939   Pre-chart

Country music knew two breeds of cowboy singers during the years immediately before and after World War II. On the one hand were the likes of Carl Sprague and Jules Verne Allen, men who'd actually done some roping and herding before they became recording artists. Their coarse, parched voices and easy way with cowboy slang left little doubt they'd known the rigors and isolation of the life they sang about. On the other hand were Hollywood stars like Gene Autry and Roy Rogers, some of whom

(though not Autry) had never seen the inside of a bunkhouse before they walked onto their first movie set. Nevertheless, it was the romanticized portrayal of riding the range proffered by these impersonators, and not the dusty, grueling life of the real ranch hands, that came to symbolize the spirit of freedom and adventure that people now associate with the old West.

"Back in the Saddle Again" is the quintessential cowboy anthem from the quintessential silver screen cowboy. It also hinges on a brilliant conceit. By suggesting that he was hopping *back* on his mount, Autry heads off questions about whether he'd ever been on a horse in the first place. Or, for that matter, about what he and his fellow buckaroos are doing carting along an orchestra with them on the trail. Not that anyone minded. The point was entertainment, not authenticity. When Gene, his voice splitting the difference between his heroes Jimmie Rodgers and Bing Crosby, croons genially about his horse, his six-gun, and sleeping under the stars, it's entertainment at its best. Especially with that jaunty accordion conjuring images of him bouncing up and down on his mount.

"Back in the Saddle" soon became Autry's signature song, as well as the theme for his radio and TV shows, which, along with his many movies and records, made him one of the most successful performers and entrepreneurs in country music history. The record's timing was perfect, coming as it did when many were still struggling to recover from the ravages of the Depression. Not only did Autry's reverie offer millions a budget-friendly, three-minute escape; with the saddle as a metaphor for prosperity, it gave countless breadwinners and their families hope that they too would soon be sitting pretty.—bfw

31

I Wanna Be a Cowboy's Sweetheart, Patsy Montana
Produced by Art Satherley; Written by Patsy Montana
OKeh 03010, Vocalion 03010,
Conqueror 8575   1935   Pre-chart

Well before she borrowed its melody for "I Wanna Be a Cowboy's Sweetheart," Patsy Montana had been performing "Montana Plains," a one-word revision of her old boss Stuart Hamblen's

"Texas Plains," as a kind of namesake theme song. The faintly polka-sounding western number must have been a real crowd pleaser for her out on the road, but you can easily imagine how it might have furrowed a few brows. Playing guitar and decked out in a cowboy hat and western skirt, she'd plant one leg up on a chair and sing Hamblen's original words—"I want to feel a saddle horse between my legs, ridin' him out on the range / Just to kick him in the side, just to show his step and pride"—followed by one of her exhilarated, Jimmie Rodgers–styled yodels. Quite a titillating picture. Maybe that's one of the

reasons that, in 1934 while a member of Chicago's National Barn Dance, she recast the song's melody and content in a way that toned down her independence and sexuality while playing up the romantic attachment her audience would have expected.

On the other hand, she didn't exactly overemphasize that attachment. Years later Montana explained that she actually wrote "Cowboy's Sweetheart" because she was a "love-sick lonely 'cowgirl,'" out on the road and missing her new husband. Well, maybe, but that's not what the record sounds like. Even when she says she wants to be a cowboy's sweetheart, the cowboy comes off as just a means to an end. In the first verse she says she wants to be some cowboy's sweetheart, but she proceeds to sing longingly and at length of her heart's real desires: roping and riding on the plains, hearing the coyote's howl, watching the setting western sun. All pieces of a life good little girls were denied—at least without men by their sides (a state of affairs of which Montana, the only daughter among eleven children, would have been keenly aware). During the second verse, her cowboy doesn't even get a mention; it's all riding Ol' Paint, feeling the wind in her face, sleeping out under the moon, strumming her guitar, and singing yodel-ay-hee-hee. "Oh *that's* the life that I love," she concludes, and the only thing more unrestrained than her yodel is the smile you know is just beaming off her face.

Sweetheart, schmeetheart. What Patsy really wants is to *be* a cowboy. Free and self-sufficient, unbound. That her single is reputed to be the first-ever million seller by a female country artist—during the Depression, no less—shows that more than a few folks, male and female alike, wished they could ride along.—dc

32

Don't Come Home A'Drinkin' (with Lovin' on Your Mind), Loretta Lynn
Produced by Owen Bradley;
Written by Loretta Lynn and Peggy Sue Wills
Decca 32045   1966   #1 country (1 week)

33

The Pill, Loretta Lynn
Produced by Owen Bradley;
Written by Loretta Lynn, Don McHan, and T. D. Bayless
MCA 40358   1975   #5 country; #70 pop

It happens all the time. A guy goes out with the boys for the night, comes home drunk and horny, and heads straight for his woman's bed. Loretta Lynn knows the story only too well. As she relates in her autobiography, *Coal Miner's Daughter,* her husband "Mooney" often stumbled into their bedroom after a night of revelry in search of satisfaction. By the time she and her sister wrote "Don't Come Home A'Drinkin' (with Lovin' on Your Mind)," Loretta—a mother of six and, at twenty-nine, a grandmother—had had enough.

"Liquor and love they just don't mix, leave the bottle or me behind," she warns in her feistiest back-hollow drawl while the A-Teamers working the session weigh in on hubby's options. Pig Robbins's pealing piano and Hal Rugg's slurring steel make the case for the high times to be had in the honky-tonks, but as their voices give way to Grady Martin's stinging guitar barbs, there's little doubt Loretta's man will be hanging around the house more often. At least if he knows what's good for him.

It was no coincidence that Lynn's growing assertiveness coincided with the first stirrings of the women's movement. Betty Friedan's *The Feminine Mystique* came out just as Loretta's career was taking off, and the National Organization for Women (NOW) came into being three years later, right as "Don't Come Home A'Drinkin'" became her first #1. Lynn has always rejected the feminist tag in interviews (she once nodded off while sharing a couch with, *and listening to*, Friedan on *The David Frost Show*). Yet there's no denying that many of her recordings tapped the heady spirit of the early women's movement.

Loretta's sexual politics took an even more proactive turn with "The Pill," a song she recorded in December 1972. Nevertheless, perhaps fearing that its plug for the reproductive rights of women would put off male radio programmers, MCA didn't release the single till 1975. It's easy to see why—rather than just fending off a licentious lover, Loretta seizes control of the bedroom. Bemoaning all those years she had to sit home with the kids while her man was out running wild, she tells him, "There's gonna be some changes made, right here on nursery hill / You've set this chicken your last time, 'cause now I've got the pill." Judging by the way she bolts for the chorus as the rhythm section scrambles to keep up, Loretta's ready for some high times of her own. Exulting in more than just her freedom from raising babies, she's relishing the prospect of worry-free sex, and lots of it. Granted, and as she admits in *Coal Miner's Daughter*, Loretta didn't start taking the pill until after Mooney got clipped (her term for his vasectomy), and then she used it just to regulate her periods. But when she clucks, "The feeling good comes easy now," you can bet it's because she knew the release of which she sings.—bfw

34

20/20 Vision, Jimmy Martin
& the Sunny Mountain Boys
Produced by Steve Sholes; Written by Joe Allison and Milton Estes
RCA Victor 5958   1954   Did not chart

In 1949, twenty-two-year-old Jimmy Martin lit out for Nashville from his Tennessee mountain home with one goal—he was going to meet Bill Monroe and win a spot in his band. In preparation, Martin says he learned every Blue Grass Boy guitar lick by heart. He even memorized each lead vocal, not to mention all three harmony parts, so he'd be prepared to fill any hole Monroe might have. As luck had it, Monroe was looking to replace his lead singer, Mac Wiseman, who was planning to depart for a solo career. After glad-handing his way backstage at the Opry, Martin confronted his hero for an audition, and when it was over, fiddler

Chubby Wise reportedly exclaimed, "Ah Lordy, Bill, I thought Lester [Flatt] had it, but he can't touch this boy." Martin got the job.

He quickly began contributing changes to his new boss's sound. Martin had an energetic and bluesy singing style, influenced as much by honky-tonkers as bluegrassers—he liked to throw a sharp break into his voice on key words; he'd slide from one note to the next on others—and he sang higher leads than earlier Blue Grass Boys had. Impressed, Monroe began to break and slide his vocals too and to push his already sky-high harmonies up into the stratosphere. Additionally, Martin's hard-driving rhythm guitar style inspired Monroe to develop his trademark "chop" rhythm on the mandolin to keep up. Today, when bluegrass fans talk about "high lonesome," they're referring to the sound Monroe refined with Jimmy Martin on haunting early fifties sides like "I'm Blue, I'm Lonesome," "In the Pines," and "Sitting Alone in the Moonlight," among many others. Any fair accounting of the bluegrass creation story must reserve a place at Bill Monroe's right hand, alongside Flatt and Scruggs, for Jimmy Martin.

Though they would continue to record together sporadically through 1955, Martin left his mentor for a solo career in 1951. Eventually, he wound up in the Detroit area and, working with Bobby and Sonny Osborne, became a favorite of the southerners who'd left the cotton fields back home for the assembly lines up north. "20/20 Vision," cut in 1954 at Martin's first (and only) session for RCA, was one side of the new band's first single. The song's classic cheating theme and fiddler Red Taylor's honky-tonkish kick off, together with Martin's vocal attack, illustrates his debt to more commercial forms of country music. Bending notes and biting down on key words, he sounds something like a young George Jones might've if he'd ever fronted a bluegrass band with a sore throat.

On the record, Martin says he's been to the doctor to have his vision checked. He's sure he must be blind to have missed the way his lover cheated, but the doc says his eyes are just fine. "I knew that she cheated, I knew all the time," Martin chokes out, feeling his way over every word. Still, he hadn't seen it coming—hadn't *allowed* himself to see it—a clear case of the sort of denial sociologist Diane Vaughan calls knowing without knowing. "Twenty-twenty vision, and walkin' 'round blind," he concludes over and over, as Bobby and Sonny commiserate with him to create softly piercing trio harmonies. It's a hell of a thing, though. Now that she's gone, he can't help but see it all perfectly, a high-lonesome movie playing over and over through "the eyes of [his] mind."—dc

35

Blue Yodel (T for Texas), Jimmie Rodgers
Produced by Ralph Peer;
Written by Jimmie Rodgers
Victor 21142   1928   Pre-chart

36

Cool Drink of Water Blues, Tommy Johnson
No producer credited;
Written by Tommy Johnson
Victor 21279   1928   Pre-chart

Country music and the blues have always been close kin. This was most obviously the case during the Depression, when cowboy songs, blues, and stringband stomps could be heard side-by-side from the stages of variety theaters and traveling tent shows. All of them, as well as Tin Pan Alley and vaudeville favorites, turned up in the repertoires of the era's black and white songsters, who were only too quick to borrow and steal from each other. Tracing the lineages of these tangled strains of music, of attributing ownership of what to whom, is often tricky, to say the least.

One of the most striking cases of these uncertain origins came to light in Peter Guralnick's interview with Howlin' Wolf in *Feel Like Going Home*, in which the blues man claims that the yodeling of Jimmie Rodgers was the source of his hair-raising wail. Wolf surely heard the Singing Brakeman during the late twenties when, as a teenager, he lived and worked on the Dockery plantation in northwestern Mississippi. Yet Wolf's trademark howl also owes a debt to Tommy Johnson, a tremendously influential, if today relatively unsung, Delta blues singer. Johnson's lilting 1928 recording of "Cool Drink of Water Blues" provided the blueprint for Wolf's 1956 Chess single, "I Asked for Water (She Gave Me Gasoline)," right down to its lupine moan. Play Johnson's blues back-to-back with Rodgers's "Blue Yodel," and the similarities between the two records, released just

months apart, render arguments about Wolf's "real" source as so much academic hairsplitting.

Their shared twelve-bar, AAB format (swap out lines from one record and see if they don't fit perfectly into the other) is obvious enough. So is the way the two Mississippians draw on the same storehouse of verses and lyric fragments that virtually all of their blues and songster contemporaries did. Furthermore, in something of a reversal of roles, "Blue Yodel" finds Rodgers playing an outlaw akin to Stackalee, an antihero more popular with black than white audiences, while in "Cool Drink" Johnson adopts the persona of a freight-hopping rounder much like the one who frequents many of Rodgers's railroad songs. What's truly uncanny, though, is the resemblance between Johnson's crying, field holler–inspired falsetto and Rodgers's blue yodel, singular devices that each man tacked onto the end of vocal lines to heighten their emotional impact.

Of course, Rodgers's more measured diction, something of a cross between the parlor singing of Vernon Dalhart and the blackface minstrelsy of Emmett Miller, evinces fewer of the hallmarks of African-derived music—the coarse, dirty timbres and such—employed by Johnson. Rodgers's "Blue Yodel" also sounds jauntier than the bluesman's rhythmically heavier "Cool Drink," although Johnson's music is quite lyrical, even country-sounding, compared to the brooding, declamatory style of his Delta counterparts. Indeed, as accompanied here by Ishman Bracey and Charlie McCoy on mandolin and guitar, Johnson's music resembles that of black stringbands like the Mississippi Sheiks, who not only played hillbilly material at white dances, but also recorded tunes based on those of the Singing Brakeman and other country and pop acts. In other words, despite their differences, "Blue Yodel" and "Cool Drink of Water Blues" display an undeniable affinity, most notably between Rodgers's and Johnson's vocal contortions, and melodicism, and their manifest theatricality.

None of this is all that surprising considering that the two men were born just a year apart and grew up a few miles from one another in central Mississippi. It's almost certain that each would have heard the other's records, even if establishing direct influence at this point is impossible. What we do know for sure is that, after 1928, the two singers' careers diverged greatly. Rodgers's "Blue Yodel" sold more than a million copies, making him a celebrity and affording him the chance to leave behind a sizable body of work before his death from tuberculosis in 1933.

Johnson, by contrast, worked just one more session, despite the fact that he was a star of the magnitude of Delta heavy hitters Charley Patton and Son House, and that he performed publicly pretty much until he died of complications related to chronic alcoholism in 1956.—bfw

37

Singing the Blues, Marty Robbins

Produced by Don Law;
Written by Melvin Endsley
Columbia 4-21545   1956   #1 country (13 weeks); #17 pop

"What kind of singer are you?" Marion Keisker asked Elvis Presley when he first showed up at Memphis's Sun Records. "I sing all kinds," he said. Nearly a decade earlier in Arizona, a young Marty Robbins was himself trying to break into the music business, and it's easy to imagine him answering that question the same way. As Robbins, a musical kindred spirit to Presley if ever there was one, explained to writer Bob Allen in a 1981 interview, "The first road show [I did], I did everything. Western songs, Perry Como songs, Johnny Ray songs, Ernest Tubb songs, Roy Acuff, Eddy Arnold. Everybody's songs." Robbins pursued such wide-ranging instincts throughout his career. By the time he died in 1982, he'd recorded songs by everyone from Sammy Cahn and Hank Williams to Fats Domino and the Beatles.

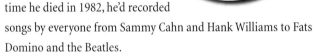

This willingness to follow his interests all over the musical map helps explain why it was Robbins—before virtually any of his country contemporaries—who saw the emergence of rock & roll as an artistic opportunity rather than a threat. Specifically, he grasped that the problems Presley posed for country music came with built-in solutions. In late 1954, Marty cut a fiddle-fueled version of "That's All Right," a cover that retained the phrasing and much of the easy energy of Elvis's regionally successful Sun debut. Given Presley's well-documented and nearly immediate impact on the country scene, this move hardly seems prescient today—until you remember that when Marty's "That's All Right" cracked the country Top Ten, Presley remained all but unknown on country radio, his first charting single still a couple of months

away. And Robbins once again had his ear to the ground for his follow-up to "That's All Right," a rollicking country version of "Maybelline" (# 9 country) the very week that Chuck Berry's single ("Maybellene") debuted on the R&B chart.

By the time Robbins recorded his next single in the fall of 1955, he'd completely absorbed the new rock & roll into his own brand of country music. From its first notes (a staggering lick on acoustic guitar), "Singing the Blues" sounds like it could have come from Memphis, particularly that nifty little electric guitar solo and that flight across the keys, courtesy of Floyd Cramer, which might've been a Jerry Lee rip-off if only "Whole Lot of Shakin'" hadn't still been more than a year away.

Not that you'd ever mistake this for anything but a country record. After all, there's a steel guitar wanging away throughout, and while it's clear this singer already knows Elvis by heart, it's equally clear that Robbins has sung his share of western songs and songs by Ernest Tubb, Eddy Arnold (check out that catch in his voice as he breaks into a near yodel), Roy Acuff, and, yeah, even Perry Como. It doesn't go far enough, then, to observe that Marty Robbins sang all kinds. Like Elvis, he sang all kinds *all at once*—even when he was singing the blues.—dc

38

(There'll Be) Peace in the Valley (for Me),
Red Foley with the Sunshine Boys Quartet

Produced by Paul Cohen;
Written by Reverend Thomas A. Dorsey
Decca 9–46319   1951   #5 country

Most discussions of Red Foley's ballad style focus on his velvety, Bing Crosby–inspired crooning. That influence is certainly evident, and gloriously so, in his rendition of "Peace in the Valley." But that's not all there was to Foley's style. His recording of the old gospel standard suggests he was also conversant with the vocal techniques of black gospel quartets like the Dixie Hummingbirds and the Rebert Harris–led Soul Stirrers, both of which were widely popular when Foley moved to Nashville to join the Grand Ole Opry in 1946.

Foley's reading of the song owes as much to the Hummingbirds' 1948 recording of "We Shall Walk through the Valley in Peace" (an earlier version of which Thomas A. Dorsey rewrote as "Peace in the Valley") as it does to Crosby or anyone else. Granted, Foley's record lacks the pressing rhythms, the groaning and falsetto vocals, and the ad-lib testifying that are hallmarks of black gospel singing. But he does make liberal use of melisma, and the Sunshine Boys achieve a vocal weave more akin to the era's black quartets than to white southern gospel groups like the Blackwood Brothers or the Stamps Quartet. And there's no mistaking Grady Martin's bluesy guitar work here as anything but R&B on its way to becoming rockabilly and, after that, rock & roll.

It's a safe bet that it was this blend of black and white styles that drew a young Elvis Presley to Foley's music and that later moved Elvis to make "Peace in the Valley" his own. But Elvis—and, for that matter, Foley and the members of his predominantly white audience—probably missed the dual meaning the song held for black listeners. Red might have been referring to his heavenly reward when, with a mix of sorrow and hope, he sang, "Oh, well I'm tired and so weary, but I must go along / Till the Lord will come and call me away." But the spiritual from which Dorsey, formerly a ribald bluesman, cribbed "Peace in the Valley" wasn't just alluding to some pie-in-the-sky hereafter. Like so many of their black counterparts, the "black and unknown bards" (to borrow poet James Weldon Johnson's phrase) who created the spiritual were engaging in masking or double voicing. They were speaking of both eternal glory *and* the here-and-now, about liberation, and about God's role in their struggle to change and, ultimately, dismantle the social and political structures that kept black people down. (For the record, Dorsey always maintained he wrote "Peace in the Valley" while thinking about World War II.)

This tension between "the already and the not yet," between the real and the ideal, has long been a central theme in black preaching and spirituals, and one that you can hear in Rebert Harris's sublime groaning on the Soul Stirrers' earlier recording of "Peace in the Valley." It's just ironic that Foley, a noted conservative (and Pat Boone's future father-in-law) would have helped carry this message at a time when the freedom movement was about to start loosening the grip that Jim Crow had on black southerners. And yet, as they say, God works in mysterious ways.—bfw

39

A Satisfied Mind, Porter Wagoner
Produced by Si Siman and Porter Wagoner;
Written by Red Hayes and Jack Rhodes
RCA Victor 47-6105   1955   #1 country (4 weeks)

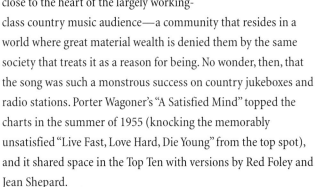

"A Satisfied Mind" expresses one of country music's defining sentiments—money can't buy happiness, and, at any rate, "I'm richer by far with a satisfied mind." While people at every rung of the American class ladder give lip service to this sentiment, it lies particularly close to the heart of the largely working-class country music audience—a community that resides in a world where great material wealth is denied them by the same society that treats it as a reason for being. No wonder, then, that the song was such a monstrous success on country jukeboxes and radio stations. Porter Wagoner's "A Satisfied Mind" topped the charts in the summer of 1955 (knocking the memorably unsatisfied "Live Fast, Love Hard, Die Young" from the top spot), and it shared space in the Top Ten with versions by Red Foley and Jean Shepard.

It's Wagoner's version, though, that remains best known today. That's good because it's just plain the best. There is a mournfulness to this recording that's missing from so many of the others, a palpable sense of frustrated yearning that emphasizes the circular nature of the song's advice—the path to satisfaction, Wagoner says, is to have a satisfied mind. But how do you achieve that? Clearly, money isn't the answer. Friendship, love, and faith all seem important, but we knew that going in. Whatever the secret, Porter's not telling.

Probably because he doesn't know. If he did, everything here, from those pained trio harmonies and Don Warden's sobbing steel guitar to Porter's own strained delivery, wouldn't sound so beat down. That's why it's hard to believe Porter when he asserts at the close, "When it comes my time, I'll leave this old world with a satisfied mind."—dc

40

Blue Moon of Kentucky, Bill Monroe
& His Blue Grass Boys
Produced by Paul Cohen; Written by Bill Monroe
Decca 9-29289   1954   Did not chart

41

Blue Moon of Kentucky, Bill Monroe
& His Blue Grass Boys
Produced by Art Satherley; Written by Bill Monroe
Columbia 37888   1947   Did not chart

42

Blue Moon of Kentucky, Elvis Presley, Scotty & Bill
Produced by Sam Phillips; Written by Bill Monroe
Sun 209   1954   Did not chart

Working with guitarist Scotty Moore, bassist Bill Black, and producer Sam Phillips, Elvis Presley had already cut "That's All Right," a cover of Arthur Crudup's blues original that didn't sound a thing like the blues or, for that matter, like anything they'd ever heard. When DJ Dewey Phillips played an acetate of the recording over the radio, the phone lines lit up. Sam said they needed a B side before it could be released as a single. Elvis, Scotty, and Bill needed to prove "That's All Right" hadn't been a fluke.

But nothing seemed to click. They'd tried out practically every song they knew and were beginning to wonder if they'd ever again catch the spark when Black started slapping his bass and singing "Blue Moon of Kentucky" in a silly falsetto. He was only playing the clown—as bassist/comedian in the Starlite Wranglers, a western swing styled band that he and Scotty were in, this wasn't unusual for him. But this time Elvis joined in the fun, Scotty too, and all of a sudden they knew they had it. "Hell, that's different," Sam Phillips famously told the trio after one early take that July. "That's a pop song now, nearly about."

"Different" understates the case considerably. In the original 1946 recording of the song, Monroe asks a blue moon to shine on a woman who has cheated on him, wherever she may be. Precisely why he wants the moon to shine on her is uncertain. It's quite clear, however, that he feels hopeless. Blue moons only come along once in a, uh, blue moon, after all, and he knows this one isn't going to stick around any longer than his girl did. The sheer futility of his request reveals why Monroe's simple mandolin solo sounds like it's crying and why Monroe himself sings "blue

moon" like he's sobbing "boohoo." The record is a waltz, but Monroe sounds like he'll never dance again.

Presley, on the other hand, sounds like he can barely stand still long enough to finish the song. In their version, Elvis, Scotty, Bill, and Sam add a giddy and unforgettable opening ("Blue moon, blue moon, blue moon / keep-a shinin' bright"), provide an explanation for the request (Elvis wants the moon to light the way for his lover's return), and delete any mention of the woman's infidelity. Singing around Scotty's Chet Atkins–inspired fills, Elvis bangs out the rhythm on his guitar, carrying on as if he has the world on a string, as if the moon and the girl are all behind him. The point of the performance becomes its own sense of discovery. This "Blue Moon of Kentucky" doesn't invest itself in the words, as Monroe's did; it ignores them. It revels in taking a song Elvis had loved all his life and reinventing it with a rocking sound even he didn't quite understand.

Supposedly, it took several years for country music to come to terms with rockabilly records like Elvis Presley's "Blue Moon of Kentucky." It took Bill Monroe 'til Labor Day. When he heard Elvis's debut record that summer, he grasped its importance immediately. Partly he was just a savvy businessman. After all, he'd written "Blue Moon of Kentucky" in an attempt to recapture the Top Five chart success of his biggest hit, "Kentucky Waltz." When Monroe played Presley's record for Carter Stanley that August ("You better do that number tomorrow if you want to sell some records," Monroe reportedly advised), he was doing the Stanley Brothers a favor, sure, but he was also working his publishing. Monroe was present the next day when the Stanley Brothers cut a marvelous 4/4 recording of "Blue Moon of Kentucky," one that retains Presley's repeated "Blue moon, blue moon, blue moon" at the top and spotlights the boogie-woogie picking of Charlie Cline, one of Monroe's Blue Grass Boys.

Next it was Monroe's turn. The performance he turned in the following weekend proves he wasn't only out to cash in on a fad. The new interest in "Blue Moon of Kentucky" must have stroked Monroe's ego a bit—cutting his song was certainly a compliment, and Presley hadn't merely copied the Blue Grass Boys' sound either, as had certain other admirers. On the other hand, the song had become one of his signature numbers over the years, and all the attention being paid to someone else's recording of it surely must have challenged Monroe's competitive personality, not to mention motivated the musician in him. He had something to prove. His new version of "Blue Moon of Kentucky" would not only need to out-lonesome his classic original; it would need to out-rock, to use the language of our times, this Presley kid.

Monroe began the song once again as a waltz, but it wasn't the same. For one thing, there are three fiddles sawing away now, not one, and they sound like the wind picking up just before a storm. Monroe's singing has a new assurance and force, the result of eight more years of living and hard work. So when he goes high and lonesome here, he sounds both more in charge of his emotions and more enslaved to them. Then, turning on a thrillingly thin dime, the song floors it to 4/4. Sick of waiting for this girl to return, he roars down the road to bring her home, the moon racing to keep up. Monroe's mandolin, locked into the record's new fierce rhythm, fires off a solo that starts to cry, like his original, then changes its mind, dances a step or two, and shouts, "Look what I can do!"

At the end of the record, Monroe still hasn't found his love, but he's found a new way to look. When his mandolin snaps the record to a whiplash close, it feels as if earth's rotation has been halted. That blue moon hovers in place, shining there in the Kentucky sky under Monroe's control. In the glow you can imagine the father of bluegrass music grinning to himself and thinking: "Top *that*."—dc

43

Blue Suede Shoes, Carl Perkins

Produced by Sam Phillips; Written by Carl Perkins
Sun 234   1956   #1 country (3 weeks); #2 pop; #2 R&B

Carl Perkins counts it off as his band skitters along behind, all of them full of a nervous energy that's bound to cut loose. Dancing across the room to the accompaniment of his own bluesy country-boogie licks, Perkins defines the rockabilly ethos about as clearly as it can be: "You can do anything, but lay off-a my blue suede shoes." Instantly it's as if everyone in the joint has known him for years, lived next door to him, worked beside him, dated his sister, maybe even smiled at him in the mirror. They know full well he's so crazy about these shoes because they're about the only material thing he has that's worth a damn, and they know the reason they're blue suede is the same reason he's shouting at the top of his lungs—he wants the world to notice. Everything else he has—his house (which he doesn't even own) and his car (which doesn't run but half the time), even his name (which his boss apparently thinks is Damnit Perkins)—is strictly no account. But, man, check out those shoes! He deliberately exaggerates the braggadocio for comic effect, forcing everyone to smile when he comes bouncing by. Just the same, they're careful with him, too. Because they know him so well, they understand that around a man who needs to invest so much in something so small, you want to watch your step.

To the southern working-class audience of 1956, this hell of a fellow would have been a part of everyday life. Carl Perkins heard the key line from Johnny Cash and then heard it used again by a fan at one of his own shows just a few weeks later. So while it's tempting to say that a twangy eruption like "Blue Suede Shoes" sounded like the future, the truth is that Carl Perkins and his brothers had been burning down honky-tonks with this same crazed brand of country music, more or less, for a couple of years already. Very soon, this new sound would be dubbed rockabilly, and it would help create a whole new world. But when Perkins hit with "Blue Suede Shoes," the biggest reason it climbed to the top of virtually every known chart was because it spoke so intimately, and without condescension, about what many folks were already living.—dc

44

I Can't Stop Loving You, Ray Charles
Produced by Sid Feller; Written by Don Gibson
ABC-Paramount 10330   1962
#1 pop (5 weeks); #1 R&B (5 weeks)

Like so many southerners, Ray Charles grew up loving the Grand Ole Opry. When he landed his first professional gig at fifteen, it was pounding keys for a hillbilly outfit called the Florida Playboys. In 1959, when he was twenty-nine and already an established star, Charles scored with a thundering version of Hank Snow's "I'm Movin' On," two years before Solomon Burke put an R&B spin on the country standard "Just out of Reach." So it wasn't exactly a surprise that Charles might release an album called *Modern Sounds in Country and Western Music*. It was unexpected, though, and potentially controversial. For a black man to embrace in 1962, at the height of the civil rights movement, the music most identified with white southern racism sent a statement of racial unity that anyone paying attention could hardly have missed. That Charles chose to make that music his own, transforming it with heaping helpings of soul, pop, and jazz, must surely have struck listeners, whether sympathetic or hostile, as a kind of musical miscegenation, an attack on segregation itself.

The track chosen to be the album's first single was "I Can't Stop Loving You," a minor crossover hit for Nashville Sound singer-songwriter Don Gibson four years earlier. But Brother Ray's version comes off like the Nashville Sound to the tenth power, plus Atlantic soul, plus Tony Bennett pop. Charles is enveloped here by a sultry rhythm track, a full choir, and an orchestra that sets new standards for lushness. But it's the slowly increasing intensity of his gospel-born phrasing that rivets your attention and that pushes the record to its climax. The single was a phenomenon, selling over a million copies, inspiring countless covers, and topping both the pop and R&B charts that summer. It did not, however, make a dent on country radio.

That would come. Though Charles continued to have success with country covers for several years, it wasn't until he began recording straight-up country with producer Billy Sherrill in the early 1980s that he finally cracked country radio. In 1983, he was nominated for a Horizon Award, the Country Music Association's way of honoring the best new talents in the country field. The irony was that, by then, white country singers had already been embracing the modern sounds of "I Can't Stop Loving You" for twenty years.—dc

45

Once a Day, Connie Smith
Produced by Bob Ferguson; Written by Bill Anderson
RCA Victor 47-8416   1964   #1 country (8 weeks)

46

Burning a Hole in My Mind, Connie Smith
Produced by Bob Ferguson; Written by Cy Coben
RCA Victor 4-9335   1967   #5 country

Connie Smith has few peers when it comes to plumbing the depths of heartache. Her boundless alto doesn't just convey hurt; when backed by the knifing runs of steel guitarist Weldon Myrick, it throbs with a vengeance. It's certainly not the voice you'd expect to come from the bright-eyed, honey blonde smiling out at you from the pastoral backdrops of such perkily titled albums as *Cute 'n' Country*.

Doubtless that was just how Smith's record label wanted it. After all, what better way to hype Nashville's latest Cinderella story than by playing up the happy ending? But Smith *wasn't* happy. She was a conflicted soul—a wife, mother, entertainer, and woman of faith nearly torn apart by her inability to fit the pieces of her life together. Not even sudden stardom, or billing as "The Sweetheart of the Grand Ole Opry," could alleviate Smith's afflictions. Then there were the scars of her troubled childhood.

Smith was born Constance June Meador in Elkhart, Indiana, one of fourteen children of migrant farm-worker parents. Her father, an alcoholic, was a brutish man; to escape his abuse, young Connie would often dig up a sassafras root, climb a tree, and, from that protected perch, sing for hours. Smith was a singing housewife when Bill Anderson discovered her, at age twenty-three, performing at a Columbus, Ohio, talent contest. By the summer of 1964, Anderson had sold Chet Atkins on the idea of signing her to RCA. "Once a Day" hit the streets in August; by November it topped the charts, where it stayed for eight straight weeks.

Set to a jaunty, tic-tac shuffle, the song's half-winking lyrics find Smith playing a jilted lover who's thankful she only hurts once a day, albeit all day long. Yet Connie suffuses even this joke with sorrow. Indeed, everything she sang at this point came out sounding like the blues, her few moments of transcendence coming from the life-affirming power of her own indomitable voice. Even that wasn't enough to sustain her for long, though, what with the road keeping her away from her kids, not to mention the roving hands of DJs and her male peers keeping her constantly on edge. In fact it was all Smith could do *not* to lose it, which she finally did. She suffered a nervous breakdown in 1968 after sending out an SOS with "Burning a Hole in My Mind."

"Burning" begins unassumingly. The champagne piano, swooning strings, cantering brushes, and creamy background crooners are more akin to Owen Bradley's work with Patsy Cline than to the gale force honky-tonk Smith made with Myrick at the steel. "Burning" is almost buttery enough to soothe the pain in Smith's voice, but not quite. "Though I try to forgive, every moment I live, is a torture the devil designed," she sings, fighting back tears. The song's lyrics might be about a love gone bad, but the hole that's burning in Connie's mind seems more transcendental in nature, so deep-seated that no earthly music could make it go away.—bfw

47

I'm So Lonesome I Could Cry, Hank Williams
Produced by Fred Rose; Written by Hank Williams
MGM 10560   1949   Did not chart

No record in his catalog makes as strong a case for Hank as the Hillbilly Shakespeare as "I'm So Lonesome I Could Cry." There's the evocative imagery: the call of the blue whippoorwill, the whistle of the midnight train, the falling star that lights up the purple sky. There's Williams's economical use of language, as well as the interplay between sound and sense—the way, to cite but

one example, he draws out the first syllable of the word "crawling" while wringing his hands over his seemingly endless dark night of the soul.

More than just great poetry, "I'm So Lonesome I Could Cry" marked the arrival of the confessional singer-songwriter in modern country music. Williams wasn't the first honky-tonker to write and sing songs based on personal experience. Both Floyd Tillman and Ernest Tubb, for example, were doing it for nearly a decade before Hank saw the inside of a recording studio. But no one who came before or after Williams embodied the persona of the solitary hillbilly bard as completely or as indelibly as he did. "I'm So Lonesome I Could Cry" might have first appeared only as the B side of "My Bucket's Got a Hole in It," but few records in any genre have conveyed spirit-crushing desolation as vividly.

Williams's approach to the lyrics is deceptively simple. He sets each verse to a waltz-time rhythm and the sparest of sawdust-and-steel honky-tonk. In each he invokes an image—usually drawn from nature and always in language of disarming immediacy—which plumbs the barren recesses of his heart. "I've never seen a night so long when time goes crawling by / The moon just went behind the clouds to hide his face and cry," he moans in a lump-throated drawl in the second verse. Jerry Byrd plays the bluesy steel solo that follows, and Tommy Jackson takes the mournful fiddle break that comes after the third verse. Both men echo Hank's despair with the understated eloquence of the songwriter himself.

Which raises the question of the song's authorship. Producer Fred Rose, a veteran of Tin Pan Alley, often worked closely with Williams on his writing, even to the point of tweaking his lyrics and helping him flesh out ideas. From time to time the relationship has had critics wondering whether it was Hank's or Rose's muse that's evident here. But does it matter? As much as anything in his unassailable body of work, Williams inhabited—*and lived*—the exquisitely bruised lyrics of "I'm So Lonesome I Could Cry." That's a kind of ownership very few want to claim.—bfw

48

Hank and Lefty Raised My Country Soul,
Stoney Edwards
Produced by Earl Ball and Biff Collie;
Written by Dallas Frazier and A. L. "Doodle" Owens
Capitol 3671   1973   #39 country

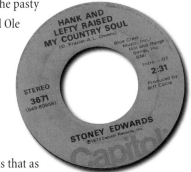

You'd never know it from the pasty faces you see on the Grand Ole Opry or Country Music Television, but "hillbilly" music has never been the sole province of white people. Recent research conducted by the Country Music Association suggests that as much as 20 percent of the adult black population in the United States tunes in country radio, and history confirms they do more than just listen. African Americans have been making crucial contributions to the idiom since at least 1926, the year harmonica player DeFord Bailey made his Opry debut, and much further back if you consider the African origins of the banjo. Jimmie Rodgers, the "Father of Country Music," and Bob Wills, the "King of Western Swing," drew on black blues, jazz, and stringband music, while Hank Williams and Bill Monroe learned at the feet of black pickers Rufus "Tee-Tot" Payne and Arnold Shultz. That's just a sampling of the musical cross-pollination that's been taking place between black and white southerners since the days of slavery. African American country singer Cleve Francis, alluding to the racism that's pervaded the industry since its inception, observed, "You can't shake the tree and in seventy-five years have only one black man fall out who can sing country music."

Francis, of course, was referring to Country Music Hall of Famer Charley Pride, one of Nashville's best-selling artists during the sixties and seventies. Oklahoma-born Stoney Edwards is a distant second to Pride among black country singers, charting a mere fifteen singles from 1971 to 1980, only two of which reached the Top Twenty. With this record, however, Stoney testifies not only to the roots of *his* raising, but to those of countless African Americans who came before and after him.

Edwards didn't write "Hank and Lefty Raised My Country Soul," but he might as well have, having come up listening to the Opry on weekends and to Wills and his Playboys weekdays on Tulsa's KVOO. "I learned to sing and shuffle my shoes / Listening to Hank sing the 'Lovesick Blues,'" Stoney sings, backed by fiddle and piano, in a molasses, Lefty-inspired baritone. It's a lovely and loving tribute, right down to Pete Drake's swirling steel figure, which copies Curly Chalker's work on Frizzell's "Always Late (with Your Kisses)" just as Stoney starts to reminisce about it.

Too bad Frizzell didn't respond in kind the one time he and Edwards met. According to an interview published in a 1992 issue of the *Journal of Country Music*, Frizzell was off at a table by himself in a Music Row dive in 1973, just two years before his death, when Edwards approached him. "Hank and Lefty" was playing on the jukebox. "Lefty was sitting there crying and he was listening to that song," Stoney told interviewer Jeff Woods. "He said, 'Boy, I tell you, that song just tears me up. That song's a tribute to me. I didn't think anybody cared nothing about me anymore.' And then out of the clear blue, Lefty says, 'And wouldn't you know it? It had to be by a nigger.' Well, then he shook my hand, but I don't think he ever did know who he was talking to."

Thirty years later, the country music industry still doesn't know who it's talking to, much less appreciate the richness of its diverse legacy.—bfw

49

Lovesick Blues, Emmett Miller & His Georgia Crackers
No producer credited; Written by Cliff Friend and Irving Mills
OKeh 41062   1928   Pre-chart

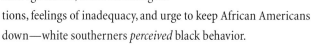

Ridicule? Worship? Exploitation of the vilest sort? Blackface minstrelsy was all of these things—a truly peculiar institution born of white southerners' fascination with how black slaves walked, talked, and otherwise acted. Or at least how—fueled by their ignorance, overactive imaginations, feelings of inadequacy, and urge to keep African Americans down—white southerners *perceived* black behavior.

Stephen Foster, Al Jolson, and Emmett Miller were the best known practitioners of this infamous art, one that dates back to the day, in 1828, that Thomas "Daddy" Rice stumbled onto a black stable hand amusing passersby on the street in Charleston, South Carolina. Seeing a chance to make his fortune, Rice bought the man's song and dance for fifty bucks there on the spot. He promptly smudged his face with burnt cork, started aping the black man's shtick, and, before long, was packing music halls around the nation and, later, in England as well. Rice wasn't the only one. An early rival of his, George Washington Dixon, did his part to establish minstrelsy as a popular form of entertainment, a medium that thrived on its caricatures of "darkies" as infantile, superstitious, sex-crazed rubes.

Ironically enough, and as opprobrious as they indeed were, burlesque figures like Dixon's "Zip Coon" and Rice's "Jim Crow" often depicted black people in terms more human than most white folk had ever seen. In many cases these characters supplied whites with the *only* pictures of blacks they had, a circumstance that has prompted some to argue that minstrelsy helped pave the way, however indirectly, for greater appreciation of black culture by whites. Muddying the waters still further, former slaves themselves began "blacking up" after the Civil War, with African American vaudevillians like Billy Kersands and Bert Williams going on to become stars in their own right, albeit less well paid than their white counterparts.

The blackface minstrel who had the greatest impact on country music was Emmett Miller, a preternaturally gifted white man born in Macon, Georgia, in 1903. Miller's stature in country circles would have been secure if all he had done was record early versions of "Anytime" and "Right or Wrong," songs that became classics of the genre. But much more than that, Miller's artistry induced country pioneers like Jimmie Rodgers and Bob Wills to don black face. His "vocal contortions" provided Rodgers with the grist for his blue yodel, while Miller's mannerisms furnished Wills with the blueprint for his hotdog antics and jive asides. And then there's Miller's 1928 recording of "Lovesick Blues," a tune that twenty-some years later gave Hank Williams not just his breakthrough hit but the biggest hit of his meteoric career.

A vaudeville favorite, "Lovesick Blues" first appeared on record in 1922. Miller subsequently cut the song twice for the OKeh label, but the earlier version, recorded for A&R man Ralph Peer in 1925, has long been lost. The remaining take, made in New York three years later, is a stunning testament not just to Miller's vision and virtuosity, but to how his dialectical approach to blackface bridged disparate worlds and even subverted much of what made minstrelsy so odious.

Cut with a hot bunch of syncopators that included guitarist Eddie Lang as well as brothers Jimmy and Tommy Dorsey, "Lovesick Blues" highlights more than one facet of Miller's art. A comic dialog (Emmett plays both parts) is followed by a sentimental ballad, a progression that both personifies Miller's awareness of the conflicts inherent in donning blackface and strikes at the heart of the rift between the races. In the record's droll intro, an authoritative voice, presumably that of a white man, asks a lovelorn black schlub named Sam how he can feel blue when the birds are singing and the sun is shining. How, in other words, can a happy-go-lucky Stepin Fetchit like Sam have such feelings—that is, be fully human?

Sam, of course, is no fool; he knows he's got the blues all right, the very existence of which certifies his humanity. But since his straight-man companion can't seem to grasp the notion (he assumes Sam is brooding because the cops locked up his bootlegger), Sam makes his case by launching into a tragicomic version of "Lovesick Blues" that's of a depth and beauty worthy of Shakespeare or the ancient Greek playwrights. As his clarinet-like falsetto slurs and slides, extending heartsick vowels over stop-time passages à la Louis Armstrong, Miller's vocals run the gamut of human emotion and ultimately transcend it, presenting black Sam as the very embodiment of the self-surpassing human spirit.

Miller's nearly twenty-year run lasted well into the thirties and, alongside contemporary Al Jolson, he influenced everyone from Bing Crosby to Roy Acuff. Yet unlike his friend Lasses White, who with partner "Honey" Wilds performed in blackface on the Grand Ole Opry, Miller wasn't able to make the transition from the vaudeville stage to radio and film. After years out of the limelight, he resurfaced as part of a traveling minstrel troupe in 1949, and then again two years later in the musical *Yes, Sir, Mister Bones*. But minstrel shows began dying out as the freedom movement gained momentum and many blacks and whites denounced minstrelsy as a racist institution. Of course, from *Hee Haw* to the rapper Eminem, vestiges of the idiom, minus the blackface, persist today. Few song-and-dance men, though, have approached the art with Miller's subtlety, grace, or singular humanity.—bfw

50

I Love You a Thousand Ways, Lefty Frizzell
Produced by Don Law and Art Satherley; Written by Lefty Frizzell
Columbia 4–20739   1950   #1 country (3 weeks)

Lefty Frizzell was by all accounts a real tough—a guy who could booze and brawl with the best of them (his nickname was a tribute to his devastating southpaw hook). Yet much like his hero Jimmie Rodgers, another singer known for his rough and rowdy ways, Lefty could also be a real softy—an out-and-out sentimentalist who wrote paeans to undying love like "I Want to Be with You Always" and "Mom and Dad's Waltz," songs as moving and enduring as any in country or pop music. What makes Frizzell's records more than just maudlin weepers, though, is the way they express idealized visions of the intimacy, stability, and trust that were utterly absent from his own life.

With a voice as expressive as Lefty's, there is no way that dissonance isn't going to bleed through, and nowhere does it come across more vividly than in "I Love You a Thousand Ways," the first song he claimed to have written. On the surface, "I Love You" is just another sentimental number, a pledge of fidelity that, despite what's happened in the past, he vows he'll prove and keep right on proving. Yet the record—and the regret in Lefty's voice—cuts much deeper when you know that it was one of several songs Frizzell, then eighteen, wrote to his wife and the mother of his firstborn. Stewing in a New Mexico jail awaiting trial on charges of statutory rape, he had no one to talk to but the blues.

"I love you, I'll prove it in days to come / I swear it's true, darlin', you're the only one," Lefty pines to a lightly chopping shuffle beat, the mix of tears and tenderness in his liquid baritone striking just the right balance to prove he's sincere. Bittersweet fiddle and steel plead his case, while Madge Sutee's piano break makes nice and sweet—just like Frizzell promises he'll be if his wife takes him back. Lefty's got to know he has his gal where he wants her when, moving in for his final appeal, he implores, "So darlin' wait, please wait until I'm free / There's been a change, a great change in me." Judging by the ache in his voice, he desperately wants to believe it too.—bfw

51
Your Good Girl's Gonna Go Bad, Tammy Wynette
Produced by Billy Sherrill;
Written by Billy Sherrill and Glenn Sutton
Epic 10134   1967   #3 country

When Tammy Wynette walked past an unattended receptionist's desk and into the office of Epic Records producer-songwriter Billy Sherrill in 1966, she was looking to become a star. But she could never have dreamed just how enormous a star she was about to become or how she and Sherrill would change the face of country music. Years later, Sherrill would describe Wynette that day as "a pale skinny little blond girl who looked like she was at her rope's end," which must've been exactly right. Separated from a husband who had recently tried to have her committed, the twenty-three-year-old Wynette Pugh was, in effect, a single mother of three girls. She'd packed her daughters into the car and moved to Nashville, trading away her life in Alabama—which included the relative security of shelter in a government housing project and a steady income as a hairdresser—for the indignities of a twelve-dollar-a-week room in a motor court and a series of rejections from the producers up on Music Row.

It's hard to say why Sherrill didn't just run her out of his office that day. Never a soft touch, he certainly didn't need to be bothered with a skinny kid who hadn't brought so much as a guitar, let alone a demo tape. Maybe he liked that she knew Haleyville, the little Alabama town where he'd grown up. Maybe, having just produced and co-written David Houston's "Almost Persuaded" (a country chart topper for nine straight weeks) the thirty year-old producer was feeling invincible or lucky. Maybe he was bored. Maybe he just thought this Pugh kid was a cute little number. Whatever the reason, he let her play, listening as she strummed a couple of her own songs on his guitar, then a couple of George Jones and Skeeter Davis hits. The emotional, naturally breaking cry he heard in her voice—he'd later dub that break "the teardrop"—made him tell her he'd record her if she could land some better original material.

He must have been even more impressed than he let on because when she called him a week later, he'd already found her a song: "Apartment #9," a Johnny Paycheck–penned weeper that had given Bobby Austin a minor hit the year before on tiny Tally Records. Sherrill thought it might score big with an Epic-sized push. He was wrong about that—Wynette and Sherrill's version did worse than Austin's had, not even cracking the country Top

Forty. In retrospect, that's not surprising. Tammy's "Apartment #9," while gorgeously played and sung, sounds like a lot of other country ballads—one more weary acoustic guitar shuffle backing a lazy piano and pedal steel. In an era when the only really big female country star was Loretta Lynn, and when "girl singers" were still just one small part of a male star's road show, it took more than a good record to break a new woman singer; it took a great one.

Tammy's great record was "Your Good Girl's Gonna Go Bad." Hurtling out of the speakers, "Your Good Girl" throbs through its verses, bouncing with fed-up determination upon a rhythm bed that borrows heavily from the pop, rock & roll, and R&B records Sherrill had produced at Phillips Recordings Studios earlier in the decade. But while the single announces itself as pure pop—that opening rubberband riff could've been lifted from a Dick Dale record—Wynette's wrought twang, plus those fierce pedal-steel fills, are unmistakably country. And when a tambourine shifts the whole thing into a rousing camp meeting at the chorus (Tammy had spent time in a southern gospel trio as a teen; Billy had spent his adolescence playing gospel piano at his preacher dad's tent services), you can hear that Wynette and Sherrill have discovered their sound.

In time, that sound would be labeled countrypolitan, a style of country music that Wynette and Sherrill helped create by marrying a brand of country pop with the steel guitar and southern accents that the old Nashville Sound had abandoned—and also by making the record pulse and scoot with soulful rhythm. The song itself is a fed-up declaration of how things are going to have to be from now on, and Wynette sings it just like that. She's pissed off and uninterested in idle threats; this new state of affairs is just a matter of fact. Behind her, Sherrill's arrangement and production make it crystal clear that this good girl gone bad is gonna have one hell of a good time turning the tables.—dc

52
Make the World Go Away, Ray Price
Produced by Don Law; Written by Hank Cochran
Columbia 42827   1963   #2 country; #100 pop

53
Night Life, Ray Price
Produced by Don Law; Written by Willie Nelson
Columbia 42827   1963   #28 country

Ray Price has long insisted there's no substantial difference between singing a good song with country backing and performing it with a pop arrangement—to him, "it's the same thing." Here that argument is distilled down to one absolutely perfect two-sided single.

"Night Life," the single's B side, has long been recognized as Price at his hardcore best. And it's true—honky-tonk doesn't get any better this. Even so, some of the best touches in this slow shuffle aren't hardcore at all. Buddy Emmons's bluesy, horn-like pedal steel swaps sad tales throughout with Pig Robbins's weary piano ("Listen to what the blues are saying," Price instructs), and their smoky, jazz-inspired conversations lend the record a decidedly uptown feel, something like a honky-tonk version of Sinatra's saloon classic "Only the Lonely." And the cut's driving force—the brushwork of Buddy Harman—bears witness to the lessons he'd learned studying Buddy Rich, Gene Krupa, and other jazz drummers.

Recorded just four months later, "Make the World Go Away" is regularly cited as one of the earliest examples of Ray Price, pop singer. But, as with "Night Life," things aren't that simple. Price had originally recorded "Make the World Go Away" in his patented shuffle style but, unsatisfied with the results, he quickly rearranged and rerecorded it on his way to releasing a version with overdubbed strings and a backing chorus. Still, lurking beneath the Nashville Sound trappings was a loping rhythmic base that was decidedly country in feel—at least country in the way it was defined on a honky-tonk classic such as "Night Life." Ignoring the record's lush and sweeping string arrangement for a moment (and for *just* a moment, since the strings make the record), the standout instrumental features on "Make the World Go Away" are Harman's drumming and Robbins's lonely, wandering piano, each an obvious descendant of the pair's performances on "Night Life."

"Make the World Go Away" begins in a way that would have been unexpected for a Ray Price record in 1963: a flourish of strings, followed by the title phrase sung by a loud and echoing vocal chorus. But when Price then enters to complete the line—"and get it off my shoulders"—his singing is quiet, a striking contrast to those backing singers and the strings swirling extravagantly about him. Because he opens near a whisper, he can build to something like a scream. By the time he unleashes the line again at the choruses—"just get it *off, off* of my shoulders" he practically yelps in pain—we can feel just how oppressively the world presses down upon this man and how much power he has granted to the woman he believes can relieve the burden. The strings seem to push the singer to greater and greater heights, and they'd better do the trick, too. For if this plea fails, his life will be crushed. His existence will be reduced, as he puts it in "Night Life," to a never-ending sequence of taverns filled with "lonely people just like me."

What really makes these two sides of a piece, thematically and musically, is the way Price sings them. One side is pop-influenced Nashville Sound, the other is the hardest of honky-tonk, but he delivers them in exactly the same pop-meets-country voice. Uptown or downtown, Price makes clear, misery's all the same.—dc

54

I Take It on Home, Charlie Rich
Produced by Billy Sherrill; Written by Kenny O'Dell
Epic 10867   1972   #6 country

The standard knock against Billy Sherrill–produced records is that they're *over*produced. The truth is that the best of them (usually the ones that were hits) were models of purposeful restraint, thrilling testaments to how the contrast between large and small can strengthen the emotional punch of a song. One exceptional example of Sherrill's work is "I Take It on Home," the Top Ten hit that finally broke Charlie Rich to country radio.

As the song begins, it's just Rich and his piano. First, he explains how he likes to stop for a drink after work before heading home to his wife and, later, how there's always some gal or other there trying to hit on him. A soft bass line and the barely audible tapping of a woodblock and high hat enter, keeping time and ticking off the minutes until Charlie knows he needs to take it on home. And that's it for the first verse. With Rich's conversational voice way out front in the mix, it sounds like he's right there at the table with you, sheepishly explaining why he can't stay for another round.

For one thing, he's out of town often enough as it is; for another there's this one buddy who Charlie knows isn't beyond hitting on his wife, just like those ladies who are always tempting him. It ain't easy to be out and alone, you know? While he's explaining all this in a tone more offhand than confiding, the Jordanaires sneak in behind him. But Rich's voice is so commanding, and they sing so softly, you barely notice them. Way back in the mix, they're nearly indistinguishable from the small, hushed string section that's also entered—the singers and the strings fuse into an intimate, atmospheric hum you might miss altogether if you weren't listening carefully. What mainly stands out in the first two verses is how much space there is, how many moments there are on the record where there is no sound at all.

So it's a jolt when everything explodes at the chorus. With Sherrill's strings punching each word of the title as if someone's banging on the table for emphasis, Rich insists at full volume, "I take it on home, to the woman who sticks by me." His voice, pushed by those banging strings, lets us know just how hard that can be. Then, just as suddenly, the strings hush, Charlie recalls how much he loves and trusts his wife, and the song's main point hangs there in the air, underlined by Sherrill's dynamic arrangement: " 'Cause I believe she'd do the same if she was me." Just as Sherrill's arrangement has, Rich delivers those words like the prayer they are—because he "wouldn't know where to turn to if she was gone." And *that*'s when he finally packs it on up, turns it around, and takes it on home.—dc

55

My Heart Skips a Beat, Buck Owens
Produced by Ken Nelson; Written by Buck Owens
Capitol 5136   1964   #1 country (7 weeks); #94 pop

The Beatles' "I Don't Want to Spoil the Party"? The Byrds' version of "A Satisfied Mind"? Nah, if you're looking for the birth of country rock, look no further than the early sixties hits of Buck Owens and his Buckaroos. The buoyant twang of "Act Naturally" and "Love's Gonna Live Here," both country chart toppers from 1963, paved the way with their "freight-train" rhythms. But it was the irrepressible "My Heart Skips

a Beat," with Willie Cantu's palpitating toms way up in the mix and Don Rich's leads making Chuck Berry's "ringin'-a-bell" guitar safe for the barn-dance circuit, that brought it all back home. "You came into my life without a warning / And you turned my cloudy skies from gray to blue / You're my sunshine that comes up every morning / Yes, you are my every dream come true," Buck beams, and he isn't just crowing about his new love. He's singing about the thrill of discovering a brand new beat. Not that Owens, who to this day remains the most cagey of businessmen, would ever cop to being a rock & roller. Never mind that he apprenticed with wildcats Gene Vincent and Wanda Jackson and cut his first singles—rockabilly sides no less—for a label with an incriminating moniker like Pep Records. Talk about having a tiger by the tail.—bfw

56

Galveston, Glen Campbell
Produced by Al DeLory; Written by Jimmy Webb
Capitol 2428   1969   #1 country; #4 pop

Countrypolitan's ability to cross over in the late sixties and early seventies provided country music with a voice in a Top Forty mix in which some of the era's most pressing issues were being addressed. Vietnam, for example. Although it's rarely given credit, country music took its part in this debate seriously. Before Creedence Clearwater Revival railed against a system that sent working-class boys off to die in a war LBJ promised we'd never fight, before Edwin Starr screamed war was good for nothing, before Freda Payne demanded we "Bring the Boys Home," Glen Campbell and songwriter Jimmy Webb had already shown us one of those boys, up close and personal.

"Galveston" focuses on the individual costs of war, so unlike those other antiwar anthems, its politics emerge only between the lines. A typical country response to politics, this approach both comforts and works against the very audience that inevitably does a good bit of the dying. In 1966, for instance, Loretta Lynn's "Dear Uncle Sam" bared the grief of a woman learning her husband has died overseas, as a bugle honors his sacrifice to the greater good. Merle Haggard's "I Wonder If They Ever Think of

Me," from 1973, presents a POW who can only "take his memory trips and try to fight the pain" but who nevertheless isn't sorry to be fighting for Uncle Sam.

By contrast, "Galveston" doesn't try to soothe its anguish with any patriotic purpose. "I am so afraid of dying," Campbell sings, and Al DeLory's thrilling arrangement booms and shakes like cannons exploding just a hill or two away. There's no flag waving on the record, no glory. Just a poor kid cleaning his gun in 'Nam, scared to death and dreaming of the girl he left behind—praying he'll make it back home.—dc

57

The Little Old Log Cabin in the Lane,
Fiddlin' John Carson
Produced by Ralph Peer; Written by William Shakespeare Hayes
OKeh 4890   1923   Pre-chart

Commercial country music starts right here.

In 1923, OKeh A&R man Ralph Peer was looking to buoy sagging record sales in the face of competition from the burgeoning radio industry. Noting that sales of so-called race records geared to

black, predominantly southern record buyers were as high as ever, Peer contacted Polk Brockman, an Atlanta businessman who sold 78s in his furniture store (the better to sell the machines that played them), and instructed him to identify promising blues, jazz, and gospel performers for a June recording session. It was Brockman who guessed that a similar market might exist among white, working-class southerners, if they were offered the right kind of music. To that end, he convinced Peer to record a couple of sides by fifty-five-year-old John Carson, a well-known regional fiddle champ.

The introduction of the condenser microphone was still three years into the future, so Carson sang and played his fiddle into a large acoustic horn set up to record his performances, which OKeh execs later declared to be "pluperfect awful." At Brockman's insistence, however, Peer agreed to press 500 copies for local sales only. Brockman sold out of Carson's record almost immediately thanks to a simple but flawless marketing strategy—Carson would play the songs before a live audience; then just as the applause began to die away, Brockman played the record. "We sold them just like hotcakes," Brockman said, "right there in the hall." As Brockman reordered the disc every few weeks, Peer finally woke up to what was going on. He added Carson's title to the label's catalogue, and "The Little Old Log Cabin in the Lane" (backed with "The Old Hen Cackled and the Rooster's Going to Crow") became the first "country" record ever released.

It still holds up, too. Carson's fiddling is nothing fancy (next to the work of someone like Clayton McMichen, you might even call it primitive), but he delivers the song's insistent melody with a sweet, casual lyricism that's tough to resist, even when shrouded by the pops and cracks of an early twentieth century recording. Carson's vocals—vibrant and distinctive, not exactly demonstrative but still brimming with emotion—are the record's prime selling point. All these decades later, Carson's individual grappling with the human condition—change, loss, death—still commands attention.

Despite its historical position, however, "The Little Old Log Cabin in the Lane" doesn't completely support the myth of country music's benighted-but-pure rural origins. For one thing, Fiddlin' John was hardly some isolated hillbilly, even though he did learn to play in the north Georgia hills on an instrument his Irish grandfather brought from the old country. By the time he cut "Little Old Log Cabin," Carson had already lived in Atlanta or its suburbs for nearly a quarter century, ever since he found mill work there, and he was a popular radio performer. Similarly, the song itself wasn't a folk relic transported to America from the British Isles. Rather, it was a minstrel number written by William Shakespeare Hayes in 1871 (Carson's version drops the blackface dialect of the original) and already recorded by the Romanian-American opera singer Alma Gluck, among other popular performers, in the early twentieth century.

An old country record like this one is also supposed to be nostalgic, but that's not accurate here either. This old house Carson is singing about—its chimney falling down, its roof caving in, its doors falling off their hinges—is not a log cabin of memory but the one he lives in right now. He certainly remembers, and misses, the way life used to be. His parents are dead and gone now, as are the black sharecroppers who used to sing as they worked the fields and who used to visit his cabin to hear him strum his banjo, an instrument he's now too feeble to play. Still, he's not wasting his time yearning for, or cursing, the past. "I ain't got long to stay here," he sings, his voice every bit as brave as it is

lonely. "And what little time I got, I'll try and be contented to remain till death shall call my dog and me to find a better home."

Like thousands of country records to come, "The Little Old Log Cabin in the Lane" struggles with change, loss and death—and it doesn't deny their inevitability for a second. At the song's end, Carson's fiddle leaps unexpectedly from the melody to one sharp, shrieked note of surprise before the record just stops dead in its tracks. It sounds like Fiddlin' John has kicked the bucket right there and then.—dc

58

How Can a Poor Man Stand Such Times and Live,
Blind Alfred Reed
Produced by Ralph Peer; Written by Alfred Reed
Victor V-40236   1929   Pre-chart

Like many blind men in the early part of the twentieth century, fiddler Alfred Reed supported his family as best he could by hiring himself out for parties and church events and by playing for change on the streets. So he knew what he was talking about when he recorded "How Can a Poor Man Stand Such Times and Live." Its 1929 recording date would seem to identify this as a Depression-era number, but Reed's protest appears to be more general. It's likely, for example, that he would have already written the song well before anyone knew there was a depression occuring. His lyrics certainly don't mention the stock market crash, and at any rate, although he recorded the song for Ralph Peer just five weeks after Black Tuesday, the crises of Wall Street would've been pretty much irrelevant to the rural—and *already* poor—West Virginia audiences that Reed counted upon for his living.

The troubles Reed rails against are longstanding and close at hand: money-grubbing doctors and preachers, trigger-happy law enforcement, corrupt schools, and, most of all, inflation so bad he feels like making out his will every time he goes to the grocery store. Reed's feisty baritone is plainly fed up, but he still grins at the absurdity of it all. His springy fiddle tune and his son's guitar, geared for getting folks to push back the furniture and cut a rug, encourage listeners to release the frustrations and agonies that come with being poor—particularly in a time not of depression but of ostensibly wide-spread prosperity, like the Roaring Twenties. It seems a safe bet that "How Can a Poor Man Stand Such Times and Live" will be revived periodically (as roots rockers the Del Lords did during the so-called boom years of the 1980s) for exactly as long as its question remains relevant— as long as some people struggle in poverty while others prosper.—dc

59

Hungry Eyes, Merle Haggard & the Strangers
Produced by Ken Nelson; Written by Merle Haggard
Capitol 2383   1969   #1 country (1 week)

Merle Haggard wasn't alive in 1935, the year his parents packed up their two kids and joined the swarms of Dust Bowl refugees who migrated west to find fortune in the orchards and oil fields of Southern California's San Joaquin Valley. But he came along in 1937, soon enough to have known the backbreaking labor and subsistence wages that his folks and thousands of other squatters in Kern County's squalid tent cities reaped as their reward.

"A canvas-covered cabin in a crowded labor camp / Stands out in this memory I revive / 'Cause my daddy raised a family there / With two hard-working hands / And tried to feed my mama's hungry eyes." Merle croons these lines softly, backed only by the bluesy strains of a lightly picked acoustic guitar. There isn't a hint of bitterness or judgment in his voice. There isn't even much overt social commentary, despite what some who hear the record only as a populist anthem would have us believe. And yet the picture Merle paints transcends mere reportage. It may be just three minutes and twenty-three seconds long,

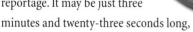

but "Hungry Eyes" is as monumental—and artful—as the Dust Bowl photos Dorothea Lange took for the Farm Security Admin- istration during the Depression. In "Hungry Eyes," Merle gets inside the hardscrabble life his parents knew, a life plagued not just by a soul-sucking grind, but by the gnawing certainty that there would always be another class of people around to remind them of their wretched estate.

The ache in Hag's voice amply makes this point, but the lush string arrangement that caresses his parents' shattered dreams drives it home. Those swelling violins are, on the one hand, a nod to the sacrifices made by Merle's father, a railroad carpenter who, among many other things, gave up his own fiddle before he brought his family west. On the other hand, those strings represent the luxury Merle's mother couldn't afford to let herself desire; "she only wanted things she really needed." The entire record hinges upon this notion of privation, and if there's anything that makes the withering effect it has on people real, it's Flossie Haggard's hungry eyes. Those dignity-starved spheres— windows into the soul as piercing as those of Lange's "Migrant Mother"—are the point at which the personal and the political converge.—bfw

60

Are They Gonna Make Us Outlaws Again?
James Talley
Produced by James Talley and Steve Mendell;
Written by James Talley
Capitol 4297   1976   #61 country

Most country singers would have us believe that music and politics don't mix, and that any hint of the latter in their records is really about their personal lives. Loretta Lynn downplayed the feminism writ large in "The Pill" and "One's on the Way," while Merle Haggard dismissed the right-wing sloganeering of "Okie from Muskogee" as an inside joke run amok. James Talley's songs take the opposite tack; even his first-person narratives about growing up in post–Dust Bowl Oklahoma illuminate larger social and political realities. Like the best of Woody Guthrie, this recession-era broadside—loaded with cannon fodder like, "Now, there's always been a bottom / And there's always been a top / Well, that may be the way it's been / But that don't mean it's right"—moves beyond commentary to activism.

Talley says his inspiration for "Outlaws" came from a long-haul trucker he saw being interviewed on the TV news during the Arab oil embargo of the early 1970s. Taking part in an interstate blockade somewhere in Kentucky, the driver was protesting the skyrocketing gas prices that were driving indepen- dent truckers out of business. The reporter asked if the man was aware that what he was doing was illegal, to which the trucker, getting up in the guy's face, shouted, "Let me tell you something, mister. When a man can't make a living and provide for his wife and kids, he's *gonna* break the law!"

Associations flooded Talley's head—Woody Guthrie's "Pretty Boy Floyd," John Steinbeck's *The Grapes of Wrath*, the Dust Bowl stories Talley's parents and grandparents told him when he was a kid. "Well, I guess I see why Pretty Boy Floyd done the things he did / Are they gonna make us outlaws again?" he wonders, connecting the dots between the Depression and the stalled global economy of the seventies that was disinheriting his working-class peers. Talley phrases the issue as a question, but spurred on by Johnny Gimble's searing fiddle and the record's locomotive rhythm section—a sound akin to that of a train leaving the station—he transforms the question into a threat.

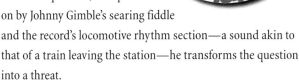

Talley underscored the point in a conversation that author Peter Guralnick recounted in *Lost Highway*. Wanting there to be no mistaking his lyrics for an allusion to the prevailing musical movement spearheaded by "Outlaws" Waylon Jennings and Willie Nelson, Talley explains, "I'm talking about breaking the fucking law!" In the process he sounds as relevant and righteous a call to leftist populism as country music has ever known.—bfw

61

This Land Is Your Land, Woody Guthrie

Produced by Moses Asch;
Written by Woody Guthrie
Folkways 2481   1945   Did not chart

It's more than a little ironic that "This Land Is Your Land," a song sometimes cited as a more suitable national anthem than the bellicose "Star-Spangled Banner," began life as a proletarian rebuttal of Irving Berlin's "God Bless America." And it's both ironic and appropriate that Woody Guthrie would have written this ode to the potential beating within the nation's breast not in a redwood forest or diamond desert but in a Times Square flophouse. As profound a statement of America's unresolved desires as any ever written, the sweeping reverie Woody wrought while holed up there brims with imagery of sunshine and lifting fog, with an irrepressible sense of possibility and hope.

"As I went walking that ribbon of highway / I saw above me that endless skyway / I saw below me that golden valley / This land was made for you and me." So goes the first verse. On paper the lines read like something out of a Horatio Alger primer, which is just how the Weavers, the Kingston Trio, and nearly everyone else on the hootenanny circuit of the fifties and sixties sang them—as a rousing paean to both the promise of prosperity and the power of solidarity.

That's not how Woody sings them. Scratching out the tune to the Carter Family's "When the World's on Fire," he betrays none of the exuberance of his acolytes or peers. Rather, he sings as if he's still stuck in that dingy room, deadpanning the lyrics, imbuing their enthusiasm with an equally pervasive sense of loss—with the realization that, despite America's storehouse of riches, most people, particularly the millions left unemployed by the Depression, aren't as "blessed" as the lucky few. He also seems to be aware that given human greed, an impulse that had assumed institutional proportions since the rise of capitalism, things might very well stay that way.

This isn't to say that those who hear "This Land" as an anthem are wrong, not entirely anyway. Woody exults in America's natural splendor every bit as much as Walt Whitman does in *Leaves of Grass*. He expresses plenty of faith in what human solidarity can achieve, too. But his is a far more politicized understanding of solidarity—a taking sides with those the rich and powerful would have us believe God *hasn't* blessed, a taking sides that sees every injustice as an affront, a taking sides that means getting organized and joining disenfranchised people in the fight to take back their inheritance.

Of course, by the time Woody wrote "This Land," he wasn't one of the common folk anymore. Even though he'd known the hard-knock life of the people he ran with and sang about, he was a self-conscious artist, an adept manipulator of his own image, like Jimmie Rodgers before him. Woody was also a member of the era's intelligentsia and had a regular column in the weekend edition of the *Daily Worker* to prove it. None of which lessens the punch of this populist wonder, a conflicted meditation that for decades has given voice to the struggles and aspirations of millions who, no matter how much it's betrayed them, have clung to the promise inherent in the American dream.—bfw

62
Tramp on the Street, Molly O'Day
& the Cumberland Mountain Folks
Produced by Art Satherley; Written by Grady and Hazel Cole
Columbia 4-52013   1947   Did not chart

The knock against backwoods piety is that it's hopelessly backwards—all judgment and no grace. That's often the case, but it's hardly true of the tender mercies shown here by Molly O'Day & the Cumberland Mountain Folks. "He was some mother's darlin', he was some mother's son / Once he was fair-haired, once he was young," O'Day begins. "Some mother rocked him, her darlin' to sleep / But they left him to die like a tramp on the street." Before the record's over, Molly applies these lines not just to this forgotten soul, but to Jesus, and in connecting the two—a natural move given that Jesus was born in a barn and hung out with drunks and prostitutes—she anticipates third-world liberation theologians by a good twenty years. The message: God takes sides, and God's loyalties lie with poor people. The force of Molly's plangent alto alone would be enough to drive the point home. But there's also the compassion that flows from the fiddle of her brother, Skeets Williamson, and the dobro of Speedy Krise, both of whom play like the dead tramp was their brother, which as a member of God's family he was.

Not that there isn't a word of exhortation here as well. "If Jesus should come and knock at your door / For a place to come in, or bread from your store / Would you welcome him in or turn him away?" Molly asks. It's an admonition that would be just as righteous ringing out from some dark hollow as it would from the pulpit of some big-city congregation, especially one of those giant cathedrals in the shadow of which the homeless huddle all week long as the "faithful" walk on by.—bfw

63
King of the Road, Roger Miller
Produced by Jerry Kennedy; Written by Roger Miller
Smash 1965   1965   #1 country (5 weeks); #4 pop

A friend who's spent the past fifteen years fighting to change the conditions that create homelessness rankles every time he hears

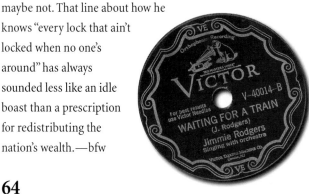

"King of the Road." He insists that the record romanticizes life on the streets, that it makes homelessness seem like a choice, a situation people can opt out of if they just pull themselves up by their bootstraps. Roger Miller's wacky wordplay and the finger-popping of Thumbs Carlisle and Buddy Killen don't help matters, reinforcing my friend's complaint by making hoboing seem like livin' large.

Yet Miller's boxcar bravado is just a front. The way he exults in his Huck Finn–like knack for living by his wits—and in his freedom from being under anyone's thumb—is his way of wresting a shred of dignity, however illusory, from a life that affords him none. Of course, had Roger come along twenty years later, when homelessness was reaching epidemic proportions in the United States, he'd doubtless have been singing a different tune. Or maybe not. That line about how he knows "every lock that ain't locked when no one's around" has always sounded less like an idle boast than a prescription for redistributing the nation's wealth.—bfw

64
Waiting for a Train, Jimmie Rodgers
Produced by Ralph Peer;
Written by Jimmie Rodgers
Victor 40014   1929   Pre-chart

"King of the Road" for the 1920s, complete with train whistle and yodel. Next stop: the Great Depression.—dc

65
I've Been Everywhere, Hank Snow
Produced by Chet Atkins; Written by Geoff Mack
RCA Victor 47-8072   1962   #1 country (2 weeks); #68 pop

When Hank Snow sang that he'd been everywhere, and done everything, he wasn't just blowing smoke. Though he hasn't acquired the hip quotient of contemporaries such as Hank

Williams, George Jones, and Ray Price, that's the company he deserves to keep.

By nearly any standard you can name, Snow excelled. He was a prolific artist—in his autobiography, he estimates he recorded over 1,000 sides—and he was a successful writer, too. His music, which featured elements of everything from honky-tonk to rumba, calypso, boogie, pop, and even, eventually, Outlaw country, showed him to be a synthesizer of the first order. He was influential too. His signature recordings were important links in the chain connecting Jimmie Rodgers with, say, Jimmie Dale Gilmore. His earliest hits anticipated elements of rockabilly and served as prototypes for the Nashville Sound, both in terms of Snow's singing (think Marty Robbins, think post–"Danny Boy" Ray Price) and their means of production. Additionally, Snow was a remarkably astute music-biz figure who played a key role in the early development of Elvis Presley, and he was a guitar picker accomplished enough to record four instrumental albums with Chet Atkins.

And what a singer! At first listen, his nasal croon sounds a bit brittle and easily mimicked. Listen a bit more closely, and you'll realize Snow possessed a rare dexterity with lyric, melody, and rhythm. Like Price, Red Foley, Tommy Duncan, and other masters of the country croon, Snow could express pain or joy without breaking a sweat, the vocal equivalent of knocking out your opponent with both hands tied behind your back. And unlike those other singers, he could caress a ballad without sacrificing any of his twang.

But Snow was at his best when he floored it to highway speed. He made a specialty of bouncing playfully in and around the beat on impossibly uptempo romps, always maintaining impeccable enunciation no matter how fast he went. On "I've Been Every-where," he outdid even himself. Snow, once again the Jimmie Rodgers–worshipping rambler, is remembering the time he bragged to a trucker of all the places he'd been, but he's also bragging to us. At breakneck speed, Snow lights into a tongue-twisting itinerary. He's been to Reno, Chicago, Fargo, Minnesota, Buffalo, Toronto, Winslow, Sarasota, Wichita, Tulsa, Ottawa, and Oklahoma before he even makes it through the first verse. Initially this may seem like a parlor trick—yep, he's fast all

right—but with every key change the song seems to accelerate. The backing singers don't even bother trying to keep up; they just add another "ohhh" at the end of each verse, intensifying the momentum and sounding like they're the ones in need of a deep breath. Then Snow's moving on again—Kalamazoo, Kansas City, Sioux City, Cedar City, Dodge City, What-a-pity! If you can make it to the end of this record without reaching for your car keys, it's only because you're heaving for breath from trying to sing along.—dc

66

Detroit City, Bobby Bare
Produced by Chet Atkins;
Written by Danny Dill and Mel Tillis
RCA Victor 47-8183   1963   #6 country; #16 pop

By 1960, one in six white Americans born in the south had left the region. Mostly these uprooted southerners set off in search of better paying jobs and, they hoped, the better lives that would come with them. So they left the Ozarks for factory work in Kansas City and Chicago, Wichita and Southern California; they abandoned the coal mines of Kentucky for plants in Cincinnati and Cleveland; they traded rows of cotton in the Deep South for assembly lines in Michigan. Many sent a part of their paychecks back home to their families even as they dreamed of returning themselves one day. That usually didn't happen—after all, if they hoped to secure some measure of material comfort or financial security for themselves and their children, what was there to go back to?

In many ways these southerners were like immigrants, and since so much of this strange land was disorienting—the pace of life, the landscape, the way people talked, even the weather—they congregated in the same neighborhoods, nurturing the culture they'd brought with them, creating pockets of the south in the north. As historian John Shelton Reed has noted, the south is anywhere you find southerners, even if that's on the streets of Baltimore or Detroit. Of course, the hard truth was that no matter how much of the south these transplants brought with them, "up North" wasn't home. The result for many was intense homesickness—for an idealized Southland, certainly, but more realistically for a place where all the stresses and limits at least had the advantage of being familiar.

This tug-of-war between the desire for home and the practical benefits of staying put is conveyed in every element of Bobby Bare's early sixties crossover hit, "Detroit City." The quintessence of homesick longing, Mel Tillis's languid melody is clearly southern yet also suggestive of the late fifties urban folk revival's most commercial moments. Charlie McCoy's unforgettable guitar riff, equal parts lazing-around and bouncing-off-the-walls, clashes with a Nashville Sound string motif that, like an automobile assembly line, comes off as uniform, relentless, and not a little violent. "By day, I make the cars / By night, I make the bars," Bare sings, as beat-down weary as that grim ritual would suggest. "Oh, how I want to go home."—dc

67

What Would You Give in Exchange?
The Monroe Brothers
Produced by Eli Oberstein;
Written by J. H. Carr and F. J. Barry
Bluebird 6309   1936   Pre-chart

68

Atlantic City, Bruce Springsteen
No producer credited; Written by Bruce Springsteen
Columbia C4-8513 (Canada)   1982   Did not chart
Video single only in U.S.

"What Would You Give in Exchange [for Your Soul]?" was an epochal record, both in terms of music and message. Charlie and Bill Monroe had just moved to Charlotte, North Carolina, where they'd signed on to host a radio show sponsored by the makers of Crazy Water Crystals, a popular, Depression-era laxative. In Charlotte the duo came to the attention of A&R rep Eli Oberstein, who talked them into cutting a few sides for Victor's Bluebird imprint. Oberstein had already signed two other sibling duos, the Delmore Brothers and the Blue Sky Boys, but as celebrated as each of them would become, neither matched the success the Monroes achieved on their very

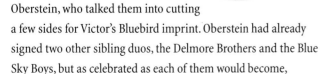

first single. "What Would You Give in Exchange" not only became one of the best-selling records by an old-time act to date, it helped establish the brother duet style that would hold sway over country audiences for years to come.

The song had been in circulation since just before the First World War, when it started appearing in shape-note hymnals, which is where the Monroes learned it. The question it raises, intended as an admonition against storing up riches on earth rather than in heaven, comes from the teachings of Jesus as they appear in the first three Gospels. Charlie sings lead, as he did on all of the duo's Bluebird recordings. But it's Bill's eerie harmonies, especially the "echo" on the chorus, in which he intones "in exchange" as if he were the ghost of Jacob Marley from Dickens's *A Christmas Carol*, that gives the record its pallid cast. Bill's mandolin further heightens this effect, jangling over Charlie's gloomy guitar rhythms as if shaking the chains the avaricious Marley forged while on earth.

But "What Would You Give" is more than just a homily about the ills of lusting after mammon, particularly coming as it did during the Depression, a time when broke and hungry rural folk sought work, even fortune, in the big city. For many it was the first time they'd set foot off the mountain or out of the hollow where they grew up. To these transplants the Monroes' message—a theme echoed by "Honky Tonk Blues," "Streets of Baltimore," and countless other country (and pop) records that came in its wake—spoke to issues that went beyond theological concerns. It tolled a warning about the risks of losing one's self amid the bright lights, temptations, and would-be palliatives of the city.

It's not always that simple, though. Sometimes, as we learn in Bruce Springsteen's "Atlantic City," you've got to hock your soul in order to hang onto it. Singing against stripped down backing that brings his country roots to the fore, Springsteen is beset by danger, debt, and corruption; just as the Monroes said it would, trouble surrounds him on all sides. Why, they're even "busin' [it] in from outta state," Bruce moans, his disembodied wailing reminiscent of Bill's chilling echoes on "What Would You Give." But in contrast to the moral questions the Monroes pose, Springsteen's character faces challenges that can't be reduced to good or evil, to paradise or perdition; "it's just winners and losers and [not getting] caught on the wrong side of that line."

Or about getting out. Not the breathless escape of Springsteen's "Thunder Road," but the simple attempt to get out alive and, in the long run, if you're lucky, with your soul intact.

Even if, in the short run, that means doing something wrong, a dilemma Bruce's character, a guy with "a debt no honest man can repay," wrestles with here. "Atlantic City" hews close to the antediluvian sounds of the Monroes, right down to the homey interplay of guitar and mandolin and Bruce's ghostly, overdubbed harmonies, but don't let these similarities fool you. The harrowing picture of urban desperation it paints is straight out of "In the Ghetto," "Living for the City," and "The Message." It's a last grasp at survival and hope—"Maybe everything that dies someday comes back"—by a man for whom eternity is now.—bfw

69
Independence Day, Martina McBride
Produced by Paul Worley, Ed Seay, and Martina McBride;
Written by Gretchen Peters
RCA 62828   1994   #12 country

In the fall of 1999, the Dixie Chicks released "Goodbye Earl," a song whose main characters, Mary Anne and Wanda, decide they have no alternative but to kill Wanda's wife-beating husband. The recording stirred a mini controversy—a few country stations refused even to play the song— partly because it appeared to defend vigilante justice but mainly because it reduced an all-too-common situation to an 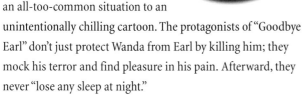 unintentionally chilling cartoon. The protagonists of "Goodbye Earl" don't just protect Wanda from Earl by killing him; they mock his terror and find pleasure in his pain. Afterward, they never "lose any sleep at night."

Released six years earlier, "Independence Day" is a great record, in part because it rejects such trouble-free fairy-tale endings. It never received anywhere near the criticism "Earl" did, though—and not because its abusive husband winds up any less dead. Maybe this was because songwriter Gretchen Peters isn't interested in the physical deaths of her characters so much as the spiritual consequences. She tells the story from the point of view of the abused woman's daughter who, in the years since the tragedy, has experienced not sweet-dream happy endings but pained ambivalence at the terrifying cost of her mother's independence. Was the mother arrested or committed? Did she

die in the fire she set to kill her husband? The song leaves the details unclear, keeping the song's narrative tension alive. All the singer reveals before blasting back into the song's anthemic chorus is one hell of a complex truth: "Now I ain't sayin' it's right or wrong, but maybe it's the only way." You wonder if she'll ever sleep peacefully again.

All of which is to say that "Independence Day" rocks harder than "Goodbye Earl," in every possible way. And, for once, diva-wannabe Martina McBride finds a subject that's the perfect emotional match for her vocal fireworks.—dc

70
Pistol Packin' Mama, Bing Crosby & the Andrews Sisters, with Vic Schoen & His Orchestra
Produced by Jack Kapp; Written by Al Dexter
Decca 23277   1943   #1 country (5 weeks); #2 pop; #3 R&B

Bing Crosby did for music in the first half of the twentieth century what Elvis Presley did in the second—he changed it all. This isn't to say Crosby was the most innovative musician of his time (that was Louis Armstrong) or that he was the era's finest singer (though arguably he was). Rather, like Elvis, Bing was the door through which many of the period's most potent musical forces walked into the popular consciousness. With Crosby, white music meets black, Tin Pan Alley goes nationwide, and the vaudeville tradition enters the recording studio to be transformed for a modern world. The effect of his perfection of microphone techniques alone, which allowed him to sing conversationally, quietly even, instead of having to shout to the back row like Al Jolson, is simply staggering. By expanding his career to include work in radio and film—and developing a winning persona that tied these endeavors together—he modeled for an entire century what it would mean to be a "star." In this regard, even Elvis is unimaginable without him.

Crosby also played an important role in the evolution of country music. His hit recordings of Johnny Mercer's "I'm an Old Cowhand" and Cole Porter's "Don't Fence Me In," among many others, were key moments in the assimilation of western themes and sounds into the pop music of Hollywood and Broadway. Of course, in what amounts to returning the favor, Crosby's croon would deeply influence not just Tin Pan Alley but the creation and performance of cowboy music itself, not to mention honky-tonk and western swing. Bing had a great knack for identifying the pop potential in country music. In the decade surrounding

World War II, Crosby cut songs associated with Bob Wills, Red Foley, and Ernest Tubb. He forged his most significant country connection with Gene Autry, from whose catalogue he frequently borrowed. Ever on the lookout for crossover possibilities, Bing recorded both the singing cowboy's own compositions and many of the numbers that Autry himself had borrowed from the likes of Floyd Tillman, the Sons of the Pioneers, Jimmie Davis, and the Carter Family.

Crosby's first Decca release following the musicians' strike of 1942–43 was "Pistol Packin' Mama," and it stands among his most successful forays into the country repertoire. Typically, Crosby's record reworks Al Dexter's original from the ground up, kicking the memorable, sing-along chorus to the front for maximum impact; adding two new verses; and sharing the stage completely with the Andrews Sisters, who sail through a new bridge—from the point of view of the jealous, gun-toting mama, no less.

The fundamental difference between the versions, though, shows up in the way Bing's record tinkers so playfully with meter and arrangement, stopping and starting the music in ways that are quite unpredictable (which was not really an option for Dexter, of course, bound as he was by the needs of a dance floor full of two-steppers). The result is that this "Pistol Packin' Mama" clearly distinguishes itself from Dexter's hit. It finds more humor in the punch lines and even creates a few of its own ("Lay that thing down before it goes off and hurts somebody," Bing ad libs in his patented burbling baritone), as well as managing, behind blaring trumpets and trombones, to swing as fiercely as anything to the pop side of Count Basie. Crosby's "Pistol Packin' Mama" is a charming, freewheeling lark of a record. More to the point, it captures the modern sounds of country and western music, way ahead of its time.—dc

71
Ommie Wise, G. B. Grayson
No producer credited; Written by G. B. Grayson
Victor 21625   1927   Pre-chart

72
Down on the Banks of the Ohio, Blue Sky Boys
Produced by Eli Oberstein; Traditional
Bluebird B-6480   1936   Pre-chart

73
Knoxville Girl, The Louvin Brothers
Produced by Ken Nelson; Traditional
Capitol 4117   1959   #19 country

The tales of murder and mayhem that made their way from England to America during the eighteenth and nineteenth centuries couldn't have landed on more fertile ground than the rugged mountains of central Appalachia. The region's savage, beautiful terrain—looming hills and dark hollows—teemed with the shadowy forces that seemed to conspire against the characters in the old Anglo-Celtic ballads. The ever-present threat of death posed by disease, violence, and hazardous work reminded mountain folk of what those ruinous British narratives had always known—that life was brutish and short. The old ballads were more than just lively, moralistic tales to the people living in Appalachia during the nineteenth and early twentieth centuries. They were a reflection of the human condition and of the world as many knew it—a harsh, forbidding place that offered few comforts. Too often, only death, whether in the bosom of the church or not, promised a way out.

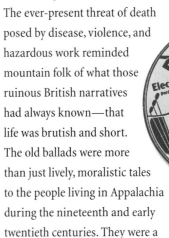

This sense of being trapped pervades all three of these murder ballads. The names and places are different, but the archetypal drama is unchanging—a young man lures his fiancé to a remote spot and does her in, either by drowning, stabbing, or bludgeoning her, and *then* throws her into the river. In "Down on the Banks of the Ohio" it's because she wants to break off their engagement; in the other two the motives aren't as clear. Maybe the bride-to-be is pregnant, and her fiancé doesn't want the baby. Maybe he just doesn't want to marry her. Or, as one might infer from "Ommie Wise," he may fear her love of "money and fine things" will be his undoing.

Each story leaves much to the imagination, its skeletal plot unfolding relentlessly, as if in a nightmare or feverdream. In "Knoxville Girl" and "Banks of the Ohio," both of which are told in the first person, the killer shows no remorse, betraying a disturbing lack of emotion. The same is true of "Ommie Wise," although perhaps more understandably, given that it's narrated by a third party. But even here we have no reason to believe the killer feels any compunction over what he's done. This isn't to say that any of these men welcomes the consequences of his deed, which in each case lands him in jail. The predominant emotion in these ballads is that of feeling stuck in a situation and reckoning that taking some action, any action, no matter how dire, is better than taking none at all.

None of which excuses the misogyny, the utter disregard for women's lives, inherent in these ballads. Each is ultimately too bleak to be called tragic, at least not in the Greek sense of a tale that affirms life as meaningful, or even beautiful, in the face of irrevocable loss. Each does, however, testify to an ethic of resistance—a fundamental instinct, however reprehensible its expression, that finds its protagonist unwilling to succumb to resignation despite his seeming inability to transcend his circumstances. His desperate straits are not so different from the grim lives most mountain folk knew, and they're not nearly as cruel as those known by many of the workers who spent their lives entombed in the mines.

Despite their common wellspring, these records are hardly interchangeable. "Ommie Wise" is the earliest and most primitive of the recordings, with G. B. Grayson's unvarnished tenor accompanied only by the rough sawing of his baleful fiddle. It's also the least embellished of the three; Grayson's narrative gives us no more information about Ommie's ruin than he likely heard in the historical account of her murder, which was his source. The Blue Sky Boys' "Banks of the Ohio" augments the proceedings with a second voice (Bill Bolick's tenor harmonies to brother Earl's lead) as well as instrumentation that features both mandolin and acoustic guitar. But perhaps the biggest change is the song's graphic depiction of the murder in question. The killer doesn't just shove his victim into deep water; he first pulls a knife on her and threatens to slit her throat. Even that pales, however,

compared to the grisly scene that unfolds in the Louvin Brothers' latter-day recording of "Knoxville Girl" where, backed by a full stringband, the killer describes how he beat his victim bloody and senseless before dragging her *by the hair* and tossing her into the river.

Musically, there's an evolution of sorts here, one born, in the Louvins' case, of technological advances in recording, and reinforced by the need to deliver a performance vivid enough to compete with television and the movies. But it would be rash to see a progression in the increasingly graphic content of these ballads, one that has them presaging, among others, the cold-blooded killer in Johnny Cash's "Folsom Prison Blues," or the rapper Eminem's recorded fantasies about murdering his estranged wife. One problem with arguing for such a progression, as some critics might want to do, is that "Knoxville Girl," the most explicitly violent of the three ballads, is likely also the oldest, an East Tennessee rewrite of the eighteenth-century ballad "Wexford Girl." Better then to view these records as prototypes. That is, as stories of a more timeless sort that, whether set in nineteenth-century Appalachia or twenty-first century Detroit, enable people to vent, if only vicariously, their feelings of stuckness, as well as the dark, murderous impulses that surface with them.—bfw

74

Life to Go, Stonewall Jackson
Produced by Don Law and Frank Jones; Written by George Jones
Columbia 41257   1958   #2 country

Merle Haggard sang of doing life in prison and praying every night for death to come; after hearing Stonewall Jackson sing George Jones's "Life to Go," it's easy to see why. Jackson's character is nearly twenty years into a life sentence for stabbing a drinking buddy to death during a row the two men had one night while out hitting the bars. The convicted man owns his guilt; it's not as though he thinks he shouldn't be paying for his crime. But that doesn't make his isolated, mind-, body-, and spirit-numbing existence any less of a living hell.

"I've been in here eighteen years, a long, long time I know /

But time don't mean a thing to me because I've got life to go," Stonewall sings, his doleful tenor droning away like the tedious march of his sentence. The record's gutbucket rhythms likewise reflect the caged man's circumstances, plodding along without the slightest change in tempo. Each verse is the same as the one that comes after it, as repetitious as the hours, days, and years that stretch out ahead of him. His wife doesn't visit anymore; his daughter doesn't know him; he has no connection to the outside world. His body and soul are withering away, a fate that befalls virtually everyone who spends life behind bars. Their skin turns sallow; their teeth fall out; their eyes sink into their faces, becoming little more than sockets holding dim, distant balls. With no one but the guards to notice or care, death would indeed be better, Jackson reckons, than rotting in "prison 'til [his] body's just a shell."—bfw

75

Green, Green Grass of Home, Porter Wagoner
Produced by Bob Ferguson; Written by Curly Putman
RCA Victor 8622   1965   #4 country

Prison songs are among the most wrenching in the country canon, and few if any are as devastating as Porter Wagoner's reading of "Green, Green Grass of Home." All we hear as the record opens is his sonorous baritone. "The old hometown looks the same," reckons Porter as Buck Trent's gutstring guitar creeps in midway through the line. We don't know whether the place looks good to Porter or not, at least not until the bum-bum-bum of the rhythm section puts a spring in his step and he hops off the train into the arms of his parents who 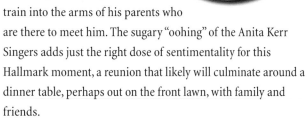 are there to meet him. The sugary "oohing" of the Anita Kerr Singers adds just the right dose of sentimentality for this Hallmark moment, a reunion that likely will culminate around a dinner table, perhaps out on the front lawn, with family and friends.

The scene is pure Americana lifted straight from an episode of *The Andy Griffith Show*. It also sets the stage for the plot to unravel, in every sense of the word. After Porter sizes up the house and yard and takes his sweet Mary out for a stroll, we learn,

as he swallows hard in the recitation that follows, that he was only dreaming. He's not among loved ones back home but alone in a prison cell waiting for the guard and the chaplain to escort him on his final walk as the Kerr Singers, sounding like angels, summon him *from* his earthly home. Not once during the first two verses has Wagoner given away this ending; his delivery remains as measured as the steps that will lead his character to his doom.

Songwriter Putman deserves equal billing with Wagoner. Much as he (and co-writer Bobby Braddock) did with "He Stopped Loving Her Today," Putman lets us see precisely what we need to see, and not a second before we need to see it. His taut narrative conveys as much through what it doesn't tell us as through what it does. There aren't many prison songs that don't mention bars or a cell, or even the condemned man's crime or how he'll be executed. None of this seems to matter to Putman, who, inspired by director John Huston's *The Asphalt Jungle*, forces us to deal with the prisoner's humanity—and the inhumanity of the situation.

"Green, Green Grass of Home," at least in Tom Jones's Top Twenty pop remake, loses something the third or fourth time we've heard the clincher. But *this* record never loses its immediacy, not with Wagoner and company putting us right inside its protagonist's throbbing heart, deep enough inside that we utterly empathize with him, even to the point of being scared for our own lives—whether it was meant that way or not. That's about as powerful a statement on the death penalty as we're ever going to hear.—bfw

76

Sing Me Back Home, Merle Haggard & the Strangers
Produced by Ken Nelson; Written by Merle Haggard
Capitol 2017   1967   #1 country (2 weeks)

Written for a friend of Merle's from San Quentin who actually did go to the chair, this takes up where "Green, Green Grass of Home" leaves off. The condemned prisoner is about to meet his fate and wants a fellow inmate, a guitar player and the song's narrator, to sing him something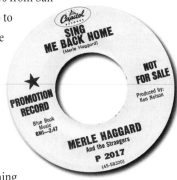

that'll bring back memories of home. We never know what the man did or how he'll be executed. We don't even know his name, but we know he's got a guitar-playing buddy who thinks his memory's worth keeping alive.

He's not the only one. In the song's final verse we learn that the man's mama used to sing him gospel hymns when he was a boy. And while Merle doesn't tell us as much, from the ache in his tender tenor we know he's seeing the doomed man's mama sitting at home, wracked with grief, desperately trying, just like he is, to keep memories of happier times alive.—bfw

77

Sweet Dreams (of You), Patsy Cline
Produced by Owen Bradley; Written by Don Gibson
Decca 31483   1963   #5 country; #44 pop

78

Coal Miner's Daughter, Loretta Lynn
Produced by Owen Bradley; Written by Loretta Lynn
Decca 32749   1970   #1 country (1 week); #83 pop

You can make a strong argument that Owen Bradley is country music's greatest producer, but somehow even that doesn't go far enough. His best records sounded richer and warmer than the competition; they were hook filled, lush without being fussy, and all about rhythm. Working with acts as diverse as Ernest Tubb and Red Foley, Kitty Wells and Brenda Lee, Bill Monroe and Conway Twitty, Bradley mastered virtually every style of country music predominant in his era. And what an era—stretching from 1947, when he was hired to supervise Decca's Nashville recording sessions, through 1976, when he stepped down as the head of MCA Nashville, with occasional returns in the eighties and nineties when young divas like k.d. lang and Mandy Barnett coaxed him out of retirement. Owen Bradley did it all, he did it longer, and he did it better. To get a proper sense of his accomplishments, you have to understand that his peer group wasn't just country producers but producers of all types of American popular music. Even on those sweeping terms, it's doubtful anyone has produced more great records than Owen Bradley.

Bradley is best remembered for his elegant pop-country work with Patsy Cline, and "Sweet Dreams" marks the apotheosis of their partnership. The opening bars are emotionally fitting, instantly arresting, and truly unforgettable. A plummeting string glissando, the brainchild of arranger Bill McElhiney, spirals

dizzily out of the speakers. When those strings finally hit bottom, they cushion Cline as she cries through the title phrase. She wants to forget the man who has hurt her, or at least bring herself to hate him. Instead, in the most wonderful dreams, she spends each night in his arms. Bemoaning her inability to resist these visions, she modulates her voice as if she's mimicking a weeping pedal-steel guitar, and then drummer Buddy Harman, pianist Floyd Cramer, and bassists Bob Moore and Harold Bradley lay down a stunningly spare rhythm bed that bounces and swings Cline, ever so gently, from memory to memory, climax to climax (these dreams are sweet for a *reason*). All the while, the Jordanaires and those strings swathe her voice in gossamer sheets. Earlier versions of the song by Faron Young and composer Don Gibson were memorable enough, but Bradley's record haunts like a phantom, perilous precisely because it offers you no way to resist.

Most great records are the result of collaboration, and there can be no denying that singer and players made huge contributions to "Sweet Dreams (of You)." In the end, though, this was Bradley's baby. As A-Teamer Bob Moore has stressed, Owen Bradley, alone among his peers, regularly arrived at the studio with a specific idea of what he wanted. And "Sweet Dreams" bears the unmistakable uptown stamp of the man who for more than a decade fronted the Owen Bradley Orchestra.

On the other hand, Bradley was easily capable of creating the illusion of down-home music when the song and artist required it. "Coal Miner's Daughter," Loretta Lynn's signature hit about her Appalachian youth, sounds down-home from the ground up, especially when it emphasizes Lynn's East Kentucky accent ("The work we done was hard / At night we'd sleep cause we were tard") and strips the music down to a foot-stomping beat and a relaxed, front-porch banjo.

Of course, this simplicity is just as much the careful creation of Owen Bradley as was an ostensibly more-produced record like

"Sweet Dreams." Bradley helped Lynn edit her song down from nine verses to a more succinct six; he made sure the Jordanaires were there to "oooh" and "aaah" in a way that underscored that Lynn's remembrances are also sweet dreams; he lets the rhythm section almost imperceptibly pump up that simple beat as the arrangement progresses, and although Hal Rugg kicks the record off with pedal steel, Bradley places Bobby Thompson's over-dubbed banjo in the spotlight—at least until Lynn declares "A lot of things have changed since way back then." At this point, the sudden return of Rugg's pedal steel yanks the listener back into the musical present. A present created, in large measure, by Owen Bradley.—dc

79

Statue of a Fool, Jack Greene
Produced by Owen Bradley; Written by Jan Crutchfield
Decca 32490   1969   #1 country (2 weeks)

Emerging from the same Atlanta scene that produced the likes of Jerry Reed, Roger Miller, steel man Pete Drake, and many others, Jack Greene landed his first big break in 1962 when he became a Texas Troubadour. As Ernest Tubb's drummer, Greene spent the next several years honing his chops on the road, where he sometimes warmed the crowds up for his boss with an emotional reading of "The Last Letter." An even bigger break came along four years later, when Greene and

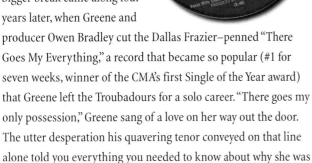

producer Owen Bradley cut the Dallas Frazier–penned "There Goes My Everything," a record that became so popular (#1 for seven weeks, winner of the CMA's first Single of the Year award) that Greene left the Troubadours for a solo career. "There goes my only possession," Greene sang of a love on her way out the door. The utter desperation his quavering tenor conveyed on that line alone told you everything you needed to know about why she was leaving.

In 1969 Greene's fifth and final country chart topper, "Statue of a Fool," catapulted listeners to a whole other level of anguish by offering a return visit from what appears to be the same guy—only now he's had the time to realize just how foolish he's been. Bradley crafts an absolutely unique setting for the song. The

record's dreary, collapsing opening notes sound like a Patsy Cline record on hallucinogens. Then, after a piano augmented by marimba and a staccato electric guitar have fidgeted in and out of the mix, those jarring opening notes return out of nowhere, shuddering the song nearly to a halt even as they herald the climax.

First, though, Greene has his own work to do. In trembling voice, he begins by insisting that someone really ought to erect a statue in tribute to "the man who let love slip through his hands." On one cheek, he says, there should be a lone golden tear ("to honor the million tears he's cried"). Greene sings each line with the kind of fragile caution and supreme self-pity that are the sure signs of a shattered heart. You can imagine him standing as still as that statue as he makes his request, but even if it's been reduced to rubble, his is no heart of stone. By the time Bradley's arrangement ascends to its thrilling conclusion, Greene's composure is shattered. All he can do is shout, in an operatic cry even Marty Robbins or Roy Orbison might have envied, that this statue of "the World's Greatest Fool" should be named after *him*.

Mission accomplished. If it's a monument to heartbreak that Greene and Bradley were after, a great record beats a statue any day.—dc

80

There Stands the Glass, Webb Pierce
Produced by Paul Cohen;
Written by Russ Hull, Mary Jean Shurtz, and Audrey Greisham
Decca 28834   1953   #1 country (12 weeks)

One of the quintessential honky-tonk drinking songs, but oddly enough, one in which Pierce seems scared to death to down that first shot. You'd think that Jimmy Day's opening steel slur, or Floyd Cramer's saloon-style piano atop the ensuing gutbucket shuffle, would be enough to induce anyone to start throwin' 'em back. And from what he tells us in the first verse Webb knows only too well that the whiskey can help "settle his brain" and "ease all his pain." So why such trepidation? Why the catch in his throat when, contemplating that first drink, he moans, "There sta-a-ands the glass"? Could be his boozing

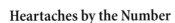

made his woman leave in the first place. Or maybe he's not ready to blot out her memory; he'd rather keep on "wondering" where she is and whether she's coming back, no matter how much that means white-knuckling it. Then again, maybe Webb already knows what Merle Haggard would later discover—that the bottle will only let him down. Whatever the case, the fear and trembling in Pierce's high, out-of-control tenor suggest that even before he touches that glass, he's got one bad case of the shakes.—bfw

81

Pop a Top, Jim Ed Brown

Produced by Felton Jarvis; Written by Nat Stuckey
RCA Victor 9192   1967   #3 country

Awash in memory and Pete Drake's swirling pedal-steel guitar, Jim Ed Brown sits at a bar, popping open one can of beer after another. It's either that, he says, or head home to remember the woman who's left him flat. Of course, it's not as if he could concentrate on anything else just now, regardless of where he was. But at least here he's not alone, he's not sober, and he's got a jukebox cranking out a loud, hard-driving shuffle. We know he's not going anywhere soon because we can hear him, literally, popping a top again at the start of each chorus.

Hard-core honky-tonk at its finest, right? Well, sure, but it also sounds suspiciously like a Nashville Sound classic. Besides commiserating with a bartender, Jim Ed is comforted by a female chorus, and he sings his stylized lines ("Did you ever hear / Of a clown with tear / Drops streaming down his face?") in a genial croon that's awash in more echo than beer. Even those popped tops, meant to signify a tavern, mostly wind up screaming: recording studio!

How about we just say it's softcore and hardcore at once? Whatever you call it, "Pop a Top" is a record shrewdly designed to make the beers go down easy when you hear it calling from the jukebox.—dc

82

Misery Loves Company, Porter Wagoner

Produced by Chet Atkins; Written by Jerry Reed
RCA Victor 7967   1962   #1 country (2 weeks)

If you're searching for a litmus test of "true" country fandom, look no further than Porter Wagoner. Porter's career spotlights just about everything that would normally be praised in a country musician side by side with everything the rest of the world judges as just plain corny. Porter's blinding Nudie suits may have acquired a hip cachet outside country circles, but his architecturally unsound hairdo is, for many, the very definition of kitsch. He is a master of the story song, be it a murder ballad, a barroom bawler, or a sweet remembrance of his Ozark youth, but he's also a purveyor of that most derided of country expressions, the recitation. He's a successful producer, publisher, bandleader, talent scout, and live performer, but he can also be a relentlessly ingratiating show-man. On the upside, his groundbreaking work in television paved the way for *Hee Haw* and The Nashville Network; his ragged-yet-right voice recalls a time when sincerity mattered as much as technique; and his hits explicitly connect country's urban present with its rural past. Yet on the downside, we're told, he paved the way for *Hee Haw* and The Nashville Network; his singing recalls a time when technique mattered only as much as sincerity; and he's just too damn traditional.

"Misery Loves Company" is Porter all over, a chart topper that was the first concrete evidence his syndicated *The Porter Wagoner Show* might actually pay off. It was penned by an up-and-comer by the name of Jerry Reed, and it combines unabashedly twangy guitars with Nashville Sound touches like echo and backing female singers. All of which, song and sound, were just what Wagoner wanted. For despite the official credit to Atkins, Porter was the one who handled every aspect of the session's produc-tion. His friendly, conversational baritone threatens to go flat here and there—in fact, it does more than threaten—but that's what renders Wagoner an instantly convincing narrator. "Gather 'round me," he pleads, enlisting a crowded honky-tonk to "break out the bottle," share a few jokes, and help him get over a broken heart.

And so we do, singing and laughing along, more than willing to help the fellow out. And if you can understand that misery *does* love company, that backslapping and laughing your troubles away beats the hell out of keeping them pent up inside, then you can also understand why the seeming contradiction between Porter the down-home teller of sad tales and Porter the smiling, over-the-top showman is no contradiction at all.—dc

83
She's Actin' Single (I'm Drinkin' Doubles),
Gary Stewart
Produced by Roy Dea; Written by Wayne Carson
RCA Victor 10222   1975   #1 country (1 week)

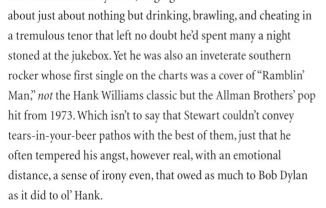

Gary Stewart often gets lumped in with the small band of hard-core country singers (Mel Street, Vern Gosdin, Gene Watson) who seemed like an endangered species during the Nashville bland-out of the mid-to-late seventies. Stewart certainly had one foot in the honky-tonk, singing about just about nothing but drinking, brawling, and cheating in a tremulous tenor that left no doubt he'd spent many a night stoned at the jukebox. Yet he was also an inveterate southern rocker whose first single on the charts was a cover of "Ramblin' Man," *not* the Hank Williams classic but the Allman Brothers' pop hit from 1973. Which isn't to say that Stewart couldn't convey tears-in-your-beer pathos with the best of them, just that he often tempered his angst, however real, with an emotional distance, a sense of irony even, that owed as much to Bob Dylan as it did to ol' Hank.

Stewart's one and only #1 hit finds him playing the cuckold, drowning his troubles in some dive while his wife is off in another bar coming on to a stranger. The title conceit is clever enough to pass for vintage Harlan Howard or Roger Miller and, with the Jordanaires and steel guitarist John Hughey crying in their drinks along with him, Stewart plays the self-pitying chump to the hilt. " 'I'm not weak,' I tell myself, 'I stay because I'm strong' / The truth is that I'm not man enough to stop her from doing me wrong," he blubbers as he picks himself up off the floor for a final run at the record's over-the-top chorus. It's almost as if, struck by

how pathetic, even silly, he is, Stewart is laughing at himself. Almost, but not quite. He's hurting like hell; besides, even if he was laughing, it would only be to disguise his real weakness—the whiskey's going down as smoothly as the rhythms laid down by Harold Bradley's A-Teamers, and there, on the bar, stands yet another glass.—bfw

84
The Battle, George Jones
Produced by Billy Sherrill;
Written by Linda Kimball, Norro Wilson, and George Richey
Epic 50187   1976   #16 country

One weakness of a song-centric approach to country music is that it doesn't explain how so many mediocre songs wind up as great records. Take "The Battle," for instance. If the song's all that matters, this bit of bathos can't even aspire to mediocrity. Melodically, it's almost nonexistent. Lyrically, it takes a romance-as-war conceit (deployed with a self-deprecating sense of play in something like Arthur Alexander's rock & soul classic "Soldier of Love") and invests it with an epic self-importance that's damn near embarrassing. Billy Sherrill's production, replete with martial snare, shots of bass drum to simulate cannon fire, and violins that play "The Battle Hymn of the Republic," only ratchets up the melodrama. This thing is hopeless.

But then along comes Jones. "Dawn breaks on the battlefield" is George's opening salvo, and his emotional presence is so powerful that, against all odds, every line that follows is simply . . . true. Every ridiculous line of it, including "I fire the guns of anger once again" and "with teardrops as her weapon, she easily destroys my battle plan." Even the bit about "her soft, satin armor." Both the lyrics and Sherrill's snowballing arrangement suggest at each moment that the record is set to explode, yet Jones resists. He holds his rage in check throughout, though from the way he clenches his teeth he must only just barely pull it off. The result elevates cheap melodrama into the dramatic, larger-than-life way that lovers experience a quarrel.

So here's a corollary to that old saw "It all begins with a

song"—great singers can trump everything else. That's why by the time you get to the end of "The Battle," the only thing to do is surrender.—dc

85

Rose Garden, Lynn Anderson
Produced by Glenn Sutton; Written by Joe South
Columbia 45252   1970   #1 country (5 weeks); #3 pop

The opening strings, lots of them, ominous and unforgettable, snap your head back like a slap in the face. "I beg your pardon," Lynn Anderson sings calmly enough but surprised nonetheless. "I never promised you a rose garden." The man she's with wants her word that nothing bad will ever happen to them, that she'll never be with another man, that she'll stand by him forever. But that ain't her, babe. Either you "come along and share the good times while we can," she tells him, or you can just "let go" right now. That's the deal. No promises, no strings (well, not counting the ones in the orchestra), no plan, and no telling what's next. The most pinched, manic pedal-steel guitar you've ever heard argues back, but that string arrangement, bolstered by an immense and impatient backbeat, never even blinks.

Anderson crosses her arms, taps her foot, and smiles in sunny defiance. Well? What'll it be? Are you in or are you out?—dc

86

The Cattle Call, Eddy Arnold
Produced by Steve Sholes; Written by Tex Owens
RCA Victor 6139   1955   #1 country (2 weeks); #42 pop

Originally the B side of his debut Bluebird single in 1944, "The Cattle Call" became Eddy Arnold's signature song. He chose it as his radio theme in the forties and fifties and returned to the number throughout his career, rerecording it in 1949, 1955, 1961, and 1996 (with LeAnn Rimes). Small wonder he couldn't get enough of "The Cattle Call"—its pop-western melody and yodeled choruses provide a perfect showcase for Arnold's lithe, lustrous tenor.

The song's writer, cowboy singer Tex Owens (brother of Texas Ruby) wrote "Cattle Call" while a cast member on the *Brush Creek Follies* radio show in Kansas City, Missouri. Corresponding with historian Dorothy Horstman, Owens's wife, Maude, described how her husband recalled the song's origins: "I was sitting . . . on the eleventh floor (of a K[ansas] C[ity] hotel and office building), waiting to do a broadcast . . . Snow began falling. Small flakes at first, then big ones, so big they blotted out my view of the buildings through the windows. Now, I grew up on a ranch . . . and in winter I could never help feeling sorry for the dumb animals out in the wet and cold. Sitting there, watching the snow, my sympathy went out for cattle everywhere." Owens's guitar-and-voice-only recording of the song in 1934 nails perfectly that image of a cowboy calling in the cattle.

Somehow, though, Arnold's hit recording of the song twenty years later more fully captures the song's inspiration—not Owens's empathy for livestock but the snow-globe wonder of his view out that big city window. From the sparkling harp and lonesome flugelhorn that announce the record, there is something nearly surreal about Arnold's 1955 recording. Its rubbery, in-the-saddle rhythm track bounces us through a lush dreamscape that was devised by New York pop arranger Hugo Winterhalter to accent Arnold's ethereal falsetto. Arnold's pristine yodeling feels practically Tyrolean, especially compared to the rough-and-ready blue yodels of Jimmie Rodgers. And, unlike Owens's sad call, Arnold's record isn't about cattle at all but something more intangible: the ineffable pleasure provided by a beautiful human voice, unbound by melody from language's limits, and floating free.—dc

87

Tumbling Tumbleweeds, Sons of the Pioneers
Production credited to "Mr. Rush"; Written by Bob Nolan
RCA Victor 20-1904   1948   #11 country

"Home on the Range" as cowboy mysticism.

"Cares of the past are behind / Nowhere to go but I'll find / Just where the trail will wind / Drifting along with the tumbling tumbleweeds." Sounding less like saddle tramps than Buddhist monks, the Sons of the Pioneers intone these lines in the most sublime four-part harmonies, and with tropes like "I know when the night has gone / That a new world's born at dawn," they sure have their Zen poetry down. "Tumbling Tumbleweeds" in fact began as a poem, an ode to freedom through detachment called "Tumbling Leaves" written by Sons cofounder Bob Nolan. All Nolan did was swap out a few words, notably "leaves" for "tumbleweeds," and he had a made-to-order theme for the 1935 Gene Autry picture of the same name.

Autry sang the movie version of the song, itself a remake of the Sons' original 1934 recording for Decca. But it's the quartet's ineffable, violin-rich rendition from 1948—hooked by Ken Carson's otherworldly whistling on the break—that best captures the transcendental bent of Nolan's lyric. Were it not for its lightly clip-clopping rhythms, high lonesome steel guitar, and ubiquitous tumbleweed references, the record could be set anywhere. And that's the point—Nolan's meditation ultimately transcends time and place, giving voice to nothing so much as a tumbling state of mind.—bfw

88

Dallas, The Flatlanders
Produced by Royce Clark; Written by Jimmie Dale Gilmore
Plantation 92   1972   Did not chart

Lone Star mystics par excellence, the Flatlanders were the Sons of the Pioneers for the post-Aquarian age. With Jimmie Dale Gilmore's numinous quaver, Butch Hancock's metaphysical ballads, and the unearthly whirring of Steve Wesson's saw, the group's mind-expanding stringband music did more than evoke the wind-swept plains and endless horizons of their native Lubbock. It conveyed just how isolated and alienated a body can feel, stuck out there among the tumbleweeds. Here, on their first and only single, the Flatlanders turn their attentions to the bright lights of "Big D," 350 miles to the southeast.

"Did you ever see Dallas from a DC-9 at night / Well Dallas is a jewel, well yeah Dallas is a beautiful sight," Gilmore muses in a voice that's equal parts Gene Autry and the Dalai Lama. The observation's prosaic enough; what's not is the string of elo-

quently plainspoken aphorisms that follows. The first finds Gilmore personifying Dallas as a fickle and cruel mistress, the second as "a rich man who tends to believe his own lies," a third as a "steel-and-concrete soul in a warm-hearted love disguise." Set to the keening wail of Wesson's saw and Joe Ely's harmonica, this web of images constitutes a Zen-like cautionary tale about the risks of losing one's spiritual and emotional compass amid the glitter and snares of the city.

More than just an abstract meditation, "Dallas" would prove a cruelly ironic portent of the tangle the Flatlanders found themselves in after succumbing to the allure of another city—Nashville. In 1972 the group signed with the fledgling Music City–based Plantation Records, for which they cut an album's worth of material, including "Dallas." Owing, however, to a combination of poor promotion and the record's surreal imagery and instrumentation, the single stiffed on country radio. Plantation decided not to press copies of the group's album, although the record eventually surfaced for awhile on eight-track tape. By then, disillusioned, the group's members returned to Texas. Worst of all, their contract with Plantation prevented them from recording together for years, ensuring that, to paraphrase the title of the first stateside reissue of their debut album (in 1990), the Flatlanders would be remembered as more of a legend than a band.

Meanwhile, Gilmore, Ely, and Hancock (the group's principal singer-songwriters) all went on to perform the band's material as solo artists, enabling the mirage-like Flatlanders to exert considerable sway over subsequent generations of progressive country types, especially in their home state of Texas. Through it all, the trio's transcendental ethos never waned, achieving its ultimate expression in Gilmore's 1993 recording of Hancock's "Just a Wave" where, pondering humanity's place in the cosmos, he sang, "You're just a wave, you're not the water."

Cowboy song-poet Bob Nolan—or, for that matter, the Buddha himself—could hardly have said it better.—bfw

89

Amarillo by Morning, George Strait
Produced by Blake Mevis; Written by Terry Stafford and P. Fraser
MCA 52162   1983   #4 country

In the classic western *The Searchers*, John Wayne helps restore a community he can never be part of; in the final scene, his family celebrates a wedding as he walks away, alone again, into the sunset. But at least he has a community to save. The modern-day cowboy in "Amarillo by Morning" doesn't even have that. He's a rodeo cowboy, "bucking at the county fair," who's long since lost both wife and girlfriend. His future, always

somewhere further down the road, is another rodeo just like the last one. Maybe, if his luck and his body hold up, he'll scratch out enough prize money to make it to the next town, the next rodeo, the next eight seconds when he'll feel most alive.

"I ain't got a dime, but what I got is mine / I ain't rich but Lord I'm free," George Strait sings, and as the music rises up defiantly around him, he almost convinces you he believes it. But then he stops singing, a lone fiddle takes the melody, and this pop-inflected tune turns suddenly desolate. Eventually the rest of the band drops out until it's just that lonely fiddle. When even that fades away, you know this oasis was just a mirage all along—the freedom to be broke and alone is no freedom at all.—dc

90

Makin' Believe, Kitty Wells
Produced by Paul Cohen; Written by Jimmy Work
Decca 29419   1955   #2 country

Unable to get beyond the loss of a man she loves, Wells spends her days pretending he still cares. She's not trying to fool anyone that he's really coming back, least of all herself. But since she knows she'll never have the future she planned, and since she can't yet imagine any other future—can't believe, that is, in her own power to create any tomorrows that don't just repeat this painful today—she's determined to make believe, forever. Her voice quakes at the very thought of such an existence, but though a steel guitar coaxes her to let go and cry, she never sheds a tear. If she lets the tears come now, they might fall forever and that would be a fate even worse than pretending.—dc

91

How Long Will My Baby Be Gone,
Buck Owens & the Buckaroos
Produced by Ken Nelson; Written by Buck Owens
Capitol 2080   1968   #1 country (1 week)

92

Together Again, Buck Owens
Produced by Ken Nelson; Written by Buck Owens
Capitol 5136   1964   #1 country (2 weeks)

This double shot points out just how much more there was to the Buckaroos' sound than its patented "freight-train" shuffle. The first skips lightly along atop the delicately propulsive brushwork of Willie Cantu, the nearly flamenco acoustic guitar

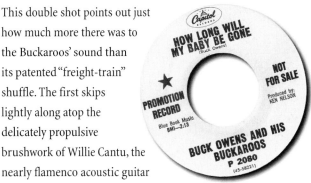

licks of Don Rich, and a sunny chorus hooked by handclaps. The second moves at a virtual crawl, as a dispirited Buck engages in a duet with Tom Brumley's cheerless steel guitar.

These chart toppers also underscore that Owens's records could be a lot more complicated than their seemingly simple lyrics let on. The ostensibly distressed "How Long Will My Baby Be Gone" feels airy and carefree, while "Together Again," a song that on its face should be happy as can be, sounds ready to cry. At the end of each chorus, Buck notes that he and his ex are indeed "together *again*," and each time his voice hardens and drops. He sounds like maybe he should be careful what he wishes for.—dc

93

We Must Have Been out of Our Minds,
George Jones & Melba Montgomery
Produced by Harold "Pappy" Daily;
Written by Melba Montgomery
United Artists 575   1963   #3 country

Temporarily insane, George Jones and Melba Montgomery fell in love with someone else, or at least thought they had. Back in their right minds, they're reconciling. So you'd think this would be a happy record. But then why in the world do their harmonies sound so inconsol- able? And why is that dobro throwing off tears like their reunion is also a funeral?

Well, first off, they may very well be settling for the best they can get, not getting what they really want—the only reason they're back together, after all, is that their new lovers "turned out to be the wrong kind." The real clue, though, is in the choice of that dobro. It would have sounded ancient on country radio in 1963, amid that era's orchestras, backing choirs, and electric guitars, so each wailing fill can't help but suggest the past— specifically, George and Melba's past together. They'll have to "forgive and forget" every petty slight, every ugly fight, every betrayal, if they're going to make this reconciliation work. In other words, like a lot of country music, "We Must Have Been out of Our Minds" is a song about second chances. George and Melba sound sad because, now, they know firsthand just how often people need them, and why.—dc

94
Ring of Fire, Johnny Cash
Produced by Don Law and Frank Jones;
Written by June Carter and Merle Kilgore
Columbia 42788   1963   #1 country (7 weeks); #17 pop

June Carter was hardly ready for her future husband Johnny Cash to know about her feelings for him when she immortalized them in "Ring of Fire." Cash was in the throes of a wicked addiction to booze and pills when June, who started singing and doing stand-up in his show in 1961, began falling for him. Rather than fanning those flames, she gave the song to her sister Anita, for whom it sank without a trace when released as "Love's Burning Ring of Fire" in 1962.

The "Ring of Fire" that June wrote (with encouragement from Hank Williams cohort Merle Kilgore) was a mix of desire and trepidation, the confession of a woman terrified of her passion burning out of control lest it, or its object, consume her. June, a devout Christian who disapproved of Johnny's bad habits even as she feared for his soul, had every reason to be wary of falling into a flaming pit with a hell-raiser like Cash—she could very well have been burned alive.

Johnny's swaggering version of "Ring of Fire" couldn't be more different from what June originally had in mind. Spurred on by the galloping rhythms of the Tennessee Three—and particularly, by Luther Perkins's giddy-up guitar—Johnny sounds like he couldn't wait to jump into the inferno. "I fell into a burning ring of fire / I went down, down, down / And the flames went higher," he sings in a robust baritone as the Mariachi trumpets of Karl Garvin and Bill McElhiney fan the blaze. Johnny must have suspected what lay behind the lines he was singing; he sure inhabited them as if he did, abandoning himself to the purifying love he somehow knew would eventually save him from him- self.—bfw

95
Baby, It's Cold Outside,
Homer & Jethro with June Carter
Produced by Steve Sholes; Written by Frank Loesser
RCA Victor 21-0078   1949   #9 country; #22 pop

Nothing has hampered country music in its perennial quest to be taken seriously more than its hillbilly pedigree, and nothing embodies the legacy the industry wants to live down more than the corn-pone comedy of *Hee Haw*.

There was a time, though, when *Hee Haw's* barnyard shtick, itself a throwback to minstrel shows and vaudeville, was an integral and much-loved part of the radio barn dances and traveling revues that put country on the map. The gags of comedians like Whitey Ford, Minnie Pearl, and Rod Brasfield afforded rural folk much the same release from the grind of farm and factory life as a good fiddle tune or sad ballad. The main difference was that while their picking and singing counterparts induced people to dance and drink away their blues, these country cutups had folks laughing to keep from crying.

Homer & Jethro were perhaps postwar country's most popular

comedy act, placing two singles in the Top Ten and three more in the Top Twenty shortly after signing with RCA in 1949. This was no mean feat for a subgenre of country music that's never made much headway with radio. Parodies à la Spike Jones were the duo's specialty ("Poor Ol' Koo-Liger," "Hart Brake Motel"); here, with help from twenty year-old June Carter, they subject Frank Loesser's Tin Pan Alley standard to their hillbilly high jinks.

June, who honed her bumpkin improv as part of the Carter Family's act when they worked on border radio in San Antonio during the late thirties and early forties, plays the role of the gingham-clad hayseed to the hilt. She's just spent the day at Homer & Jethro's cabin, whiling away the hours flirting and sipping something that sure ain't "sasperilly." "I got to git home, fellers / I can't stay here all night," she demurs in an "aw shucks" drawl. June's got plenty of reasons for leaving—it's getting dark; the snow's started falling; her pa's fixin' to come after her with his shotgun. But every time she reels off one of her excuses, Homer & Jethro are ready with another ploy to keep her there—they'll hold her hand; they'll pour her another drink; they'll put on some Eddy Arnold records.

June, of course, has no intention of braving the cold, not with the prospect of imbibing that homebrew ("Maybe just a half-a-jug more," she titters) or of hearing the ember-like crooning of the Tennessee Plowboy on the Victrola. Then again, maybe it's the way Jethro Burns's mandolin heats up things on the break that's keeping her there. Or maybe June just can't resist the wordless advances of Chet Atkins's guitar that spark their conversation. Whatever it is, it's plain that everyone here is having a ball. It's a testament not just to great picking and comedic timing, but to a time when country folk still knew how to laugh at themselves and weren't ashamed to do so.—bfw

96
Single Girl, Married Girl, The Carter Family
Produced by Ralph Peer; Written by A. P. Carter
Victor 20937A   1927   Pre-chart

Most discussions of this record, which comes from the Carter Family's epochal Bristol Sessions, revolve around Sara's stunning solo vocal. And well they should; bereft of the group's signature harmonies, her forlorn alto could well have been the inspiration for Hank's heartsick whippoorwill. Yet "Single Girl, Married Girl" is also a strong dose of protofeminist sexual politics, minus the comic relief of Loretta's "One's on the Way." The fact that Sara's

husband A. P. adapted it from an antediluvian favorite doesn't for a minute lessen its punch.

"Single girl, single girl, she's going dressed fine . . . Married girl, married girl, she wears just any kind," Sara broods, commiserating with the poor married girl as Maybelle's dogged picking invests her lines with the force of fate. Sara herself was a new mother at the time and was often stuck home alone with the baby while A. P. was out combing the hillsides for folk songs. Her feelings of frustration could hardly help bleeding through here, and doubtless the thousands of married women who spent a few pennies from their meager dress fund to buy this record detected as much. Surely they also understood, the constraints of the era being what they were, that those fancy things they used to buy were but a precursor to rocking the cradle—and crying, right along with the child.—bfw

97
Don't Touch Me, Jeannie Seely
Produced by Fred Foster; Written by Hank Cochran
Monument 933   1966   #2 country; #85 pop

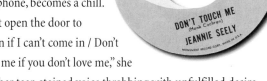

"Your hand is like a torch each time you touch me," Jeannie Seely moans, her body trembling as the tingle, frozen by a chiming vibraphone, becomes a chill. "Don't open the door to heaven if I can't come in / Don't touch me if you don't love me," she begs, her tear-stained voice throbbing with unfulfilled desire.

The arrangement—slip-note piano, sighing steel, silky background singers—is the Nashville Sound on the cusp of its soul-inflected successor, countrypolitan. The same is true of Seely's aching vocals, on the one hand a nod to the torchy burn of Patsy Cline ("Don't Touch Me" was written by Seely's future husband and former Cline collaborator Hank Cochran), on the other a precursor to the down-home sobbing of Tammy Wynette. Tammy cut "Don't Touch Me" with Billy Sherrill the following year, but as good as her version is, it's not in the same league as Seely's, a performance that earned Jeannie the appellation "Miss Country Soul."

And how. "To have you, then lose you, wouldn't be smart on my part," she groans in a ravaged quaver, torturing the word "part" for an agonizing eight counts until at last her voice breaks and, with it, her heart.—bfw

98
Begging to You, Marty Robbins
Produced by Don Law; Written by Marty Robbins
Columbia 42890   1964   #1 country (3 weeks); #74 pop

On "Begging to You," Marty Robbins outdoes even himself. "What a pitiful sight I must be tonight," the singer known as Mr. Teardrop admits to the woman he hopes will take him back. Judging by the story he tells, even that painful description is probably generous. That very morning he announced he was leaving for good; she laughed in his face, predicting he'd come crawling soon enough. And now here he is, right on cue, begging for another chance. He can't figure out why a woman who he knows doesn't love him, need him, or even respect him, would keep him hanging around.

That's a no-brainer. He's still in the picture because she swoons every time she hears Marty's baritone unwind, like the most beautiful ribbon, across a blue melody. Because she breaks out in goose bumps when his voice catches and moves into falsetto, contradictorily conveying abjection by flying high. And maybe even because when she hears him admit just how pathetic he's become—"To you, it don't matter *what* you cause me to do"—she feels a twinge of guilt. But just a twinge. Mainly, she keeps Marty hanging on for the same reason anyone would. She likes to hear him sing.—dc

99
Turn Around, Carl Perkins
Produced by Sam Phillips; Written by Carl Perkins
Flip 501   1955   Did not chart

Thought ol' Carl was a one-trick rockabilly? This gutbucket shuffle finds him moaning the lovesick blues like he was the second coming of Hank Williams. Or the first of George Jones.—bfw

100
For the Good Times, Ray Price
Produced by Don Law; Written by Kris Kristofferson
Columbia 45178   1970   #1 country (1 week); #11 pop

Country music is often called music for grown-ups, and no record better illustrates the point than Ray Price's "For the Good Times." The foundation is Kris Kristofferson's song, which is every bit as complex and conflicted as any real-life adult breakup.

"Don't look so sad," Price begins. You figure he's comforting a woman to whom he's just delivered bad news. But as the scene unfolds, you learn that he's the one getting the bad news; she's leaving him, and the song is his attempt to get her to go to bed with him just once more. You know, "for the good times." Price could have delivered these lines in all sorts of ways. He could have sung as if the man were unable or unwilling to let go. He could leave the man wallowing in self-pity or nostalgia, or he could have let the man believe he just needs someone to help him make it through the night. It could have been a last ditch effort to get her to stay, or maybe he's just a creep who wants to get laid. The miracle of Price's delivery—he croons elegantly in one breath, all pathetic in the next—is that he never allows us to choose between these interpretations. Kristofferson's words and melody and Price's delivery combine to let the man be all these things at once. No wonder Price has frequently gone out of his way to identify "For the Good Times" as among the best songs he's ever sung.

The reason he even has to point this out at all is the record's arrangement. Its clopping drum and tic-tac bass are unmistakably country in feel, but the problem for some listeners is the Cam Mullins string arrangement intertwined with that pulsing rhythm—as every purist knows by heart, string arrangements don't belong on country records. Whatever. There's really no accounting for such reactions, particularly to a record like "For the Good Times," where the strings so clearly aid both the singer and the song. It's true that on some records strings are needlessly stitched onto perfectly serviceable country rhythm sections (think of those Frankenstein monster overdubs of Hank Williams's hits), but that's not the case here. "For the Good Times" was clearly conceived with an orchestra at its center. As a result, the strings give the song its mournful tone and sonic thrust; they suggest, in their call-and-response with the singer, all the history that stands between this couple. Most of all, they assist Price in his seduction even as they point to the man's inevitably lonely future.

Because she's going to tell him no, right? "Don't look so sad," he begins. Every time you hear Price sing those lines, you wonder anew just what it is he has done to make her give him that look. Has he moved to hold her in his arms as she was packing to leave? Touched his lips to her neck as she pulled away? "Make believe you love me," he purrs, then pauses ever so slightly before adding "one more time." And that's where you finally understand why her eyes have filled with tears—she's remembering all those nights when making believe was precisely what she had to do.—dc

101

Blue Eyes Crying in the Rain, Willie Nelson
Produced by Willie Nelson; Written by Fred Rose
Columbia 10176   1975   #1 country (2 weeks); #21 pop

Willie Nelson's *Red Headed Stranger* is widely hailed as the apotheosis of country's outlaw movement, and for obvious reasons. There was his choice of where and with whom to make the record: in a small studio in Garland, Texas, with his road band rather than in Nashville, where he could have availed himself of hotshot producers and first-call session pros. There was the spare, crepuscular sound of the album, an almost demo-like quality that had Columbia Records exec Billy Sherrill urging the label to block its release. There was the project's organizing concept, an ambitious, mystical-existential plot line that owed more to the films of John Ford and Sergio Leone (and to the self-conscious albums of the era's progressive-rock bands) than to anything dreamt of in Chet Atkins's philosophy. Finally, there was Nelson's reincarnation as a bearded longhair, a transformation born of his retreat to Austin and his identification with the

hippies who hung out at the Armadillo World Headquarters. After fifteen years of watching others run his songs up the charts but having next to no success singing them himself, Willie decided to cut his ties to the Nashville hit mill.

Or did he? The one thing lost in the rush to crown Willie prince of the Nashville dissidents—and, ironically, the most radical thing about *Red Headed Stranger*—is that the first single from the album, "Blue Eyes Crying in the Rain," was a song firmly entrenched in the Nashville machine. Written in 1945 by Music Row publisher Fred Rose, "Blue Eyes" had been recorded by Grand Ole Opry stars Roy Acuff and Eddy Arnold, and Willie makes no effort to disguise that fact. As he tenderly croons the song's lyrics—his voice a mix of the rough and smooth tones of Acuff and Arnold (with dollops of Crosby and Sinatra thrown in as well)—Willie sounds like he's paying homage to, not disparaging, his predecessors. Much the same is true of the record's understated arrangement. Mickey Raphael's accordion-like harmonica fills, Bee Spears's dewdrop bass, and Willie's gauzy gut-string guitar have more in keeping with the "less is more" aesthetic of the Nashvile A-Teamers who played on Arnold's version of "Blue Eyes" than with the rock-edged sounds favored by Waylon and Hank Jr.

Make no mistake, Willie was still casting judgment on the records that were then rolling off the Nashville assembly line, he was just using Music Row's own gold standard to critique them. "Love is like a dying ember / Only memories remain / And through the ages I'll remember / Blue eyes crying in the rain," he pines in a mournful baritone. These lines, of course, are about the love gone wrong at the heart of the *Red Headed Stranger* narrative. Yet they also convey Willie's longing for an alternative to the slick impersonal music that, in the early years of what would become the *Urban Cowboy* style, was fast becoming the Nashville norm. By playing a time-honored song in a new, but hardly unheard-of way, Willie, always a consummate dialectician, was at once reaching backward and looking forward. Doubtless it was this combination of conservative and progressive impulses that resonated with so many people who tuned in country and pop radio in 1975 and made "Blue Eyes" Willie's first #1 single as a recording artist.—bfw

102

Walking the Floor over You, Ernest Tubb
Produced by Dave Kapp; Written by Ernest Tubb
Decca 5958   1941   Pre-chart

E.T. might have been out of his
head pacing the floor over the
woman who'd just walked
out on him. But this ultra-
lean wonder—little more
than skipping rhythms and
the cornet-like spurts of
electric guitarist Smitty
Smith—had everyone waltzing, or
at least shuffling, through Texas, and across
the South, heading for points beyond.—bfw

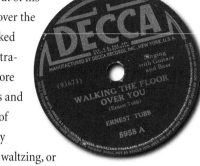

103

Oh Lonesome Me, Don Gibson
Produced by Chet Atkins; Written by Don Gibson
RCA Victor 7133   1958   #1 country (8 weeks); # 7 pop

The story goes that Don Gibson wrote "Oh Lonesome Me" and "I
Can't Stop Loving You," its Top Ten B side, during the same
afternoon. Too often that part of the Gibson bio, as well as his

pioneering role with producer
Chet Atkins in the evolution of
the Nashville Sound, is all
that most people know.
That's not to say these
things aren't hallmarks of
Gibson's career. He has, after
all, written scores of hits,
including "Sweet Dreams," that
have sold millions of records the world

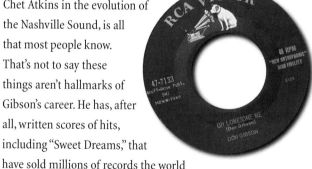

over. And this recording, on which he and Atkins eschewed the
then-obligatory fiddle and steel guitar in favor of the backing
vocals of the Jordanaires, certainly helped chart the course for
country's late-fifties move uptown.

But Gibson was also a terrific and highly nuanced singer, one
whose phrasing evinces a deep affinity with what Ralph Ellison
calls "the blues impulse." The "impulse to keep the painful details
and episodes of a brutal experience alive in one's aching
consciousness, to finger its jagged grain, and to transcend it, not

by the consolation of philosophy but by squeezing from it a near-
tragic, near-comic lyricism."

This tragicomic lyricism is writ large in "Oh Lonesome Me," a
song that's proven elastic enough to work in radically different
versions by both Neil Young and the Kentucky Headhunters.
"Everybody's goin' out and havin' fun / I'm just a fool for stayin'
home and havin' none / I can't get over how she set me free / Oh,
lonesome me," Gibson moans, shaking his head both at his
lovelorn state and at his pathetic response to it. Yet as pitiful as he
is, at least he's able to sing about it—in itself an act of self-
affirmation. And as he listens to the record's swinging rhythms
and Chet's pick-me-up guitar on the break, Don even indulges in
a moment's transcendence. Sure, it's only a vicarious triumph, but
it's a moment of truth nonetheless, and one that ultimately
enables him to say "there must be some way that I can lose these
lonesome blues."

It's also just the kind of self-deprecating, "laughing to keep
from crying" sensibility that Roger Miller perfected a few years
later in a song like "The Last Word in Lonesome Is Me." Which,
come to think of it, owes enough to "Oh Lonesome Me" that
maybe it should be added to Gibson's long list of songwriting
laurels.—bfw

104

Bye Bye Love, The Everly Brothers
Produced by Archie Bleyer;
Written by Boudleaux and Felice Bryant
Cadence 1315   1957   #1 country (7 weeks); #2 pop; #5 R&B

And hello world. Memphis rockabilly pioneer Elvis Presley had
recorded in Nashville as early as 1956, but the Everlys were Music
City's first homegrown rock & roll act to land a major hit on pop
radio.

Don and Phil Everly were just twenty and eighteen years old,
respectively, when "Bye Bye Love" turned them into overnight
stars, but they were already seasoned professionals. They'd been
performing a "family-style" radio show with their parents for a
decade when in 1955 their folks decided to move to Nashville and
give big-time country music a try. In just a few months, rock &
roll would explode across the land. Don and Phil—talented boys
with plenty of teen sex appeal who now resided in a town that
was scrambling for just that profile—were in the right place at
the right time.

They were also the right boys for the job. After all, their father, former Kentucky coal miner Ike Everly, was one of the guitarists who'd taught the young Merle Travis a thing or two. The so-called "Travis-pickin'" style, adopted quickly by Chet Atkins, then by Scotty Moore and countless others, would help shape the guitar attack on hundreds of rock & roll hits to come. Ironically, the Everlys rarely employed the sound on their own early hits, even when Atkins played the session. It's as if what had thrilled them most about the band on Presley's Sun records wasn't Scotty Moore's licks—hell, their daddy could do that—but the rocket thrust blasting from Presley's own acoustic rhythm guitar.

"Bye Bye Love" is *all* about rhythm guitar. Phil and Don sing in the same piercingly sweet close-harmony style (inherited from the brothers Delmore and Louvin, and later adapted by Lennon and McCartney, and Simon & Garfunkel, as well as the O'Kanes and the Judds) that they'd been using in the family act all along. But it's that jolting first note that commands instant attention—just that one quick, sharp pass across the strings, and you're theirs forever. Augment Don's visceral, aggressive strumming (he chops away at the strings like an acoustic Bo Diddley) with drummer Buddy Harman and stand-up bassist Floyd "Lightnin'" Chance, and you've got a rhythm engine that could power the world.

Add the elegant parallel rhymes of Boudleaux and Felice Bryant's great song (wave goodbye to "happiness" and "sweet caress"; say hello to "loneliness" and "emptiness"), and how could the thing miss? "Bye Bye Love" was a country smash, quickly crossed over pop, and heralded a string of Everlys hits that remain among the finest Nashville has ever produced. The Everlys' chart run clued in the world to the secret that Nashville was a great place to cut a hit, country or otherwise. After all, Nashville's not just the country music capital of the world; it's Music City, U.S.A.—dc

105

Oh, Pretty Woman, Roy Orbison & the Candy Men
Produced by Fred Foster; Written by Roy Orbison and Bill Dees
Monument 851 1964   #1 pop (3 weeks)

Mention Roy Orbison's "Oh, Pretty Woman," and everyone instantly recalls that giant, snarling guitar riff. No wonder, since

it's actually *four* guitars—played by Orbison, Wayne Moss, Jerry Kennedy, and Billy Sanford—plus bassist Henry Strzelecki, plus the saxophones of Boots Randolph and Charlie McCoy, all laying down the same monster riff. Even so, when the record comes on the radio, it's the fierce, drill-press drumming of Buddy Harman that snaps your head back and demands you listen in the first place.

After studying for three years at Chicago's Roy Knapp School of Percussion, Harman returned to his hometown of Nashville in 1952 and quickly found work as the drummer in the original edition of Carl Smith's band, the Tunesmiths. One of the few country drummers in town, Harman couldn't have known how perfect his timing would turn out to be. Drums were still a rarity on country records in the early fifties, but in just a few years, after rock & roll triggered the Nashville Sound, drums would be as much a staple of country recording as fiddles had been for the previous three decades.

Almost always, Harman would be the one playing them. It has been estimated that, from the fifties through the seventies, Harman provided the backbeat on anywhere from 15,000 to 18,000 recordings. It should come as no surprise, then, that so many of the recordings in this book feature Buddy Harman on drums. Still, the mind boggles at the number of musically distinctive and emotionally fitting ways Harman found to lay down a beat. Like Al Jackson Jr. in soul music, Buddy Harman set the standard, both quantitatively and qualitatively, for what a great country drummer should be—and that's taking "country drummer" in the broadest possible sense. Harman kept expert time on all sorts of records—everything from swooning Patsy Cline classics and hard Ray Price shuffles to rock and pop hits by the Everly Brothers, Elvis Presley, and Simon & Garfunkel.

His work with Orbison might be his most impressive. On "Oh, Pretty Woman," Harman makes the whole preposterous situation seem nothing short of inevitable—the shy, nerdy Orbison is out hitting on strange women as they pass him on the street. He tosses a smarmy come-on at one ("Mercy!"), growls his approval at another, and then, just as he's ready to hang it up for the night, one of these women actually turns around and comes back to him! Then again, with Harman slamming away in the background, not to mention offering fills as offhand cool as a smile and a wink, it's a wonder she doesn't have to stand in line.—dc

106

Great Balls of Fire, Jerry Lee Lewis
Produced by Sam Phillips;
Written by Jack Hammer and Otis Blackwell
Sun 281   1957   #1 country (2 weeks); #2 pop; #3 R&B

Jerry Lee Lewis could've been one hell of a preacher. He certainly had the credentials. He came up in the Holiness Church/ Assembly of God and attended Bible college in Waxahatchie, Texas, just outside Dallas. He even claims to have done some evangelizing while he was a student there. Then again, he wasn't exactly a prime candidate to minister to straying souls. Among other things, he was too much of a lech to have been able to hold onto a pulpit for long (not that fornicating with a member of the flock got his cousin Jimmy Lee Swaggart defrocked or anything).

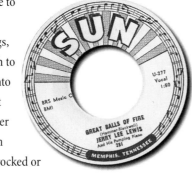

Thing is, the Killer could be speaking in tongues and it would still sound like lust, and he sure doesn't leave much to the imagination here. Lines like "you shake my nerves and you rattle my brain" and "you broke my will, but what a thrill" might seem like they're describing the neurological and psychological effects of being possessed by the Holy Ghost. But from the way he bangs away at the piano as he proclaims them, the spirit that's got hold of him is of a more carnal, and infernal, variety. Those aren't tongues of Pentecostal fire that are kissing him—that's for damn sure.—bfw

107

Great Speckle Bird, Roy Acuff
& His Crazy Tennesseans
Produced by Art Satherley; Written by Guy Smith
Vocalion 04252, OKeh 04252, Conqueror 8740
1936   Pre-chart

What the hell is this song about?

Acuff claims he bought it for two bits from a man named Charlie Swain, a singer with ties to the Church of God, a fundamentalist denomination based in East Tennessee. The title invokes a passage of scripture, Jeremiah 12:9, in which a dappled bird, likely a hen, is beset by hawks. The hen represents Israel's heritage; the perilous state it's in is a sign that the Hebrew people are letting outside forces sully their inheritance. The lyrics of Acuff's recording paint the bird as a metaphor for the Bible, and its avian attackers as the Good Book's detractors. What any of it meant to Roy, a pious fellow but no theological adept, remains a mystery.

What is clear is that "Great Speckle Bird," which borrows its melody from the Carter Family's "I'm Thinking Tonight of My Blues Eyes," is a momentous record, and not just as a showcase for Clell Summey's swooping dobro or Acuff's stirring Sacred Harp–inspired singing. It was also Roy's ticket to the Grand Ole Opry. After his Crazy Tennesseans (who, at the suggestion of Opry founder George Hay, soon changed their name to the less pejorative Smoky Mountain Boys) performed the song for their Opry debut, they became fixtures on the show. More than that, their popularity helped solidify a shift in the Opry lineup away from the hoedown bands that dominated its first ten years toward groups fronted by "star"

vocalists, a development that paved the way for Acuff to become the show's focal point for decades to come. Meaning that whatever its theological import, Roy, who went on to become the "King of Country Music," rode the wings of this "Bird" straight to glory.—bfw

108

His Hand in Mine, The Blackwood Brothers Quartet
Produced by Steve Sholes; Written by Mosie Lister
RCA Victor 5709   1954   Did not chart

109

This Ole House, The Statesmen Quartet
with Hovie Lister
Produced by Steve Sholes; Written by Stuart Hamblen
RCA Victor 5850   1954   Did not chart

White gospel is as important to the development of country music as almost anything else you could name—every bit as important, say, as black gospel is to soul. It was largely through the nineteenth-century traditions of Sacred Harp and shape-note singing, for example, that the use of harmony was introduced to country music in the first place. Ever since, from A. P. Carter to Elvis Presley to Iris DeMent, the history of country music has been filled with artists who first learned to sing in church. Until very recently, in fact, it would have been all but impossible to find a major country act who *hadn't* recorded at least a few gospel sides in his or her career, and it would have been only slightly less difficult to name one who didn't sometimes include a few gospel numbers during live performance.

Still, gospel music's place within the country tradition remains underrated today—that is, when it's not being over-looked altogether, especially by those rock critics who write about country music from a postpunk sensibility. As Cheryl Cline has pointed out in her satiric essay "20 Easy Rules for Writing About Country Music: The Way the Pros Do It!," the tendency among many such writers is to "Play up Johnny Cash as an outlaw" and rockabilly, for example, but to "play down Johnny Cash as a Bible scholar" and gospel singer.

But if the music's gospel side remains a neglected part of the story, southern gospel might as well not even exist. Related to but distinct from bluegrass gospel and country gospel, southern gospel emerged from a publishing-house marketing ploy—set quartets loose upon the south like packs of spiritual Fuller Brush men, then have them demonstrate to rapt congregations the songs and arrangements the companies had for sale. These quartets were so enthusiastically received that many of them eventually set out on their own. None of them, however, could rival either the Statesmen Quartet or the Blackwood Brothers.

Recorded in their heydays, when these quartets were so popular that a major label like RCA could actually be bothered to release dozens of their singles and albums, "This Ole House" and "His Hand in Mine" are representative of the stylistic extremes that defined southern gospel. On "This Ole House," the Statesmen move through Stuart Hamblen's standard at breakneck speed while the Blackwoods render at a crawl "His Hand in Mine," written by southern gospel songwriting legend Mosie Lister. Both recordings also feature prayer-to-a-shout dynamics, vocal arrangements that shift suddenly between intense solo leads and intricate harmonies, and individual voices that run the gamut from higher-than-heaven first tenors to bone-rattling basses.

Yet these singles aren't here merely because they're represen-tative. Rather, they resonate with a depth of human aspiration and spirit that's undeniable, even if you're not a Christian. "This Ole House" is as ecstatic a musical embrace of death as there is. Lead Statesman Jake Hess shouts in a voice that's downright frisky, even though he's already feeling the chill of death in his shaky knees. His body's falling apart, his house is falling down, but he doesn't care anymore. He doesn't need anything; he's getting ready to meet the saints. Then, when first tenor Denver Crumpler takes the quartet through a thrilling chorus of "When the Saints Go Marching In," you realize he really is dead and gone. The miracle of the record is you want to go with him.

The Blackwoods manage something even more amazing on "His Hand in Mine." Rather than joyously flying away, they nurture the sublime right here, right now. "You may ask me how I know my Lord is real," James Blackwood sings at the beginning of "His Hand In Mine." "You may doubt the things I say and doubt the way I feel." There is no way, though, that anyone could doubt the sound in his soaring, breathtaking tenor. It sounds like you might imagine an angel's—mighty yet forgiving and high without the lonesome; it sounds like peace.—dc

110

Be-Bop-a-Lula, Gene Vincent
Produced by Ken Nelson; Written by Gene Vincent and Tex Davis
Capitol 3450   1956   #5 country; #7 pop; #8 R&B

111

It's Only Make Believe, Conway Twitty
Produced by Jim Vienneau;
Written by Conway Twitty and Jack Nance
MGM 12677   1958   #1 pop (2 weeks); #12 R&B

Today's Elvis impersonators preserve Elvis's physical persona and revere his music as a monument to a mythic past. Presley's finest contemporary imitators, Gene Vincent and Conway Twitty, seized the spirit of the Elvis moment and then sprinted ahead with it, lunging headlong into an exhilarating future.

By the time Gene Vincent recorded "Be Bop-a-Lu-La," he was already a big fan of Presley's first recordings at Sun Records. He'd also been blown away by Elvis live when, fresh from the Navy and still recuperating from a leg injury that left him limping and in pain for the rest of his life, he'd seen the young singer on a Hank Snow package show in 1955. Inspired, Vincent began playing his own version of this new sound, a number called "Be Bop-a-Lu-La." Despite this history, though, the record Vincent and producer Ken Nelson made owes less to the Sun sound of the earliest Elvis recordings than it does to Presley's first RCA single, "Heartbreak Hotel," the smash that transformed Elvis from a regional rumor into a national obsession. Fittingly, that very record sat atop both the pop and the country charts when Nelson, Vincent, and his Blue Caps entered Nashville's Bradley Studios to record "Be Bop-a-Lu-La" in May of 1956.

"Heartbreak Hotel" and "Be Bop-a-Lu-La" each begin at a barely restrained crawl. Slurred and bluesy voices fight against the slow, spare rhythms, and both records seem ready to explode if they have to keep their emotions a secret even a moment longer. The only thing keeping them from going over the edge is the will of their singers, and even then, Vincent's will completely caves in about every four lines—which must be the difference between a caution born of heartbreak and despair and a love so new and thrilling it can't yet admit despair as a possibility. Losing his breath, screaming, so horny and in love he can't keep quiet or still, Vincent turns "Be Bop-a-Lu La" into a showcase for the sort of calculated emotional spontaneity that was among Elvis's greatest talents. The Blue Caps' attack-and-retreat arrangement—particularly guitarist Cliff Gallup's demented licks and drummer Dickie Harrell's sledgehammer beats—matches Vincent's emotional intensity step for step.

Country music's notorious response to records like this was the smoother, pop-influenced style now called the Nashville Sound. But the flipside of this story is that country didn't just run away from rockabilly; it quickly absorbed it into hits by Johnny Horton, Webb Pierce, George Jones, Carl Smith, Marty Robbins, and, soon enough, Buck Owens (who briefly played rhythm guitar with Vincent in a 1959 studio version of the Blue Caps) and Merle Haggard and Waylon Jennings and on and on. Even as "Be Bop-a-Lu-La" helped assure a future for rock & roll, it helped create country music's future. "Let's rock again now," Vincent insists near the end of his biggest hit, and that, in different ways and to varying degrees, is exactly what country radio has been doing ever since.

The Nashville Sound, on the other hand, was drawing its own inspiration from Elvis, specifically from softer, poppier hits like "Don't Be Cruel" and "Don't." Elvis's more intimate side left its

brand on country-pop hits like Sonny James's "Young Love," for instance, as well as the dramatic ballad styles of singers such as Robbins, Jack Greene, Gene Watson, T. G. Sheppard, Ronnie McDowell, Billy "Crash" Craddock, Ronnie Milsap, Dwight Yoakam, The Mavericks' Raul Malo, Brooks & Dunn's Ronnie Dunn, and, of course, Conway Twitty.

Like Vincent's, Twitty's world exploded when he heard Elvis's Sun singles. Those early rockabilly sides inspired Twitty to travel from his Mississippi home (only a few miles from where Presley grew up) to Memphis in 1956, where he worked briefly with the label's head Sam Phillips. None of these recordings were ever released, though, and it wasn't until he and sideman Jack Nance wrote "It's Only Make Believe" two years later that Twitty scored a hit.

As critic Dave Marsh has noted, "It's Only Make Believe" is "one long crescendo whose title seems to be an internal pun because it's probably the greatest ever impersonation of Elvis's early ballad style . . . right down to the Jordanaires." Not that you can't tell the difference. Even at this early stage in his career, Twitty's voice is huskier than his hero's, and so he's unable, as Elvis could do when he chose, to make it appear as if all those booming crescendos came easily. What's most remarkable in hindsight, though, is just how little Twitty's style would have to change when, a few years after the international success of "It's Only Make Believe," he decided to give up rock & roll for country. Though he grew even more soulful through the years, the basic outlines of Twitty's distinctive vocal approach, right down to his trademark growl, were right here from the get-go in this blatant and unforgettable homage to the King.—dc

112
Live Fast, Love Hard, Die Young, Faron Young
Produced by Ken Nelson; Written by Joe Allison
Capitol 3056   1955   #1 country (3 weeks)

The arrival of Elvis posed a serious threat to Nashville's old guard. Partly because of his wild music, but that wouldn't have bothered country music's powerbrokers if he hadn't been such deadly business competition. During Elvis's first year of radio success—roughly from the middle of 1955, when he debuted on the country charts with "Baby Let's Play House," until the two-sided hit "Don't Be Cruel" and "Hound Dog" solidified his national celebrity the following summer—several established chart careers were stopped in their tracks. In some cases, this was only temporary, but sometimes it was for good. It was during this period, for instance, that Red Foley saw his career as a hit maker suddenly come crashing down like a bowling ball rolling off a table. To varying degrees, the same fate befell Eddy Arnold, Red Sovine, Tennessee Ernie Ford, Lefty Frizzell, and Porter Wagoner.

There was no way to predict who'd go down and who wouldn't. Jim Reeves and Webb Pierce weathered the rock & roll storm by fine-tuning what they'd been doing all along (the former went Nashville Sound; the latter beefed up his beats). But how do we account for the persistent chart dominance of a twangy matron like Kitty Wells, for whom the hits just kept coming as if that kid from Tupelo had never been born? Or, to flip the question, why didn't they keep coming for Faron Young?

If any pre-Presley country star was ideally suited to cross into the new rock & roll world unscathed, it was Faron. He was movie-star handsome; in fact, he enjoyed a moderately successful second career in TV and film. He was young, just three years older than Elvis himself, and he'd already established himself as something of a hillbilly rebel. "Live fast, love hard, die young, and leave a beautiful memory" sounds like it should be carved on some rockabilly's tombstone.

What really should've made him a lock for rock-era success, though, was his voice, a piercing, energetic tenor that was unmistakably Hank-derived. But on ballads such as "Just Out of Reach (Of My Two Open Arms)" or "In the Chapel in the Moonlight," he could croon and swoon as dreamily as any of the teen idols that followed Presley's lead. The honky-tonk bounce of his earliest hits gets him lumped in with old-school acts like Hank, Lefty, and Carl Smith. But, at least as far as his pipes were concerned, Young's closest relatives were Ray Price and Marty Robbins, two pop-aware country singers who managed to establish themselves as stars at the very moment that rock & roll was threatening Young's career.

Not that Faron fell off the earth or anything, but he did fall off his game, at least as far as the charts were concerned. (In the four years prior to "Don't Be Cruel," Faron's charting singles had never failed to crack the Top Ten; in fact, all but one had made it into the Top Five. In the four years after "Don't Be Cruel," Young's singles fell outside the Top Ten ten times; six of his "hits" in those years didn't even score Top Twenty.) Before the slump, however, and again a few years down the road (thanks to an early sixties comeback launched by his Nashville Sound classic "Hello Walls"), Young was as big a country star as there was.

None of his early records was bigger than "Live Fast, Love

Hard, Die Young." It's an unabashed anthem to lovin' 'em and leavin' 'em, but Young delivers it with an easy friendliness that makes it feel more eager and innocent than cruel or bitter. It's as if Hank's "Hey, Good Lookin' " were casting a wider net—in fact, Young pulls off a pretty swell imitation of Williams during the verses. But it's the choruses where Young cuts loose, bouncing easily through a melody that demands far greater range than his effortless delivery lets on, adding curlicues to the ends of words, punching certain phrases to drive home the rhythm, building to a big finish that, despite Faron's pronounced twang, is as much Tony Bennett as Hank Williams. Even on a "hard-core" masterpiece, Young shows he could sing it both ways—like Hank and, if not like Elvis exactly, then at least like the pop singers who lined up to try on his shoes.

It makes sense then, or maybe it's just poetic, that Faron Young was from Shreveport, Louisiana, where he sang on the *Louisiana Hayride* between the tenures of Hank Williams and Elvis Presley. Prophetic, too. Faron Young's "Live Fast, Love Hard, Die Young" began its slide down the charts during the very weeks that "Baby Let's Play House" announced Elvis's country chart debut.—dc

113

Brain Cloudy Blues, Bob Wills & His Texas Playboys
Produced by Art Satherley;
Written by Bob Wills and Tommy Duncan
Columbia 877   1947   Did not chart

"You can change the name of an old song, rearrange it, and make it swing," Tommy Duncan sang on the Texas Playboys' "Time Changes Everything."

Few lines capture the inventive spirit of Bob Wills and his band better, and few records in their catalog demonstrate it more than "Brain Cloudy Blues," a tune based on "Milk Cow Blues," a popular "race" recording cut by Kokomo Arnold in 1934. The first thing that Wills and the Playboys did to Arnold's brooding, declamatory blues was to overhaul it for the dance halls—stepping up the tempo, sugar-curing its melody line with a trio of fiddles, and, most of all, making it swing. Wills and Duncan also tone down the lyrics to let the singer express confusion instead of the less palatable menace of Arnold's original. Bob's blithe asides, a trick he picked up from blackface minstrel Emmett Miller, further lighten the mood, all but begging listeners not to take Duncan's bruised vocals seriously; the only real bite comes from

Junior Barnard's fat, dirty-toned guitar break. In other words, Wills and company soup up an old song for maximum entertainment value, making it an ideal vehicle for the weekend revelry of hard-working men and women who didn't want to wallow in their blues so much as stomp all over them.

Lost in the process, however, was Arnold's name in the songwriting credits, where it should have been alongside those of Wills and Duncan. This omission wasn't unusual; the publishing industry was a lot looser then, and many blues singers treated melodies and lyrics as common property—a repository of a shared oral tradition. Even so, Wills should have known better; not only was Arnold's record a big hit in the Southwest, but Wills was an astute businessman who knew how the royalty system worked. "Brain Cloudy" was also the B side of the Playboys' best-selling "Sugar Moon," a fact that underscores the lines "Darkies raise the cotton, white man get the money" from Wills's "Take Me Back to Tulsa" in a harshly ironic way. Seven years later, Elvis Presley and Sam Phillips balanced the scales some, assigning sole songwriting credit for Elvis's 1954 recording "Milkcow Blues Boogie" to Arnold, despite the fact that the King kicks off his single with the second verse of the Wills-Duncan rewrite.—bfw

114

Chattanoogie Shoe Shine Boy, Red Foley
Produced by Paul Cohen; Written by Harry Stone and Jack Stapp
Decca 46205   1950   #1 country (13 weeks); #1 pop (8 weeks)

Virtually every cowboy singer, western swinger, country crooner, and early honky-tonker was deeply influenced by Bing Crosby. None of them absorbed the Crosby style more completely than Red Foley. An absolutely monster crossover hit for him in 1950, "Chattanoogie Shoe Shine Boy" is a veritable Crosby clinic. Foley scoots along with effortless cool, phrasing within and around the beat and tossing off jive patter between the verses, all the while crooning in a flawless baritone. It's all derived straight from Der Bingle, who himself was heavily enamored of jazz players and vocalists, particularly Louis Armstrong.

Small wonder then that Crosby immediately covered "Chattanoogie." He couldn't compete with Foley's original, though, not even on the pop charts. Crosby didn't have a thrilling Grady Martin guitar solo backing him up, for one thing. He didn't have drummer Farris Coursey, either. Simulating the joyous pop and snap of the shoeshine boy's rag, Coursey slaps his leg throughout with such force his thighs must've stung for weeks. As for the listener, "You'll feel as though you wanna dance when he gets through."

Of course, it should be noted that the title character here probably wasn't a boy at all but a full-grown black man struggling to earn a living at a nickel a shoe, a realization that taints this stereotypical portrayal of a rhythmic, perpetually happy "darky." Then again, at some point you just have to trust the truth of a record more than the prejudice of its creators (despite the credit above, the song was most likely penned by Fred Rose). No doubt about it, Red Foley's "Chattanoogie" is a record head over heels in love with hot licks, crooning, and the beat, man, the beat.—dc

115

It's Mighty Dark to Travel,
Bill Monroe & His Blue Grass Boys
Produced by Art Satherley; Written by Bill Monroe
Columbia 20526   1947   Did not chart

Bill Monroe's inspiration for "It's Mighty Dark to Travel" came halfway through a shave and a haircut. "I was getting some barber work done down on Broadway in Nashville one time, and a colored man came to the door," Monroe recalled in an interview. "Somebody had been giving him an awful hard time—I don't know if it was a white man or not—and he shook his head and said, 'It's mighty dark to travel.' I had my song right there."

It wasn't the first time a black man inspired the Father of Bluegrass. Arnold Shultz, the son of a former slave and the principal source of the thumb-style guitar later made famous by Merle Travis and Chet Atkins, had played with Pendleton Vandiver, Monroe's "Uncle Pen." Bill himself had apprenticed with Shultz's band, playing at house parties and other gatherings in and around their native Kentucky. But it was the banjo, an instrument of African origin, that ultimately transformed Monroe's music into what would become known as "bluegrass."

Monroe was already redefining his group's sound by the time he joined the Grand Ole Opry in 1939. Among other things, he'd pitched the vocals much higher than usual and opted for a hopped-up stringband sound that was scarcely recognizable alongside the blues and mountain-ballad style he and his brother Charlie helped popularize during the thirties. The metamorphosis wasn't complete until 1945, when—along with guitarist Lester Flatt, fiddler Chubby Wise, and bass player Howard Watts—Monroe brought twenty-one-year-old banjo whiz Earl Scruggs into the Blue Grass Boy fold.

Scruggs's syncopated three-finger technique made the prevailing old-time frailing style of playing seem quaint by comparison; his banjo was certainly in overdrive the day he went into the studio with the Blue Grass Boys to cut "It's Mighty Dark to Travel." Lead singer Lester Flatt might be singing about being lost on a dark, gravel road since his baby left him, but from the fevered breakdown Scruggs and company are laying down behind him, you'd swear he was racing along just fine.

Monroe and his contemporaries didn't always acknowledge their debt to black musicians. But from Bill's soulful high tenor, to the galvanizing effect of the African-derived banjo, to the story behind this song, the influence is undeniable. As bluegrass-leaning singer-songwriter Steve Earle put it, "There's no way that Monroe could have arrived at this on his own. The blues—and other black traditions—are definitely part of this music. The name 'bluegrass' wasn't just about Kentucky; the word 'blues' was in there, and it was intentional."—bfw

116

Pan American Blues, DeFord Bailey
No producer credited; Written by DeFord Bailey
Brunswick 146   1927   Pre-chart

You might not know it from reading most histories of the music, but DeFord Bailey, and not Charley Pride, was the first black star in country music. "The Harmonica Wizard" had been a hit on the Grand Ole Opry a good ten years before Pride was born; he was also the only African American to star on a radio barn dance before World War II.

Bailey's fifteen-year tenure on the Opry, however, was a conflicted one. He was among the show's best-loved performers; one year he appeared on forty-nine broadcasts, at least twice as many as any of the Opry's other regulars. Yet the Opry brass

also dubbed him the show's "mascot," an epithet that implied he was less than a full member of the cast, if not somehow less than human. Then there were the circumstances surrounding his firing from the show in 1941, an incident that might very well have been racially motivated. Bitter and disillusioned, Bailey went back to shining shoes for a living and rarely performed in public again.

"Pan American Blues," the song that inspired the naming of the Opry (formerly the *WSM Barn Dance*) in 1927, was Bailey's signature number, a solo harp workout that mimicked the rattle and hum of an old L&N passenger train. The tune opens with a pair of short, sharp whistle blasts. Then, as Bailey simulates the mounting clickety-clack of the train pulling out of the station, it picks up speed until it's chugging along full throttle, its roar punctuated with harp squalls that sound like locomotive puffs and whistle cries. With nothing but his Hohner Marine Band harmonica, Bailey conveys the wide-eyed wonder he must have felt when, as a boy growing up in rural Smith County, Tennessee, he used to cover his eyes and stand beneath the railroad trestle on his walk to school, listening in awe to the thunderous roar of the passing trains.

Despite its title, "Pan American Blues" really isn't a blues, but rather a mix of old-time musical styles, a hybrid of black and white country-dance rhythms that Bailey learned from his grandfather, a fiddle champion and former slave. Bailey called it "black hillbilly music," a term that encompassed the singing and banjo and guitar playing he performed but never recorded commercially. Doubtless perceived as quaint, Bailey's style of music faded from popularity soon after the Second World War, although examples of it persist today. One in particular, "Orange Blossom Special," a song written by a white, vaudeville fiddler named Ervin Rouse, sounds like it's barreling down the tracks right behind Bailey's train.—bfw

117

Freight Train Boogie, The Delmore Brothers
Produced by Henry Glover; Written by Jim Scott and Bob Nabor
King 570   1946   #2 country

They called it hillbilly boogie, but this cross between "Orange Blossom Special" and "One O'Clock Jump" might just as well have been tagged barnyard jazz.

The sons of Northern Alabama tenant farmers, the Delmores were country to the core; how they sang and what they sang about were as down-home as the back forty. But this record's locomotion, fired by Wayne Raney's fat, "choke-style" harmonica and Merle Travis's syncopated, piano-like guitar licks, could almost have come from Louis Jordan's Tympany Five or Count Basie's Kansas City rhythm section. Swing and jump bands had been laying down this kind of boogie for years, but for country, it qualified as a brand new beat.

The Delmores certainly didn't start out sounding this way. They emerged, in the mid-thirties, as a close-harmony, guitar-and-mandolin duo akin to their early label mates the Blue Sky Boys and the Monroe Brothers. But during wartime, with honky-tonk and its amplified twang gaining a foothold in the beer joints and dance halls, mountain harmonies began to sound dated and the Delmores faded in popularity. That is, until they reinvented themselves, with the help of Henry Glover, staff producer at King Records and an arranger for orchestra leader Lucky Millinder, as a hillbilly boogie band.

"Freight Train Boogie," which just missed the top spot on the country charts in 1946, was the first successful postwar single in this new style, and soon everyone from Red Foley to Ernie Ford to Arthur "Guitar Boogie" Smith was beating it eight-to-the-bar as well. The Delmores' hot-wiring of hillbilly music and jazz (by way of R&B) even held its own with honky-tonk for a while, after which it became rockabilly and flat surpassed it.—bfw

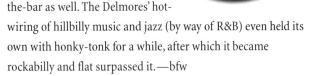

118

Sixteen Tons, Tennessee Ernie Ford
Produced by Lee Gillette; Written by Merle Travis
Capitol 3262   1955   #1 country (10 weeks); #1 pop (8 weeks)

119

Black Land Farmer, Frankie Miller
Produced by Don Pierce; Written by Frankie Miller
Starday 424   1959   #5 country

Merle Travis wanted what became his most famous number to sound something like an old public-domain folk song. After Tennessee Ernie Ford got a hold of it, though, "Sixteen Tons" was

a very modern-sounding pop record—one of the biggest crossover country hits of all time. Built around a swinging rhythm bed so spare it's barely more than the singer snapping his fingers in front of a small horn section, the record dreamed up by Ford and arranger Jack Fascinato allowed a wide, contemporary audience to connect Travis's tale about life in the mines to their own jobs. The record remains so up to date, in fact, that it can still do that, whether your job has you racing to keep up with an assembly line or spending all day in a cubicle staring at a computer screen.

"Sixteen Tons" is about any job, really, that leaves you "another day older and deeper in debt." Tennessee Ernie's Sisyphean task is loading coal, and faced with such a backbreaking, soul-robbing existence, his best defenses offer nothing but cold comfort. Even his braggadocio presents him as more machine than man (he wields "one fist of iron, the other of steel"), and his sense of humor has grown every bit as dark and poisonous as the mine in which he slaves. Even if he could manage to load sixteen tons of coal a day—and that's a job for two dozen men, not one—he would still owe money for food and rent to the very people for whom he labors; he literally can't dig himself out of debt. "St. Peter, don't you call me 'cause I can't go," he prays, "I owe my soul to the company store." He can't afford to die. Some joke.

Frankie Miller's work is labor intensive too, but his life couldn't be more different. Sounding like a peaceful Hank Williams out plowing his pappy's fields, his "Black Land Farmer" also features vocals over a simple rhythm track—just an acoustic guitar and the clip-clop-clop of his mule. But instead of the misery and grim humor of Ford's record, the effect here is to recall some simpler, idealized era when people's labor was not for sale. "I feel like I'm a-gettin' closer to you, God" is the prayer Miller offers, "a-plantin' the ground and breakin' up the sod."

God linked to work? These days the logic of twenty-first century capitalism—specifically, that computer chips should be dedicated to profit rather than to human need—has rendered the idea of work as a form of spiritual aspiration all but incomprehensible. Miller's record, despite its nostalgia, holds fast to the ideal. To the extent that our very humanity resides in our work, in our ability to imagine and create a world that serves our needs and fulfills our potentials, maybe human labor needn't be alienated from nearness to God. Maybe, in a different, better world, they're the same thing.—dc

120
Workin' Man Blues, Merle Haggard & the Strangers
Produced by Ken Nelson; Written by Merle Haggard
Capitol 2503   1969   #1 country

"I ain't never been on welfare, and that's one place I won't be," Merle Haggard sings on "Workin' Man Blues." During the first months of the Nixon administration, this line could be heard as code for a series of racist and elitist swipes of which Haggard could not have been unaware. As is usually the case with his songs, though, "Workin' Man Blues" is a good deal more conflicted than it initially seems. For one thing, it helps to hear the line in context. Hag's narrator won't be on welfare for a very specific reason. "I'll be working," he explains, 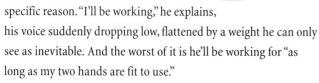 his voice suddenly dropping low, flattened by a weight he can only see as inevitable. And the worst of it is he'll be working for "as long as my two hands are fit to use."

If you don't know the anxiety, not to mention the pain, of hoping your body can simply hold out until you can retire (or longer, if retirement isn't an option), then count yourself lucky. Everyone in Hag's audience would've known firsthand the burden of an economy that proclaims human beings are worthless unless they work, work, work. So there's no doubt that the groove the Strangers smoke here turns the record into a celebration—we've earned this barstool by making it through to another Friday! But it's the certainty that those Mondays will just keep on coming down, like that hammer striking incessantly in the background, that makes this the working man *blues.*—dc

121
They'll Never Keep Us Down, Hazel Dickens
No producer credited; Written by Hazel Dickens
Rounder 4511   1980   Did not chart

People said that hearing Delia Byrd sing was like hearing heartbreak in a whole new key. Her voice could make you sweat, make you move, make you want to lift your hands and pull justice out of the air.

—Dorothy Allison, *Cavedweller*

Allison is talking about a fictional rock & roller in the Janis Joplin mold, but she could just as easily be describing the mountain tenor of Hazel Dickens: a piercing wail that can evoke the sound of a woman in childbirth, a mother wracked with grief, or a prophet crying out in the wilderness; or, at its most lovelorn and blue, the doleful moan of Hank's lonesome whippoorwill. This broadside, a pro-union rafters rattler Dickens wrote for Barbara Koppel's documentary of the same name, finds her trying to harvest justice from the salt of the earth.

"United we stand, divided we fall . . . Working people use your power, the key to liberty / Don't support that rich man's style of luxury," Hazel trumpets to open the record. This is more than just a call to arms; with febrile strains of bluesy banjo fueling her ardor, it's the very sound of resistance itself. Shoring up the bottom is a marching upright bass, its unwavering stride matching Hazel's resolve step for bulldog step.

The plight of those who toiled in the coal pits in and around Dickens's native West Virginia was her first and perhaps greatest passion; like her rabble-rousing sisters in the struggle Aunt Molly Jackson and Sara Ogun Gunning before her, Dickens witnessed the miners' hardships firsthand. Her father, a Primitive Baptist preacher and a stirring singer in his own right, eked out a living hauling timber and coal. Her sisters cleaned house for the company bosses; her brothers worked in the mines.

The factories of Baltimore where Hazel labored after she left home at sixteen were hardly less grueling—or exploitative. Still, it wasn't until nearly twenty years later when she and Alice Gerrard, her partner in the pioneering folk duo Hazel & Alice, started touring with singer/activist Ann Romaine's Southern Grassroots Revival Project that Dickens began writing about her experiences. "Black Lung," her first—and still most wrenching—composition, recounts how the coal dust in her oldest brother's lungs ate clear through his body to the sheets of his death bed. (Another of Dickens's brothers also died of the disease.)

In 1976, Koppel used Hazel's recording of "Black Lung" in her Oscar-winning documentary *Harlan County, U.S.A.*, and then asked her to write and perform a song for the film's successor. Rife with salvos like "Got a contract in our hands signed by the blood of honest men" and "They'll never shoot that union out of me," "They'll Never Keep Us Down" found Dickens making the shift from personal to political in her music complete. "They can cheat, lie, frame or kill / But we'll stop that big wheel," she shouts on the final chorus, hammering home the syllables "cheat," "lie," "frame," and "kill" on successive beats before testifying, banjo and bass backing her all the way, that "there ain't no way they can ever keep us down."

Harlem Renaissance poet and civil rights leader James Weldon Johnson once dubbed black preachers "God's Trombones." Dickens's voice is no trombone—it's more of a raspy cornet—and her gospel has always been wholly of this world. Yet the moral, almost biblical force with which she wields her indomitable tenor could hardly be more prophetic. As with Moses or Elijah, there's never any doubt that Hazel, in solidarity with her working brothers and sisters, can pluck justice out of the air, even air choked with dust from the deepest, darkest mine.—bfw

122

One's on the Way, Loretta Lynn

Produced by Owen Bradley; Written by Shel Silverstein
Decca 32900   1971   #1 country (2 weeks)

Bruce Springsteen might have had "One's on the Way" in mind when he sang, "We learned more from a three-minute record, baby, than we ever learned in school." Lynn's single clocks in at two minutes and thirty-seven seconds, but it's hard to imagine a roomful of sociologists saying as much about class and gender as she does here. They sure wouldn't be able to match her righteous mix of humor and ire. The licks that guitarist Grady Martin (biting) and steel player Hal Rugg (playful) trade to open the record set an appropriately tragicomic tone. Pregnant and bewildered at the site of kids crawling the

walls and the housework piling up, Loretta is laughing in the face of hardship, but she's also mad as hell.

She bemoans how glamour gals like Elizabeth Taylor and Jackie Onassis are free to jet around the globe while she's stuck in Topeka, where the screen door's slamming, the faucet's dripping, the baby's crying, and the wash needs hanging. But Loretta has more on her mind than just the disparity between her domestic servitude and the splendor-filled lives of the jet set. Her husband's just phoned from a bar to announce—surprise!—that he's bringing some old army buddies to dinner. Making matters worse, he doesn't even bother to ask if he can pick up anything from the market on his way home. Then there's the mix of guilt and outrage Loretta feels when she turns on the TV and sees all those "girls in New York City," doubtless free of the drudgery she shoulders, marching "for women's lib." It's not like holding a rally is going to scrub the floor for her or like that new pill they're pushing is going to do anything about the baby that's already on the way.

That Lynn was a big star by the time she made "One's on the Way"—and that it was written by a man, and a *Playboy* cartoonist at that—in no way undermines the record's working-class feminism. Loretta knew the harried life she laments only too well, having given birth to and cared for four children while still in her teens. She'd earned the right to sing "One's on the Way," the message of which isn't that she doesn't love her husband and kids (witness the tenderness in her voice), or even appreciate the aims of the Women's Movement. She's just sick and tired of having to be all things to all people. You also get the feeling the situation's about to change.—bfw

123

Little Pink Mack, Kay Adams
with the Cliffie Stone Group

Produced by Cliffie Stone;
Written by Chris D. Roberts, Jim Thornton, and Scott Turner
Tower 269   1966   #30 country

The closest Kay Adams ever came to driving an eighteen-wheeler was to have brothers who did. No matter. With "Little Pink Mack" she made one of the greatest trucking records ever, one that packed added punch by expressing a woman's view of what the world looked like through a windshield at a time when most long-haul truckers were men.

Sporting pink polka-dot curtains and a blushing paint job,

Kay's rig might be the frilliest on the road, but it also has every trucker within miles choking on her dust. "I cut my baby teeth on a set of Spicer gears / I'm a gear-swappin' mama and I don't know the meaning of fear," she taunts, ready to take on all comers. "When you see a flash of pink go flying by / The next thing you know there's a taillight in your eye," she adds; the skid marks left by the torqued-up pedal steel and electric-guitar breaks that follow make it obvious she means business.

Adams's raven beauty, working-class virtues, and fetching, down-home soprano made her the odds-on favorite to become the West Coast's answer to Loretta Lynn. She won the Academy of Country Music award for Most Promising Female Vocalist in 1965 (Merle Haggard was her male counterpart). After that she signed on as the featured "girl" singer in Buck Owens's touring show, and later in Haggard's, and she released a number of singles and albums in the hard-driving Bakersfield style patented by those two men. Adams's body of work, which includes *Wheels and Tears*, the first—and, to date, only—female concept album about trucking, is relatively small. But galvanized as it was by ace songwriting, as well as the keening pedal steel of Ralph Mooney and the bluesy electric-guitar barbs of James Burton, it stands with the best West Coast country of its era.

Ironically enough, given the white-line fever of "Little Pink Mack," by the late sixties, the pressures of the road started to get the better of Adams. The booze, drugs, and sexual come-ons of her male peers proved too much for the sheltered, Texas-bred singer, and before long she'd all but retired from performing. Had she been as dauntless as the gear-jammer of her sole Top Forty hit or even just a bit more worldly, Kay might very well have joined the ranks of the honky-tonk angels of the late sixties and early seventies.—bfw

124

Truck Driver's Blues, Cliff Bruner & His Boys
Produced by Dave Kapp; Written by Ted Daffan
Decca 5725   1939   Pre-chart

125

Six Days on the Road, Dave Dudley
Produced by Dave Dudley;
Written by Earl Greene and Carl Montgomery
Golden Wing 3020   1963   #2 country; #32 pop

Time was when truck driving was among the most popular and explicitly working-class topics in country music. That's been a while, though. Trucker songs haven't shown up on country radio with any regularity since the seventies, and nowadays, you can tune in your local country station for weeks without finding so much as a skid mark's worth of evidence that the genre ever existed. Still, it's been a long road.

It began in the late thirties when, touring the Southwest, songwriter and steel guitarist Ted Daffan observed how often this new breed of worker would stop at some roadside diner and make a beeline for the jukebox. (Intercity trucking didn't come to prominence in the south until the thirties and then only with stiff resistance from the railroads.) Though Daffan and the Bar X Cowboys performed his new "Truck Driver's Blues" on the road for several months, it was former Milton Brown fiddler Cliff Bruner who first cut the song in 1939. It was a huge hit, thanks in large part to the many truckers who bought and requested it. In truth, though, it was probably the depressed, bleary-eyed mood of the record, rather than any specific trucking references, that ensured its widespread appeal. "Ride, ride, ride on in to town / There's a honky-tonk gal a-waitin', I got troubles to drown," moans Bruner's pianist Moon Mullican. Really, these could be any blues at all, and based on the impact of Moon's jazzy, ragged solo, they're about as low-down as it gets.

Despite the popularity of Bruner's hit, truck-driving numbers didn't really become commonplace until 1963 when Dave Dudley's "Six Days on the Road" made the pop chart. For the next several years, it was the rare country singer who didn't cut at least a couple of records loaded high with details of life over the road—truck-stop waitresses and speed-trap smokies; diesel fumes and dangerous curves; equal measures of independence, hyper-masculinity, and tedium. Dudley himself returned to the theme only slightly fewer times than there are mile-markers on I-70, while acts such as the Willis Brothers ("Give Me 40 Acres to Turn This Rig Around"), Dick Curless ("Tombstone Every Mile"), Kay Adams ("Little Pink Mac"), and Red Simpson ("I'm a Truck") discovered in the genre the highest-charting records of their careers.

In the mid-to-late seventies, the truck-driving genre rolled off country radio and into American mythology behind a few nationally publicized Teamsters' strikes, a brief CB craze fueled by C. W. McCall's crossover hit "Convoy," the film *Smokey and the Bandit* and its Jerry Reed theme song "Eastbound and Down," and the TV series *Movin' On*, with a title song courtesy of Merle Haggard. By then, though, the genre's glory days were mostly in the rearview mirror. (A book subtitled *Country Music's 500 Worst Singles* would have to include two of 1976's biggest trucker-themed hits, Red Sovine's maudlin "Teddy Bear" and Rod Hart's homophobic novelty recitation, "CB Savage.")

Dudley's "Six Days on the Road" established the model and set the standard for everything to follow. Set to a chugging electric riff, a hard-driving Bakersfield-style backbeat, and a chorus that mimics the hum of an eighteen-wheeler flying by you on the left, "Six Days" has all the specificity missing from "Truck Driver's Blues," and no wonder. Songwriters Earl Greene and Carl Montgomery weren't imagining a life; they were literally living it—the pair composed "Six Days" while hauling freight from Pittsburgh on "down that eastern seaboard," just like the song says. Along the way, Dudley dodges scales because his rig's overweight and his "log book's way behind." He speeds every chance he gets, letting his truck slip into "Georgia overdrive" and "taking little white pills" so he can stay awake to keep driving.

All are details, one assumes, of the life lived by Daffan's depressed trucker three decades earlier. With one huge exception. At the end of his run, Dudley turns his deep, rumbling voice into a cry of delight: "My hometown's a-comin' in sight / If you think I'm happy, you're *right*!" Happy to see his wife again, he means. Unlike Daffan's trucker, Dudley has a reason for driving all those miles—and somewhere he wants to be when his work week is through.—dc

126

Howlin' at the Moon, Hank Williams with His Drifting Cowboys
Produced by Fred Rose; Written by Hank Williams
MGM 10961   1951   #3 country

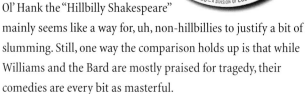

Besides the obvious fact that they're both great and written in English, the songs of Hank Williams and the works of William Shakespeare wouldn't seem to have anything very specific in common. Dubbing Ol' Hank the "Hillbilly Shakespeare" mainly seems like a way for, uh, non-hillbillies to justify a bit of slumming. Still, one way the comparison holds up is that while Williams and the Bard are mostly praised for tragedy, their comedies are every bit as masterful.

"Howlin' at the Moon" is Williams at his most uproarious. Singing to his best girl, he explains how he's been running around crazy lately, plumb out of his head in love; he's been treeing coons, chasing rabbits, even walking around on his hands like a damn fool. Behind him, Drifting Cowboy Jerry Rivers howls away, literally, and Don Helms skips and zips through a steel solo that sounds positively delirious. This is, in other words, a daffy, loopy, loony, screwy, just plain goofy song about the overwhelming power of love. But behind the one liners and physical humor (Hank asks a station attendant to fill his horse up with gas, and the guy smacks him upside the head with a wrench) stands an artist who takes very seriously the power of love to make human beings act daffy, loopy, loony, screwy, and goofy. Williams suspects he's gone and lost what little common sense he once had—he's asking the girl to marry him, for goodness sake—but he also understands that love has given him access to a new sort of sense, one that's precious precisely because it's so uncommon.

Or, as the "Elizabethan Hank Williams" once phrased it, "Lovers and madmen have each seething brains . . . that apprehend more than cool reason ever comprehends."—dc

127
How Far to Little Rock, Stanley Brothers
No producer credited; Written by Ruby Rakes
King 5306   1960   #17 country

"Howdy, neighbor" this ain't.

Many of the old country comedy
routines cast rural folk as
rubes, affording the music's
primary audience a laugh at
its own expense. But this
one, a take-off on "The Arkansas Traveler" published
under the name of the Stanley
Brothers' half-sister, turns the
tables a bit. That's not to say that Carter

Stanley, who plays the country bumpkin to brother Ralph's
straight-man traveler, doesn't come off a tad daft at times. With
each of their exchanges punctuated by a barreling banjo-guitar-
bass run (the sonic equivalent of vaudeville's bada-bing, bada-
boom), some of Carter's responses to Ralph's smart-aleck
questions suggest he hasn't followed their drift at all. Or hasn't
wanted to follow, judging by the way his increasingly pointed
punch lines swing around—like the old "duck the 2 x 4" gag—to
smack Ralph in the ass. The moment of truth comes on their final
give-and-take when Ralph, having endured Carter's hayseed
banter long enough, again asks how far it is to Little Rock.
Carter's response: "Well, I'm sure glad to tell you buddy. It's three
lengths of a fool. If you don't believe it, lay down and measure it
sometime."

Moral of the story—there's smart and then there's country
smart.—bfw

128
Amos Moses, Jerry Reed
Produced by Chet Atkins; Written by Jerry Reed
RCA 9904 1970   #16 country; #8 pop

Jerry Reed had been a successful songwriter and hotshot guitar
man for nearly a decade before this crossover smash set him on
the road to more hits, a movie career, and his own summer
variety series on CBS. His most notable moment, though, will
always be "Amos Moses," a hilarious slice of southern storytelling
about a larger-than-life Cajun who can catch the nastiest gator in
the swamp with just one hand. Good thing too because as Reed

points out, all wide-eyed and grinning, "That's all he got left
'cause the alligatuh *bit it.* Left arm gone clean up to the elbow!"

Reed doesn't actually believe this line of jive; he just knows
the story's too good not to share. You won't believe it either, but
the exaggerated charm of his good-ole-boy
delivery, not to mention a juke-joint
band that spotlights Reed's
own chicken-scratched,
Chet-Atkins-meets-Tony-
Joe-White licks, will leave
this much beyond question:
when he finishes this tall
tale, you'll beg him to tell it
again.—dc

129
If I Lose, I Don't Care, Charlie Poole
& the North Carolina Ramblers
No producer credited; Traditional
Columbia 152 15-D   1927   Pre-chart

130
Up on Cripple Creek, The Band
Produced by John Simon and The Band;
Written by Robbie Robertson
Capitol   2635   1969   #25 pop

Charlie Poole & the North Carolina Ramblers reportedly worked
more breakdown dances in their home state during the 1920s
than any stringband around. It's no
wonder; galvanized by Poole's
thumb-and-three-finger
banjo and the devilish
fiddling of Posey Rorer, the
trio played with as much
lyricism and abandon as
anyone on record.

Poole was also a souse and
a rounder of Rabelaisian propor-
tions—his reputation confirmed by the titles of two of the
Ramblers' most requested numbers, "Take a Drink on Me" and
"Can I Sleep in Your Barn Tonight Mister?" No record presents
Charlie at his most feckless, though, better than "If I Lose."
Returning home from a spree that took him from the Piedmont
to New York and Cincinnati, he shamelessly throws himself into

the arms of his sugar mama, ready to gamble her money away. "If I lose, let me lose / I don't care how much I lose," Charlie shrugs with a sly, self-deprecating nod as Rorer conspires with him on the fiddle. "If I lose a hundred dollars while I'm tryin' to win a dime / Well, my baby, she keeps money all the time."

Poole lost his gamble with the bottle at age thirty-nine, after a celebratory, three-month binge triggered by an invitation to supply the music for a Hollywood movie. Nearly forty years passed before the rake of "If I Lose" resurfaced, and then it took four Canadians and an Arkansan— collectively known as The Band—to revive the gambler and his larger-than-life benefactress. "Up on Cripple Creek, she sends me / If I spring a leak, she mends me / I don't have to speak, she defends me / A drunkard's dream if I ever did see one."

Drummer Levon Helm crows these lines with the randy glee of a lecher set loose in a whorehouse.

To their credit, The Band don't try to recreate Poole's sound, even if the title of "Up on Cripple Creek" invokes the old-time staple "Cripple Creek," a version of which Poole recorded as "Shootin' Creek." Instead, opening with a serpentine bass line that pays homage to Motown bassist James Jamerson, the group uses clavinet, tuba, and assorted arcane instruments to make latter-day jug-band music born more of Beale Street than the Great Smoky Mountains. Then again, after hearing Helm's vocals on The Band's 1967 take of "If I Lose" (from *The Basement Tapes* sessions), it's likely that Toronto-born Robbie Robertson, the group's carpetbagging guitarist, was conjuring "Up on Cripple Creek" even then.—bfw

131
Keep My Skillet Good and Greasy, Uncle Dave Macon
No producer credited; Written by Uncle Dave Macon
Vocalion 14848   1924   Pre-chart

Few people mention Uncle Dave Macon, "the Dixie Dewdrop," in the same breath as his fellow Country Music Hall of Famers Jimmie Rodgers, Roy Acuff, or Earl Scruggs. They should. Macon's repertoire, which included everything from vaudeville, parlor, and country dance tunes to barnyard hokum, black blues, and

old-time hymns, was as vast, varied, and affecting as that of the Singing Brakeman. Macon was also a stentorian-piped Opry star (the show's first) of the magnitude and charisma of Acuff, despite being in his mid-fifties when the radio barn dance made its on-air debut in 1925. And he was a brilliant banjoist whose early three-finger approach to the instrument, while hardly as influential or virtuosic as Scruggs's, encompassed nearly twenty discernible styles. Most importantly, Macon did as much as anyone to transform the folk and minstrel songs of the 1800s into the commercial country music of the twentieth century. "If people call yodeling Jimmie Rodgers 'the father of country music,'" wrote historian Charles Wolfe, "then Uncle Dave must certainly be 'the grandfather of country music.'"

Born in 1870 and raised in the hills of Middle Tennessee, Macon displayed an omnivorous appetite for music early on. As a young boy he learned the popular folk songs of the day as well as the blues played by the black field hands who worked in the area. As a teenager (he got his first banjo when he was fourteen), Macon picked up tricks from the vaudeville and circus performers who stayed at his parents' Nashville hotel. He gleaned music from any source he could. The crux of a song like "Rock About My Saro Jane," for example, came from black stevedores who loaded and unloaded the steamers that passed through Nashville on their way up and down the Cumberland River.

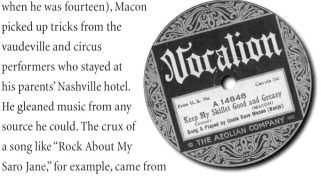

As central a part of his life as it was, playing music was just an avocation for Macon until he was well into middle age. After marrying in 1889, he went into business hauling freight, something he would have kept at until retirement age had trucks not undercut his mule line around 1920. The "crisis" wrought by one technological advance, however, freed Macon to take advantage of another—the burgeoning record business. First, though, he hit the vaudeville circuit where, like a biscuit on bacon fat, he kept sopping up everything he heard.

One of Uncle Dave's earliest and most enduring recordings, "Keep My Skillet Good and Greasy" captures this appetitive spirit completely—and not just his hunger for music, but for liquor, laughter, lovemaking, and whatever else his or anyone else's larder held in store. "I be gwine downtown for to buy me a sack of flour / Gwine cook it every hour / Keep my skillet good and greasy all the time, time, time," he swaggers, before rapping out the lines on his banjo in a percussive, rolling style that fuses old-time frailing and newfangled fingerpicking techniques. Macon then liberates a sack full of chickens and a ham and, before long, lays his hands on some bootlegged brandy so as to lubricate the libido of his gal Mandy. He does it all without a whiff of compunction—that is, with much the same bravado as he lifted licks from other pickers in the service of his music and persona, both of them larger than life.—bfw

132

Don't Let Your Deal Go Down,
Charlie Poole & the North Carolina Ramblers
No producer credited; Written by Charlie Poole
Columbia 15038-D   1925   Pre-chart

In hindsight, a stringband classic like "Don't Let Your Deal Go Down" is clearly doing spadework for bluegrass—generally via the North Carolina Ramblers' whirling, rhythmic ensemble work and specifically in Charlie Poole's sprightly three-finger banjo playing which set the stage for later Carolina pickers like Earl Scruggs and Don Reno. So perhaps it seems perverse to note that there's also a fair amount of Tin Pan Alley running through this early country record.

It certainly wouldn't have seemed odd to Charlie Poole. In 1925, when he and his Ramblers quit their cotton mill jobs in Spray, North Carolina, they headed to New York for an audition at Columbia Records, the label for which Poole's idol, Al Jolson, had recorded his biggest hits. Granted, Poole sings "Don't Let Your Deal Go Down" in a slurred twang that's 100 percent Blue Ridge Mountains—given Poole's reputation, it may well be 100-proof corn liquor, too—but you can hear Jolson's influence creeping through all the same. Poole echoes Jolson's bouncy and declamatory style, and it's not hard to picture Poole, dressed in his sportcoat and bow tie, his banjo bouncing on his knee, rolling his eyes and grinning loudly as he rocks away this Dixie melody. Never more so than when he's boasting about all the places he's seen or the

way his good gal hugged his neck the last time he took off, crying "Honey, doh-on't you go!" At the end, though, he lets us in on the price he's paid for all that rambling—his "good deal" has found herself a papa closer to hand. Then he's not smiling at all.—dc

133

El Paso, Marty Robbins
Produced by Don Law; Written by Marty Robbins
Columbia 41511   1959
#1 country (7 weeks); #1 pop (2 weeks)

134

(The Man Who Shot) Liberty Valance, Gene Pitney
Produced and written by Burt Bacharach and Hal David
Musicor 1020   1962   #4 pop

The western half of country-and-western has a long and intimate relationship with pop music, particularly the pop music of Hollywood movies. Marty Robbins's "El Paso," the best-known western song to emerge from the second half of the twentieth century, came along at a time when most of the singing cowboys of the silver screen had ridden off into the sunset. But its narrative sweep and rambling length (four minutes plus, which in radio terms was practically epic) were still marvelously cinematic. And the song's plot—a romantic cowpoke falls hard for a Mexican dancer named Felina, with fatal consequences—would surely have been familiar even to the most casual admirers of the western genre.

Indeed, America's late 1950s love affair with westerns of all kinds set the scene for Robbins's career record. "El Paso" was in part inspired by the period's craze for saga songs like "Don't Take Your Guns to Town." Robbins was also looking to follow up "The Hanging Tree," the title tune for a Gary Cooper western (itself based upon a novel by Dorothy Johnson) that had been a hit earlier in 1959. On the small screen that year, the guiding rule seemed to be all westerns, all the time, what with series such as *Bonanza, Gunsmoke, Maverick, The Rifleman, Wagon Train, Have Gun Will Travel,* and *Cheyenne* dominating prime-time schedules. It was all familiar territory for Robbins who as an Arizona youth had spent his Saturdays watching Gene Autry movies and other western serials and listening to the Wild West tales of his own grandfather, a former Texas Ranger.

None of this, though, fully explains why "El Paso" became such a phenomenon. Pop-cultural trends, Marty's biography, and even his gripping, expertly crafted tale would have mattered little if Robbins, producer Don Law, and a lineup of A-Team musicians hadn't made such a perfect record. The rhythm track starts out footloose, then feels as if it's hurtling increasingly out of control. The haunting harmonies of Jim Glaser and Bobby Sykes are somehow both sympathetic and as chill as the West Texas wind. And Grady Martin provides the Mex-Tex inspired acoustic guitar that conjures up the Southwest—even as it serves as Robbins's sidekick, seconding the singer's spiraling emotions. Marty himself maneuvers through the twists and turns of story and melody with grace, passion, and a sense of overriding tragedy that renders every scene as vividly as if this were one of the greatest westerns you'd ever seen, instead of a record merely inspired by them.

"El Paso" instantly became the standard for every cowboy song recorded in its wake. Surely it was part of the inspiration a couple of years later for "(The Man Who Shot) Liberty Valance," a song written for, but not included in, what was destined to become one of the greatest big-screen westerns, director John Ford's film of the same name (yet another movie based upon a Dorothy Johnson story). Composers Burt Bacharach and Hal David certainly had good reason to be paying attention to what Marty Robbins was up to on "El Paso"—Robbins's recording of "The Story of My Life" had given the duo its first hit back in 1957. Five years later, David penned lyrics that summarized both the plot of Ford's film (in a nutshell, go west young man!) and its theme (what's lost and gained when the needs of civilization come face to face with liberty). But David and Bacharach still needed a singer to sell it.

Gene Pitney was the Brill Building version of Marty Robbins—a handsome, powerful-voiced singer's singer versatile enough to record just about anything he wanted, even country music. In addition to his many Top Forty pop hits, Pitney would, over the course of his career, release a solo album of country material, cut two country duet albums with label mate George Jones and another one with Melba Montgomery, and even record bel canto–styled, Italian-language versions of country hits for the European market. "(The Man Who Shot) Liberty Valance" allowed Pitney an early chance to explore country music in a setting that suggests what Marty Robbins might've sounded like if he'd allowed his own pop instincts to lead him further in Pitney's direction.

"Liberty Valance" starts with a creepy, solitary fiddle that's quickly replaced by an overtly cowboy-song rhythm track, except that its loping bass is exaggerated out of all proportion to what we'd expect. "When Liberty Valance came to town, the women folk would hide," Pitney begins, then carefully repeats himself, "They'd hide." Just that quick, it's unmistakable how bad an hombre this Valance character is and what the stakes are for anyone who doesn't get out of his way. For a climax, Bacharach's arrangement unleashes a cacophony of strings, backing choirs, and kettledrum, and Pitney's magnificent tenor is the equal of that swirling soundscape every step of the way. The musical journey captured on "(The Man Who Shot) Liberty Valance," a progression from sparse frontier to wide-open streets to bustling sidewalks, crystallizes Ford's themes. Like its country cousin "El Paso," "Liberty Valance" reminds us how often cowboy music and pop have ridden parallel trails.—dc

135

City Lights, Ray Price
Produced by Don Law; Written by Bill Anderson
Columbia 41191   1958   #1 country (13 weeks); #71 pop

"City Lights" catches country music in a variety of transitions. First, there's the one from honky-tonk to the Nashville Sound. Just as Ray Price's fans would've expected in 1958, "City Lights" features fiddle and Price's driving, namesake beat. But the record also features plenty of echo and the shimmering wail of a backing female vocalist—two additions that spotlight the city's "great white way" as temptingly as a siren's call.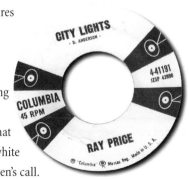

Change is afoot, too, in the songwriting. "City Lights" was Bill Anderson's first big success, joining Music City legends-to-be

Harlan Howard and Roger Miller, who also broke through in 1958 (Miller's "Invitation to the Blues" was the "City Lights" B side). Howard, Miller, and Anderson's songs—part wide-eyed and sentimental, part philosophical and just a little worldly—would provide the bridge from the deceptively simple heartaches of Hank Williams to the self-consciously poetic angst of Kris Kristofferson.

The biggest change going on here, though, is the one the song is most about: the postwar migration of rural country fans to the city. That subtext was in the song all along, but when Price replaced the question in Anderson's original lyric—"Did the God who put the stars above make those city lights?"—with a very specific answer—"But God who put the stars above, I don't believe made those lights"—he underscored the alienation experienced by transplanted rural folk as they left their homes for jobs in big industrial towns up North. Those lights "paint a pretty picture of a world that's gay and bright," Price groans. Because he knows better: "They're just a mask for loneliness in a world of city lights."—dc

136
(Sittin' on) the Dock of the Bay, Otis Redding
Produced by Steve Cropper;
Written by Otis Redding and Steve Cropper
Volt 157   1968   #1 pop (4 weeks)

Some view "Dock of the Bay" as a stylistic departure for Otis Redding, a record that hints at the pop singer he might have become had he not died in a plane crash on the eve of the single's release. From Otis's sublimely understated vocals (a far cry from his usual ravaged pleading), to the record's acoustic guitar-based arrangement, there's no denying it's different. Take away the horns and "Dock of the Bay" sounds more like John Lennon's "In My Life" or something from Bob Dylan's *John Wesley Harding* than anything else in Otis's catalog. None of which is surprising, given that he had been listening to *Sgt. Pepper* and that Dylan had been after him to cut "Just Like a Woman," which, according to producer Jerry Wexler, Otis found long-winded. Not only that, but just a few months earlier, Redding's fevered preachments had turned on the hippies at the Monterey Pop Festival, opening doors to a whole new audience.

Yet for all of that, "Dock of the Bay" is also downright country—and not just for its folk-song-from-the-hills simplicity and lyricism, or for the way the chiming fills of guitarist Steve

Cropper, who grew up in Missouri listening to the Grand Ole Opry, mimic those of a steel guitar. More than anything, it's the song's subject matter—Otis's longing for his home in Georgia—that's of a piece with hillbilly paeans to the old homeplace like Dolly Parton's "My Tennessee Mountain Home" or Jimmie Rodgers's "Miss the Mississippi and You." Granted, such songs aren't the exclusive province of country singers (they also betray more sentimentality than "Dock of the Bay"). But moreso than in blues, R&B, and rock & roll (genres of music in which men and women often have minds to ramble, rave about fast cars, or are born to run) tributes to home and hearth are quintessentially country.

Otis was staying on a houseboat just north of San Francisco in Sausalito, some 2,000 miles from his home in Macon, when he wrote "Dock of the Bay." Yet he wasn't just pining for his beloved Georgia red-clay. As the philosophical cast of the lyrics attests—note their use of the ocean's tides as a metaphor for time's ineluctable sweep—Otis is also going through a crisis of meaning; he's longing for a sense of permanence in a world that can't afford him one. What other explanation could there be for lines like "I've had nothing to live for, didn't look like nothing's gonna come my way"? Redding had *everything* to live for—a wife, kids, a ranch, a boundless musical future. But here, contemplating the transitory nature of life, he looks at a bigger picture; he's wrestling with what it's all worth if, in the end, everything fades away. Beyond being just another country song celebrating the virtues of home, "Dock of the Bay" suggests that Redding's writing was developing along the existentialist lines of Hank Williams.

Then again, in the liner notes to *Dreams to Remember: The Otis Redding Anthology*, "Dock of the Bay" co-writer Cropper claims that Otis barely had the germ of an idea, not even the bit about heading west from Georgia, when the two men sat down to finish the song. No doubt that's the case, but from the way that Otis tortures the word "home" when he moans, "I left my home in Georgia," there's no denying that the voice in "Dock of the Bay" is entirely his own. It also echoes the voice of Jimmie Rodgers who, forty years earlier in "Waiting for a Train," cried, "I'm on my way from Frisco, I'm goin' back to Dixieland."—bfw

137

Homecoming, Tom T. Hall
Produced by Jerry Kennedy; Written by Tom T. Hall
Mercury 72951   1969   #5 country

This is how "Honky Tonk Blues" might have turned out had Hank made it back to his pappy's farm. Thinking about Williams, or one of countless scufflin' musicians who walked down his mythic path, Hall casts himself as a singing star who's been away so long—and is so wrapped up in his legend—that he scarcely knows his own people anymore. Hall underscores the singer's self-absorption by making sure we never hear the father's voice; all we get by way of dialogue are the

excuses and false modesty of the man's guilt-ridden son as he breezes through town between gigs. "I'm sorry that I couldn't be here with you all when mama passed away," he apologizes as the band modulates higher, ratcheting up the tension. "I was on the road, and when they came and told me it was just too late."

Hall's deft portrayal of the isolated worlds of both father and son, triggered by the song's spare but pressing rhythms, earns him a place in a southern storytelling tradition that includes lyricists as well as great writers of short fiction. Hall never passes judgment on the son, letting him hang himself with his own words instead. Indeed, it's in the merest detail he tosses off as the song fades out—the son's request that his dad say hello to Barbara Walker (a high school sweetheart he doesn't have the time or guts to look up)—that Hall drives home his point: You can't go home again.—bfw

138

Don't It Make You Want to Go Home,
Joe South & the Believers
Produced by Joe South; Written by Joe South
Capitol 2592   1969   #27 country; #41 pop

"All God's children get weary when they roam / Don't it make you want to go home," sings Joe South as he pensively strums his twelve-string guitar. It's the story from Tom T. Hall's "Home-coming," except that now it's several years after the protagonist's

fateful visit to his daddy's farm and he's wishing he *could* go home. It's not that he can't get back to where he grew up or even face the people who looked at him funny the last time he was there. It's that the *place* has changed. There's an interstate along the creek where he went skinny-dipping as a kid, a drive-in theater in his favorite meadow, and a drag strip running through his grandma's old cow pasture.

Poorly managed growth and scattershot development have been the norm throughout the South—in Nashville, in Charlotte, and, especially, in Joe's hometown of Atlanta—since the sixties. Mimicking the whir of cranes and bulldozers, the record's swirling strings are enough to make anyone's head swim, particularly with that thumping bass hailing the inexorable march of "progress." All Joe can do is wring his hands and keep wondering aloud to himself, "Don't it make you want to go home."

Not that it'll do him any good. Not even the gospel choir that picks him up as he heads for the final chorus can transport him to a place that no longer exists.—bfw

139

By the Time I Get to Phoenix, Glen Campbell
Produced by Al DeLory; Written by Jimmy Webb
Capitol 2015   1967   #2 country; #26 pop

Jimmy Webb is best known today as the author of silly, over-inflated pop fare like "MacArthur Park," but it was the deceptively simple country songs he wrote for Glen Campbell that landed him in the Nashville Songwriter's Hall of Fame. "By the Time I Get to Phoenix" was the first of these. Los Angeles pop-rocker Johnny Rivers cut it initially, but after Campbell crossed over with the song in 1967, it was quickly covered by

country acts like Charlie Rich, Ray Price, and Marty Robbins. Less predictably, the song also went on to become one of the many country songs of its era ("Green, Green Grass of Home" and "Gentle on My Mind" were two more) that were taken into the pop repertoire, recorded by everyone from Isaac Hayes (in an eighteen-minute album version) and the Mad Lads to Burl Ives, Englebert Humperdinck, and Frank Sinatra.

It's Campbell's state-of-the-art countrypolitan (courtesy of producer Al DeLory, like Campbell a former member of Phil Spector's famed Wrecking Crew) that gets closest to the heart of Webb's song. Driving down the highway, Campbell imagines what the woman he's left behind will be doing by the time he reaches Phoenix, Albuquerque, Oklahoma. As the towns crawl slowly by, strings wash away the miles like wipers on a windshield. She's not going to believe I'm really gone, he repeats to himself. But by the end those strings stream through the mix like tears down a cheek, and we know *he's* the one who can't believe he's finally hit the road. And the one still battling the urge to turn around and go home.—dc

140

Ruby, Are You Mad?
The Osborne Brothers & Red Allen
Produced by Jim Vienneau;
Written by Cousin Emmy (a.k.a. Cynthia May Carver)
MGM 12308   1956   Did not chart

Bobby and Sonny Osborne came not to bury the bluegrass tradition but to praise it—which is to say they learned the bluegrass rules by heart, then proceeded to ignore them at will.

They certainly had great teachers— Sonny and Bobby served apprenticeships, either individually or together, with Bill Monroe, the Stanley Brothers, and Jimmy Martin. Even so, by the sixties they were going their own way, plugging in on the road and adding dobro, piano, and drums in the studio. In truth, they'd been experimenting all along. Their debut single, "Ruby, Are You Mad?" in 1956, caught Bobby laying down his mandolin temporarily to team with brother Sonny for a twin-banjo attack. With banjo notes pelting him like raindrops, Bobby cuts loose a tenor lead that could slice through the harshest storms of life. He stretches out his piercing notes for

what feels like forever. "Oh Rew-beeeeeeeeeeee-yee," he cries into the night, "are you mad?" From the way his voice is swallowed in studio echo, it's a safe wager she's not just mad; she's gone. That seems especially true at the end, when the song slows to a dramatic crawl and the now a cappella Bobby is joined in careening harmony by Sonny and guitarist Red Allen, an early preview of the high-tenor-lead trio that would soon become an Osbornes trademark.

The haunting results feel like high lonesome cubed.—dc

141

You Win Again, Hank Williams
with His Drifting Cowboys
Produced by Fred Rose; Written by Hank Williams
MGM K11318   1952   #10 country

The legend of Hank Williams is appropriated regularly as a symbol of musical and cultural rebellion, but unless alcoholism somehow counts as sticking it to the man, Hank was no insurgent. Nor was he much of an innovator. Whereas Bill Monroe, Ray Price, and Elvis Presley created sounds that heralded the next big thing, Williams trafficked in the old and familiar. The rambling blues of the Singing Brakeman, the homilies of the Carter Family, the earnest stringband music of Roy Acuff, the playfulness of hillbilly boogie and western swing, the honky-tonk rhythms and cheating songs of Tubb and Tillman—they all crystallized at mid-century with Hank Williams.

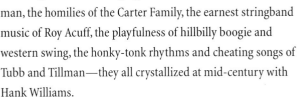

Put another way, Williams was a synthesizer of the first rank, though that hardly means he added nothing of his own to the music. Certain elements of his phrasing were distinctly his, and the way his records appeared to play out in public the problems of his private life was unique for his time (in contrast to today, when such a confessional approach is taken for granted). More than any of his peers, he composed the songs that got country music on pop radio, and his lyrics, frequently poetic yet as plainspoken as if he were just jawing with a neighbor, forever raised the bar for country songwriting.

"You Win Again" highlights each of these qualities. Conceived as a Luke the Drifter cut but released as the B side for "Settin' the Woods on Fire," the song has a smoldering pop potential that has only been suggested in subsequent versions by Jerry Lee Lewis, R&B-pop singer Tommy Edwards, and Ray Charles. From the opening "The news is out all over town," one can easily imagine each line sung, for example, by Frank Sinatra in a brassy, swinging Nelson Riddle arrangement. But this is a Hank Williams record, so he's backed not by piano and horns but by a typically spare mid-century country rhythm track. And one, it must be noted, so locked in on the misery of Hank's vocal that it never even takes so much as a solo; Don Helms just repeats, halfway through, the steel licks he's already used at the top. Surely singing to his ex-wife Audrey—the pair had officially divorced just the day before this session—Hank phrases the lyrics in ways that are both inherently musical and emotionally intense, biting down hard on certain words and stretching out "heart" and "shame" and "love" until you realize these words *are* the solos. Each moan conveys just how angry he is, how hurt, and how much he is still in love.

Dozens of country songs have essayed this same pained ambivalence. But with "You Win Again," Williams (along with Fred Rose, who suggested he revise the original title, "I Lose Again"), captured it better than anyone before or since. "I know that I should leave," he cries, before giving up completely. "But then / I just can't go. You win again." Nothing fancy there. No musical or lyrical revolution. But would you settle for perfection?—dc

142

You Don't Know Me, Eddy Arnold
Produced by Steve Sholes;
Written by Cindy Walker and Eddy Arnold
RCA Victor 6502   1956   #10 country

It's become a cliché to say that songwriters put into words things that the rest of us feel but don't know how to express. Yet like most clichés, the notion contains a kernel of truth. Case in point: the songs of Cindy Walker.

Gene Autry, Ernest Tubb, Spike Jones, Rose Maddox, Hank Snow, Ray Charles, and Roy Orbison are just a few of the stars who flocked to record Walker's songs. In a recent interview with John Morthland, Walker estimated that her songs have accounted for more than 400 Top Forty country and pop hits since the early 1940s. That was when the Central Texas native, already a compulsive amateur songwriter, accompanied her father, a cotton broker, on a business trip to Hollywood. She talked her way onto the set of a Bing Crosby movie, pitched him "Lone Star Trail," and Crosby promptly recorded the tune. Before the decade was out, stars like Margaret Whiting, Jo Stafford, Patti Page, and Bob Wills had scored Top Ten hits with Walker's songs as Cindy went on to become one of Hollywood's most in-demand writers, especially among the silver screen cowboys.

Walker also enjoyed a brief career as a performer, first as a star in the early music videos called "Soundies," and then on radio, where her remake of "When My Blue Moon Turns to Gold Again" for Decca reached the country Top Ten in 1944. But Cindy soon abandoned singing to focus on songwriting. In the early fifties she moved back to Texas and started making regular trips to the annual Disc Jockey Convention in Nashville. There, with her mother Oree at the piano, she would set up shop and write for virtually all of country's biggest stars, including Eddy Arnold.

Arnold supplied Walker with the title and the gist of "You Don't Know Me," the story of a guy who can't bring himself to divulge his feelings to the woman he loves, only to watch her walk away with someone who can. Cindy took it from there, and Eddy rode the song into the country Top Ten, no mean feat at a time when his unprecedented chart success had all but run its course. Nevertheless, it's surprising the record didn't crossover over and go pop. Recorded in New York with uptown session pros, it was closer in style to the dreamy doowop and teen ballads crowding the jukeboxes of the era's roller rinks and malt shops than the honky-tonk that still prevailed in Nashville.

"I never knew the art of making love, though my heart ached with love for you," Walker has Eddy confess on the bridge, as a shimmering piano, subdued electric guitar, and sighing background choir hang on his every word. "Afraid and shy, I let my chance go by, the chance you might have loved me too," he continues, caressing each syllable just as he does the thought of the love that slipped past the tips of his fingers. It's a tender, heartrending moment, one from which Ray Charles would later wring every drop of pathos in the process of granting the song immortality. Over the years, "You Don't Know Me" would also come to define Walker's singular gifts as a songwriter, above all her mastery of the art of putting words into the mouths of singers, the better to take us closer to the unspoken stirrings of our own hearts.—bfw

143

She's Got You, Patsy Cline

Produced by Owen Bradley; Written by Hank Cochran
Decca 31354   1962   #1 country (5 weeks); #14 pop

Hank Cochran wrote "She's Got You" late one afternoon while coming up as a writer and song plugger for Pamper Music. It was a heady time at the fledgling Nashville publishing company, home to Harlan Howard and Willie Nelson, Cochran's fellow lunchpail (but soon to be legendary) songwriters.

Everyone else had knocked off for the day when Hank, sitting alone in a small garage out back of the Pamper office, spied a photo of a woman in his desk drawer. The face in the frame (an old flame?) must have hit him hard; in less than a half-hour he'd finished writing "She's Got You." And none too soon either. Patsy Cline was just coming off long chart runs with "Crazy" (written by Nelson) and "I Fall to Pieces" (a Howard-Cochran co-write) and was looking to Pamper for her next big hit. Hank knew he had a smash on his hands, so he called Patsy, who invited him to come over and play it for her, but not before he'd stopped off and picked up a bottle of something. A good thing, too; the lovelorn lyrics and smoldering melody he was about to sing for her cried out for whiskey.

Built around a simple lyrical conceit—"I've got your picture / She's got you"—the song might not have looked like much on paper. But with Floyd Cramer's teardrop piano, Buddy Harman's nagging brushes, and those moping basses and sighing Jordanaires egging her on, Patsy turned "She's Got You" into a pop-country tour de force, a rarely matched monument to heartache. "I've got your memory," she pines on the bridge, halfheartedly consoling herself with the knowledge that at least she's got that, before adding, "Or has it got me," lingering on the word "or" as if struck for the first time that her lover's memory is possessing her. "I really don't know," she continues, not wanting to face the truth before wailing, "but I know it won't let me be,"

drawing out the word "be" so that it's painfully clear who, or rather what, has got who. It's not some old memento she's mooning over, it's the memory of her ex, very much alive in the here and now, that's burning a hole in her mind.

"She's Got You" was Cline's second (and last) #1 country single and Cochran's first as a songwriter, promising only good things for future collaborations. There's no telling the string of hits they might have had together had Patsy not gone down in the 1963 plane crash that also killed Cowboy Copas, Hawkshaw Hawkins, and Randy Hughes. But at least we've got this stunner. Or rather, it's got us.—bfw

144

She's All I Got, Johnny Paycheck

Produced by Billy Sherrill; Written by J. Williams Jr. and G. Bonds
Epic 10783   1971   #2 country; #91 pop

Johnny Paycheck first gained attention in the mid- to late sixties when he recorded an often deranged body of work that, even in a genre known for extremes in mental anguish, stands out as memorably unhinged. But despite the creepy intensity of a modern-day murder ballad such as "(Pardon Me) I've Got Someone to Kill," or maybe because of that intensity, the records he recorded for the Hilltop and Little Darlin' labels didn't sell squat. By the end of the decade, Paycheck had hit bottom, reportedly singing for drinks in the dives of L.A.

Back in Nashville, however, producer-songwriter Billy Sherrill had wanted to work with Paycheck for years. In 1971, when Johnny's money and alcohol problems had seemingly rendered him unsignable in Nashville, Sherrill took a chance and had the singer record "She's All I Got," a number co-written by Jerry Williams (a.k.a. Swamp Dogg) and Gary U. S. Bonds for Nashville soul singer and DJ Freddie North.

On its face, "She's All I Got" looks like a simple love song, the antithesis of Paycheck's darker, earlier work. With Sherrill's not quite manic arrangement thumping away, Paycheck begins by politely asking someone, in his rubbery baritone, to please not take his woman; she's all he has in the world. At first you figure he's just another goofy good ol' boy, head over heels in love. But then the band drops to a hush, and it's hard to be so sanguine. "She is life," he sings, before adding a caveat that reads like a warning sign for depression: "When I want to live." And then he just keeps on going. "She's everything to me in life that life can give . . . the only thing to me that's really real." Pretty soon you realize that this guy's out there, obsessed, maybe a little scary. He needs more from his lover than anyone could ever possibly deliver, a state of emotional affairs that is not only unrealistic and unhealthy but potentially dangerous. "(It's a Mighty Thin Line) Between Love and Hate," Paycheck sang on one of those Little Darlin' sides, and this guy, believing a lover is his only link to everything else, is that same crazy man, sinking into that same hopeless vision. Only here we glimpse him *before* it's left him with no option but to kill his rival, his woman, or himself.—dc

145

Chug-a-Lug, Roger Miller
Produced by Jerry Kennedy; Written by Roger Miller
Smash 1926   1964   #3 country; #9 pop

146

One Dyin' and a Buryin', Roger Miller
Produced by Jerry Kennedy; Written by Roger Miller
Smash 1994   1965   #10 country; #34 pop

"Things for him were funny and sad at the same time," D. H. Lawrence once observed about the stories of Anton Chekov, "but you would not see their sadness if you did not see their fun, because both were linked up." You could say something similar about country music, but nowhere does this tragicomic sensibility come through more clearly than in the work of Roger Miller.

When Miller was just one year old, his father died; when he was three, his mother took ill and, unable to support her family, was forced to divvy up Roger and his two brothers among relatives. Taken in by an aunt and uncle, Roger grew up on an Oklahoma farm, a profoundly lonely child. By his account, "We were dirt poor. What I'd do is sit around and get warm by crawling inside myself, and make up stuff." In high school he began running away—during one adventure, he stole a guitar, a move that landed him in Korea by way of avoiding a jail sentence. "I always wanted attention," he said of his youth. "Always was reaching and grabbing for attention."

He got it with music. As a boy Miller had fallen in love via the radio with the mournful songs of Hank Williams and the

showmanship of Bob Wills; he also tagged after a neighbor friend, Sheb "Purple People Eater" Wooley, who taught him his first guitar chords. That trio of musical influences encompasses the Miller aesthetic to a T. When he moved to Nashville in 1957, he began writing hits for everyone from Ray Price and Faron Young (he played for a time in both their bands) to Ernest Tubb and Jim Reeves. Compositions like "Invitation to the Blues" were typical of the period in every respect, save their rare quality. But when Miller's recording of "Dang Me" became a British Invasion–era crossover hit in 1964, it was clear his solo career would be anything but typical. Scatting, swinging, off-kilter, with melodies as unpredictable as they were unforgettable, Miller's best songs veered between joyous lunacy and near suicidal depression. And while one extreme or the other would normally take the fore, its opposite always threatened to burst from between the lines.

"Chug-a-Lug" showcases Miller's comedic talent at its peak. It's a record in love with sound, as heard in its bounding acoustic rhythm track and Miller's own inebriated sound effects (apparently, George Jones's white lightning was mere Kool Aid compared to what Roger's chugging). It's also a record in love with language, as witnessed by its wide-eyed drinking tales and cracker-barrel lyrics like "we uncovered a covered-up moonshine still" (the deliberate redundancy being a particularly Millerian device). Full of belly laughs and high times, "Chug-a-Lug" is both sophisticated and hilarious. Then again, "Chug-a-Lug" also recounts the not-funny-in-the-least history of a man who's been getting tanked since he was a kid and who still doesn't know when to say when. The record ends, don't forget, with the gurgling moan of the guy puking.

Miller's songs nearly always had that extra layer. His zaniest novelties express states of mind that are practically Zen ("You can't roller skate in a buffalo herd, but you can be happy if you've a mind to" is a good example), and his saddest numbers are filled with the darkest humor around. For instance, in the spare acoustic opening to "One Dyin' and a Buryin'," Miller says of some deep lingering hurt that "I think I finally found a way to forget," and you instantly perk up because, of course, you'd like to know how to do that too. But you quickly realize his solution is just a joke, a punch line so demented you can't help but laugh even as its harrowing elegance has the hair rising on your neck—"All it takes" to forget "is one dyin' and a buryin' / Some cryin', six carryin' me / I wanta be free." The level of song craft in those lines, not to mention the sheer emotional presence it requires to pull off a sentiment every bit as earnest as it is playful, is nothing short of awesome.—dc

147

He Stopped Loving Her Today, George Jones
Produced by Billy Sherrill;
Written by Bobby Braddock and Curly Putman
Epic 50867   1980   #1 country (1 week)

148

Today I Started Loving You Again, Sammi Smith
Produced by Jim Malloy; Written by Merle Haggard
Mega 1236   1975   #9 country

It's impossible at this late date to hear "He Stopped Loving Her Today," George Jones and Billy Sherrill's Wagnerian ode to undying love, with anything like fresh ears. We know how its gut-wrenching plot will unfold. We know that George's gloriously maudlin recitation will come after the first chorus,

and we know that his measured, barely contained vocals will build to that chorus, and that Sherrill's exacting arrangement will gradually unfurl on its way to sweeping up George's unbounded wail with a gust of swirling strings. Nevertheless, even after we've played the record a hundred times, it can still render us defenseless. It doesn't matter how often we've heard George's line about seeing his lovesick friend smile for the first time in years. Those violins that surge at precisely the moment it hits us that his buddy's peaceful grin is the handiwork of the undertaker still have the power to stand our every last nerve strand on end. All of

these things, along with Pete Drake's unhinged steel and George's unwavering commitment to what he's singing about (his love for Tammy?), explain why "He Stopped Loving Her Today" is one of the most beloved country singles of all time.

Just as riveting, though, are the story and pathos the record doesn't divulge—that of the woman who, nearly twenty years earlier, assured George's late friend that he'd get over her in time, but who now confronts her own unresolved feelings as she stands over his open casket. The only real clue we have as to what she's feeling is the ghostly female voice, that of the unsung Millie Kirkham, moaning grievously during the recitation. The dead man may be over her for good, that voice is saying, but crying time for her has just begun. Or at least that's the case if we imagine that the woman at the funeral is the Sammi Smith of "Today I Started Loving You Again," her fate hinging upon the word "Today" no less than her departed lover's did.

"I should have known that the worst was yet to come," Sammi tells herself, less angst ridden than in a state of shock on the opening chorus. The entire record aches with this desolation, notably Sammi's nicotine-steeped alto, country's closest answer to Billie Holiday. The way Sammi sings behind the beat makes it seem like she's too weary to go on. The strings and guitars that enter on the record's sole verse prop her up some, but just enough to let her see that she's right back where she's always been. "I got over you just long enough to let my heartaches mend / And then today I started loving you again," she pines, just as the pallbearers shut the lid on her barren heart.—bfw

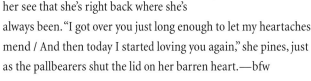

149

Love Hurts, Gram Parsons with Emmylou Harris
Produced by Gram Parsons; Written by Boudleaux Bryant
Reprise 1192   1974   Did not chart

Gram Parsons's outsized myth often masks the fact that—as good, even great, as some of them are—a fair number of his records are too slapdash to live up to his grandiose visions and pronouncements. Not so with the ten sides that compose his posthumous, second solo LP, *Grievous Angel*.

Parsons and his band, the Fallen Angels, which included

guitarist James Burton and a couple of other hired guns from Elvis's post-comeback combo, had been on the road for a year and a half at this point, and Gram was singing better than ever. Just as crucial, background vocalist Emmylou Harris had emerged as a full-blown duet partner. She and Gram had become the latter-day equivalent of close-harmony sibling acts like the Louvin and Everly Brothers, and their repertoire reflected this change.

For the *Grievous Angel* sessions, they cut three songs popularized by the Everlys and two by the Louvins, all of them first-rate. Only one cover from each duo, though, made it onto the album, and "Love Hurts" was the best. Where the Everlys' original was wistful, combining teen naïveté with youthful resiliency, Gram and Emmylou's remake sounds ravaged and world-weary, older and more bereft spiritually than either of the singer's twenty-something years should have allowed. "Love hurts, love scars / Love wounds and mars," they mourn, their desolate voices intertwining, Gram's tenor breaking all over the place, Emmylou's spectral soprano as bracing as cold mountain air. Burton's searing leads and Al Perkins's bleeding steel cut marrow deep while the rhythm section throbs away behind them, confirming that Gram and Emmylou aren't just bemoaning betrayal and heartbreak as transitory conditions, but as givens, the birthright of every man and woman who's ever dared to love.—bfw

150
(Now and Then There's) A Fool Such as I, Hank Snow
Produced by Steve Sholes; Written by Bill Trader
RCA Victor 5034   1952   #3 country

Hank Snow adored Victorian parlor songs, and this record is as poignant an evocation of that era's weepers as anything this side of Vernon Dalhart. "Pardon me if I'm sentimental when we say goodbye / Don't be angry with me should I cry," Snow croons in a brandy-smooth baritone while fiddle and steel guitar whimper quietly in the background. Hank's lover is bidding him a final farewell, and it's killing him to watch her go. But from the way his guitar and the fiddle lightly dance together on the break, it's also clear he wants to savor the moment's sweet sorrow.

"Now and Then" came out just as the golden age of honky-tonk was reaching its peak, a time when the gutbucket records

of Lefty Frizzell, Webb Pierce, Hank Thompson, and Kitty Wells were all over the country charts. Snow's hit must have sounded positively antediluvian by contrast, a throwback to prewar Tin Pan Alley pop. All of which invests the words "Pardon me if I'm sentimental" with added freight, turning them into Hank's apology for indulging his softer side.

At his core, however, Snow was always an astute traditionalist—one eye trained on the past, the other on the future. That's doubtless what drew him to a song that recast the Victorian era's most mawkish tendencies in a distinctly modern light. "Now and Then" might *sound* like an old-time parlor tune, but that's hardly true of its message. Seeking refuge in neither philosophy nor the institutions that comforted his predecessors, Hank abandons himself to his hurt as if that's *all* he has to cling to.

So no matter what the song's title says, Snow, who took the record to #3 (Elvis had a #2 pop hit with it in 1959) is no fool. "Now and Then" is as bracing a shot of hillbilly existentialism as anything in Hank Williams's catalog; the only difference is that it goes down a whole lot smoother.—bfw

151
Ode to Billie Joe, Bobbie Gentry
Produced by Kelly Gordon;
Written by Bobbie Gentry
Capitol 5950   1967   #17 country; #1 pop (4 weeks)

If "I'm So Lonesome I Could Cry" earns Hank the title of Hillbilly Shakespeare, then this slice of Southern Gothic qualifies Bobbie Gentry as country-soul's answer to Carson McCullers. Yet not even McCullers could have crafted as taut and riveting a tale as this account of the murky events surrounding the suicide of young Billie Joe McAllister. Of course, Gentry's medium gives her an edge over McCullers. The itchy guitar lick Bobbie plays to open the record—the sonic equivalent of someone picking a scab or scratching a mosquito bite—suffuses her story with foreboding; aggravated by Jimmie Haskell's acerbic string arrangement, the music speaks volumes before she utters a word.

"It was the third of June, another sleepy, dusty Delta day / I was out choppin' cotton and my brother was balin' hay," Bobbie drawls in a languid alto, heightening the tension. From that point until near the end of the narrative Gentry's protagonist falls silent. By turns gossipy, distracted, and suspicious, the young woman's mama, papa, and brother proceed, over Sunday dinner, to comment on Billie Joe's death as if they were talking about the weather. Of all the lines that get passed back and forth with the biscuits and the black-eyed peas, the one that grabs most folks, and on which the story pivots, is an offhand remark the mother makes while going on about having

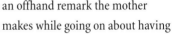

"that nice young preacher Brother Taylor" to supper. "Oh, by the way," she begins, paying no more attention to what she's saying than her husband and son do. "He said he saw a girl that looked a lot like you up on Choctaw Ridge, and she and Billie Joe were throwing something off the Tallahatchie Bridge."

Everyone has a theory about what went into the water that day—the main contenders being an unwanted baby and a spurned engagement ring, although neither makes much sense. Wouldn't the narrator's family have noticed if she'd been pregnant? And why, if she had rejected Billie Joe's marriage proposal, would they *both* be flinging the ring he bought her into the river?

From the war in Vietnam to race riots up North, the nation was being torn apart as "Ode to Billie Joe" hit #1 during the ironically dubbed Summer of Love. Citing this turmoil, writer Ron Carlson submitted as good an answer as any in the *Oxford American*'s 1998 southern music issue, contending that what went over the side of that bridge was the collective innocence of the American people. Yet not even that accounts for the indifference of the narrator's family to her grief over Billie Joe's suicide. Her papa wouldn't have noticed anyway, but her mama certainly should have suspected something was wrong from the way the young woman picks at her food.

Likely it was out of grief for this apathy, as well as for the indifference of a nation that sat down to dinner each night talking around but never about what was going on in its midst, that Gentry had her narrator take to tossing flowers into the Tallahatchie's muddy waters.—bfw

152
Don't Let Me Cross Over, Carl & Pearl Butler
Produced by Don Law; Written by Penny Jay
Columbia 42593   1962   #1 country (11 weeks); #88 pop

153
Don't Let Me Cross Over, Jerry Lee Lewis &
Linda Gail Lewis
Produced by Jerry Kennedy; Written by Penny Jay
Smash 2220   1969   #9 country

What a difference a decade makes, or the better part of a decade anyway. From the emerging feminist movement to the sexual revolution, the sweeping social changes that took place during the seven years between the releases of these two versions of the same song mark the passing of an era.

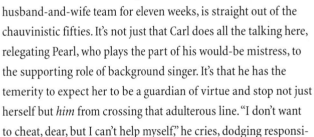

Although it bears a 1962 recording date, Carl and Pearl Butler's original version of "Don't Let Me Cross Over," a country #1 for the husband-and-wife team for eleven weeks, is straight out of the chauvinistic fifties. It's not just that Carl does all the talking here, relegating Pearl, who plays the part of his would-be mistress, to the supporting role of background singer. It's that he has the temerity to expect her to be a guardian of virtue and stop not just herself but *him* from crossing that adulterous line. "I don't want to cheat, dear, but I can't help myself," he cries, dodging responsibility for what he's about to do while providing Tammy Wynette with all the fodder she'd need for her controversial aside, "After all, he's just a man." In the process, Carl sets up Pearl to take the blame no matter what happens between them. If she keeps him from cheating she's denying him a taste of heaven. If she doesn't she's damning him to a living hell—not to mention breaking the heart of the man to whom she's already married.

The whole affair, or at least Carl's participation in it (Pearl never speaks her mind or heart), is as pathetic as the whimpering strains of fiddle and steel guitar that plead his case in the background—unabashed hillbilly music that couldn't have been more at odds with the then-reigning Nashville Sound. Yet it's just this pathos that gives the record its power. No matter how much Carl deserves our reproach, his anguish is real. As a man who came of age in the honky-tonking, Bible-thumping postwar era, he's genuinely tortured about crossing "love's cheatin' line" because, deep down, he knows there will be hell to pay regardless of what he does or doesn't do.

By contrast, the Lewises' version of "Don't Let Me Cross Over"—a bona fide duet, and one between a brother and a sister no less—finds the tables turned. Embracing the sexual freedom unleashed by the Summer of Love, Linda Gail is positively on the prowl, and it's no confession of weakness or cheater's prayer when she belts, "I'm tempted, my darling, to steal you away." She's got a mind to snatch Jerry away from his woman and is putting him on notice, or at least flirting with serious intent. Not that the Killer, crooning the second verse, seems to mind. Judging by the way their ecstatic moans fuse on the chorus, crossing that line doesn't feel like cheating to them at all.—bfw

154
Back Street Affair, Webb Pierce
Produced by Paul Cohen; Written by Billy Wallace
Decca 28369   1952   #1 country (4 weeks)

The town calls Pierce a cheating husband, says his young girlfriend's a homewrecker, and dismisses what they're up to as a cheap "back street affair." Pierce says these busybodies don't know what the hell they're talking about. His wife cheated first, this girl didn't know he was married until she'd already fallen for him, 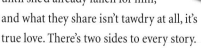 and what they share isn't tawdry at all, it's true love. There's two sides to every story.

And with more chapters than you can know. Pierce says they'll disprove the naysayers when they're "free to love . . . (and) when all the talk has died away." But that's only what he hopes right now, and Pierce, who's apparently making this prediction while awaiting his final divorce papers, knows firsthand how today's promises can twist into tomorrow's regrets. When he and his lover are no longer innervated by the thrill of sneaking around and when they're no longer buoyed by the need for a united front against "the unfair judgment of gossip," they'll indeed be free to love and make a life for themselves. But, as Pierce should understand as well as anyone, that's when the hard part starts.—dc

155
Walk on By, Leroy Van Dyke
Produced by Shelby Singleton; Written by Kendall Hayes
Mercury 71834   1961   #1 country (19 weeks); #5 pop

Time was when cheating situations were country music's most dependable cash crop. Even in a crowded field, though, Leroy Van Dyke's "Walk on By" stood out. This monstrously popular 1961 hit avoids all the expected approaches to infidelity (the ecstatic stolen moments, the anguished eternities apart, the consequences, the children, the guilt) and instead details the logistics of not getting caught. If we should pass each other on the street, Van Dyke croons conspiratorially to his lover, "just walk on by" like I was any other stranger. Then, in a whisper, "Wait on the corner."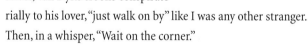

The Nashville Sound arrangement—a rhythm track that's sunny and confident, a halting guitar riff that sneaks about on tiptoe—says that this is just how it's got to be when the dark passions of a backstreet affair meet the light of day.—dc

156
Slipping Around, Floyd Tillman
Produced by Art Satherley; Written by Floyd Tillman
Columbia 20581   1949   #5 country

World War II wreaked havoc on domestic tranquility in the United States. The physical distance that separated husbands and wives was bad enough, but for many couples, thousands of them newlyweds, the lack of emotional warmth—and sex—was unbearable. Those who couldn't endure the isolation sought comfort where they could find it. There certainly was no shortage of temptation, what with the men away in far-off lands and women entering the labor force where they worked alongside the men who remained at home. The upshot of all this infidelity was an unprecedented rise in the divorce rate and a lot of conflicted feelings. Victorian attitudes toward sex and marriage might not have held sway any longer, but the nation was still a generation away from the sexual revolution of the sixties, leaving the many who did stray to wrestle with a prickly mix of freedom and guilt.

None of this was lost on the era's songwriters. "One Has My Name (the Other Has My Heart)," a 1948 hit for Jimmy Wakely that was co-written by singing cowboy Eddie Dean, was perhaps the first record to explore the phenomenon. But whereas it merely got inside the head and heart of a guy whose emotional loyalties had shifted, Floyd Tillman's "Slipping Around" got down to the nitty gritty of cheating.

The record finds Tillman talking with his lover in the back booth of some dimly lit bar, or at least that's the image conjured by Ralph Smith's honky-tonk piano as it peals away in the background. Yet as the endless weeping of twin fiddles and steel attests, there's nothing cozy or exhilarating about this rendezvous; it's pure hell. "I know I can't forget you and I gotta have you near / But we just have to slip around and live in constant fear," Floyd tells his outside woman, slurring his lines as if he were indeed spilling tears in his beer. Both, you see, are stuck in relationships they're unable to break. And as much as Floyd hopes they'll be together for good someday, he can't shake his suspicion that the pain of living a lie—and perhaps of getting caught—isn't really worth the pleasure of their furtive couplings.

Doubtless many of the millions who heard "Slipping Around" could relate, what with three different versions of the song making the Top Ten within the span of four months in 1948. Tillman's original reached #5, while those of Ernest Tubb and Jimmy Wakely—the latter a duet with pop singer Margaret Whiting—went to #1, with Wakely and Whiting's staying there seventeen weeks and eventually crossing over to top the pop charts as well. But neither of these subsequent versions, as good

as they were, could match Tillman's aching baritone as it twisted its way through the words "tied up" on the chorus, a sound that's the embodiment of the song's binding dilemma.—bfw

157

On the Other Hand, Randy Travis
Produced by Kyle Lehning and Keith Stegall;
Written by Paul Overstreet and Don Schlitz
Warner Bros. 28962   1986   #1 country (1 week)

George Jones's "Who's Gonna Fill Their Shoes" voiced a question on the minds of many country fans in the spring of 1985—in a radio world that seemed increasingly disconnected from the country traditions of "ol' Marty, Hank and Lefty," "blue suede shoes and Elvis," who would carry on?

Climbing just to #67 on the country charts that summer, Randy Travis's "On the Other Hand" must have sounded, at least to the handful of folks who actually heard it, like the answer to a prayer. Its classic "Almost Persuaded" theme ("But on the other hand, there's a golden band") and the relaxed twang of Travis's delivery identified the record as close kin not only to Lefty but to George himself (not to mention Ernest Tubb). Combined with a lone acoustic guitar strum fleshed out by pedal steel and a loping rhythm track, "On the Other Hand" pays brilliant tribute to a rich history of hard-core classics. When it climbed to the top of the charts upon re-release the next summer, it became not just homage to a tradition but a prime example of that tradition at its very best.

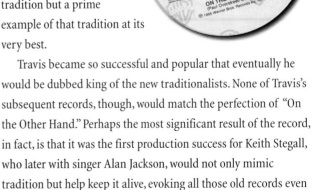

Travis became so successful and popular that eventually he would be dubbed king of the new traditionalists. None of Travis's subsequent records, though, would match the perfection of "On the Other Hand." Perhaps the most significant result of the record, in fact, is that it was the first production success for Keith Stegall, who later with singer Alan Jackson, would not only mimic tradition but help keep it alive, evoking all those old records even as they rocked the jukebox.—dc

158

Mule Skinner Blues, Bill Monroe & His
Blue Grass Boys
Produced by Frank Walker;
Written by Jimmie Rodgers and George Vaughan
Bluebird B-8568   1940   Pre-chart

159

Mule Skinner Blues (Blue Yodel No. 8), Dolly Parton
Produced by Bob Ferguson;
Written by Jimmie Rodgers and George Vaughan
RCA 9863   1970   #3 country

It's often said that country values its past more than other genres, that this backward-looking bent is what makes it such a traditional music, and that the way for the country tradition to survive is for its adherents to leave the music unchanged. If this static definition of tradition described anything like the reality of the country story, then the Dixie Chicks would sound like the Carter Family and Garth Brooks would be valued as the latest in a sixty-year procession of Blue Yodelers. In truth, the country music story is one of perpetual change—its tradition doesn't reject dynamism but it does explicitly connect the music's present, however altered, to its past.

One way country musicians move forward while remaining in touch with where the music's been is through repertoire, as in the case of Bill Monroe's 1940 recording of Jimmie Rodgers's "Blue Yodel No. 8," better known as "Mule Skinner Blues." The charm of Rodgers's original lay in its lazy, off-the-cuff sound; Jimmie is asking for work as a mule driver but you can tell he would just as soon pick and yodel his version of the country blues. A decade later, Monroe honored the Father of Country Music by covering one of the records he'd worn out in his brother Charlie's record collection as a young man, and by recording it in a stringband style clearly influenced by another of his early favorites, Charlie Poole's North Carolina Ramblers.

But no stringband ever sounded like Monroe's new Blue Grass Boys. Monroe kicks it off himself with a bluesy guitar lick, then the band follows his lead through an arrangement that's fiercely rhythmic and bass driven, frenetically paced, completely modern.

Monroe's yodels aren't sweetly, intimately bluesy like Rodgers's, either; they're cocky and razor sharp. Rodgers came off as if he could take the work or leave it, but Monroe (who'd auditioned with "Mule Skinner" to land a spot on the Opry just a few weeks before this session) desperately wants the job, and from the sound of that laughing, stretched-out yelp of a yodel he tacks on at the end, he knows it's his for the asking. How could it not be? There's never been anyone like him. The caricature of country music presents tradition as a weight that crushes artistic freedom and flattens individuality like biscuit dough under a rolling pin. But in a great country record such as Monroe's "Mule Skinner Blues," there's something quite different going on. For Monroe, glancing back doesn't limit who he can be; it inspires him to write his singular chapter in a story that will continue long after he's gone.

Forty years later, Dolly Parton did the same thing with "Mule Skinner Blues," a recording that recalls Monroe's version, points to the Dixie Chicks at their twangiest, and yet doesn't exactly sound like either. Dolly's stringband is plugged in and studio slick— its beat nailed down by a drummer—and she says good morning to Monroe and Rodgers before flying past them like a jet past a model A. She's thoroughly rooted in

her tradition, yet thoroughly modern too. Sick of a husband who takes every dollar she earns as a waitress, this would-be muleskinner is a country music woman at the dawn of the feminist era demanding a life of her own creation; she's as giddy and tough as the yodels she stretches out like Blue Ridge mountain arias. Like Monroe before her, Parton uses Jimmie Rodgers's song to link her music to a tradition even as she declares that she's her own person now.—dc

160

The Dance, Garth Brooks
Produced by Allen Reynolds; Written by Tony Arata
Capitol 44629   1990   #1 country (3 weeks)

"The Dance" wasn't Garth Brooks' first hit; it wasn't even his first #1. But it was the record that broke him out of the hat-act pack and set him on the road to superstardom. Brooks's earliest singles—"Much Too Young (To Feel This Damn Old)," "If Tomorrow Never Comes," "Not Counting You"—were typical eighties country, the sorts of twangy, pop-inflected records Brooks's biggest country influence, George Strait, had been scoring with for years. "The Dance," on the other hand, was a pop record through and through. From the Elton John-ish piano that starts it off, through the Dan Fogelberg–inspired lyrics and melody, to the strings that spring the song skyward, everything here opens its arms to a suburban, middle-class rock audience that had previously imagined itself too sophisticated for country music. "The Dance" didn't merely predict Nashville's pop future; it practically invented it.

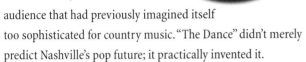

It's ironic, then, that "The Dance" created that future with a message as old as the hills. When Garth sings to a departed lover that "I could've missed the pain, but I'd've had to miss the dance," he's simply restating in his admittedly new-agey fashion a truth that defines the heart of country music. Not just that life is inevitably filled with both joy and pain but that the two are hotwired together. Even more than country's recurring topics (loving and cheating; working, drinking, and dying), this dialectical vision of life explains why the country music tradition has so often been described as "adult." Not to mention why an increasingly youth- and rock-centered culture has so regularly mistaken the acceptance in country music for resignation, or even fatalism.

Coming of age in 1970s Oklahoma to a soundtrack that combined album-oriented rock radio with the old-time country tunes of a mother who'd once sung on Red Foley's *Ozark Jubilee*, Brooks seems never to have made this mistake. Even though he sings "The Dance" in exactly the fashion you'd expect from someone who grew up loving Kenny Loggins and James Taylor, he still invests the song with the strengths of his country forebears—the unabashed sincerity of Conway Twitty, the unironic emotionalism of Roy Acuff, the humble wisdom of Luke the Drifter. And he does it with barely a whiff of the smug posturing that would soon come to define Garth Brooks, superstar.—dc

161

The Gods Were Angry with Me,
Margaret Whiting & Jimmy Wakely
Produced by Lee Gillette; Written by Bill and Rona Forman
Capitol 800   1950   #3 country; #17 pop

Now *this* is a fatalistic country song. Blasting the fates in accursed harmony, Jimmy Wakely and Margaret Whiting tell us they'd found not just love but heaven on earth in each other's arms. And since that's apparently far too much joy for mere mortals, the gods have shown them who's boss by dousing the sun and commanding the winds to whirl them forever apart. See, that's what you get for being happy.—dc

162

When You're Smiling (the Whole World Smiles with You), Cliff Bruner's Texas Wanderers
Produced by Dave Kapp;
Written by Mark Fisher, Joe Goodwin, and Larry Shay
Decca 5660   1938   Pre-chart

When Bob Dunn decided to electrify his steel guitar sometime in the early 1930s, it changed country music forever. But Dunn isn't a legend today just because he got there first—after all, somebody was bound to plug in, sooner or later. Rather, Dunn's considered a "steel colossus" (in writer Kevin Coffey's apt phrase) because of records like "When You're Smiling."

Like so many musicians of his generation, Dunn fell in love with the sound of the Hawaiian steel guitar the first time he heard it. But when he heard a black musician at Coney Island playing the steel with a homemade pickup, he absolutely flipped. Back home in Texas, he began experimenting with a loud, frenetic sound of his own, and in 1934 he landed a spot with western swing pioneer Milton Brown & His Musical Brownies. Dunn's ringing solos were heavily influenced by the hot jazz of the day, both in the horn-like tone he coaxed from his instrument and in his ability to improvise wildly. As a result of the reputation he'd made, Dunn had no trouble finding work when the Brownies split up after their founder's death. He eventually landed in the band of another former Brown sideman, fiddler Cliff Bruner's Texas Wanderers.

On "When You're Smiling (the Whole World Smiles with You)," Dunn steals the show—no small feat considering the competition from fellow Wanderer Moon Mullican. Louis Armstrong, one of Dunn's heroes, had scored a hit with "When You're Smiling" back in 1930, and Dunn and his bandmates seem to have that record in the backs of their minds. They begin where Armstrong and his orchestra leave off, with the song's exquisite melody. After Mullican sings a verse, the solos fire up. First Dunn tosses notes around as if he's never heard the melody in his life but just might invent rock & roll if you give him a second. Bruner and Mullican each take a quick turn (Armstrong's record also featured fiddle and piano solos), and Dunn roars back in, his steel sounding like he's blowing on an electrofied trumpet. By the end, Dunn must've been smiling big indeed, while the rest of the world picked its jaw up off the floor.—dc

163

Slowly, Webb Pierce
Produced by Paul Cohen; Written by Webb Pierce and Tommy Hill
Decca 28991   1954   #1 country (17 weeks)

Bud Isaacs worked just one session with Webb Pierce, but it forever changed the way country records sounded. Sitting in for Pierce's regular steel player Sonny Burnette, Isaacs decided to use the double-necked Gibson Electraharp he'd been monkeying with since he was a teenager. The instrument's pedals (and knee lever) not only enabled him to play smoother chord changes; they also made it easier for him to mimic Pierce's swooping, swooning voice as he sang of plunging ever deeper in love. The move proved a masterstroke, producing the breathtaking wedding of sound and sense that accounted for the sacks of fan mail that poured in once the record hit the airwaves—and for its nearly four-month run at the top of the country charts.

Today, of course, pedal steel is little more than a garnish on most country records, a fading whisper of the music's tenuous link to its honky-tonk past. But that was hardly the case with "Slowly." Pierce had already decided not to release two earlier

versions of the song before heading into the studio in November 1953, the day Isaacs's fluid modulations finally gave him what the record needed—a hook.

Isaacs wasn't the first to record with a pedal steel. That honor goes to West Coast prodigy Speedy West, who used a soon-to-be-outmoded four-pedaled model on recordings dating as far back as 1949. Isaacs, however, introduced the pedal steel to the Nashville studio scene, effectively unleashing it upon the rest of the world as lap steel players all over town scurried to rig their guitars with pedals. The devices soon became common currency among country session pros, constituting a sea change as crucial as Earl Scruggs's introduction of his three-finger banjo style to Bill Monroe's band in 1945.—bfw

164

Always Late (with Your Kisses), Lefty Frizzell
Produced by Don Law;
Written by Lefty Frizzell and Blackie Crawford
Columbia 4-20837   1951   #1 country (12 weeks)

Steel players working in Nashville didn't start outfitting their guitars with the pedals fancied by their West Coast counterparts until Bud Isaacs played on Webb Pierce's "Slowly" in 1954. Yet it would be a mistake to discount the impact of Lefty Frizzell's molasses phrasing, which had been ringing out from jukeboxes and radios for four years before Isaacs's landmark effort. More than just inspiring generations of singers from George Jones and Merle Haggard to Stoney Edwards and Randy Travis, it's a safe bet that Frizzell's slurring, sliding vocals induced plenty of steel players to augment their musical palettes as well. Anyone looking for evidence need only hear "Always Late," a bluesy heart-to-heart between Lefty and lap-steel player Curly Chalker.

The solitary whorl of Chalker's strings opens the record before giving way to Lefty who, singing a cappella, completes the call-and-response. "Awl-way-ay-ayz-lay-yate . . . with your kisses," he sings. Every bent and tortured note intensifies the doubt at the heart of the lyrics—Lefty's suspicion that his baby's reluctant kisses mean she no longer cares for him. The real gutwrencher, though, comes when, in a single breathless run, Lefty, unwilling to break off the line for fear of letting her go, moans, "Why-oh-why do you want to do me this way-ay?" Chalker's steel answers him on the break, but, deft as his modulations are, it doesn't wring quite the same depth of emotion as Lefty does from the lyrics. That's likely why it wasn't long after this, his recording debut, that Chalker got himself some of those newfangled pedals.—bfw

165

I Don't Believe You've Met My Baby, The Louvin Brothers
Produced by Ken Nelson; Written by Autry Inman
Capitol 3300   1956   #1 country (2 weeks)

166

When I Stop Dreaming, The Louvin Brothers
Produced by Ken Nelson;
Written by Ira Louvin and Charles Louvin
Capitol 3177   1955   #8 country

The Louvin Brothers were born Ira and Charlie Loudermilk in the Sand Mountain region of northern Alabama, and they grew up just as country music's great tradition of brother duets was at its commercial and artistic zenith during the Great Depression. At church, Charlie and Ira sang and worshipped among fervent Pentecostal congregations. At home, they huddled around the family radio, soaking up their favorite duets: the sweet, close harmonies of Bill and Earl Bolick (better known as the Blue Sky Boys), the high-and-lonesome harmonies of Charlie and Bill Monroe, and, most of all, the smooth harmonies and boogie songs of fellow Sand Mountain natives Alton and Rabon Delmore. Emulating these models, the Loudermilk boys

taught themselves to pick and harmonize—Ira on mandolin and high-as-heaven tenor, Charlie on guitar and a tenor more down-to-earth.

Gospel was all they recorded until they finally persuaded producer Ken Nelson to let them cut one of their own secular songs, the waltzing "When I Stop Dreaming," a Top Ten country hit in 1955. Speaking to the woman who has broken his heart, Ira confesses a detail so private and vulnerable it's hard to listen yet impossible to turn away—when she told him she was leaving, he wanted to die. And when, on her way out the door, she begged his forgiveness, he told her no way—he won't forgive her until he stops dreaming, by which he means until he's dead and has no more hope for reconciliation. He tries hard to explain how disheartened he will be without her ("I'd be like a flower unwanted in spring / Alone and neglected, transplanted in vain / To a garden of sadness where its petals would fall in the shadow of undying pain"), but all he has to work with is flailing language. That is, until Charlie enters at the chorus to give him harmony in a voice that sounds taciturn next to Ira's mournful wail.

Perhaps to draw a loose thematic tie to their initial hit, or at least to capitalize on its success, Ira added a verse to the beginning of their next single "I Don't Believe You've Met My Baby." His addition transformed the waking action of Autry Inman's song (the singer's sweetheart introduces him to a man he fears is her lover) into a dream. That dream articulates the hopes for an out-of-the-blue happy ending that the guy in "When I Stop Dreaming" was unable to give up. This connection reveals why Ira can sing that he was already feeling "sad and blue" before he even went to sleep. It also explains the level of paranoia that lets Ira assume the worst when his girlfriend introduces him to this new man. One glance into the stranger's smiling face and he imagines "that his eyes were filled with victory"; a second later, he realizes the man is just delighted to see his sister wed. This time when Charlie and Ira join voices, the sound is pure joy—even if it is based in nothing more substantial than dreams.

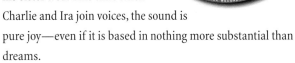

Harking back to the Delmores and predicting the Everlys, those harmonies embody the pain that arises when desire comes face to face with loss. If you were to claim that Ira and Charlie's harmonies were the closest anyone has ever come to catching all that hope and insecurity on tape, you might well be right. But you still wouldn't be doing them justice. —dc

167

In the Pines, Bill Monroe & His Blue Grass Boys
Produced by Paul Cohen;
Written by Bill Monroe and Jimmie Davis
Decca 28416   1952   Did not chart

Talk about having a grip on the human imagination; some 200 different acts, everyone from Lead Belly to the grunge band Nirvana, have recorded "In the Pines" since 1925. Typically rendered as a blues, the song is a composite of old lyric fragments, notably the "in the pines" chorus and the stanza that begins with the line "the longest train I ever saw." Many versions contain a verse depicting a gory death by decapitation (a murder?) under the wheels of a passing train. Others, such as Lead Belly's, include a scene in which a jealous lover confronts his woman about where and, presumably, with whom she slept the night before. Bill Monroe's 1952 recording leaves out these bits of bloodshed and betrayal, rendering the narrative at once more enigmatic and more harrowing in the process.

It's a vivid, surreal picture, especially the long train that takes an incredible three hours to pass and the unbounded sense of time symbolized by the watch the mysterious captain (the engineer?) has "throwed" away. Haunted as they are by the disembodied wailing and whooshing noises made by Monroe and lead singer Jimmy Martin—and that ghostly fiddle and mandolin—these images suffuse the record with an air of dreamlike foreboding. Martin sings of being on his way home, but the dissonance created by Monroe's eerie harmonies suggests otherwise. More than a real place, those sunless pines cast their shadow over Jimmy's subconscious—a dark, frigid, terrifying realm into which he finds himself rapidly descending. Something his woman has done, some grave wrong, has jarred him from the comfort of their familiar, taken-for-granted lives, forcing him to confront a chilling new reality—far from being her lover, he's a rank stranger, a frostbitten victim of her cold, cold heart. —bfw

168

Cold, Cold Heart, Tony Bennett
Produced by Mitch Miller; Written by Hank Williams
Columbia 39449   1951   #1 pop (6 weeks)

When Mitch Miller first asked Tony Bennett to record Hank Williams's "Cold, Cold Heart," the pop singer wanted nothing to do with it. "Don't make me do cowboy songs!" he complained. Bennett's prejudices against country music were typical of Tin Pan Alley music makers at mid-century. In 1951, New York A&R men should have been on a sharp lookout for country songs— that spring, "The Tennessee Waltz" sat atop the national charts for three months on its way to becoming the biggest-selling record of the year. But when Fred and his son Wesley Rose (as in Acuff-Rose, the publishing company that owned "The Tennessee Waltz") traveled to New York to capitalize on this breakthrough with a handful of Hank Williams tunes, no one showed any interest in a bunch of old hillbilly songs. No one, that is, except Columbia's Miller, who a short time later would be busy keeping rock & roll off the label for as long as he could afford to (which wasn't long). Not yet committed to pop purity, at this point he was still willing to patronize hillbilly music when he saw a chance to make a buck off it.

Bennett had as little power to call his own shots as you'd expect of a singer still searching for his first hit, so he let Miller talk him into it. To his credit, once Bennett decided to record "Cold, Cold Heart," he put aside his prejudices and flat nailed the thing. Backed by a full string section and a loping rhythm arrangement (courtesy of Percy Faith), and belting his rough bel canto at the very top of his range, Bennett sounds desperate to know the answer to Hank's famous question. "Why," he asks, stretching out the word as he reaches for a note higher than any you'd have thought he could hit, "can't I free your doubtful mind and melt your cold, cold heart?"

Tony Bennett's "cowboy song" topped the pop charts, sold one and a half million copies, and triggered a stampede of pop singers eager to cover Hank Williams. In the short time before he died, Williams saw his songs become hits for Rosemary Clooney ("Half As Much"), Frankie Laine and Jo Stafford together ("Hey,

Good Lookin' "), and Jo Stafford solo ("Jambalaya"), among many others. The record's most lasting legacy, though, was the way it blurred the seemingly clear line between pop and country music.—dc

169

Harper Valley P.T.A., Jeannie C. Riley
Produced by Shelby Singleton; Written by Tom T. Hall
Plantation 3   1968   #1 country (3 weeks); #1 pop (1 week)

Tom T. Hall was still punching the clock as a staff songwriter at a Nashville publishing house when Margie Singleton approached him about writing a cotton-patch *Peyton Place* along the lines of "Ode to Billie Joe." Trouble was, Singleton was on tour when Hall finished his send-up of small-town hypocrisy, so it fell into the hands of Jeannie C. Riley, a young upstart who had just signed with the fledgling label run by Margie's husband, Shelby Singleton. Turned out to be a good thing, too, because "Harper Valley P.T.A." was a perfect vehicle for Riley, a sheltered Texan who'd had most of her small-town illusions shattered after moving to Nashville in 1966. According to historians Mary Bufwack and Robert K. Oermann, Riley was seduced by a scheming record exec, turned on to liquor, and got a close-up look at the slimy underbelly of the music business—all within two years of arriving in Music City. By the time she went into the studio to record "Harper Valley P.T.A.," they wrote, "she felt like a cheap floozy."

That's just the label the powers-that-be at Harper Valley Junior High tried to pin on the widow Johnson, the record's headstrong protagonist. The action begins with Johnson's daughter bringing home a note from the P.T.A. dressing down her mama for drinking, wearing miniskirts, and "running around with men and going wild"—that is, for being a poor excuse for a mother. Bob Moore's strutting bass and Jerry Kennedy's biting dobro suggest that the P.T.A. won't be having the final say, though. There are no choruses here, just one verse marching inexorably to the next, just as Mrs. Johnson does when she bursts into the P.T.A. meeting unannounced and, in a salty drawl, proceeds to sock it to the group's members for being the boozing, sex-starved,

transparently jealous hypocrites they are. No one escapes unscathed, either from Riley's lashing tongue or from Kennedy's stinging barbs; the coup de grace comes in the final verse when the narrator shifts from third to first person and identifies herself as Johnson's prouder-than-punch teenage daughter.

But "Harper Valley P.T.A." is more than just the slice of middle-American dysfunctionality it at first appears to be. The themes of hypocrisy and prejudice that Hall weaves through the record reflect the dis-ease that pervaded the nation during the summer of 1968, especially among those who suffered at the hands of the country's systemic bad faith: the women who were earning sixty cents on every dollar made by men for comparable work; the young black men and poor whites who paid the ultimate price in Vietnam while middle-class white kids finagled college deferments; the welfare moms whose babies went without while the war in Asia depleted the coffers pledged to the war on poverty. Hypocrisy reared its head at every turn, and everyone caught in the crossfire was as pissed off, but rarely as articulate, as the widow Johnson.—bfw

170

Son-of-a Preacher Man, Dusty Springfield
Produced by Jerry Wexler, Tom Dowd, and Arif Mardin; Written by John David Hurley and Ronnie Stephen Wilkins
Atlantic 2580   1969   #10 pop

Dusty claims that only one boy, a southern preacher's kid named Billy Ray, ever really moved her, but the rapturous groove that transports her here suggests she's holding out on us. From Gene Chrisman's rocking backbeat to Bobby Emmons's tingling electric piano, from Tommy Cogbill's bumping bass to Reggie Young's grinding guitar work, it sounds like at least four of the reverend's boys had a hand in taking her higher.

Working with these Memphis pickers—a crew whose names later turned up on Nashville recordings by the likes of Waylon Jennings and George Strait—triggered a great change in the English-born Springfield. She'd always made deeply emotive, if at times girlish records, but here we find her born again as a natural woman, a country-soul singer of the first rank.

A big reason for the transformation, she told Stanley Booth in the liner notes to her landmark *Dusty in Memphis* LP, was her exposure to the impromptu or "head" arrangements favored by her southern counterparts.

It was an approach to playing that valued feeling over thinking, and it was the norm in studios from Nashville to Muscle Shoals at the time. It's also a lot like what had long taken place in black and white churches throughout the south where, instead of writing down what they were going to say, deacons and elders abandoned themselves to the spirit's pull, riding its ebb and flow as they worked worshippers into a lather. Where else did that preacher's boy learn the art of "takin' time to make time" but from watching his daddy wait for an infusion of the spirit in church?

"Son-of-a Preacher Man" proves that Dusty was just as capable of inciting desire as her memorable tutor. At first she takes things slow and easy, her humid alto—her link to the high-cotton eroticism of Bobbie Gentry and Sammi Smith—straddling the lusty groove anchored by Cogbill's voluptuous bass lines. But on the final chorus, when she testifies that Billy Ray was the only one who could ever reach her, Dusty's declaiming like a sanctified preacher herself, engaging her studio congregation—not just the rhythm section but the juking horns and amen corner as well—in a carnal call-and-response.

Oh, and to set the record straight, "Son-of-a Preacher Man" isn't just about the boys teaching the girls. While the line "learnin' from each other's knowin' " confirms that Dusty taught Billy Ray a thing or two, those are preacher's *daughters*, the aptly named Sweet Inspirations, egging her on throughout.—bfw

171
Satisfied, Martha Carson
Produced by Ken Nelson; Written by Martha Carson
Capitol 1900   1951   Did not chart

Martha Carson was a veteran of the stringband circuit, having sung and played guitar with the Amburgey Sisters and the Coon Creek Girls before she started working as one-half of a southern gospel duo with her husband James Roberts, the son of Fiddlin' Doc Roberts. Billed as "the Dixie Sweethearts," the couple was popular on radio and as a touring act during the mid-forties; they also recorded for Capitol from 1947 to 1950. But James didn't walk it like he talked it, and after he'd stepped out on Martha one time too many, she filed for divorce. She took heaps of grief for

her decision, too, finding herself all but drummed out of the gospel fold for "failing" to stand by her man. Carson told historian Robert K. Oermann she felt that her career was over. Then, while driving to a show with future Opry star Bill Carlisle, she had an epiphany. "All of a sudden it just seemed like I heard a voice that said, 'What are you crying for? I'm satisfied, and you're satisfied.' And the words to that song just almost split me open."

All was forgiven when people heard the good-rocking version of "Satisfied" that Martha cut for Capitol in 1951. "Satisfied, satisfied, no trouble can ever get me down," she belts out to the sound of slap bass, spanking brushes, and tongues-of-fire fretwork; minus the thundering handclaps and Pentecostal piano, the sound would later become the rockabilly of Elvis, D. J., Scotty, and Bill.

Despite its popularity in gospel circles and on the Opry, "Satisfied" never made the charts. But it soon became a standard, as did a half-dozen or so of Martha's other compositions, including "Rock-a My Soul" and "I Can't Stand Up Alone," which has been covered by everyone from Jesse Winchester to Clyde McPhatter. Elvis and the boys even tried their hand at "Satisfied" but, according to biographer Peter Guralnick, erased the tapes because "they just weren't going anywhere." Or maybe because they knew Ms. Martha had gotten there first.—bfw

172
Swingin', John Anderson
Produced by Frank Jones and John Anderson;
Written by John Anderson and Lionel Delmore
Warner 29788   1983   #1 country (1 week); #43 pop

John Anderson's "Swingin' " sometimes gets labeled a novelty record. The only way that makes sense is if you think there's something trifling about a man "feelin' love down to [his] toes." "I can't believe I'm out here on her front porch in this swang, just a-swangin'," Anderson brays, amazed he's managed to get close to an angel like Charlotte Johnson and plumb flabbergasted she could love him back.

The novelty tag probably comes from folks being thrown by a

country record that blasts off with Hammond B3 organ and Stax/Volt-inspired horns, especially when it comes from one of the decade's founding new traditionalists.

Then again, "Swingin' " was cut at the final recording session at Columbia's famed Studio B—a.k.a. the Bradley brothers' Quonset Hut—home of any number of swinging little country hits by Patsy Cline, Ray Price, Marty Robbins, Charlie Rich, and a host of others. What could be more perfect than that?—dc

173

I Walk Alone, Marty Robbins
Produced by Bob Johnston; Written by Herbert Wilson
Columbia 44633   1968   #1 country (2 weeks); #65 pop

Talk about singing the blues. This lonely heart's lament sounds a whole lot more like what was happening in Memphis, especially at Stax Records, during the late sixties than on Nashville's Music Row. Bill Pursell's organ, by turns smoky and slinky, could easily pass for that of Booker T. Jones; Grady Martin's snarling-but-circumspect leads recall those of guitarist Steve Cropper; and although the drummer's offbeats are a tad heavy, the groove they cut is nearly as deep as that patented by Al Jackson Jr. Or if not the Stax rhythm section, then its counterpart across town at Chips Moman's American Studios, where months after Robbins made this record, Elvis cut some of the best sides of his career.

Indeed, much of "I Walk Alone," and particularly the emotional and technical command Robbins displays vocally, anticipates Elvis's post-comeback recordings. And not just *Marty's* singing, but that of Conway Twitty, Charlie Rich, Jack Greene, and Joe South, all of whom likely influenced Elvis as well. The King, of course, inspired each of these men back in the fifties, but while he was off making movies during the sixties, each developed his own country-soul croon, a style that, in aggregate,

became the blueprint for Elvis on records like "Stranger in My Own Home Town" and "Long Black Limousine." None of them, though, could've attacked and nailed that fourth note, that ascending second syllable of the word "a-*lone*" in this record's opening line, the way Marty does. Not even the King himself.—bfw

174

The Year That Clayton Delaney Died, Tom T. Hall
Produced by Jerry Kennedy; Written by Tom T. Hall
Mercury 73221 1971   #1 country (2 weeks); #42 pop

Tom T. Hall is known as "the Story Teller," but "the Narrator" is more like it. So many of Hall's best-known songs forgo actual stories in favor of in-the-moment character sketches. They aren't narratives per se, so much as they're emotionally wrought interior monologues (think of "Margie's at the Lincoln Park Inn" and "I'm Not Ready Yet," two great Hall songs that were hits for Bobby Bare and George Jones, respectively) or half of a revealing conversation (Hall's hit recordings of "Ballad of Forty Dollars" and "Homecoming"). Even when his songs do recount stories, in the strictest sense, Hall still favors point of view over plot—"Harper Valley P.T.A." becomes a different song if told by Mrs. Johnson instead of her daughter.

Hall's most famous recording is "The Year That Clayton Delaney Died," but it isn't really about the guitar-picking boozer that Hall had trailed after twenty years before as "a barefoot kid." (The real Delaney wasn't much more than a kid himself when he died of tuberculosis at nineteen.) Instead, the song gives us a glimpse of what it feels like to be Tom T. Hall, all grown up in 1971, as he struggles to understand how in the world that Kentucky kid ever became a famous singer-songwriter with money in his pocket in the first place. "I remember," Hall begins with a drawl, sounding like he's just dropped by to nurse a beer, shoot the breeze, and laze away the afternoon. It's a credit both to his songwriting and his relaxed vocal style that he conjures an illusion of offhandedness out of a lyric that's as chiseled as a statue, its lyrics as compressed as a good poem. So much regret, guilt, and joy are conveyed without ever being stated. The memory of Delaney warning him off the musician's life ("It'll lead you to an early grave") leads Hall directly to the bittersweet and self-implicating lines, "I guess if I'd admit it, Clayton taught me how to drink booze / I can see him, half-stoned, a-pickin' out the 'Lovesick Blues.'"

The music around Hall is designed to leave you hanging on his every word. The arrangement's accented here and there by a Dixieland trumpet, but producer Jerry Kennedy creates the simplest of settings: a Jimmie Rodgers–style guitar run at the top, an occasional ringing dobro lick, a steady and spare, momentum-less acoustic rhythm track—the record feels like Jeannie C. Riley's "Harper Valley P.T.A" in a rocking chair. These minimalist surroundings put you right there on the porch with Tom T., rocking and listening at his side, as he reminisces. It's easy to picture him squinting as he talks, the better to see more clearly back through all those years.—dc

175

Lord Is That Me, Jack Greene
Produced by Owen Bradley;
Written by Dallas Frazier and Sanger D. Shafer
Decca 32631   1970   #16 country

Here we have Elvis's "Long Black Limousine," except the body in the back of the hearse belongs to a man instead of a woman. The preacher's frowning, the stiff's mother and his widow are distraught, and no one's saying much or lingering long. They're a pious lot and, because the guy died a sinner, they don't as much grieve his loss as shudder at his fate. "I can see that long line of cars quickly drive away / I can see an old gray-haired mother linger behind by the grave," Greene begins, slowly unfolding the scene to a descending, dobro-flecked chord progression like the one from "The Dark End of the Street." 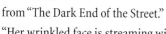 "Her wrinkled face is streaming with tears as she stands there trembling in fear / She knows that only a chosen few can meet up there," Greene continues, as the Nashville pickers working the session wrap his husky, murmur-turned-sob in just the sort of gospel-cured, country soul that Elvis had been making since his return to Memphis. Then, as a timpani thunders a note of

judgment, it hits Greene that these are *his* people. "Lord, is that me / Tell me about this vision I see," he sings, recoiling in disbelief. "Lord, if it is, have mercy, have mercy on me," he begs as a choir of voices chimes in to prop him up.

Talk about there goes my everything. Where Greene's headed isn't good, but from the dread in his voice here, it'll be nothing compared to the hell he's putting his loved ones through.—bfw

176

(You've Been Quite a Doll) Raggedy Ann,
Little Jimmy Dickens
Produced by Harry Silverstein; Written by H. R. DeLaughter
Decca 32644   1970   #75 country

Though he was an accomplished singer of sad and tender ballads, Little Jimmy Dickens will forever be remembered as the four-foot-eleven shouter of high-energy knee-slappers like "Take an Old Cold Tater (and Wait)," "A-Sleeping at the Foot of the Bed," and crossover smash "May the Bird of Paradise Fly up Your Nose"—precisely the sort of country novelties you'd expect from an artist who began his career billed as "The Singing Midget." As his over-the-top persona shouts in one song, "I'm puny, short, and little—but I'm *loud*!"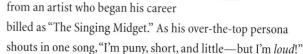

Unexpectedly, then, Dickens's greatest moment—a recitation called "(You've Been Quite a Doll) Raggedy Ann"—is as heartwrenchingly poignant, and as terrifying, as they come. Which is amazing, given the recitation's preposterous premise—an old man visits his daughter's grave to thank her favorite doll (who has apparently watched over the grave for decades) for being such a source of strength to him. Dickens makes you believe every line, every precious memory and gulped-down tear, with a performance as in-the-moment as any by the finest Actor's Studio graduate.

It's one hell of a sad and scary moment, too. Consumed with mourning the loss of his daughter—and his wife's death too, which is to say the loss of both the life he'd lived and the future he'd planned—the old man is reduced to confiding intimately, insanely, to a doll; his only remaining handle on reality is the knowledge that his own days on earth are also numbered. By contrast, the sheer commitment of Dickens's reading makes the supposedly more hip expressions of uncontrollable grief in, say, David Lynch's *Twin Peaks* seem as realistic as an episode of *Scooby-Doo*.

It's hard to believe such an earnest, over-the-top recitation could've been recorded as close to our irony-armored times as 1970, but what makes "Raggedy Ann" hold up even today is the way it asks a survivor's most desperate questions: How do you move on when you lose the ones you love? And what happens if you can't? The Jordanaires, softly humming their way through "Farther Along," provide the record's only answer.—dc

177
The End of the World, Skeeter Davis
Produced by Anita Kerr and Chet Atkins;
Written by Sylvia Dee and Arthur Kent
RCA Victor 8098   1962   #2 country; #2 pop

Self-pity writ large.

Skeeter, newly in the throes of heartbreak, takes a cue from the metaphysical poets and colors the entire world with her blues. She's astounded that the sun goes on shining, the birds keep singing, and the stars still glow in the night sky. "Don't they know it's the end of the world?"

Producers Anita Kerr and Chet Atkins nestle Skeeter's bruised, doubled-tracked alto in tearful strings, undulating piano, and lightly throbbing rhythms—the Nashville Sound at its most

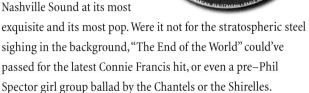

exquisite and its most pop. Were it not for the stratospheric steel sighing in the background, "The End of the World" could've passed for the latest Connie Francis hit, or even a pre–Phil Spector girl group ballad by the Chantels or the Shirelles.

Of course, Skeeter is no teenager, but that hardly matters, as the break in her voice during the recitation on the final chorus attests. It makes no difference how old you are; when you're hurting the way she is, you really *can't* understand why life goes on the way it does.—bfw

178
The Cold Hard Facts of Life, Porter Wagoner
Produced by Bob Ferguson; Written by Bill Anderson
RCA Victor 9067   1967   #2 country

Fans of "hard-core" country music often write off Bill Anderson as a softy, citing his whispered vocal style and penchant for corn pone and schmaltz as proof. Those leanings are there all right, but from "City Lights" to "The Lord Knows I'm Drinking," songs that topped the charts for Ray Price and Cal Smith, respectively, Anderson has demonstrated an equal talent for writing sawdust-and-steel honky-tonk. His tale of cheating and murder, "The Cold Hard Facts of Life," is downright transgressive. Of course, it took a master narrator like Porter Wagoner to put it across; Bill's breathy quaver just wouldn't have cut deep enough for that knife.

The events unfold as Wagoner returns from a trip a day early, eager, as both he and the song's cantering shuffle-beat tell us, to surprise his wife. Primed for an evening of lovemaking, he stops off for a bottle of champagne and overhears a stranger boasting how he's been sleeping with a woman whose husband's away. The twin fiddles of Mack Magaha and Johnny Gimble chime in, heightening the tension as Porter follows the guy out of the liquor store. He doesn't put two and two together, though, until, behind the wheel of his car, he realizes he's following the man into his—that is, Wagoner's—driveway. After circling the block a few times and downing a fifth of courage, Porter bursts in on the adulterous couple, pulls a knife and, deaf to their pleas for mercy, kills them.

The scene shifts to Porter in prison—"I guess I'll go to hell, or I'll rot here in this cell / But who taught who the cold hard facts of life?" Background singers join him as he repeats the final line, stabbing the point home, the lack of remorse in his voice as chilling as that of the protagonists in many a mountain murder ballad or gangsta boast. Needless to say, it also recasts writer Anderson's reputation for being a simp in a radically different light.—bfw

179
I Saw the Light, Hank Williams
with His Drifting Cowboys
Produced by Fred Rose; Written by Hank Williams
MGM 10271   1947   Did not chart

The story goes that Hank wrote "I Saw the Light" after sleeping
one off on his way back to Montgomery after a gig. His mother
was at the wheel, and when she saw the beacons at Dannelly
Field, she roused Hank from his muddled slumber to tell him
they were almost home. Hank
proceeded to turn the vision of
those airport lights into one
of the most enduring and
beloved hymns in the
country gospel canon.

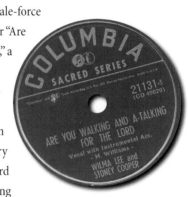

Set to the irrepressible
melody of the Chuck Wagon
Gang's "After the Sunrise," "I Saw
the Light" opens with Brownie
Reynolds's trotting bass and Tommy Jackson's blazing fiddle
racing Hank down to the altar. "I wandered so aimless, life filled
with sin . . . Then Jesus came like a stranger in the night / Praise
the Lord, I saw the light," he testifies as he gets there, shouting
"Praise the Lord" as if he'd just won the lottery. It's the most
moving kind of testimony—that of the prodigal returned to the
fold.

Williams must have known, if only fleetingly, the rapture of
which he sings; there's just no denying the release he feels when
he assures us that there's "no sorrow in sight." But even if he
didn't, there's still plenty of cause to praise the Lord here; with "I
Saw the Light," Hank gave us as rousing a paean to the possibility
of redemption as any ever recorded. Not bad for a guy best
known as an avatar of unremitting gloom.—bfw

180
Are You Walking and A-Talking for the Lord,
Wilma Lee & Stoney Cooper
Produced by Art Satherley; Written by Hank Williams
Columbia 21131-8   1953   Did not chart

181
When God Comes to Gather His Jewels,
Molly O'Day & the Cumberland Mountain Folks
Produced by Art Satherley; Written by Hank Williams
Columbia 20389   1947   Did not chart

Proof not only that Hank Williams saw the light but also that he
grasped the different stages of faith, no matter how hard he found
it to live them.

The first of these Williams originals brims with the evangeli-
cal ardor of the new convert, the second radiates the blessed
assurance that takes root only after years of being nurtured in the
faith. Wilma Lee Cooper's gale-force
alto is the perfect vehicle for "Are
You Walking and A-Talking," a
rousing call-and-response
admonishing the faithful to
cleave to the straight and
narrow. "Are you traveling in
His light every day and every
night," she shouts as the third
chorus gives way to pounding

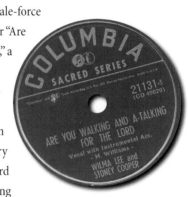

Pentecostal piano. Hands clap and feet stomp in time, loosening
floorboards and drumming home the message, which includes
the sure knowledge of what befalls sinners who don't heed the
call, an exhortation that must have
tweaked Hank's conscience sorely
when he wrote it.

"When God Comes to
Gather His Jewels" is
subdued by contrast,
especially coming from
Molly O'Day, a belter whose
piercing wail had people calling
her the "female Hank Williams."

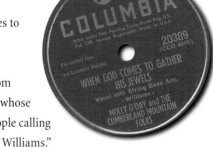

O'Day's connection to Hank ran deep. She was the first singer to
record his material, and when Fred Rose convinced Art Satherley
to sign her to Columbia, he went so far as to tender Hank a
publishing deal with Acuff-Rose just so he could start pitching
his songs to O'Day.

"When God Comes" opens with O'Day assuming the character
of a young man who's grieving the loss of a woman he's loved for
years. It's not clear who the woman is; she could be his wife,
sweetheart, sister, or mother, but as the fiddle and dobro spill

buckets of tears in the background, it's obvious the loss is killing him. The only comfort the man has is his faith, just as it would be faith in which O'Day and her husband/fiddle player Lynn Davis took refuge four years later, right before they started their own church and radio ministry.

Therein lay the difference between their epiphany and Hank's—O'Day and her husband saw the light and kept walking in its glow, whereas Hank got sidetracked down the lost highway.—bfw

182
Sowing on the Mountain, Coon Creek Girls
No producer credited; Traditional
Vocalion 04278, Conqueror 9113   1938   Pre-chart

The abandon with which the Coon Creek Girls attack this exhortation to follow the narrow way makes walking and a-talking for the Lord sound like having a natural ball, more fun even than sinning. "Sowin' on the mountain, reapin' in valley," shout out sisters Lily May and Rosie Ledford on the opening chorus, repeating the line twice, before lowering the boom: "You gotta reap just what you sow." Lily May nails down the melody while Rosie's high tenor soars above it, the two women's voices plunging precipitously each time they allude to the snares that await the drunkards, gamblers, liars, and gossips who sow their seeds in the valley—that is, in the gutter. Although the Ledfords and guitar player Violet Koehler hold the tempo steady enough, their zeal is so irrepressible you'd swear they were gaining momentum with each successive verse. Or maybe that's just the quickening footfall of the parade of sinners who, goaded by Lily May's frailing banjo, are making a beeline for the church-house door.

There were no all-female stringbands on the radio when the Coon Creek Girls started sending out freewheeling racket like "Sowing on the Mountain," "Shortenin' Bread," and "How Many Biscuits Can You Eat" over the airwaves during the late thirties. Lily May had already been a solo star (after the fashion of banjo-toting cut-up Cousin Emmy) on the WLS National Barn Dance in Chicago. When in 1937 Barn Dance producer and emcee John

Lair tapped members of that show, including Red Foley and the Girls of the Golden West, for his fledgling Renfro Valley Barn Dance, Lily May headed south with the gang to Cincinnati and made history. At Lair's suggestion she assembled an "all-girl" stringband, recruiting her sister Rosie, guitarist Koehler, and bass fiddle player Daisy Lange, and it wasn't long before the four women with flowers for nicknames were headliners on Lair's show on WLW, as well as on packaged tours that played schoolhouses and auditoriums all over the south and midwest.

The Coon Creek Girls cut nine sides for Vocalion in 1938, including "Sowing on the Mountain" and "Banjo Pickin' Girl," the latter becoming a hot licks anthem for aspiring female pickers (like future Coon Creek Girl Molly O'Day) tantamount to what "Johnny B. Goode" later became for would-be rock & rollers. In 1939, Eleanor Roosevelt invited the band to play at the White House, where they performed for the king and queen of England. Not bad for a bunch of "girls" who, however much they admonished listeners to sow on the mountain, reaped a bumper crop down in the Renfro Valley while having the time of their lives.—bfw

183
Wildwood Flower, The Carter Family
Produced by Ralph Peer; Written by A. P. Carter
Victor V-40000   1929   Pre-chart

What could be more country than the Carter Family doing "Wildwood Flower"? More than just one of the half-dozen or so records that helped define this Clinch Mountain clan as the first family of country music, "Wildwood Flower" was among the trio's biggest hits, eventually becoming a folk and bluegrass standard. There's also its reputation as *the* showcase for Mother Maybelle's signature thumb-brush guitar technique, a widely imitated style of playing in which guitarists pick the melodic line on the bass strings and strum the rhythm on the treble strings. Were it not for the thematic richness and reach of "Can the Circle Be Unbroken," "Wildwood Flower" would have a legitimate claim to being the quintessential country anthem.

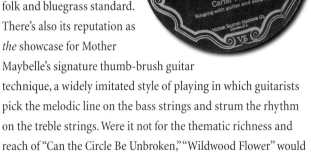

That's no mean feat for a sentimental pre–Tin Pan Alley pop song first published as "I'll Twine Midst the Ringlets" in 1860. Judging by the way Sara mistakes the word "ringlets" for "mingles" in the opening line, it's a safe bet the Carters didn't learn this lovelorn ballad from a piece of sheet music. Likely as not, they came by it via oral tradition, much as they did most of the songs A. P. dug up for the group to sing—that is, only after "Wildwood Flower" had *become* a mountain folk song.

So much for country purity.—bfw

184
Sallie Gooden, Eck Robertson
No producer credited; Traditional
Victor 18956   1923   Pre-chart

Eck Robertson and fellow fiddle champion Henry Gilliland must have been quite a sight when they turned up at the New York offices of the Victor Talking Machine Company on June 30, 1922, requesting an audition. Fresh from a Confederate veterans' reunion and clad in period attire (seventy-four-year-old Gilliland had fought in the war), the two fiddlers doubtless looked as quaint as all get-out. The dozen or so tunes they recorded over the next two days, however, were anything but, the most sizzling—and enduring—being Eck's solo romp through "Sallie Gooden."

Robertson probably didn't think twice about launching into yet another rendition of the breakdown he'd played countless times at fiddle contests back home in Texas. The brass at Victor, though, must have stood slack-jawed as Eck, his fingers rampaging all over his fiddle's fingerboard, reeled off variation upon variation on the tune's basic theme. Along the way he sawed off everything from syncopated runs and blue notes, to single-string/double-string harmonies and clusters of quicksilver grace notes with a horn-like timbre.

Robertson's display of down-home virtuosity notwithstanding, "Sallie Gooden"—the first country recording made for the commercial market—didn't sell well when Victor issued it the following spring. (The label, it turned out, had no experience marketing or distributing records in the rural south or southwest.) By then Robertson had returned to Texas, where the tune soon became a standard, a test for the mettle of aspiring fiddlers for decades to come. Indeed, by the time Byron Berline introduced it to a new generation of pickers on the Decca recording he made with Bill Monroe's Blue Grass Boys in 1967, "Sallie Gooden"

had become a permanent part of the American musical vernacular. Back on that summer day in 1922, however, the uncanny magic coaxed by that lonesome Confederate from the strings of his fiddle must have sounded like the charge of a rebel brigade.—bfw

185
Uncle Pen, Bill Monroe & His Blue Grass Boys
Produced by Paul Cohen; Written by Bill Monroe
Decca 46283   1950   Did not chart

Bill Monroe's "Uncle Pen" was inspired by his mama's brother, Pendleton Vandiver—an old-time Kentucky fiddler who played dances for part of his living and who took a teenage Bill into his own cabin after Monroe's father died. "Uncle Pen" honors the man who taught Monroe so much about music, and not just because it tips its hat to the old-time tunes his uncle favored ("Soldier's Joy," "Boston Boy," and "Jenny Lynn" all get mentioned) or brags on the way Pen's playing would "talk" and "ring" (you could say the same for his nephew's harmonies here with Jimmy Martin). Not even just because Monroe turns over so much of the spotlight to his band's fiddler, Red Taylor (to whose tune Monroe set his lyrics). No, what really makes this a perfect tribute is that—even as it marks that "mournful day when Uncle Pen was called away"—it makes you want to get up and dance.—dc

186
Second Fiddle (to an Old Guitar), Jean Shepard
Produced by Ken Nelson; Written by Betty Amos
Capitol 5169   1964   #5 country

"I'm tired of playing second fiddle to an old guitar," declares Jean Shepard on her first hit single after her husband, country singer Hawkshaw Hawkins, went down in the 1963 plane crash that also killed Cowboy Copas and Patsy Cline. In press coverage of the tragedy, Shepard's grief—as well as that of Copas's daughter, who lost both her father and her husband, pilot Randy Hughes—took a backseat to the news of Cline's death. It wasn't the first time that

Shepard had played second fiddle to one of her female counterparts, nor would it be the last.

Throughout the 1950s, the fiery honky-tonker was a perennial runner-up to Kitty Wells for top female vocalist honors in the country trade magazines. In the sixties, Shepard's star was eclipsed first by Cline and, later, by Loretta Lynn and Tammy Wynette, two women whose plucky, emotionally direct styles owed a considerable debt to Jean's hard-hitting approach. It was also during the sixties that the Opry's management dubbed newcomer Connie Smith, a petite blonde in the Shepard mold, the "Sweetheart of the Grand Ole Opry," even though Jean had been winning the hearts of the show's fans ever since she joined its cast in 1955.

Shepard—one of ten kids born to Oklahoma sharecroppers—nevertheless stands tall among the pioneering women of country music. Still a regular on the Opry, where, since Minnie Pearl's passing, she reigns as the show's indisputable matriarch, Jean was the first country female of the postwar era to launch a successful solo career on her own—that is, without a man at her side. Wilma Lee Cooper made her way as part of a husband-and-wife team; Kitty Wells had been the featured "girl singer" in the road show of her husband Johnnie Wright, one-half of the popular duo Johnnie & Jack. But when Shepard braved country's boys' club, she opened her own doors. And while Wells may have been the first to unmask the double standard applied to good-timing women in "It Wasn't God Who Made Honky Tonk Angels," Jean did more than just shine a light on the matter. With "Two Whoops and a Holler," she had the gumption to dress down the men who'd come up with that ridiculous idea in the first place.

Shepard got her big break in 1952 while singing and playing bass fiddle with the Melody Ranch Girls, an all-female band that worked the West Coast dance hall circuit. Hank Thompson & His Brazos Valley Boys were appearing at a local night spot, and Thompson, riding high at the time with "The Wild Side of Life," invited Shepard onstage to sing with him. Surprised that she didn't have a recording contract, Thompson took Jean's case to Capitol Records A&R man Ken Nelson. By fall Nelson had the eighteen-year-old in the studio with some of the West Coast's

finest pickers, including steel player Speedy West and guitarist Jimmy Bryant. "A Dear John Letter," a Korean War tearjerker featuring a recitation by a then unknown Ferlin Husky, topped the charts the following summer, establishing Jean as a gutsy young singer who wasn't afraid to tackle taboo themes—in this case, infidelity.

Over the years, Shepard, whose bell-like alto was tailor-made for sobbing steel guitars and pealing piano, would sing many songs that found her in cheating situations. "The Other Woman" and "A Thief in the Night" are perhaps the best known, but "Color Song (I Lost My Love)," in which she guns down her wayward lover, crosses way over most lines you'd care to name, especially for 1960. Jean, however, was never one to shy away from controversial topics, and her penchant for adult material sung from a strong woman's point of view paved the way for the frankly sexual recordings later made by Tammy Wynette, Tanya Tucker, and Sammi Smith.

A bluegrass-tinged ramble written by banjo player Betty Amos, "Second Fiddle" was something of a departure for Shepard, who had for the most part always been an unreconstructed honky-tonker. Still, listening today, it's hard not to hear it as her theme song, particularly if you hear it as Jean's refusal to play second fiddle to her female counterparts. From the fire in her voice to the way Jerry Kennedy's bluesy flatpicking blazes away behind her, it's plain that Jean never intended to settle for being anything but the best. To drive the point home, she caps the song with one of the most electrifying yodels this side of Rosalie Allen—a dazzling display of vocal dexterity that none of her female contemporaries could have hoped to match.—bfw

187
Wichita Lineman, Glen Campbell
Produced by Al DeLory; Written by Jimmy Webb
Capitol 2302   1968   #1 country (2 weeks), #3 pop

Critics often slam the presence of strings on country records, even on overtly pop-leaning singles like this one. It's a common prejudice, one that usually boils down to the assumption that records that opt for violins are somehow less "real" or "authentic" than those that employ fiddles. Even as prejudices go, it's a ridiculous one. Country music is no more or less predisposed to good or bad orchestration than pop. Besides, the string arrangements on Glen Campbell's late sixties crossover hits, most of them written by producer Al DeLory, are typically first-rate; in the case of "Wichita Lineman," DeLory's arrangement defines the sonic and conceptual heart of the record.

There's the crystalline wash of strings early on, a moment of clarity akin to what the song's pole-sitting protagonist must feel, his head above the wires, surveying the horizon. The dark rumblings that follow the words "overload" and "strain," however, suggest pressure on the lines—and stormy times at home. Then there's the way the violins echo the whine of his lover's siren call as it surges through the telephone lines; the repairman's desire positively smolders in the round, lusty guitar tones on the break.

So the question isn't what the strings are doing here; they convey the lineman's conflicted heart clearly enough for listeners who don't speak English to know what he's feeling. No, the big mystery is why the guy is still stuck up on that pole. Could be he needs the job; he certainly sounds like he means it when he says he's ready for a vacation. Or it could be he can't go home yet. But whatever the tension keeping him up there is, if he doesn't deal with it soon, it'll be *his* circuits, not the ones he's working on, that'll overload.—bfw

188

Take Me Back to Tulsa, Bob Wills & His Texas Playboys
Produced by Art Satherley and Don Law;
Written by Tommy Duncan and Bob Wills
OKeh 06101   1941   Pre-chart

The hoedown fiddling at the top gives this one away. So free-wheeling is the abandon with which Wills and his seven Playboys attack this breakdown that no one would believe Tommy Duncan's tale of heartbreak if he paid them. The reason Wills and company, several of whom chip in with vocals on the chorus, are itching to get to Tulsa isn't that they're "too young to marry"; it's that they've got a regular paying gig there. Fresh from the Light Crust Doughboys, a band that formerly included his friend and rival Milton Brown, Wills and his newly christened Playboys (including new lead singer Duncan) had just landed a daily spot

on KVOO in Tulsa and couldn't have been more jazzed about it. Al Stricklin's barrelhousing piano solo, Louie Tierney's swinging fiddle lick, and the by turns torrid and wailing breaks taken by guitarist Eldon Shamblin and steel player Leon McAuliffe certainly attest as much. Even Duncan, unwilling to keep up the ruse any longer, joins the party on the last verse when, with transparent delight, he beams, "We always wear a great big smile, never do look sour / Travel all over the country, playing by the hour." Never did a lyric have less do to with what was going on in a song— and say *more*—than it does here.—bfw

189

Oklahoma Hills, Jack Guthrie & His Oklahomans
Produced Lee Gillette and Cliffie Stone;
Written by Woody Guthrie and Jack Guthrie
Capitol 201   1945   #1 country (6 weeks)

Woody Guthrie's best-known odes to Oklahoma are his Dust Bowl ballads, songs in which he chronicles how the great winds of the thirties swept away the houses and farms of his fellow Okies—their inheritance—and set in motion their vast migration West. There's no mention of the Depression here though. Instead, we find Woody, or rather his cousin Jack (who, unbeknownst to Woody, rearranged and cut the song for Capitol), longing for the Oklahoma of an earlier, more bountiful time. Not an Oklahoma ravaged by dust storms, but a place "where the oak and blackjack trees kiss the playful prairie breeze." An Oklahoma where oil flowed and snow-white cotton grew, and where ranch hands like Jack once dotted the range. "Way down yonder in the Indian nation, riding my pony on the reservation, in those Oklahoma hills where I was born," the former rodeo cowboy sings in a warm, nasal tenor. Porky Freeman lays down some hot hillbilly-jazz guitar licks and

Tex Atchison fiddles all over this swinging boogie, testifying to the better days alluded to in Woody's lyrics.

"Oklahoma Hills" spent six weeks at #1 on the country charts during the summer of 1945, a time when the nation, still in the glow of V-E Day, was experiencing a renewed sense of hope and possibility. It would be awhile, though, before Jack would enjoy either that euphoria or his newfound popularity. He was drafted into the army and posted to an island in the South Pacific during 1945 and 1946, a turn of events that gives added meaning to the yearning he expresses here. Compounding matters further, while overseas he contracted malaria, a condition that likely heightened his susceptibility to tuberculosis, the disease that soon took his life, just as it did that of his hero Jimmie Rodgers.

That isn't to say that Jack Guthrie didn't taste the fruits of his success before he succumbed to TB in early 1948. "Oakie Boogie," his first hit after returning to the States, reached #3 on the country charts in 1947, and Jack made the most of his celebrity, touring and, thanks to Ernest Tubb, earning a cameo in the movie *Hollywood Barn Dance*. "Happiness was never out of [the] reach of Jack Guthrie," wrote his pal and fellow West Coast star Merle Travis in the liner notes to an early posthumous collection of the sides Guthrie cut for Capitol. "He held it with strong hands . . . he cherished it with a light heart . . . he lived each precious day to the hilt." In other words, however briefly, Jack Guthrie knew the good life he pined for here.—bfw

190
The Ballad of Ira Hayes, Johnny Cash
Produced by Don Law and Frank Jones; Written by Peter LaFarge
Columbia 43058   1964   #3 country

Johnny Cash has always been the best kind of patriot—the kind, for example, who loved his country fiercely enough to speak out against the Vietnam War. Unlike the self-appointed guardians of freedom who rail against evil empires and foreign terrorists, Cash knows that, even more than defending America's borders, national security depends on strengthening communities here at home. This knowledge, Cash's self-mythologizing aside, explains his decision to shroud himself in

mourner's black until the government pays more attention to domestic matters of social and economic justice.

"The Ballad of Ira Hayes" may well be the most patriotic recording in Cash's voluminous canon. Written by folk singer and Korean War veteran Peter LaFarge, the song recounts the tragic story of its namesake, a Pima Indian who returned home from World War II a hero (one of twenty-seven survivors who planted the flag at Iwo Jima), only to be forgotten, hit the bottle, and die in the gutter.

"Call him drunken Ira Hayes, he won't answer anymore / Not the whiskey drinkin' Indian nor the marine that went to war," Cash drawls as guitarist Norman Blake scratches out a melody akin to that of Woody Guthrie's "Pretty Boy Floyd." Johnny's stentorian baritone—his timbre uncannily reminiscent of John Wayne—contrasts sharply with Blake's dour flatpicking. Their message comes through clearly. Instead of being cast aside like an outlaw—a rank stranger disowned both by his people and the country he fought to save—Hayes should have been held up, like the Duke, as a flag-waver's icon.

The larger social issue here, though, revolves around the images of thirst that tie the song together, linking Hayes's craving for whiskey with the parched land of the Pima, whose fields had been fertile until the federal government rescinded the tribe's water rights. The clincher is the picture of Ira lying dead after passing out drunk in two inches of ditch water. The coroner listed the cause of death as alcohol poisoning, but Cash's snarling response—"his ghost is lyin' thirsty"—confirms that the patriotic Indian's unquenched thirst for justice was what really did him in.—bfw

191
Cool Water, Sons of the Pioneers
Produced by Dave Kapp; Written by Bob Nolan
Decca 5939   1941   Pre-chart

Staggering lost through the desert, the Sons of the Pioneers pray for water in voices that are fevered, feeble, and . . . beautiful? The lyrics to this terrific Bob Nolan song suggest that any water these cowpokes might find will be a mirage, but it's the group's voices

that let you know this cowboy song is pure hallucination. There's just no other way to explain how harmonies this perfectly liquid could emerge from the throats of men so desperate for even one drop of cool, clear water.—dc

192
Big River, Johnny Cash & the Tennessee Two
Produced by Jack Clement; Written by J. R. Cash
Sun 283   1958   #4 country

Johnny Cash heads down the Mississippi in search of the woman he loves, but from the sound of things what he actually discovers—a few years before the world heard of the guy—is Bob Dylan. Or at least his toolbox: the bluesy, doomsday imagery and playful infatuation with language; a wanderlust that's all tangled up in blue; and even Dylan's phrasing, when Johnny sings, "I met her, accidentally, in St. Pawwwl, Minnesota."

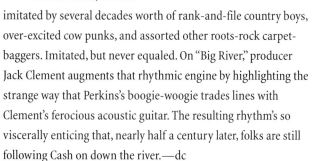

The driving power behind this epic search, though, is provided by the boom-chuck of Cash and the Tennessee Two's Luther Perkins and Marshall Grant, a sound imitated by several decades worth of rank-and-file country boys, over-excited cow punks, and assorted other roots-rock carpetbaggers. Imitated, but never equaled. On "Big River," producer Jack Clement augments that rhythmic engine by highlighting the strange way that Perkins's boogie-woogie trades lines with Clement's ferocious acoustic guitar. The resulting rhythm's so viscerally enticing that, nearly half a century later, folks are still following Cash on down the river.—dc

193
Electricity, Jimmy Murphy
Produced by Steve Sholes; Written by Jimmy Murphy
RCA Victor 21-0447   1951   Did not chart

Why would you doubt the existence of God, Jimmy Murphy wants to know, just because you can't see Him? "You can't see eee-leck-a-tricity a-movin' on the line" either, but I bet you don't go around doubting the existence of alternating current, now do you? For Murphy, belief's just that simple.

"Electricity" is usually seen as something of a throwback, but that has less to do with the song itself than with Murphy's bygone, two-piece arrangement. Lit up with a full country combo, "Electricity" would've been perfect for the Louvin Brothers in their "Cash on the Barrelhead" mode. Here, though, Murphy is band enough. Assisted by only Anita Carter (who races to keep up on upright bass), Murphy provides his own rapid acoustic rhythm and sparking, bluesy fills. He scrambles through the song like a man possessed, or at least like a man 100 percent confident of who he is and in what he believes. It's that electricity in Murphy's performance that finally clinches his argument, however dubious his logic may be. Give him debating points, too, for the way the single stands as its own proof. After all, even to hear him make his case you have to plug in the record player.—dc

194
Foggy Mountain Breakdown, Lester Flatt, Earl Scruggs, and the Foggy Mountain Boys
No producer credited; Written by Earl Scruggs
Mercury 6247   1949   Did not chart

Country music, and especially bluegrass, gets a bad rap when it comes to innovation. Critics revere rock as the essence of rebellion and tout jazz as the quest for the new, but country, they insist, looks backward, obsessed with preserving the past.

Try telling that to bluegrass pioneer Earl Scruggs, a picker who's ushered in as many major shifts in his idiom as any rock iconoclast or jazz lion. The three-finger banjo technique he patented, later dubbed "Scruggs-style picking," transformed the instrument from a quaint, droning helpmeet to a fleet, emotionally expansive voice that could handle leads with as much facility as the fiddle. In fact, as heard during his two-year stint with Bill Monroe & His Blue Grass Boys, Scruggs's three-finger roll crystallized the sound that later became known as bluegrass. With their own band, Earl and fellow Monroe alum Lester Flatt expanded the voicings of the standard stringband to include the dobro resonator guitar of Uncle Josh Graves. Whether fusing bluegrass and rock with his sons, or jamming with sitar master Ravi Shankar or R&B saxophonist King Curtis, Scruggs has perpetually stretched himself and the boundaries of his music.

No performance embodies Earl's self-surpassing drive more than Flatt & Scruggs's 1949 recording of "Foggy Mountain Breakdown," a tune widely hailed as the bluegrass national anthem. The two men subsequently cut studio versions of the song in 1965 and again in 1968 (#58 country, #55 pop) at the bidding of Warren Beatty, who used it as the theme song for the movie *Bonnie and Clyde*. But neither of those could touch the original, a whitewater rush of notes and emotion. And that's just the first break. After fiddler Benny Sims takes his turn at the mike, Earl storms back with even greater fury—it sounds as if he's playing with ten fingers instead of three. A far cry from the drop-thumb frail of old-time stylists, the cascade of melody and rhythm pouring out of his banjo is the sound of one man plunging headlong into the future. Uncle Dave Macon, who could play in twenty different styles, was so blown away when he heard Scruggs on the Opry with the Blue Grass Boys in 1946 that he swore he was going to make a hen's nest out of his banjo.—bfw

195

Are You Missing Me, Jim & Jesse
and the Virginia Boys
Produced by Ken Nelson; Written by Ira and Charles Louvin
Capitol F2233   1952   Did not chart

Bill Monroe's Blue Grass Boys provided a proving ground for up-and-coming bluegrass musicians ever since the time Lester Flatt, Earl Scruggs, and Cedric Rainwater decided to quit their boss and form their own band, which is to say since the dawn of the genre. By and large, though, the younger bluegrass outfits, which copied the Monroe sound in so many other ways, rarely featured a lot of mandolin fills and solos in their arrangements. Perhaps it came down to person-nel—after all, the Blue Grass Boys cranked out mandolin players at the same rate Christian-ity produces saviors. Then again, maybe these new groups gave so many more breaks to the banjo for a far less practical reason. In the late forties and early fifties, Scruggs's

ferocious banjo style just sounded brand-spankin'-new—and irresistible.

Just ask Jesse McReynolds, one of the few bluegrass founding fathers to play the mandolin, but whose unique cross-picking technique on the instrument was designed to mimic the thrilling rolls and runs of a bluegrass banjo rather than Monroe's work on the mandolin. Jim & Jesse's version of the Louvin Brothers–penned "Are You Missing Me" offers a stellar example of the McReynolds mandolin style. Session fiddler Sonny "Young Love" James kicks off the song, and then Jesse starts in pining for a woman whose lips promised love but who betrayed him while he was away looking for work. When guitarist brother Jim McReynolds adds high-tenor harmony at the chorus, it defines lonesome—although the brothers still manage to maintain their composure. But then Jesse explodes on the mandolin, cross-picking his way through the first break, and the record suddenly sounds manic, desperate, eerily hollow, like a banjo with its heart ripped out.—dc

196

You Don't Know My Mind, Jimmy Martin
Produced by Owen Bradley; Written by Jimmie Skinner
Decca 31157   1960   Did not chart

"You Don't Know My Mind" is appropriately enigmatic. On the one hand, Jimmy Martin could be putting a lover on notice. "When I find that I can't win, I'll be checking out again," he tells her—and from what she can know of his thinking, which according to Jimmy is nothing at all, he could take off any time, just you watch. On the other hand, Jimmy may just be spitting in the direction of anyone who thinks they've got him figured out. After all he's been through—he's been homeless, ridden the rails, "slept in every dirty jail"—he ain't much concerned with folks who judge him without first having walked in his shoes. It's an ideal theme song for the irascible Martin's entire career.

Either way, though, this bluegrass puts its emphasis on the blues, of both the musical and existential variety—the record reveals the deep-down lonesome "feeling of human separateness," as author Craig Werner puts it, that is simply part of being alive. Martin endows every line with bluesy feeling, especially at the close when he worries over the title phrase with a George Jones–inspired flourish. Meanwhile, bruised yet hardy solos by Benny Martin and J. D. Crowe, on fiddle and banjo, respectively, empathize with every hard thing Martin might be thinking, even if they can't quite put it into words.—dc

197

Delta Dawn, Tanya Tucker
Produced by Billy Sherrill;
Written by Alex Harvey and Larry Collins
Columbia 45588   1972   #6 country; #72 pop

People find themselves homeless for all sorts of reasons, but most are grieving a loss, whether of a loved one, a job, or a place to live. Many who spend any length of time on the streets get stuck there, succumbing to depression or schizophrenia, or otherwise losing their hold on reality. It's not clear whether Delta Dawn is homeless, but she certainly fits the profile of those whom society used to call "street people." Emotionally, she shares a burden similar to that of the legions that haunt the nation's park benches, bus stations, alleys, and deserted downtowns.

The portrait we have of Dawn is pretty sketchy. We know she used to be a beauty and that twenty years ago (she's now forty-one), a stranger passing through town promised to marry her and take her away, presumably to a life of luxury. We also know that she's been dressed and waiting, suitcase in hand, for him to come back for her ever since—and that everyone thinks she's crazy.

It's not an entirely plausible story, especially the bit about Dawn still wearing the rose the guy gave her back when they first met. But what's even more unlikely is the empathy thirteen-year-old Tanya Tucker musters to tell Dawn's story; her tart, twangy soprano evinces a pathos that not only belies her tender years, but shames Helen Reddy's smarmy remake of the song, a #1 pop hit in 1973.

Billy Sherrill's roomy production—weary rhythms, forlorn harmonica, gospel-derived piano—is equally sympathetic,

leaving Tanya plenty of space to unfold her tale. Sherrill coaxes just the right mix of kindness and ache from the musicians working the session, particularly the solemn background choir of the Nashville Edition and the Jordanaires. The record hinges upon the hymn-like grandeur with which these singers imbue the ending, revealing that Dawn isn't pining for her earthly suitor anymore. Tired of walking the streets mourning what might've been, she's now waiting for God to come and take her away "to his mansion in the sky."—bfw

198

Release Me, Ray Price
Produced by Don Law;
Written by Eddie Miller, Dub Williams, and Robert Yount
Columbia 21214   1953   #6 country

Ray Price's early Columbia recordings were often little more than Hank Williams imitations, and no wonder.
Hank's Drifting Cowboys played on most of Price's early sessions, and when the pair toured together, Price sometimes stood in for Williams when the singer was too drunk to perform. It was partly upon the strength of Price's recording of "Weary Blues (From Waiting)," a song Williams wrote specifically for his protégé, that Price first appeared on the Grand Ole Opry in 1952. And when Hank's wife Audrey left him for good, the two men shared a house for a time.

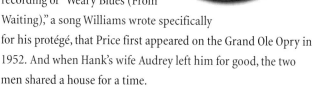

As he emphasizes in a story he's told repeatedly through the years, it was a fan's compliment in the fall of 1953—"You sound more like ol' Hank everyday"—that finally prompted Price to decide he wanted to be more than someone else's clone. It couldn't have been the first time he heard such a comment. For years, he'd sung Hank's songs at Hank's gigs and had toured with Hank's band, all the while singing in Hank's style—even hunching over the mike in mimicry of his mentor. Perhaps then it wasn't the comparison, per se, that troubled Price, but the way that five failed singles, each released in the wake of his friend's death and each a flop, told him that the comparison was becoming a liability. "It hit me at the right time," he now says. "I finally *heard* it."

Whatever the reason, when Price next entered the studio, he took his first serious step toward a sound of his own. Though still recording with a core group of Drifting Cowboys, Price now highlighted guitarist Grady Martin and the other session musicians, encouraging the band to decorate their honky-tonk with touches of western swing. Martin joined Jerry Rivers on twin fiddles to kick it off, then quickly switched instruments to join Don Helms and Sammy Pruett for the Texas Playboys–inspired "twin"-guitar attack at the break. And Price sang "Release Me" in a style that took as much from Playboy vocalist Tommy Duncan as it did from Hank. Price's voice sounds looser here, less pinched, and he is more likely to hold a note rather than twist it, even hinting in a couple of spots at the vibrato that soon became his calling card. "Please release me," he croons, "let me go," and it's in that croon that you can feel the legend of Hank Williams beginning to do just that.—dc

199

You Gave Me a Mountain, Johnny Bush

Produced by Pete Drake and Tommy Hill;
Written by Marty Robbins
Stop 257   1969   #7 country

200

I Wish I Was a Mole in the Ground,
Bascom Lamar Lunsford

No producer credited; Traditional
Brunswick 219B   1928   Pre-chart

Johnny Bush faced the biggest mountain of his life in 1974 when he literally lost his voice. He was touring in support of his hit "Whiskey River," a song that would later become a concert staple for fellow Cherokee Cowboy alum Willie Nelson, when he contracted spastic dysphonia, a rare neurological disorder that caused his vocal cords to shut down without warning. The disease left Bush unable to tour or record, a devastating blow for a singer whose multi-octave range had earned him the nickname the "Country Caruso." Bush eventually learned to live with the condition, for which there is no cure; he was able, with the help of breathing and vocal exercises, to make

records again and return to the Texas dance-hall circuit where he first made his name.

"You Gave Me a Mountain" casts Johnny as a modern-day Job, a man who's undergone a series of trials and who, beseeching the Almighty, wonders just how much more he can stand. His mother died while bringing him into the world, and his father went out of his mind with grief; Johnny's also served time in prison for a crime he didn't commit. And he's endured each ordeal in turn. *This* time, however, God has placed an insurmountable peak in his path. Johnny's wife, tired of the hardship and strife they've known together, has left him, and she's taken his "reason for living"—his baby boy. All seems lost as the strings swell and Pete Drake's steel starts raining down notes like hail—that is, until Johnny, singing in a neo-operatic style reminiscent of Elvis or Roy Orbison, tells God the mountain's no longer there. He draws out the word "longer" as if soaring above the clouds, which he is, not because he's scaled the summit, but because, brokenhearted and unable to go on, he's given up the fight.

Forty years earlier and faced with his own set of problems, Bascom Lunsford envisioned another way out. Fed up with his designing woman, as well as the threats of the rough and rowdy men who swear they'll kill him and "drink [his] blood for wine," Lunsford imagines he's a mole who can burrow into the mountain that stands before him and root it down. From the way he pours his frustration and rage into his flinty tenor and his stammering but unrelenting banjo, you'd swear he could pull it off, too.

It's a surreal, even phantasmagoric, picture, one that couldn't have been further from the staid life that Lunsford made for himself as an Asheville, North Carolina, attorney and collector of ballads, banjo and fiddle tunes people knew as the "Minstrel of the Appalachians." What will come as more of a shock to those who ascribe a centuries-old philosophy of resignation to Lunsford's Anglo-Celtic stock is the resolve he conveys here—a determination that enables him to conceive of and create a reality other than the one he inherited. In other words, one that just might enable him to root that mountain down.—bfw

201

Faith Unlocks the Door, The Statesmen Quartet
with Hovie Lister
Produced by Chet Atkins;
Written by Samuel Scott and Robert Sands
RCA Victor 6723   1956   Did not chart

"One of Elvis's idols when he was young was Jake Hess of the Statesmen Quartet," singer Johnny Rivers told Presley biographer Jerry Hopkins. "He was playing some of their records one day and he said, 'Now you know where I got my style. Caught—a hundred million records too late.' "

Elvis wasn't just being humble. The inspiration for much of Presley's vocal style—the earnest energy; the dramatic, whisper-to-a-scream dynamics; and especially his ballad phrasing—can be traced directly to the Statesmen's lead singer. One of the finest vocalists ever to emerge from within the American tradition of popular singing, Hess was a performer that a teenage Presley first thrilled to at Memphis's famed "all-night sings" in the early 1950s. Anyone who's ever heard Hess sing will recognize this Elvis connection immediately. When Hess testifies, though, the only influence that matters is the one he's having on you.

On "Faith Unlocks the Door," the players mostly just get out of his way. The spare accompaniment provided by guitarist Chet Atkins, pianist Hovie Lister, and the other Statesmen is so ethereal and unobtrusive that Hess could almost be singing a cappella. Good gospel singers regularly transform their yearning into contentment, their egos into humility, contemplation into action. But Hess works on a higher plane. Considered and spontaneous at once, his tenor feels both infinitely flexible and solid as a rock, transcending all worldly oppositions as he flies to his final line, "prayer is the key to heaven, but faith unlocks the door." What's left is unmitigated humanity and the mystery of grace.

And the record's only half over. The rest of "Faith" features a recitation by Statesmen bass singer "Big Chief" Wetherington and a stirring finale from high tenor Denver Crumpler. Still, even though his light hides under a bushel for half the record, "Faith" was rightfully considered Jake Hess's signature number, a judgment that in itself bears witness to his heavenly gifts.—dc

202

I Love You Because, Leon Payne
Produced by Lee Gillette; Written by Leon Payne
Capitol 40238   1949   #1 country (2 weeks)

"I Love You Because" was one of the songs that Fred Rose's son Wesley had in his briefcase in 1950, the first time he tried selling New York on the pop potential of hillbilly music. Four years later, Elvis Presley cut "I Love You Because" during the same weekend he recorded the monumental Sun sides, "That's All Right" backed with "Blue Moon of Kentucky." As it turned out, the Big Apple A&R reps weren't interested in the song, and Presley's version wouldn't see the light of day until RCA released it on an album in 1956. Just as well. It would've been tough to beat Leon Payne's beguiling original.

Born in Texas and blind since childhood, Payne delivers his lilting melody in a gentle, earnest tenor that's the ideal vehicle for poignant sentiments like "I love you because my heart is lighter every time I'm walking by your side," "You're always there to lend a helping hand, dear," and "I know your love will always see me through." Next to his darker compositions ("Lost Highway," for example, or "Psycho," a bent cult favorite), "I Love You Because" sounds unabashedly sentimental. "I love you for a hundred thousand reasons," Leon beams in a song inspired by his wife. "But most of all I love you 'cause you're you." Now isn't that just sweet as can be?

Which is not to be confused with mawkish or simple-minded. Surely, there's nothing more complex than loving people for what they are, rather than for what you'd like them to be. Unless maybe it's learning to trust that someone might love you in return, just because you're you.—dc

203

Any Day Now, Elvis Presley
Produced by Chips Moman;
Written by Burt Bacharach and Bob Hilliard
RCA Victor 47-9741   1969
(B-side of "In the Ghetto") #60 country; #3 pop

An ode to dread as hair-raising as "Suspicious Minds," although you'd never expect it from the upbeat note on which the record begins. Reggie Young's sunny guitar figure, Tommy Cogbill's scooting bass line, and the punchy Memphis Horns exude hopeful anticipation, as do the first three words that come out of Elvis's mouth. "Any day now," he croons in a swaggering baritone, as if eagerly expecting something. Then the bottom drops out—"I will hear you say, 'Goodbye my love' / You'll be on your way." Huh? These lines barely register amid the record's surging arrangement, coming clear only in the second verse, when Elvis imagines his lover leaving him when all she's done is glance at another guy. Paranoia strikes deep. Why else would he be talking himself out of a relationship he desperately wants to keep?

Or at least that's how it seems until the bridge, where a trembling Elvis, sounding as naked and scared as he ever did, sings, "I know I shouldn't want to keep you / If you don't want to stay / Until you're gone forever / I'll be holding on for dear life / Holding you this way / Begging you to stay." Cogbill's bass tolls a dirge-like pace while Young's scratchy guitar and Gene Chrisman's nagging cymbal echo Elvis's fear—no, his certainty—that even though he holds his lover, he's already lost her. A swirl of strings and voices close in on him like his obsession and then it hits you—Elvis isn't talking about a relationship with a woman here, he's talking about himself. He's fighting with everything he's got to hang on to some sense of who *he* is while living in the vast blue shadow of his own myth.

In other words, Elvis transforms Burt Bacharach and Bob Hilliard's study in romantic dissolution—a Top Forty hit for soul singer Chuck Jackson in 1962 and a country and pop smash for Ronnie Milsap twenty years later—into a presentiment of his impending demise.—bfw

204
Rockin' Chair Daddy, Harmonica Frank
Produced by Sam Phillips; Written by Frank Floyd
Sun 205   1954   Did not chart

Harmonica Frank (Floyd) was Sam Phillips's Elvis prototype, the proverbial "white man who had the Negro sound and . . . feel." The main reason that Frank, a grizzled veteran of the medicine show curcuit, wasn't the one who made Phillips his million bucks was that he was already in his forties when Sam met and recorded him in 1951. Plus, Frank's blend of hillbilly music and R&B was too raw and primitive. Here was a guy who did imitations of barnyard animals and played two harps at the same time, one with his mouth, the other with his nose. Whereas Elvis's influences were fairly sophisticated, including crooners like Dean Martin and Eddy Arnold, Harmonica Frank's musical instincts were born of the miscegenation of black and white cultures that took place on plantations and in prisons and sideshows—that is, out on the margins where they were destined to remain.

Witness "Rockin' Chair Daddy," an extended rant in which Frank, playing the big-balled bull-cow, exults in the unadulterated joys of fucking. "I rock 'em over and I rock 'em down / I rock 'em in the country and I rock 'em in the town," he crows in a gruff warble, seemingly dissociated from the crude hillbilly boogie he's cranking out on his harmonica and guitar. The record is pure attitude, an id-driven subversion of rhythm, melody, and middle-class decency that threatens to fall apart at every turn.

Yet there's also an undeniable theatricality at work when Frank, assuming the voice of one of his paramours, cries, "Rock it, boy," in a campy falsetto. Judging by lines like "Well I never went to college, I never went to school / But when it comes to rockin' I'm a rockin' fool," as well as by Frank's closing boast that his ability to satisfy women is why he "don't have to work," there's considerable attention to issues of class here too.

In other words, Phillips's ears didn't fail him; he knew it wouldn't be long before these sexy, dangerous sounds—a mix of music at once black and white, urban and rural, old and new—would blow things wide open. It's just that when Phillips finally released "Rockin' Chair Daddy" after sitting on it for three years, the world still wasn't ready for someone to get real, real gone. Not even for a change.—bfw

205
Flyin' Saucers Rock & Roll,
Billy Lee Riley & the Little Green Men
Produced by Sam Phillips; Written by H. R. Scott
Sun 260   1957   Did not chart

It was bound to happen, someone claiming, while the music was still in its infancy, that rock & roll sounded so weird it must have come from outer space. Billy Lee Riley, the most far-out comet in the Sun stable, was just the guy to do it, despite the fact that his own origins couldn't have been more down-to-earth.

Riley grew up poor, a sharecropper's son, in Arkansas and Mississippi, where he learned to play harmonica from his father, and guitar from the black field hands who chopped cotton and cut spinach alongside him. Riley dabbled in honky-tonk during a hitch in the army, but it wasn't until he hooked up with Jack Clement in Memphis in the mid-fifties that he came to the attention of Sam Phillips, then the owner of Sun Records. Phillips had been keeping an eye out for a singer who could fill the shoes of Elvis Presley, whose contract Sam had sold to RCA. Billy Lee might've fit the bill had Jerry Lee Lewis not cut "Great Balls of Fire" at Sun just as orders to press copies of Riley's first single "Red Hot" were going out the door. Convinced that Lewis was his man, Phillips put "Red Hot" on hold, effectively derailing Riley's recording career at Sun, which amounted to a mere six singles, supplemented by a crucial though behind-the-scenes gig as a studio guitarist.

History vindicated Phillips's decision as Jerry Lee went on to give Elvis a run for his money. But it's also likely the public wasn't ready for a singer as unhinged as Riley. Lewis's early sides, some of them backed by Billy Lee and his aptly named Little Green Men, might have been wild, but none quite shifted into the interstellar overdrive of "Flyin' Saucers Rock & Roll." Not with guitarist Roland Janes's laser-like leads, drummer J. M. Van Eaton's unearthly thrashing, and the Killer's own propulsive piano sending a screaming Riley, who sounds like he's downed a fifth of rocket fuel, into orbit. "Well the news of the saucers been flyin' around / I'm the only one who saw it on the ground," Riley raves, his words scarcely more intelligible than those of the Martians with whom he claims to have had contact. You can bet that's just how Phillips thought the public would have heard it too—as a close encounter with an alien species.—bfw

206

Stratosphere Boogie, Jimmy Bryant & Speedy West
Produced by Ken Nelson; Written by Jimmy Bryant
Capitol 2964   1954   Did not chart

Few records are as aptly titled as this—the only possible explanation for the way West and Bryant's nimble digits defy the laws of physics here is that they actually made the record in outer space where such rules don't apply. As it turns out, they really did use a little rocket science. Take the four pedals on West's triple-necked Bigsby—devices that enable him to make chord changes

that no lap-steel guitarist, however dexterous, could have played. Then there's Bryant's "Stratosphere Twin," an experimental guitar (he usually played a solid-body Fender) with six- and twelve-string necks which, according to historian Rich Kienzle, "was tuned in thirds, so it sounded like twin lead guitars played in harmony." That sleight-of-hand—no overdubs—is just what we hear on the quicksilver run that kicks off this record. Then, switching over to the other neck, Bryant reels off a boppish break until West jumps in, crash bar in hand, and unleashes a flurry of notes that swoop up and down and dart in and out like a hawk challenging the wind for dominion. Everything here is head-arranged—just two intrepid virtuosi, their unbounded imaginations, and a go-cat rhythm section taking the twin-guitar approach of Eldon Shamblin and Leon McAuliffe to its farthest extreme.

West and Bryant evinced much the same inventiveness and abandon on the thousands of sessions they worked during the fifties, playing on records by everyone from Ernie Ford and Spike Jones to Bing Crosby and Frank Sinatra. Brought together by West Coast impresario Cliffie Stone, who dubbed them "the Flaming Guitars," the duo sold plenty of their own records as well, including "Stratosphere Boogie." It never made the *Billboard* charts, but you can bet it was #1 throughout the rest of the galaxy.—bfw

207

Maybellene, Chuck Berry
Produced by Leonard Chess; Written by Chuck Berry
Chess 1604   1955   #5 pop; #1 R&B (11 weeks)

Elvis Presley and other early rock & rollers such as Buddy Holly, Carl Perkins, and the Everly Brothers are routinely cited as examples of the way white musicians borrowed ideas and inspiration from rhythm and blues. But this interracial exchange went the other direction too—that's what made it rock & roll— as even a cursory examination of the biographies and recordings of Fats Domino, Ray Charles, and Chuck Berry reveals.

Berry wasn't merely familiar with country music; he was a fan. Perkins, who toured with Berry in the fifties, remembered

Chuck as a traveling companion who enjoyed singing along with him in the car to "Blue Moon of Kentucky" and "Knoxville Girl." Berry even corrected Perkins about which verses went with which of Jimmie Rodgers's Blue Yodels. In his St. Louis days, Berry entertained his audiences by changing the words to songs like "Mountain Dew" and "Jambalaya." And tinkering with the words to the western swing favorite "Ida Red" sparked Berry's discovery of the melody and rhythm for his breakthrough smash, "Maybellene." In fact, what made Berry distinctive, more than just a second-rate Louis Jordan or Muddy Waters, were the country elements in his music: his twangy guitar (basically, country licks performed blues style—or was that the other way around?) and his stories.

Berry's narrative for "Maybellene"—he's racing his V-8 Ford down the highway in hot pursuit of an unfaithful, Cadillac-driving lover—would've fit in at most any postwar honky-tonk, right next to, say, one of the four versions of "Hot Rod Race" that made the country charts in 1951. Berry's attention to detail ("Rain water blowin' all under my hood / I knew that was doing my motor good") sparkles even at this early stage of his career. It's that great big sound, though, that keeps driving you on—the relentless thwack of the rhythm section and, especially, Berry's guitar, which floors it through the first half of his solo like the booziest rockabilly, and the second half like he's become a slurred pedal-steel guitar.

Country music had long had its own version of a backbeat you couldn't lose. But after Chuck Berry hit, it was the rare country boy who didn't at least occasionally play his guitar just like he was a-ringin' a bell.—dc

208

Big in Vegas, Buck Owens & the Buckaroos
Produced by Ken Nelson;
Written by Buck Owens and Terry Stafford
Capitol 2646   1969   #5 country; #100 pop

In 1965, Buck Owens placed a full-page ad in *Music City News,* heralding a "Pledge to Country Music": "I shall sing no song that is not a country song . . . I shall make no record that is not a country record." That same month he released an album that included a cover of Chuck Berry's "Memphis," a rockin' little take on the song that borrowed heavily from Johnny Rivers's pop hit from the year before. To those for whom "country music" implied specific and established boundaries, the juxtaposition seemed a

blatant contradiction. But to Buck, a pledge to country in no way implied that he couldn't expand those boundaries, the better to follow his own instincts and to find a wider audience for his music.

Through the years, those ambitions led Owens to modify his country with elements of rockabilly, folk-rock, R&B, and country-rock and to cover songs associated with Berry, the Drifters, and Simon & Garfunkel. Those ambitions must have drawn him to a Terry Stafford pop song called "Big in Dallas," which Buck transformed into the countrypolitan smash "Big in Vegas." "My will is strong and I've got to make it big in Vegas," Owens attests. "I'll get a standing ovation from the people when I . . . turn 'em on in Vegas." It's a safe bet. If his trademark twang doesn't get the crowd on its feet, then the stirring chorus and Al DeLory–inspired string arrangement certainly will.

What else is new? Buck's determination to accept no definition of country music but his own made him big all over the world.—dc

209

Fancy, Bobbie Gentry
Produced by Rick Hall; Written by Bobbie Gentry
Capitol 2675   1969   #26 country; #31 pop

A slice of Southern Gothic about getting over—that is, about learning the rules of the game and moving up in the world.

Fancy's story begins *in medias res* in a seedy one-room shack on the outskirts of New Orleans; she's just turned eighteen. Her father has walked out on the family, her destitute mother is dying, and the people from social services are coming to take away her baby sister. The tensive strings and skittish rimshots of producer Rick Hall's cottonfield soul set an appropriately forbidding tone for the scene as Fancy, singing in a steamy, self-possessed drawl, recalls the day her mama sent her out into the streets to earn her keep. "Just be nice to the gentlemen, Fancy, and they'll be nice to you," the dying woman tells her precocious daughter. "Here's your one chance Fancy . . . your mama's gonna help you move uptown."

So Fancy slips into the red dress and heels her mama bought

her with the money she got from cashing her welfare check. Fancy knows what she has to do, but she makes herself a promise as she does it. She "might have been born just plain white trash," but, true to her name, she's going to be a "lady" someday. That's exactly what happens; buoyed by Jimmie Haskell's ascending string arrangement and a surging horn riff reminiscent of Sam & Dave's "Hold On, I'm Comin', " Fancy ultimately realizes her dream of owning both a "Georgia mansion and an elegant New York townhouse flat."

It's all a bit, well, fanciful, especially the part about Fancy entertaining a king and a congressman. Yet it *does* make for good drama, not to mention for one hell of a fine record. It's also, loosely, autobiographical. Born Roberta Streeter, Gentry grew up poor in the Deep South—Greenville, Mississippi—where her grandmother traded a milk cow for the upright piano on which young Bobbie taught herself to play. Years later, after she moved to Los Angeles to study music, Gentry worked as a Vegas showgirl. No, she didn't turn tricks on her way to the top of the pop charts (with "Ode to Billie Joe" in 1967). But nightclub dancing certainly revolves around pleasing men, and doubtless that explains the venom in Bobbie's voice when, counting the cost of getting over, she spits: "In this world there's a lot of self-righteous hypocrites who would call me bad."

Reba McEntire glossed over this venom when she played Fancy in her hit remake of the song from 1991. When Reba trumpets, "And I ain't been back," it's merely a victory cry, a declaration of independence from a life of prostitution. By contrast, when Gentry tells us she ain't been back, we know better than to believe her; the reason she's telling us her story in the first place is that she's been back on those mean streets all too often, even if only in her mind.—bfw

210
Just Like Real People, The Kendalls
Produced by Brien Fisher; Written by Bob McDill
Ovation 1125   1979   #11 country

Some might write off Jeannie Kendall's character here as a victim of bad socialization—a woman who doesn't believe she can be

complete without a man, a woman whose self-esteem is so low she doesn't deem herself worthy of being loved. "Well before we go any farther, there's something that you oughta know," Jeannie says to the man she loves, before going on to confess that she's "been around some" and "made a mistake or two." But as she also tells him, she's a dreamer, an idealist. While she's never found much worth holding onto, Jeannie clings to her faith in love and thinks she might be looking at it now. "I believe if you'd only have me / I could start a new life with you / Just like real people," she sings, her silvery tremolo sounding like a prayer against the hymn-like strains of the piano.

There's no denying that Jeannie's acting like damaged goods here—that's how she feels. She's been hurt before, but so have most people, and it's precisely that solidarity that gives this record such resonance. Jeannie's got a hole in her heart and is seeking the kind of renewal, at once sexual and spiritual, that Madonna sings of in "Like a Virgin" when she talks about feeling "shiny and new." It's a far cry from Jeannie's often-cheating persona but hardly less credible. The only flaw in her logic, or rather that of songwriter Bob McDill, is the implication that real people aren't flawed or broken, that they can't, or don't, make mistakes. Nevertheless, the beauty of Jeannie's gutsy, heart-in-throat performance—bereft as it is of the support her dad's harmonies usually provided her—gainsays that fallacy. Indeed, it proves that "real people" can be, and often are, broken and beautiful at the same time.—bfw

211
I'm Sorry, Brenda Lee
Produced by Owen Bradley;
Written by Ronnie Self and Dub Albritten
Decca 31093   1960   #1 pop (3 weeks)

"Little Miss Dynamite" begs, Owen Bradley's strings leak tears down around her, and though decades come and go, nothing changes. Brenda Lee says she's sorry over and over and over—despite the fact that the lover she's hurt has already forgiven her. "You say mistakes are part of being young / but that don't right the wrong that's been done," she responds before apologizing yet again. It makes you wonder—just how many years will have to pass before she forgives *herself*?—dc

212

A Wound Time Can't Erase, Stonewall Jackson
Produced by Don Law and Frank Jones; Written by Bill D. Johnson
Columbia 42229   1962   #3 country

"Is it power you've won for the things you have done / What you've gained I guess I'll never see."

On the surface, these lines find Jackson expressing heartache and disbelief over the cruelty of the woman who's shamed and then walked out on him. Yet heard in light of the harrowing abuse he suffered at the hands of his stepfather while growing up, it's hard not to imagine that what drew Stonewall to these lyrics was just how directly they spoke to his shattering boyhood in South Georgia.

According to *From the Bottom Up*, an "as told to" memoir available through Jackson's fan club, Stonewall's stepfather, a sharecropper who feared the boy was coming between him and his mother, worked him like a dog, mercilessly beating and ridiculing him every chance he could. "I'd been known to just walk up to where he was and have him slap me upside the head and knock me clean across the field," Stonewall told interviewer Billy Henson, later explaining how his brutish stepdad once battered him senseless and left him for dead. "I've still got scars in places that I got back in those days. And some of the scars are inside of me, in my heart and in my mind; not trusting anyone and not believing there was anything such as love or happiness."

Those wounds bleed through on this fusion of unvarnished barroom country and high-gloss Nashville Sound, a synthesis akin to the sound that Jackson's label mates Ray Price and Lefty Frizzell were perfecting at the time. "What did you have in mind, when you broke this heart of mine / Are you laughing in my face?" Stonewall agonizes, as if confronting the man whose own

feelings of powerlessness drove him to seek a measure of control, however misplaced, by terrorizing a helpless kid.

At fourteen, after ten years of hell, Jackson finally ran away. The police caught up with him in Atlanta, but Stonewall escaped his stepfather, first going to live with relatives and later making it to Nashville, where he immediately landed a publishing deal with Acuff-Rose and became a member of the Grand Ole Opry. Those last two strokes of fortune happened overnight, but it's taken a lifetime for the injuries Jackson suffered as a boy to mend. Nevertheless, as he told Chris Dickinson in a 1998 issue of the *Journal of Country Music*, the minute he got his big break he wasted no time getting started with his recovery. He drove his brand new pickup down to Georgia, tracked down his stepfather, and handed him the keys, as if to say "you've got no hold over me now." Having taken control of his life, Stonewall hitchhiked his way back to Nashville to heal as best he could.—bfw

213

Better Man, Clint Black
Produced by James Stroud and Mark Wright;
Written by Clint Black and Hayden Nicholas
RCA 8781   1989   #1 country (1 week)

This is what the best country music sounded like in 1989, after yet another decade spent cherry picking what it could use off rock radio. "A Better Man" retains an undeniable sawdust feel, but its stinging Bakersfield licks are surrounded by airy piano fills that occasionally push into Bruce Hornsby territory, not to mention a chorus brimming with new-wave bounce and subtle synth washes that sound like something off Bruce Springsteen's *Born in the U.S.A.*

The record's most profound updating is a thematic one. Where generations of honky-tonk singers have greeted the end of romance either with tears in their beer or a curse of good riddance, the man that Black and co-writer/guitarist Hayden Nicholas have created actually claims to be better off for having known the woman he's singing to, even though he's sad to realize that their relationship is better off over. Clearly, he's read a self-help book or two in his time, but what's remarkable is that he actually seems to have helped himself. "Things I couldn't do before, now I know I can," Black concludes, and suitably enough for such a pronouncement of emotional growth and healthy resolution, his voice sounds just like a young Merle, minus the haggard.—dc

214
Wide Open Spaces, Dixie Chicks
Produced by Paul Worley and Blake Chancey;
Written by Susan Gibson
Monument 79003   1998   #1 country (4 weeks)

"I Wanna Be a Cowboy's Sweetheart" for a new generation of woman. First, we dump the cowboy. Then, instead of a girl who dreams of riding her horse beneath western skies, imagine a young woman who's leaving home, headed west for a college dorm room or maybe her first apartment. When the girl's mother, who's given her daughter a lift to this fresh start, turns to drive off without her, she gulps, "I'm leaving my girl." Then she immediately recalls the time when *she* needed the space to forge "a dream and a life of [her] own," the "room to make her big mistake."

   "Who doesn't know what I'm talking about," lead singer Natalie Maines begins. "Who's never left home? Who's never struck out to find a dream and a life of their own?" It's almost as if she's both rejoicing and singing the blues, preemptively, for this young woman and the thousands like her, for all the joys and mistakes to come. Martie Seidel's fiddle encourages the girl on to some unknown future even as Emily Irwin's banjo reassures her that home is still there, if she ever needs it. Not now, though. Somehow she's already figured out what it takes some folks a lifetime to learn—mistakes and freedom go hand in hand. Pack that message onto a wistful, swelling melody, delivered over gently percolating country-rock, and you've got a sing-along anthem for women everywhere.

   Men too, assuming they're smart enough to sing along.—dc

215
Deep in the Heart of Texas, Gene Autry
Produced by Art Satherley;
Written by June Hershey and Don Swander
OKeh 06643   1942   Pre-chart

Gene Autry rustles a Texas anthem away from the city slickers.

   "Deep in the Heart of Texas" dominated Your Hit Parade with five charting versions in early 1942. The most popular were a chart-topping treatment by Alvino Rey (the steel guitar–playing bandleader whose brainstorm, in this case, was to waste his instrument on cheesy sound effects) and a swinging stampede of a record by Bing Crosby.

   It was Autry's version, though, recorded within days of Rey's and Crosby's chart debuts, that finally provided "Deep in the

Heart" with an appropriately Lone Star setting. With a lyric that includes only the most stock "Texas" details (coyotes, cacti, and the like) and a sing-along melody that punctuates each rhyme with handclaps, the song itself is little more than a schoolyard chant. But Autry's campfire croon summons visions of wide-open spaces, and the small combo that leads him down the trail suggests, via horn, accordion, and a loping, danceable rhythm, the sounds of western swing, Tex-Mex, cowboy music, even honky-tonk. When it's the heart of Texas you're shooting for, that's a bull's eye—even if Autry was aiming it from deep in the heart of a Hollywood recording studio.—dc

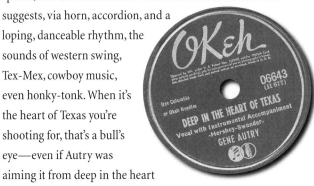

216
Waltz Across Texas,
Ernest Tubb & His Texas Troubadours
Produced by Owen Bradley; Written by Billy Talmadge Tubb
Decca 31824   1965   #34 country

You can drive all day, the saying goes, and never leave Texas. So when ol' E.T. offers to *dance* across the state, you know he's floating on air—and in it for the long haul. To a lover who gazes at him with stars in her eyes, he avers, "With your hand in mine, dear, I could dance on and on."

   That's Texan for "Will you marry me?"—dc

217
Golden Ring, George Jones & Tammy Wynette
Produced by Billy Sherrill;
Written by Bobby Braddock and Rafe Vanhoy
Epic 50235   1976   #1 country (1 week)

In her autobiography *Stand by Your Man,* Tammy Wynette recalls being in the middle of a fight with her second husband Don Chapel when a recently divorced George Jones showed up unexpectedly at their door. The year was 1968. George and Tammy hadn't known each other long, having only worked a few dates together. But when George saw the way Chapel was treating Tammy and heard the names he was calling her, he jumped up from the couch and threw over the coffee table in a jealous rage. "You don't talk to her that way," he screamed, and when Chapel told him to mind his own business, George blurted out "I love her!" And then, to Tammy, "And you love me, too, don't you?" "Yes, yes, I do," she responded, surprising even herself. "Okay," said George, "Let's go." And they did.

Two of country's great romantics, George Jones and Tammy Wynette charted their stormy six-year marriage with a series of confessional duets, "Take Me," "The Ceremony," "We're Gonna Hold On," and "We Loved It All Away" among them. But none of those pathos-drenched hits conveyed the couple's faith in love's power the way "Golden Ring" did. "By itself it's just a cold metallic thing / Only love can make a golden wedding ring," they sing, fittingly enough, to a melody reminiscent of "Can the Circle Be Unbroken." By the final verse, when the ring, like their marriage, has lost its luster and rests again in the pawnshop window, their voices throb with sorrow. It's enough that they've caused each other pain; the sting of knowing that love itself has failed them is just too much to bear.

Yet judging by the way their voices soar on the gospel-inspired chorus, George and Tammy have as much faith in the transformative power of music as they do in their romantic ideals. What else but the rapture they convey here kept them making records together, even after their embattled relationship became tabloid fodder—indeed, long after it had fallen apart?

"Golden Ring" went to #1 in 1976, the year *after* George and Tammy divorced.—bfw

218

Would You Lay with Me (in a Field of Stone), Tanya Tucker
Produced by Billy Sherrill; Written by David Allan Coe
Epic 45991   1974   #1 country (1 week); #46 pop

Country music's version of "Will You Love Me Tomorrow," right down to the teen girl singer, the should-I-or-shouldn't-I sexual tension, and the giving-in-as-they-go string arrangement and

rhythm track. Except that Tanya Tucker (and here lies a big chunk of what *makes* this a country version) isn't only asking about tomorrow morning. She wants to know if this guy will love her forever, through all the years ahead and all the troubles those years will inevitably bring— on even into eternity.

What? You thought the stones in that field were just rocks?—dc

219

Tonight I'll Be Staying Here with You, Bob Dylan
Produced by Bob Johnston; Written by Bob Dylan
Columbia 45004   1969   #50 pop

Biographer Robert Shelton called Dylan's *Nashville Skyline* "a retreat from significance," but that's only half right. The album, the third Dylan made in Music City yet the first he conceived as a country record, indeed marked a major shift in perspective, though not so much *away* from significance as from one type of meaning to another. Gone are the grand statements, as well as the vitriol, irony, and abstruse metaphors, of his previous albums. In their place are heartfelt declarations of love and paeans to domesticity. More than anything, Dylan was reveling in a world enfolded in harmony and contentment, one that offered him a break from the discord and dissent—and pretensions—of the previous decade.

"Tonight I'll Be Staying Here with You" brims with the sense of freedom Dylan felt as he unloaded that baggage. "Throw my ticket out the window / Throw my suitcase out there too / Throw my troubles out the door / I don't need them anymore," he tells the woman he's about to go home with as he steps off his train. At first it sounds like he's just planning to spend the night, but he doesn't re-book passage on a later train, and he instructs the porter to give his ticket to some "poor boy" on the street. Bob's staying all right, and from the ease in his fluid, newly nicotine-free voice, he's ready to settle in for a while.

He's also getting back to the basics of love, and his Johnny Cash–coached croon, a voice that split the difference between those of his heroes Hank Snow and Bill Anderson, couldn't be better suited to this latter-day heart song. The same goes for the elegantly straightforward playing of the Nashville cats working the session; every flat-picked note, piano obbligato, and surge of steel guitar tossed off by Norman Blake, Pig Robbins, and Pete Drake tugs at Bob's heartstrings and bids him to stay.

"Tonight I'll Be Staying Here with You" didn't chart country, and neither did "Lay, Lady, Lay," the other single from *Nashville Skyline,* despite a resounding endorsement from the Man in Black in the album's liner notes and an appearance by Dylan on Cash's ABC variety show. "Tonight" did, however, help anoint country as cool with the rock crowd, in the process confirming what country folk had always known—even the most modest and unassuming of gestures can signify plenty.—bfw

220
Absolutely Sweet Marie, Jason & the Scorchers
Produced by Terry Manning; Written by Bob Dylan
EMI X-7111   1984   Did not chart

A lot of people thought Jason & the Scorchers were mocking country music when they first heard the band's thrashing covers of hits by Hank Williams and Faron Young. Indeed, the Scorchers' fusion of punk and twang sounded, as their fellow insurgents the Mekons put it, like they'd been "listening to the country boys and dancing on their graves." But unlike the spate of Southern-lit-majors-turned-trailer-park dilettantes they spawned, the Scorchers' renegade take on honky-tonk was anything but ironic or condescending. One reason was that the band's members grew up tuned to Nashville's WSM, the station that broadcasts the Grand Ole Opry. Their hillbilly pedigree was also legit—singer Jason Ringenberg was raised on an Illinois hog farm; guitarist Warner Hodges's folks worked with Johnny Cash; drummer Perry Baggs's father sang southern gospel.

The Scorchers, however, had no intention of playing mama and daddy's music. They were bent on making their own noise, and in the beginning that meant running country chestnuts like "Hello Walls" and "Jimmie Rodgers' Last Blue Yodel" through their punk-rock blender. It was a natural enough tack for four crackers (including bass player Jeff Johnson) who came up slam-dancing to the Sex Pistols and the Ramones. And it wasn't such a far cry from what Bob Dylan did a generation earlier when he took a wrecking ball to "Lost Highway" (a song the Scorchers would later trash) and recast it as "Like a Rolling Stone."

The Scorchers' blistering assault on "Absolutely Sweet Marie," a snarling record Dylan cut with a handful of Nashville session pros in 1966, pays the erstwhile folkie back in kind. Baggs and Johnson pump like hyperkinetic pistons, bashing away in what feels like double time. Hodges slashes all over the place like a Dixie-fried Eddie Van Halen, while Ringenberg rages as if the hellfire of cousins Jerry Lee Lewis and Jimmy Lee Swaggart is burning in his veins. "To live outside the law you must be honest," Jason yowls, transforming Dylan's exhortation into a rallying cry.

No catchphrase ever captured the Scorchers's firebrand aesthetic better. Arriving after the country-rock gold rush of the seventies and before the alt-country boomlet of the nineties, the band never cashed in, but their particular seizure of country music was as righteous as any before it or since.—bfw

221
James Alley Blues, Richard "Rabbit" Brown
No producer credited; Written by Richard Brown
Victor   1927   Pre-chart

Little is known of Richard "Rabbit" Brown other than that he was a black street singer from New Orleans and an early exponent of the twelve-bar blues. He cut just five sides for Victor (with Ralph Peer) in March of 1927, mostly ballads and vaudeville-derived fare; this ominous account of one-sided romance, though, was singularly auspicious.

Anticipating the confessional songwriting of Hank Williams—notably the ultimatum of "You're Gonna Change (or I'm Gonna Leave)"—as well as the apocalyptic admonitions of Bob Dylan, "James Alley" was twenty to thirty years ahead of its time. Dylan left the most obvious clue as to the record's impact when he lifted its biblical "sugar for sugar, salt for salt" passage to form the backbone of "Down in the Flood." You can also hear "James Alley" as a precursor (along with the old plaint "Hard Times") to "Maggie's Farm," with Brown playing the role of the bumpkin who ain't gonna work for his cruel mistress no more.

" 'Cause I was born in the country she thinks I'm easy to rule," he grouses, his groaning voice as emphatic as the notes he doggedly plucks from his guitar. "She try to hitch me to her wagon, she wanna drive me like a mule." Brown's done everything for his woman—bought her groceries, paid her rent, and now she's trying to get him to do her laundry as well. It all smacks of

Dylan's gripe in "Maggie's Farm"; "it's a shame the way she makes me scrub the floor."

Of course, Dylan was protesting alienation in a broader sense, but it's not hard to imagine "James Alley" as an inspiration for his sardonic screed. Especially the grim revolution implied in the record's final couplet, in which Brown turns to his mean mistreater with deadly cool and twice warns, "Sometimes I think you're too sweet to die / Other times I feel like you should be buried alive."—bfw

222

The Long Black Veil, Lefty Frizzell
Produced by Don Law;
Written by Danny Dill and Marijohn Wilkin
Columbia 41384   1959   #6 country

Songwriter Danny Dill drew inspiration from a quartet of unconnected sources: an unsolved New Jersey murder; a gospel song titled "God Walks These Hills with Me"; the story of a woman who for years visited the grave of Rudolph Valentino; and the old ballads of folk-revival singer Burl Ives. When Marijohn Wilkin set Dill's lyrics to an elegiac melody, the result was exactly what they'd been looking for—"an instant folksong." It's been subjected to countless versions since Lefty Frizzell introduced the song in 1959.

Because it begins by telling us that, "ten years ago . . . someone was killed 'neath the town hall light," the song sometimes gets labeled a murder ballad, but it's a murder ballad without a murder—the only death we witness is the narrator's execution for a crime he didn't commit. "The Long Black Veil" can more accurately be described as a ghost story, but even that doesn't speak to the song's enduring appeal—the shock that comes with learning that the narrator is singing from beyond the grave is only good the first time through, after all. More than anything, "The Long Black Veil," in which a man can't clear his name because to do so would require admitting that he'd been "in the arms of [his] best friend's wife," is a gothic cheating song—where love and guilt stretch beyond the grave and mourning never ceases. Over a haunting, barren arrangement, Frizzell foregoes his trademark melisma, and the effect is as eerie as the final image: "Sometimes at night, when the cold wind moans / In a long black veil, she cries o'er my bones."—dc

223

Just Out of Reach (of My Two Open Arms),
Solomon Burke
Produced by Jerry Wexler and Bert Berns;
Written by V. F. Stewart
Atlantic 2114   1961   #7 R&B; #24 pop

Rhythm-and-blues does the Nashville Sound. The backing choir that kicks off this soul music version of the country standard might as well have been the Anita Kerr Singers; the piano and vibes that double one another throughout create an effect that's reminiscent of Floyd Cramer's famous slip-note style; and when a sax takes the melody during Solomon Burke's sober recitation, it does what a string arrangement would if Chet Atkins had produced the record instead of Jerry Wexler.

It's doubtful Burke had heard earlier versions of the song by Faron Young and Patsy Cline (neither were hits), but we do know he later claimed to be a big fan, in his youth, of cowboy stars such as Roy Rogers and Gene Autry. No wonder, then, that this self-proclaimed "King of Rock and Soul" knew exactly how to ride the record's loping, western rhythm. Instead of building to an explosive release as he would on later hits, Burke embodies restraint, 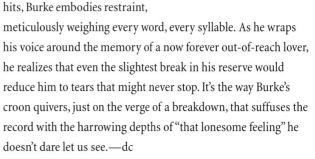 meticulously weighing every word, every syllable. As he wraps his voice around the memory of a now forever out-of-reach lover, he realizes that even the slightest break in his reserve would reduce him to tears that might never stop. It's the way Burke's croon quivers, just on the verge of a breakdown, that suffuses the record with the harrowing depths of "that lonesome feeling" he doesn't dare let us see.—dc

224

Don't Worry, Marty Robbins
Produced by Don Law; Written by Marty Robbins
Columbia 41922   1961   #1 country (10 weeks); #3 pop

"Don't Worry" is remembered today mainly for its famous guitar solo. When a malfunctioning pre-amp caused Grady Martin's six-string electric bass to distort, producer Don Law decided that the resulting noise—something like a hoarse and heartsick foghorn bouncing across a trampoline—was too cool to pass up. Within a few years, the new "fuzztone" effect had become a staple in rock & roll.

What makes "Don't Worry" more than just the answer to some guitar-tech trivia question, though, is that Martin's solo remains as fitting as it was innovative. Marty Robbins's song has him trying to keep a stiff upper lip, insisting to his ex-lover that he'll be okay when she's gone. "Love can't be explained, can't be controlled," Robbins offers in a wavering croon, letting her off the hook. "Don't worry 'bout me." Belying his every word, Grady Martin's bass blares and bounds through its solo, each distorted note a sob suppressed too long.—dc

225

A Good Year for the Roses, George Jones
Produced by Harold "Pappy" Daily; Written by Jerry Chesnut
Musicor 1425   1970   #2 country; #112 pop

George Jones recorded "A Good Year for the Roses" in 1970 just before he left Musicor for Epic Records and a successful two-decade-long partnership with producer Billy Sherrill. Yet Sherrill might as well have produced this record too, what with its atmospheric choir and pedal-steel guitar, its mournful piano accents and throbbing quiet-loud-quiet dynamics, all caressing Jones's every strangled note. "A Good Year for the Roses" stands as the sonic and narrative prequel for later Jones and Sherrill collaborations such as "The Grand Tour," "These Days I Barely Get By," and "The Door."

While those records would find Jones mourning a departed wife as he wanders about a Home Sweet Home that suddenly is neither, "A Good Year" gives us the breakup in progress—she's literally packing to leave while he sings. As he sits numbly watching her from the couch, each mundane domestic detail becomes an object lesson in his own worthless-

ness. The cigarette she lit but didn't finish, the "lip print on a half-filled cup of coffee that you poured and didn't drink," the bed that for the first time in their marriage he'll be making—everything speaks of a love that's withering away. Everything, that is, except the roses blooming outside his window. "Many blooms still linger there," he observes, speaking as much about his heart as the garden. But so what? It may have been a good year for the roses, but love's been dying on the vine.—dc

226

The Last Thing on My Mind,
Porter Wagoner & Dolly Parton
Produced by Porter Wagoner; Written by Tom Paxton
RCA Victor 9369   1967   #7 country

When you hear Dolly sing "I've got reason aplenty for going," then hear Porter plead "Please don't go, please don't go," it's impossible not to flash to the pair's infamous mid-seventies breakup. But "The Last Thing on My Mind" is from 1967, not 1976, and what's most remarkable about it is how perfectly, how universally, this Tom Paxton song nails the slow dissolution of a failing relationship. Neither singer can believe the other's really leaving, and yet, pushed along by highway-speed picking on top of a bustling country groove, you know they're both in a hurry to be gone. "I could've loved you better, didn't mean to be unkind," they insist to each other, but the next line unwittingly reveals why they didn't love better and why they were unkind, all the same: "You know that was the last thing on my mind."

Parton's pretty, soaring lead and Wagoner's much lower, raggedy tenor come together on that line to make exquisite harmony. But they still sound very far apart.—dc

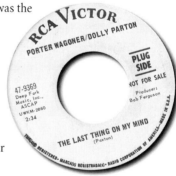

227

As Soon As I Hang Up the Phone,
Loretta Lynn & Conway Twitty
Produced by Owen Bradley; written by Conway Twitty
MCA 40251   1974   #1 country (1 week)

The record startles you to attention with the ringing of a telephone. A woman answers "Hello." A man says, "Hello,

Loretta?" As he reveals that he's found someone else, we hear him speaking rather than singing his lines, phoning it in, literally. She sings her responses, at first not really hearing what he has to tell her, then finally crying out in anguish, "Ohh nooo, ohh nooo.""Goodbye, Loretta," he gulps, and the connection clicks dead.

A lot of folks would call that the very definition of hokey and contrived. But those folks wouldn't be the country music fans who turned "As Soon As I Hang Up the Phone" into one of Twitty and Lynn's most popular duets. And anyway, allowing for the necessities of rhyme, melody, and backing band, this is about as close to cinema verité as a two-and-a-half minute single is ever likely to come. And thank goodness for rhyme, melody, and—most of all—the band. The record's softly pulsing rhythm, John Hughey's moaning pedal steel, and Tommy Jackson's mournful fiddle will lull even the least sentimental country fans into suspending disbelief long enough to experience the shock of recognition. The way a choked-up Conway feels obliged to tell the woman whose world he has destroyed that this "hurts me *too*" is infuriatingly true to life. Most accurate of all, though, are those sobbed "Oh no"s. You can practically hear Loretta's heart breaking in two. If that ain't real, nothing is.—dc

228

He'll Have to Go, Jim Reeves
Produced by Chet Atkins;
Written by Joe Allison and Audrey Allison
RCA Victor 7643   1959   #1 country (14 weeks); #2 pop

An international star with large followings in parts of Africa and the British Isles, Jim Reeves was maybe the most popular country singer ever. A staggering thirty-five of his eighty charting country singles—including eighteen Top Tens and six #1s—came *after* he died in a 1964 plane crash.

Reeves's first recordings were twangy romps typical of early fifties country singers. His first #1 was an undistinguished near-novelty called "Mexican Joe" that earned the East Texan a gig as an announcer and performer on the *Louisiana Hayride*. It could have been recorded by Carl Smith, Hank Thompson, a young

Eddy Arnold . . . almost anyone. But when he began working with RCA producer Chet Atkins in 1956, Reeves found a sound to call his own. He slowed the tempo to a crawl, eliminated the fiddles, added the Jordanaires on swooning harmony, and dropped his own already deep voice to a velvety baritone croon. The result, "Four Walls," topped the country charts and barely missed the pop Top Ten. Furthermore, "Four Walls" became one of the basic templates for the Nashville Sound, as well as for virtually everything else Reeves recorded. Unfortunately, this was often a bad thing. "Four Walls," like many of Gentlemen Jim's hits, sounds more concerned with the sonorous perfection of its croon than with any emotional connection to the lyric.

"He'll Have to Go" was a meaningful exception and an even bigger crossover hit (the result, in part, of an intense RCA promotional campaign directed at northeastern pop stations). Inspired by a phone conversation in which songwriter Joe Allison asked his wife Audrey to please speak up, Reeves purrs the song's opening couplet—"Put your sweet lips a little closer to the phone / Let's pretend that we're together, all alone"—so sensuously it almost sounds like an invitation to phone sex. Of more immediate concern, Reeves is out to convince his lover that she needs to ditch the guy lingering in the background: her husband, most likely, since Reeves is the one reduced to calling from a bar. Even from across town, though, Reeves's accomplices in seduction—particularly the vibraphone of Marvin Hughes and the buttery bottom of Bob Moore's electric bass—make his plea irresistible. Not that Reeves needs the help; for once, his dream-deep voice is the perfect vehicle for the song. When he asks his lover to make up her mind and choose already, he delivers his lines with the smooth air of someone who sounds pretty damn confident he'll get the answer he wants.—dc

229

The Coo-Coo Bird, Clarence Ashley
No producer credited; Traditional
Columbia 15489   1929   Pre-chart

Clarence Ashley claimed he learned this deceptively simple ditty as a boy growing up in East Tennessee. According to historian

Charles Wolfe, Ashley, a veteran of medicine-shows and an Uncle Dave Macon disciple, called it a "lassy-makin' tune," one of several commonly known numbers he picked up during molasses-making time back home. The seemingly

unrelated verses he quilts together here had likely been in circulation for centuries, the cuckoo being a harbinger of spring in the English ballads in which the image first gained common currency. Nevertheless, there's a fixity of resolve, a vested interest and unfolding drama, in Ashley's piercing vocals and banjo runs that suggest there's more of a narrative thread to these verses than there first might appear. Critic Greil Marcus hears something akin to the "comic worry" of the American people, the discomfort of displaced folk who, despite their status as a commonwealth, remain strangers in a strange land. Citing the female cuckoo's imperialistic habit of laying its eggs in the nests of others—and of uprooting them in the process—Marcus sees Ashley's cuckoo "as the specter of the alienation of each from all."

It's an inspired reading of an otherwise unassuming folk song, but there's at least one more story here, a grittier tale rooted in the other image for which the cuckoo has long been a symbol—the cuckold. Ashley seems to be more than just acquainted with this "pretty bird [who] wobbles as she flies." The way he changes the word "warbles," as it appears in older versions of the song, to "wobbles" conveys a knowing sensuality; it suggests he's been intimate with the woman. So does the way he divulges how she "never says coo-coo / Till the fourth day [of] July," an allusion perhaps to how she doesn't holler or moan during sex till she sees fireworks—that is, till she reaches orgasm. Trouble is, there's no lovemaking here—at least not for Clarence, who suspects his bird is cuckolding him and is out to even the score. From the resolve with which he hums "mm, mm, mm" to the intractable gait of his "sawmill" banjo (Ashley's term for the mix of what sound like Asian and blues tonalities in his playing), no doubt he'll go to any lengths to catch her in the act. He'd even, as he sings in the first verse, build a cabin on a mountain top to spy "Willie" (or Jody, or whatever his cuckoo's back-door man calls himself) on his way to or from their furtive couplings. When he vows "I'll beat you next game," it's no idle boast about his cunning at the card table. It's a threat.—bfw

230

Poison Love, Johnnie & Jack
and their Tennessee Mountain Boys
Produced by Steve Sholes; Written by Mrs. Elmer Laird
RCA Victor 48-0377   1951   #4 country

Johnnie & Jack were just another duo working in the tradition of brother acts like the Delmores and the Monroes when they went into the studio to cut "Poison Love." They were fairly popular throughout the south during the forties; besides hosting their own radio shows, they cut a number of sides for the King, Apollo, and RCA labels. But apart from Jack Anglin's thrilling high tenor, nothing distinguished them from the brother teams that preceded them. At least not until bass fiddle player Ernie Newton suggested they try something different at the "Poison Love" session. Strapping some maracas around his wrist, Newton asked if either Johnnie (Wright) or Jack could play a calypso rhythm on the guitar. Neither man was up to the task, but jack-of-all-trades Eddie Hill stepped in and hammered out something along the lines of what Newton was after. The exotic, rhythmically charged attack that resulted catapulted Johnnie & Jack into the Top Five, transforming the lines, "And I know my life will never be the same," into a self-fulfilling prophecy. "Poison Love" earned the journeyman duo an invitation to join the Grand Ole Opry. It also gave them a signature sound that predated Hank Snow's "Rhumba Boogie" and the Latin-inflected records Jerry Leiber and Mike Stoller would soon be producing for doo-wop groups like the Coasters and the Drifters.—bfw

231

You Ain't Woman Enough, Loretta Lynn
Produced by Owen Bradley; Written by Loretta Lynn
Decca 31966   1966   #2 country

"You ain't woman enough to take my man," Loretta Lynn declares, and you can easily picture her rearing back, getting ready to send her rival straight to "Fist City." Of course, the problems with Lynn's attitude here are obvious, starting with her premise—you can't, barring kidnapping, "take" an adult who doesn't want to be taken, so if her man's been giving her rival a second look, the person she should be singing at is her husband. "Are You Man Enough to Keep Your Woman?" How about, "These Boots Are Made for Walkin'"?

But the problem with leaving it at that is everything such a dismissal overlooks. For one thing, we need to account for the way the self-assured strut of Hal Rugg's steel seems directly at odds with the record's anxious, racing-pulse of a rhythm section. Furthermore, Loretta's pumped-up reaction to the situation ("It'll be over my dead body / so get out while you can") is all out of proportion to her professed lack of concern ("He took a second look at you / but he's in love with me"). Lynn's song captures, in other words, a real and conflicted human response; the very irrationality is part of what makes it so painful. That Lynn gets us to see the dignity in this defensive-ness, rather than reveling in her character's pain as they would on, say, *The Jerry Springer Show*, is what turns a song that's all about being pissed off at the wrong person into one about being scared your world is falling apart.

Scared to death, judging by the way Lynn's voice trembles almost out of control on that final note.—dc

232
Jolene, Dolly Parton
Produced by Bob Ferguson; Written by Dolly Parton
RCA Victor 0145   1973   #1 country (1 week); #60 pop

A woman with whom Dolly can't compete in the beauty depart-ment? Fat chance, unless, of course, the temptress who's out to take her man is some sort of mythical creature or goddess. The image Dolly paints of Jolene—a smile like a breath of spring, a voice that's soft as summer rain—certainly suggests as much. So does the music here, particularly the way that gusting steel and those howling harmonies conjure an apparition out of *Wuthering Heights* or, closer to home, some mountain hollow. Dolly's lover may have muttered Jolene's name in his sleep, but she just can't be real. No natural woman could strike fear in another's heart this way, much less in the breast of a beauty like Dolly.

But unattainable illusions could. Those frantic guitar rhythms and the panic in Dolly's dread-filled soprano suggest that what's haunting her isn't so much a flesh-and-blood rival as her own fear of measuring up to the idealized specter that visits her lover in dreams.—bfw

233
Jole Blon, Harry Choates
No producer credited; Written by Amadie Breaux
Gold Star 1314   1946   #4 country

Harry Choates wasn't the first fiddle player to mingle hillbilly styles and western swing with Cajun music; that laurel goes to his mentor and former boss, Leo Soileau. But with his flamboyant, Hank Williams–like persona and his flair with the fiddle, Choates flashed the sort of star power that enabled him to lift Soileau's Cajun-country hybrid out of the bayous and piney woods of Louisiana and into the national spotlight.

"Jole Blon," the 1947 hit with which Choates made his mark, had been around for years; accordionist Amadie Breaux was the first to record it, under the title "Ma Blonde est Partie," in 1928. Breaux's version, as well as countless others that soon rang out from the region's porches and beer halls, featured fiddle and accordion as lead instru-ments, as was the practice among Cajun dance bands at the time. Choates's recording, however, dispensed with the accordion and, with it, some of the song's regional flavor. His record could have passed for the latest release by most hillbilly or western swing bands, which is likely why it became a coast-to-coast hit.

Eager to cash in, country stars Moon Mullican, Roy Acuff, and Red Foley rushed to release covers of "Jole Blon," but none matched the heady splendor of Choates's original. With Joe Manuel's chopping banjo rhythms and B. D. Williams's high-stepping bass spurring him on, Choates woos the strings with his bow, sliding in and out of notes as if he's positively drunk with love. His garbled patois may not be comprehensible to other than Cajun or Creole ears, but the lusty exuberance in his voice makes it plain that the pretty blonde in question is worth shouting about.

Choates, who'd been deep into the bottle since his early teens, never managed to parlay his breakout success with "Jole Blon" into greater fame before his death under mysterious alcohol-related circumstances in a jail cell in Austin, Texas, in 1951. But several of his counterparts did, notably fiddler Doug Kershaw and singer Jimmy C. Newman, both of whom went on to become stars on the Grand Ole Opry. (Kershaw would later introduce Cajun music to rock audiences.) The biggest winner of all, though, was "Jole Blon" itself. The song soon emerged as the equivalent of the Cajun national anthem, one that's a whole lot easier to dance or hum along to than, say, "The Star-Spangled Banner" or "La Marseillaise."—bfw

234
Dixie Fried, Carl Perkins
Produced by Sam Phillips;
Written by Carl Perkins and Curly Griffin
Sun 249   1956   #10 country

Fellow name of Dan hits a roadhouse just before dawn, ready to drink, fight, and rave on till he gets good and Dixie fried. First off, he pulls a quart bottle from his hip pocket, and when he's finished that, he pulls a razor ("but he wasn't shavin'). Everyone knows enough to step away. Pretty soon, the cops come busting in to haul Dan off, but not before he shows the crowd "that he wasn't scared of the law." Carl Perkins tells this story over a hard rockabilly beat, pausing just twice to toss off guitar solos that burn like whiskey going down, and cut clean and deep, just like that razor. "Get fried!" he barks. It sounds like he already is.

Many Americans, up north and down south too, would likely have responded to a story like this with a slur: poor white trash. Or with a phrase that comes down to the same thing: no better than niggers. Such racist epithets were, no doubt, all too familiar to a poor, white southerner like Perkins. As a child, Perkins had worked shoulder to shoulder with black sharecroppers in Tennessee cotton fields. One of those workers, John Westbrook, taught Perkins to play guitar.

No wonder then that, by the end of "Dixie Fried," Perkins sounds as crazed and tetchy and cocksure as if he were Dan himself. He knew firsthand what it was to be poor and despised. He understood what it felt like to spend all week bent over or on your knees in someone else's field and to know each new week promised more of the same for at least as long as your back and knees held out. Where Perkins grew up, getting shit-faced wasn't

a proof of your immaturity. It was a way to numb the pain and feel more alive. A man with a family to feed can't tell his boss to take his damn job and shove it, so it helps at least to shove something.

"Dixie Fried," like all the best rockabilly, rocks the twang. But what makes it a truly great record is how it identifies with its characters. Perkins includes himself among the folks who are impressed when Dan resists arrest and who continue raving after Dan's locked up. Perkins allies himself completely with this grim weekend ritual—its absurdity, its danger, and its allure. That's why, even today, when deriding the poor remains in fashion, "Dixie Fried" can amaze for its absolute lack of condescension toward "white trash" lives.

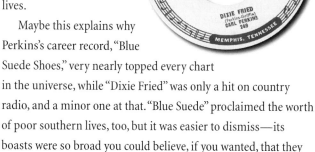

Maybe this explains why Perkins's career record, "Blue Suede Shoes," very nearly topped every chart in the universe, while "Dixie Fried" was only a hit on country radio, and a minor one at that. "Blue Suede" proclaimed the worth of poor southern lives, too, but it was easier to dismiss—its boasts were so broad you could believe, if you wanted, that they were played strictly for laughs. "Dixie Fried" wasn't playing.—dc

235
Fais Pas Ca, Hackberry Ramblers
Produced by Eli Oberstein; Traditional
Bluebird 2040   1938   Pre-chart

236
One Step Des Chameaux,
Dennis McGee & Amede Ardoin
No producer credited; Traditional
Brunswick 559   1930   Pre-chart

Cajun music conveys a mixture of melancholy and high spirits born of the persecution and resiliency of the Acadian people. Forced by the British to flee their homes in Nova Scotia during the mid-1700s, many Acadians migrated to French-speaking Louisiana, where they absorbed the cultures of, and intermarried with, people of Spanish, African, and American-Indian descent. Inevitably, the music they made expressed the commingled sense of possibility and loss that grew out of their experience of uprooting and resettlement.

Translated back into English, the lyrics of "Fais Pas Ca," a French-language version of the blues standard "Trouble in Mind," epitomize this outlook: "Trouble in mind, I'm blue / But I won't be blue always / The sun's gonna shine in my back door someday." Yet even more than what "Fais Pas Ca" says is how the Hackberry Ramblers, one of the earliest and most durable Cajun stringbands, play it. The way Luderin Darbone's lilting fiddle "sings" the opening lines of the record is practically all we need to hear. Witness how, with one downward slide of his bow, he emits a wincing cry at just the point in the melody where he would have sung "I'm blue." Or how, a few bars later, the grace notes he coaxes from his strings leap for joy precisely when he would have been claiming that the sun was gonna shine in his back door someday. Mandolinist Edwin Duhon engages in a knowing call-and-response with Darbone throughout, his bittersweet fills the musical equivalent of shout-outs like "Sing the blues" and "I hear you, brother."

"One Step des Chameaux," a collaboration between Amede Ardoin, a black Creole accordionist, and Dennis McGee, a white Cajun fiddler, achieves much the same emotional effect. Driven by McGee's fierce bow strokes on the offbeats, Ardoin's heavily syncopated chording is ripe for the dance floor, yet the minor key he's playing in also betrays a deep sadness. A similar tension pervades Ardoin's feral vocals; without understanding Creole, it's impossible to know whether he's howling in agony, ecstasy, or both.

Each of these records sheds light on the complex Acadian temperament and also on the cultural cross-pollination that has shaped Cajun life over the past 200 years. "Fais Pas Ca" grew out of the convergence of Acadian and African American traditions, while "One Step" folds Ardoin's Creole heritage into the mix. The latter is one of the dozen or so sides Ardoin and McGee, who met while sharecropping, cut from 1929 to 1934; their recordings are now considered to have given birth to modern Cajun music, as well as to Zydeco, the music of the region's black Creole population. It's easy to see why their records gained this reputation. As "One Step" attests, Ardoin and McGee played with a singular intimacy, testifying to the possibility not just of musical harmony but of a deeper racial accord, one that transcended the shame of segregation.—bfw

237

Midnight Special, Lead Belly

No producer credited;
Written by Huddie Ledbetter, John Lomax, and Alan Lomax
RCA Victor 27266   1940   Pre-chart

Critics argue about whether Huddie Ledbetter, a.k.a. Lead Belly, should be considered a blues or a folk singer. The truth is he was both and a lot more besides. He sang the blues with Blind Lemon Jefferson on the street corners and in the brothels of Dallas's barrelhouse district during the years immediately following World War I. After folklorist John Lomax "discovered" him in the early thirties, he reemerged, a twelve-string guitar in hand, as something of a folk singer—a darling of the Old Left and, later, of insurgent folk revivalists like the Almanac Singers and the Weavers. Ultimately, however, Lead Belly's music can't be confined to a specific genre or genres. Its influence extends to country (Johnny Cash), garage pop (Creedence Clearwater Revival), and grunge (Nirvana). No less than that of his friend and sometime companion Woody Guthrie, Lead Belly's legacy stands as an example of Americana at its unbounded best.

"Midnight Special" speaks to confinement of a different sort. Written while he was doing time at Sugarland Prison Farm in Fort Bend County, Texas, during the 1920s, the record finds Lead Belly playing the part of the worried man. No longer shackled on the banks of the river, he's behind bars dreaming of his freedom, when yonder comes his Rosie with a piece of paper, a request for his pardon, in hand. "I'm goin' and askin' the governor / He's turnin' loose my man," Lead Belly hears her cry only to have the prison bell jar him from his reverie as he wakes to find himself, still locked up, staring down at a plate of slop. Things go from bad to worse as he gets the very real news that his wife is dead. All he can do now, it seems, is pray for the chance to hear the whistle and see the lights of the midnight train as it speeds past the prison each night, a reminder, as John Rumble writes, "of the freedom that lay beyond [his] reach."

That light finally shone on Lead Belly in 1932; he was serving another sentence, this one at the Louisiana State Farm in Angola, when John Lomax, there to do some field recording, heard him sing. Knocked out by the power of his voice, Lomax helped secure Lead Belly a pardon and whisked him away to New York, where his trumpet-like cry of "Let the midnight special, shine a light on me" became a beacon of freedom for the thousands who heard it. The song also went on to achieve immortality, over the years appearing on dozens of country, folk, and rock albums, including those by everyone from the Delmore Brothers and Odetta to Andy Griffith and CCR.—bfw

238
Mystery Train, Elvis Presley
Produced by Sam Phillips; Written by Junior Parker
Sun 223   1955   #11 country

Musicologists can cite antecedents for Elvis's version of "Mystery Train" till the milk cows come home, but this, the King's last single for Sun, is as sui generis as any record he ever made.

The main source for R&B singer Junior Parker's 1953 "original" for Sun was the Carter Family's "Worried Man Blues," a recording of an old folk song that finds sisters Sara and Maybelle stolidly bemoaning the "long, black train" that carried their baby from town. Parker tacks a new ending onto the tale—those sixteen coaches bring his lover home, but from his record's funereal, sax- and guitar-driven arrangement, it's clear she's coming back in a box.

Elvis wants no part of either the Carters' surrender or Parker's blues, setting his sights instead on an outcome—a future—of his own making. "Train, train, comin' rou-ound the be-end / Well it took my baby, but it never will again / No, not again," he vows as the chugging rhythms laid down by guitarist Scotty Moore, drummer Johnny Bernero, and bassist Bill Black send him barreling headlong down the track. Nothing—not God, not fate, not even the laws of physics—is going to keep Elvis from bringing his baby back. If he can't outrun her

train, you get the sense he'll jump on board, slam on its brakes, jump out, and, like the second coming of John Henry, pull up the track, snapping it like a ribbon until it heaves her into his outstretched arms.

"Mystery Train" was like no hillbilly record before it (and maybe since). More than just some torqued-up, phantom train, Scotty Moore's lashing guitar, Elvis's Olympian defiance, and that boundless Sun echo must have sounded like a whole new set of tracks.—bfw

239
Little Sister, Elvis Presley
Produced by Steve Sholes;
Written by Doc Pomus and Mort Shuman
RCA Victor 47-7908   1961   #5 pop

Two minutes and thirty-two seconds of A-Team studio perfection. Drummer Buddy Harman, working with D. J. Fontana, slams home a beat so potent that the record's mid-tempo pace feels positively breakneck. The Jordanaires provide low, low harmonies. Hank Garland throws down some of the most memorable electric guitar ever caught on tape; his blue and funky licks snarl through the recording with such immediacy you'd almost swear you could reach out and touch them. Meanwhile, Bob Moore's bass notes, tic-tacked up by Scotty Moore on the acoustic guitar, pop out of the speakers with such force you're afraid they might reach out and touch *you*. And don't forget to thank engineer Bill Porter. With his hands on the knobs, every musician's note explodes from the speakers clear, separate, alive— *present*.

The singer's pretty good too, though that doesn't matter here quite so much as it normally would. The "little sister" that Elvis is charming (though only if she'll promise that kissing and taking off doesn't run in the family) would likely follow him anywhere, even if he never opened his mouth. That's because the music here sounds every bit as playful, sexy, and dangerous as the King himself.—dc

240
Sugarfoot Rag, Red Foley
with Hank "Sugarfoot" Garland
Produced by Paul Cohen;
Written by Hank Garland and George Vaughan [Horton]
Decca 46204   1950   #4 country; #24 pop

The artist credit notwithstanding, this is a Hank Garland record all the way, a rare instance of this sideman par excellence getting his turn in the spotlight.

Garland grew up in South Carolina, where he taught himself guitar listening to the records of Mother Maybelle and Arthur "Guitar Boogie" Smith. In 1946, when he was just sixteen, he landed a featured spot in Opry star Paul Howard's band. In Nashville for good, Hank quickly gained a reputation as a hotshot hired gun. He graduated from playing in Howard's Arkansas Cotton Pickers to touring with Eddy Arnold and Cowboy Copas. Even off the road, he was always playing his guitar. If he wasn't wood shedding with his favorite Charlie Christian

and Django Reinhardt records, joining in all-night jam sessions with fellow jazz hounds like drummer Buddy Harman and sax man Boots Randolph, or hanging out in Nashville's R&B clubs, he was in a recording studio. Occasionally he worked on his own releases (including a couple of jazz LPs), but mostly he found himself in the role of supporting musician. Until a 1963 auto accident forced him into early retirement, Garland was among the most sought-after session guitarists in Music City, contributing to Nashville Sound–era hits by everyone from Arnold, Copas, and Lefty Frizzell through Patsy Cline, Don Gibson, and Jim Reeves to Roy Orbison, the Everly Brothers, and Elvis Presley.

Garland earned himself a nickname with "Sugarfoot Rag," a guitar workout that's long since earned a spot in the country-picking pantheon alongside Maybelle's "Wildwood Flower." Basing its melody on a fiddle tune called "Pretty Little Widow," Garland originally conceived the number as a good finger exercise, but soon he'd cut the song for release. His solo version went nowhere, but when A&R man Paul Cohen had words added to Garland's instrumental, gave it to Red Foley to sing, and placed it on the flipside of "Chattanoogie Shoe Shine Boy," the number

became a country crossover hit. Ostensibly Foley's cutting a rug here because he's just won big at the track, but the words hardly matter with that rapid-fire electric guitar laying down big, twangy licks that sound every bit as fierce as they do light-hearted. "Dig a little jig, then a zig and a zag," Foley sings, and the zag and the zig he's digging belong to none other than Hank Garland picking out the "Sugarfoot Rag."—dc

241
Hillbilly Fever, "Little" Jimmy Dickens
Produced by Don Law; Written by Vaughn Horton
Columbia 20677   1950   #3 country

"Sweet Soul Music" hillbilly-style, and the tribute could hardly have been more timely. The country recording industry was a good quarter-century old and had recently survived wartime shortages of labor and shellac; now, "with a new honky-tonkin' sound," fiddles and guitars again blared from jukeboxes. And not just in the south or Texas either. Soldiers who lived outside the twang belt got bit by the bug while serving overseas; buoyed by the goodwill of ambassador Bing and the Hollywood "cowboys," along with the national syndication of the Grand Ole Opry, country records were crossing over to the pop charts. Hillbilly fever was contagious all right, and here Little Jimmy and his band call the roll of several of the era's biggest hits. "Slippin' Around," "Lovesick Blues," "Sugarfoot Rag," "Chattanoogie Shoe Shine Boy" all get their due, with Red Taylor even chiming in with the "Sugarfoot" fiddle break and someone in the studio snapping the hell out of that shine boy's towel. From the bugged-out guitars of Grady Martin and Jabbo Arrington to Jimmy proving he's more than just little and loud, the record couldn't be more infectious. Hell, it *would* have started an epidemic if that mountain fever hadn't already spread so far and wide.—bfw

242
Midnight, Red Foley
Produced by Paul Cohen;
Written by Boudleaux Bryant and Chet Atkins
Decca 28420   1952   #1 country (1 week)

From the time Grady Martin was fifteen years old—when, in 1944, he convinced his folks to let him leave the family's East Tennessee farm to play country music in Nashville—he was a professional musician. Initially, he was a fiddler for Big Jeff & His Radio Players. Quickly, though, he made a name for himself as a hot young guitarist, first as one-half of the twin-guitar attack behind Opry western swinger Paul Howard and then, as the fifties dawned, as lead guitarist for Little Jimmy Dickens's touring band, the Country Boys. When Martin died at age seventy-two, he left behind an unrivaled legacy as one of the most recorded musicians in history, and as flat-out one of the best guitarists ever to strap on a six-string.

It was Martin's work as one of Nashville's A-Team of studio musicians in the fifties, sixties, and early seventies that made him a legend—at least among the singers, songwriters, and producers he helped make famous as picker and session leader. Martin provided the unforgettable

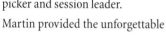

licks for records such as Dickens's "Hillbilly Fever," Red Foley's "Chattanoogie Shoe Shine Boy," Johnny Horton's "Honky Tonk Man," Ronnie Self's "Big Fool," Lefty Frizzell's "Saginaw, Michigan," Jeanne Pruett's "Satin Sheets," and Ray Price's "For the Good Times," among countless others. He cut some sides of his own too, fronting a breezy jazz combo called Grady Martin & the Slew Foot Five that once backed Bing Crosby.

That none of the records above really sound like one another—and that they each sound unmistakably country—is all the evidence you need to conclude that, besides being prolific, Grady Martin was among the most important and innovative musicians in country music history. When we say today that some guitar part or other sounds "country," we could just as well say that it sounds like something borrowed from Grady Martin.

Of course, Martin borrowed techniques and licks himself. Like A-Teammate Hank Garland, Martin's playing was strongly influenced by jazz and all kinds of blues. Both sides of that equation are evident on Red Foley's "Midnight," where Martin establishes the record's dark mood with nothing more than a disarmingly dissonant strum of his electric guitar. Walking the floor in the wee, small hours of the morning, Foley is crying and moaning over the baby he misses, but he doesn't sound as miserable as Martin's solo, which alternates between stark, jazzy little figures and blues so deep and urban you've got to figure Martin had a few Chess Records in his collection. Thanks to Grady, it's enough nowadays just to say it sounds country.—dc

243
The Shot Gun Boogie, Tennessee Ernie Ford
Produced by Lee Gillette; Written by T. E. Ford
Capitol F1295   1950   #1 country (14 weeks); #14 pop

After "Sixteen Tons" turned Tennessee Ernie Ford into a household name, it wasn't long before the ol' pea picker took up permanent residence in the middle of the road. Before that, though, Ford made his name with some of the fleetest country boogies ever put to tape. "Shot Gun Boogie" was the best of an explosive bunch, custom made for Ernie Ford's greatest gifts—a rib-splitting, disarmingly down-home persona deployed via phrasing that's all about nailing down that beat. Then again, *Henry* Ford could swing with this group behind him: pianist Billy Liebert having fun with "Boogie Woogie Bugle Boy" on the first solo; Speedy West cracking up on the pedal steel on the second; the whole thing goosed by guitarist Jimmy Bryant and jazz drummer Roy Harte, who makes the record recoil every time Ernie gets off another blast. Damn but this dog hunts!—dc

244
Roly Poly, Bob Wills & His Texas Playboys
Produced by Art Satherley; Written by Fred Rose
Columbia 36966   1946   #3 country

In this Fred Rose–penned novelty, "Daddy's little fatty" spends his days hustling all over town on chores for his old man. In the process, he works up a voracious appetite, eating biscuits, whole pies, "bread and jelly twenty times a day"—and those are just the snacks to keep him going till supper. But don't get too sidetracked by all the jokes about youthful corpulence. Better just to dance your ass off.

This version of Bob Wills's Texas Playboys features a somewhat stripped-down lineup, thanks in part to World War II and the draft, but even so, the band's firing on all cylinders. They perform "Roly Poly" with an intensity and abandon that anticipates rock & roll, but this baby's brilliance has nothing to do with its predictive qualities. Twin guitars, skipping into place one at a time, kick it off as the rhythm section fans a groove hot enough to leave every two-stepper west of the Mississippi dripping with sweat. Steel, fiddle, and piano trade good-natured solos punctuated by shots in the arm and slaps on the back. The swinging blasts of trumpeter Alex Brashear hit you like bellows of "Hey, how's about one more round of drinks anyway?"

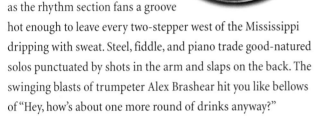

"Bet he's gonna be a man someday," beams lead singer Tommy Duncan. Someday? "Roly Poly" is made *by* adults *for* adults. Hell, after a week busting tail in a Texas oil field or some California defense plant, even grown-ups need to run and play.—dc

245

Honky Tonkin', Maddox Brothers & Rose
Produced by unknown; Written by Hank Williams
Four Star 1238   1949   Did not chart

The Maddox family—two parents, four brothers, and sister Rose—fled Depression-scarred Alabama for California at a time when such migration was still so rare that they actually made the papers ("Family Roams U.S. for Work") when they hopped off a freight at the Oakland rail yards in 1933. The promised land that awaited them there wasn't promising at all, at least not at first. The family picked fruit, even panned for gold, but times were so hard that they briefly had to send Rose to stay with friends— "They couldn't afford to feed me," she later told writer Nicholas Davidoff. By 1937 the family was back together, picking cotton, when Fred Maddox suggested to his brothers that they quit the fields and play music for a living. Fred smooth-talked a Modesto furniture dealer into sponsoring a radio show for the aspiring

group—but only if they got themselves a girl singer. They enlisted their little sister, a mere eleven years old, and the Maddox Brothers & Rose were off and running.

They were the perfect band for their time and place. In the decade since the family's arrival in the state, the Depression and the Dust Bowl had combined with California's growing agriculture and defense industries to send southerners west in unprecedented numbers. The Maddox Brothers & Rose's music was tailor-made for this milieu. Their rip-snortin' racket could slice through the din of the most packed honky-tonk or dance hall, and their eclectic, fun-loving sets (not to mention their dazzling western stage dress) were just the thing for jump-starting hearts and minds numbed by repetitive hours in field and factory. Following World War II, the group's rocket-powered rhythms and electric guitar breaks stood out as state-of-the art hillbilly boogie—and as a foreshadowing of the rockabilly and Bakersfield sounds to come.

At the center of it all was Rose, whose voice Hank Williams once said could sound "like an angel that's pure as the drifted snow" one moment and "a gal that's straight out of a cat house" the next. Regarding that last descriptor, Williams was specifically referring to Rose's work on his own "Honky Tonkin'," where "The Sweetheart of Hillbilly Swing" and her rowdy siblings transform Hank's sly come-on into an entire Saturday night's worth of hot times. The propositions and the cutting up, the dancing, drinking, and dirty jokes—they're all here, crammed into one whirlwind single. Rose graces the end of the song with her flirty, lighthearted giggle, but the whole record sounds like a laughing, boisterous crowd: the stomping rhythm section of Henry and Fred Maddox, brother Don's wild fiddle, boot-scooting solos from hired hands Jimmy Winkle on lead guitar and Brad Duncan on steel. Sister Rose brays through each riotous chorus like "a honky tonkin' donkey." She's bucking in her stall, ready to go, ready for *anything*, and all her brothers can do is race along behind as she leads the Maddox clan through another wild weekend.—dc

246

Let's Have a Party, Wanda Jackson
Produced by Ken Nelson; Written by Jessie Mae Robinson
Capitol 4397   1960   #37 pop

Loads of singers rave about how Elvis shaped their music, but few can back up the claim like Wanda Jackson. Bit by the singing bug early (she grew up listening to her father's hillbilly band), Jackson had her own radio show on Oklahoma City's KPLR while barely in her teens. At age seventeen she scored a Top Ten country hit—a duet with Billy Gray, an alum of Hank Thompson's Brazos Valley Boys. But it wasn't until Wanda signed a solo deal with Capitol in 1955 and started touring with—and dating—the King, who urged her to make the shift to rock & roll, that she really started shaking things up.

Spurred on by the white-hot picking of Joe Maphis and Speedy West, Wanda's feral growling on early rockabilly singles like "I Gotta Know" and "Honey Bop" proved wilder than anything her female counterparts, and most of the men, were doing at the time. In 1957 she went head-to-head with her mentor and ex-boyfriend, taking "Let's Have a Party" (a song Elvis had cut earlier in the year for the movie *Loving You*) over the top and making it her own. "I never kissed a bear / I never kissed a goose / But I can shake a chicken in the middle of the room / Let's have a party," Wanda crows, whooping and ripping it up like a cross between Little Richard and proto-rockabilly Rose Maddox. Jackson's vocal is pure attitude, exactly the kind of defiant, sexually charged boast that most of the era's parents dreaded their kids would hear, especially with those lines about sending someone to the store conjuring images of midnight beer runs. But the song's words hardly mattered; Vernon Sandusky's turbo-charged guitar, Big Al Downing's hammering piano, and the pile-driving rhythm section shouted that the kids were doing a brand new boogie.

Even so, neither "Let's Have a Party," nor any of Jackson's other rock & roll hits, fared as well as the records she made upon returning to the country fold after the rockabilly well dried up in the early sixties. It's hard, at this late date, to say why that was the case, but doubtless it had something to do with the fact that Wanda's unhinged records were coming from a woman. It was enough that the likes of Carl Perkins, Gene Vincent, and Elvis were detonating bombs this raw, sexy, and intense. The idea of a female Elvis must have been too much.—bfw

247

White Lightning, George Jones
Produced by Harold "Pappy" Daily; Written by J. P. Richardson
Mercury 71406   1959   #1 country (5 weeks); #73 pop

George Jones is rightly revered as country music's master of the sad ballad. But he possesses an equal gift for the most madcap tongue twisters imaginable. Whirlwind numbers like "The Race Is On," "I'm a People," "Nothing Ever Hurt Me (Half as Bad as Losing You)," and a dozen more besides would be amusing, albeit slight, romps if performed by almost any other singer. When Jones throws himself into them with headlong conviction, the term "novelty" doesn't begin to do them justice.

"White Lightning," for example, is a hilarious celebration about the innervating joys of a moonshine buzz—"Mighty, mighty pleasin' / Pappy's corn squeezin'," Jones grimaces, even as he smacks his lips. Beyond that, the song's about how those jugs of homemade mountain dew are filled with rural pride and poor-white ingenuity. Near the end, a city slicker says "I'm tough / I think I want to taste that powerful stuff," then collapses moaning to the floor. Throughout Jones taunts "The G-Men, T-Men, Revenooers too," as they search unsuccessfully for his old man's still. Perhaps because he was toasted himself when he recorded "White Lightning" (that's why he stumbles over "suh-slug," legend has it), or perhaps because he'd grown up around the stuff, Jones sings the Big Bopper's song as if it presented nothing more than the thirst-quenching facts of the matter. He exploits each punch line to its fullest even though the only time he plays it for laughs is at the end of each chorus, when he sputters and shudders through the title phrase.

Born during the Depression in the wild East Texas region known as Big Thicket (home to dense forests, dismal poverty, and his father's drinking problem), George Jones grew up listening to the Opry and singing at Pentecostal churches. When the Joneses moved to the bustling port city of Beaumont, young George began busking for spare change on street corners with his "Gene Autry" guitar. Running away at the age of fourteen, he eventually hooked up with husband-and-wife country duo Eddie & Pearl. It was with them, in the blood-bucket joints of East Texas, that he graduated from Acuff and Monroe to Hank Williams, and from beer to the hard stuff.

That background is about as country as it gets, and it helps explain how Jones, even as late as 1959, could make a record as hillbilly twangy as "White Lightning." Compared to many Nashville Sound hits of the era, Jones's record really does sound like it's from "way back in the hills." It also sounds like rockabilly, which is what happens when hardcore country roots like Jones's get spiked with rhythm and blues. If the nearest big town to where Jones grew up had been Memphis (as it was for Carl Perkins and Johnny Cash) instead of Beaumont, then he might have come by this transition more naturally than he did on the cartoonish rockabilly sides he'd once recorded as "Thumper" Jones.

Here, though, Jones just rears back and sings it like he knows it, and the session team races along with him like a ridge runner with the law in hot pursuit. Buddy Killen slaps his bass like he's auditioning for the Blue Caps; Pig Robbins breaks free for a piano solo that's on intimate terms with Chuck Berry's main man, Johnnie Johnson; and Floyd Jenkins sends his electric guitar out for another jug, by way of Memphis. Added up, it's Jones's novelty masterpiece, the most wildly hillbilly record he ever made, and the most rockin'. "White Lightning," in every sense of the phrase.—dc

248
A Six Pack to Go, Hank Thompson & His Brazos Valley Boys
Produced by Ken Nelson;
Written by Hank Thompson, Dick Hart, and Johnny Lowe
Capitol 4334   960   #10 country

Hank Thompson's specialty was the "heart" song. Literally. In many of his quirky hits, Hank stands in the lobby of his lover's heart, waiting futilely for her to buzz him in; or his tears have erased "I love you" from the blackboard of his heart; or he has a Humpty-Dumpty heart that no one can put together again. One thing that saves these numbers from sheer preposterousness is Thompson's band. Among the finest country outfits ever, the Brazos Valley Boys blasted a tight, hard-driving dance beat that sounded like they only dimly recalled the differences between honky-tonk and western swing. The other thing Thompson had going for him was his own agreeable, ordinary-guy persona: his steady baritone sounds a lot like an eager Ernest Tubb, only after vocal cord surgery and diction lessons. Thompson and his Boys can make even the most bizarre conceit sound perfectly reasonable, or at least like nearly reasonable drunk talk rather than full-fledged foolishness.

Nothing foolish about "A Six Pack to Go." After drinking all day, Thompson's fixing to call it a night, but not before he asks the bartender for "one more round, and a six-pack to go." The former is to drown his anxiety over being so broke he can't even pay his rent. As Thompson nurses his last cold one, the Brazos Valley Boys make sure it goes down smooth, especially thanks to the easy electric-guitar strut of Thompson studio staple, Merle Travis. Still, Thompson's headaches ain't going anywhere—he's got debts that Curly Lewis's dizzy fiddle, producer Ken Nelson's pounding echo at the chorus, and drummer Billy Stewart's merciless thwack make sure he won't forget. That's why he needs a six to go—as a hair-of-the-dog insurance policy against the hangover to come.—dc

249
If We Make It through December, Merle Haggard
Produced by Ken Nelson; Written by Merle Haggard
Capitol 3746   1973   #1 country (4 weeks); #28 pop

Merle Haggard has always claimed that "Okie from Muskogee" started out as a spoof of small-town provincialism. If you want to know the kind of life experiences that led many working-class Americans to hear a proud anthem in that joke (and one in which they were the punch line, no less), listen to "Hungry Eyes." But if you want a clear-eyed picture of the fear at the core of those experiences, check out "If We Make It Through December."

Ostensibly a holiday song, "If We Make It through December" presents a Christmas of a particularly blue variety. "Got laid off down at the factory," Haggard informs us, and his "little girl don't understand why Daddy can't afford no Christmas cheer." Crafting lyrics as unadorned and poetic as everyday speech, and deploying a melodic gift equal to George Gershwin's or Paul McCartney's, Haggard conveys an anxiety that remains a year-round by-product of the U.S. economy—one that's especially unbearable amid the materialistic glitter of what's supposed to be "the happy time of year."

From his window, Haggard watches the snow pile up on an early seventies America where everything that used to seem so certain has lately been thrown up for grabs. He looks at his daughter and tries to imagine a better life. But the truth is he's not even sure he'll make it through the month. He shivers to his very bones, and it ain't because of the temperature.—dc

250

Blue Christmas, Ernest Tubb

Produced by Paul Cohen;
Written by Billy Hayes and Jay Johnson
Decca 46186   1949   #1 country (1 week); #23 pop

For almost as long as there have been records, there have been Christmas records; the first is believed to be a barbershop version of "Silent Night" recorded by the Hayden Quartet in 1902. Christmas releases didn't become a holiday tradition in their own right, though, until the Second World War, when Bing Crosby forever established the pop potential of Yuletide recordings with his version of Irving Berlin's "White Christmas." It topped both the pop and R&B charts in 1942, then repeated the feat on the pop side in 1945 and 1946. In fact, Crosby's "White Christmas" returned to the pop Top Ten every holiday season for the rest of the decade and continued to make appearances on the chart (albeit it at increasingly lower levels) until 1962. With commercial appeal that broad and enduring, it was hardly surprising that other artists would follow Crosby's lead—and it was all but

inevitable that a longtime Crosby acolyte like Gene Autry would be one of them. Certainly, it was the cowboy singer's continued attention to the Crosby model that encouraged Autry to release "Here Comes Santa Claus" in 1947, followed by "Rudolph, the Red-Nosed Reindeer" in 1949. Each made

the country Top Ten, each was a major pop hit, and each returned to both the pop and country charts the winter following its initial release.

Unlike "White Christmas," though, Autry's Christmas hits were playful novelties, aimed at children of all ages rather than adults longing for reunited families during wartime. In the world of country music, it would be left to Ernest Tubb and his recording of "Blue Christmas" to capitalize on the tension that had made "White Christmas" hit home—the often gaping divide between the Christmases we wish for and the ones we get. And since the holiday season merely intensifies desires we feel all year, we could just as easily replace that "Christmases we wish for" with, say, the "marriages" or "lives we wish for." Tubb's "Blue Christmas" has stood the test of time so well because, like "White Christmas," it

understands that the most powerful Christmas songs are the ones that ring true all year.

Two New York composers wrote "Blue Christmas" during the war as a take off on the ubiquitous "White Christmas" (besides Crosby's record, there had been five other versions on the pop charts during the war alone). The song wouldn't become a hit, though, until 1949 when Ernest Tubb's single topped the country charts and briefly crossed over before returning to the country Top Ten in 1950 and 1951. Over a standard shuffling Texas Troubadour beat, Owen Bradley provides a bit of organ and guitarist Billy Byrd marks his debut on an E.T. session. But it's steel man Don Davis who makes the most striking contribution, dropping notes that shimmer like the bluest snowflakes. Meanwhile, the Beasley Sisters, billed here as the Three Troubadettes, provide a convincing imitation of the Andrews Sisters—indeed, they're mimicking the impromptu pop-country approach already achieved with the real Andrews, when label mate Crosby failed to show for an L.A. session with Tubb earlier that year.

Reigning over all of this is Ernest's singular voice, which trembles and nearly chokes on the miserable irony of a Christmas spent alone: "Decorations of red on a green Christmas tree won't mean a thing dear if you're not here with me." Tubb's "Blue Christmas" hones in on the furtive longing of Berlin's classic, then strips it bare of even the dim hope that dreams might actually come true. Today, of course, "Blue Christmas" is best known as an Elvis song. But perhaps because the King at least has his own gorgeous voice to keep him warm, his record doesn't sound nearly so lonesome, let alone so emotionally country, as Tubb's. Which stands to reason. Sung any other day of the year, "Blue Christmas" is called "Walking the Floor Over You."—dc

251

Heartaches by the Number, Ray Price

Produced by Don Law; Written by Harlan Howard
Columbia 41374   1959   #2 country

Heartache number one was when Ray's lover left him. Number two was when she returned, even though she had no intention of hanging around. Number three was when she called saying she "was coming back to stay," then didn't bother to show. Added up, Ray tells us, this is "a love that I can't win." Still, "the day that I stop counting, that's the day my world will end."

In other words, the only reason Price stops the count at three is because he runs out of record.—dc

252
Sing a Sad Song, Merle Haggard
Produced by Fuzzy Owen; Written by Wynn Stewart
Tally 155   1963   #19 country

Merle Haggard is such a commanding, penetrating songwriter, and his voice seems so entwined with the melody and rhythm of his best compositions, that it's sometimes easy to forget he's also a great singer. Haggard didn't write "Sing a Sad Song," but his first hit reveals just how affecting a vocalist he was from the start. His phrasing and intonation betray infatuations with Lefty Frizzell, Jimmie Rodgers, Gene Autry, Tommy Duncan, and Wynn Stewart, but even at this early date Merle is his own man. Compared to those other singers, there is greater range here between Haggard's loudest moments and his quietest, and he can already move from caressing a line to belting it within the space of just a few syllables.

Merle's at a bar feeling sorry for himself; his woman has had the temerity to say she's "unhappy with" him. Truth be told, though, he's enjoying the chance to do a bit of wallowing. Everything around him underscores the self-pitying mood, from the loping, singing-cowboy rhythm track and Ralph Mooney's boohoo-ing steel to the way the overdubbed strings come in hard at one self-absorbed internal rhyme ("if a tear should appear / it's because she's not here") and then return just as Haggard alludes to Skeeter Davis's monster hit from the year before ("Let's pretend it's 'The End of the World' "). "Sing a Sad Song" is a smart record.

What makes it great, though, is the way its melody gives Haggard room to fly. He must have known it, too, or he would never have asked Stewart (for whom Hag was playing bass at the time) if he could record the boss's new song. "Sing me a

song of sadness, and sing it as blue as I feel," he pleads, then proceeds to fill his own request. On the word "sadness" his voice floats higher and higher until he's singing falsetto, practically yodeling. Finally, he reaches a height that renders the word inconsequential. All that matters is the beautiful, heart-wrenching sound of Merle Haggard's voice.—dc

253
Ridin' My Thumb to Mexico, Johnny Rodriguez
Produced by Jerry Kennedy;
Written by Johnny Rodriguez
Mercury 73416   1973   #1 country (2 weeks); #70 pop

Juan Raoul Davis Rodriguez was the first Latino singer to break into the country mainstream, preceding Freddy Fender onto the charts by a good two years. Rodriguez listened to all kinds of music while growing up in South Texas, but Merle Haggard was his hero, and you can certainly hear Hag's influence in Johnny's molasses baritone here. The record's lyrics, though, have more in common with the quotidian existentialism of Kris Kristofferson and Tom T. Hall (the latter discovered Rodriguez and gave him his first break). "This old highway seems so lonesome when you're going where you've been / And a lonesome song can make you cry time and time again," Johnny begins, the mix of longing and regret in his voice born of blown opportunities and commitments. Weighing heaviest on his mind, however, is the woman who walked out on him, even though he won't admit to himself that his rambling ways were what drove her off. No, he's merely "a traveling kind of man [who] just need[s] a change of atmosphere." Yeah, well, not even the record's undulating rhythms and gently sighing strings, or Harold Bradley's tender gutstring guitar, can sugarcoat the fact that Johnny's white-line fever has cost him everything. Sometimes freedom really is just another word for nothin' left to lose.—bfw

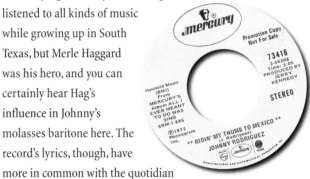

254
Mi Unico Camino, El Conjunto Bernal
No producer credited; Traditional
Ideal 1637A   1958   Did not chart

Tears in your beer music, cantina style, replete with doleful waltz-time rhythms and an accordion weeping in the background.

"Traigo una pena clavada / Como puñalada / En mi pensamiento," weep Eloy Bernal, Paulino Bernal, and Ruben Perez in the aching three-part harmonies that begin the first verse. In English these lines translate as "I have a sorrow / Nailed like a stab / In my thoughts," as grievous and vivid an image as any painted by Hank Williams. Yet the picture pales compared to the way the throbbing voices of the three men, confessing they've driven away the one they love, crescendo on the chorus, where we learn that the "only path" alluded to in the record's title is a life steeped in wine and regret.

In some respects, "Mi Unico Camino" anticipates the tortured romanticism of fellow Texans Roy Orbison and Johnny Bush, singers who, like many others, were inspired by the Tejano music of the Bernal brothers and their peers. But not all conjunto, the accordion-driven music played by working-class Chicanos who live in South Texas, is as wrenching as "Mi Unico Camino." Much of it is upbeat and full of life—the perfect tonic for dancing away yet another corrosive week spent slaving in some rich boss's field or factory.

Bands like Los Lobos and the Texas Tornadoes have given conjunto greater exposure in recent years, but the music's roots date back to the late nineteenth century when German and Czech immigrants introduced the accordion to people living along the border of Texas and Mexico. Conjunto didn't start taking on its current form, though, until after World War II, when rising stars like Tony de la Rosa and Villerio Longoria began augmenting the traditional lineup of accordion and bajo sexto (a giant twelve-string guitar) with bass, drums, and amplifiers. El Conjunto Bernal, a Kingsville, Texas–based combo led by two brothers, didn't come along until the early fifties (the height of the honky-tonk era), but the group immediately became a mainstay of the postwar Tejano music scene.

At least two things set the Bernals apart from their contemporaries: the group's close harmonies (at times reminiscent of the Louvins or the Everlys) and the dazzling finger work of accordionist Paulino Bernal. Though conversant with the styles of prewar pioneers like Narcisco Martinez and Bruno Villareal,

Bernal broadened the instrument's sonic palette with bold, jazzy chords and improvised solos, the latter very much like those that Flaco Jimenez, the then-future "King of Conjunto," would soon start playing as well. At times, Paulino's fills sound uncannily like those of a steel guitar, an effect heightened by the Bernals' penchant for rancheras ("country songs"), and something that made the group's jukebox hits the most honky-tonkin' of all the conjuntos. Those wanting to know where the border lilt from "El Paso" or any number of Buck Owens's biggest hits came from need look no further than El Conjunto Bernal.—bfw

255
Crying, Roy Orbison
Produced by Fred Foster;
Written by Roy Orbison and Joe Melson
Monument 447   1961   #2 pop

256
Before the Next Teardrop Falls, Freddy Fender
Produced by Huey P. Meaux;
Written by Vivian Keith and Ben Peters
ABC/Dot 17540   1975   #1 country (2 weeks); #1 pop (1 week)

Two Latin-inflected records that wouldn't convey half the anguish they do were it not for the spit and polish they got in the studio. Both should be required listening for anyone who thinks that raw emotion can't be served by slick arrangements and production.

During Roy Orbison's brief tenure at Sun Records (which came after he released a single back home in Texas), producer Sam Phillips tried, unsuccessfully, to squeeze him into the rockabilly shoes Elvis had left behind when he ran off to RCA. This isn't to say the sides Roy cut at Sun weren't good jukebox fodder; they were, especially "Ooby Dooby," "Rock House," and "Domino." But they didn't afford his multi-octave range a chance to soar the way it did when, hooking up with Nashville A-Teamers and producer Fred Foster during the early sixties, Roy fashioned a series of string-drenched monuments to dread. Foremost among them were "In Dreams," "It's Over," "Running Scared," "Only the Lonely," and "Crying," a record that invokes the pseudo-classical splendor of Leiber and Stoller's work with the Drifters even as it anticipates Phil Spector's Wall of Sound. It's not even a half step from "Crying" to the tortured romanticism of the Righteous Brothers' "You've Lost that Lovin' Feelin'."

Like many great ballads, "Crying" begins slowly, leaving plenty of room for the drama to ebb and flow. A light bolero beat, a plinking vibraphone, and a wash of cymbals—the last of these lapping like waves onto a beach at low tide—set a subdued tone as strings and background singers enter midway through the first verse. Orbison's baritone is a marvel of restraint, at least until the second chorus, where, bursting into an angst-ridden falsetto, he finally admits to himself how lost he is without his lover. The strings swirl and swell, and the tom-toms begin to pound as Roy, who comes utterly unglued on the final chorus, wails, "from this moment on, I'll be crying, crying,

crying, cry-ing, yeah cryyy-ing, cryyy-ing oh-oh-oh-oh-ver you." Not even his titanic outpouring of pathos can quell the sheets of strings and cries that rain down on him, pummeling him like breakers until both his voice and his throbbing heart fall silent.

Like Orbison, Freddy Fender (born Baldemar Huerta) got his start belting out blues and rockabilly in Texas, where he was known as the "Mexican Elvis." And like Roy, Fender became a star by singing lovelorn weepers that summoned or fought back great wells of emotion. But that's pretty much where the similarities between the two men and their music end. Witness Fender's breakthrough hit, "Before the Next Teardrop Falls"; heard alongside a rococo, neo-operatic ballad like "Crying," the record's impeccable adornment and Freddy's pinched vibrato sound positively minimalist.

That's just how Freddy must have felt—like he'd been reduced to nothing—while talking to the woman who'd just left him for another man. "If he brings you happiness / Then I wish you all the best," he sings, promising to be there for her if her new lover makes her cry. The tender brushstrokes and tearful marimba in the background, though, suggest that *Freddy* is the one who feels like crying. Yet even at the risk of breaking down in front of the woman he's just lost, he gets more intimate with her on the second verse, crooning it in Spanish (the loving tongue), and *still* doesn't betray his heartache. Remarkably, he manages, like the

steady rhythms that have propped him up all along, to keep it together till the end of the record.

Yeah, well, you can bet that when he gets home and locks the door behind him he'll put on "Crying" and absolutely fall to pieces.—bfw

257
Hot Burrito #1, The Flying Burrito Brothers
Produced by Jim Dickson;
Written by Gram Parsons and Chris Ethridge
A&M 1067   1969   Did not chart

258
You Don't Miss Your Water, William Bell
Produced by Chips Moman; Written by William Bell
Stax 116   1962   #95 pop

Gram Parsons envisioned a countercultural fusion of country, soul, rock, and gospel he called "Cosmic American Music," but ultimately, his approach to playing was too intuitive for a scheme as grand and calculated as that. What he did, in his offhand way, was treat country as white soul music, and at his best, he created records that wed the vulnerability of "Mr. Pitiful" with the stolid resolve of "Crying Time."

Take this far-from-cosmic ballad Parsons recorded with the Flying Burrito Brothers, the short-lived country-rock band he fronted after his even briefer stint with the Byrds. "You may be sweet and nice / But that won't keep you warm at night / 'Cause I'm the one who showed you how / To do the things you're doing now," he pines over an aching backbeat and the hymn-like strains of piano and steel guitar. It's a bruised, almost over-the-top pronouncement, one that finds Gram imagining his true love with her new man, and it could easily have succumbed to melodrama, even self-pity, were it not for the mix of tenderness and acceptance in his cracked, magnolia drawl. Gram wants things to be the way they were; he wants to undo the words they've said and the wrongs they've done, but he knows that's not possible. So there's no pleading for second chances here, no bitterness or blame—just a broken man holding the love of his life in his heart even as he knows he'll never hold her in his arms again.

Parsons must have had soul singer William Bell's rueful "You Don't Miss Your Water" in mind when he wrote the lyrics to "Hot Burrito #1" (reportedly to his wife Nancy after the couple had separated). The Byrds, with Gram on board, had cut "You Don't Miss Your Water" for the *Sweetheart of the Rodeo* album the year before. The group's stiff reading hardly did the song justice, but the churchy horns and country lyricism of Bell's record doubtless struck Parsons as the epitome of his cherished "Cosmic American Music," minus the psychedelic and rock overtones. Not only that, Bell's original, which was likewise addressed to the woman who'd left him, evinces much the same lump-throated stoicism as "Hot Burrito #1." "Now I sit and wonder / How can this be / I never thought / You'd ever leave me," Bell muses, as Marvell Thomas's piano and Booker T. Jones's organ echo his plaint in a gospel-derived call-and-response. Bell admits he's driven his love away, even tells her he's cried and lets out a wail or two to prove it. But rather than letting his tears fall and begging her to stay, rather than promising to change his ways, he merely sifts through the ashes of their love and clings to the moral of the record's title—in other words, to precious little at all.—bfw

259

Fifteen Years Ago, Conway Twitty
Produced by Owen Bradley; Written by Raymond Smith
Decca 32742   1970   #1 country (1 week); #81 pop

They say affairs are mostly about the keeping of secrets, and if so, Conway Twitty is keeping a doozy. He has "a lovely wife" who he tries to make happy, but when a friend mentions the name of an old lover, the facade collapses. He's instantly thrown back fifteen years, yet again, to the woman whose love he's never been able to shake. "Oh Lord, don't let it show," he gulps, as if his wife might be about to discover a ghostly trace of lipstick on his collar or an ancient book of motel matches in his pocket. It would take a very great love indeed, he admits, "a *real* love," to get a man over a connection this powerful, and what he feels for his wife clearly hasn't done the trick, though "so far she doesn't know." So even though he hasn't seen his old lover in years, let alone held her in his arms, this is still a cheating song.—dc

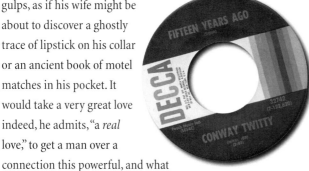

260

Just Between the Two of Us,
Merle Haggard & Bonnie Owens
Produced by Ken Nelson; Written by Liz Anderson
Tally 181   1964   #28 country

In many country songs, once you get through the first verse and chorus—where the premise is established, then cleverly reversed—you pretty much know what's coming. Take "Just Between the Two of Us." In the verses, songwriter Liz Anderson introduces us to what appears to be a perfect couple; in the chorus, she reveals that the only reason the couple gets along so well is that they no longer care enough even to disagree with each other, let alone get pissed off.

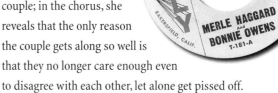

As with many country records, though, that's only the half of it. To really appreciate just how emotionally detached Anderson's couple has become, you have to hear the way drummer Helen "Peaches" Price makes the beat drag ever so slightly, like she can't be bothered anymore to keep time. And you have to hear the listless harmonies of Merle Haggard and Bonnie Owens, too. Bonnie comes off particularly weary. Her deep, full twang usually sounded like Kitty Wells crossed with a horn, but here the former Mrs. Buck Owens (and Merle's bride-to-be) sounds like she's just about ready to pack it in, if she can only get through this song.

Merle sounds good too, of course, but this time out, his female collaborators—Liz, Peaches, and Bonnie—steal the show. Like they say, behind every great man are three great women.—dc

261

Passionate Kisses, Lucinda Williams
Produced by Lucinda Williams and Gurf Morlix;
Written by Lucinda Williams
Rough Trade 66   1989   Did not chart

262

Did I Shave My Legs for This? Deana Carter

Produced by Chris Farren;
Written by Deana Carter and Rhonda Hart
Capitol 58672   1997   #25 country; #85 pop

Women who want it all—romance, family, career—often get a bad rap. They find themselves labeled "difficult" or "demanding," blamed for going after things most men take for granted.

Just ask singer-songwriter Lucinda Williams. When she emerged from L.A.'s roots-country scene in the late eighties purring "Is it too much to demand / I want a full house and a rock & roll band / Pens that won't run out of ink / And cool quiet and time to think," fans and critics didn't bat an eye. "Of course not," they swooned. Who, after all, could resist the seemingly modest demands of "Passionate Kisses," especially when delivered in Williams's willowy drawl and set to an irrepressible backbeat and jangly guitar runs that blur the line between country and rock?

But nearly ten years later, a decade that yielded just one album and loads of hype about its elusive successor, some of Lucinda's fans, most of them men, had changed their tune. Now when she sang, "Do I want too much / Am I going overboard," many uttered a resounding "Yes," charging her with taking too long between albums, with being a perfectionist—a head case who wasn't able to bring anything to closure. Never mind that her male counterparts like Bruce Springsteen and John Fogerty had taken just as long to write and record albums of new material. And never mind that when Williams's *Car Wheels on a Gravel Road* finally did come out in 1998, the album was an unmitigated triumph, an unflinching tour of the back roads of her aching southern heart.

That's ultimately all that really mattered to Williams, who, unlike her more commercially minded peers, has never compromised her music. It's an attitude she comes by honestly, having breathed the somewhat rarefied air of the writers and painters that her father, poet Miller Williams, was always bringing by the house while she was growing up. It certainly isn't a world that country radio's core audience, that proverbial army of soccer moms, readily identifies with, despite the fact that they bought enough copies of Mary Chapin Carpenter's wooden version of "Passionate Kisses" to land it in the country Top Five and earn Lucinda a Grammy.

Deana Carter's "Did I Shave My Legs for This?" is another story altogether, one that hits home for countless women stuck with a man whose idea of a perfect evening is to veg out in front of the TV with a six-pack. Forget wanting it all, Carter just wants to get *some*—that is, to get laid. And she's willing to compromise plenty, even to the point of cooking dinner and prettying herself up even though *she*, and not her husband, has been at work all day. "I bought these new heels, did my nails / Had my hair done just right / I thought this new dress was a sure bet / For romance tonight," Carter grimaces as she sizes up the situation. "Well it's perfectly clear, between the TV and beer / I won't get so much as a kiss."

Fortunately, from the over-the-top sobbing of Dan Dugmore's steel and the bada-bing, bada-boom drums on the chorus, to Carter's self-deprecating lyrics and the puckish lilt in her husky alto, there's no shortage of humor here. But just like Roger Miller and Shel Silverstein at their winking best, "Did I Shave" cuts close to the marrow. Carter, you see, is singing her song on the way out the door and she's not coming back. Not that the jerk on the couch will notice, at least not until he hollers for another cold one.—bfw

263

Success, Loretta Lynn

Produced by Owen Bradley; Written by Johnny Mullins
Decca 31384   1962   #6 country

You have no time to love me anymore
Since fame and fortune knocked upon our door
Now I spend all my evenings all alone
Success has made a failure of our home.

It's an old story, the way success can destroy a marriage. But when Loretta sings these couplets in a keening, Kitty Wells–style whine, the quiet desperation of thousands of women whose love lights went out after years of playing second fiddle to their husbands' careers feels absolutely new.

Loretta must have seen it coming in her own life even before she recorded "Success," only it wasn't Loretta, but her husband, Mooney, who would sit home alone living its lines. Granted, he was the one who pushed her to become a star, dragging her to honky-tonks and radio stations so people could hear her sing. But not long after the release of "Success," her first single for Decca, Loretta engaged the Wilburn Brothers, who, besides being stars in their own right, had their own talent agency, to manage her affairs. She didn't need her husband for that anymore.

Never an easygoing guy, and certainly not one to play the part of the kept man, Mooney continued trying to control his wife's career. When she fought back—such as the time she wore makeup onstage against his wishes—the couple scuffled; things even came to blows on occasion. Mooney was also given to fits of jealousy, despite the fact that it was he, not Loretta, who had the roving hands and eyes. Eventually he withdrew, turning to the bottle, until he finally refused to go out on the road with her anymore.

Remarkably, the couple stuck it out and remained fiercely loyal to each other for nearly fifty years until Mooney's death in 1996. Their marriage had ups and downs from the outset, but never so much as after they moved to Nashville in 1960, just a year before Loretta cut "Success," its weeping twin-fiddles and brooding tic-tac bass foreshadowing the heartaches and tears to come.—bfw

264

(Remember Me) I'm the One Who Loves You, Stuart Hamblen

Produced by Art Satherley; Written by Stuart Hamblen
Columbia 4-20714   1950   #2 country

If it weren't for one line about remaining true "right or wrong," "(Remember Me) I'm the One Who Loves You" could easily be heard as a country gospel number, a reminder from a loving God rather than a romantic pledge. Since this is Stuart Hamblen we're talking about, that's no accident.

Texas born and bred, Hamblen arrived in Los Angeles in 1930. He was briefly a member of the radio group the Beverly Hill Billies (the act most responsible for establishing a beach head for country music in California), and he soon established himself among the first cowboy singers, fronting a western band called the Covered Wagon Jubilee. Hamblen also did film work in these years, more than once playing the villain to Gene Autry's white hat, a role that often spilled over into real life—Hamblen is said to have regularly found himself jailed for fighting, drinking, and gambling. All that changed in 1949, though, when Hamblen was "saved" during a Billy Graham tent revival. From then on, he focused on modeling his version of the Christian life; he even campaigned for president in 1952 on a return-to-prohibition platform.

It's fortunate that he didn't give up music because his conversion seems to have inspired his finest work. With its churchy organ, hymnal tempo, and, especially, its promise of a love eternal, "(Remember Me) I'm the One Who Loves You" clearly marked a transition for Hamblen. His only previous charting single had been the bird-dogging "(I Won't Go Huntin' Jake) But I'll Go Chasin' Women," while his only Top Ten hits afterward were the country gospel classics "It's No Secret" and "This Ole House."

Witness how Hamblen croons "When you're all alone and blue" as if he knows a thing or two about how that feels and then, like a preacher inviting a congregation to an altar call, quietly adds, "I'm the one who loves you." There's no explicit attempt to save souls here, but the record's exquisite string arrangement—sprinkled with heavenly xylophone and washes of that coaxing organ—create an effect that's truly divine.—dc

265

It's a Sin, Eddy Arnold

Produced by Steve Sholes; Written by Zeb Turner and Fred Rose
RCA Victor 20-2241   1947   #1 country (5 weeks)

The records made by pop panderer Eddy Arnold and honky-tonk avatar Hank Williams couldn't sound *less* alike, right? Listen to Eddy moan "It's a sin to say that I don't miss you / When people know I'm still in love with you" alongside Hank's "I Can't Help It If I'm Still in Love with You" and you'll be singing a different tune. Sure, Arnold's Bing Crosby– and Pete Cassell–inspired vocals aren't as down-home as Hank's, and the playing on "It's a Sin" isn't quite as gutbucket as that of the

Drifting Cowboys on "I Can't Help It." Yet the differences are just matters of degree. The structure and theme of these records—the way they *feel*—are virtually identical. Arnold's employs not just honky-tonk fiddle and whining Hawaiian-style guitar but mandolin to boot. He was also working in this vein a good five years *before* Hank got down to business with MGM and came up with that indelible opening couplet, "Today I passed you on the street / And my heart fell at my feet," to kick start his thinly veiled rewrite of Zeb Turner's and producer Fred Rose's original.

Fred Rose, huh? Could it be that the Tin Pan Alley tunesmith turned Nashville publishing mogul was in fact the "Hillbilly Shakespeare's" muse? Or that Arnold and Williams drank from the same existential wellspring more than history would have us believe? Both questions merit consideration. Ultimately, of course, these men's lives and careers couldn't have differed more, Arnold and Rose enjoying prosperity while Williams's star went nova. Nevertheless, Rose and Arnold sound an unmistakably Hank-like note here when they equate denying one's feelings, however tortured, to sin. Or, more to the point, Hank couldn't have echoed Arnold and Rose more clearly when, a few years later, he plumbed those very same depths.—bfw

266

You Are My Sunshine, Jimmie Davis
Produced by Dave Kapp;
Written by Jimmie Davis and Charles Mitchell
Decca 5813   1940   Pre-chart

It's hard to hear this putatively sentimental ballad with fresh ears now, but it's an oddly swinging ditty coming from a guy whose worst nightmare is about to come true. As Jimmie Davis awakens from a dream born of his fear that his woman is about to leave him, his trumpet player and clarinetist, seemingly oblivious to his dread, blithely improvise over a bed of freewheeling rhythms akin to those that came from the band of Jimmie's former associate Milton Brown. The steel run that co-writer Charles Mitchell tosses off during the first break is conspicuously upbeat too. Bereft of the mournful tone that marked Gene Autry's version of "You Are My Sunshine" (a pop hit

the following year), the accompaniment here just doesn't add up—not as backing for this lovelorn precursor to "There Goes My Everything" and "The End of the World."

Or maybe, as the final lines of the second verse suggest, it adds up to something different. After pleading with his sweetheart not to forsake him for another, Davis slips in what sounds like a threat: "If you leave me to love another / You'll regret it all someday." He could just be trying to get his woman to think twice about breaking up with him, but when, on the third verse, he reminds her of how she promised to be true, it's as if he's holding that pledge over her head. With those sauntering rhythms steeling his resolve, it's as if Davis is determined to *make* her love him, even against her will.

Of course, that's not what happens. The story ends with sunshine walking out the door, leaving Jimmie's dreams of love in tatters. Even so, the tension between "Sunshine's" doleful lyrics and imperious arrangement—notably the vaguely menacing undercurrent that tension creates—gives the lie to the record's reputation as a maudlin parlor ballad turned state song of Davis's native Louisiana.

Not that baser emotions were foreign to him. Before he reinvented himself as the gentlemanly Eddy Arnold prototype heard here, Davis was a Jimmie Rodgers disciple who cut some of the lewdest double-entendre blues country music has ever known. The most infamous of the lot, "Red Nightgown Blues," flirts with rape. But when Davis went into politics, forcing his will on people became more than just something to sing about. He not only built his second successful run for governor of Louisiana on a pro-segregation ticket, he nearly shut down the New Orleans public schools in a bid to block black students from enrolling. Ain't no sunshine in any of that, that's for sure.—bfw

267

Just Between You and Me, Charley Pride
Produced by Jack Clement; Written by Jack Clement
RCA Victor 9000   1966   #9 country

When Charley Pride began recording in 1966, his record company worked hard to hide the fact that he was a black man in a white industry. His photograph was absent from early press materials, and he was always referred to as "Country" Charley Pride. In concert, though, he had no choice but to address his blackness directly, joking about his "permanent tan," verbalizing what his audience was already thinking. "Charley, how'd you get into country music," he asks aloud on his 1968 live set *In Person*, "and why you don't sound like you supposed to sound?" The short answer was that he grew up in Sledge, Mississippi, the son of a sharecropper who disdained the Delta blues but loved the Grand Ole Opry. Still, many country fans were shocked to discover that their new favorite singer was a black man. On the same album, Pride tells the story of a woman who insists to friends that there's no way Charley could be black—she has the records, after all. But when she hears the man on stage begin the chorus to "Just Between You and Me," she instantly shouts, "It's true! It's true!"

It's true all right. One listen to his chart debut, and there's no mistaking Charley Pride for anything but country. Pride sings with far less adornment than many country singers, George Jones or Lefty Frizzell, say, or even his hero Hank Williams. But he has a deceptively wide range and his twangy baritone reverberates with sincerity—all qualities, no doubt, that led Red Sovine and Red Foley to recommend he make a go of it in the country music business. Pride eventually took their advice to heart (his first love was baseball), even in the face of some DJs who described him on air as that "good nigra." He refused, wisely, to heed the early suggestion that he go the novelty route and perform under the name George Washington Carver III. Pride had no intentions of playing anybody's fool. Least of all on records like this one, where Pride (assisted by Lloyd Green on pedal steel) confesses that, "just between you and me," he has his doubts he'll ever get over the woman who broke his heart, no matter what anyone tells him. He could just as easily be confessing his continued passion for a music that was never supposed to love him back.—dc

268

Are You from Dixie? The Blue Sky Boys
Produced by Eli Oberstein;
Written by Jack Yellen and George L. Cobb
Bluebird B-8294   1939   Pre-chart

Something about the mournful, close-harmony singing of country's brother duos has always lent itself to the South's tragic songs of life. But none of the great sibling acts, not even the

Louvin Brothers, who released an entire album of centuries-old odes to murder and mayhem, sang of bloodshed and ill-fated love more convincingly than Bill and Earl Bolick, a.k.a. the Blue Sky Boys. That's not all the Bolicks sang about, though. Their repertoire also included sacred and popular material, as well as this sprightly paean to the sunny Southland. A tune that, from its nostalgic portrayal of plantations to its highly stylized word-play—"You seem surprised, I recognize / I'm no detective, but I just surmise"—can't help betraying its Tin Pan Alley origins. Not that that stopped "Are You from Dixie?" from becoming the Bolicks' theme song for most of the fifteen or so years they had their own radio show.

From Jimmie Rodgers's "Somewhere Down Below the Mason Dixon Line" to Hank Jr.'s "Dixie on My Mind," tributes to the south have long occupied a prominent place in the country canon. Many of them, like Rodgers's number and this record, depict transplanted southerners with hearts aching for home. "Are you from Alabama, Tennessee, or Caroline / Anyplace below the Mason-Dixon Line?" Earl asks a stranger, as Bill's fluttering mandolin and high tenor harmonies palpably convey his yearning for home. Still, the fact that he's been away so long—since 1889, and thus for decades—begs the question of what drove him away in the first place. A sweetheart? A job? Some unspoken shame? We never find out. No matter how sweetly Earl and Bill sing, there remains a doleful quality, an underlying sadness in their harmonies that suggests the land of cotton isn't the idyll the song's writers make it out to be.—bfw

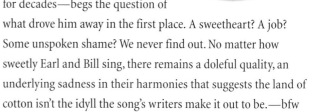

269

I Been to Georgia on a Fast Train, Billy Joe Shaver
Produced by Kris Kristofferson; Written by Billy Joe Shaver
Monument 8580   1973   #88 country

Conventional wisdom has it that the Outlaws made country palatable to the rock crowd, and there's no denying it. There was their focus on albums instead of singles, their fondness for Woodstock-style festivals like Willie Nelson's Fourth of July picnics. There was their long hair, their anti-establishment stance, their casual attitudes toward drink, drugs, and sex. But that's not all there was to the movement. The music and values of Nashville dissidents like Waylon Jennings and Billy Joe Shaver also spoke to people who were as country as cornbread and collard greens. People who flocked to church on Sundays and worshiped their mothers. People who prided themselves on putting their backs into their work, on hailing from rural stock, on the wisdom they gleaned from their elders. People who spoke their minds and had no use for those who put on airs. People who weren't about to let anyone tell them they weren't as good as anyone else, even if in their heart of hearts they believed it to be true. The Outlaws offered something for everyone or—looked at from another angle—embodied a mass of contradictions.

Perhaps nowhere were these disparate threads woven together with as much ragged glory as in Billy Joe Shaver's sweeping, autobiographical "I Been to Georgia on a Fast Train." The record clocks in under two-and-a-half minutes, but with the locomotive, neorockabilly rhythms of Tommy Cogbill, Kenny Malone, and Jerry Shock springing him loose, Billy Joe, sounding as country as all get-out, reels off a lifetime's worth of detail. "Hell I just thought I'd mention, my grandma's old-age pension / Is the reason I'm standin' here today / I got all my learnin', milkin', and a-churnin' / Pickin' cotton, raisin' hell, and balin' hay." Billy Joe's Texas-bred drawl isn't pretty; it's the sort of voice Woody Guthrie said "sound[ed] like the ash cans of the early morning." Even when it goes flat or sharp, at once rock hostile and country proud, its aim is always true.

Not that any of that helped Billy Joe sell a fraction of the records sold by the scads of singers, from Waylon and Willie, to Elvis and Bob Dylan, who covered his songs. But neither does it diminish the unassailable dignity in Billy Joe's raspy growl when, over "Fast Train's" chugging beats, he proclaims, "I got a good Christian raising / An eighth grade education / Ain't no need in y'all treating me this way."

Which makes Shaver's "Train" a latter-day version of an aphorism the Singing Brakeman was so fond of: "The underest dog is just as good as I am—and I'm just as good as the toppest dog."—bfw

270

Me and Bobby McGee, Janis Joplin
Produced by Paul A. Rothchild;
Written by Kris Kristofferson and Fred Foster
Columbia 45314   1971   #1 pop (2 weeks)

271

Midnight Train to Georgia, Gladys Knight & the Pips
Produced by Tony Camillo and Gladys Knight & the Pips;
Written by Jim Weatherly
Buddah 383   1973   #1 pop (2 weeks)

Neither of these records charted country, but both—one by a hippie icon, the other by an Atlanta soul group—are steeped in down-home arrangements and sensibilities that could easily pass for country. "Me and Bobby McGee" in fact was a country hit for Roger Miller in 1969. It was written by a pair of Nashville tunesmiths during Kris Kristofferson's five-year flash of brilliance, a period in which he was infusing country songwriting with the fevered inspiration of Bob Dylan and the Beat Poets. "Midnight Train to Georgia," now a fixture in Trisha Yearwood's live show, came from Jim Weatherly, a Jimmy Webb acolyte who provided several albums' worth of country material to Ray Price, among others.

Both songs plumb an enduring country theme—the conflict between and the variable pull of the urges to be free and to settle down. Heard back to back they tell the story of a southern odyssey come full circle.

"Me and Bobby McGee" starts out celebrating the heady rush of getting out—of hopping freight cars, thumbing down semis, and embracing a way of life in which "feelin' good is good enough" and where "nothin' ain't worth nothin' if it ain't free." The euphoria lasts long enough for Janis Joplin, a country girl from East Texas, to hitch her way out to California, only to discover—once her lover and traveling companion ditches her—that feelin' good *wasn't* good enough. While having nothing left to lose can be freeing, it can just as easily leave you holding on to nothing.

"I'd trade all my tomorrows for one single yesterday / To be holdin' Bobby's body next to mine," Janis winces in her nicotine- and Southern Comfort–steeped drawl. The twangy guitar that snakes in and out of the background is enough to remind her of Nashville, the mile-wide groove and smoky organ of Muscle Shoals. And judging by her wordless wailing on the coda, she really wants to be back down South, where she and Bobby might not have felt as free but where at least they shared a life together.

That's how Jim Weatherly must have heard it when he picked up the story's thread and gave it new resolution in "Midnight Train to Georgia." When Janis's Bobby slipped away near Salinas, he could have been following the same dream as Gladys's guy, who leaves his home in Georgia to make it as a singer in L.A. Yet as signaled by the momentous breath Knight takes after she utters "L.A." to open the first line, we soon learn that the city of angels "proved too much for the man." Looking to reclaim the life he left behind, he's bought himself a one-way ticket on the red-eye home.

He's not alone either. Gladys is with him; she's tracked him down and isn't about to let him get away this time. "I'd rather live in his world / Than live without him in mine," she vows, the conviction in her voice that of a woman who, far from making a concession, knows what she wants and isn't afraid to make sacrifices in order to get and hang on to it. From the way she bites down on the line "I got to go" as she rides out the final chorus, there's little chance she'll lose her nerve. Not as long as that choir of voices behind her (horns, strings, and the Pips) testifies to the possibilities—indeed, the freedom—inherent in commitment. —bfw

272

L.A. Freeway, Jerry Jeff Walker
Produced by Michael Brovsky; Written by Guy Clark
MCA 40054   1973   #98 pop

The side of country-rock that has become so closely associated with the Austin music scene is more interested in songs—and, to a lesser degree, albums—than singles, which accounts for why so little of it shows up on country radio (or in this book). Over the years, many of the genre's finest moments (from the likes of Townes Van Zandt, Ray Wylie Hubbard, Jimmie Dale Gilmore, and Robert Earl Keen) have been rambling story songs that are long

on verses and short on hooks, and that have stripped-down, static arrangements that aren't much concerned with holding their own at radio. Add in the Nashville brass' bias against anything produced away from Music Row, and the style's minimal commercial success was all but inevitable. Appropriately too, mostly, since great *records* require a heck of a lot more than a singer and a good song.

Take Jerry Jeff Walker and Guy Clark, two Austin-associated singer-songwriters whose best compositions have been turned into superior records—hit singles even— by other acts. Walker's "Mr. Bojangles" was a major pop smash for the Nitty Gritty Dirt Band in 1970; Clark's songs produced country hits throughout the eighties (for Ricky Skaggs, Rodney Crowell, and John Conlee, among others). In Walker's case, the lack of solo radio success isn't hard to explain. On the recordings that have amounted to his "greatest hits," he's a rather faceless singer, his reputation as a free-spirited live performer and one-time boozehound notwith-standing. His reading of Guy Clark's "L.A. Freeway" is typically unremarkable. Walker's voice has little range; his phrasing is predictable, his affect mostly flat. There are literally hundreds of singers across America, probably a few dozen in Austin alone, who could sing it better.

On the other hand, songs are important too, and Clark's is a *great* one. Something like "Midnight Train to Georgia" told from the man's point of view, "L.A. Freeway" is about a musician and his wife who are leaving the big city for some land they still "ain't bought, bought, bought." Clark's lyrics find the music in everyday language ("Leave the key in the old front door lock / They will find it likely as not"), and his melody, no matter who's singing it, lets the singer stumble through the verses before exploding with another chance, or the possibility of one, at each chorus. But what makes Walker's recording of the song so amazing is everything that's not part of the song as such: Weldon Myrick on slicing pedal steel, Kelly Dunn on organ, the alternately pulsing and banging percussion team of Donnie Dolan and Kenny Buttrey, John Inmon's jamming guitar, and especially the soulful female backing singers who ride the groove all the way out of town. Working together, Walker, Clark, and the band make moving on, and pissing on the memory of what you're leaving behind, sound like freedom.—dc

273

Blue Yodel No. 4 (California Blues), Jimmie Rodgers
Produced by Ralph Peer; Written by Jimmie Rodgers
Victor 40014   1928   Pre-chart

Biographer Nolan Porterfield identifies the Singing Brakeman's tragicomic persona as one of his great gifts to country music; it's certainly writ large in this ironic pre-Depression ode to the West Coast's pastures of plenty.

"I'm going to California where they sleep out every night," Rodgers crows, yodeling away his blues like he's whistling "Dixie." Jimmie's leaving his mistreatin' mama behind and the implication—he's worried now but he won't be worried long—is that he'll not only find an abundance of available women out West, but loads of work as well. He puts on a good front, too, especially with the swinging rhythms of that hot jazz combo putting a swagger in his step. Only problem is, John Westbrook's sorrowful slide refuses to let Jimmie believe that a change in geography can cure his blues—he ain't sleepin' out every night just 'cause the weather's fine; hard luck and trouble are following him as he chases that receding golden horizon.

That's one of the reasons why these are the California—not the Mississippi or Texas or wherever he is now—blues.—bfw

274

The Tennessee Waltz, Patti Page
No producer credited; Written by Pee Wee King and Redd Stewart
Mercury 5534-X45   1951   #2 country; #1 pop (13 weeks)

"The Tennessee Waltz" began simply enough. If Bill Monroe could write a "Kentucky Waltz," then Pee Wee King figured he could certainly write a waltz for his own home state. But what King's song started went way beyond state rivalry. First, King cut the song with his Golden West Cowboys, and the subsequent single, featuring the lead vocals of co-writer Redd Stewart, became a Top Five country hit in 1948; it even cracked the pop charts for a week

and spawned another successful country version by Cowboy Copas. Next, bandleader Erskine Hawkins recorded a version of the song that became a decent-sized R&B hit in 1950. Then, after A&R man Jerry Wexler suggested the idea to her manager, Patti Page recorded the song.

The Oklahoma-born Page had begun her career singing country material, but by 1950, she was pop all the way. What limited success she'd achieved was partly based upon novelty; her early singles, the first ever to feature vocal overdubs, let Page sing harmony with herself. Her version of "The Tennessee Waltz" repeated this gimmick, but it quickly became clear that there was something special about the record that had nothing to do with studio tricks. It entered the pop charts in November of 1950. By Christmas it was #1, where it stayed until March. By May, the single had sold nearly five million copies, spawned six cover versions on the pop charts alone, and ushered King's original back into the country Top Ten. Today, Patti Page's recording of "The Tennessee Waltz" has sold over ten million copiesmaking it one of the best-selling singles of all-time.

With a song this good, Page didn't need to be spectacular. Backed only by strummed acoustic guitar, a small horn section that sticks to the changes, and piano notes that blink in and out like stars, all she needed to do was to voice that unforgettable melody, provide those sad harmonies, and sing that bittersweet refrain: "Yes, I lost my little darling the night they were playing the beautiful Tennessee Waltz."

As the last song to sell over a million copies of sheet music, "The Tennessee Waltz" marked the end of an era, but it pointed to the future, as well. In the second half of the century, Americans didn't make their own music at home; they bought and played studio recordings of the songs they'd fallen in love with on the radio. "The Tennessee Waltz" helped ensure that a lot of those records, even ones played on big city radio stations, were going to be country songs.—dc

275
Kentucky, Sammi Smith
Produced by Jim Malloy; Written by Sammi Smith
Mega 0056   1972   #38 country

Singing from a Tennessee studio,
Oklahoman Sammi Smith
recalls the "lost and lonely
Texas" evening when she fell
in love with a country singer
called Kentucky. Don't let all
that geography fool you. The
heart of this country-soul
masterpiece was provided by a
man straight out of Muscle
Shoals, Alabama: drummer Jerry Carrigan.

On "Kentucky," Carrigan uses every skill he learned in Muscle
Shoals and then some. At the start, as Smith begins to sing over
Chip Young's gutstring guitar, Carrigan doesn't play at all. But as
the bricks in this wall of sound pile up—a thrilling Bergen White
string arrangement, a backing choir, Weldon Myrick going nuts
on the pedal steel, David Briggs pounding his piano—Carrigan
assembles a beat to match. First, it's just two quick punches of
bass drum, then a high hat to keep time, then woodblock fills.
Eventually, huge splashes of cymbal that rock like thunder also
pass across the kit, all of it lying back just behind the beat. At one
point, the whole thing explodes to a hush, only to build and
explode again. Somehow, not one of these tricks detracts from
Smith's vocals; every strike of a drumhead reinforces how blessed
she feels to know this man Kentucky. By the end, Carrigan's bass
drum and Smith's heartbeat . . . well, who can tell the difference?—dc

276
Only Daddy That'll Walk the Line, Waylon Jennings
Produced by Chet Atkins; Written by Ivy J. Bryant
RCA Victor 9561   1968   #2 country

In the early seventies, as he was unwittingly contributing to the
creation of the Outlaw movement, Waylon Jennings fought long
and hard for artistic autonomy; he wanted to record the songs he
liked when he wanted to record them, with musicians he chose,
rather than acquiescing to the unwritten rules like all the other
Nashville bums. This battle seems to have been fought mostly

over creative process (and control of publishing) rather than
actual product. That's because the Outlaw records Jennings made
post-independence remained remarkably of a piece with the ones
he'd been making all along. If you didn't know the history behind
them, you likely would be unable to identify any fundamental
changes at all.

That's not just hypothetical, either. It's common knowledge,
for example, that the album that broke the movement, *Wanted:
The Outlaws*, was composed of previously released material.
What's usually forgotten is that the album included several cuts,
including a version of "Suspicious Minds" by Waylon and wife
Jessi Colter, which had been recorded before the singer gained his
freedom. That is, back in the bad old assembly-line days when all
Jennings could do was take orders from Chet Atkins while
recording with a bunch of "wind-up
session hacks," to quote critic
John Morthland. Marketed as
a catchy new brand, though,
no one noticed.

That's partly because the
"hacks" had already helped
Jennings realize the basics of
his sound. Waylon's distinctive
musical characteristics certainly would be
more emphasized in later years (now and then they were even
exaggerated, you might say), but they're already front and center
on "Only Daddy That'll Walk the Line"—driving, bass-heavy
rhythm and a smoking tempo, a wicked and unmistakably
rocking electric guitar solo (from Wayne Moss), bluesy harmonica (Charlie McCoy), squawling organ (Pig Robbins), and, of
course, Waylon's inimitable baritone, especially when he stretches
"You got the ohhhhhhhhhhhhhhh-nly daddy that'll walk the line"
into a yowl of discontent. In 1968, who else was cutting records
that sounded like this? Jennings couldn't stand to "walk the line"
for long, but while he did, boy, he sure made some great
records.—dc

277
Nashville Cats, The Lovin' Spoonful
Produced by Erik Jacobsen; Written by John Sebastian
Kama Sutra 219   1966   #8 pop

Right story, wrong city. Those "yellow Sun records" John
Sebastian dotes on here came out of Memphis, not Nashville. In

fact, Sun didn't establish a presence in Music City until Shelby Singleton bought the label's catalog from Sam Phillips and moved it 200 miles east in 1969, nearly three years *after* "Nashville Cats" reached the pop Top Ten. Even the chugging rhythms and Zal Yanovsky's hiccupping bass-string leads suggest these folk-rockers from Greenwich Village used some of the sides that were cut at Sun in Memphis as a template for their record. But hey, Memphis, Nashville, what's the difference? They're both hillbilly towns down in Tennessee, right?

Sebastian's historical gaffe notwithstanding, he gets just about everything else right, and his reference to those 1,352 pickers leaves no doubt he's talking about Nashville, and the Nashville Sound in particular. Not so much as a style of music but as an attitude or vibe—a laid-back, less-is-more approach to playing and a spirit of camaraderie—that had been producing great music for years. Most rockers first got wind of it when Bob Dylan cut *Blonde on Blonde* in Nashville in early 1966. Soon everyone from Joan Baez and Buffy Sainte-Marie to Rick Nelson and the Byrds was recording down there, lending hip cachet to "hillbilly" pickers like Charlie McCoy, Pig Robbins, and Pete Drake, whose names soon started turning up in the credits of albums by a host of folk, rock, and pop singers.

Oddly enough, this was also right about the time the Nashville Sound, as both a definable style of music and an approach to making records, was growing formulaic and, in some cases, just plain stale. But how were the Spoonful, outsiders in every sense of the word, to know that? To them the simple, uncluttered playing of those Nashville cats ("clear as country water") doubtless was a tonic for the arty pretensions and indulgent soloing that were creeping into the music of the incipient psychedelic era. Still, where Sebastian got that bit about the pickers on Music Row playing "wild as mountain dew," a description that was true not of the Nashville Sound but the Memphis rockabilly it initially reacted against, is anybody's guess. But then, based on the evidence here, Sebastian wasn't one to let the facts get in the way of a good story.—bfw

278
I Walk the Line, Johnny Cash & the Tennessee Two
Produced by Sam Phillips; Written by Johnny Cash
Sun 241   1956   #1 country (6 weeks); #17 pop

Johnny Cash told writer Dorothy Horstman that he wrote "I Walk the Line" as a pledge of fidelity to his first wife Vivian Liberto. No doubt that's the case. But over the years the song took on much greater significance as Cash emerged as one of the most iconic and complex figures of the second half of the twentieth century. A mass of contradictions, he was an addict and an evangelist, a protester of the Vietnam war who palled around with Richard Nixon's pet preacher Billy Graham, a singer of grim odes to murder like "Delia's Gone," and an aficionado of clodhopper corn pone who once released an LP called *Everybody Loves a Nut*. Indeed, with Walt Whitman, Cash can say, "Do I contradict myself, very well then, I contradict myself. I am large, I contain multitudes."

So it's more than a little vexing to hear latter-day tastemakers reduce the Man in Black to a one-dimensional avatar of darkness who's part prototypical Outlaw/punk-rocker and part forerunner of the modern gangsta MC. The soul of the man lies instead in his heroic struggle—not nearly as easy as he claims in "I Walk the Line"—to remain true to that unruly heart of his. That's just what Cash is driving at when, over this record's obdurate beat, he sings of keeping the ends out for the tie that binds—he's confessing just how desperately he wants to unite the disparate strands of his conflicted self in hopes of subduing the beast within.—bfw

279
Sittin' and Thinkin', Charlie Rich
Produced by Sam Phillips; Written by Charlie Rich
Phillips International 3582   1962   Did not chart

"No matter what, Charlie Rich was going to tell you the truth," Sam Phillips once said. If you need evidence, this record, a barroom weeper that Rich easily could have subtitled "The Story of My Life," might as well be exhibit number one. Charlie grabs you from the outset—"I got loaded last night on a bottle of gin / And I had a fight with my best girlfriend." Set to a creaky roadhouse shuffle, this couplet alone would've been enough to make "Sittin' and Thinkin' " a jukebox staple, but it's Charlie's next confession, "When I'm drinking I am nobody's friend," that knocks you off your barstool.

Rich knew this kind of guilt all too well. One of the more public incidents took place after the success of "Behind Closed Doors," when Charlie drank himself senseless during the taping of a Burt Reynolds television special at the Governor's Mansion in Nashville. The most notorious scene, however, unfolded before a national TV audience when Rich was a presenter at the 1975 Country Music Association awards. After announcing that pop singer John Denver had won the award for Entertainer of the Year, Charlie, who looked as if he *was* loaded on a bottle of gin, took out his cigarette lighter and torched the envelope. He apologized profusely afterwards, and no one questioned his remorse, but this time it seemed like the last straw with his wife Margaret Ann, who was ready to file for divorce. The couple soon reconciled though, and they stuck together until Rich's death (of a heart attack) in 1995.

Most drunks are quick to make excuses for their behavior, blaming just about everyone but themselves for their actions: the boss, the wife, the kids. But not Charlie, at least not in "Sittin' and Thinkin'." Here he's begging his baby to wait for him until he gets out of the drunk tank, but he's not about to lie to her by making some pledge he can't keep. "I won't promise the same thing won't happen again," he cautions in a bruised baritone steeped in self-knowledge. He's gotten sloppy before, and with the nagging rhythm section and acerbic strings revealing just how much it pains him to admit it, he knows he'll get that way again. That's a hard thing for a husband to admit, but it's doubtless even harder for a wife to hear and accept. Then again maybe Margaret Ann stood by Charlie precisely because of the honesty and humility—the nobility of spirit—his admission shows.—bfw

280

Flowers on the Wall, The Statler Brothers
Produced by Don Law and Frank Jones; Written by Lewis DeWitt
Columbia 43315   1965   #2 country; #4 pop

Gospel quartets have been a pervasive influence on country singing for decades, but actual quartet appearances on country radio, particularly in their purest southern gospel form, have been next to nonexistent. For years, country's highest profile quartet was the Jordanaires, and their harmonies, while essential to the Nashville Sound, were as much doo-wop as gospel and used almost exclusively as background. Until the Oak Ridge Boys and Alabama broke out circa 1980, the only country quartet with any real commercial success was the Statler Brothers, a Virginia-based southern gospel group that got their break when Johnny Cash asked them to join his package show in 1964. Even their harmonies were often closer to those of the Kingston Trio, or the Mamas and the Papas, than the Blackwood Brothers or Brown's Ferry Four.

Motivated by their popularity with the college kids Cash was drawing, the Statlers hoped "Flowers on the Wall" would help them connect with the pop side of the folk revival. Though the group would eventually cultivate one of the most nostalgic catalogues in country music ("What Ever Happened to Randolph Scott," "The Class of '55," "Do You Remember These"), "Flowers on the Wall" is an absolutely credible and up-to-date take on hipster heartache. The Statlers are trying to convince an old flame that life is exciting as ever since she's gone, but no matter how much glee they manufacture, it's clear their days couldn't be emptier. They pass the time chain-smoking, counting flowers on the wallpaper, and "playing solitaire with a deck of fifty-one." Gone folk-pop, the Statlers come off as stir crazy as the record's banjo-meets-bass drum arrangement, and their pinched harmonies bounce off the walls with a hysteria only barely restrained.—dc

281

Looking at the World through a Windshield,
Del Reeves
Produced by Bob Montgomery;
Written by Jerry Chesnut and Mike Hoyer
United Artists 50332   1968   #5 country

Musicians and truckers share a familiarity with the joys of life on the road—those great all-night country stations, for instance. But they also share a realistic knowledge of the hardships behind the romance. The long weeks away from home and family; the road food that's routinely terrible and always unhealthy, even when it's delicious; crumbling blacktops and treacherous weather conditions; itineraries that bounce you like a pinball between destinations hundreds if not thousands of miles apart; and the way that seeing big stretches of country through the windshield can leave you feeling like you're nowhere at all, like life is literally passing you by. Or as Del Reeves puts it here, like he's "watching [the world] fly by me on the right."

Singing along with the radio to records like "Looking at the World through a Windshield" won't get Del home any faster to that "sweet little thing that I'm wanting to see in Nashville," not when the next job has him hauling all the way from L.A. to Baltimore. But when this record's frenetic rhythm track kicks in—it sounds like the Strangers on little white pills—it sure feels like it.—dc

282

Wreck on the Highway, Roy Acuff & His Smoky Mountain Boys
Produced by Art Satherley; Written by Dorsey Dixon
OKeh 6685   1942   Pre-chart

283

Wabash Cannon Ball, Roy Acuff & His Smoky Mountain Boys
Produced by Art Satherley; Written by A. P. Carter
Columbia 37008   1947   Did not chart

Sometime around 1940, a young Ira and Charlie Louvin were working the fields when an unfamiliar car came racing down the dirt road that passed the family farm, kicking up a long cloud of dust. "I'll be damned if there wasn't a car that looked to us as long as a three-quarter ton truck," Charlie Louvin told historian

Charles Wolfe. "On the side were the words, 'Roy Acuff and the Smoky Mountain Boys.' I'd never seen anything like that . . . [W]hen we saw Acuff pass in his car that day, we knew that's what we wanted to do."

Roy Acuff had a similar inspirational effect on a lot of southerners. In the years before rock & roll, Acuff was that rare son of the south who approached household-name status across the nation. He didn't do it with recordings, either—Acuff had only a handful of hits, most of them coming during World War II or in the two years immediately following. But behind the scenes, as half owner of the publishing company Acuff-Rose; and over the airwaves, as a longtime star of the Grand Ole Opry (after the war, *the* star); and as a reminder of home to thousands of southern soldiers during World War II, Acuff became something of an ambassador not just for country music but for the entire South. He was so widely known, the story goes, and considered so archetypically American, that the Japanese would taunt U.S. soldiers by shouting, "To hell with FDR! To hell with Babe Ruth! To hell with Roy Acuff!" Roy's career seemed proof positive that a southern boy could venture beyond the horizon, and succeed, without forsaking his roots.

Part of why Acuff was so adored below the Mason-Dixon was simply that he was so unambiguously southern; he was one of "us" in a popular culture where southern accents remain few and far between. When he offered up the unshakable imagery and despairing melody of "Wreck on the Highway," for example, he was speaking a language his fans knew well. At a time when honky-tonk, hillbilly boogie, and other amplified urban styles dominated country music, the record's stringband arrangement reminded listeners of a shared rural history. Grounding the Smoky Mountain Boys' sound, Bashful Brother Oswald's wailing dobro bespoke a past that was only *just* past, and Acuff's voice (which he called "a country tenor without training, performing in the Old Harp singing style") did the same. "Wreck" has Acuff coming upon an automobile accident where whiskey, blood, and glass are scattered all over the road. "I heard the groans of the dying, but I didn't hear nobody pray," he cries, and his voice is despairing precisely because he and his listeners agree on the stakes. No prayer means no forgiveness; no forgiveness means you burn.

That sort of old-time religion doubtless seemed exotic, if not downright preposterous, to many Yankees who stumbled across it. Though Acuff would've been reasonably well known up North, his very southernness ensured that he would remain a mystery there, as is evidenced by the countless commentators over the years who've been amazed to learn that Acuff could shed real tears while singing such a song. Or, for a more recent example of regional condescension, think of Robert Duvall's fine *The Apostle*, which surprised many viewers simply by offering a sympathetic portrait of a southern "Holy Roller" preacher. There's a scene in that film where the title character comes upon a wreck on the highway; ministers to one of its trapped, groaning victims; then skips off ecstatic because, even if the person dies, a sinner has been saved. Acuff's "Wreck on the Highway" is exactly that scene, minus the happy ending.

No wonder the rousing "Wabash Cannon Ball," a number with less regional distinctiveness, has become the song most associated with Acuff, in the south and everywhere else. "From the great Atlantic ocean to the wide Pacific shore," Acuff's train takes the listener on a coast-to-coast tour of America, with stops in New York, St. Louis, Chicago, and Minnesota, as well as Tennessee and Alabam'. The song had originally been associated with the Carter Family, and in 1936 Acuff himself had already cut a popular version that appeared briefly on the national charts. On that recording Acuff delegated the vocal chores to one of his Smoky Mountain Boys, but in 1947, it's Acuff who proclaims the glory of this train, "mighty tall and handsome," and about the dear departed it's carrying southward to eternal "victory." The best parts are that rooster's-crow dobro that kicks off the record and Acuff's whining impersonation of a train whistle. There's something universal in those sounds, an unmistakable suggestion of new dawns and far horizons—and the Something More they herald. It must've been just that sense of possibility that the Louvins sensed as they watched Acuff's touring car speed down the road and out of sight.—dc

284

Sweet Home Alabama, Lynyrd Skynyrd

Produced by Al Kooper;
Written by Ed King, Gary Rossington, and Ronnie Van Zant
MCA 40258   1974   #8 pop

"Sweet Home Alabama" was written both as a joke and as a pissed-off rejoinder to charges of southern racism found in Neil Young's "Southern Man" and "Alabama." Skynyrd frontman Ronnie Van Zant, who wasn't about to accept Young's demonology, went after Young for painting with too broad a brush. In the process, he also exhibited a classic southern impulse to defend himself against outsiders who neither know nor love the land he calls home. The result was a regional anthem, albeit one that could easily be heard as a defense of precisely the sort of racist, insular populism—specifically, Alabama governor and presidential candidate George Wallace—that Young was attacking in the first place. Or rather the record was an anthem that could easily be *mis*heard as all that: "The lyrics about the governor of Alabama were misunderstood," Van Zant said in 1975. "The general public didn't notice the words 'Boo! Boo! Boo!' after that particular line, and the media only picked up on the reference to the people loving the governor."

In other words, this is the southern rock equivalent of "Okie from Muskogee"—its politics are plenty boneheaded, but there's also more going on here than first meets the ears. As much as anything else, Skynyrd's breakthrough hit is a love song to the South. Recorded in Georgia by a bunch of good ol' boys from Jacksonville, Florida, "Sweet Home Alabama" is just a rocking version of "Are You from Dixie," "My Window Faces the South," or "Hey Porter." "Singin' songs about the Southland," indeed.

Surely it was such intense regional pride—coming at a moment when southern culture was being both vilified and widely assimilated by the nation at large—that accounted for the way the record quickly became a hit throughout the South. As for the rest of the nation? Well, who could resist the searing lurch of the Skynyrd's white-boy blues, not to mention a chorus that is absolutely impossible not to sing along with, even if you've never been south of, say, New York's Houston Street.

Even after twenty-five years of AOR and classic rock airplay in every part of the nation, the record continues to scream its southern distinctiveness. So it makes sense that, over that same quarter century, much of the southern rock sound would be absorbed into contemporary country music, one of the few forums where hailing from Dixie was still a point of pride. "Turn it up," Van Zant urges at the outset, and through the years acts like the Charlie Daniels Band, Waylon Jennings, Hank Williams Jr., Travis Tritt, the Kentucky Headhunters, Confederate Railroad, Montgomery Gentry, and the alt.country Bottle Rockets have, to varying degrees of commercial and artistic success, done just that. And that's saying nothing about the generations of country singers and pickers for whom, like Skynyrd, Muscle Shoals went along with blue skies, mama's sawmill gravy, and those redneck triple guitars.—dc

285

You Better Move On, Arthur Alexander
Produced by Rick Hall; Written by Arthur Alexander
Dot 16309   1962   #24 pop

286

Soul Song, Joe Stampley
Produced by Norro Wilson;
Written by George Richey, Norro Wilson, and Billy Sherrill
Dot 17442   1972   #1 country (1 week); #37 pop

The most important development in country music history, between Elvis and Garth, was the arrival in Nashville of the original Muscle Shoals rhythm section. After bassist Norbert Putnam, pianist David Briggs, and drummer Jerry Carrigan left Alabama for Nashville in late 1964, they anchored a second-generation A-Team that would help fashion a new soul-and-pop-inflected country music. The record that set all this in motion was Arthur Alexander's "You Better Move On." Alexander's chart debut paved the way for producer Rick Hall and a talented cast of northern Alabama musicians to make a success, first, of FAME Studios and, later, of what became known as the Muscle Shoals Sound—home of

classic hits by everyone from Aretha Franklin and Wilson Pickett to Paul Simon and Lynyrd Skynyrd.

Fact is the Muscle Shoals gang was on its way to changing country music before those famous records were even made. Convinced they had a hit with "You Better Move On," Hall and Alexander had unsuccessfully made the rounds of the Nashville labels, but until Dot took a chance on the record, it was always the same thing—good song, but the singer's too black. Or so they were told. Heard today, Alexander's work on "You Better Move On" puts one very much in mind of Charley Pride, which makes sense for a kid who'd grown up on singing cowboys and the Grand Ole Opry. With Alexander delivering his lines in a soulful twang that's part C&W restraint, part good old boy threat, "You Better Move On" sounds like a southern, down-home take on Ben E. King's "Stand by Me." The strings are gone, the backing vocals suggest the Nashville Sound more than urban R&B, and the groove has lost its Afro-Cuban feel. In its place Briggs, Carrigan, and Putnam, along with guitarist Terry Thompson (who died of a drug overdose, in 1965), have laid the foundation for country soul.

Prior to Alexander's hit, the Muscle Shoals rhythm section had been busy backing singer/songwriter Dan Penn in the legendary blue-eyed soul outfit the Mark V's. But after the Alexander record took off, they began spending even more of their time at FAME, laying down a country-soul groove for Jimmy Hughes, Tommy Roe, Joe Simon, and a host of others. At least that's what they did until friends began telling them they could be making a lot more money, in a lot less time, by doing the same thing 100 miles to the north in Nashville. So that's what they did. On thousands of sessions over the next decade, both together and as parts of other configurations, the members of the original Muscle Shoals rhythm section played country music. The stirring results can be heard on scores of country classics, many included in these very pages.

Briggs, Carrigan, and Putnam didn't effect this transformation all by themselves, of course. Producer Billy Sherrill, who himself had been present at the birth of FAME Studios before moving to Nashville, played an inestimable role in this shift. Also important was the influx throughout the late fifties and early sixties of other rock-and-soul-bred musicians, songwriters, and producers, particularly those from Atlanta's Lowery Music group like Chip Young, Joe South, and Jerry Reed. But the more or less en masse arrival of Briggs, Carrigan, and Putnam established critical mass, and by the early seventies, the more soulful rhythms and quiet-loud-quiet pop dynamics that the Muscle Shoals boys had helped transport across state lines were *the* dominant sound on country radio.

One example of how these influences played out is the career of Joe Stampley. Prior to becoming one of the most successful country stars of the seventies, Stampley had admired, and once met, Hank Williams. But he'd also recorded R&B sides for both Imperial and Chess before being produced by Dale Hawkins in a pop-rock outfit called the Uniques. These strands came together on his biggest hit, "Soul Song." From the a cappella shout of the title phrase that seems to summon the song out of thin air, it's clear Stampley has heard his fair share of R&B and soul. But it's been filtered through Elvis and Jerry Lee, Conway Twitty and Charlie Rich, which is to say it's R&B and soul as country singers had already been absorbing them for a decade. Behind Stampley, the rhythm section (including Carrigan on drums) is a more recent hybrid—straight-up-and-down country with pulsing soul. That's how something called "Soul Song" could top the country charts without ever risking charges of false advertising. From either direction.—dc

287

At the Crossroads, Sir Douglas Quintet
Produced by Doug Sahm; Written by Doug Sahm
Smash 2253   1969   Did not chart

They say you can set out driving across Texas before dawn and still be in the state long after dark. And not just on your way from El Paso in the west to Nacogdoches in the east, but also from Amarillo in the northern Panhandle to Harlingen down south in the valley. No less expansive than the seemingly boundless Texas horizon, though, is the music that's taken root there: blues, R&B, rock & roll, honky-tonk, western swing, and all manner of Cajun, German, and Mexican dance tunes. These strains of American roots music don't just exist side by side in the Lone Star State; they melt all over and season each other like ingredients wrapped up in a burrito deluxe.

No single Texan, not even syncretistic Bob Wills or Willie-nilly Nelson, embodied this musical ecumenism with more relish and imagination than the late Doug Sahm. A guitar prodigy who as a kid sat on Hank Williams's knee, Sahm was a visionary, if at times half-cocked, savant who could and seemingly did play it all. With the Sir Douglas Quintet he cranked out everything from faux–

British Invasion garage pop to blissed-out stoner rock to punchy, horn-driven Cajun and border rhythms. With the Last Real Texas Blues Band he did T-Bone Walker and Bobby "Blue" Bland covers. Under the pseudonyms Wayne Douglas and Doug Saldaña he made 190-proof honky-tonk, including "Be Real," a shoulda-been-country smash he cut with Jerry Kennedy and a half-dozen first-call Nashville session pros in 1970. And he made Tejano music *in excelsis* with the Texas Tornados, a Mexican-American supergroup featuring Freddy Fender, accordion master Flaco Jimenez, and Sir Doug organist Augie Meyers.

"At the Crossroads," a languid, Farfisa-steeped ode to love's dissolution, finds Sahm and the Quintet doing a slow-burning Ray Charles impersonation by way of Bob Dylan's "Sad-Eyed Lady of the Lowlands." The record also features as sharply drawn a statement of purpose as Doug ever uttered—"You just can't live in Texas if you don't got a lot of soul." It's a sweeping claim, as big as the outsized Texas ego it betrays, but in this case Sahm delivers, as he often did, drawing on a musical palette as vast and kaleidoscopic as the geography and mythos that define his home state. Gram Parsons might have preached the gospel of Cosmic American Music, but Sir Doug, who talked as good a game as anyone, personified Parsons's beloved synthesis like no one else—be they from Texas or the dark side of the moon.—bfw

288

The Dark End of the Street, James Carr
Produced by Quentin Claunch and Doc Russell;
Written by Chips Moman and Dan Penn
Goldwax 317   1967   #10 R&B; #77 pop

In the mid-sixties, a generation of white session players from Atlanta and Muscle Shoals were busy transforming the country music scene by mixing in a little bit of soul. The same thing was taking place across the tracks where R&B vocalists Ray Charles, Percy Sledge, Joe Simon, William Bell, and others were creating the country soul ballad. In *Say It One Time for the Brokenhearted: Country Soul in the American South*, a history of this sub-genre, Barney Hoskyns describes the style as "really a black gospel foreground, with all the vocal improvisation and intensity that implies, superimposed on a white country background." Or, in writer Geri Hershey's memorable phrase, "part church, part hills."

Country-soul songs don't get any better than "The Dark End of the Street" by Dan Penn and Chips Moman, two more southern white boys who cut their teeth on black gospel and Hank

Williams records. A decade earlier, they probably would have had careers in country, but the changing currents of the sixties drew them to black music, despite having grown up in a society where black and white were supposed to be segregated. It's hardly surprising, and definitely not insignificant, that this civil rights era ballad alludes to cheating songs out of both Muscle Shoals (Jimmy Hughes's "Steal Away") and Nashville (Leroy Van Dyke's "Walk on By").

Despite recordings of the song by Aretha Franklin, the Flying Burrito Brothers, Percy Sledge, the Kendalls, and a score of others, the best version of "Dark End" remains James Carr's original. Typical of country soul, it features a black soul singer crying in front of a white southern band that was every bit as familiar with country music as with rhythm and blues. That band was the American Studios house band in Memphis (here working across town at Hi Studios, on a session for the Goldwax label). Reggie Young, who would later move east and become a Nashville session legend, kicks the record off with a fragile, echo-y electric guitar part that predicts the anguish to come. Bassist Tommy Cogbill, who would one day log his own share of country sessions, keeps the whole thing tied down to earth no matter how fiercely Carr testifies. "Living in darkness to hide our wrong. . . . Oh but our love keeps coming on strong," Carr moans to the woman with whom he's having an affair.

Then again, considering the era and the context in which this record was created (not to mention Memphis's hard-earned reputation as a place where the South's racial rules could be stretched and broken), who is to say that Carr isn't sneaking around because his lover is white—a "sin" that in the light of day would have been a whole lot more dangerous than mere adultery? Whatever the theory, the single's glorious gospel-schooled cries coupled with its spare and steady country backbeat challenge the line between black and white in a way that can't be denied.—dc

289

Lovin' on Back Streets, Mel Street
Produced by Dick Heard; Written by Hugh H. King
Metromedia 901   1972   #5 country

"The Dark End of the Street," honky-tonk style, except that for the couple sneaking around here, the passion isn't worth the pain. At least not for Street, who isn't just agonizing over the prospect of getting caught; he's suffering like a man who's *already* been found out. Mel's guilt stems from the fact that he and his outside

woman are actually cheating, whereas the furtive couple in "The Dark End of the Street" loves in the shadows because society leaves them no other choice. In other words, and as Mel's clench-jawed, George Jones–inspired delivery attests—especially when he sings of lying to his wife—there's nothing righteous about their situation at all. Unlike James Carr's version of "The Dark End of the Street," in which gospel choruses mingle agony and glory, or even the Kendalls' rendition of the song, in which forbidden love sounds like heaven on earth, this backstreet affair is pure hell.—bfw

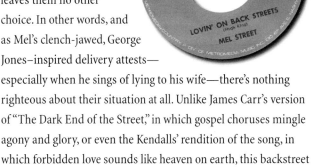

290

Bouquet of Roses, Eddy Arnold
Produced by Steve Sholes;
Written by Steve Nelson and Bob Hilliard
RCA Victor 20-2806   1948   #1 country (19 weeks); #13 pop

Eddy Arnold was originally heralded as the Tennessee Plowboy, a moniker he later rejected as too rural-sounding for a country singer courting crossover sales. But even when the young Arnold actually walked behind a mule on his family's land, he was on his way to becoming a country-pop crooner. Arnold grew up during the pre-Depression heyday of the stringband, but like the country audience generally, he quickly gravitated toward singers—in Arnold's case, it seems, the more pop the better. When he began learning guitar at age seven, the first song his mother taught him was a nineteenth-century song called "My Darling, Nelly Gray." As a teenager, he regularly sent off for the latest Bing Crosby and Gene Austin sides along with 78s by Jimmie Rodgers and Gene Autry. Arnold's rural background and commercial instincts would eventually place him at the vanguard of country music as it journeyed from the field to the city, from folk music to the Nashville Sound.

In 1930, the death of his father and the Great Depression conspired to turn Arnold's family into sharecroppers. Four years later he was a sixteen-year-old, sixth-grade dropout, working the fields during the day and playing dances, church socials, and other local events for a buck a night. At seventeen, he was a professional musician, following radio work from Jackson, Tennessee, to Memphis, St. Louis, and, in 1940, Nashville. There he spent the next three years as lead singer for Opry star Pee Wee King & His Golden West Cowboys. When he quit King, he embarked upon a solo career the likes of which country music hasn't seen since.

The Tennessee Plowboy's brand of country music ("The Southeast's answer to Gene Autry" is how critic John Morthland described it) was irresistible and unmistakably modern. Arnold's records showcased his fluid, self-confident crooning; the distinctive "ting-a-ling" steel guitar of another former Golden West Cowboy, Little Roy Wiggins; and some of the most beautiful melodies in country music. After his second single, "Each Minute Seems a Million Years," went Top Five in 1945, everything Arnold released for the next decade was a hit—fifty-seven consecutive Top Ten singles, nineteen of them chart toppers. Primarily under the guidance of Colonel Tom Parker, Elvis Presley's future manager, Arnold was so staggeringly popular that he left the Opry and dared (though only briefly) to place his "Hometown Reunion" radio show in head-to-head competition with the Opry on Saturday nights.

The peak was 1948, when Arnold had five #1 country hits (plus three more in the Top Five), the most redolent of the bunch being "Bouquet of Roses." Written by New York tunesmiths Steve Nelson and Bob Hilliard, the song sets a story of romantic dissolution to an aching melody. Arnold's reading is appropriately bittersweet. He's saying goodbye to a woman who won't be true by sending her a bouquet of roses, "one for every time you broke my heart." If you don't listen too closely, you'd swear his dulcet croon was almost ebullient, but this front is undercut by the way Wiggins's steel throws off notes that fall like wilted petals—and by the way Arnold, straining ever so slightly at the top of his natural range, has to fight to transform his tears into a dignified retreat.

"Bouquet of Roses" stayed on the country charts for over a year, including nineteen weeks at #1. It also just missed the pop Top Ten, a crossover success that Arnold would begin to pursue on every front. Ahead for Arnold were more crossover hits, Las Vegas concert appearances, four TV series, and significantly less

and less steel guitar. Then in the mid-sixties, after rock & roll kept him virtually hitless for five years, Arnold returned for a second career of Chet Atkins–produced Nashville Sound country hits that landed him on the pop charts nearly as often as they did on Johnny Carson's couch. The Plowboy had left the fields where he was raised, but by then, so had country music.—dc

291

Slow Poke, Pee Wee King & His Golden West Cowboys
Produced by Steve Sholes
Written by Pee Wee King, Redd Stewart, and Chilton Price
RCA Victor 48-0489   1951
#1 country (15 weeks); #1 pop (3 weeks)

Who's the most underrated act in country music history? There'd be plenty of potential nominees, but you'd be hard pressed to name a more important figure with less name recognition, let alone critical attention, than Pee Wee King.

An influential accordionist, bandleader, singer, and songwriter, King grew up in Wisconsin, the heart of polka country. In 1937, after a few years in Gene Autry's band, King joined the Grand Ole Opry, where over the next decade he and his Golden West Cowboys helped introduce that conservative radio program to everything from drums, amplified guitars, and horns to western music and Nudie suits. In the forties, his band provided an early testing ground for both Eddy Arnold and Cowboy Copas, and in the fifties, he become one of the first country performers to explore television, eventually hosting the short-lived *Pee Wee King Show* on ABC. At mid-century, three of King's songs, "Bonaparte's Retreat" (a popular fiddle tune to which he and partner Redd Stewart added lyrics), "Tennessee Waltz," and "You Belong to Me" were among the first from a country-associated songwriter to become pop hits, for Kay Starr, Patti Page, and Jo Stafford, respectively. King had major country hits with the first two of those songs as well, but hands down the most successful recording of his career was "Slow Poke," a country #1 for almost four months that eventually landed at the top of the pop charts as well. Not to mention the half dozen other versions of the song that cracked the pop Top Twenty in 1951 and 1952.

"Slow Poke" is King and the Golden West Cowboys at their country-pop finest. The record begins with King's accordion and the tick-tock-tick of a woodblock; throughout, the song's melodic elegance and breezy rhymes highlight the pop songcraft of King and collaborators singer/fiddler Stewart and Chilton Price. The lyric has Stewart complaining about the way his new slower-than-molasses girlfriend always leaves him checking his watch, often for hours at a time, while he waits for her to show. "I wait and then / Late again," Stewart croons sweetly, his tone more affectionate than perturbed. "Eight o'clock, nine o'clock, quarter to ten." It must be early in the relationship, since her chronic lateness still seems like an endearing quirk rather than proof of, at best, her insensitivity or, at worst, some kind of passive-aggressive power play. "I guess I'll have to learn to be a slow poke too," Stewart concludes, and at least for now, he seems to mean it. But it's worth noting that when King's accordion brings the song to a close, he's still waiting, and that woodblock is still counting off the seconds with an impatience that's bound to grow.—dc

292
Shame on You, Spade Cooley
Produced by Art Satherley; Written by Spade Cooley
OKeh 6731   1945   #1 country (9 weeks)

293
Smoke! Smoke! Smoke! (That Cigarette),
Tex Williams & His Western Caravan
Produced by Lee Gillette;
Written by Merle Travis and Tex Williams
Capitol Americana 40001   1947
#1 country (16 weeks); #1 pop (6 weeks)

West Coast fiddler and bandleader Spade Cooley hopped on the swing train of Milton Brown and Bob Wills and rode it all the way uptown. Spade and his big, sleek, Nudie-suited ensemble even cut Wills in a battle of the bands after Bob moved to southern California in 1943. And they did it with one hand tied behind their backs, or at least without the aid of the trumpet, trombone, and sax players Wills had in his employ.

After inheriting the band of his former boss, singer Jimmy Wakely, in 1942, Cooley promptly jettisoned his horn section and hired more fiddlers. The dense, orchestral weave they created—a sound, to invoke Cooley's contemporary Merle Travis, so round,

so firm, so fully packed—was more than enough to subdue the din of the dance halls. Especially with the bell-like tones of Spade's electric and steel guitarists punctuating the proceedings.

"Shame on You," a lilting mid-tempo ballad that has velvety crooner Tex Williams giving his philandering sweetheart a good tongue-lashing, shows what all the fuss was about: the tidal wash of fiddles, Joaquin Murphey's brassy steel, John Weis's cornet-like guitar comping all over the place. The record capped Cooley's ascendancy out west (a reign that lasted well into the fifties) and not just in the dance halls but on TV and at the movies as well. Always a volatile man and hard drinker, Spade bottomed out in 1961 when, in a drunken rage he beat his wife Ella Mae to death while their teenage daughter looked on.

Back in 1946, Cooley's hot temper also cost him the group that played on "Shame on You." When he fired Tex Williams after Capitol A&R man Lee Gillette offered the singer a solo contract, most of the rest of Spade's band defected to the affable Williams's new orchestra, the Western Caravan. Tex and company foundered for nearly a year without their old boss; then Merle Travis gave them "Smoke! Smoke! Smoke! (That Cigarette)," a novelty talking blues about that tyrannical master, tobacco. It quickly became Capitol's first #1 hit.

"Nicotine slaves are all the same / At a pettin' party or a poker game / Everything's gotta stop while they have that cigarette," Tex raps in a tar-stained baritone as juking rhythms, propelled by an infernal squeeze box, puff along in his wake. It makes for a breathless ride, especially with that jazzy trumpet and fiddle lighting up those breaks. It's addictive, too, just like those damn cigarettes.—bfw

294
Brown's Ferry Blues, The Delmore Brothers
Produced by Eli Oberstein; Written by Alton Delmore
Bluebird B-5403   1933   Pre-chart

The story goes that after almost losing to a novelty act at an old-time fiddlers contest, Alton Delmore told his brother Rabon something to the effect of: if they want funny, I'll give 'em funny. What he came up with was the blues.

And not just his or his brother's blues, but those of an entire community. The Delmores start this Depression-era number by joking about a "Hard luck papa, standin' in the rain / If the world was corn he couldn't buy a grain." They go on to laugh at and with women who're not only single but lonely, with folks who've cheated only to find themselves abandoned, and with anyone else along the Delmores' stretch of the Tennessee River who knows what it's like to declare "Lord, Lord, got them Brown's Ferry blues." As Langston Hughes wrote,

"Sad as the blues may be, there's almost always something humorous about them—even if it's the kind of humor that laughs to keep from crying."

That's something that's easier to pull off when the blues are backed up by proto-boogie guitar licks and airy harmonies that leave your soul skipping more lightly, like a flat rock over troubled waters.—dc

295

The Bridge Washed Out, Warner Mack
Produced by Owen Bradley; Written by Warner Mack
Decca 31774   1965   #1 country (1 week)

"When I awoke this morning" is how Warner Mack starts, but he might want to pinch himself to make sure he's not still sleeping. "The Bridge Washed Out" sounds for all the world as if Mack is still tossing and turning through a nightmare that any psychotherapist would have a field day with. Mack's beside himself because it's his wedding day, and because the only route to the ceremony—and his baby—is currently underwater. "The preacher and my bride's awaitin', and the wedding bells are startin' to chime," he blurts, frantic that he's going to be late. On a literal level, of course, that's silly; in the waking world, weddings tend to get postponed when there's a flood. Mack paces along the bank, staring at the deep water,

desperate to cross over but afraid he'll drown. Meanwhile, the music behind him—fever dream licks on the pedal steel, the jittery pulse of bass and drum, the Jordanaires Mr. Sandman-ish *buh buh bums*—produces an air of barely repressed anxiety while Mack drops details that are easy enough to interpret. "I can't kiss and hold her, and it's driving me out of mind," he blurts, and we know how much he wants marriage and all that comes with it. But then he cries, "I got one foot in the river, one foot solid on ground," and we know he's scared to death, too.

At some level, every relationship is a leap of faith. Looks like Mack will just to have to dive in.—dc

296

Milwaukee, Here I Come,
George Jones and Brenda Carter
Produced by Harold "Pappy" Daily; Written by Lee Fikes
Musicor 1325   1968   #12 country

297

What's Made Milwaukee Famous
(Has Made a Loser Out of Me), Jerry Lee Lewis
Produced by Jerry Kennedy; Written by Glenn Sutton
Smash 2164   1968   #2 country; #94 pop

It's Friday night, George and his wife have just picked up their paychecks at the brewery, and they've decided, spur of the moment, to hightail it down to Nashville for the Saturday night Opry. When they hit Music City, though, it turns out that the Mrs. (played here by Brenda Carter, a Houston-

based singer making her only chart appearance) has a plan of her own, and it doesn't include the Ryman. She's going to leave Jones at the motel while she heads out to find "the man for me," Ernest Tubb. "I love him, there's no doubt," she growls as if the old Troubadour were the most mouthwatering beefcake around. Not that she won't compromise if she has to: "If I can't find him, I'll settle for that bluegrass Lester Flatt." The George Jones of today, scrounging as he is for Young Country airplay, might be a bit more forgiving of a woman whose concept of a desirable male centers on a pair of fifty-four year-olds. But this is 1968, not 1998, and George is in no mood to play second fiddle. Who's it gonna be, he fires back. "Them Opry stars or me?"

Maybe neither, if some sexy newcomer should show up to turn his gal's head. On country radio in 1968 that likely would've been Jerry Lee Lewis, barely thirty-five and just setting out on a second career on country radio. Just a few months prior to Jones and Carter's duet, Lewis had followed up his breakthrough country single (the Top Five "Another Place, Another Time") with "What's Made Milwaukee Famous (Has Made a Loser Out of Me)," where an alcoholic realizes what a shambles he's made of his marriage. He knows he should take it on home to his wife; she's threatened to leave if he doesn't. Yet here he sits at a tavern, popping the tops off can after can of Schlitz, listening to the jukebox, unable to pull himself away. Twisting and stretching the notes of the title phrase, he unleashes a lamentation of pure anguish. Either Lewis is on intimate terms with the song's misery or he's a George Jones fan. Most likely both.

With records as powerful as Lewis's calling from the radio, it seems all but predictable that, back in "Milwaukee, Here I Come," Jones's character would face stiffer competition than E. T. and Lester. "I'm gonna leave this town till you decide which one you love the best," Jones barks. Half-mocking, half—"Hell, I can sing better than that clown," his voice descends to a thin, rubbery bass as he draws a line in the sand—"Me or Jerry Lee?" From the agitated sound of Lloyd Green's pedal steel, plus the way this frenzied revival-meeting arrangement puts the pedal to the metal, it's pretty clear she's made her choice. "O-o-o-ohh Milwaukee here I come," Jones moans through gritted teeth, all alone and racing north out of town. If Jerry Lee's single came on the radio just now, he'd probably drive off the road. Or catch an exit for the nearest bar.—dc

298

Motel Time Again, Johnny Paycheck
Produced by Aubrey Mayhew; Written by Bobby Bare
Little Darlin' 0016   1966   #13 country

Dilettantes who discover the sides Johnny Paycheck cut for the Little Darlin' label during the sixties often fixate on the most warped and sensational numbers, notably "He's in a Hurry (to Get Home to My Wife)" and "(Pardon Me) I've Got Someone to Kill." This puerile delight in Paycheck's zonked-out honky-tonk is ultimately reductive, painting him as a titillating novelty act, not as the tortured and tragic soul he indeed was. Apart from Lloyd

Green's *Twilight Zone*–inspired steel work, the eeriest thing about these records isn't their bent plot lines but the matter-of-fact, even dissociative, tone with which Paycheck renders them.

"Motel Time Again" was one of the few undeniably "out there" records Paycheck made for Little Darlin' that the label actually released as a single; it finds Johnny looking at the world through bloodshot eyes. "Oh I sit here on this stool / Drank so much I blew my cool / And now they're closin' up the world I'm living in," he sings, twisting the word "living" into knots like his boozing buddy George Jones while Green's bluesy steel blubbers away in the background. It's closing time, and Johnny, in the middle of a wicked bender, doesn't even know what *town* he's in. Still, he remains unfazed; he's been through the drill so often he's confident he'll be able to find his way back to his motel room.

That's the scary thing about this record. Sounding less disgusted than sure of himself, Johnny seems right at home two steps from the gutter. Or maybe he's just oblivious to how far from home he really is. Even scarier, though, is how this single— as well as Paycheck's "If I'm Gonna Sink (I Might as Well Go to the Bottom)"—became self-fulfilling prophecies when, down and out in L.A. in the late sixties, Johnny became the real life embodiment of his former boss Porter Wagoner's "Skid Row Joe."

Scary yes, but hardly titillating.—bfw

299

Pistol Packin' Mama, Al Dexter & His Troopers
Produced by Art Satherley; Written by Al Dexter
OKeh 6708   1944   #1 country (3 weeks); #1 pop

Alternate title: "Don't *Go Out* A'Drinkin' (With Lovin' on Your Mind)." At least not unless you want to get yourself killed.

Al Dexter was an aspiring singer when he wrote this cautionary tale in the late thirties. He was running a honky-tonk called the Round-Up in Longview, Texas, when a jealous wife packing a six-gun showed up looking for her two-timing husband. We don't know what happened after that, but Dexter goes for maximum dramatic effect here, having his hacked-off heroine shoot out the lights and kick in her husband's windshield as prelude to gunning him down there on the sawdust floor. Al's good-natured delivery and the record's jaunty accordion-and-trumpet-driven arrangement, the latter played by Gene Autry's Melody Ranch band, certainly mitigated the song's murderous intent. But how else could Dexter and producer Art Satherley have expected to get the record played on the radio *unless* they toned down its dicey themes? Of course, it didn't hurt that "Pistol Packin' Mama" sounded a whole lot smoother than the gutbucket sides Al had cut for ARC in the thirties, or that the song's melody was based on a much-loved favorite, Bob Wills's "Take Me Back to Tulsa."

All of these instincts proved good ones, as "Pistol Packin' Mama" quickly sold a million copies and topped both the country and the pop charts, becoming the first honky-tonk record ever to do so. The song was also a hit for pop stars Bing Crosby and Frank Sinatra, with Crosby's cover (a collaboration with the Andrews Sisters) staying at #1 on the country chart for five weeks and at #2 on the pop hit parade for four. Before its run was over, Bing's single had gone a long way toward etching country and western music into the pop consciousness. Yet in contrast to Dexter's record, which was ultimately tragicomic, Crosby's was all yucks, right down to Bing's boozy asides and the mess of zany sound effects, most of them lifted straight from the gag bag of Spike Jones. Crosby's is a great record, make no mistake. But while it captures the outrageousness of having a jealous lover shoot up a honky-tonk, Dexter's original never quite lets us forget the sober aftermath of scenes like the one he witnessed in that beer joint back in the thirties.—bfw

300

Bubba Shot the Jukebox, Mark Chesnutt
Produced by Mark Wright; Written by Dennis Linde
MCA 54471   1992   #4 country; #121 pop

"Dixie Fried," again. Except it's forty years later, and there's an emotional distance between story and storyteller that wasn't present in Carl Perkins's earlier version of the tale. Partly that's because of the songwriter. The perpetually winking Dennis Linde does his damnedest to make sure we're laughing at Bubba, not with him (his name is Bubba, for God's sake), when he takes out the jukebox for playing "a sad song that made him cry." But this

new distance also suggests the distances traveled by the country audience since the birth of rock & roll. Compared to the mid-fifties, the early nineties audience was far more likely to live in the suburbs and to identify itself as middle class. Or at least to believe that middle-class respectability was a possibility, which just wasn't an option for Perkins and his peers.

What makes the song more than just a caricature are all the musical touches that make it a record—and a first-rate example of the country audience's changing tastes. The single's heavy arena-rock backbeat, bluesy guitar figures, and rocking fiddle licks remind us that good old boys like Bubba now expect some Charlie Daniels and Lynyrd Skynyrd alongside the country weepers on their jukeboxes. The record's over-the-top harmonies and visceral string arrangement hint that they like a little Aerosmith on there, too. Most revealing, Mark Chesnutt twangs through his story in an accent that's unmistakably southern. Hot New Country may have been taking the music uptown in 1992, but as far as the rest of the world is concerned, that accent means only one thing—singer, songwriter, and audience ain't so far removed from Bubba as they'd like to think.—dc

301

Miller's Cave, Hank Snow
Produced by Chet Atkins; Written by Jack Clement
RCA Victor 7748   1960   #9 country; #101 pop

Mid-century pulp fiction, delivered Nashville Sound style. As Hank Snow tells us how his girl cuckolded him with "a man they called Big Dave," and how he subsequently murdered them both, an echo-y backing choir follows along behind like a taunting Greek chorus or maybe voices in his head. Yet it's Snow's vocals that make the record truly scary. The mocking contempt with which he delivers his threat—"I said, 'You'll pay, both you and Day-vee,'"—and the coolly mad way he makes good on it—"They laughed at me, and then I shot 'em"—comes straight out of an EC Comic or a Jim Thompson novel. At the end, Snow wanders lost in the very cave where he's fled to stash "their cheatin', schemin' bones," and his voice bounces off the walls like ironic laughter in *The Twilight Zone*.—dc

302
Stackalee, Frank Hutchison
No producer credited; Written by Frank Hutchison
OKeh 45106   1927   Pre-chart

Stagolee was, undoubtedly and without question, the baddest
nigger that ever lived. Stagolee was so bad that the flies wouldn't
even fly around his head in the summertime, and snow
wouldn't fall on his house in the winter. He was bad, jim.
                                                    —*Julius Lester*

Like those of Casey Jones, John Henry, and High John the Conqueroo, the myth of the Stagolee (a.k.a. "Staggerlee" or "Stackalee") is as outsized as any folk tale ever told. The particulars of the story, which may or may not be based on a murder that took place in Memphis around 1900, are few, but nearly every version shares a handful of details and the same skeletal plot.

The narrative revolves around a back-alley scuffle between Stagolee and a man known, among other things, as Billy Lyons or Billy the Lion. The two fight over a Stetson hat until Stag pulls a gun and shoots Billy dead, but not before the poor guy begs for mercy, whimpering that he has a wife and small children to support. Other than that, the only limits imposed upon the teller of the tale are those native to his or her imagination. Some have Stag arrested, but it usually turns out that no sheriff, jail, or noose can hold him. How it all ends depends almost entirely on the moral the narrator wishes to impart.

Stagolee's myth has had greatest resonance among black communities in the South, and perhaps never more than at the height of Jim Crow, when being able to identify with someone who did whatever he damn well pleased afforded black people both a measure of self-affirmation and a vicarious taste of freedom. From Chuck Berry's "Brown-Eyed Handsome Man" and Curtis Mayfield's "Superfly" to gangsta MCs like Ice-T and the Notorious B.I.G., shades of Stagolee have been manifesting themselves in the form of black outlaw-heroes ever since.

Curiously, one of the earliest recordings of Stagolee came not from a black singer but from a white man named Frank Hutchison, a songster from West Virginia who cut a harmonica-sweetened version of the ballad under the title "Stackalee" back in 1927. Hutchison, who is also known for the popular Depression-era number "The Train That Carried My Girl from Town," learned to sing and play bottleneck guitar as a boy from black railroad workers, and it was doubtless from them that he first heard "Stackalee."

Nevertheless, from its poetic opening lines ("It was out in an alley, one dark and drizzly night") to the way he has Stack roguishly promise to care for Billy's wife just as he pulls the trigger, Hutchison gives the song his own distinctive stamp. In fact, it's a testament to his narrative that so much of it resurfaces some thirty years later in a #1 pop single by R&B singer Lloyd Price. The big difference between the two records, besides their arrangements, is that whereas in Hutchison's account Stack ends up in prison haunted by Billy's ghost, Price's "bad man" gets away with murder. Hutchison's isn't the only version in which Stackalee gets his comeuppance, and as Mississippi John Hurt's 1928 rendition attests, it doesn't just happen in recordings of the ballad made by whites.—bfw

303
Wild and Blue, John Anderson
Produced by Frank Jones with John Anderson;
Written by John Scott Sherrill
Warner Brothers 29917   1982   #1 country (2 weeks)

Neither of Anderson's neotraditionalist counterparts George Strait or Ricky Skaggs could have handled this bizarre tale of dissipation so deftly. Strait's croon is too staid, Skaggs's mountain tenor too clean, but Anderson's guttural slurs and coon-dog whine— backed here by the sobbing vocals of his sister, a woman whose drawl is so down-home it almost makes John sound like Jim Reeves— make it sing.

Anderson's lover is about to step out on him, the record's waltzing rhythms and rolling banjo are propelling her out the door. Lloyd Green's steel and the twin fiddles whimpering in the background tell us it's killing John to sit idly by. But he loves his woman and believes it's just her nature to cheat. That's why, at four in the morning, after her crosstown tryst is over, the cuckolded chump is ready to welcome her back home.

Or is he? Green's steel takes on an eerie feel during the last verse, and Pig Robbins's piano sounds like a death knell. When on the final chorus John wails, "They could just take you up yonder," it's as if he's stumbled onto an idea—maybe *he* could launch his high-flying angel into oblivion and let her know what it feels like to be *black* and blue.—*bfw*

304

Little Maggie, The Stanley Brothers & the Clinch Mountain Boys
Produced by Don Pierce; Traditional
Starday 45-522   1960   Did not chart

Ralph Stanley's voice is a force of nature. That's a cliché, sure, but it's still true. And not just because comparing Stanley's bracing, hog-call tenor to, say, a gale storm or a hurricane feels like an apt metaphor. Hearing that voice can raise goose bumps on your arms or the hair on your neck as surely as a sudden chill wind.

This 1960 recording of an old folk song the Stanleys first cut in the late forties is Ralph at his most affecting. He's convinced that "Little Maggie" was made for him, just as "pretty flowers were made for blooming [and] pretty stars were made to shine." But since he's caught her dancing for the favors of other men, he also knows his hopes will never be realized. "Go away, go away little Maggie," he implores, delivering the line like it's the most painful he's ever spoken.

Then again, the force of Stanley's phrasing is so great, his expert use of tone and texture so compelling, that the words almost don't matter. When he lets loose those high, cutting notes, then holds them, his voice has a distressed quality that's practically tactile. It's as if grief itself could flash like lightning or hang like a damp mist in the day's final light.—*dc*

305

Who Will Buy the Wine, Charlie Walker
Produced by Don Law; Written by Billy Mize
Columbia 41633   1960   #11 country

306

Charlie's Shoes, Billy Walker
Produced by Don Law; Written by Ray Baham
Columbia 42287   1962   #1 country (2 weeks)

It's always been easy to mix up the names of Charlie and Billy Walker. They were both Texans with the same last name (though they weren't related). They shared a record label and a producer, were on the charts at the same time, and were about the same age. Muddying things further, Billy found his signature hit with a song called "Charlie's Shoes." Billy's "Charlie's Shoes" is about wishing you could have someone else's life—in this case, wishing you were lucky enough to be married to Charlie's *wife*—only to find out you should be careful what you wish for. "Now I'm wearing out the shoes that Charlie wore," Billy sings, "walking back and forth across the floor / the troubles that drove him away I've got for company."

That's a theme that might've been pulled straight from the Charlie Walker songbook. In fact, "Charlie's Shoes" sounds a lot like Billy Walker might be agonizing over the very gal that caused Charlie Walker to walk the floor just a couple of years prior. In "Who Will Buy the Wine," Charlie's wife leaves him at home each night to hit the bars. "Not long ago you held our baby's bottle / but the one you're holding now's a different kind," Charlie complains. "You just sit and wait to be somebody's baby / and it all depends on who will buy the wine." Yikes! As Billy would learn soon enough, Charlie's shoes are jammed full of tacks.

Such comparisons only get you so far, though, and Billy and Charlie Walker were ultimately quite different recording acts. "Who Will Buy the Wine," with a twin fiddle kickoff, a driving shuffle beat, and C. Walker's piercing, twangy tenor, is post-rockabilly honky-tonk at its finest. "Charlie's Shoes," on the other hand, features B. Walker's smooth

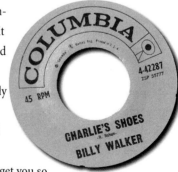

croon, a catchy backing chorus, a springy acoustic rhythm bed, and a hook that's whistled rather than picked or bowed.

Or to sum up succinctly, Billy walked around in Marty Robbins's shoes, Charlie in Ray Price's.—dc

307
The Image of Me, Conway Twitty
Produced by Owen Bradley; Written by Wayne Kemp
Decca 32272   1968   #5 country

A classic tale of dissolution and regret, but with a twist; instead of bemoaning *his* lost innocence, Conway rues the way he's corrupted the love of his life, a "simple, old-fashioned" girl he remade in his own hard-drinking, fast-living image.

The story begins unassumingly enough. Grady Martin's after-hours guitar, Lew Houston's woozy steel, and David Briggs's tinkling piano place Conway in a bar. Talking with some of the regulars, he agrees with the general consensus that his gal is the life of the party, but he reminds them, and himself, that there's more to her than meets the eye. "Don't be fooled by her laughter," Conway sings, his resolute baritone betraying a hint of desperation. "She has her sad times, she knows how to cry."

That desperation builds as Joe E. Lewis and the Jordanaires enter on the chorus, and Conway, hesitating a bit, reveals that "she drinks and she talks just a little too loud." Lewis's high harmonies on the word "little" intensify this anguish as Conway, through clenched jaws, confesses, "Yes I know I'm to blame, and I feel so ashamed, that I made her the image of me." The realization that he dragged her down—and that it's because of *him* they've drifted apart—is eating him alive.

A sobering cautionary tale, one that offers a chilling amen to Kitty Wells's claim that when you get down to it, it's usually men who make honky-tonk angels.—bfw

308
A Picture of Me (without You), George Jones
Produced by Billy Sherrill;
Written by Norro Wilson and George Richey
Epic 10917   1972   #5 country

George hopes to win his baby back by tugging at her heartstrings. It's a simple, even simplistic, ploy—he paints nine different scenarios depicting just how incomplete his life is without her. They're all pretty hackneyed—a garden with no flowers, heaven with no angels, and so on. It's a good thing producer Billy Sherrill doesn't lay the music on too thick. He makes liberal enough use of strings and background choruses, but it's all very understated, the only other audible sounds being Pig Robbins's teardrop piano, Pete Drake's sighing steel, and the heartbeat pulse of the A-Team rhythm section. It all builds to a swelling crescendo, but surely George must have won her back

before that—indeed, before the end of the first verse when, with a tender ache in his voice, he invites her to "imagine a world where no music's playing." Odds are, not a word George sings registers with her after that, not with the ba-bum of the bass, piano, and drums burning that terrible image into her mind—that picture of how empty *her* world would be without the sound of his voice.—bfw

309
Wondering, Webb Pierce
Produced by Owen Bradley; Written by Joe Werner
Decca 9-46364   1952   #1 country (4 weeks)

"Wondering," Webb Pierce's debut single for Decca and first #1, finds him updating the Cajun music he heard while growing up in Louisiana. In this case, it's a lovelorn waltz the Hackberry Ramblers recorded in 1936 as the Riverside Ramblers, the name under which Bluebird released the sides the group cut in English.

Pierce and producer Owen Bradley stick fairly close to the Ramblers' fiddle-sweetened arrangement, but this being the golden age of honky-tonk, they augment that stringband sound with Jimmy Day's woeful steel and Hank Garland's bluesy electric guitar fills. Not even these jukebox adjustments, though, nor the whiff of cheating in the line where Webb speculates about who might be kissing his girl, make "Wondering" sound like anything other than a sentimental old parlor song. We don't even have reason to believe Webb is off drowning his sorrows in some bar; just the opposite, he sounds like he's home every night beseeching the Almighty to bring back the one he loves—that is, praying for a miracle, and not just to the Lord above. The way his whining tenor pierces the thick bayou air, you can bet he's hoping against hope that his long-gone lover will hear him as well.—bfw

310

Pine Grove Blues, Nathan Abshire

Produced by George Khoury; Written by Nathan Abshire
O.T. 102A   1949   Did not chart

The accordion might be one of the cornerstones of Cajun music, but it hadn't been invented when Acadian exiles began resettling in French Louisiana during the latter half of the eighteenth century. It wasn't until Cajuns heard German immigrants playing the instrument around 1850 (it first appeared in 1829) that they started pairing it with the fiddle. Able to produce a louder, fuller sound than its bowed counterpart, it wasn't long before the squeeze-box took the spotlight in most Cajun dance bands.

The accordion predominated at the tail end of World War I when Nathan Abshire first started messing with it as a kid. The instrument's vogue, though, didn't last, not after the advent of radio and the building of major highways, which brought an influx of sounds from outside Cajun country, notably hillbilly music and western swing. Soon accordion-driven acts were being supplanted by fiddle-spurred stringbands like the Hackberry Ramblers and Leo Soileau's Three Aces. It wouldn't be till after the Second World War, in the years just before the first burst of rock & roll, that the instrument finally made a comeback—in large part due to the recordings of Iry LeJeune and Abshire's "Pine Grove Blues."

A bayou cousin of DeFord Bailey's "Pan American Blues" and Ervin Rouse's "Orange Blossom Special," "Pine Grove Blues"

evokes the sound of a train picking up a head of steam and barreling down the track. Abshire kicks off the commotion with a swaggering flurry of notes, the rush of air between the bellows of his button-boxes making a chugging sound as the whistle-like drone of Will Kegley's fiddle pierces the din. "Yaa, let's go," Abshire roars, hailing the rest of the band to hop on board as the upright bass lays down a crude, jug-like rhythm. Whoops, hollers, and a steel guitar punctuate the ride while Abshire—equal parts jump-blues shouter and carnival barker—crows the song's Cajun lyrics in a beer-soaked yawp before guiding the train back into the station.

Small wonder Abshire's backwoods locomotion incited an accordion revival. It anticipates the ravings of Little Richard and Jerry Lee Lewis and, at its most frenetic, makes those wild men almost sound tame.—bfw

311

My Wife Died Saturday Night, Dr. Humphrey Bate & His Possum Hunters

No producer or writer credited
Brunswick 271   1928   Pre-chart

Uncles Dave Macon and Jimmy Thompson were easily the most flamboyant stars of the early Grand Ole Opry. Yet it was Dr. Humphrey Bate & His Possum Hunters who embodied, even more, the ebullient *esprit de corps* of the emerging Opry; their rendition of "There'll Be a Hot Time in the Old Town Tonight" often opened the show's eight o'clock segment. According to the history books, Bate and company were also the first stringband to perform on the show, the first to play hillbilly music on Nashville radio, and the first Opry act to tour.

Bate, an M.D. with a degree from Vanderbilt Medical School, grew up thirty miles outside Nashville, where he learned to play old-time dance tunes on harmonica and guitar from the former slaves who worked on his father's plantation. He put together his first band around 1900 and, for the next twenty-five years, played a wide-ranging repertoire, à la fellow Opry star DeFord Bailey, at social gatherings throughout Middle Tennessee. Bate's ensemble typically included one or two fiddles, but this 1928 recording for Brunswick features just him on harmonica and vocals, backed by Walter Liggett's rampaging banjo, Staley Walton's rhythm guitar, and Oscar Albright's feverishly bowed bass fiddle.

Bate's harmonica and Liggett's banjo chase each other around the stump a couple times before Bate belts out the first chorus: "My wife died Saturday night, Sunday she was buried / Monday was my courtin' day and Tuesday I got married." The doc delivers these lines with next to no emotion, and doubtless his seeming indifference generated its fair share of laughs, including a few nervous titters. But as the pickers break it down a couple more times it's clear that words aren't the point here. This romp ain't nothin' but a party or, as Opry founder George Hay put it, a good-natured riot.—bfw

312
If You've Got the Money I've Got the Time,
Lefty Frizzell
Produced by Art Satherley and Don Law;
Written by Lefty Frizzell and Jim Beck
Columbia 4-20739   1950   #1 country (3 weeks)

In the early fifties, when Lefty Frizzell stepped to the mike at honky-tonks and dance halls across the Southwest, teenage girls and grown women would blush and scream and rush the stage, the better to listen as his sensual voice curled its way through his biggest hits. But not just to listen. Lefty's boyish good looks (including a roguish grin and dark, curly hair that the singer was smart enough not to hide under a cowboy hat) provided an enticing frame for that dreamy voice. In person, the total Lefty package oozed emotional sensitivity, easy charm, and undisguised sexuality in just about equal measures.

Surely only a singer with Frizzell's charisma could've succeeded with a proposition as crass as "If You've Got the Money I've Got the Time." Lefty's pockets are empty in his chart debut but, if some pretty new friend wants to pay his way . . . well, hell, he's all hers. "We'll go to the park where it's dark / we won't fool around," he entices, his voice both winking and earnest while fiddle and piano dance and skip to a seductive beat. Still, Lefty

wants to make sure she understands that when it comes to "you with no more money, honey, I've no more time." In other words, Lefty's a male gold digger, a scrub in today's parlance, and one who's completely up front about what he's offering. Irresistible, too. Bewitched, country fans across the land, male and female alike, heard Lefty's terms and responded, "Let's go." Then they took off for the record store, handed over their hard-earned money, and demanded, "Lefty please!"—dc

313
Above and Beyond, Buck Owens
Produced by Ken Nelson; Written by Harlan Howard
Capitol 4337   1960   #3 country

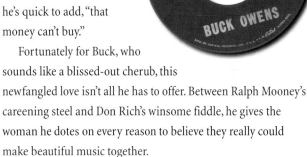

As clever a play for a woman's hand as any committed to tape. Poor boy Buck meets the girl of his dreams and, sensing that "All I Have to Offer You (Is Me)" ain't gonna cut it, promises her something that no man has—something that Buck didn't know existed till he made it up there on the spot. "Love beyond the call of love," he calls it—a love, he's quick to add, "that money can't buy."

Fortunately for Buck, who sounds like a blissed-out cherub, this newfangled love isn't all he has to offer. Between Ralph Mooney's careening steel and Don Rich's winsome fiddle, he gives the woman he dotes on every reason to believe they really could make beautiful music together.

A Texas-born sharecropper's son who as a kid picked peaches and cotton in the fields outside Bakersfield, Owens wouldn't be courting women empty-handed for long. On the strength of early Top Ten records like this one and "Under Your Spell Again," Owens scored a total of twenty #1 country singles over the next twelve years. He used the royalties to build an entertainment empire that would eventually induce people to rechristen his adopted home "Buckersfield."

Harlan Howard, the guy who wrote this song and co-wrote other hits such as "I've Got a Tiger by the Tail" with Buck, didn't make out too shabbily either—doubtless above and beyond *his* wildest dreams. While Owens and his Buckaroos were in the studio cutting this record, Howard was watching singer Guy

Mitchell take his "Heartaches by the Number" (a #2 country hit for Ray Price in 1959) to the top of the pop charts. The success of Mitchell's record prompted Howard, still an aspiring tunesmith, to move to Music City, where he immediately fell in with drinking and writing buddies Willie Nelson and Hank Cochran and, later, became known as the "dean" of Nashville songwriters.—bfw

314
Kiss an Angel Good Mornin', Charley Pride
Produced by Jack Clement; Written by Ben Peters
RCA 0550   1971   #1 country (5 weeks); #21 pop

Had a rake like Lefty Frizzell sung this in his slippery, blue drawl, it would've positively oozed sex and sounded like a come-on. But crooned in a cozy baritone by gentle-

manly and sincere-beyond-doubt Charley Pride, it's a recipe for romance. Stir in Jerry Carrigan's heartbeat pulse, Gene O'Neal's wooing steel, and those sweetly lowing twin fiddles; let that good mornin' kiss simmer all day; "and love her like the devil when you get back home." Attend to every tender detail, Charley is saying; make intimacy, not sex, the focus of lovemaking because, as he knows, few things are sexier than intimacy. Which is doubtless why Charley can sing about having a satisfied grin on his face all the time. He's getting good home cookin' every morning *and* every night.—bfw

315
If You Ain't Lovin' (You Ain't Livin'), Faron Young
Produced by Ken Nelson; Written by Tommy Collins
Capitol 2953   1954   #2 country

A Cadillac, a forty-room shack, a bucketful of money, and a tree full of honey. You can have all that, reckons Hank acolyte Faron Young, but "If you're gettin' no huggin', no kissin' or a-muggin' "—that is, "If you ain't lovin' "— "then you ain't livin'."

Young couldn't match his hero's poetic genius, but he comes off like some kind of cracker-barrel philosopher on this unsinkable, Hank-style shuffle, and with a big helping of "Hey Good Lookin' "–inspired corn pone to boot.

Yeah, well, look at the songwriting credit here, and it'll come as no surprise. "If You Ain't Lovin' " was written by the great Tommy Collins, perhaps the only man who could number everyone from wise guys Roger Miller and Harlan Howard, to the typically less sanguine Merle Haggard, as protégés.—bfw

316
This Kiss, Faith Hill
Produced by Byron Gallimore and Faith Hill;
Written by Robin Lerner, Annie Roboff,
and Beth Nielsen Chapman
Warner Bros. 17247-2   1998   #1 country (3 weeks); #7 pop

"Unstoppable" was how this record's hook-rich chorus put it and, as much as any country hit of the nineties, "This Kiss" and its country-pop Wall of Sound (the "Rose Garden" of its era?) seemed destined to cross over and go pop. Even if the insistent backbeat and chugging guitars of the first few bars didn't grab you, there was no resisting the cascade of emotion in the polysyllabic romp that followed. "It's a pivotal moment / It's (ah) subliminal," Hill purrs on the chorus. She may be singing about the first stirrings of desire, but with that steel rampaging behind her, she might as well have been talking about the way the sound of a great single, like true love, sweeps you off your feet. "Unsinkable," indeed. Here was a case of the cream rising to the top and spilling all over the place.—bfw

317
Cuddle Buggin' Baby, Eddy Arnold
Produced by Steve Sholes; Written by Red Rowe
RCA Victor 48-0342   1950   #2 country

Eddy Arnold's "Cuddle Buggin' Baby" is everything you want in a novelty song. It's musically captivating (check out Vic Willis's snazzy little piano solo, which barely lets Little Roy Wiggins's steel guitar get a word in edgewise), melodically irresistible, and crooned like a dream come true. So long, that is, as the dreamer in question is horny as hell. That's Eddy all over, and it's a good thing, too—he's fallen for a young woman who'd rather, um, "cuddle bug" than anything else.

Nowadays, many retro-minded alt-country types like to perform just this sort of mid-century country-boogie novelty. Their clear admiration for the material, though, is sometimes curdled by a begrudging wink—the joke apparently being that this is charming and all but, hey, we know it's pure corn pone. Arnold is winking as well, but only enough to confirm that he and his gal are interested in more than snuggling. Eddy's croon stays lighthearted simply because his heart is light; his voice floats on pure gladness. "Oh, I love my little darlin', and I guess I always will," he sings with a grin that stretches ear to ear. "When it comes to cuddlebuggin', I just never get my fill." Proof positive that feeling playful is not the same thing as kidding around.—dc

318

Elvira, Rodney Crowell
Produced by Brian Ahern; Written by Dallas Frazier
Warner Bros. 8637   1978   #95 country

If you only know this song in its wooden, antiseptic Oak Ridge Boys' monster of a 1981 crossover hit, you don't know what you're missing. When the Oak Ridgers do those *Giddy-up-oom-poppa-oom-poppa-mow-mows*, you can't help but visualize Sha Na Na soldiering through their third or sixth theme park performance of the afternoon. When Rodney Crowell sings 'em, it's hard not to blush; he wrings every drop of sweaty, nasty, horny glee there is from this Dallas Frazier classic.

Over the next decade, Crowell would establish himself as one of Nashville's most sought-after songwriters and producers, eventually attaining stardom in his own right. His first charting (just barely) single leaves you dumbfounded it took so long. Here, he stokes his down-home country soul with the playfulness of the Coasters and the libido of Jerry Lee. "El-vy-ruh, my heart's on fire-ruh," he yelps like a glowing hunk of burning love. That's to be expected when you're riding steamy Emmylou Harris harmonies and a smoldering rhythm bed stoked by guitarists James Burton and Ry Cooder, pianist Glen D. Hardin, and bassist Emory Gordy Jr. Giddy up, indeed. And oom-poppa-oom too!—dc

319

Whole Lot of Shakin' Going On, Jerry Lee Lewis
Produced by Jack Clement;
Written by Dave Williams and Sonny David (Roy Hall)
Sun 267   1957   #1 country (2 weeks); #3 pop; #1 R&B

To anyone who came of age when rock & roll was simply a fact of life, it can sometimes be hard to understand what was so terrifying to some listeners about the first generation of hep cats and their music. But check out "Whole Lot of Shakin' Going On," even today, and part of that threat still shoots out of the speakers—the Killer, sweaty and leering and getting it on.

From note one, Lewis's famous "Pumping Piano" does just that. Drummer J. M. Van Eaton furiously slams his kit until you'd almost swear those aren't drums he's playing at all—more like a headboard against a wall. "Aw, let's go," Lewis screams, but Van Eaton's already gone, so carried away with the moment that, like a simultaneous climax, he's still banging out his fill a bar into the beginning of Jerry Lee's own wild solo. Momentarily catching his breath, Jerry Lee entices his lover to "shake, baby, shake" and "wiggle it around just a little bit" and "take the bull by the horn." "Come all over, baby," he shouts more than once, plain as day. Right there on the radio!

The Pelvis was about sex too, of course, but more in the bump and grind of his stage act than on his records. Jerry Lee's "Whole Lot of Shakin' Going On" was another matter entirely. It didn't just suggest sex; it rubbed it all over you. Still does.—dc

320

Everybody's Truckin', The Modern Mountaineers
Produced by Eli Oberstein; Written by Babe Fritsch
Bluebird 6911   1937   Pre-chart

Not about an increase in over-the-road freight.

You can spot the influences of vaudeville and minstrelsy, Tin Pan Alley pop, and the blues in "Everybody's Truckin'," but they're all swirled together by a mighty beat. In other words, you hear jazz, which by the late thirties had reached out to touch just about every spot on the American musical landscape. When pianist

Smokey Woods shouts "Everybody's doin' it now," he's explaining why a band of self-described Mountaineers, recording in San Antonio, would be throwing themselves so uproariously into the music of Harlem "darkies" singing "Hy-dee-ho." No question about it—these western swingers are "modern." Just check out that series of hot improvisations on the fiddle, sax, piano, and steel guitar.

Might've been a major hit too, if only Woods hadn't replaced "truckin' " about every third time with "fuckin'." Which *is* what it's about.—dc

321
Pussy, Pussy, Pussy, Light Crust Doughboys
Produced by Art Satherley; Written by Marvin Montgomery
Vocalion 04560   1938   Pre-chart

Me-*ow*! Double-entendre isn't as common in country music as it is in blues or jazz, but the likes of Milton Brown's "Easy Ridin' Papa" and Jimmie Revard's "Cake Eatin' Man" helped make risqué numbers all the rage during the golden age of western swing. This blue material was pretty much the province of the dance halls and jukeboxes; certainly no radio stations down South, the heart of the Bible Belt, were going to touch it.

"Pussy, Pussy, Pussy" is a vaudevillian mess-around from a late-thirties edition of the germinal Light Crust Doughboys. Judging by the sounds of Knocky Parker's prancing piano, Ramon DeArmon's ass-slapping bass, and Zeke Campbell's randy, single-string guitar breaks, it could have been recorded in a cathouse. It's also as transparent as "dirty swing" gets. One of the band's members, he of the outrageous falsetto, has lost his cherished feline and enlists his mates in a pillar-to-post search. Their incessant cries of "pussy, pussy, pussy" turn up stray after stray, but none of them fits the

bill, least of all the last, which neither looks nor *smells* like their bereft buddy's, um, cat.

Doubtless some found the Doughboy's brazen cavorting obscene, and there's no denying they're objectifying women. But with music this transporting and gags this over the top, only a prude could take real offense. Indeed, only a stick-in-the-mud could resist reeling off a Bob Wills–like "Aaah-Hah!" Or maybe even joining in on a chorus or two of "Here, kitty, kitty!"—bfw

322
Love's Gonna Live Here, Buck Owens
Produced by Ken Nelson; Written by Buck Owens
Capitol 5025   1963   #1 country (16 weeks)

The sound of a new day dawning, and not just romantically for Buck in the wake of divorce. With Don Rich singing those outrageous harmonies and teasing that twang out of his Telecaster, it's the start of something new for rock & roll as well. Soon the records of the Beatles, then the Byrds, and later those of CCR and The Band would all bear the Bucka-roos' stamp. In other words, Buck, Don, and the boys knew what they were doing. They could see the music's future looking out their *front* door.—bfw

323
Everybody's Talkin', Nilsson
Produced by Rick Jarrard; Written by Fred Neil
RCA Victor 447-0838   1969   #6 pop

Country musicians borrow ideas from the pop field all the time, but the trade works both ways. "Everybody's Talkin' " was written by a veteran of the Greenwich Village folk scene and recorded in 1968 by a singer-songwriter the Beatles once named as their favorite. Somehow, though, Nilsson's recording of Fred Neil's song ended up sounding exactly like the next Glen Campbell single. Its hard-traveling lyrics, backed by a front-porch rhythm track driven by twangy acoustic picking, echoed Campbell's break-through record from the year before, "Gentle on My Mind." And just a few months after Nilsson's single first "Bubbled Under" the Billboard Hot 100, Campbell hit with the Al DeLory–produced

"Wichita Lineman," which featured a high, sustained string part that easily could've been inspired by the one on "Everybody's Talkin'."

These connections are no stretch either. Those strings on "Everybody's Talkin'" had been arranged by George Tipton who, like Campbell, had once worked with the Beach Boys; Nilsson himself had written songs for Phil Spector, whose Wrecking Crew studio team included both Campbell and DeLory. Yet, despite all this pop pedigree, it was the country atmosphere of "Everybody's Talkin'" that stood out— and that made it the perfect choice to play over the poignant final scene of the 1969 movie *Midnight Cowboy*. "I'm going to where the weather suits my clothes," Nilsson sang to that road-song rhythm. On screen, the cowboy of the title and his New York friend fly along in a Greyhound, fleeing New York and headed south.—dc

324
You Ain't Going Nowhere, The Byrds
Produced by Gary Usher; Written by Bob Dylan
Columbia 44499   1968   #74 pop

325
She's Gone Gone Gone, Lefty Frizzell
Produced by Don Law and Frank Jones;
Written by Harlan Howard
Columbia 43256   1965   #12 country

"You ain't going nowhere" sums up the Nashville establishment's response when the Byrds took the country plunge with their 1968 *Sweetheart of the Rodeo* LP. The group recorded the album at Columbia Studios on Music Row, the same place country giants Ray Price, Lefty Frizzell, Marty Robbins, and others had cut some of their biggest hits. The Byrds even enlisted a few Nashville ringers like banjo man John Hartford, bass player Junior Huskey, and steel guitarist Lloyd Green for the sessions. Yet the reception that greeted the band when they appeared on the Opry that week in March was icy to say the least. Gram Parsons's last-minute decision to play "Hickory Wind," a homesick original, instead of a second Merle Haggard cover as agreed upon, didn't exactly go over big with the show's brass. And DJ Ralph Emery, none too impressed with the gatecrashers' take on country, gave Parsons and McGuinn the cold shoulder when they visited his all-night show on WSM. As a belated rejoinder, the two men wrote the send-up "Drug Store Truck Drivin' Man," slyly casting the repressive Emery as the "head of the Ku Klux Klan."

The old guard's reaction to the Byrds "gone country" was hardly surprising. Even if they weren't viewed as carpetbaggers, the group's playing didn't hold a candle to the A-Teamers who graced records by the likes of Price, Robbins, and Frizzell. And while the Byrds' remakes of material made famous by Gene Autry, Merle Haggard, and the Louvin Brothers were heartfelt enough (after all, Chris Hillman got his start in bluegrass and Parsons worshipped at the altar of country music), their versions were no match for the originals. To top it all off, the record's first single, a stately cover of Bob Dylan's abstruse "You Ain't Going Nowhere," wasn't exactly aimed at the Opry crowd, not even with Green's shimmering steel bringing it all back home. The Byrds weren't kidding, though. When McGuinn sang, "Strap yourself to a tree with roots / You ain't going nowhere," he wasn't just parroting Dylan; he was saying, "*We* ain't going nowhere—this is *our* music too."

History bears out McGuinn and company, at least in terms of their legacy. Along with Dylan's earlier Nashville recordings (also made at Columbia Studios) and some of those made by Parsons and Hillman's subsequent band, the Flying Burrito Brothers, *Sweetheart* introduced country music to a new generation of rock fans. The ensuing country-rock movement spawned at least three generations of acolytes: laid-back groups like the Eagles and Poco in the seventies, cowpunks like the Long Ryders and Jason & the Scorchers in the eighties, and alt-country bands like Uncle Tupelo and the Jayhawks in the nineties. Much of the music these groups and their peers made wasn't really country, involving little more than the wedding of down-home themes and instrumentation to what was ultimately rock music. But the best of it, notably the records of the Scorchers and the Jayhawks, revealed a deep affinity with the sounds that inspired *Sweetheart*, advancing both country and rock traditions in the process.

Of course, what made *Sweetheart* such a watershed event was its claim to being the first overt—and in large part successful—attempt to cross over to country from rock. Whatever. For all the "pioneering" rhetoric writers have heaped on the album over the years, what the Byrds were doing sonically had been going on up and down Music Row—and out in Bakersfield—at least since the arrival of Elvis and Jerry Lee. Lefty Frizzell's "She's Gone Gone Gone" is a case in point. Recorded at Columbia Studios three years before the Byrds invaded Nashville, it combines the core elements of "You Ain't Going Nowhere"—the rockin' backbeat, the sprightly flatpicking, that careening steel. All of the Byrds' "innovations," plus that far out fuzz-toned guitar, heard not just that summer on the Rolling Stones' "Satisfaction," but on Marty Robbins's 1961 smash "Don't Worry" when a glitch in the board distorted Grady Martin's guitar mid-take. All of which is to say that maybe the tepid reception those seemingly Luddite Nashville cats gave "You Ain't Going Nowhere" was just their way of saying, "Been there, done that . . . and better too."—bfw

326

Last Train to Clarksville, The Monkees
Produced by Tommy Boyce;
Written by Tommy Boyce and Bobby Hart
Colgems 1001   1966   #1 pop (1 week)

The greatest country-rock record ever available on the back of a cereal box.

For that matter, it'd take a pretty stunted definition of the genre not to hear "Last Train To Clarksville" as a great country-rock record, period. Of course, the cult of Michael Nesmith would have us believe his work with the Monkees was a mere diversion—entertaining at best, embarrassing at worst—from the mildly influential yet largely unheard country-rock he would later create with his First National Band. It's "Last Train," though, that should be heralded as an early country-rock classic, even if Nesmith's contribution was nothing more than standing and watching while Mickey Dolenz dubbed lead vocals over a track cut by L.A. session pickers the Candy Store Prophets.

From the jangly-meets-twangy riff that kicks it off, through a rhythm track that sounds more than a little conversant with the Buckaroos' famous sound, this train chugs along irresistibly, stopping to board passengers in Liverpool and Bakersfield. And if you can resist any knee-jerk anticommercial biases long enough to stay on board, you can follow the tracks to "Bowling Green," where the Everly Brothers are waiting on the platform, and on to "Galveston," so Glen Campbell can catch a ride to the top of the charts.

In the case of "Galveston," the connections are literal—Campbell played guitar both on "Bowling Green" and the Monkees' debut LP (though not on "Last Train")—but they're also thematic. After all, the most likely reason this Clarksville boy is begging his girl to catch the last train to see him, the reason he fears he might never be back, is that he's been drafted. Maybe he's off to boot camp or being shipped overseas. Either way, he's another young soldier praying he makes it home.—dc

327

Ruby, Don't Take Your Love to Town,
Kenny Rogers & the First Edition
Produced by Jimmy Bowen; Written by Mel Tillis
Reprise 0829   1969   #39 country; #6 pop

"It all begins with a song," the saying goes. The operative word is "begins." Because, when we're talking records, the song's just one factor among many. "Ruby, Don't Take Your Love to Town," for instance, has been cut many times over the years, including fine versions by Johnny Darrell and by the song's composer, Mel Tillis. Yet while the song remains the same, it's the 1969 version cut by Kenny Rogers & the First Edition that stands out.

The single screams tension from its first notes—a frenetic, propulsive rhythm part that's all high-hat and bass drum. Then the percussion abruptly falls silent and Rogers delivers the song's first line a cappella before the entire band backs him for the second. This dramatic, stop-start introduction highlights the painful contrast of the opening couplet—Ruby's getting all dolled up, but not for Kenny. We soon learn that Rogers is playing a man paralyzed and impotent due to injuries incurred during that "crazy Asian war" and that his wife has taken to finding satisfaction elsewhere—in short, *Lady Chatterly's Lover* done up country style.

Still, it's all the choices made in the studio that turn a good song into a record you want to hear again and again. That nifty little circular guitar riff sounds absolutely mad with anxiety. Rogers's breathy rasp, augmented by just a touch of reverb, aches with need and worry. The whole record emphasizes movement—every step the woman takes as she readies herself to leave, every step the man wishes he could take to stop her—and this kinetic quality is most apparent in that irresistible rhythm, courtesy of Mickey Jones, a former drummer for Johnny Rivers and Bob Dylan. Jones keeps a rock-steady groove even as its velocity seems to increase right along with Rogers's pulse. And yours.—dc

328

Garden Party, Rick Nelson & the Stone Canyon Band
Produced by Rick Nelson; Written by Rick Nelson
Decca 32980   1972   #44 country; # 6 pop

Rick Nelson began his musical career as Ricky Nelson, the heartthrob who made the little girls squeal on his parents' 1950s sitcom, *The Adventures of Ozzy and Harriet.* All that TV exposure positioned him perfectly to cash in on the lucrative youth market Elvis had created. But with songs as strong as Gene Pitney's "Hello, Mary Lou"—and with James Burton firing off blistering Telecaster solos at his side—Nelson could never be wholly contained within a diminutive like "teen idol." Still, the term dogged Nelson throughout his career, even after he began fronting the Stone Canyon Band in 1969. A decidedly unteen-oriented outfit that the singer had formed in the wake of country-rock breakthroughs by the Byrds and Bob Dylan, the Stone Canyon Band scored its most enduring success with "Garden Party," a song inspired by a particularly hellish gig at a Madison Square Garden oldies package show.

The Rick Nelson of "Garden Party" is flabbergasted to discover Dylan and John Lennon have actually turned out to see him play, and he's enough of a fan to be impressed that Chuck Berry still

plays his guitar "like a-ringin'-a-bell, looking like he should." The by then shaggy-haired and country-rockin' Nelson, on the other hand, neither looked nor sounded like the teen idol the crowd expected. He'd changed and was booed for it.

At least that's how Nelson experienced it. Tom Brumley, the legendary pedal-steel man that Nelson recruited from the Buckaroos, remembers things differently. "During our segment of the show, somebody booed," Brumley recounted to the country fanzine *Maybelle.* "[Rick] zeroed in on that one little boo. . . . We found out later that the cops were taking somebody out for smoking pot or something . . . and people were booing the cops. Rick thought they were booing him. . . . But the people actually loved him."

So did radio listeners. His first real hit in nearly a decade, "Garden Party" entered the pop charts at virtually the same moment as "Take It Easy," the Eagles' first country rock hit. "Garden Party" took it even easier. "But it's all right now / I've learned my lesson well / You can't please everyone / so you got to please yourself," Nelson decides, at peace with the changes he's made. And why not? With the peaceful, easy feeling of Tom Brumley's pedal steel working behind you, who wouldn't conclude that, "If memories were all I sang, I'd rather drive a truck"?—dc

329

You Could Know As Much about a Stranger,
Gene Watson
Produced by Russ Reeder and Bob Webster;
Written by Nadine Bryant
Capitol 4214   1976   #10 country

Relationship Ossification 101. Gene Watson tells us that he and his wife know all the details about the superficial surface of their lives—the hair styles, pet peeves, and conversational pleasantries that by now have settled into predictable routines. But when it comes to digging a bit deeper, they leave the important things unspoken until even their indifference has ceased to bother them.

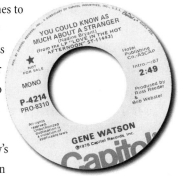

"We're so used to things this way, tomorrow's just like yesterday," Watson

declares, "and there lies the danger." There's no denying he's right. So you wonder—if he's aware enough to know what can cause a relationship to calcify, then crumble, why's he wasting his time talking to us? Behind him, the rhythm just rolls along comfortably, propelled by its own easy, inevitable momentum. And there, as the song says, lies the danger.—dc

330
Faded Love, Patsy Cline
Produced by Owen Bradley;
Written by John Wills and Bob Wills
Decca 31522   1963   # 7 country; #96 pop

Several musicians working the session at which Patsy Cline cut "Faded Love" recalled how she cried off and on that night. Listen closely to the last time she sings the word "love." "That wasn't a breath," Jordanaire Ray Walker told historian John Rumble. "That was a weep."

No doubt about it. The pickers and singers drop out, leaving only a bed of billowy violins for Patsy to lean on the second time she approaches the final line of the chorus. "I re-mem-ber our fa-ded . . . ," she simmers, suspending the second syllable of "faded" with a low moan to keep from breaking it off mid-verse. Then, after heaving a gasp-inducing sob, she softly croons the word "love," transforming her tearful quaver into a heart-stopping tremolo. Producer Owen Bradley reportedly considered removing Patsy's "breath" from the recording but ultimately thought better of it. It's a good thing, too, because that seeming glitch helped make "Faded Love" one of the greatest heart songs ever recorded.

Heart songs, earnest declarations of love and fidelity, came to prominence after the Second World War, a time when sincerity, even to the point of unabashed sentimentality, wasn't scorned as sappy or maudlin. Everyone from honky-tonker Ernest Tubb and crushed-velvet crooner Jim Reeves, to the western swing bands of Bob Wills and Milton Brown, recorded heart songs. In fact, Wills released the first version of "Faded Love," a Top Ten country hit in 1950 featuring Rusty McDonald and the Playboy Trio on vocals.

The song had begun life as an instrumental, a tune that Wills and his father worked out when Bob was still a young boy. The lyrics didn't come along until 1950; Bob's kid brother Billy Jack added them, and then the Playboys cut "Faded Love" for Decca. It was Cline's reading of the song though, a record bathed in Bill McElhiney's swirling string arrangement, that set the standard for subsequent renditions. Thirty-seven years later we can only

speculate about what, or who, made Patsy cry that night, a mere four weeks before her death. All we know for sure is that she sang "Faded Love" as if she'd lived it.—bfw

331
I Will Always Love You, Dolly Parton
Produced by Porter Wagoner; Written by Dolly Parton
RCA 0234   1974   #1 country (1 week)

Whitney Houston's enormously popular 1992 recording of "I Will Always Love You" showcased a preposterous attachment to static, stentorian vocal pyrotechnics. The result was an impressive performance but one that lacks any warmth or human-scale emotion. It's like Aretha Franklin had taken singing lessons from Al Jolson.

By contrast, Parton's 1974 original is fragile, dynamic, forward-looking. Written in anticipation of ending her partnership with mentor Porter Wagoner, Dolly's song is presented here in a spare, light-as-air arrangement that owes more than a little to the country-soul of Tammy Wynette, Bobbie Gentry, and Sammi Smith. At the chorus, Dolly's voice sounds confident even as it sheds tears; she knows it's time to strike out on her own but her departure will be bittersweet just the same. Pledging her undying gratitude in a voice that flutters, ever so delicately, with emotion, Dolly sings, "I will always love you." What an intimate thing to say.

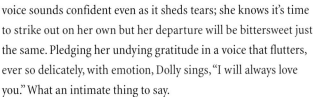

Accept no substitutes.—dc

332
'Til I Get It Right, Tammy Wynette
Produced by Billy Sherrill;
Written by Red Lane and Larry Henley
Epic 10940   1972   #1 country (1 week); #106 pop

"Stand by Your Man," with an eye to the long view. With " 'Til I Get It Right," Tammy insists that love's not a call for submission but a lifelong process of personal growth. One that demands perpetual maintenance and plenty of fresh starts, too—and not always with the same partner. Here, stung by yet another broken heart,

Tammy still has enough hard-won wisdom to declare, "If practice makes perfect, then I'm about as perfect as I've ever been in my life." If you can see how that line is sad while also being the very model of hopefulness, then you already know what Tammy's singing about.

It's become common in recent years for big-voiced female country singers to enroll at the If-You-Ain't-Screaming-You-Ain't-Singing School of the Pop-Country Diva. But on " 'Til I Get It Right," Tammy takes a different tack. She sings loudly but also oh-so soft. She crawls through a minefield of possible mistakes on some lines while sprinting confidently through others. She even pauses at times, in silence, to consider what she's learned, and she never belts it full blast for more than a word or three at a time. In other words, she takes everyone else to school—the lesson being that it takes a lot more than a big voice to be a great singer.—dc

333
Good Hearted Woman, Waylon Jennings
Produced by Ronny Light;
Written by Waylon Jennings and Willie Nelson
RCA Victor 0615   1972   #3 country

This Outlaw paean to the ultimate stand-by-your-man woman is hardly the good-timin' anthem all Waylon's rowdy fans heard it as. Granted, Jennings and pal Willie Nelson put their co-dependent heroine up on a pedestal, and they can't resist invoking that bit from "Stand" about men doing things women don't understand. But as Waylon's matter-of-fact delivery and his shift to the first person on the final chorus reveal, this is more confession than boast. With the record's throbbing

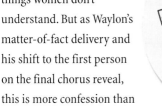

bass echoing the guilt pounding in his head, Waylon laments everything—from dreams to the good life—that his wicked ways have cost her.

All of which is commendable enough, and perhaps his self-awareness—albeit a day late and a dollar short—explains why Waylon's good-hearted woman is still at his side. But she ought to know better, especially after Waylon trots out that tired "boys will be boys" excuse—proof that, despite all he's put her through, he has no intention of changing.—bfw

334
XXX's and OOO's (An American Girl),
Trisha Yearwood
Produced by Garth Fundis and Harry Stinson;
Written by Alice Randall and Matraca Berg
MCA 54898   1994   #1 country (2 weeks); #114 pop

Some hear this fiddle-charged ode to womanly resilience as the aural equivalent of a "chick flick." There's no denying that the middle-class everywoman Yearwood plays here, a put-upon working mom who's trying to earn a living and have a life, is putting on her game face. But to say that's all she's doing is to miss the record's tragicomic underpinnings and with them its cutting edge. As much as anything, Yearwood's "American Girl" (the co-creation of a black Jane Austen scholar and a white show-biz kid) voices the frustration and sense of betrayal known by countless women who came of age in feminism's wake. Specifically, it captures the sting of defeat felt by those who believed they were finally entitled to the same shot at the American Dream as their male counterparts, only to find themselves obliged to make many of the sacrifices their

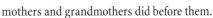

mothers and grandmothers did before them.

"Phone rings, baby cries, TV diet-guru lies, Good mornin' honey / Go to work, make up, try to keep the balance up between love and money," Yearwood sighs, the resolve in her caffeine-fueled soprano firmed up by the clock-like ticking of Eddie Bayers's rimshots. Trisha values the life that her mama, a heels-and-pearls, June Cleaver–style housewife, had, but she wants to get paid like her daddy did—that is, she wants both stability and a career. Not to mention romance. Barring that, she'll keep the job and seek comfort in God, good wine, and the records of her go-to girls, Aretha Franklin and Patsy Cline. Not that it won't pain her to have to make do that way. But judging by the grit in her voice as she enumerates those would-be surrogates at the song's bridge, Trisha realizes it might be the only way to define life on her terms and make it in her daddy's world. —bfw

335
Amanda, Waylon Jennings
Produced by Jack Clement; Written by Bob McDill
RCA 11596   1979   #1 country (3 weeks); #54 pop

Songwriter Bob McDill says that when Waylon Jennings first heard this working musician's grateful apology to his longsuffering wife the singer told him, "Hoss, that's the story of my life."

No hyperbole there. Even before he played bass on Buddy Holly's final tours, Jennings had lived the life of a professional musician, struggling to earn a living on the road or playing till all hours even when toiling close to home. In fact, his dream of making it as a singer, and the resulting neglect of his home life, helped end his first three marriages. After he married fourth wife Jessi Colter in 1969, she too stayed home with the kids while Jennings was out singing and playing, as well as participating in less job-related activities. As the index to his own autobiography sums it up, "Jennings, Waylon . . . alcohol consumed by . . . drugs used by . . . womanizing of." As Jessi put it, Waylon was a night walker.

All the same, Colter supported her husband's drive to make it in the music business. In "Amanda's" best line, Waylon notes, "It's a measure of people who don't understand the pleasures of life in a hillbilly band." Jessi Colter wasn't one of them. She sporadically pursued her own musical career all through their marriage—recording duets and touring with her husband, releasing a number of solo albums—efforts that resulted, if only briefly, in a crossover success with "I'm Not Lisa" that outstripped even her spouse's.

Jennings cut "Amanda" as an album track in 1974 and released it as a single five years later—same version, but with one overdubbed line to account for his being forty rather than thirty. "Amanda, light of my life," Waylon sings to the woman who's suffered along with him all these years. He's just checked himself in the mirror where, amazingly, the wrinkles around his eyes have helped him understand how his hard choices have aged his wife as well. "Fate should have made you a gentleman's wife," he tells her. Not a musician's. Behind him there's not much more than a humble acoustic guitar strum and the haunting cry of a woman's voice. She's got plenty to cry about, but apparently she's going to see it through.—dc

336
A Lesson in Leavin', Dottie West
Produced by Randy Goodrum and Brent Maher;
Written by Brent Maher and Randy Goodrum
United Artists 1339   1980   #1 country (1 week)

A lesson in country soul is more like it. Producer Brent Maher had previously engineered sessions by Sly & the Family Stone and Ike & Tina Turner, but this date with Dottie West was his first real country gig. At least it started out that way. Then drummer Kenny Malone started laying down, in Maher's words, that "funky, little half time groove," at which point it turned into a mighty fine Nashville facsimile of an R&B recording session.

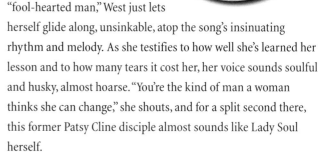

Predicting that what goes around will come around for her love-'em-and-leave-'em, "fool-hearted man," West just lets herself glide along, unsinkable, atop the song's insinuating rhythm and melody. As she testifies to how well she's learned her lesson and to how many tears it cost her, her voice sounds soulful and husky, almost hoarse. "You're the kind of man a woman thinks she can change," she shouts, and for a split second there, this former Patsy Cline disciple almost sounds like Lady Soul herself.

This is great news. Because if a singer whose resume includes dueting with Kenny Rogers and penning the Coca-Cola jingle "Country Sunshine" has an inner Aretha, then that means we all must have one. Just takes the right groove to bring it out.—dc

337
Dreaming My Dreams with You, Waylon Jennings
Produced by Waylon Jennings and Jack Clement;
Written by Allen Reynolds
RCA 10270   1975   #10 country

Has country radio ever aired a quieter record than "Dreaming My Dreams with You"? Waylon Jennings and co-producer Jack Clement take the already hushed sound of records like Sammi Smith's "Help Me Make It through the Night" (Jennings called Smith his "Girl Hero") and reduce it to whispers: an acoustic guitar strum placed *way* back in the mix, Waylon's humbled delivery, violins and cellos that rise up only to slink quietly away. Amazingly, those whispers communicate every scream that's paved the way for this goodbye. "Someday I'll get over you," Waylon tells the woman on her way out the door. "But I'll always miss dreaming my dreams with you."

That's not a pin you hear echoing in the quiet; it's the other shoe.—dc

338
The Door, George Jones
Produced by Billy Sherrill;
Written by Billy Sherrill and Norro Wilson
Epic 50038   1974   #1 country (1 week)

It's fitting that a song *about* a sound would get a wall-of-sound treatment. In "The Door," George Jones recalls all manner of noises: his mother's terrified sobs, the roar of the train that took him from her side, the battlefield explosions it took him to. None of those painful noises, however, has sent him crashing to his knees quite like the sound that punctuated the night he lost his reason for living. That sound, "the closing of the door," still rings in his ears.

Literally. Sherrill's arrangement escalates slowly as Jones struggles to hold himself in check. But after we actually hear a door shut (the one in Sherrill's office, because it closed with a coldly hollow "k-lup" instead of a dull thud), the singer breaks down altogether, and the producer says bombs away. Good move, too, because once you've actually included a closing door in the mix, sonic subtlety isn't really an option anymore. Or a smart emotional choice, either, since this psychodrama is all about memories that scream so loudly they drown out the world.

Jones bears down masterfully on some words and stretches out others for emphasis; when he sings "that lonely sound," his voice feels like the loneliest sound imaginable. At least until Sherrill clears out a moment's quiet for him to bawl, "Through tear-stained eyes I watched her walk away." From the anguished trek Jones makes across that line alone, you know that even now he sees nothing else. Then the record blows up into a noisy symphony—strings whiz like missiles through the sky, backing singers whine like a distant train, drum shots resound like the closing of a door. Loudest of all is that silence after Jones's final lonely note.—dc

339
Gone, Ferlin Husky
Produced by Ken Nelson; Written by Smokey Rogers
Capitol 3628   1957   #1 country (10 weeks); #4 pop

Ferlin Husky might have been the first country star to come out of Bakersfield, but his biggest and best hits ("Gone," "Wings of a Dove") were pure Nashville Sound. Historians, in fact, usually cite "Gone" and *not* Jim Reeves's "Four Walls" or Patsy Cline's "Walkin' after Midnight" (both also from early 1957), as the breakthrough smash of the new crossover sound. It's easy to see why; Husky's neo-operatic "There Goes My Everything" prototype is a towering monument to regret.

At first, the only sound we hear is Husky's echo-laden tenor. Then, two-thirds of the way through the opening line, a crescendo of voices—the Jordanaires and soprano Millie Kirkham—sweeps Husky's confession skyward, where the sun, moon, and stars already know why he cries. He's acted the fool and made his baby leave him. Yet as heart-rending as these first few bars are, they're simply a prelude to the bridge where Husky pines, "Oh what I'd give for the lifetime I've wasted," stretching the word "oh" out eight agonizing syllables as that soul-drenching echo, nagging piano, and snare reverberate with the emptiness he feels in the pit of his heart.

This, by the way, was Husky's second crack at "Gone"; the first was a more stripped-down version (featuring Speedy West on pedal steel) he cut under the pseudonym Terry Preston in Hollywood in 1952. While that record never went anywhere and began a four-year semi-dry spell for him, this recording put Husky *and* the Nashville Sound on the map. Of course, none of this had happened when Husky went into the studio in Nashville to make "Gone," which likely explains the urgency in his voice when he beats himself up on the bridge for the seeming lifetime he'd wasted out West.—bfw

340
That'll Be the Day, The Crickets
Produced by Norman Petty;
Written by Jerry Allison, Buddy Holly, and Norman Petty
Brunswick 55009   1957   #3 pop; #2 R&B

"That'll Be the Day," Buddy Holly's chart debut, came too late to make it on country radio. If this recording had come out even a few months earlier (Holly had already cut another version of the song for Decca that flopped), Holly likely would've climbed the country charts as swiftly as Elvis Presley, Jerry Lee Lewis, Carl Perkins, and Gene Vincent. By the summer of 1957, though, the Nashville Sound had been building momentum for a year already—"Don't Be Cruel," "Gone," "Young Love," and "Four Walls" had all been major hits. Consequently, rockabilly acts were in the process of being banished from country play lists; even established stars like Elvis and Jerry Lee wouldn't be on country radio much longer.

Holly wouldn't be around much longer either. His 1959 death in the same plane crash that killed Ritchie Valens and the Big Bopper meant that, in addition to coming along too late for country success, he was gone too early to witness the country and country-associated music that he and his band the Crickets inspired. Buddy Holly's influence is all over the Bakersfield sound, for instance—Wynn Stewart's stabs at rockabilly clearly use Holly as their model, and there's plenty of "That'll Be the Day" in the "freight-train" rhythm tracks of the Buckaroos. It's also easy to draw fairly straight lines from the rockin' country-pop of Buddy

Holly to the music of Roy Orbison, Bob Dylan, and, of course, the Beatles.

In other words, Holly is a far more significant artist than his innocent, *Happy Days* reputation let's on. There's nothing innocent about "That'll Be the Day," which, depending on what Buddy lets his voice reveal at any given moment, is either about a man who's certain he'll die if his gal ever dumps him or about a man threatening his girlfriend that the only way she's leaving is over his dead body. Holly's pinched vocals (country phrasing decorated with Elvis-derived affectations like hiccups and dramatic drops in register); his flaming Scotty Moore–inspired electric guitar solo; the Crickets' typically edgy, coiled rhythms—it all feels anxious and a little desperate, even though Holly says, over and over, how confident he is this will never end.

"The Day the Music Died" is what some call the anniversary of Holly's death, but the truth is that the power and influence of this west Texan's music has never diminished, much less passed away. You can hear Buddy Holly in the jangly guitars of folk and country rock, and in the Outlaw country of his former bassist Waylon Jennings. He's there in the sounds of Linda Ronstadt, Mickey Gilley, and Ray Price (each had hits with Holly songs), as well as Dave Edmunds and Nick Lowe, Bruce Springsteen, the Blasters, Marty Stuart, Nanci Griffith, Joe Ely, Rodney Crowell, the Mavericks, Jim Lauderdale, and Steve Earle.

Buddy Holly's music *die*? That'll be the day.—dc

341
Walkin' after Midnight, Patsy Cline
Produced by Owen Bradley; Written by Don Hecht and Alan Block
Decca 30221   1957   #2 country; #12 pop

Patsy Cline's legacy will always be tied to the creamy, pop-leaning Nashville Sound that helped country music fend off the initial onslaught of rock & roll. But during the mid-to-late fifties when her career was just taking off, Cline, who'd always seen herself as a hillbilly singer, frequently expressed misgivings about performing pop material set to uptown arrangements. A letter to her fan club president Treva Miller describing the session at which she cut "Walkin' after Midnight" strongly suggests Cline didn't think of the record as country at all. "'Pick Me Up on Your Way Down' is the only real country song I did this time," she wrote to Miller, as if the other three sides she did with producer Owen Bradley on November 8, 1956, including "Walkin'," involved some sort of compromise. Maybe they did, but what a trade-off it was. Patsy and the A-Teamers working the session split the difference between country and pop, transforming "Walkin'," a lovelorn blues à la "I'm So Lonesome I Could Cry," into a swaggering romp. Spurred on by Bradley's all but rocking rhythm section (the only outwardly twangy thing here is Don Helms's seductive steel), Patsy sounds like she's not so much pining for her long-gone daddy as hoping to hook up with that Presley boy everyone in Nashville was so up in arms about. Judging by her swinging 1961 remake of the song (this time with the bop-bopping Jordanaires on board), she did.—bfw

342

Angel Band, The Stanley Brothers
Produced by W. D. Kilpatrick; Traditional
Mercury MG20349   1955   Did not chart

With a little help from his friends, Bill Monroe invented what eventually became known as bluegrass. But it was the Stanley Brothers who turned Monroe's sound into a genre. Or at least they got the ball rolling when, in 1948, they recorded "Molly and Tenbrooks," a song Monroe had been playing on the Opry. At that point, he'd already recorded the number (a nineteenth-century song about a famous horse race), but Columbia hadn't released it. So he was plenty pissed to discover that Ralph and Carter Stanley had beaten him to the draw with their own rendition of the song. Well, not exactly their own—the Stanleys' recording was nearly identical to Monroe's version, which wasn't surprising since they'd most likely learned it studying their hero's radio performances or catching Monroe live when his itinerary took him near the Stanleys' Clinch Mountain home. The record even features mandolin player Pee Wee Lambert pushing his lead vocals way up high in unabashed imitation of Bill Monroe.

Recorded seven years later, "Angel Band" is still marked by Big Mon's shadow. Its arrangement is built around a very Monroe-like mandolin, rather than Ralph's banjo, and it features a quiet bluegrass quartet of the sort Monroe had been favoring on gospel numbers for years. But by this point in their development, the brothers knew full well that it was Carter's emotional lead vocals and Ralph's holler-bred harmonies that made them distinctive.

Carter begins "Angel Band," a commonplace of old southern gospel songbooks, preparing to fly away. "My strongest trials now are past, my triumph has begun," he sings, stoic and passionate at the same time. When Ralph and his bracing tenor join Carter on the chorus—"Oh bear me away on your snow white wings to my immortal home"—you understand those trials have been strong indeed but that peace is close at hand. Ralph and Carter's voices stand well in front of the rest of the quartet, and when the brothers sing "Oh come, Angel band," it's as accurate a description of their own harmonies as we're likely to get.—dc

343

Crying in the Chapel, The Orioles
Producer unknown; Written by Artie Glenn
Jubilee 5122   1953   #1 R&B (5 weeks); #11 pop

Another case of pop-goes-the-country, this time via the R&B chart.

In the summer of 1953, country singer Darrell Glenn scored his only hit with "Crying in the Chapel," a song his father had written. Immediately the Orioles—a prototype doo-wop outfit from Baltimore—covered Glenn's single for the rhythm and blues market. Soon their single was a hit on pop radio, too, where it competed for airplay with yet another country version of the song—this one from stentorian-voiced singing cowboy Rex Allen. Twelve years later, Elvis revived the song for another run up the charts.

Despite the competition, it's the Orioles' recording you can't shake; lead singer Sonny Til is the one who sounds the most, and least, like he's found peace of mind. Appropriately for a song about spiritual redemption, Til and his band mates sing in a hushed, elegant style akin to that of Jubilee gospel groups like the Golden Gate Quartet (a favorite of southern gospel singers the Statesmen Quartet, who themselves were a Presley favorite). Til bears witness that, having searched the world over, he's finally seen the light here in this "plain and simple" church. As if he were kneeling before an altar at that very instant, he sings in a voice that's sweet, clear, and content, yet tentative and oh-so-quiet. The conversion's still new, shimmering with mystery, and he doesn't dare break the spell.—dc

344
He Touched Me, Elvis Presley
Produced by Felton Jarvis; Written by Bill Gaither
RCA 74-0651   1972   Did not chart

That was what gospel was meant to do—make you hate and love yourself at the same time, make you ashamed and glorified. It worked on me. It absolutely worked on me.

That's Bone Boatwright speaking, the narrator of Dorothy Allison's stunning southern coming-of-age novel, *Bastard Out of Carolina.* It's a sure bet, though, that she wasn't talking about the finest work of gospel quartets like the Statesmen and the Blackwoods, or about the gospel recordings of their most famous disciple, Elvis Presley.

If only Bone could have heard "He Touched Me." Accompanied by the Imperials Quartet and their pianist Joe Moscheo, Presley sings this Bill Gaither composition in an earnest style that would've resonated immediately with generations of southerners, who'd been exposed to the music in church and traveling tent revivals, just as Bone was. Whether or not she's correct about what gospel music was *meant* to make her feel, Presley's voice achieves another effect altogether. "Shackled by a heavy burden, 'neath a load of guilt and shame," Elvis croons, his voice blending into the group. "Then the hand of Jesus touched me and now I am no longer the same"—and, at least for that moment, all-too-common ailments of the spirit like self-hatred give way in his voice to a cleansing humility. "Something happened and now I *know*," he declares. Suddenly being glorified means more than merely loving yourself in some abstract way; rather, it allows us to sense, if only fleetingly, that the irreducible parts of ourselves are the most precious. Or as critic Greil Marcus once phrased it, writing about the power of Elvis's singing in terms secular rather than sacred, "No man is better than I am . . . [and] I am better than no man." In Elvis's song of praise, you can hear all of this.

"He touched me and made me whole," he testifies at the electric finale. Elvis's voice soars above the quartet, blending harmoniously and standing distinctive as well, humble and special at once, and it works on you. It absolutely works.—dc

345
His Blood Now Covers My Sin, The Lewis Family
Produced by Don Pierce; Written by Fred Rich
Starday 801   1967   Did not chart

"Sinners in the Hands of an Angry God" this isn't. The record opens, as many gospel numbers do, with a confession of unworthiness, but that's just a liturgical formality. All the First Family of Bluegrass Gospel wants to do here is testify to the joys of salvation. "Yes, the precious blood of Jesus is so won-der-ful," they shout on the chorus, their stout harmonies and frenzied picking taking a page out of the good book of Wilma Lee and Stoney Cooper and their Clinch Mountain Clan. Spurred on by Talmadge's quicksilver fiddling and Little Roy's juking banjo fills, the Lewises abandon themselves to a house-rocking call-and-response that, were it in church, would have had the deacons checking to see if the pews were bolted down. And it never lets up. With the three brothers and three sisters trading lines back and forth as they modulate to the final chorus, they ride Pop's jug-like bass (upright, naturally) all the way to the promised land.—bfw

346
The Lord Knows I'm Drinking, Cal Smith
Produced by Owen Bradley; Written by Bill Anderson
Decca 33040   1972   #1 country (1 week)

When the church busybody threatens to tell the whole congregation she's seen this former Texas Troubadour out drinking in a bar, Cal Smith lays into the "self-righteous woman." By extension, he also tells off every nosy neighbor and holier-than-thou hypocrite from here to Harper Valley. After all, the only reason Mrs. Johnson knows he's backsliding (and with a "young lass" who isn't his wife!) is that she's there doing the same thing. They've got company, too. The soundtrack to this showdown sounds like the church pianist stopped in for a drink, then decided to join the house band for a honky-tonk number or two, and, of course, the good Lord is watching as well. That's why Smith can insist so strongly that he and Jesus have their own thing going on. It's also why he "knows" what he's up to is a sin in need of forgiveness.—dc

347
Friends in Low Places, Garth Brooks
Produced by Allen Reynolds;
Written by Dewayne Blackwell and Bud Lee
Capitol 44647   1990   #1 country (4 weeks)

After "The Dance" went to #1 in 1990, Garth Brooks wasted no time distancing himself from the other hats vying for dominance on the country charts, and it was this boozy mess-around that put him on top for good. "Low Places" finds Garth, sporting cowboy boots and feeling no pain, crashing his ex's black-tie affair, snatching her new hubby's glass of bubbly, and toasting, "Honey, I know we're through / But you'll never hear me complain." Then he launches into the sing-a-long chorus half the world knows by heart, his "Swingin' "–inspired slur swimming in Bruce Bouton's mercurial steel while Chris Leuzinger's gutter-bent guitar break beckons him to rejoin the rowdy crowd back at their favorite dive.

In real life, of course, Brooks didn't crawl back into his hole; he shot straight to the top of the heap. *No Fences*, the album anchored by "Low Places," went on to sell more than sixteen million copies; Brooks's next record, *Ropin' the Wind*, shattered pop's glass ceiling by becoming the first country album to debut at #1 on the pop charts. It also made Garth as huge an icon as Elvis or Madonna.

In other words, "Low Places" not only belied its "Don't Get Above Your Raisin' " message, it signaled the end of Garth's "Hey, I'm one of us" phase. Not that he minded; the titles of his next three albums (*No Fences*, *Ropin' the Wind*, *The Chase*) rendered his all-consuming quest for megastardom explicit. Meanwhile, his songs grew more mannered, while his live shows turned into three-ring circuses. It was as if Brooks, his image now verging on abstraction, figured he had to exaggerate his voice and gestures to bridge the ever-widening gap between him and his audience. Which kinda makes you wonder if he isn't just stating his ambitions here when he vows, "Just give me an hour and then / Well, I'll be as high / As that ivory tower / That you're livin' in." It really makes you wonder.—bfw

348
Sitting on Top of the World, The Mississippi Sheiks
Produced by Polk Brockman;
Written by Lonnie Carter and Walker Jacobs
OKeh 8784   1930   Pre-chart

Question: When did black American musicians first influence white American musicians? And vice versa?

Answer: The first time black musicians heard their white counterparts and liked what they heard. And vice versa.

Many music fans remain invested in the idea that black people make black music and white people make white music, but it's rarely been so simple. The truth is that the history of American music is the story of cultural miscegenation. What we now call country music wouldn't even exist if it weren't for the persistent influence of so-called black music; at the same time, if blacks had never encountered European-derived styles—hadn't been forced via slavery to encounter them—America never would've gotten the blues. In the first decades of the twentieth century, any reasonably well-traveled musician, black or white, would've been exposed to spirituals, chain gang chants, Tin Pan Alley songs, ballads from the British Isles, Tyrolean yodelers, German marching bands, the blues, ragtime, Hawaiian string bands, hot jazz, and what we now call old-time music, as well as various forms of minstrelsy and vaudeville—not to mention records and, soon afterward, radio. If a lyric, lick, or melody, an instrument or a technique, sounded good, it got swiped. And since everyone was serving themselves from the same great big pot of stew, each style of music became, to varying degrees, dependent upon all the others for its flavor, meaning, and—when you get down to it—its very existence. The differences mostly depend on who was doing the ladling.

Often the differences weren't all that great anyway. Case in point: the Mississippi Sheiks. Their best known song, "Sitting on Top of the World," has gone on to become a blues and country standard, recorded by everyone from Howlin' Wolf and Johnny Shines to Bob Wills and Bill Monroe. But it's tough to beat the Sheiks' original. Fiddlers Lonnie and Bo Chatmon and guitarist Walter Vinson were all black sharecroppers who'd fled farming for music. They were contemporaries of fellow Mississippians Robert Johnson and Jimmie Rodgers who, more or less splitting the difference, played bluesy stringband music. Whenever they could, they played for white square dancers because that's where the money was.

The Sheiks got their name from "The Sheik of Araby," a song they liked that had twice been a pop hit back in 1922, and their most famous song was inspired by another pop hit, Al Jolson's blustering 1926 smash "I'm Sitting on Top of the World." There are a couple of possible explanations for the song's distinctive feel. The Sheiks might've hated Jolson's upbeat, straight-faced performance and devised a new song with a more ironic edge in response; or they might've received a request for a song they didn't know and set new words to an old Tampa Red melody on the spot; or maybe it was some combination of the two. However they came to it, there's no mistaking that when they draw out the lines, "Now she's gone, I don't worry / I'm sitting on top of the world," they ain't on top of nothing. Buried under a mountain is more like it.

If you didn't already know that the Mississippi Sheiks were black men, that particular detail might slide right past you, especially with those weeping twin fiddles and a guitar part that would've sounded right at home in the Appalachians. No way, though, could you, or any of their black or white descendents, miss that they've got the blues.—dc

349

I'm a Lover, Not a Fighter, Lazy Lester
Produced by J. D. Miller; Written by Lazy Lester
Excello 2143   1959   Did not chart

More musical miscegenation from the margins, this time from the bayous of South Louisiana. Producer J. D. Miller was a musical omnivore who, from the late forties until the early sixties, recorded everything from Cajun, country, and zydeco to blues, rockabilly, and western swing. Invariably, elements of each seeped into others, and "I'm a Lover, Not a Fighter," a rollicking swamp-blues by harmonica ace Lazy Lester, was no exception. Take the record's juking rhythms, which owe as much to the hillbilly boogie of the Delmore Brothers as to the jump blues of Wynonie Harris. Or Guitar Gable's go-cat guitar-licks, inspired as much by Elvis's main man Scotty Moore as by the barrelhouse piano of Pete Johnson. Or Lester's languid harp playing, with its nods to both Slim Harpo and Wayne Raney, and his liquid drawl,

which invokes not just Jimmy Reed but Moon Mullican. You can cite whole genealogies of musical antecedents, both black and white, till you're blue in the face, but no matter how you cut it, all of the sounds in question were getting it on in the same down-home swamp.—bfw

350

A Boy Named Sue, Johnny Cash
Produced by Bob Johnston; Written by Shel Silverstein
Columbia 44944   1969   #1 country (5 weeks); #2 pop

351

Okie from Muskogee, Merle Haggard & the Strangers
Produced by Ken Nelson; Written by Merle Haggard
Capitol 2626   1969   #1 country (4 weeks); #41 pop

It's not the difference of age now / Everybody's talkin' about / It's all those no-no's that make up the generation gap.

Jeannie C. Riley must have had Merle Haggard's "Okie from Muskogee" in mind when she belted out those lines on her 1970 single "The Generation Gap." Haggard's record had come out the previous year, at a time when the social tensions of the sixties were reaching their peak. The hippie movement—with its celebration of sex, drugs, and long hair—was in full flower; the outcry against the Vietnam War was at fever pitch. Yet most of the nation watched uneasily from the sidelines, and it was that "silent majority"—a group that tacitly embraced the ideals of the previous generation—that heard Haggard's paean to heartland values as its anthem.

"We don't smoke marijuana in Muskogee / We don't take our trips on LSD / We don't burn our draft cards down on Main Street / We like livin' right and bein' free." Hag declares these lines to the meat-and-potatoes twang of the Strangers; together, they paint a picture of a life that's as safe as it is secure. But Merle's message also carries a hard edge. He's saying that anyone who doesn't live the way *his* people do isn't "livin' right"; his testimony to what they *don't* do is tantamount to a litany of "no-no's" aimed squarely at the counterculture.

Hag's are fighting words; his digs about beads, shaggy manes, and Roman sandals amount to out-and-out hectoring, calling into question, among other things, the masculinity of those craven hippie boys he thinks should have been over in Vietnam defending the flag. Merle later dismissed "Okie" as a joke, an attempt to get inside the heads of members of his father's generation. Granted, he threw the hippies a bone in 1971 with "Big Time Annie's Square," a song about a romance between an Oklahoma farm boy and a tie-dyed mama "who don't agree on nothin'," but make one hell of a pair. Nevertheless, there's no getting around Hag's crack about the squirrelly guy who won't go to war in "The Fightin' Side of Me," a jingoistic salvo from 1970 that proved the hard-nosed stance he adopted in "Okie" was more than just a joke.

Johnny Cash's "A Boy Named Sue," on the other hand, was a joke that rang out like an anthem. Recorded live at San Quentin, the California prison in which Haggard turned twenty-one, Cash's hit, a talking blues written by *Playboy* cartoonist Shel Silverstein, is a rib-splitting tale of a son's quest to exact vengeance on the absentee father who saddled him with his girlish moniker. The record is also a thinly veiled allegory about how communication, even to the point of conflict, is the best way to breed the tolerance and mutual understanding needed to bridge the generation gap.

Things come to a head during the final scene in which Cash, happening on his father dealing poker in a dingy saloon, thunders across the room: "My name is Sue, how do you do? / Now you gonna die!" (How he manages to make those lines sound scary, after all the punch lines that have come before them, is an honest-to-goodness marvel.) A brawl of Rabelaisian proportions ensues, the two men kicking, gouging, and bloodying themselves beyond recognition as the Tennessee Three's jabbing rhythms and Carl Perkins's guitar provide rollicking ringside commentary. It isn't until Cash pulls his gun that the old man finally explains why he named him Sue (although not why he abandoned him and his mother in the first place).

"Son, this world is rough and if a man's gonna make it he's gotta be tough . . . And it's that name that's made you strong," his father tells him. The implication is that by giving him a name like Sue—its "sissy" connotations just the sort implied in "Okie's"

gibes at hippies—he's made Cash the man he's become. The kid relents after the old man says his piece, and the two reconcile, but it's not so much because Cash believes his father made him who he is, a claim that countless parents of baby boomers doubtless made to their children. No, it's that after mixing it up with him and hearing him out, Cash finally knows, right or wrong, where the man he now calls "Pa" is coming from.

All of which couldn't be further from the sloganeering of "Okie from Muskogee." "A Boy Named Sue" nearly topped both the country and pop charts, speaking not only to the silent majority who presumably tuned in country radio, but to the long hairs who listened to rock stations as well. By contrast, "Okie" spoke only to one side of the debate and stalled just outside the pop Top Forty.—bfw

352

Take This Job and Shove It, Johnny Paycheck
Produced by Billy Sherrill; Written by David Allan Coe
Epic 50469   1977   #1 country (2 weeks)

With a title that expresses a universal sentiment in bullshit-free language, "Take This Job and Shove It" is the epitome of a working-class anthem. Everyone knows the song's impossibly catchy refrain because it's so perfect for singing along with in the car as you drive home from work or for selecting on the jukebox at a Friday afternoon happy hour. But it's the number's more-easily-forgotten verses that provide the refrain with its real-world depth.

First off, the verses make plain that Johnny Paycheck isn't actually quitting his job. Rather, over an itchy rhythm track of nothing more than electric bass and hand drums, he's wishing he had the guts to quit. Hardly a new fantasy, most likely, but one that's particularly tempting today since his wife ("all the reasons I was working for") has just told *him* to shove it, and left. The verses are also where Paycheck remembers all the tears his wife has cried since he got on at the factory and all the loved ones he's seen die in those years. David Allan Coe's lyrics make a clear connection between all the crying, dying, and leaving, and this guy's miserable job—where for fifteen years he's had to put up with cruel and condescending bosses in exchange for a paycheck that still leaves him scrambling to pay the bills.

Johnny's pissed-off vocal makes it all work. Sounding like he'll kick in the teeth of anyone who stands in his way, he voices the all-too-common daydream of working stiffs everywhere.

All together now: "Take this job and shove it. I ain't a-workin' here no more!"—dc

353

Another Day, Another Dollar, Wynn Stewart
Produced by Joe Johnson; Written by Wynn Stewart
Challenge 9164   1962   #27 country

Viewed from the audience, the life of a musician looks like glamour and fun, but the reality is that it's hard work and, in some respects, not all that different from other working-class gigs. For most professional musicians, the job means sporadic employment, grueling hours, and long stretches away from home and family in exchange for stingy pay. Benefits are mostly nonexistent, as is any real shot at either fame or fortune.

Just ask Wynn Stewart. He was one of the founding fathers of Bakersfield country. Merle Haggard, steel man Ralph Mooney, and guitarist Roy Nichols all served time in his band, and it was with songs Stewart had written ("Sing a Sad Song") or first recorded ("Above and Beyond") that Haggard and Buck Owens had their breakthrough singles. His "Wishful Thinking" became a Top Five radio success in 1960 (the record's hyper rhythm section anticipates the sound for which Bakersfield would soon be known—it plays like Ray Price's Cherokee Cowboys on pogo sticks), but Stewart never managed the leap to the next level. He spent the early sixties working an open-all-day-all-night club in Las Vegas. According to writer Colin Escott, Stewart received one-third interest in the club in exchange for his body and soul—he worked the bandstand from 9 P.M. to 3 A.M. during the week, and until six in the morning on Saturday nights.

That's the sort of backbreaking schedule that likely inspired "Another Day, Another Dollar," in which Wynn's entire existence consists of dragging himself out of bed and going to work. Well,

not quite entirely—he gets to see his loved ones once in a while, when he's not sleeping or slaving, and it's for them he keeps at it. "My family is my thanks-giving," he sings, his bluesy voice momentarily free of weariness. His wife and kids are probably also why he can still respond to the grind with a pissed-off sense of humor ("The boss told me I'd get paid weekly, and that's exactly how I'm paid") instead of just being pissed. Behind him a hammer strikes an anvil (foreshadowing Merle's "Working Man Blues"), and Roy Nichols lays down some truly wicked licks, as Wynn sings, "Another day, another dollar, working my whole life away." And then, to prove the point, he sings it again.—dc

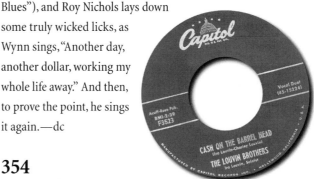

354

Cash on the Barrel Head,
The Louvin Brothers
Produced by Ken Nelson; Written by Ira and Charlie Louvin
Capitol 3523   1956   #7 country

355

Busted, Ray Charles
Produced by Sid Feller; Written by Harlan Howard
ABC-Paramount 10481   1963   #4 pop; #3 R&B

Country singers have long sought refuge from hard times in humor, and perhaps nowhere has this strategy of "laughing to keep from crying" worked better than when they've sung of being broke or in tight financial straits. Two classic examples, "Cash on the Barrel Head" and "Busted," speak directly to the issue of class, specifically to how tough it is for working people to get credit.

"Cash on the Barrel Head" finds Ira Louvin playing the role of a footloose fellow who's down on his luck. Arrested for loitering, he gets thrown in jail because he can't pay his fine. "No money down, no credit plan / No time to chase you 'cause I'm a busy man," the judge tells him, the rhythm section rapping like a gavel as Paul Yandell's hotfoot guitar conjures images of the bailiff hustling Ira back to his cell. Ira's bad-luck streak continues when he tries to make a toll call and, after he gets out of jail, to bum a ride on the bus. These are funny scenes, sharpened by the mock weeping of the steel and Yandell's "free as you please" guitar rubbing Ira's nose in his misfortune. But they're also degrading scenes. Louvin's a nobody; he's got no friends or relatives to extend him credit; hell, he doesn't even have his brother Charlie to sing harmony with him this time around.

Not being able to get credit is humiliating for anyone, but as Brother Ray testifies in "Busted," it can drive a man struggling to feed his family to crime. The record begins with Ray wringing his hands over a stack of overdue bills he has no way of paying. His cotton won't grow, his cow won't give milk, his hen won't lay, and the wolves are at his door in the form of the county, which is set to haul off everything he owns and sell it to pay his debts. Desperate, he swallows his pride and asks his brother for a loan, but the poor guy's in the same shape Ray's in, maybe worse. *His* wife and kids are down with the flu and can't pick whatever's left of their cotton crop. If they don't work, they don't eat.

Yet it's not all "gloom, despair, and agony on me," as the old *Hee Haw* gag would have it. For starters, Ray plays Harlan Howard's self-deprecating lyrics for maximum comedic effect. Not only that, Benny Carter's brassy arrangement swings hard enough to lift anyone out of the dumps. Anyone, that is, except Ray, who knows those unpaid bills are just going to hunt him and his family to the next town.—bfw

356

In the Good Old Days (When Times Were Bad),
Dolly Parton
Produced by Bob Ferguson; Written by Dolly Parton
RCA Victor 9657   1968   #25 country

"The past is never dead. It's not even past," William Faulkner wrote in *Requiem for a Nun*, stressing that we carry our personal and collective pasts with us through every step of life. Even when we try to leave them behind, we're shaped by the facts of our history and the stories we tell to make sense of them. In Faulkner's version of the South, the past presses down with an oppressive weight that crushes any possibility of change or real freedom. In the best country music, the past more often serves as a buoy—a legacy with which one is in perpetual conversation, gleaning lessons that can shape a future.

Dolly Parton's finest recordings highlight this distinction as well as anyone's in the country tradition. At least during the first decade of her career, Parton's intimate, nuanced relationship with the past—her own, the South's, country music's—provides a sharp rebuttal to the simplistic nostalgic-for-a-time-that-never-was tag so often trotted out by rock-centric critics. The Tennessee mountain memories that Parton recounts in "In the Good Old Days (When Times Were Bad)" are hardly nostalgic: months of labor rendered worthless by a storm that destroyed the family crops, ice on the cabin floor in the winter, sick family members who had to tough it out for want of funds to pay a doctor. "Anything at all was more than we had," Parton concludes, and she's glad those days are gone. But she also appreciates just how helpful her hardscrabble origins have been to her since she left those mountains to create a different life for herself.

"No amount of money could buy from me memories that I have of then," she sings in a fluttering, modern keen. "No amount of money could pay me to go back and live through it again." Around her, a studio rhythm section driven by drummer Jerry Carrigan propels Dolly down the highway toward some future she's busy making. At the same time, the acoustic twang of Pete Drake's dobro tells her that, whenever she needs some perspective or advice, or just a reminder of how far she's come, well . . . that's what the good old days are for.—dc

357

Have I Got a Deal for You, Reba McEntire
Produced by Jimmy Bowen and Reba McEntire;
Written by Michael P. Heeney and Jackson Leap
MCA 52604   1985   #6 country

Talk about elevating selling yourself to an art form. Taking the opposite tack Jeannie Kendall did when she meekly passed herself off as damaged goods in "Just Like Real People," Reba, riding high on a train of two-stepping rhythms, markets her second-hand self as a bargain that's too good to be true. "Have I got a deal for you," she bids her would-be lover, curling her supple alto around every word. "A heart that's almost like brand new / And I'll let it go so cheap / You'll think you stole it 'fore you're through." Buoyed by the record's unsinkable fiddle and steel guitar, Reba glides right over the question of how much mileage she's got on her heart. "Well, sure, well I'll admit that it's been used a time or two," she allows, setting up her final pitch. "But have I got a deal for you."

It was just this sort of moxie, plus loads of ambition and an unflagging work ethic, that enabled McEntire to go from

Oklahoma tomboy to country superstar and prosperous entrepreneur. It took her a good ten years to do it, but in the pre-Shania eighties and nineties, Reba was the only female country singer who could hang with hunks like George Strait, Vince Gill, and Garth Brooks when it came to selling records, filling arenas, and racking up awards. At the end of the last century, she took Broadway by storm playing the lead role in *Annie Get Your Gun*; at the start of the new one, she starred in her own TV sitcom.

Along the way Reba has sold herself as everything from a neotraditionalist torchbearer to a single-monikered show queen, in each case laying it on the line with the same pull-no-punches aplomb she displays here. Her brazen self-confidence can seem shamelessly over-the-top at times, as well as detrimental to her music, but it's an approach from which she hasn't wavered since seizing control of her career right before she made this record: "I've got me this ol' heart that I'm putting on the market / And I'll make you a deal you can't turn down."—bfw

358

Any Man of Mine, Shania Twain
Produced by Robert John "Mutt" Lange;
Written by Shania Twain and Robert John "Mutt" Lange
Mercury 856448   1995   #1 country (2 weeks); #31 pop

All you hear at first is a lone acoustic guitar, and then a bomb goes off; Rob Hajacos's fiddle detonates a mongrel hoedown stomp the likes of which had yet to come out of Nashville. In place of the knee-slapping, toe-tapping rhythms that made Music City famous comes a blitz of "We Will Rock You" beats and handclaps as Canada's answer to Reba and Dolly, letting out a whoop and then a giggle, demurs, "This is what a woman wants." Shania's tone may be coyly apologetic, but the martial cadences and list of demands that follow are anything but. "Stand by Your Woman" and snap to it is more like it. "Any man of mine better walk the line," she declaims as Paul Franklin's high-spirited steel do-si-dos right in time. "I need a man who knows how the story goes / He's gotta be a heartbeatin', fine-treatin' / Breathtakin', earthquakin' kind."

Shania's terms of endearment—she's echoing the demand for romance and respect Loretta issued on "Don't Come Home A' Drinkin' "—don't exactly break new ground. What does, though, is her *other* message—one that serves notice to the men who run her record label and, by implication, the rest of Music Row's boys club, that she's taken control of her career.

And a good thing too, judging by the quantum leap in quality between Shania's 1993 debut, a record on which her label saddled her with uninspired production, and *The Woman in Me*, the album that contains "Any Man of Mine." Hooking up with Mutt Lange, a producer who'd worked with rockers Bryan Adams and Def Leppard, and a man who fit the bill well enough to become her husband, Shania hotwires hockey-rink hooks to down-home twang for a sound that's at once more pop *and* more country than the Nashville norm. "This is what a woman wants," she laughs knowingly as the record fades. Indeed, Shania went on to release *Come on Over*, which, at sales of 17 million and counting, is the best-selling album in the history of country music.—bfw

359

Don't Rock the Jukebox, Alan Jackson
Produced by Scott Hendricks and Keith Stegall;
Written by Alan Jackson, Roger Murrah, and Keith Stegall
Arista 2220   1991   #1 country (3 weeks)

In "Don't Rock the Jukebox" (the song) a lovelorn Alan Jackson declares that sad country ballads are better suited for dealing with heartbreak than rockers. "I wanta hear George Jones," he begs the guy who's about to feed another quarter into the Wurlitzer, "my heart ain't ready for the Rolling Stones." "Don't Rock the Jukebox" (the record) assures Jackson that he doesn't have to choose. Not with Brent Mason's rubber-band Telecaster sharing space with Paul Franklin's pedal steel. And definitely not when the drums push the shuffle this hard.

Of course, in the real world, this is the last lesson Alan Jackson would ever need. It's his knack for synthesizing country with the supposedly incompatible elements of rock that has kept him sounding up to date and competitive on country radio all these years, even when he's celebrating tradition.—dc

360

Family Tradition, Hank Williams Jr.
Produced by Jimmy Bowen; Written by Hank Williams Jr.
Elektra/Curb 46046   1979   #4 country; #104 pop

Just a chip off the ol' Hank. And don't you forget it, either.

Not that there's much chance of that happening, what with Hank Williams Jr. bringing it up just about every other song for the last thirty-five years. Hank Jr.'s public life has at times seemed like one long wrestling match with his father's legacy. His album titles regularly trade on his daddy's fame (*Songs of Hank Williams*, *The Era of Hank Williams*, *Songs My Father Left Me*, and several others) or allude to its crushing weight (*Country Shadows*, *In My Own Way*, *Removing the Shadow*, etc.). Partly this was his mama's doing—Audrey Williams had Bocephus taking the stage to sing the songs of a father he'd never really known when he was still just a third grader (Sr. died when Jr. wasn't even four). On the other hand, as he sings here, try to "put yourself in [his] unique position." Hank Jr. isn't merely the son of a famous man. He's the descendent of an icon, a whiskey-bent, hell-bound genius who looms—for fans and detractors alike—as the very definition of country music. What's a poor boy supposed to do with *that*?

What Hank Jr. did, eventually, was say, "Fuck it." Sort of. On "Family Tradition," he's still proudly dropping his daddy's name while behind him someone lays down a steel part that's pure Don Helms. And he's still buying into the rowdiest parts of the myth. He's nearly killed himself drinking, for one thing, just like dear old dad; he even hints that it's been the stress of living up to a legend that's led him to drink so heavily in the first place. But "Family Tradition" catches Williams in that brief moment after he discovered a sound and persona that wasn't just inherited—basically, a twangy, two-steppin' brand of southern rock—but before he devolved into a good-old-boy caricature. As he's careful to point out from the first, he's pursued this new direction at the risk of being disowned, specifically by those members of the country family who believe the only way to extend a tradition is to imitate it. Yet he went ahead and broke their tradition anyway, and in the coming decade he would become one of the biggest country stars ever. Those bluesy electric guitar licks, not to mention his boozy snarl, are living proof that these honky-tonk blues are his very own.—dc

361

Streets of Bakersfield, Dwight Yoakam & Buck Owens
Produced by Pete Anderson; Written by Homer Joy
Reprise 27964   1988   #1 country (1 week)

Nothing Dwight Yoakam has recorded better captures his outsider ethos than this 1988 duet with Buck Owens. "I came here looking for something I couldn't find anywhere else," Dwight declares to open the record, and despite the fact that Buck first sang the line sixteen years earlier, it's plain that Yoakam identifies with it as if it were telling his own story. Which, of course, it was. Yoakam had doors slammed in his face when he tried to make it as a singer in Nashville in the late seventies, after which he lit out for the West Coast. He found north Hollywood's cow-punk scene much more receptive to his expansive artistic vision, which wed country and rock, hungering to see how far each could bend without breaking.

It's an approach that's certainly evident here, as Yoakam and producer Pete Anderson reinvent Owens's sprightly original as a slashing, accordion-driven polka worthy of L.A. post-punks Los Lobos. But whereas Yoakam came to California to find a new ethic, the Dust Bowl émigrés who gave birth to the Bakersfield Sound that inspired him journeyed West to start new *lives*. They were looking to feed 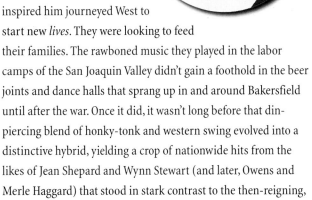 their families. The rawboned music they played in the labor camps of the San Joaquin Valley didn't gain a foothold in the beer joints and dance halls that sprang up in and around Bakersfield until after the war. Once it did, it wasn't long before that din-piercing blend of honky-tonk and western swing evolved into a distinctive hybrid, yielding a crop of nationwide hits from the likes of Jean Shepard and Wynn Stewart (and later, Owens and Merle Haggard) that stood in stark contrast to the then-reigning, smooth Nashville Sound.

The streets of Bakersfield did in fact give rise to something you couldn't find anywhere else, even if it was hardly the pure twang that revisionist historians, or even Owens, would have us believe. The way they hot-wired crying fiddle-and-steel and gutbucket guitars to jumpy rockabilly rhythms was, in many ways, as insurgent as big-beat rock & roll, a countervailing ethos that informed not just Yoakam's aesthetic but the hard-driving music of the Byrds, the Flying Burritos Brothers, X, Los Lobos, and the Blasters before him.—bfw

362

I'll Sail My Ship Alone, Moon Mullican

Produced by Henry Glover; Written by Henry Bernard [Glover], Morry Burns, Sydney Nathan, and Henry Thurston

King 830   1950   #1 country (4 weeks); #17 pop

Hailed as the "King of the Hillbilly Piano Players," Moon Mullican was pretty much the *only* hillbilly piano player of note during the 1940s. A good ten years ahead of its time, his barreling blend of honky-tonk and R&B anticipated the first burst of rock & roll; it also provided Jerry Lee Lewis with a blueprint for his trademark pumping piano style.

Mullican first learned to play the blues from a black sharecropper while growing up in East Texas. As a teenager, he logged time in the beer joints and brothels of Houston before landing his first real paying gig with Leon "Pappy" Selph's Blue Ridge Playboys, a pioneering western swing outfit that included Floyd Tillman and Ted Daffan. Mullican subsequently played with Jimmie Davis's Sunshine Boys and Cliff Bruner's Texas Wanderers, for whom he sang the epochal "Truck Driver's Blues." Though he never received credit, Moon also co-wrote Hank Williams's "Jambalaya," reportedly trading his publishing to Hank for the spot on the cast of the Grand Ole Opry that Hank finagled for him.

Devouring everything from country and Cajun music, to blues, jazz, and Tin Pan Alley standards, Mullican's own body of work evinced an appetite as voracious as his taste for liquor and food. He made his best recordings during the forties and fifties at King Records, where staff producer Henry Glover was fostering a heady cross-pollination of hillbilly music and R&B heard not just in Moon's hits but in those of jump-blues singers Roy Brown and Wynonie Harris. Glover, an African American, told historian John

Rumble that until he met Mullican he "hadn't seen a white man play the boogie woogie piano that the early black pianists were famous and known for." Add to that a voice that oozed lusty exuberance (witness the salacious "Pipeliner's Blues"), and Moon was practically unstoppable. Had he not been bald, middle-aged, and pudgy when rock & roll first erupted in the mid-fifties, he doubtless would have been there to detonate that new beat right alongside Little Richard and the King.

"I'll Sail My Ship Alone," Mullican's only #1 single, is standard issue honky-tonk—that is, except for Moon's rollicking piano and his patented "East Texas Sock," a tricked-up two/four rhythm he liked to boast could make "those bottles bounce on the table." That bounce is toned down some on this ode to heartbreak—it's nothing compared to his juking "Cherokee Boogie"—but it still rocks the house. "I'll sail my ship alone, though all the sails you've torn / And if it starts to sink, then I'll blame you," Moon warns the woman who's left him, his voice, oddly enough, bereft of bitterness. Then again why shouldn't it be? Buoyed by those lighter-than-air rhythms, Moon not only knows he can keep his boat afloat, he rightly suspects he can walk on water.—bfw

363

Angel of the Morning,

Merrilee Rush & the Turnabouts

Produced by Tommy Cogbill and Chips Moman; Written by Chip Taylor

Bell 705   1968   #7 pop

In which the hunter gets captured by the game.

At first, this promise of sex without strings sounds like a commitment-fearing snake's dream. That's likely how writer Chip Taylor (who also penned the garage-rock come-on "Wild Thing") intended it. Singer Merrilee Rush has other plans though. Granted, she plays the stoic "other woman" to the hilt, promising not to beg her lover to stay if he'll only call her angel and tenderly caress her cheek on his way out the door the morning after.

Yet the reason Rush can be so magnanimous, as noble as the stately horn choir that plumbs her deepest yearnings, is that she knows she won't have to beg. From the mix of poise and eroticism in her sultry alto, Rush sounds like she's woman enough to hang on to any man. Not only that, she's got the "Turnabouts," the studio pros assembled by producers Chips Moman and Tommy Cogbill, standing by her. By the time those gauzy strings, that harp-like finger-picking, and Gene Chrisman's momentous cadence have erected their country-soul wall of sound, Rush and her consorts have transformed Taylor's chauvinistic fantasy into a billowy siren song no lover in his right mind would ever walk away from.—bfw

364
Lonely Women Make Good Lovers, Bob Luman
Produced by Glenn Sutton;
Written by Freddy Weller and Spooner Oldham
Epic 10905   1972   #4 country

What gets you first is the sound of the thing, how producer Glenn Sutton has refocused the drama and sexual energy of Bob Luman's rockabilly origins onto a seductive countrypolitan soundscape. What keeps you listening, though, is trying to figure out whether or not the record is offering advice to would-be pick-up artists (Great news, boys! Lonely women are "all at the mercy of a good-lookin', smooth talkin' man") or a warning to any man in love (Careful there, fella! "If you got a woman, better treat her just as good as you can.")

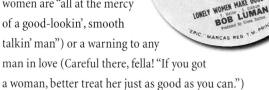

The answer's revealed by the sounds that charmed you in the first place. Throughout, Luman's earthy baritone makes it plain that he's played the role of the handsome operator himself a time or two and that he's also lost women for lack of respect. And when the music swells over and over with breathless excitement only to collapse suddenly into an echoing, solitary hush, you get the sense that what Luman's really telling us is that taking advantage of women and losing their love are intimately linked.—dc

365
I Met a Friend of Your's Today, Mel Street
Produced by Dick Heard;
Written by Wayland Holyfield and Bob McDill
GRT 057   1976   #10 country

There's hardly a male country singer in the past three decades who hasn't cited George Jones as a major influence. Not one of them has been a better singer than Mel Street. This particular Jones apostle didn't have as much to work with as most; Street's voice is nowhere near as rich and distinctive as his hero's, and his pinched range held his lyrical flights close to earth. But then, Street's strengths as a vocalist were those very limitations.

On "I Met a Friend of Your's Today," Street tells his wife that he has, quite by accident, discovered her infidelity. On his way home from work, he stopped off at a tavern for a beer where he overheard one of the patrons discussing his own spouse in terms far too intimate. "I introduced myself, and you should've seen his face," he tells his wife, though if she glanced in the mirror just then

she'd get the picture. Street switches back and forth between singing and talking throughout the record, but his narrow range and thick Smoky Mountain twang make every word sound like he's just speaking, albeit with phrasing borrowed straight from George Jones. If it weren't for the south-of-the-border acoustic guitar punctuating his sentences, you'd swear we were eavesdropping.

Street had sporadic chart success throughout the seventies, bouncing as he did from one small label to another. When he signed to major label Mercury in 1978, it looked like stardom might be within his grasp. It wasn't to be, though. That year, Street shot himself dead on his forty-fifth birthday, just as his father and grandfather had done before him. At his funeral, George Jones sang "Amazing Grace."—dc

366
Why Me, Kris Kristofferson
Produced by Fred Foster; Written by Kris Kristofferson
Monument 257 4577   1973   #1 country (1 week); #16 pop

Kris Kristofferson stands as one of country music's most incisive, memorable, and influential songwriters; he's the brains behind such masterpieces as "For the Good Times," "Help Me Make It Through the Night," "Me and Bobby McGee," and "Sunday Morning Coming Down." Kristofferson is also one of country music's most God-awful singers—a point that wouldn't be worth mentioning if only the unprecedented crossover success of his songs hadn't allowed him to secure a recording contract in the first place.

Then again, on "Why Me," Kristofferson's vocal liabilities are the very qualities that make the record sing. "Why me, Lord?" he prays. "What have I ever done to deserve even one of the pleasures I've known?" His voice is so cracked you figure every note must hurt. His range is cramped yet still uncontrollable, his interest in phrasing appears negligible, and his relationships with pitch and key are downright abusive. That's why, when he croaks "Lord, help me Jesus . . . I know what I am," we know just what he means without him having to finish. He's just a man—deeply flawed but humbled, and amazed.—dc

367

I Can Help, Billy Swan
Produced by Chip Young; Written by Billy Swan
Monument 8621   1974
#1 country (2 weeks); #1 pop (2 weeks)

Chip Young began his career playing pop and soul music alongside Joe South, Jerry Reed, Ray Stevens, and the other musicians who gravitated toward Atlanta's Lowery Music Group in the late 1950s. After he moved to Nashville in late 1963, Young established himself as a first-rate country picker, a fixture of the second generation A-Team that would transform the sound of Music City.

Probably the most memorable lick Young ever put down, the indelible waterfall riff that puts over Billy Swan's "I Can Help," almost never made it to vinyl. When guitarist Reggie Young (no relation to Chip, but a marvelous country-soul guitarist in his own right) played the riff that kicked off the record, Chip Young, who was producing the session, told him to leave the solo alone. He already had an idea, and he'd overdub it while Swan was out on the road playing rhythm guitar and singing harmony for Kris Kristofferson.

When Swan returned to Nashville and heard his producer's overdubbed guitar part, Young remembers, "he said 'I hate that. It needs some blues on there.' 'Billy, blues is not gonna get that I don't think.' He said, 'I think it needs blues. I got to tell you I hate it. Take it off.' So . . . we erased it off the sixteen track. And I tried from one morning about seven o'clock . . . to about seven at night playing every blues lick I'd ever heard, ever thought I'd hear, ever wanted to hear, and nothing fit . . . It just cried for that lick that was on there. And Billy finally put his head down and said, 'I tell you one thing: I hate it, but you can put it back on there.'" Young did just that, and when his kinetic part joined Swan's own roller-rink organ and a vocal and melody reminiscent of solo Ringo Starr, the record became one of the most irrepressible pop-country crossovers of the seventies.

On the road again a short time later, Kristofferson and Swan were driving through California when they heard a DJ play "I Can Help" two or three times in a row. Then the DJ came back yet again, Young says, and declared, " 'I just got to hear this guitar break one more time,' and he played just the guitar break. [Kristofferson and Swan] pulled over and called me right then. 'You win,' they said. 'You win.' "—dc

368

Hey Joe! Carl Smith
Produced by Don Law; Written by Felice and Boudleaux Bryant
Columbia 21129   1953   #1 country (8 weeks)

That Carl Smith sure is a mover. Within the span of one month—May 1950—the smooth-voiced honky-tonker went from being an unknown Knoxville demo singer and bass player (for Molly O'Day and comedian Archie Campbell, among others) to signing a record deal, cutting his first single, and joining the Grand Ole Opry. In the twenty years that followed, Smith would notch seventy-nine country hits—during that stretch third only to Webb Pierce and Eddy Arnold in a field that also included giants like Ray Price, Marty Robbins, and Lefty Frizzell.

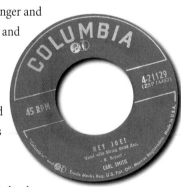

But the charts weren't the only thing Smith was homing in on. "Hey Joe! Where'd ya find that pearly girly / Where'd ya get that jolly dolly / How'd ya rate that dish I wish was mine," Carl gushes here, and he's doing a whole lot more than wishing. Johnny Sibert's fluttering steel and the Bryants' breathless wordplay ooze innocent infatuation, but Grady Martin's bluesy fills tip Carl's hand. He means business, and those souped-up rhythms—proto-rockabilly and then some—suggest he isn't wasting any time. And not just to grab Joe's girl, but to take liberties with the honky-tonk of his late pal Hank Williams as well.—bfw

369

No Help Wanted, The Carlisles
Produced by D. Kilpatrick; Written by Bill Carlisle
Mercury 70028   1953   #1 country (4 weeks)

Originally the Carlisles were Cliff and Bill, Kentucky-born brothers who together and separately recorded an impressive string of popular country-blues sides during the thirties and forties. Both Carlisles were fine guitarists (Cliff being instrumental in the adaptation of the Hawaiian steel style to country music); both were singers heavily influenced by the blue yodels of Jimmie Rodgers (Cliff even

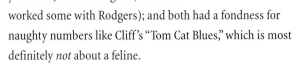

worked some with Rodgers); and both had a fondness for naughty numbers like Cliff's "Tom Cat Blues," which is most definitely *not* about a feline.

By the early fifties, Cliff had mostly retired. On his own, Bill had dropped the dirty stuff and was working with a full band—smart moves for a mid-century hillbilly act with one eye on the charts and the other on the Opry. On the Carlisles' biggest hit, "No Help Wanted," what's been lost in bawdiness and country-blues austerity has more than been replaced by a love for just plain goofy language and boogie-based beats. Over skittering rhythms, Carlisle cavorts through this novelty with all the spazzed-out energy of Little Jimmy Dickens loaded up on coffee and crossed with a horny jumping bean.

He's in love, see. ("No-oh help wanted," he hollers at anyone who even asks about the gal he calls his "little thing-a-majiggy.") So in love, evidently, that he's plumb out of his head. "She's got a

cute little walk with a hippety-hop / She's big at the little and bottom at the top," he gushes like a nut, and if you aren't paying attention, you might miss that the old sexual themes were being refashioned as fun for the whole family.—dc

370

Thanks a Lot, Ernest Tubb
Produced by Owen Bradley;
Written by Eddie Miller and Don Sessions
Decca 31526   1963   #3 country

By the early sixties, it looked like Ernest Tubb's time in the spotlight was finished. He was fast approaching his fiftieth birthday; his brand of hard-core Texas honky-tonk had largely passed out of favor, at least on the airwaves; and his quavery singing voice, which hadn't been a particularly supple instrument since back in his days of imitating the Blue Yodeler, could now regularly be counted upon to go flatter than road kill. If you didn't know better, you'd swear the guy was singing into an electric fan. But just when it seemed like this prewar relic's radio career was at an end, things changed. Honky-tonk, which had never really gone away, made a comeback via the recordings of Buck Owens and George Jones. At the same time, Tubb's booking agent Hal Curtis (co-owner of Nashville's hot publishing company Pamper Music, home to Willie Nelson, Harlan Howard, Hank Cochran, and others) provided the singer with his strongest material in years. And all of this coincided with Tubb's putting together the finest band he'd ever had.

Given that Tubb's Texas Troubadours had previously spotlighted musicians such as lead guitarist Billy Byrd and pedal-steel ace Buddy Emmons, that's no faint praise. But whether working a one-nighter in Tulsa, or laying down tracks with producer Owen Bradley in Nashville, the new line-up gave Tubb a crack rhythm section—including bassist Jack Drake, drummer Jack Greene, and guitarist/front man Cal Smith—and a pair of hotshot soloists in pedal-steel man Buddy Charleton and lead guitarist Leon Rhodes. When this group attacked a song as memorable as "Thanks a Lot," the result was Tubb's highest-charting single since 1952.

"Thanks," Ernest huffs. "Thanks a lot." For breaking his heart, he means, and his ragged, conversational approach is absolutely right for this expression of good-natured bitterness. Good-natured because Tubb's gruff voice comes off like the crochety old uncle you've loved all your life. Bitter because the band (supplemented in the studio by pianist Pig Robbins and tic-tac specialist Harold Bradley) scoots the crowd over the sawdust with a finger-jabbing vengeance. Meanwhile, Rhodes's back-sassing licks and Charleton's self-pitying whine on pedal steel suggest all the words Tubb couldn't have said on the radio even if he'd wanted.

No wonder Tubb biographer Ronnie Pugh refers to this edition of the Troubadours simply as "the Great Band." When you hear that old Troubadour announce "Aw, Leon" or "Aw, Buddy, now," it's as close as C&W has ever come to a "Good Honky-Tonkin'" seal of approval.—dc

371

Jingle Jangle Jingle, Tex Ritter & His Texans
No producer credited;
Written by Joseph J. Lilley and Frank Loesser
Capitol 110   1942   Pre-chart

A significant record both for country music (it was an early success by the primary purveyor of West Coast country, Capitol Records) and for Tex Ritter. "Jingle Jangle Jingle" helped the singing cowboy begin his transition from stage and screen (where he'd starred in sixty movies) to radio, where he'd notch hits off and on for the next two decades.

What a way to start anew: "I've got spurs that jingle, jangle, jingle as I go riding merrily along / And they sing 'Oh ain't you glad you're single' / and that song ain't so very far from wrong." In other words, Tex is saying no thanks and so long to all the girls that, in the heat of the moment, he'd maybe, kind of, sort of said he'd marry. He names Lily Bell, Mary Ann, Sally Jane, and Bessie Lou, but you get the feeling the list could go on a ways if only singles weren't so darn short. Perhaps one of the extra names on the list could've been Patsy Montana? Assisted by square dance fiddle and a rhythm section that includes spurs that

really do jingle, jangle, jingle, Tex jubilantly insists that he wants to be a cowboy too. But nix the sweetheart.—dc

372

D-I-V-O-R-C-E, Tammy Wynette
Produced by Billy Sherrill;
Written by Bobby Braddock and Curly Putman
Epic 10315   1968   #1 country (3 weeks); #63 pop

Why Tammy feels compelled to spell out anything remains one of country's great mysteries. Her volcanic sobbing is all that four-year-old J-o-e needs to hear to know that it's the e-n-d of the w-o-r-l-d.—bfw

373

Mommy for a Day, Kitty Wells
Produced by Owen Bradley;
Written by Harlan Howard and Buck Owens
Decca 30804   1959   #5 country

Kitty Wells wrote very little, but she sure knew how to get inside a song. Her plaintive whine was best suited to weepers, mournful laments like "I Heard the Jukebox Playing" and "A Woman Half My Age" in which she plays the long-suffering lover or housewife who's stuck with a faithless man. Here, however, the shoe is on the other foot. *Kitty* is the one who's been accused of sleeping around, or so goes the loose talk around town. There's also a kid in the picture, a daughter whom she can visit only on Sundays. "She's much too young to realize why mommy can't come home / And that her daddy wanted things this way," Kitty sings, bemoaning her custody arrangement as fiddles snivel above a chopping shuffle beat. Of course, Wells, in real life a mother of three and happily married to country singer Johnnie Wright, is only making believe. Maybe that explains why "Mommy" is such a gutwrencher. Terrified at the prospect, much less the consequences, of a D-I-V-O-R-C-E, Kitty can only imagine the agony she'd feel if, cut off from her kids, she found herself relegated to the role of mommy for a day.—bfw

374
Daddy Come and Get Me, Dolly Parton
Produced by Bob Ferguson;
Written by Dolly Parton and Dorothy Jo Hope
RCA Victor 9784   1970   #40 country

Here's what became of Dolly's character in "Down from Dover" after her parents exiled her from the homeplace, unwed and pregnant. Upon giving birth to a stillborn child, Dolly tracks down the dead baby's father, only to go crazy with jealousy when she discovers he deserted her for another woman. Wanting to keep her quiet (Dolly admits she cried and carried on for days), the guy has her locked away in a mental hospital, leaving her no choice but to appeal to her father to come get her out.

"Yes I need help, but not this kind / He didn't love me from the start / But it's not my mind that's broken, it's my heart," Dolly cries in a tortured vibrato as a weepy fiddle and a downright creepy-sounding steel guitar plead her case in the background. We never learn how her father responds, if at all. What's clear, though, is that men—Dolly's ex-lover, her father, her doctor—have all the power. And that they're using her "hysteria" as an excuse to control her, much as men have been doing since the ancient Greeks first attributed the condition to a malady of the uterus, the female reproductive organ from which the word derives.

Ironically, while the men at Dolly's record label felt "Dover" was too illicit to release as a single, they didn't think twice about working this record to radio, despite the fact that it uncovers a far greater sin.—bfw

375
Little Bessie, Darby & Tarlton
Produced by Frank Walker; Traditional
Columbia 15492-D   1929   Pre-chart

Darby & Tarlton were a breed apart from other prewar duos like the Blue Sky Boys and the Monroe Brothers. Whereas the latter employed close harmonies, tight arrangements, and drew heavily on mountain and centuries-old British sources, this Georgia twosome favored an improvisational approach to singing and playing, as well as a far-reaching repertoire, that was more in keeping with those of the early songsters and blues singers than anything else. And in Jimmie Tarlton they had one of the first (along with Ellsworth Cozzens of Jimmie Rodgers's band), and best, steel guitarists in the history of country music.

The son of sharecroppers, Tarlton mastered everything from the banjo to the accordion while growing up in the Southeast; by the time he was twelve, he'd taken up the guitar, which he learned to play bottleneck style from black field hands. After meeting famous Hawaiian-style guitarist Frank Ferera, he started using a steel bar, finally settling on a wrist pin he liberated from a cast-off engine block. Tarlton met Tom Darby, a similarly blues-derived singer and guitarist some ten years his senior, at the urging of a Columbus, Georgia, record-store owner who suggested the two men perform as a duo.

Darby & Tarlton cut their first sides together for Columbia in 1927, just a few months before Ralph Peer's fabled Bristol Sessions. But it was a record the two men made toward the end of that year, "Columbus Stockade Blues" backed with "Birmingham Jail," that was their biggest hit, selling around 200,000 copies as both songs went on to become standards. The duo released dozens of other sides for Columbia over the next seven years, but none of them matched this success and before long their rough-hewn records started sounding quaint, if not a little crude, compared with those of streamlined brother teams like the Sheltons and the Monroes. Darby & Tarlton nevertheless left behind a body of work that's as soulful as it is riveting, and nowhere was that more the case than with their 1929 recording of "Little Bessie."

Not to be confused with the mawkish, child death ballad that's been done by everyone from the Stanley Brothers to the Country Gentlemen, *this* "Bessie" is a weeper in which a young soldier bids his sweetheart farewell before he goes off to war. Set to a variant of "Don't Forget Me Little Darling" (of which the Carter Family's 1935 version is perhaps the best known), Darby & Tarlton's "Little Bessie" might have been just as maudlin as its more famous counterpart if not for its otherworldly aura.

"Don't forget me, Little Bessie, when from me you're far away / Just remember, Little Bessie, none will love you like I do," Darby wails as Tarlton's eerie harmonies hover above his baleful lead like a ghost floating in the ether. It's an image that sounds less and less fantastic the longer you listen to Tarlton's numinous slide and spellbinding falsetto, the latter a vocal effect closer to that of Delta bluesmen Skip James or Tommy Johnson than the western-style yodeling associated with most country singers. By the time

Darby sings of bugles sounding and cannon shots screaming, it's as if he's telling Bessie that he knows he's going to die overseas and that she'd best forsake all others since no one will ever match his love for her. More than that, he'll carry that love with him to his grave and will be there to haunt her, even when "her hair has turned to silver and her eyes have faded too."

It's at that point that the tingle in this would-be sentimental ballad becomes a chill.—bfw

376

Blues Stay Away from Me, The Delmore Brothers
Produced by Henry Glover; Written by Alton Delmore,
Rabon Delmore, Wayne Raney, Henry Glover
King 803   1949   #1 country (1 week)

377

Those Memories of You, Dolly Parton,
Linda Ronstadt, Emmylou Harris
Produced by George Massenburg; Written by Alan O'Bryant
Warner Bros. 28248   1987   #5 country

One of country music's most persistent subjects deals with a theme every human knows by heart—love hurts. Keeps right on hurting, too. Memory lugs our broken hearts with us through the years, and all we can really hope is that we develop muscles capable of shouldering the burden—as well as brains and hearts big enough to share the load when we can.

Music helps. Whether love's pain comes from death, betrayal, or a long, almost invisible uncoupling, great music confirms the universal nature of our hurt—reminding us that there is a community, a whole world even,

with which to share the pain. Music may coax tears from the eyes of those who can't will themselves to cry, just "as dancing allows the tongue-tied man," to borrow from author Andre Dubus, "a ceremony of love." Perhaps that's the secret to how "Those Memories of You," a song that on paper should be nothing but sad ("I'll always love you, little darling / Until the day they lay me down"), manages instead to provide real comfort. When Dolly Parton joins with Linda Ronstadt and Emmylou Harris in sad, sweet harmony, lyrics and voice together evoke just about all

there is to say about the way loss lingers. At least that's the way it seems until you encounter the single's video, where a new widower (portrayed by Harry Dean Stanton) putters alone about his house, feeding the dog, sweeping the floor, watching TV, retiring to bed, remembering.

By comparison, the Delmore Brothers sound so haunted by the past you wonder how they're able to find a reason to get out of bed each morning. Working from a slowed-down boogie riff supplied by King records A&R man Henry Glover, and accompanied by harmonica wiz Wayne Raney, the Delmores join their voices in beautiful, pitiful close harmony to recall a lover whose memory brings no peace. "Years don't mean a thing to me," Alton and Rabon cry. "Time goes by and still I can't be free."—dc

378

I Never Go around Mirrors, Lefty Frizzell
Produced by Don Gant;
Written by Sanger D. Shafer and Lefty Frizzell
ABC 11416   1974   #25 country

Lefty Frizzell was always an old soul. He grew up fast in the rough-and-tumble oil towns of Arkansas, East Texas, and Louisiana; he was singing in beer joints and dance halls before he was old enough to drink; he got married and became a father at sixteen. He even acknowledged his older-than-his-years disposition when, at twenty-four, he wrote and had a Top Five hit with "I'm an Old, Old Man (Tryin' to Live While I Can)". And live he did, going through booze, money, and women like there was no tomorrow, and never really relenting, even into middle age.

Written with future songwriting great Whitey Shafer, this doleful twin-fiddle shuffle finds Lefty, at age forty-six, reckoning with his lifetime of debauchery not long before his death from a stroke. "I can't stand to see a good

man go to waste / One who never combs his hair or shaves his face / A man who leans on wine," he sings, his purling tones wrapping around Pete Drake's gently weeping steel guitar. Yet something more than Lefty counting the cost of his excesses is going on here, something more tragic. Lefty's singing about the void he has tried to fill since his wife Alice left him; he sings of not being able to get over losing her to save his life. The reason he never goes around mirrors, then, isn't just that it tears him up to see what he's doing to himself. It's that he can't bear to behold himself without Alice by his side, making this less *The Picture of Dorian Gray* than a harrowing variation of "A Picture of Me (without You)."—bfw

379
I Want to Live (So God Can Use Me),
Brother Willie Eason
No producer credited; Traditional
Regent 1043   1951   Did not chart

Most folks associate the keening, voice-like whine of the steel guitar with country music, but the truth is, the laptop instrument first started appearing on pop recordings when the "Hawaiian" guitar craze swept Tin Pan Alley after World War I. Boosted by mail-order and door-to-door sales, the resophonic, steel-bodied guitars soon caught on with the rest of the nation—for a while selling at a faster clip than conventional guitars. Yet apart from country music, the only place where their popularity has persisted has been inside the House of God, an African American Pentecostal denomination also known as the Church of the Living God. There, for more than sixty years, steel guitars have filled the place occupied by the piano and organ in other churches.

Georgia-born Willie Eason was living in Philadelphia when he introduced the steel guitar to House of God worship during the mid-1930s. Forgoing the then-popular Hawaiian sound he'd heard his brother dabbling with at home, Eason worked more in the vein of the era's bottleneck-blues guitarists, musicians whose hyper-intuitive "talking" style mimicked African American vocal techniques. In Eason's hands the steel did more than just provide accompaniment for congregational hymns. It developed a voice of its own, emitting flurries of whoops, hollers, and melismatic cries and moans that expressed as wide a range of emotion as those conveyed by the most dynamic preachers or singers.

Eason's approach to the instrument, now commonly referred to as "sacred steel," immediately caught on; it wasn't long before the steel guitar became the dominant instrument in House of

God worship. Styles varied widely among players, some opting for the jazzy, legato phrasing patented by the great Lorenzo Harrison, others for the "hot," syncopated style pioneered by Eason. A few guitarists (most of them of the old school like Eason) prefer the lap steel to the pedal steel. Even though it's harder to control than a guitar with pedals, they say the lap steel better enables them to abandon themselves to the pull of the Holy Spirit. Which, as the title of Eason's 1951 solo recording of "I Want to Live (So God Can Use Me)" attests, is the reason they play in the first place.

From its pressing rhythms to Eason's breathtaking lyrical runs, "I Want to Live" bears more than a passing resemblance to a country gospel record. It's built upon a call-and-response between Eason's vocals and talking guitar not unlike those heard in Don Helms's work with Hank Williams or Curly Chalker's playing with Lefty Frizzell. The principal difference—and the main thing that places Eason's record more on the blues than the country continuum—is the coarse African-derived timbre of his groaning vocals; it's singing closely akin to that of bluesmen Charley Patton or Blind Willie Johnson.

Eason worked as a street musician during the late thirties and forties, for a time billing himself as "Little Willie and his Talking Guitar." He also toured with a small band called the Gospel Feast Party and recorded a handful of 78s, including two sides with the Soul Stirrers (pre–Sam Cooke). After that—and until he and other sacred steel guitarists like the Campbell Brothers started recording again and appearing at festivals—the music was only heard inside House of God churches. It's unlikely, in other words, that sanctified pickers exerted much influence on the steel players of country's honky-tonk heyday. That said, and despite developing their own blues- and jazz-based styles early on, Eason and his peers admit to listening extensively to the playing of country steel greats over the years, everyone from Jimmy Day and Jerry Byrd to Buddy Emmons and Lloyd Green. And they aren't averse to working snatches of country standards like "Rolling in My Sweet Baby's Arms" and "I Saw the Light" into the lengthy offertory marches they play during worship.

Lately, though, the pendulum has swung back as a new generation of country steel guitarists, including in-demand Nashville session men like Paul Franklin and Bruce Bouton, have been plugging in to sacred steel. It's doubtless an affinity that wasn't lost on Eason when, a half-century before, he prophetically decided to arrange the lyrics of his recording of "I Want to Live" to the tune of "Can the Circle Be Unbroken."—bfw

380
After the Sunrise, The Chuck Wagon Gang
Produced by Art Satherley;
Written by J. R. Baxter Jr. and Eugene Wright
OKeh 05682, Columbia 37450   1940   Pre-chart

A vision of glory so vivid it erases whatever sorrow's in sight.

"Even the planets together will hum / After the sunrise how happy we'll be," Dad Carter and his three children proclaim in the crispest vocal blend this side of the Stamps Family Quartet. It's not just the Chuck Wagon Gang's four-part harmonies (Rose on soprano lead, Anna on alto, son Jim helping Dad shore up the bottom) that tie them to the Stamps camp. J. R. Baxter Jr., co-founder of Stamps-Baxter publishing, co-wrote this rousing testimony—as much the melodic source of "I Saw the Light" (by way of the Carter Family's "Worried Man Blues") as the Gang's oft-cited "He Set Me Free." Not only that, the Chuck Wagon Gang did as much as anyone to popularize the songs of Stamps-Baxter mainstay Albert E. Brumley, the author of "I'll Fly Away" (among dozens of other gospel standards).

Taking their name from a flour company that sponsored their early performances, the Chuck Wagon Gang emerged in the mid-thirties, and it wasn't long before their close harmonies and penchant for lusty sing-a-longs made them one of country's most beloved gospel quartets. Along the way they incorporated amplified instruments into their sound, paving the way for today's modern country-gospel groups. The only accompaniment they have here, though, is the Mother Maybelle–inspired guitar of Howard Gordon (Rose's husband). Not that they need anything else, not with Rose leading the Gang in a call-and-response that conjures up visions of heaven on earth.—bfw

381
Worried Man Blues, The Carter Family
Produced by Ralph Peer; Written by A. P. Carter
Victor 40317   1930   Pre-chart

382
I Washed My Hands in Muddy Water,
Stonewall Jackson
Produced by Don Law and Frank Jones; Written by Joe Babcock
Columbia 43197   1965   #8 country

In *This Stubborn Soil: A Frontier Boyhood*, William A. Owens recounts his coming-of-age in rural East Texas during the first decade of the twentieth century. Compiling memories by turns sweet and harsh, the book is a compelling memoir of a time and place where "the fiddle [was] as useful as the plow." The Owens clan spent many an evening entertaining themselves by telling jokes and singing old hymns and ballads while their mother chorded along, "seconding" the family singers, on a small organ. Owens writes, "The ballads were long and sad, and the tunes were as sad as the words. I soon knew the words well enough to begin feeling sad before the sad part came, and to get the lesson of the song."

The Carter Family's "Worried Man Blues" is sad from the get-go. Where the ballad originated and where the Carters learned it is murky, to say the least. Despite the songwriting credit above, and despite the words "If anyone asks who composed this song, tell 'em was I" at the close, A. P. Carter certainly didn't write the song. Most likely, he came across it during one of his many "song-fishing" trips in and around his Clinch Mountain home. The song's scenario—a man falls asleep by a river only to awaken in chains, prison bound— suggests the African American experience during slavery and Jim Crow. And its structure—a phrase repeated twice, followed by a rhyming or "punch" line to complete the verse—adheres to the standard blues pattern. Its melody resembles any number of foot-tapping, hand-clapping old-time and gospel tunes that likely would've been familiar to white and black southerners alike.

Whether "Worried Man Blues" was sung around old southern

home places before it was recorded in 1930 is unclear, but the Carter Family sure sing it that way. Though Sara, Maybelle, and A. P. all join in every word of the way, they don't bother to edit the song out of first person; although it's Sara singing lead, these are a man's blues, not a worried woman's. The Carters offer it not as autobiography but simply as a sad reminder of life's nearly Kafkaesque absurdity—when you can fall asleep, minding your own business, and wake up with "twenty-nine lengths of chain around [your] leg, and on each link, the initials of [your] name," it's a fate that can no more be explained than it can be escaped. During the Great Depression, when so many families were hitting the road after being thrown from their homes, "Worried Man Blues" expresses a worldview that likely would have had country folk everywhere singing along.

Thirty years or so down the line, family sing-a-longs had given way to radio, records, TV, and film, but Stonewall Jackson's "I Washed My Hands in Muddy Water" tells what amounts to the same sad tale. He robs a man and winds up in jail, but it all still feels out of his control. He doesn't choose trouble, he "falls in with bad companions." He tries to stay clean of the law just as his father, a criminal himself, has warned him to; he really has tried, but he must've washed his hands in a muddy stream. By the end, Stonewall's busted out of the Nashville jail, and he's racing for Macon and home. But just as he hears dogs on his trail, bluesy electric guitar licks grasp at his heels. The groove pulls him onward, like an undertow or something else beyond his power to resist. It's easy to imagine this worried man will at some point lie down to rest—you have to rest *sometime*—only to find himself once again deprived of his freedom.

Through the years, Jackson's recording of "I Washed My Hands in Muddy Water" (we know who wrote *it*: Marty Robbins's backing vocalist Joe Babcock) has been followed by well-known versions by Elvis Presley, Charlie Rich, Johnny Rivers, and Hank Snow, among others. And it's had whole new generations of worried minds singing along to car radios and record players, learning its sad lesson. Can't win for losing.—dc

383

Ways to Be Wicked, Lone Justice
Produced by Jimmy Iovine;
Written by Tom Petty and Mike Campbell
Geffen 29023　1985　#71 pop

The song was written by Tom Petty and his guitarist Mike Campbell, two Florida boys who grew up in the heart of south-

ern-rock territory but preferred the folk-rock of Dylan and the Byrds. The singer is giant-voiced Maria McKee, an L.A. girl who was raised on Zappa and the Doors but, in her teens, found herself in an early 1980s "cow-punk" scene that was home to a varied and impressive group of roots rockers (the Blasters, Los Lobos, and X, as well as transplanted hillbilly singer Dwight Yoakam). Place all those influences in the hands of an AOR-ready producer like Jimmy Iovine, and you get a country rock masterpiece. "Ways to Be Wicked" feels something like what might have happened if Janis Joplin and Dolly Parton had gone down in a church basement and got good and drunk—not to mention royally pissed off.

See, as it turns out, "wicked" is precisely the way that McKee's being treated. Her man doesn't just hurt her; he hurts her on purpose in order to get off on her pain. Just plain sick of it ("You know so many ways to be wicked," she sings, "Oh, but you don't know one little thing about love"), McKee throws a righteous tantrum at the jerk, egged on by guest Campbell's twangy, threatening-to-walk riff.

That doesn't mean she's leaving right this minute, though. And if you want to know why she's holding on, listen to the way she both spits out and delights in the line, "No, you ain't afraid to stick it in."—dc

384

Evil on Your Mind, Jan Howard
Produced by Owen Bradley; Written by Harlan Howard
Decca 31933　1966　#5 country

Most cheating songs dwell on the infidelity of the man who's running around. There are exceptions, but even a quick survey of the country canon reveals that, at least on record, a whole lot more women have suffered at the hands of wayward men than vice versa. Which doesn't mean that women don't sing about the times they have cheated or been tempted to cheat; it's just that they tend to be less transparent about it. What else, after all, is Tammy Wynette talking about in "Stand By Your Man" when she confides, "Sometimes it's hard to be a woman / Giving your love to just one man"?

Much the same subtlety, albeit expressed less as a burden than a threat, is evident in Jan Howard's "Evil on Your Mind." While the record's chugging rhythms and jaunty melody imply that everything's rosy at home, Jan's husband suggests that an out-of-town holiday might do her good. She's not buying his line for a minute, though. She's been with him long enough to know he's packing her off so he can meet up with the woman he's got on the side. Yet instead of calling her husband on it, Jan reminds him that two can play that game. "Don't think that other men don't look at me that certain way from time to time / Don't think you're the only one who must contend with evil on your mind," she warns, giving him plenty of reason to rethink his immodest proposal.

The irony of it all is that "Evil on Your Mind" proved to be something of a self-fulfilling prophecy for the Howards when, a year or so later, Jan surprised her husband Harlan, who wrote the song, in bed with another woman. It wasn't long before the couple split up, but doubtless by then Jan didn't view those wayward thoughts of hers as quite so evil anymore.—bfw

385
The Chokin' Kind, Joe Simon
Produced by John Richbourg; Written by Harlan Howard
Sound Stage 7 2628   1969   #13 pop; #1 R&B

This country-soul million-seller, also written by Harlan Howard (who originally pitched it to Ray Charles), plays out the scenario from "Evil on Your Mind" in another way. Here it turns out that the guy wasn't fixing to cheat, and that his gal was messing with his head so he wouldn't suspect that *she* was stepping out on *him*. "Why couldn't you be content with the love I gave / I gave you my heart, but you wanted my mind," Simon pleads in response to his woman's charges that he's thinking of cheating.

"The Chokin' Kind" shares a bouncy groove with "Evil," except that in place of that record's bright guitar melody are horns and a nagging, chicken-scratch guitar riff (the soul-music equivalent of a tic-tac rhythm?) that gnaws away at Joe like the wound his woman has inflicted on his heart. Yet even though it feels like she took his pride and ruined his life, the tone of Joe's voice (*another*

demonstration of husky, Elvis-meets-Brother-Ray-inspired crooning à la Charlie Rich, Conway Twitty, and Joe South) is more bewildered than bitter. In fact, the second time he starts to tell his woman just how suffocating her love is, all he can cough out is "It make me wanna hmm, mm-mm-mm, oh yeah."—bfw

386
Your Cheatin' Heart, Hank Williams with His Drifting Cowboys
Produced by Fred Rose; Written by Hank Williams
MGM 11416   1953
#1 country (6 weeks)

Heed this man's warning when he moans, "Your cheatin' heart will tell on you." His tell-tale heart haunted him to an early grave.—bfw

387
Don't Cheat in Our Hometown, Ricky Skaggs
Produced by Ricky Skaggs; Written by Ray Pennington
Sugar Hill/Epic 04245   1983   #1 country (1 week)

Ricky Skaggs is a child of the rock era—he came into the world exactly two weeks after Elvis shook things up with "Blue Moon of Kentucky"—but he's always lived and breathed for bluegrass.

Born and raised in the hills of eastern Kentucky, he grew up in a family that toured regionally as the Skaggs Clan. By the age of five, he was already well enough known as a mandolin-picking prodigy that when Bill Monroe came to town, the audience clamored for little Ricky to get his turn at the mike; when Monroe obliged, Skaggs delivered a version of the Osborne Brothers' hit "Ruby," using Big Mon's own mandolin. In 1970, at age fifteen, he and friend Keith Whitley joined the Clinch Mountain Boys after Ralph Stanley overheard them doing Stanley Brothers impersonations. Skaggs spent the rest of the decade coming of age as a featured member in some of

bluegrass' premiere bands: the Country Gentlemen, J. D. Crowe's the New South, the Seldom Scene—each band more progressive, more New Grass, than the last. All deliberately broke, or at least bent, some of the bluegrass rules in the direction of folk, rock, and country music proper. From there, it was more or less a straight line for Skaggs to Emmylou Harris's Hot Band, a folk-rock-country outfit that was merely bluegrass-influenced. Eventually, he stepped outside the bluegrass fold entirely for a career as a mainstream country singer.

By the end of the century, Skaggs had returned to bluegrass full-time, but he'd never left the music completely behind. Probably more than anyone before or since, Skaggs won a place for bluegrass-inspired sounds on country radio—today, when Diamond Rio, Vince Gill, and Lee Ann Womack get radio play with bluegrass-inflected country, they have Ricky Skaggs to thank.

"Don't Cheat in Our Hometown" illustrates how he pulled it off in an era when the music of Urban Cowboys and New Traditionalists alike included heaping helpings of rock & roll. The Stanley Brothers had recorded the song first in 1963 (Skaggs and Whitley cut another version in 1971), and Skaggs delivers it here in the earnest tenor he perfected singing harmony with the masters. But now the number's been spiked with the pedal-steel fills and the boot scooting, drum-driven beat of latter-day honky-tonk. Still, when a humiliated Skaggs pleads with his wife not to add insult to injury—"If you're gonna cheat on me, don't cheat in our hometown"—there's no mistaking those high, lonesome harmonies prove the roots of his raising.—dc

388

One Has My Name (the Other Has My Heart),
Jimmy Wakely
Produced by Lee Gillette;
Written by Eddie Dean, Dearest Dean, and Hal Blair
Capitol 15162   1948   #1 country (11 weeks); #10 pop

Jimmy Wakely's "One Has My Name (the Other Has My Heart)" had to be in this book if only because it's widely identified as country music's first cheating song. True enough, but the cheating described here seems as much emotional as physical—a relatively benign reading not allowed by, say, "Slipping Around," the Floyd Tillman song that duet partners Wakely and pop singer Margaret Whiting would place atop both the country and pop charts the following year.

Really, it's the musical virtues of "One Has My Name" that make the record stand out. Wakely's break came when Gene Autry offered the singer work in Hollywood. As a result, the Jimmy Wakely Trio (including Johnny Bond and Dick Reinhardt) backed Autry for a time, but when Wakely set out on his own, the move eventually led him to a singing cowboy career that included dozens of film appearances and even his own comic book. "One Has My Name" features effortless harmonica, Hawaiian steel guitar, and effervescent accordion—western staples polished to the highest levels of craftsmanship without sacrificing any of their campfire charm. What really puts it over the top, though, is Wakely's easy-going croon, which reveals again the tremendous debt the singing cowboys owed Bing Crosby (note, for example, the way Wakely delivers "One has brown eyes, the other's eyes are blue"). And when an uncredited female vocalist sneaks in behind Wakely for the final verses, only the most naïve listeners could hear in those seductive harmonies anything other than a cheating situation.—dc

389

Heaven's Just a Sin Away,
The Kendalls
Produced by Brien Fisher;
Written by Jerry Gillespie
Ovation 1103   1977   #1 country (4 weeks); #69 pop

390

It's a Cheating Situation, Moe Bandy
Produced by Ray Baker;
Written by Curly Putman and Sonny Throckmorton
Columbia 10889   1979   #2 country

A double shot of proof that "hard-core" country music never has to disappear. Not when it can survive a period as uninspired as the late seventies, when radio trafficked in soft-core come-ons like Eddie Rabbitt's "Every Which Way but Loose" and the Bellamy Brothers' "If I Said You Have a Beautiful Body Would You

Hold It against Me." In that dismal context, Moe Bandy's twanging moan and the guilty fiddle that sneak through "It's a Cheating Situation" evoke a rich history of honky-tonk balladry. Telling a similar story from a female perspective, "Heaven's Just a Sin Away" features traditional touches like a recurring Bakersfield riff and the gorgeous close harmony singing of Royce and Jeannie Kendall. Together, these songs pinpoint the most classic of country dilemmas—Jeannie Kendall's imagined heaven is pretty much the same thing that's making Bandy's life a living hell.

Although "hard-core" sounds need never die, in order to survive they will always need to find ways to connect with new audiences while maintaining their connection to older audience members. To that end, it's the honky-

tonk elements of "Cheating Situation" that get the spotlight, but they're fused with a contemporary country-soul rhythm section and soft washes of church organ, which hang over Bandy and backing vocalist Janie Fricke like the threatening clouds of judgment. "There's no use pretending there'll be a happy ending," Bandy sings of his affair, and though he knows it's wrong, it's the only ending he can imagine.

In "Heaven's Just a Sin Away," on the other hand, Jeannie Kendall gives new meaning to the concept of a "fortunate fall." Though she struggles some along the way, she finally decides to give in to the earthly heaven her sin will provide. Even with such a secular theme, however, "Heaven's Just a Sin Away" managed to receive spins on some gospel radio stations, in addition to all its country and pop airplay. One can imagine a program director's arguments about object lessons and the like. But you can bet what really made that crossover possible was the irresistible clavinet bouncing along with Kendall as she rushes to her lover. That joyous melody and thumping backbeat—100 proof 1970s southern gospel—didn't hurt either.—dc

391
Don't Let the Green Grass Fool You, O. B. McClinton
Produced by O. B. McClinton and Tommy Strong;
Written by Jerry Akines, John Bellmon, Victor Drayton,
and Reginald Turner
Enterprise 9059   1972   #37 country

It's the artist . . . who sets the mode of the song. Johnny Cash can make a blues song a country song, and Muddy Waters can make a country song a blues.

O. B. McClinton made the above observation during a mid-eighties interview with historian Rob Bowman, and this record proves his point. Wilson Pickett had scored a Top Twenty pop hit with the song in 1971, but even set against the limber pop-leaning groove that Philly producers Kenneth Gamble and Leon Huff supplied him, Pickett's ravaged pleading was undeniably that of a backwoods soul shouter. Laced with bittersweet dobro and pedal steel, McClinton's version is, by contrast, flat-out country. His intimate, conversational delivery on this lover's prayer was just what you might have expected from a down-home singer who, like fellow Mississippi native Conway Twitty, grew up listening to Red Foley and Hank Williams on the Grand Ole Opry.

Of course, that wasn't all that McClinton—the sixth of seven children in a family of black cotton pickers—heard while growing up in Senatobia, Mississippi. Like Twitty, he tuned in Nashville's WLAC, where DJs Gene Nobles and John R played blues and R&B; he also listened to Memphis's WHBQ, where Dewey Phillips would spin the latest rockabilly hits.

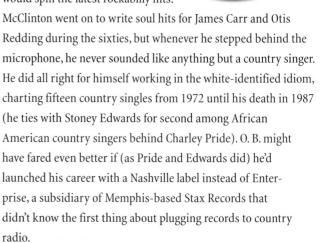

McClinton went on to write soul hits for James Carr and Otis Redding during the sixties, but whenever he stepped behind the microphone, he never sounded like anything but a country singer. He did all right for himself working in the white-identified idiom, charting fifteen country singles from 1972 until his death in 1987 (he ties with Stoney Edwards for second among African American country singers behind Charley Pride). O. B. might have fared even better if (as Pride and Edwards did) he'd launched his career with a Nashville label instead of Enterprise, a subsidiary of Memphis-based Stax Records that didn't know the first thing about plugging records to country radio.

Then again, maybe not. McClinton recorded his first album for Enterprise in Nashville with producer Jim Malloy and some of Music City's hottest pickers, only to watch it stiff. Later O. B. said he felt hamstrung by the way Malloy kept urging him to sound more country—that is, less *black*—than Charley Pride. But whatever the reason—and somewhat ironically given Malloy's expansive body of work—the producer's sessions with McClinton rarely exploited his country-soul strengths. Maybe that's why, after letting the green grass of Nashville fool him the first time, McClinton enlisted engineer Tommy Strong and produced this grooveful wonder, as well as "My Whole World is Falling Down," his only other Top Forty country hit, by himself.—bfw

392

Lead Me On, Loretta Lynn & Conway Twitty
Produced by Owen Bradley;
Written by Leon Copeland
Decca 32873   1971   #1 country (1 week)

George and Tammy. Porter and Dolly. Conway and Loretta. The late sixties through the late seventies was the golden age of country duets, a time when the pairing of male and female singers wasn't just a cross-promotional ploy like today's dreaded "vocal event," but rather a chance to expand country's sonic and emotional palette.

Each of these three acts could generate plenty of sexual tension when they cozied up to each other, giving rise to speculation as to whether, or to what extent, art imitated life. George and Tammy, of course, were married and later divorced, and Porter had designs on Dolly, although she denies that the two ever slept together. The line on Conway and Loretta has always been that they were just friends, albeit close enough to make her husband fiercely jealous and to prompt fans to blame Loretta for the breakup of Conway's first marriage. If any one of their dozen or so hits gave listeners reason to believe the rumors, it was "Lead Me On," a smoldering ember that could very well have had Conway and Loretta wondering themselves.

The record starts tentatively, as do many of Twitty's records, leaving plenty of room for crescendo and climax. As he comes in, promising that he'd never lead Loretta on, you'd hardly suspect things could go anywhere at all. They start heating up, though, when Loretta enters, her anxious vibrato telling him he'll have to help her if she's going to cross that line. With Tommy Markham's drums and Harold Bradley's bass pounding in her breast, it's as if Loretta has forgotten Conway's pledge. Or maybe she just chooses to ignore it. "Lead me on and take *control* of how I feel / I can't do this on my own 'cause it's

against my will," she moans on the first chorus. Then, as John Hughey's steel fans the flames, Conway echoes her desire in a burning croon and they breathlessly repeat the swelling chorus, redoubling their resolve to lead *each other* on. At least in song.—bfw

393

I've Got a Tiger by the Tail, Buck Owens
Produced by Ken Nelson;
Written by Buck Owens and Harlan Howard
Capitol 5336A   1965   #1 country (5 weeks); #25 pop

In 1965, mop tops were way cooler, supposedly, than flat tops, but that didn't stop Buck Owens from scoring a crossover hit at the height of Beatlemania. "I've Got a Tiger by the Tail" finds Buck caught up in the whirlwind lifestyle of his new girlfriend—it's a fair bet she's a much younger gal, too, the way he's "losing weight and turning mighty pale" while she drags him from nightclub to tavern to bar. Ironic, that. While Owens was struggling to keep up with his younger lover, the era's paragons of youthful cool, the Fab Four, were paying homage to Owens. Most famously with Ringo's turn on Buck's 1963 hit "Act Naturally," but also on country-rock prototypes like "I Don't Want to Spoil the Party" and, just ahead, "Run for Your Life," the Bakersfield-ish closing track of the Beatles' *Rubber Soul*.

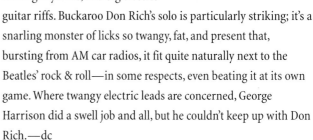

"Tiger by the Tail" could compete because of what it had in common with so many other early Beatles hits: an impossibly catchy chorus and effervescent spirit, driving rhythms, and big electric guitar riffs. Buckaroo Don Rich's solo is particularly striking; it's a snarling monster of licks so twangy, fat, and present that, bursting from AM car radios, it fit quite naturally next to the Beatles' rock & roll—in some respects, even beating it at its own game. Where twangy electric leads are concerned, George Harrison did a swell job and all, but he couldn't keep up with Don Rich.—dc

394
Honky Tonk Song, Webb Pierce
Produced by Paul Cohen; Written by Mel Tillis and A. R. Peddy
Decca 30255   1957   #1 country (1 week)

Tired of drinking or dancing his troubles away, Webb Pierce figures he'll be able to stop thinking about his baby if he can just get some sleep. So he checks into a dive, only to be kept awake "all night long" by the combo blasting away downstairs. "The band kept a-playin' with a honky-tonk beat," he complains.

Don't believe him. From the tommy-gun drums that kick it off to the "Hound Dog" guitar cop that closes it down, this is big beat rock & roll—especially that springy rhythm guitar riff that drives the record through the break. That was what helped "Honky Tonk Song" compete in a year when nearly half the singles to top the country charts were either by Elvis Presley, Johnny Cash, Jerry Lee Lewis, or the Everly Brothers. On "Honky Tonk Song," Pierce tries to shut out the noise by pulling a pillow down over his head. But as anyone listening to country radio already knew, nothing in the world was going to silence that new beat.—dc

395
I'm Coming Home, Johnny Horton
Produced by Don Law;
Written by Tillman Franks and Johnny Horton
Columbia 40813   1957   #11 country

Writers often cite "Honky-Tonk Man" as proof that, prior to his days as a purveyor of pseudo-historical ballads, Johnny Horton was one of country's great links between honky-tonk and rockabilly. It's a terrific record and one that wears well, as Dwight Yoakam's rocking cover thirty years after the release of Horton's original attests. And yet when it comes to getting real gone, "I'm Coming Home" makes "Honky-Tonk Man" sound tame. Plus, it's downright filthy. Grady Martin's growling guitar obbligato (echoes of "Train Kept A-Rollin' ") positively drips with sex, and Johnny, barreling home in his rig, broadcasts his lust all over the citizen's band. "I'm comin home / I've gotta make some love," he swaggers, his quivering vocals the aural equivalent of Elvis's thrusting pelvis. Were it not for its truck-driving conceit there's no way the record would have made it onto country radio. Not with a line as salacious—and explicit—as "I'm coming home, baby / I'm-a doggin' it in."—bfw

396
Rocky Top, The Osborne Brothers
Produced by Harry Silverstein;
Written by Boudleaux and Felice Bryant
Decca 32242   1968   #33 country

A rousing tribute to the good old days and home sweet home back in the Tennessee hills, where there was no smog and no telephone bills, just good corn whiskey, first loves, and plenty of time to enjoy 'em both. It's a sweet memory. Then again, if Bobby and Sonny Osborne really wanted to go back to Rocky Top, there's nothing stopping them. But don't hold your breath. For one thing, no smog and no telephone bills probably translate into no jobs and no modern amenities—some of the reasons why folks migrated from the hills in the first place. For another, the Osbornes' version of Felice and Boudleaux Bryant's mountain idyll has a serious crush on the sounds of the city. The brothers' radio-friendly brand of bluegrass, featuring headlong mandolin and banjo solos by Bobby and Sonny respectively, is souped up here by a team of plugged-in Nashville cats, including drummer Jerry Carrigan and pedal-steel guitarist Hal Rugg. In his piercing tenor, Bobby sings, "It's a pity life can't be simple again," and Rugg in particular leaves no doubt about the "can't" in that sentiment. His pedal steel makes this bluegrass sound as frenetic and exciting as the busiest street corner in Detroit, Dayton (where the Kentucky-born Osbornes grew up), Baltimore, Milwaukee—any city now home to generations of transplanted mountain folk.

Not that it isn't nice to remember. "Once I had a girl on Rocky Top, half bear, the other half cat / Wild as a mink but sweet as soda pop," Bobby says, shaking his head at the memory. "I still dream about that."

No doubt. Talk about how mountain girls can love!—dc

397
Don't Get above Your Raisin', Lester Flatt, Earl Scruggs, and the Foggy Mountain Boys
No producer credited;
Written by Lester Flatt and Earl Scruggs
Columbia 20854   1951   Did not chart

Bill Monroe was fit to be tied when Flatt & Scruggs quit his Blue Grass Boys in early 1948. Flatt's departure, which left the group without a lead singer and rhythm guitarist, was bad enough. But Scruggs's exit was devastating; his revolutionary three-finger banjo style played as major a role in the birth of bluegrass as Monroe's own innovations. One can easily imagine Big Mon, mad as hell after the pair gave notice, admonishing them with the colloquialism Flatt appropriated for this cautionary love song: "Don't get above your raisin', stay down to earth with me."

To hear Scruggs tell it, there was nothing uppity about the duo's decision to leave the Blue Grass Boys. "We were just riding ourselves to death, and back then Bill wasn't paying much of a salary," Scruggs explains. "I was going to go back to work in the thread mill, but Lester approached me with the idea that we both might get dissatisfied having to go back to the factory. So we formed our own group."

Flatt & Scruggs might not have consciously set out to challenge Monroe when they put together the Foggy Mountain Boys, but "Don't Get above Your Raisin' " sure sounds like they're looking to cut him. For starters, they bring in former Blue Grass Boy Chubby Wise to play fiddle. Then, forcing comparisons between the two groups, they cop the arrangement from a couple of tunes they did with Monroe, "Heavy Traffic Ahead" and Jimmie Rodgers's "Blue Yodel No. 4 (California Blues)." From Scruggs's taunting banjo lick at the start of the record to Wise's bluesy bowing and Jody Rainwater's strutting bass solo, it's hard *not* to hear Flatt & Scruggs gunning for their old boss.

It certainly wouldn't be the last time the two men challenged Monroe. In 1955 they installed Uncle Josh Graves as the Foggy Mountain Boys' dobro player, a move that broadened bluegrass's sonic palette in much the same way that Scruggs's three-finger banjo had when he joined the Blue Grass Boys ten years earlier. Later on Flatt & Scruggs took stringband music uptown by way of northeastern college campuses and Carnegie Hall; with the theme from *The Beverly Hillbillies,* they introduced the idiom Monroe "invented" to the rest of the world. Very little of which had anything to do with staying down-to-earth.—bfw

398
Big Beaver, Bob Wills & His Texas Playboys
Produced by Art Satherley; Written by Bob Wills
OKeh 05905   1940   Pre-chart

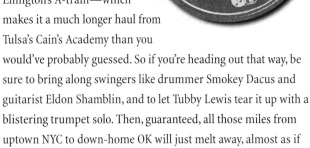

"Big Beaver" was an Oklahoma oil-pumping station that Bob Wills and his band often passed while out on the road. Weird thing, though. Judging by the sound of it, you get there by hopping aboard Duke Ellington's A-train—which makes it a much longer haul from Tulsa's Cain's Academy than you would've probably guessed. So if you're heading out that way, be sure to bring along swingers like drummer Smokey Dacus and guitarist Eldon Shamblin, and to let Tubby Lewis tear it up with a blistering trumpet solo. Then, guaranteed, all those miles from uptown NYC to down-home OK will just melt away, almost as if they didn't exist.—dc

399
Pick Me Up on Your Way Down, Charlie Walker
Produced by Don Law; Written by Harlan Howard
Columbia 41211   1958   #2 country

Ray Price's hand is all over honky-tonker Charlie Walker's breathrough hit, which also provided Harlan Howard with his first big break as a songwriter. It was Price who helped Walker land a deal with Columbia Records, in the process hooking him up with his own producer and many of the pickers who played on his records. And it was Price who suggested that Walker cut

Howard's song, a barroom variant of "Don't Get above Your Raisin'," and a shuffle no less—the very dance rhythm Price had helped establish as a durable part of the honky-tonk vernacular. Yet it's also worth pointing out that Walker had been playing two-steps in the Dallas beer halls as far back as the early forties, when he was singing and picking with Bill Boyd's Cowboy Ramblers. Walker also worked as a DJ for a number of Texas radio stations after the war, a time when Price was still crooning Bing Crosby and Frank Sinatra covers in bars for his fellow veterinary students. It's very likely, in fact, that Price heard Walker spinning shuffles and other dance tunes on the air. This isn't to diminish Price's role in jump-starting Walker's late-blooming singing career, or in the genesis of this jukebox staple, just to note that Price was likely paying tribute to an unsung shuffle-beat pioneer when he picked Walker up off the hard-wood.—bfw

400

Wasted Words, Ray Price
Produced by Don Law; Written by Don Gibson
Columbia 21562   1956   #4 country

Ray's got a problem. His woman's left him. And just when he thinks he's put her out of his head for good, someone who doesn't know any better asks him about her. Or someone else, who does know what's happened, advises him to just go out and enjoy himself or, even worse, find himself a new gal. In either case, there's not a thing in the world Ray can say that won't remind him of the very thing he aches to forget. "You don't love me," he moans as the rhythm section throbs away like a headache. "You don't care."

All the talking in the world can't change how painful *that* feels. It can't even express it, though those harmonies that Ray and guest Ira Louvin nail at the chorus must come awfully close.—dc

401

You Don't Seem to Miss Me,
Patty Loveless with George Jones
Produced by Emory Gordy Jr.; Written by Jim Lauderdale
Epic 78704   1997   #14 country; #109 pop

Singers influenced by George Jones? Let's see . . . Mel Street, Jimmy Martin, Vern Gosdin, Randy Travis, Alan Jackson, Joe Diffie, Mark Chesnutt, Sammy Kershaw. The list could go on, and often does, although almost always without mentioning a woman. Jones's female duet partners receive lip-service from time to time, notably Tammy Wynette and Melba Montgomery. Sometimes the list includes Hazel Dickens, a mountain singer known more to fans of bluegrass and folk music, who acknowledges the lessons she learned from Jones every chance she gets. But the lack of mainstream country women named each time people reel off such lists is inexplicable. Even a quick survey of the past fifteen to twenty years of chart activity yields at least a handful of country women whose singing owes a deep debt to Jones, among them Lacy J. Dalton, Shelby Lynne, Dawn Sears, Bobbie Cryner, and Allison Moorer.

And Patty Loveless. The Kentucky native's first Top Ten hit, a 1987 cover of "If My Heart Had Windows," was an early sign of her affinity with Jones (as were her early stints opening for him at state fairs across the heartland and her cameo on his 1992 single, "I Don't Need Your Rockin' Chair"). But "You Don't Seem to Miss Me," a 1997 collaboration between the two singers, is all the evidence anyone should need. There's Patty's elongated phrasing and the way she bends and swallows notes on the first few lines, all of it Jones-inspired. There's the way, when George joins her on the second and third verses, that the two singers' voices reach out for each other—and for the aching fiddle and steel—like partners who've spent decades on the dance floor together. The beauty of their performance is enough to make you forget that "You Don't Seem to Miss Me" is about the agony of discovering you're on the hurting end of a love grown cold. Well, almost enough to make you forget until you hear those pounding, "Running Scared" drums on the final chorus and the panic in Patty's voice, and you realize that, as close as those two voices are, she's still reaching out for and missing him.—bfw

402
Funny How Time Slips Away, Billy Walker
Produced by Don Law; Written by Willie Nelson
Columbia 42050   1961   #23 country

The trajectory of Billy Walker's career traces the arc of country's evolution during the first twenty years after the Second World War. The smooth-voiced Texan began singing honky-tonk in the dance halls of his home state during the late forties; he dabbled with rock & roll after Elvis emerged in the mid-fifties, and finally hit his stride in the sixties with a string of understated Nashville Sound singles for Columbia, including "Funny." A number of vocalists more gifted and expressive than Walker—including Ray Price, writer Willie Nelson, and Jimmy Elledge, who had a Top Forty hit with "Funny" in 1962—have cut good-to-great versions of the song. And soul singer Al Green's tortured reading from 1973 is absolutely devastating. Yet none of these men quite gets inside the smoldering resentment of Nelson's lyric the way Walker does here.

The record begins with Billy bumping into his old lover. Feigning indifference, he responds politely when she asks how he's doing. You almost picture him yawning and stretching when he remarks that, although it's been a while since they broke up, it seems like it was just the other day. In fact, you don't suspect he's still hurting till he asks about her new love, wondering, as nonchalant as can be, if she'll walk out on him as well. That dig, however, is nothing compared to his not-so-passive parting shot. As the walking bass and guitar follow Billy down the street, he warns, "But remember what I tell you, that in time you're gonna pay / And it's surprising how time slips away." That is, it won't be long before her chickens come home to roost.—bfw

403
I Forgot More Than You'll Ever Know,
The Davis Sisters
Produced by Chet Atkins;
Written by Cecil Null
RCA Victor 5345   1953   #1 country (8 weeks); #18 pop

Hank Cochran claims that his inspiration for "She's Got You" was a photograph he found in a desk drawer one afternoon. Doubtless that's true, but it's hard to imagine that he didn't also have the Davis Sisters' only #1 record in mind when he wrote what would become Patsy Cline's biggest hit. The only thing different, the only

thing new, is that where Hank's lovelorn protagonist is talking to the man she's just lost, Betty Jack Davis (bolstered by the high harmonies of pal-not-sister Skeeter) is telling the woman who just stole her guy that she'll never know the love they once had. Betty Jack doesn't stop there, though; she has the temerity to add that *any* love her rival could ever hope to have with her ex is doomed to fall short of the memories Betty Jack's already erased.

The truth is that Betty Jack hasn't forgotten a thing; the weeping fiddle-and-steel, as well as those tearful guitar-strokes on the second and third beats of each measure, leave absolutely no doubt of that. It's a classic study in denial masked with bravado, and one rendered all the more credible—and heartrending—by the Sisters' stolid mountain harmonies. Sandwiched historically between Johnnie & Jack and the soon-to-be-huge Louvin and Everly Brothers, the Davis Sisters might well have gone on to become a close-harmony duo on a par with the great brother acts if Betty Jack hadn't died in a car wreck just weeks before "I Forgot" topped the charts.—bfw

404
Illegal Smile, John Prine
Produced by Arif Mardin; Written by John Prine
Atlantic 45-3218   1972   Did not chart

John Prine's early reputation as the troubadour most likely to live up to the "new Dylan" hype had the unfortunate side effect of getting him tagged a "folkie." Some aspects of his music fit the bill, notably his hard-hitting lyrics and his rudimentary picking and affable croak. Still, the folkie moniker is ultimately too binding for Prine. For starters, he's toured and almost always recorded with a band. And from the American Studios crew that also played on Elvis's comeback records to the Tom Petty cohorts who backed him during the nineties, it's often been a rock band.

Prine's country colors are just as vivid, if not more so. Though born and raised in a western suburb of Chicago, he spent many a childhood summer with his grandparents in Muhlenberg County, Kentucky, the bucolic retreat that, with a nod to Merle Travis's "Kentucky Means Paradise," he immortalized in "Paradise." Prine also has fond early memories of hearing Webb Pierce and Carl Smith on Chicago's WJJD, the station his dad tuned in after work each night with a quart or two of beer. Then there are the country hits Prine's written for Tammy Wynette and Don Williams, as well as his covers of classics by everyone from the Carter Family to Lefty Frizzell. It's a connection Prine finally rendered explicit on *In Spite of Ourselves*, a 1999 album of country chestnuts done as duets with Nashville hitmakers ranging from Trisha Yearwood to Connie Smith.

"Illegal Smile," Prine's furtive toker's plaint, isn't exactly country, but with Leo Leblanc's pedal steel spreading every which way like kudzu, it's damn close. Brimming as it does with a blend of wacky humor ("A bowl of oatmeal tried to stare me down / And won") and boho existentialism ("Sometimes it seems like the bottom / Is the only place I been"), the lyrics sound as much like a Roger Miller–Kris Kristofferson co-write as a Prine original. And don't for a minute think that stoner reveries like this are foreign to the stars of the Grand Ole Opry. John probably quit smoking the stuff years ago, but, rumor has it, Willie and the Hag were still lighting up into the new millennium.—bfw

405
Whiskey River, Willie Nelson
Produced by Willie Nelson;
Written by Johnny Bush and Paul Stroud
Columbia 10877   1978   # 12 country

Willie's first crack, in 1973, at Johnny Bush's rewrite of the old blues standard "If the River Was Whiskey" found him and producer Jerry Wexler recasting Bush's hit as a woozy, country-soul shuffle. Willie sings in a rummy baritone and, with background vocalists Dee Moeller and Larry Gatlin there to commiserate with him, you'd swear he's already gone. His entreaty to the liquor isn't so much a plea for deliverance as a hymn to the juice that's even now working its stuff—in this case, wiping from his mind the memory of the woman who's just left him.

This take, recorded live when Willie was sitting on top of the world and the song had become

one of his concert staples, is desperation incarnate; it's as if he fears that not even an ocean of whiskey will be enough to dull his pain. Willie's so frantic, in fact, that he dispenses with the verses altogether, singing only the chorus as he and his band distill the song's nagging rhythmic essence. "Whiskey river, don't run dry / You're all I got, take care of me," he blurts, and this time he *is* begging. He needn't worry, though, because even if the booze fails him, the band thrashing away behind him could obliterate anything, even heartache. Hell, it's a wonder the surges coming from Mickey Raphael's harmonica and Jody Payne's galvanic guitar don't short-circuit Willie's memory banks for good.—bfw

406
Mountain Dew, The Stanley Brothers
Produced by Syd Nathan;
Written by Bascom Lamar Lunsford and Scott Wiseman
King 5347   1959   Did not chart

Preparing to record the Stanley Brothers in the fall of 1959, Syd Nathan, the head of King Records, was looking for a country music success such as he'd previously had with the Delmore Brothers, or at least Reno & Smiley. It's also likely he'd spotted dollar signs in folk-revival pop hits like the Kingston's Trio's "Tom Dooley" (winner of the first "country and western performance" Grammy) and Lauri London's "He's Got the Whole World in His Hands," both chart toppers from the year before. For their part, Carter and Ralph Stanley were ready to develop a sound that would let them stand out in the bluegrass marketplace dominated by mandolin- and banjo-centric peers.

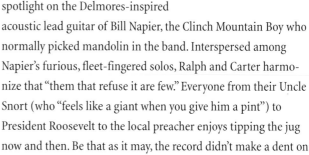

That's how the Stanleys came to cut this Prohibition-era folk standard with the spotlight on the Delmores-inspired acoustic lead guitar of Bill Napier, the Clinch Mountain Boy who normally picked mandolin in the band. Interspersed among Napier's furious, fleet-fingered solos, Ralph and Carter harmonize that "them that refuse it are few." Everyone from their Uncle Snort (who "feels like a giant when you give him a pint") to President Roosevelt to the local preacher enjoys tipping the jug now and then. Be that as it may, the record didn't make a dent on country radio, let alone crack the pop charts. On the up side, though, "Mountain Dew" was popular enough with Stanley fans to ensure that the acoustic guitar would become a distinctive element of their later sound and of bluegrass music generally.

The way Napier tears through those acoustic runs, you'd swear he's just taken a bump off something himself.—dc

407

Twin Guitar Special, Bob Wills & His Texas Playboys
Produced by Art Satherley and Don Law;
Written by Leon McAuliffe and Eldon Shamblin
OKeh 06327, Conqueror 9819   1941   Pre-chart

"No, not six guitars; that's two," Wills marvels as steel player Leon McAuliffe and electric guitarist Eldon Shamblin beat it eight-to-the-bar. But what it really sounds like is *horns*, and like nothing so much as the horn section whose incessant riffing powers Count Basie's "One O'Clock Jump." The coarse, dirty timbres McAuliffe coaxes from his steel could pass for the entire sax section, while Shamblin's punchy, Count-like arrangement pares the melody down to its core elements. If "Big Beaver" proved that Wills and company could achieve Ellingtonian splendor, then "Twin Guitar Special" showed just what they could do with a page from Basie's notebook, even with the Playboy horn section sitting one out.—bfw

408

Filipino Baby, Cowboy "Pappy" Copas
Produced by Syd Nathan;
Written by Billy Cox and Clark Van Ness
King 505   1946   #4 country

It'd be easy to conclude that dying was the only memorable thing Cowboy Copas ever did. Indeed, if he hadn't gone down with Patsy Cline, Hawkshaw Hawkins, and pilot Randy Hughes (Cline's manager and Copas's son-in-law) in that infamous 1963 plane crash, few contemporary country fans would've ever heard his name. That fate would have been almost as tragic as his death.

Lloyd Copas was a star of Cincinnati's Boone County Jamboree, the man who replaced Eddy Arnold as lead singer in Pee Wee King's Golden West Cowboys, and a fixture on the Grand Ole Opry. His affable tenor would've been right at home on the range, but despite his nickname, he was never really a western singer. He became "Cowboy" Copas only because it allowed for comic banter with his first radio partner (Lester "Natchee the Indian" Storer), but it proved such an alliteratively distinctive handle that the nickname stuck. Copas was also a substantial, albeit sporadic, hit maker; over seventeen years, he notched only fifteen hits, but each of them climbed at least as high as #14. The biggest was "Alabam," a 1961 crossover success that married old-time music to the Nashville Sound. But Copas, also known as "the Hillbilly Waltz King," was more typically a charming, unassuming singer of pop-country ballads.

The ballad that set him on the path to stardom was the unlikely "Filipino Baby," a tale of interracial romance that predates Merle Haggard's "Irma Jackson" by a quarter century (or by three quarters of a century, if you start counting from the Spanish-American War where much of the lyric originated). Copas sings of a ship full of sailors pulling out of Manila, where they spent shore leave "making love to every pretty girl they met." The song's protagonist, though, "his eyes all aglow," is missing more than just available sex. As the ship raises anchor for the states, he's showing around a photo of a "dark-faced" girl with hair "black as jet," a cherished snapshot of the girl he truly loves. So much so that by the last verse this Carolina boy has returned to marry her as his shipmates look on approvingly. Copas's single never allows, as Haggard's song would, that a lot of people think it's a sin for a man who's white to love a woman who's not. Instead, released in the giddy and oddly forgiving year after the close of World War II, Copas's single announces to the world, joyously and without caveat, that, "I love my dark-faced Filipino!" On record, it really does sound just that simple.—dc

409
Irma Jackson, Tony Booth
Produced by Dusty Rhodes; Written by Merle Haggard
MGM 14112   1970   #67 country

This should've been another Merle Haggard entry.

In 1970, Haggard was the biggest country star in the world. Amid the media storm that swirled about the controversial crossover hit "Okie from Muskogee" (the singer's third consecutive country chart topper and eighth #1 in just four years), Haggard had attained household-name status, even in homes where the closest thing to a country record was, say, Dean Martin singing Haggard's "I Take a Lot of Pride in What I Am." With that kind of popularity, he could've released whatever he wanted. What he wanted to release was "Irma Jackson."

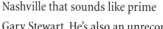

But "Irma Jackson," about an interracial love affair that the world refuses to accept, might've been even more of a lightning rod than "Okie" had been. At the very least, it would've complicated things considerably if Haggard, considered by some to be the voice of the silent majority, had so openly challenged the social strictures against so-called race mixing. "Love is color blind," the song declares—and this less than two years after Martin Luther King Jr. was assassinated for espousing similar beliefs, and just three years after the Supreme Court had declared unconstitutional any laws prohibiting interracial marriage. Furthermore, "Irma Jackson" would've been a particularly brave single to offer radio. Charley Pride's breakthrough career aside, the country format had all but ignored the issues of the civil rights movement.

"[Capitol producer] Ken Nelson never interfered with my music," Haggard says today. "But this *one time* he came out and said, 'Merle . . . I don't believe the world is ready for this yet.' . . . And he may've been right. I might've canceled out where I was headed in my career." In this context, it's not surprising that Haggard eventually chose to replace "Irma Jackson" as his next single with "The Fighting Side of Me." But it *is* disappointing; Hag's "Irma" flip-flop stands among the biggest missed opportu-

nities in all of popular music. Instead of pushing fans to confront their prejudices—"If loving Irma Jackson is a sin, then I don't understand this crazy world we're living in," the song declares—Haggard and Nelson played it safe in a land where those who challenge the status quo are greeted with that most cynical of arguments, "If you don't love it, leave it."

On the other hand, an unknown like Tony Booth (soon to be a protégé of Buck Owens) had nothing to lose by releasing such a potentially controversial single. Indeed, his dance floor-ready version of "Irma Jackson" got him just enough airplay to launch a minor career that eventually included a trio of Top Twenty hits. "I'd love to shout my feelings from a mountain high," Booth sings, sounding as if he's doing just that. "And tell the world I love her, and I will till I die." Of course, he knows good and well the world won't stand for that. He knows a white man in love with a black woman will be forced to pay a steep, even dangerous price. So he plays it safe, keeps his mouth shut, and watches her walk away.—dc

410
These Are Not My People, Swamp Dogg
Produced by Jerry Williams Jr.; Written by Joe South
Roker 505   1970   Did not chart

Musically speaking, Swamp Dogg is a man without a country. He grew up listening to the Grand Ole Opry, wrote "She's All I Got" (a Top Five country hit for both Johnny Paycheck and Tracy Byrd), and recorded his share of country material, including an unreleased 1987 album for Mercury Nashville that sounds like prime Gary Stewart. He's also an unreconstructed soul man: a former chitlin' circuit mainstay who, before his canine reincarnation, billed himself as Little Jerry Williams; the first black staff producer at Atlantic Records; and a purveyor of the greasiest fatback this side of Muscle Shoals. Yet he's never found a home in either country or soul circles, something that's doubtless due to his reliance on a singular spiritual and moral compass that's induced him, over the past thirty years, to launch an all-out assault on bigotry, greed, militarism, and other intractable stupidities. When he sang "God Bless America for What" in 1971, J. Edgar Hoover tacked Swamp's name to the FBI's list of subversives engaged in "Un-American" activities. Scrapes like that—along with broadsides like "Call Me Nigger" that undermine racism's insidious power by, among other things, noting that "we've even got ourselves a white American nigger"—have been part of Swamp's career-long commitment to speaking his mind and playing the fool, the consequences be damned.

Swamp Dogg's most devastating weapon has always been his brassy, bullhorn of a bark—a bullshit-dispelling tenor he detonates like a mountain-top Moses. He has plenty of help getting his message across here: sock-it-to-ya horns, conscience-tweaking guitar, a groove wide enough to part the Red Sea. The "don't get *beneath* your raising" sermon Swamp's preaching may not seem to warrant such fanfare, and the way he plays up writer Joe South's locker-room humor ("been a gas but I'm gonna have to pass") suggests he knows it. But "These Are Not My People" is about more than getting mixed up with the wrong crowd. Coming as it did during the conflicts over ERA, the Vietnam War, civil rights, and—after the Stonewall Riot of 1969—gay rights, it functions as an allegory about how pretenses of every stripe tear down communities. Swamp might decry some folks as "not [his] people," but it's precisely his unshakable belief in the possibility of community, as well as his unwillingness to lose sight of the humanity of those he's taking to task, that makes his rants not just palatable but righteous.

"At the time, I was thinking about all of America," Swamp explained when asked why he recorded "These Are Not My People" in the first place. "I've always considered all 'Americans' my people, regardless of how they felt about me. Naturally, I'll keep my distance from a nigger-hating klansman, but they are also part of 'my people,' for what the fuck it's worth." Would that more record companies—whether pop, country, or soul—had over the years embraced Swamp's prophetic preachments in the same spirit. Then maybe more than just the members of his cult would know how much his music, and all it promises, is really worth.—bfw

411

Night Train to Memphis, Bobby Hebb
Produced by John Richbourg;
Written by Owen Bradley, Marvin Hughes, Beasley Smith
Rich 1001   1960   Did not chart

Both peripheral to the country story and central to it, Bobby Hebb is a fairly typical example of "the black experience in country music" (as the subtitle to the box set *From Where I Stand* puts it). Hebb grew up just blocks from what would become Music Row, where from an early age he was exposed to everything from gospel, jazz, and R&B to the Grand Ole Opry. Make that a *very* early age; Hebb was performing in east Nashville clubs by the time he was three. In his teens, already a seasoned showbiz pro, he landed a spot on an early Music City television program hosted by Owen Bradley. That's where Roy Acuff spotted him and quickly hired Hebb to play the spoons for his Smoky Mountain Boys. An Opry regular for the next half decade, the young musician was taken under wing by DeFord Bailey, the radio show's first, and until Hebb arrived, only black regular.

But that was pretty much as far as a young black man could expect to rise in the country-focused Nashville music industry, especially one with an approach as ecumenical as Hebb's. "Bobby, go to New York," a friend advised. "What you're trying to do, man, you need to get to New York." Hebb did just that in 1961, and five years later he achieved one-hit wonder status by writing and recording the pop standard "Sunny."

Before heading north, he cut his first record, "Night Train to Memphis," for Nashville's tiny Rich label. He couldn't have picked a more appropriate goodbye. A tip of the hat to the country community that'd helped him on his way, "Night Train to Memphis" was co-written by Bradley, had been recorded by Acuff, and, in Hebb's version, features a relentless freight-train rhythm that recalls DeFord Bailey. Backed by a jubilant female chorus, Hebb hurtles out of town, shouting "Hallelujah all the way." He makes his exit with fierce, insistent gospel vocalizing ("SHHHOWT! SHHHOWT! HALLEY-LOO! YEAH!") that anticipates James Brown's "Night Train," an R&B hit the next year. That kind of call-and-response, coupled with Bobby's inclusive musical background, makes it plain everyone's welcome aboard Hebb's train. No matter where you're headed or what part of town you're from.—dc

412

16th Avenue, Lacy J. Dalton
Produced Billy Sherrill; Written by Thom Schuyler
Epic 03184   1982   #7 country

413

Music City U.S.A., Dick Stratton & the Nite Owls
No producer credited;
Written by Bill Beasley, Ray Anderson, and Dick Stratton
Jamboree 510   1950   Did not chart

Back in 1982, the year producer Billy Sherrill urged blue-collar belter Lacy J. Dalton to cut "16th Avenue," Nashville's music industry was hardly the corporate monolith it is today. Oh, it was big business all right; Music City had, for a good twenty-five years, been the world's country recording hub. Yet it still retained much of the loose, laid-back vibe of the grassroots picking and songwriting scenes from which it evolved. The imposing silicon-and-steel that now protects industry execs from the bearers of unsolicited demo tapes and CD-Rs wouldn't arrive for another eight to ten years. At the time, Music Row's publishing houses and record labels were still nestled in the eminently approachable bunga-lows that dotted tree-lined 16th and 17th Avenues. The Row was inviting enough in fact that, as late as 1985, a juvenile delinquent dishwasher like Randy Travis could break into the business the old-fashioned way, by singing in bars and pressing his tape into people's palms (the so-called Nashville handshake) everywhere he went. Making it as a singer or songwriter might have been a long shot, but back in the eighties, Nashville's music scene still fed dreams, and it's that Music City that Dalton, Sherrill, and songwriter Thom Schuyler toast with "16th Avenue."

The record begins with the folksy strumming of a lone acoustic guitar, a tribute to every intrepid troubadour who's ever come to Nashville because "someone told them about a friend of a friend they knew who owns, you know, a studio on 16th Avenue." As if dramatizing the unfolding of that dream, a wistful harmonica and walking bass enter on the second verse, a

steel guitar and brushes on the third. By the fourth stanza it all gives way to surging strings that announce how, "like a miracle, some golden words roll off" some solitary songwriter's tongue. It's an idealized picture, to be sure, yet it's one shaped by the realities of rejection, subsistence living, and mind-numbing labor. Sacrifices that Dalton, who'd struggled for years to make ends meet working as a waitress, a cook, and a topless dancer, knew only too well. The types of sacrifices that stopped paying off once the nineties rolled around

and consolidation within the industry caused execs along Music Row to tighten their belts, making it about as easy to break into Nashville's music business as it would be to squeeze Reba's tour bus through the eye of a needle.

None of which resembles the "come one, come all" scene that Dick Stratton guilelessly hypes in "Music City U.S.A.," the prophetically titled anthem that he and his band, the Nite Owls, cut back in 1950. "So if you're living in some distant town / Brother, pack your bags and come on down / They used to call it Nashville but I'm here to say / That now they call it Music City U.S.A." Stratton crows these lines as if he's about to bust the buttons off his overalls. Buoyed by swinging fiddle and steel guitar, the long-forgotten honky-tonker sounds like some hayseed explorer who's just discovered an uncharted land where everybody's "jumpin' to the solid beat of a guitar pickin' out an eight-to-the-bar." What he'd really happened on was a wide-open record trade dominated by independent labels with names like Republic, Bullet, and Speed run by self-made entrepreneurs who cut deals, and hit records, in back-rooms and storefronts.

Remarkably, despite its thriving jazz, country, gospel, and swing band scenes, there was no recording infrastructure to speak of, and no major label presence, in Nashville before the war. Granted, the Opry was already the envy of the nation's radio barn dances, and the show was luring more hillbilly singers to town all the time. But with the Depression cutting into record sales and the dearth of labor and shellac during wartime shutting down pressing plants, the advent of Nashville's music business would have to wait until after V-E Day. Yet come it did—not just in what would soon become known as Music City but across the rest of the nation as well.

Postwar prosperity created a bull market for entertainment everywhere, notably in the radio and jukebox industries. *Billboard* reported that more than 300 imprints, looking to give major labels like Decca, RCA, and Columbia a run for their money, sprang up from 1946 to 1948 (some of the best known being King in Cincinnati, Specialty in Los Angeles, Atlantic in New York, and Aristocrat [later Chess] in Chicago). Nashville had Tennessee, Dot, and Hickory, along with a host of smaller, fleeting labels like Delta, Select, and Jamboree. Between them, these companies put out records by everyone from whitebread Pat Boone to future R&B and blues icons Rufus Thomas and B. B. King. Among hundreds of other hillbilly titles, they accounted for the earliest recordings by Country Music Hall of Famers Chet Atkins, Owen Bradley, Ray Price, and Minnie Pearl.

Nevertheless, major labels like Decca and RCA had been holding makeshift sessions with selected country singers (Ernest Tubb, Eddy Arnold) in Nashville since the end of the war. Once indies like Bullet and Excello had established a recording infrastructure (and a track record) in the city, the pump was primed for the majors to set up their own shops in town. It wasn't long before Bradley, Atkins, and Don Law, the respective heads of the new Nashville divisions of Decca, RCA, and Columbia, were establishing Music City as the major-label hub that it is today.

As the architects of the vaunted and vilified Nashville Sound, these three men oversaw the creation of loads of first-rate music, much of it made in the loose, informal spirit of the postwar indies they put out of business. Yet as tempting as it might be at this late date to suggest that the assembly-line mentality that eventually set in on the Row compromised the quality of the records being made there, that's just not the case. From World War II until recently, Music City made inspired and insipid records in more or less equal proportions. One thing that *did* take a turn for the worse when the industry infrastructure became concentrated in a few manicured hands, though, was that it got tougher and tougher for the likes of Stratton and Dalton to get anybody to listen to them in the first place.—bfw

414
Skid Row Joe, *Porter Wagoner*
Produced by Bob Ferguson; Written by Freddie Hart
RCA Victor 8723   1965   #3 country

Recitations get a bad rap, their detractors contending that they indulge country's most maudlin tendencies, and anyone who's suffered through Red Sovine's smarmy "Teddy Bear" would have to agree. But to condemn all spoken narratives for the sins of one would be a mistake. Country music has always told stories, and the best recitations by the likes of Hank Snow, Hank Williams (as "Luke the Drifter"), Dolly Parton, and Porter Wagoner are among the most moving in the tradition's vast storehouse of yarns.

Written by country singer Freddie Hart, "Skid Row Joe" tells the story of a man who's lost everything—wife, kids, career—and hit bottom. He used to be a singing star, but when Porter runs into him on the street one night, he's filthy and unshaven, his face red from bouts of long, hard drinking. It's a familiar enough story. What's unusual is that Wagoner recognizes the man at all (most people would have averted their eyes) and that he stops to talk with him, to relate to him as a fellow human being.

Wagoner sets an empathetic tone from the outset, when he and the Anita Kerr Singers first utter the broken man's name. "Skid Row Joe," they croon in harmony, their voices betraying no hint of the pity or disgust many feel for people who are homeless; rather, their tone is warm, understanding, almost reverential. A subdued shuffle follows as Wagoner, his heart heavy, paints a clear portrait: "a mask of torture was the face of Skid Row Joe."

The rest of the record is a recitation; Porter recounts his conversation with Joe as Buck Trent's plucky electric banjo echoes the poor man's resolve to quit the bottle and get his family back. The only problem is that his wife has remarried, a detail that a conflicted Wagoner just can't bring himself to point out for fear of adding to Joe's misery. There's nothing mawkish or sentimental here; just the opposite, everything about Joe's story is tragic, except for Porter's rendering of it, which refuses to let us forget that "lost, forgotten" people have stories too.

Of course, Porter could have taken matters a step further; he could have said something about the conditions that created Skid Row Joe and people like him in the first place. He might have taken society to task for taking homelessness for granted. Nevertheless, in contrast to the indifference toward the problem that persists today, the humanity that shines through "Skid Row Joe" is at least a starting point for working on a solution.—bfw

415
The Big Rock Candy Mountains, Harry McClintock
No producer credited; Written by Harry McClintock
Victor 21704-B   1928   Pre-chart

416
Sugar Mountain, Neil Young
No producer credited; Written by Neil Young
Reprise 1065   1972   Did not chart

Two cases not so much of wishful thinking but of envisioning an alternate reality as a way to survive.

Harry McClintock's hobo paradise is far and away the most colorful of the two, a place where cigarettes grow on trees, where there's a lake of stew, and whiskey too. Where the boxcars all are empty and you never have to change your socks. Where neither the police nor their bulldogs harass you, and where there's no backbreaking work to be done—indeed, no work at all. Free of exploitation, persecution, and want, the big rock candy mountains are, literally, too good to be true.

McClintock, who went by the colorful moniker "Haywire Mac," knew all too well the desperate straits from which this mythical realm promised refuge. He started hoboing when he was fourteen, toughing it out along the way working as a cowpuncher, deck hand, mule packer, and railroad man. Those experiences lend added weight to his picture of a toil-free world where handouts grow on bushes, and that authority is no doubt why the record struck such a chord with the hard-pressed masses who heard it, particularly during the Depression. To his fellow southerners who endured either penury as sharecroppers or isolation as factory workers in strange, far-off cities, Mac's bountiful mountains must have sounded like heaven on earth.

People have been giving voice to utopian visions like this for ages, especially those who've felt disillusioned with or powerless against the prevailing social order. Yet these mythic constructs are more than just flights of fancy. To imagine such a good place, as Haywire Mac does here, is an act of resistance that affords him a measure of transcendence over his circumstances. It also

testifies to the possibility of a better world, however remote or abstract it might be.

The mountain conjured by Canadian rocker Neil Young projects a more conflicted ideal; less sanguine than McClintock's carefree domain, Young's haven is an exclusive retreat. No one twenty or older is welcome. Why that's the case isn't clear, but Young, who wrote the song on his nineteenth birthday, was doubtless pondering his fading innocence. (That was definitely how the record struck countrywoman Joni Mitchell, who wrote "The Circle Game" in response.) Yet don't count out social and political factors; between escalating racial tension and mounting opposition to the Vietnam war, Young's idyll was likely also born of a desire to flee the mess the parents of his adopted U.S. generation had made of things.

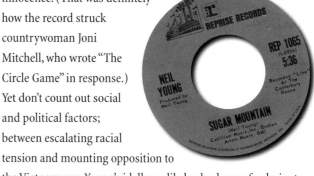

Still, for all its escapist imagery (carnival barkers and balloons await young folk on Sugar Mountain), Young's doleful performance—like McClintock's, just a solitary voice and an acoustic guitar—betrays as much loss as longing. "Now you say your leavin' home / You want to be alone / Ain't it funny how you feel / When you're finding out it's real," Neil wonders aloud, posing the question to himself and to his peers. He's talking about the weight, the responsibility, of being on one's own, as much as about any freedom from parental tyranny.

Young's music is as rooted in folk tradition and its mythic power as any rocker's this side of Bob Dylan. Echoes of Woody Guthrie, and especially the Carter Family, abound in Young's guitar playing (which owes plenty to that of Mother Maybelle) as well as in his "Worried Man" persona. Here, it's as if Neil's telling us that it's not enough to envision an imaginary place for ourselves; the only way truly to transcend our circumstances is to strive to make the world a better place here and now. And that means, out of necessity, embracing a broader community, regardless of how much more any of us might have to bear.

All of which makes Young's later support of Ronald Reagan, a president whose administration put more people on the streets than at any time since Haywire Mac's Depression, even more galling.—bfw

417
I Believe in You, Don Williams
Produced by Don Williams and Garth Fundis;
Written by Roger Cook and Sam Hogin
MCA 41304   1980   #1 country (2 weeks); #24 pop

A deceptively simplistic record. On the most basic level, Don Williams is simply expressing gratitude to his wife for believing in him (a Williams trademark). But along the way, he reels off a litany of American social problems, circa 1980. Some of these, such as decreased job security due to overseas competition and racism, he alludes to in passing. Other problems he nails down quite specifically—having to work nights just to meet "the rising cost of getting by," churches that condemn those who worship differently, and gas "shortages" he's betting are manufactured to drive up the price at the pump. It's a world of trouble out to bury this "ordinary man," and you know Williams is a regular Joe the second you hear his laconic, range-less baritone. Everywhere he looks, things are changing so fast he no longer knows what to believe, though his tempo suggests he holds to the theory that slow and steady wins the race.

His solution? "I believe in love," Williams sings. "And I believe in music," as well as in the hope of youth and the wisdom of old age. Of course, those are mostly ways of getting through life with some measure of joy, purpose, and dignity, not strategies for change. They're awfully good places to start, though. And if the singer could rally enough of his neighbors, relatives, and fellow working stiffs to sing along—"I don't believe . . . that right is right and left is wrong"—who knows what might get accomplished?—dc

418
Grandpa (Tell Me 'Bout the Good Old Days), The Judds
Produced by Brent Maher; Written by Jamie O'Hara
RCA/Curb 14290   1986   #1 country (1 week)

Who says that inheritors of country music's brother duet tradition actually need to be siblings? Or even men? Mother-daughter duo The Judds certainly plowed similar soil in the Reagan-Bush years—sowing it with touches of bright suburban blues and singer-songwriter rock—on their way to racking up fourteen #1s in less than a decade. The Judds typically lent their harmonies to songs about modern, working class women who turned to family and tradition for grounding in an uncertain world.

The Judds certainly knew about uncertainty, and about sticking together. A teen parent who, after a divorce, found herself a single mother of two, the elder Judd raised her daughters amid frequent relocations, pursuit of a nursing degree, and attempts at a movie career even as she nurtured the emerging singing talent of her oldest daughter. The Judds clearly knew a thing or two about ambition as well. After changing their names, Diana and Christina, to the more down-home sounding Naomi and Wynonna, they headed to Nashville where they hustled their demo tapes around for years before getting their crack at stardom.

The Judds' family values and rags-to-riches bio endeared them to fans, particularly during a political era invested in the myth of an earlier, simpler America. Taken at face value, the words to the duo's "Grandpa (Tell Me 'Bout the Good Old Days)" epitomize

such neoconservatism. But since this is a record, not just a set of lyrics, the way those words are presented reveal truths more ambivalent than the Judds probably intended. A frazzled Wynonna begs the family patriarch to share stories of a time when love was permanent and when there was a clear line between right and wrong. "Did lovers really fall in love to stay . . . did daddies really never go away?" this daughter of divorce asks in a voice that, in comparison to the far-fetched growl that's marked her solo career, sounds like a whispered prayer. In the end, she proclaims it all true—the faithful fathers, the kept promises, all of it. On the other hand, the mournful, home-bred harmonies she and her mother create sure don't sound very convinced. That golden age feels ephemeral, nothing but a pretty "picture of long ago."

As the record fades out to the strains of a front-porch acoustic guitar and fairy-tale piano, Grandpa still hasn't answered, which is just as well. If it's a guaranteed happy-ever-after the Judds are looking for, they're probably not going to like his stories very much anyway.—dc

419
Heaven Help the Working Girl, Norma Jean
Produced by Ethel Gabriel and Bob Ferguson;
Written by Harlan Howard
RCA Victor 47-9362   1967   #18 country

420
9 to 5, Dolly Parton
Produced by Gregg Perry; Written by Dolly Parton
RCA Victor 12316   1980
#1 country (1 week); #1 pop (2 weeks)

The women's movement might have been gathering steam, but sisters still had a long way to go when Norma Jean sang "Heaven help the working girl in a world that's run by men." Single or married, mothers or not, women were entering the workforce in droves during the 1960s. The open doors were great, but the jobs and earning power that awaited women

on the other side of the threshold weren't. Most wound up working at or just above minimum wage, waiting tables or filing and making copies for men, jobs that were little different from cooking or keeping the castle spic and span. Norma Jean (Beasler) was used to playing supporting roles; from 1960 to 1967, she was "Pretty Miss Norma Jean," the featured "girl singer" on Porter Wagoner's syndicated television show.

"Heaven Help" finds Norma Jean schlepping bacon, grits, and eggs for blue-collar stiffs in a dingy, out-of-the-way café. She's as

harried as can be, but she never lets on, her sunny smile ever ready to endure another sob story as she tops off cup after cup of coffee. Here she gracefully fends off the advances of a drunk patron. "Thank you, sir, you're very kind, I think I'll pass this time," she demurs in a sprightly Okie drawl, before giving the lout something to think about—"We'd both be sorry if I *did* go home to your wife and your kids." Set to the leanest of lunchpail twang—slicing steel and bluesy, gutbucket guitar—the record's message is clear: Norma Jean can manage well enough without heaven's help. Half a chance is all she needs to show that she could manage a business better than most men.

Thirteen years later, the song remained the same, or nearly so. "It's a rich man's game / No matter what they call it / And you spend your life / Putting money in his wallet," Dolly sings in "9 to 5," the title track from the pink-collar comedy of the same name. Even with flirtations with the Equal Rights Amendment and other advances, women still weren't getting comparable pay for comparable work in 1980; glass ceilings were just above their heads.

Dolly was an exception to the rule, proving herself to be as plucky and astute as Norma Jean's character in "Heaven Help the Working Girl." By this point she had parlayed her down-home, larger-than-life glamour (the very embodiment, as writer Chet Flippo once put it, of the Big Rock Candy Mountain) into a career that went beyond country and pop superstardom to TV, movies, and later, entrepreneurial ventures like her *Dollywood* theme park. Despite her humble Appalachian beginnings, Dolly paid her dues (she replaced Norma Jean on *The Porter Wagoner Show*), clung to her dreams, and managed to steer her own ship as it came in. That's a big reason why, spurred on by disco horns and guitar, she can strut her stuff with such abandon here. It also explains why she, and not Norma Jean (who could hardly match Dolly for moxie), went on to surpass Porter's accomplishments after having served in his employ.—bfw

421
So Round, So Firm, So Fully Packed, Merle Travis
Produced by Lee Gillette;
Written by Merle Travis, Cliffie Stone, and Eddie Kirk
Capitol 349   1947   #1 country (14 weeks)

Now here's a sentiment we could use more of today: a man extolling the beauty not of some androgynous waif but of a voluptuous (that is, grown up) woman.

It's a little ironic that such an old-school conception of female beauty would come from Merle Travis. Although he emerged from the stringband era (his first big break was as one of Clayton McMichen's Georgia Wildcats), Travis went on to become one of country music's key modernizing figures. As a musician, Travis brought an acoustic two-finger technique (where the index finger improvises around the melody while the thumb picks bass rhythm) out of the Kentucky hills surrounding his Muhlenberg County home and into country music's amplified future. His sprightly, syncopated style, dubbed "Travis pickin'," made him an immensely influential guitarist (*the* model for Chet Atkins, and a hero to nearly every Nashville cat to plug in since), and his design innovations helped Leo Fender perfect his Telecaster. As a tunesmith, Travis penned hit songs that featured cultural attitudes ("Smoke! Smoke! Smoke!," "Divorce Me C.O.D.") and an implied sense of social justice ("No Vacancy," "Dark as a Dungeon," "Sixteen Tons") that, half a century later, still feel contemporary.

To an extent, that's even true of "So Round, So Firm," which employs post–World War II advertising slogans to objectify his woman's curvaceous virtues. Merle claims his fiancé's so sexy she makes his "five o'clock shadow come around at one," "she's got the pause that's so refreshin'," and "If you don't think she's a lot of fun, just ask the man who owns one." And so on. As Travis gushes, a small honky-tonk-meets-western-swing combo, featuring accordion and muted trumpet, scoots easily along behind him. At the tail end, his own fluid guitar solo is the aural equivalent of his declaration that "From head to foot, she's perfect size." It's all very politically incorrect, of course, but at least he's not drooling over some stick-figure fantasy girl.—dc

422
Hey, Good Lookin', Hank Williams with His Drifting Cowboys
Produced by Fred Rose;
Written by Hank Williams
MGM 11000   1951   #1 country (8 weeks)

Buy into the legend and Hank Williams is nothing more or less than the most agonized man who ever lived. Outside of legends, though, no one's life can be reduced to its pain, and "Hey, Good Lookin' " has Hank feeling fine and then some. A smile beams off his face as he asks a girl if she wants to go out on the town and cut a rug; he's got a "hot-rod Ford," and, hey, it'll be his treat. As Hank opens the door to let her in, Jerry Rivers sneaks in a jazzy little fiddle lick to see them on their way, and when they reach this juke joint Williams knows, the band bounces them around the floor a few times. Before you know it, Hank's telling her he never wants it to end. He sounds randy as hell, but in a way that's never leering or threatening, and anyway, the whole future's available for whatever comes next. "How's about savin' all your time for me?" he gushes, and no one's ever sounded more comfortable in his skin, more at ease in the world, than Hank Williams.

Even out on that lost highway, you can sometimes pull off to a spot where there's soda pop and the dancing's free.—dc

423
Strawberry Wine, Deana Carter
Produced by Chris Farren;
Written by Matraca Berg and Gary Harrison
Capitol 58585   1996   #1 country (2 weeks); #65 pop

Insiders on Music Row swore this willowy ode to lost innocence would never sell. Its subject matter (premarital sex), length (4:51), and time signature (3/4), they argued, would scare off radio programmers. But when Carter's single went #1, it not only proved Nashville's bean-counters wrong, it showed just how out of touch the industry had become. After all, when *haven't* sex, waltzes, and swooning steel guitars made for great country records? Just what, after hearing the desire in Carter's steamy alto when she sings, "I was thirsting for knowledge, and he had a car," could the suits have been thinking?—bfw

424
Blanket on the Ground, Billie Jo Spears
Produced by Larry Butler; Written by Roger Bowling
United Artists 584   1975   #1 country (1 week); #78 pop

Proof that a song about a middle-aged couple getting it on can be just as sexy as a paean to forbidden fruit or the first stirrings of desire. Here we find thirty-eight year-old Billie Jo Spears, the pulse of the bass echoing the pounding in her heart, coaxing her husband out for a romp in the moonlight. "I'll get the blanket from the bedroom, and we'll go walking once again / To that spot down by the river, where our sweet love first began," she purrs, her humid, East Texas drawl transported by a wall of sound cemented by Pete Drake's surging steel guitar. "Now you know you still excite me, I know you love me as I am," Billie Jo encourages her husband, sensing his hesitation at her audacious invitation. But before she can reconsider, the giddy-up rhythms of that double-timed bass and guitar, and the lusty harmonies of the Jordanaires, betray his heart. To hell with walking. Billy Jo's hubby sweeps her up and hotfoots it down to the river, proving that "Strawberry Wine" can taste just as sweet with someone you've been sleeping with for years as it did the summer you turned sixteen.—bfw

425
Hello Love, Hank Snow
Produced by Ronnie Light and Chet Atkins;
Written by Betty Jean Robinson and Aileen Mnich
RCA Victor 0215   1974   #1 country (1 week)

In 1974, twenty-four years after his first hit on the U.S. charts, twelve years since his last country chart topper, and nearly a decade since his last Top Ten, Hank Snow scored a #1 record with "Hello Love." By then, he was just a few weeks shy of his sixtieth birthday, so he surely knew what he was talking about when he sang, "I must say I was sure surprised / You're the last thing I expected by." What's most remarkable about Snow's brief comeback, though, is that it wasn't based on any attempt to be hip. "Hello Love" succeeds because it's a good song and a good record, and one Snow could've cut, without any major changes, ten or twenty years earlier.

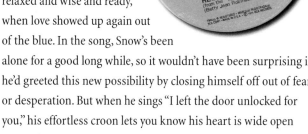

Then again, as a younger man Snow probably wouldn't have sounded quite this appreciative, this relaxed and wise and ready, when love showed up again out of the blue. In the song, Snow's been alone for a good long while, so it wouldn't have been surprising if he'd greeted this new possibility by closing himself off out of fear or desperation. But when he sings "I left the door unlocked for you," his effortless croon lets you know his heart is wide open too.—dc

426
Indian Love Call, Slim Whitman
Produced by Ken Nelson;
Written by Rudolf Friml, Otto Harbach,
and Oscar Hammerstein
Imperial 45-8156   1952   #2 country; #9 pop

Slim Whitman, yodeling in an alpine falsetto, tackles a preposterous song first popularized by sappy movie duo Nelson Eddy and Jeanette McDonald and miraculously transforms it into yearning personified. It's as if Kaw-Liga has come to life, more in love than ever.—dc

427
All the Good Ones Are Gone, Pam Tillis
Produced by Billy Joe Walker Jr. and Pam Tillis;
Written by Dean Dillon and Bob McDill
Arista 13084   1997   #4 country

The late eighties saw the emergence of a new breed of female country singer. From K. T. Oslin to Mary Chapin Carpenter, they were plucky and outspoken. Like Dolly and Loretta, they radiated independence. Yet unlike their older sisters, they'd been to college and openly embraced feminism. Oslin's "80's Ladies" was their anthem, testifying to how education and liberation, as much as the roots of their raising, accounted for the strong female points of view that defined their music. More often than not, their pursuit of meaningful romance (or even Mr. Right) wasn't so much about landing a husband as finding a partner, a soulmate with whom they could share their lives.

That's the challenge facing the protagonist of Pam Tillis's "All the Good Ones Are Gone," a single woman on the cusp of middle age. She'll turn thirty-four when the weekend rolls around. She'll go out drinking with some women friends and, from the plangent strains of John Jarvis's overripe piano, it sounds like they'll be celebrating in an upscale fern bar. Some may flirt with the guys they meet there, maybe even "get hit on" in return. But, as Sonny Garrish's bruised steel and Tillis's torchy soprano attest, what she really wants is an equal, the kind of guy her friends at the office hurry home to each night. Still, Pam's wondering if she's missed her chance, if maybe her fierce independent streak, along with her determination not to jump at the first decent guy that came along, has stranded her to play a field where all the good ones *are* gone.

The scene unfolds like an episode of the eighties TV series *Designing Women* or a more suburban version of *Ally McBeal*. Of course, the range of feelings Tillis probes—the desire to be in a committed long-term relationship without surrendering a sense of oneself—is hardly unique to straight, middle-class women. But that's doubtless the audience that responded most strongly to "All the Good Ones," not that Tillis, or the male empaths who co-wrote the song, need to apologize for it. After all, straight, middle-class women get the lovesick blues too.—bfw

428
I Know, Kim Richey
Produced by John Leventhal;
Written by Kim Richey and John Leventhal
Mercury 574184   1997   #72 country

Resiliency is a recurring theme in country music, and it's hardly the sole province of women. But dating at least as far back as the Carter Family's exhortation to "Keep on the Sunny Side," female country singers have had a special affinity for the subject. Repeatedly they've sought refuge from hard times in stoic resolve, whether rooted in faith, codependency, or denial. This has especially been the case in their dealings with men, epitomized perhaps by Tammy Wynette's long-suffering line, "After all, he's just a man," in "Stand by Your Man."

So it comes as something of a surprise when Kim Richey gives voice to another possibility. "I Know" starts out as an interior monologue, a postmortem conducted on a dead love affair. Before long, though, it's evident Richey's not just talking to herself here; she's also conversing with her country foremothers about the meaning of resiliency. When Kim alludes to the guy who's just walked out on her, it's as if, with each litany of "I know, I know," she's anticipating the advice of generations of country women who have coped with heartache. "I should fix the lock, feed the cat / Take the clothes to the Laundromat / Pay some bills and get a clue / Get up, forget about you / I know, I know," she nods, the dissonance in her bruised alto mounting right along with the song's swelling chorus.

A brokenhearted Mother Maybelle or Kitty Wells might have sought comfort, or at least tried to obliterate her pain, by throwing herself into the mundane household chores Richey enumerates. But the fact that Kim doesn't own a washing machine (that most domestic of appliances), coupled with the self-reliant tone of her lyrics and the twangy roots-rock of the record's arrangement, suggests that this isn't her mother's country music. Buttressed by unflagging drum cadences and the guitar-driven bridge that precedes the final chorus, Richey puts on a more modern face, "spinning [her] wheels just to see how bad it feels." Refusing to deny her feelings, she abandons herself to them, even to the point of self-indulgence.

Richey doesn't cast aspersions on her predecessors; she just knows that their strategies for dealing with despair can only take her so far. In the end, she understands that her only hope of emerging from her dark night of the soul, of knowing and ultimately validating herself, is to meet her sorrow head-on—or, as she puts it here, to "let the bad times roll." At some point Kim must have said to herself, "It's worked for clench-jawed male honky-tonkers—and blues singers—for decades. Why shouldn't it work for me?"—bfw

429

Don't Toss Us Away, Patty Loveless
Produced by Tony Brown; Written by Brian MacLean
MCA 53477　1989　#5 country

430

Runaway Train, Rosanne Cash
Produced by Rodney Crowell; Written by John Stewart
Columbia 07988　1988　#1 country (1 week)

Two women use love on the rocks as a metaphor for pondering the fate of country's as yet unbroken circle.

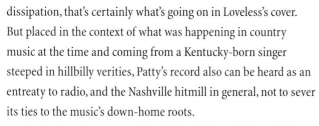

"Don't Toss Us Away" comes courtesy of L.A. roots-rockers Lone Justice, whose gloriously wasted original finds one partner appealing to another to remain steadfast in the face of love's dissolution. Minus the boho dissipation, that's certainly what's going on in Loveless's cover. But placed in the context of what was happening in country music at the time and coming from a Kentucky-born singer steeped in hillbilly verities, Patty's record also can be heard as an entreaty to radio, and the Nashville hitmill in general, not to sever its ties to the music's down-home roots.

By the time Loveless cut "Don't Toss Us Away" in late 1988, the neotraditionalist fervor that greeted the mid-eighties arrival of Steve Earle, Dwight Yoakam, and Randy Travis had cooled considerably. Her record label, MCA Nashville, was definitely feeling the chill. Apart from Patty, whose singles had just begun hitting the country Top Ten, MCA's rootsier mid-decade signees had fallen out of favor with country radio. Lyle Lovett's records no longer cracked the Top Forty; Earle and Nanci Griffith had

dropped off the singles charts altogether. "One by one they break / It's such a shame," Patty sings, as if surveying the casualties, while Mark O'Connor chimes in sympathetically on mandolin. Then, in words that seem to be speaking for the entire tradition, she turns to the industry's leaders, to the music's fans, to anyone who will listen. "Well just think of all that we've been through / The world we're building, me and you / How can all those years be tossed away / In just one moment, in just one day / Don't toss us away." Patty's prayer is that country's circle won't be broken, and the members of Nashville's vaunted class of '89 must have taken note. It wasn't long before Clint Black, Alan Jackson, and company had radio twangin' again.

Rosanne Cash approaches country's ties that bind with a whole lot more ambivalence—trepidation even—in "Runaway Train." By no means the glory-bound train or beloved community touted by Curtis Mayfield, Woody Guthrie, and Sister Rosetta Tharpe, Rosanne's singing about an engine racing out of control in the dark. And from the brooding music here, which smacks more of the roots-rock of Tom Petty & the Heartbreakers than of the boom-chicka of her father's band the Tennessee Two, it sounds like Rosanne would give anything to jump off. If only she weren't carrying so much baggage, weight that— from the legacies of her father and stepmother to her once-rocky relationship with her ex-husband Rodney Crowell—has occasioned plenty of doubt and hardship in her life. Yet judging by the empathy in her voice each time she sings, "I'm worried about you, I'm worried about me," odds are Rosanne wouldn't get off that train even if she could. Reckoning, at this point, that it would be insane to try—knowing, that is, that being a part of country's circle isn't a choice at all—she's settling in for the long haul.—bfw

431
Little Ramona (Gone Hillbilly Nuts), BR5-49
Produced by Jozef Nuyens and Mike Janas;
Written by Chuck Mead
Arista 13046   1997   #61 country

Spearheading the revitalization of downtown Nashville's Lower Broadway music scene in the mid-nineties, BR5-49 became semi-famous playing super-charged Johnny Horton and Webb Pierce covers at a time when most aspiring country acts were memorizing the Garth Brooks songbook. Outside Nashville, the band was at the center of a more far-reaching phenomenon. As their singles stiffed on the radio, the band hit the road hard, in the process winning an audience among the more twang-friendly members of the decade's loosely defined "alternative country" movement. Like the band members themselves, many of these fans had come of age in a rock & roll world that was post-Elvis, post-Beatles, and, most significantly, postpunk. They'd come of age listening to an eclectic "college rock" lineup, everything from the Clash and the Replacements to R.E.M. and Jason & the Scorchers. Once they grew up, they discovered (or rediscovered, depending on their parents' record collections) that the music of Hank Williams and his peers touched their hearts in the very same spot, if not exactly in the same way.

"Little Ramona" documents this tale perfectly, even copping to the dress-up fetish (in this case, Doc Martens are taken off, cowboy boots slipped on) endemic to so many retro-based music scenes. Retro, but not strictly nostalgic. After all, Little Ramona—who these days "only shows her tattoos one at a time"—still adores Patti Smith. It's just that now she's also gone nuts for Emmylou Harris, not to mention all sorts of older country styles: boogie woogie, hillbilly bop, western swing, honky-tonk, and rockabilly, too. The very sounds, in other words, that she once sneered at as the L7 music of her parents and grandparents. That connection makes frontmen Chuck Mead and Gary Bennett's declaration that Ramona "ain't ashamed of the way she was" kick all the harder. Sure, BR5-49's drums may be a lot further up in the mix, the pedal steel served up with a little extra "whaaang," the band's heart still bursting with punk pride. But beyond all that, "Little Ramona" finds another generation of country fans proving to the folks that they haven't got above their raising.—dc

432
Country Boy Rock 'N' Roll,
Don Reno, Red Smiley, and the Tennessee Cut-Ups
Produced by Syd Nathan; Written by Don Reno
King 1510   1956   Did not chart

Once Elvis and other early rock & rollers began to dominate pop and country radio, it was the rare country singer who didn't attempt, at least briefly, to jump on the bandwagon. Often the resulting records mimicked the music's outward characteristics—the hiccupping vocals, the hyper drums and slapped bass, the teen themes—without a real feel for the new style. Check out George "Thumper" Jones's "Rock It," for example, or Hank Snow's "Hula Rock," both from 1956, and see if you can keep from wincing.

Even bluegrass team Reno & Smiley made a nod in the direction of the new music. Don Reno was the banjo picker who'd replaced Earl Scruggs in the Blue Grass Boys; in fact, if Reno hadn't been just about to enter the army, Monroe would've hired him first. Reno's partner Red Smiley was a fine rhythm guitarist and marvelous country-influenced lead singer. At Syd Nathan's King Records in Cincinnati, the pair cut some of the best bluegrass sides of the early fifties, starting with an indelible bit of bluegrass gospel called "I'm Using My Bible for a Road Map."

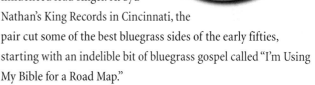

The duo's "Country Boy Rock 'N' Roll" (recorded just as Presley's "Don't Be Cruel" backed with "Hound Dog" was climbing the charts) gets the story of rockabilly just right. A country boy heads to town, hears the new music, and decides "I'd better rock it, I'd better roll it." That's just what Reno & Smiley do, telling their version of the tale via fiery harmonies, fierce fiddling, and a chopping mandolin to emphasize the rhythm—bluegrass style. Pretty much what they always did, in other words; the only concession is that Reno puts aside the banjo licks here in favor of searing boogie-woogie–inspired acoustic guitar runs that flat rock, just like the song says they should. "I guess to some folks I look foolish," they sing. "Just let him make a fool out of me."

Not a chance.—dc

433

The Train Kept A-Rollin', Johnny Burnette
and the Rock & Roll Trio
Produced by Owen Bradley;
Written by Tiny Bradshaw, Lois Mann, and Howie Kay
Coral 61719   1956   Did not chart

You've heard of a sixty-minute man, but would you believe a cross-country lover?

All the way from NYC to Albuquerque, Johnny Burnette has kept it a-rollin' with, as he puts it, "a heave and a ho." He's met a girl on the train back east and now, a thousand miles later, he and his guitar scream that "her lovin's so good, Jack, I [can't] let her go!" Along the route (though only, one assumes, from an adjoining berth), brother Dorsey Burnett slaps a furious beat on doghouse bass, assisted by hired-gun Buddy Harman on drums, and lead guitarist Paul Burlison, who unleashes fat, fuzzy licks courtesy of a busted amp.

Johnny and his girl get off the train in El Paso. Judging by the way this cat yowls, "I just couldn't let her go-oh-Oh-Oh-Oh-Oh-Oh-Ohhh-Owe," Burnette has run, finally, out of track.—dc

434

You've Never Been This Far Before, Conway Twitty
Produced by Owen Bradley; Written by Conway Twitty
MCA 40094   1973   #1 country (3 weeks); #22 pop

Conway Twitty's specialty was emotionally intense interior monologues, and here he pushes the approach to its very limits. "You've Never Been This Far Before" reveals the in-the-moment thoughts of Twitty's narrator as he prepares to make love to a new partner for the first time. "I don't know what I'm saying as my trembling fingers touch forbidden places," he moans, and then the song's unforgettable vocal and acoustic guitar hook—"Buh, buh, buh"—echoes the woman's nervous heart in reply.

That line about "forbidden places" stirred something of a controversy when the record was released. A handful of radio stations refused to play it, and some clergy, who believed the song was about scoring with a virgin, denounced the record. Yet the song makes it unmistakable that what's new for this woman is something even more scandalous—love outside the boundaries of her crumbling marriage.

For that matter, Twitty himself long argued that the song wasn't necessarily about a sexual encounter at all. "Now she's with you, this woman you've admired, and simply holding her hand has been a forbidden thing," he explained in his authorized biography. "The implication is just like putting your arm around her. Women are sensitive like that and they understand that line"—a reading that refocuses the song on the breaching of more profound emotional intimacies.

All of which is certainly there in the record. But it's also clear just where these first held hands, tentative hugs, and "tender kisses" are headed—and without delay. "Buh, buh, buh," Twitty breathes, and as the tension builds to a climax, a chorus answers with its own "buh, buh, buh." The bass pulses to the same rhythm, and pizzicato strings ring like the catching of breath.—dc

435

Burning Love, Elvis Presley
Produced by Felton Jarvis; Written by Dennis Linde
RCA 74-0769   1972   #2 pop

It's no wonder RCA decided not to release this as an A side to country radio. Country's audience might have been ready for the frank sexuality of Sammi Smith's "Help Me Make It through the Night," but "Burning Love" was something else altogether. From the opening spurts of guitar, piano, bass, and drums, to the moment Elvis moans he's "a hunka, hunka burning love," the record is pure lust. And it's downright scandalous (or maybe sinful) how J. D. Sumner & the Stamps lend their febrile gospel harmonies to the choruses, transforming "Burning Love" into something akin to a carnal camp meeting. As the record reaches its climax, the band, fanning the flames of desire that are licking Elvis's body, locks into an all-consuming groove as the King, letting out one ecstatic wail after another, testifies to the rapture of sexual salvation.—bfw

436

Nice 'n' Easy, Charlie Rich
Produced by Billy Sherrill;
Written by M. Keith, A. Bergman, and L. Spence
Epic 10662   1970   #37 country

They're trying to call Charlie a country singer now, but he isn't really. I would say he borders on being a jazz performer primarily. That's what he listens to. Brubeck, Miles Davis, Count Basie—you know, that sort of thing.

That's Margaret Ann Rich talking not long before her husband Charlie cut this record (in Peter Guralnick's chapter on Rich in *Feel Like Going Home*). And sure enough, the cocktail piano interlude after the first chorus here, a dead ringer for the playing of Stan Kenton, another of Rich's jazz heroes, bears her out. Even so, it's the way Margaret Ann qualifies her observation with the word "primarily" that gets at why her husband's records are so hard to peg. Rich's music may have roots in jazz, itself an idiom grounded in the blues, but it also encompasses soul, gospel, hillbilly music, and supper-club pop. Each is evident in this remake of his 1964 single for the Groove label: Twangy electric guitar barbs, the rhythm section's supple stroll, the Jordanaires' heaven-bound harmonies, and Rich's saloon-style crooning and jazzy electric piano are all stirred into Billy Sherrill's country-soul mix.

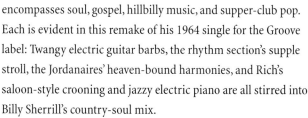

This version of "Nice 'n' Easy" is nothing like its Chet Atkins–produced predecessor; with a brisker tempo, Motown-inspired arrangements, and more straightforward rhythms, that record sounded like it was still in search of a style. What makes this take so sublime—and why it cuts even Sinatra's swinging pop version from 1960—is the way Rich and company, utterly oblivious to musical categories, apply the song's recommendations for lovemaking to the music. "The problem now of course is to simply hold your horses / To rush would be a crime," Charlie urges in his huskiest love-me-tender baritone. Indeed, you can hear the relish in his voice when, bringing those horses to a halt, he adds, "Let's make all the *stops*," before pausing for a beat and adding "along the way." And that's just what Charlie and the players here do. In absolutely no hurry at all, they wring every drop of soul from the song for the sheer pleasure of doing it.—bfw

437

Lookin' out My Back Door,
Creedence Clearwater Revival
Produced by John Fogerty; Written by John Fogerty
Fantasy 645   1970   #2 pop

After Creedence Clearwater Revival's messy split in 1972, bandleader John Fogerty regrouped and made *The Blue Ridge Rangers*, an album of mostly covers inspired by the likes of Jimmie Rodgers, Hank Williams, and George Jones. No surprise there. More than any of its contemporaries, Creedence Clearwater Revival made rock & roll rooted in southern tradition. Considering Fogerty's working-class background, populist politics, and affinity for the blues, it's easy to imagine that if he'd been born a decade earlier, in the Depression instead of the Baby Boom, he might've grown into northern California's version of Merle Haggard. Which, come to think of it, is pretty much what he was.

CCR's "Lookin' out My Back Door" suggests Fogerty was finding rejuvenation in country music all along. Arriving home after another long stretch on the road, Fogerty can't wait to park it out back and rest for a spell. "Imagination sets in, pretty soon I'm singin'," he tells us, his strangled yelp sounding uncharacteristically at ease. This being 1970, the details he reels off ("A giant doing cartwheels, a statue wearing high heels," and so on) hint he might be tripping. Yet since this is the straight-arrow John Fogerty we're talking about, it's more likely that he's just experiencing a rush of creativity now that he finally has a second to breathe. His normally snarling electric guitar work has a loose back-porch vibe (his second solo sounds like Scotty Moore doing Chet Atkins), he accompanies himself on overdubbed dobro, and all the while he's listening to Buck Owens. Toss in a cold brew and that's just the ticket to ease a tangled mind.—dc

438
Rose Colored Glasses, John Conlee
Produced by Bud Logan;
Written by John Conlee and George F. Baber
ABC 12356   1978   #5 country

One of the finest country singers of the late seventies and early eighties refuses to see the cold, hard truth. The record's lush string arrangement casts a beautiful glow over every ugly detail of his crumbling marriage, providing an exquisite frame for each failed attempt to believe the best is yet to come—just as you'd expect of rose-colored glasses. There's not a thing in the world, though, that can disguise the misery in John Conlee's doomed baritone.—dc

439
Don't It Make My Brown Eyes Blue, Crystal Gayle
Produced by Allen Reynolds;
Written by Richard Leigh
United Artists 1016   1977
#1 country (4 weeks); #2 pop

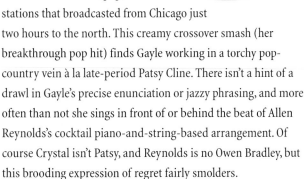

Crystal Gayle may be Loretta Lynn's baby sister, but she couldn't sound less like a coal miner's daughter. Not that that's surprising. Crystal, who was born Brenda Gail Webb, came along fifteen years after Loretta, and not in Butcher Holler, Kentucky, but in suburban Indiana, where she tuned in the folk, pop, and rock stations that broadcasted from Chicago just two hours to the north. This creamy crossover smash (her breakthrough pop hit) finds Gayle working in a torchy pop-country vein à la late-period Patsy Cline. There isn't a hint of a drawl in Gayle's precise enunciation or jazzy phrasing, and more often than not she sings in front of or behind the beat of Allen Reynolds's cocktail piano-and-string-based arrangement. Of course Crystal isn't Patsy, and Reynolds is no Owen Bradley, but this brooding expression of regret fairly smolders.

It's also one of the more enduring manifestations of the uptown aesthetic that prevailed in Nashville in the mid-to-late seventies, a time when Music Row desperately sought to live down its *Hee Haw* image. This was a period in which record labels were as open to pop incursions as they'd ever been; it wasn't long before middle-of-the-road pop singers like Anne Murray, Kenny Rogers, and Olivia Newton-John were cleaning up at the awards shows and cash registers. The trend reached its apotheosis in the early eighties with the slick come-on of *Urban Cowboy*, but in the end not even John Travolta and then-unprecedented sales could help country shake its hayseed reputation. Still, Gayle's influence had staying power, resurfacing a decade or so later as Shania Twain drew on her frothy ballad style and Garth Brooks teamed up with producer Reynolds to take country not just to New York and L.A. but to the rest of the world.—bfw

440
Don't Let the Stars Get in Your Eyes,
Skeets McDonald
Produced by Cliffie Stone;
Written by Slim Willet, Cactus Pryor,
and Barbara Trammell
Capitol F2216   1952   #1 country (3 weeks)

Whatever's got a frazzled Skeets McDonald racing out the door (perhaps he's off to Korea, this being 1952?), he finds time to slip in a quick lecture to the woman he's leaving behind. "Don't let the stars get in your eyes, so keep your heart for me for someday I'll return and you know you're the only one I'll ever love," he blurts in a single breath. It's a jumble all right but seems almost re-strained compared to the way the accompanying piano and pinched fiddle bounce frantically around his rambling plea.

That's why, when he stops babbling long enough to breathe, you listen to what comes next. "Too many nights," he sings, then takes a long pause. "Too many stars," he adds, pausing again. Then, before another pause, "Too many moons to change your mind." The pauses make the record—making you imagine every romantic moonlit night she'll be out of his sight and all those sleepless nights he'll be fretting he's out of her mind now, too.—dc

441
When My Blue Moon Turns to Gold Again,
Wiley Walker and Gene Sullivan
Produced by Art Satherley;
Written by Gene Sullivan and Wiley Walker
OKeh 06374   1941   Pre-chart

Alabama natives Wiley Walker and Gene Sullivan were a tough act to peg. During their heyday they worked at KVOO in Tulsa where Bob Wills was king, but their records weren't remotely western swing. They were a close-harmony duo, but in place of the mandolin-and-guitar format favored by brother acts like the Monroes and the Blue Sky Boys, they opted for the tearful fiddle and steel of honky-tonkers like Floyd Tillman and Ernest Tubb. Then again, the subject of this heart-rending ballad, one of the duo's biggest hits, couldn't have had less to do with the themes of cheating and drinking that would soon play so well in the era's dance halls and beer joints.

More in keeping with the sentimental Tin Pan Alley ballads that dominated the repertoires of the country singers of the twenties and thirties, "When My Blue Moon Turns to Gold Again" finds Wiley & Gene pining for the day they'll be reunited with their

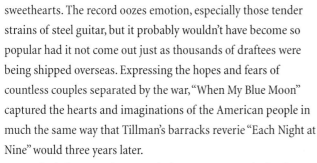

sweethearts. The record oozes emotion, especially those tender strains of steel guitar, but it probably wouldn't have become so popular had it not come out just as thousands of draftees were being shipped overseas. Expressing the hopes and fears of countless couples separated by the war, "When My Blue Moon" captured the hearts and imaginations of the American people in much the same way that Tillman's barracks reverie "Each Night at Nine" would three years later.

Yet don't discount the pigeonhole-resistant sound of Wiley & Gene's record when pinning down its appeal. Taking a page from Bing Crosby's no-fences notebook, the duo draws on old parlor songs, hillbilly brother duets, incipient honky-tonk, and crooner pop to create a modern country synthesis very much in keeping with the one that versatile stylists like Red Foley and Hank Snow would perfect after the war.—bfw

442
A Dear John Letter, Jean Shepard (with Ferlin Husky)
Produced by Ken Nelson; Written by Lewis Talley,
Charles "Fuzzy" Owen, and Billy Barton
Capitol 2502   1953   #1 country (6 weeks); #4 pop

The deck's stacked here for Jean Shepard to play second fiddle on her own chart debut. Though he was originally uncredited (at his own request) Ferlin Husky delivers the recitation that makes up the bulk of the record and, at least in theory, should earn him the lion's share of our sympathy. After all, he's John, the poor soldier who's getting thrown over via mailbag— and for his own brother, no less! But Shepard does have one advantage, a weapon so powerful it even nullifies her cruel

request that Ferlin return her picture: Jean gets to sing. One listen to her haggard journey through the line "Dear John, Oh how I hate to write," and we understand that sometimes it can be nearly as hard to write a "Dear John" letter as it is to receive it.—dc

443
Drivin' Nails in My Coffin, Floyd Tillman
Produced by Art Satherley; Written by Jerry Irby
Columbia 36998   1946   #2 country

444
10 Little Bottles, Johnny Bond
No producer credited; Written by Johnny Bond
Starday 704   1965   #2 country; #43 pop

Like Otis Campbell, the lovable town drunk on *The Andy Griffith Show*, or Dudley Moore's cackling lush in *Arthur*, Johnny Bond's spoken novelty hit, "10 Little Bottles," emerged in those final decades when public drunkenness could still be played for laughs in American popular culture. Bond's career began during the Depression—back when the distinctions between cowboy, western swing, honky-tonk, and pop singing had yet to calcify—and he had success with each of those styles. But his commercial identity was wrapped up in novelties. Sometimes that translated into pseudo-rockabilly story songs like "Hot Rod Lincoln," but usually it meant comic drinking numbers such as "Sick, Sober and Sorry," "Three Sheets in the Wind," and "The Pig Got Up and Slowly Walked Away," a comic recitation where even the title critter declines to share his gutter with a drunk.

Recorded when Bond was fifty, "10 Little Bottles" is the most indelible of the lot. It's based on a premise straight from the stage act of Foster "There's-a-reason-I'm-so-drunk-tonight-I've-been-drinking-all-day" Brooks. Bond's disapproving wife dispatches him to the basement to pour out the home brew he's been given by a friend. He does as he's told, though he makes certain to save the last drops of each bottle for himself. The results are woozily amusing: "I come from a great long line of stinkers, uh, drinkers" and "I have the wifest nice in the whole United Shtates" and so on. Nowadays, when humorless neopuritans insist that depictions of alcohol consumption must also be pious sermons on addiction or drunk-driving-related fatality, such joking wouldn't stand a chance on radio. "What's the difference between a drunk and an alcoholic?" Bond asks, then

deadpans, "Us drunks don't have to attend all them danged old meetings." That punch line would be greeted in many quarters nowadays with a stern, "That's not funny."

Even if contemporary country radio still favored swingy, fiddle-driven boot scooters, Floyd Tillman's "Drivin' Nails in My Coffin" probably couldn't get played today either. Making clear that the wages of alcoholism is death, the record certainly doesn't glorify drinking. "I'm just drivin' nails in my coffin," Tillman realizes; he "just can't quit drinkin' that old booze." But he's not going to condemn it either. Rather than functioning like a Public Service Announcement, both records seem to take for granted that the comic and tragic aspects of intoxication are worth depicting simply because they're human.

It also should be stressed that Bond and Tillman are playing characters here. Tillman retired from the spotlight at the height of his career, choosing instead to live off his royalties and

perform the occasional Texas one-nighter—a simpler lifestyle that he's pursued well into his eighties. And Bond reportedly always managed to make his family the center of his life, even while being a successful recording act, studio musician, songwriter, music publisher, scriptwriter, biographer (of Tex Ritter), and autobiographer, not to mention a film, TV, radio, and stage performer. Resumés like those aren't amassed while sitting on a bar stool and driving nails in your coffin.—dc

445

Bloody Mary Morning, Willie Nelson
Produced by Jerry Wexler; Written by Willie Nelson
Atlantic 3020   1974   #17 country

This is a book about singles, but sometimes it helps to hear a single in the context of the album on which it appears. That's certainly the case here. *Phases and Stages* was the second song cycle Willie Nelson made with fabled soul producer Jerry Wexler and the Muscle Shoals rhythm section. The first side of the album tells the story of a marriage's breakup from the woman's perspective, conveying her disgust over how her husband takes her for granted, forgetting about all the dirty dishes and laundry she's washed for him over the years. "Just pretend I never happened and erase me from your mind,"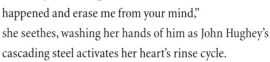
she seethes, washing her hands of him as John Hughey's cascading steel activates her heart's rinse cycle.

Cut to side two, the morning after. Eric Weissberg's galloping banjo and David Hood's hurtling bass suggest that Willie, now assuming the husband's part, is only too happy to go. But then we learn that his wife walked out on *him* during the night and that he's downing Bloody Marys on the first plane to Houston, "with forgetting her the nature of [his] flight." Judging by the way Willie's bending his notes, he must be bending his elbow pretty hard too. But not even the vodka, or Barry Beckett's pounding piano, can achieve the effect Willie's after—erasing his soon-to-be ex from his mind. Which must make his head throb all the more, considering that it was his insensitivity, his *forgetfulness*, that made his wife leave him in the first place.—bfw

446

Does Fort Worth Ever Cross Your Mind, George Strait

Produced by Jimmy Bowen;
Written by Sanger "Whitey" Shafer and Darlene Shafer
MCA 52458 1984 #1 country (1 week)

"Cold Fort Worth beer just ain't no good for jealous / I tried it night after night," rues George Strait, testifying, in his best Lefty-inspired slur, to how the bottle let

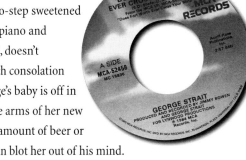

him down. The music, a chugging two-step sweetened with rolling piano and sighing steel, doesn't provide much consolation either. George's baby is off in Dallas, in the arms of her new guy, and no amount of beer or sympathy can blot her out of his mind. But then it's not *his* mind that's torturing him, but hers; specifically, he wants to know whether her thoughts ever wander back to Fort Worth and what they had together—and whether that makes any difference now at all.—bfw

447

Always on My Mind, Willie Nelson

Produced by Chips Moman; Written by Wayne Carson,
Mark James, and Johnny Christopher
Columbia 02741 1982 #1 country (2 weeks); #5 pop

"Always on My Mind" is so closely associated today with country music generally and Willie Nelson specifically that it's easy to forget its origins are in rock and

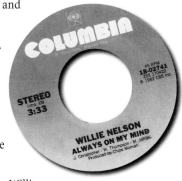

soul. Songwriters Wayne Carson, Johnny Christopher, and Mark "Suspicious Minds" James were all associated with producer Chip Moman's American Studios in Memphis, and the song's first country chart appearance was via Elvis, not Willie.

Predictably, they're very different records. The sensual sonic drive of Elvis's hit (#16, 1972–73) makes you believe him when he says

his woman was always foremost in his thoughts, even when he neglected her, hurt her, made her "feel second best." Maybe it's just that Elvis is such a powerful figure, you *want* to believe his story, or at least want to believe that *he* believes it.

Willie Nelson's version of "Always on My Mind," the CMA's 1982 Single of the Year, lacks Elvis's persuasive vocal gifts, and therein lies its own bittersweet power. Bobby Woods's tentative and brittle piano; the comparatively spare, almost naked arrangement; the way producer Moman makes every shaky line reverberate as if it were about to collapse like a house of cards—it all works to remind us that a love professed but not acted upon is, for its object, no love at all. Certainly, Willie's nervous, trebly baritone reveals that even he understands that, taken together, lines like "little things I should have said and done, I just never took the time" and "You were *always* on my mind" only cancel each other out. For the woman Willie claims he loves, such declarations will likely ring infuriatingly hollow; they're delusions at best, bald-faced lies at worst. For Willie's part, it looks like his best intentions have landed him in a lonely hell where "you were always on my mind" will at last be all too true.—dc

448

Gentle on My Mind, Glen Campbell

Produced by Al DeLory; Written by John Hartford
Capitol 5939 1967 #30 country; #62 pop

"Gentle on My Mind" might have played well during the Summer of Love—it went on to become Campbell's signature song—but was its load of bull for real? "It's knowin' I'm not shackled by forgotten words and bonds / And the ink stains that are dried upon some line," Glen sings,

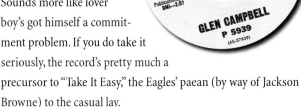

exulting in how the woman who lets him breeze in and out of her life stays "ever gentle"—that is, "ever *easy*"—on his mind. Sounds more like lover boy's got himself a commitment problem. If you do take it seriously, the record's pretty much a precursor to "Take It Easy," the Eagles' paean (by way of Jackson Browne) to the casual lay.

Yeah, well, courtesy of banjo man John Hartford at least, Glen's also got himself one hell of a line. It's one he's doubtless whipped out with countless women, and one he hopes will lead back to the beds even of those he left crying to their mothers the last time he skipped town. But who could resist that sweet tenor when in that hobo train yard he sings, "Through cupped hands 'round the tin can / I pretend to hold you to my breast and find / That you're wavin' from the back roads / From the rivers of my memories / Ever smilin', ever gentle on my mind?" And who wouldn't be undone by the sprung rhythm of that bubbly banjo roll, a sound so buoyant it could keep even the most transparent dodge afloat?—bfw

449

My Elusive Dreams, David Houston
& Tammy Wynette
Produced by Billy Sherrill;
Written by Curly Putman and Billy Sherrill
Epic 10194   1967   #1 country (2 weeks); #89 pop

In which Tammy takes "Stand by Your Man" a bit too far. She's stood by her husband (played here by Shreveport hitmaker David Houston) while he's chased pipe dreams in Texas, Utah, Birmingham, Memphis, Nashville, and Nebraska, and each time it's brought her grief. His latest scheme, a gold mine in Alaska, not only didn't pan out, it somehow cost the couple their young son. It's evident from the tenderness in Tammy's voice that she loves her man, but enough is enough, which is just what those 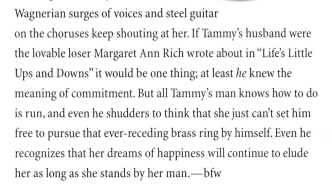 Wagnerian surges of voices and steel guitar on the choruses keep shouting at her. If Tammy's husband were the lovable loser Margaret Ann Rich wrote about in "Life's Little Ups and Downs" it would be one thing; at least *he* knew the meaning of commitment. But all Tammy's man knows how to do is run, and even he shudders to think that she just can't set him free to pursue that ever-receding brass ring by himself. Even he recognizes that her dreams of happiness will continue to elude her as long as she stands by her man.—bfw

450

My Adobe Hacienda, Louise Massey & the Westerners
Produced by Art Satherley;
Written by Louise Massey and Lee Penny
Columbia 37332   1947   #16 pop

Unlike Patsy Montana, who longed to rope and ride but never did, Louise Massey actually lived the cowgirl life she sang about. Raised on ranches in Texas and New Mexico, Massey grew up with a saddle horse between her legs and had rodeo trophies on her mantel to show for it.

It's not unusual, then, that Louise's signature song, "My Adobe Hacienda," would be different from Montana's "I Wanna Be a Cowboy's Sweetheart." What *is* surprising, even ironic, is that her biggest hit had nothing to do with the thrill of chasing the horizon or feeling the wind on her face; it was about settling down and making a home. "In my adobe hacienda / There's a touch 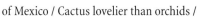 of Mexico / Cactus lovelier than orchids / Blooming in the patio," is the way Louise begins her reverie, her bell-like soprano the epitome of contentment. "The soft desert stars and the strum of guitars / Make every evening seem so sweet / In my adobe hacienda / Life and love are more complete," she continues, as strains of homey fiddle and accordion conjure images of quiet nights by the fire. And not out along the dusty trail either; Louise is picturing a cozy den or living room.

It's hardly the sentiment you'd expect from a female buckaroo. Then again maybe it's not so strange after all. By 1941, the year that Louise, her husband, and brothers first released "My Abode Hacienda," they'd been touring and singing on the radio for nearly fifteen years, including high profile gigs on the WLS *National Barn Dance* in Chicago and NBC's *Log Cabin Dude Ranch* in New York. Louise had led a life, at once glamorous and grueling, that few of her female contemporaries could have imagined; she was ready for a change—her home sweet home on the range.

As it was, Louise and her husband, bass fiddle player/composer Milt Mabie, stuck it out another six years on the road before beating it back to New Mexico. Fittingly, they settled into their own home just as this record, re-released by Columbia, was finding its place on the charts.—bfw

451

Watermelon Time in Georgia, Vernon Oxford
Produced by Bob Ferguson; Written by Harlan Howard
RCA Victor 47–8759   1965   Did not chart

A Hank acolyte from the Ozarks, Vernon Oxford was a man out of time when producer Bob Ferguson cajoled Chet Atkins into signing him to RCA in 1965. The pop-leaning Nashville Sound was at its peak, well into a ten-year run that helped country music live down its hillbilly pedigree. Witness the year's #1 singles, virtually all of which charted pop—even the burnished twang of West Coast dissident Buck Owens. Oxford's coon-dog whine, a voice as back-holler as possum stew, didn't stand a chance in this crossover climate. Even the Grand Ole Opry, an institution that's never been as chart-conscious as the rest of the industry, wouldn't book Oxford because, as Ferguson told historian Colin Escott, he sounded "a little too country."

Which is a shame, because with Ferguson and a bevy of first-call session pros playing behind him and golden boy Harlan Howard supplying him with songs, Oxford created a small but indelible body of work at RCA during the sixties, some two dozen sides that very few people heard, then or since. Few, that is, apart from record hounds and the pickers and singers who crowded into the studio while Oxford was recording them, a fan-like following that flocked to his sessions like they were club shows.

One of the knocks against Oxford was that he sounded too much like ol' Hank, but not on "Watermelon Time in Georgia," the first record he cut for RCA. Here, with the bluesy barbs of guitarist Earl Porter and steel player Lloyd Green recalling those of their Merle Haggard counterparts Roy Nichols and Norm Hamlet—and with Oxford crowing Howard's rewrite of Jimmie Rodgers's "Peach Picking Time Down in Georgia" (by way of "Detroit City")— "Watermelon Time" suggests the Singing Brakeman fronting the Strangers. "Lord it makes a country boy get down in the mouth / When his body's up North and his heart's down South," Oxford moans, more out of desire than desolation. Indeed, judging by David Briggs's rollicking piano, he's already hopped that train back to Macon.

So it's no wonder the single never charted for Oxford (it reached the country Top Fifty for Lefty Frizzell in 1970). At a time when Music Row had its sights set on the bright lights of New York and L.A., the only thing Oxford could think about was getting back down on the farm. Yet who could blame him? When he drools over those ripe melons, it's not produce that's making his mouth water and calling him home.—bfw

452

Detour, Elton Britt & the Skytoppers
Produced by Steve Sholes; Written by Paul Westmoreland
RCA Victor 20–1817   1946   #5 country

Adventures in genre definition.

In 1951, Patti Page recorded a solid version of the country standard "Detour." Following a steel-guitar kick-off that sounds exactly like it's introducing the latest Hank Williams single, Patti sings (to her own harmonies, which anticipate somewhat the sound of the Davis Sisters) over a swinging shuffle beat as that steel guitar twangs all the way to the finish. Page's "Detour" was a #5 hit on the pop charts.

Five years earlier, Elton Britt had made a much more striking and much more "pop"-sounding recording of the same song. His version also features prominent amplified steel guitar, but its "wang" is more in line with the Hawaiian style that had been a national sensation earlier in the century. Additionally, when Britt croons "Detour, there's a muddy road ahead," it's to a cowboy-movie arrangement that features a hot piano solo and a fiddle corps so lush it sounds like a full string section. Britt's record went to #5 too, but on the country charts.

Of course, we know that Page was a mid-century pop singer. And if Elton Britt is remembered at all today, it's as a country act—he's best known as a sometime yodeler and as the singer of "There's a Star Spangled Banner Waving Somewhere," a maudlin bit of World War II patriotism that became the first country record ever designated "gold" by its record company. But really now, if Patti wasn't wearing an evening gown and Elton wasn't sporting a cowboy hat, how would we tell the difference? Talk about a muddy road.—dc

453
Who Will the Next Fool Be, Charlie Rich
Produced by Sam Phillips; Written by Charlie Rich
Phillips Int. 3566   1961   Did not chart
Sun 1110   1970   #67 country

By the time he crossed over as the Silver Fox, Charlie Rich had already cut dozens of amazing though commercially unsuccessful recordings—first for Sam Phillips's Sun and Phillips International imprints, then for Groove and Smash, then Hi and Epic. All told, this decade-long collection of singles and album tracks is so varied and powerful that in order to find a superior contemporaneous body of pop music you have to start throwing around names like Elvis Presley, James Brown, the Beatles, Ray Charles, Ray Price, and Merle Haggard. Nearly all of Rich's sides in these years were jazzy and rocking, soulful and country. Indeed, they were all of these things at once. And while that made for timeless music, it didn't do the singer any favors with radio programmers, particularly in the absence of significant promotion.

"Who Will the Next Fool Be" serves as a frame for this early part of Rich's career. His vocals borrow the most soulful and intimate parts of Elvis and Brother Ray's singing, without ever imitating either—in fact, they anticipate both Presley's and 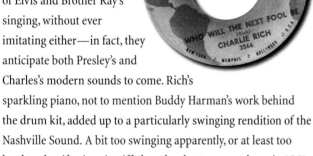 Charles's modern sounds to come. Rich's sparkling piano, not to mention Buddy Harman's work behind the drum kit, added up to a particularly swinging rendition of the Nashville Sound. A bit too swinging apparently, or at least too hard to classify, since it stiffed on the charts upon release in 1961, as did virtually everything Rich released in these years. The problem sure wasn't the song; R&B master Bobby "Blue" Bland would quickly cut his own hit-bound version of the number just a couple of months later.

By the end of the decade, though, country music had incorporated the very elements that had once placed Rich's music ahead of the pop and country curves. So when Sun (at this point owned by Shelby Singleton) re-released the record in 1970, it managed, just barely, to dent the country charts. More importantly, the second coming of "Who Will the Next Fool Be," with its country-soul rhythms and bluesy vocal restraint, provided a sneak preview of Rich's many countrypolitan hits to come. And a reminder of all the earlier ones that had gotten away.—dc

454
Danny Boy, Ray Price
Produced by Don Law and Frank Jones; Traditional
Columbia 44042   1967   #9 country; #60 pop

Most country historians plot Ray Price's career trajectory in three discrete phases: Hank Williams clone (1951–1955); hard-country pioneer (1956–1966); supper-club sellout (1967 to the present). There's more than a kernel of truth in this categorization. Price's early recordings *were* Hank Sr. knockoffs. Then, when he got sick of being told how much he sounded like his old roommate, he forged his own sound—a driving, 4/4 shuffle beat that soon became standard currency on the honky-tonk hardwood. And, as the sixties wore on, Price's music did take on a more uptown sheen, reaching its apotheosis in 1967, when he cut a string-drenched version of the Irish chestnut "Danny Boy."

Nevertheless, this standard reading of Price's musical evolution oversimplifies his story. For one thing, it obscures that Ray came up listening to the crooning of Bing Crosby and the Ink Spots. And it glosses over how Price's pop leanings could be heard as early as 1960, when, at the height of his run as a honky-tonk hero, he cut an album of gospel material steeped in strings. When Ray went into the studio to record "Danny Boy," the move was less a departure for him than a chance to delve deeper into the saloon-style singing and arrangements he'd always loved.

A sentimental war-horse based on the nineteenth century folk song "The Londonderry Air," "Danny Boy" has been sung so many times, and with such mixed results, that it's hard at this late date to hear it as anything but the worst sort of cliché—a prime candidate for karaoke night at the Holiday Inn. So it's easy to forget that back in the sixties it was a favorite at the annual Disc Jockey Convention in Nashville, where Price would close the Columbia showcase each year with his wrenching rendition of the song. Conventioneers soon came clamoring for him to record "Danny Boy," and Ray, whose sound was inching closer to Tony Bennett's all the time, took this as a license, once and for all, to erase the line between country and pop.

Price's "Danny Boy" begins with a gentle sigh of strings—the last warm breeze before summer turns to fall. Bill Pursell's circular piano figure, borrowed from some old doo-wop record, sets the stage for Ray's subdued entrance on the wings of Grady Martin's gossamer guitar. Ray's life is slipping away as the pipes call out to him, but before he can bid his Danny farewell, he must reaffirm his faith in the ties that bind. The autumnal wash of Cam Mullins's arrangement sweeps Ray up as his voice slowly gains strength on its way to the final verse, where he imagines Danny returning to this same glen to visit him after he is dead and in his grave. "You will call and tell me that you love me / And I shall sleep in peace till you come to me," Ray's operatic tenor rings out, echoing up and down the mountainside.

It's a transcendent moment on an unspeakably gorgeous record, but a lot of people didn't hear it that way when the single came out. Many of the same disc jockeys who had begged Price to cut the song wouldn't play it, accusing him of forsaking his hillbilly roots. Some of his fans booed and even spit on him. Yet Ray forged ahead in this crushed-velvet country vein and never looked back. Like the protagonist of "Danny Boy," he trusted that his circle—in this case a tradition that had long embraced both twang and pop—could not be broken.

What's happened since then certainly bears Price out. You'd be hard pressed to find a mainstream country album released in "Danny Boy's" wake, even those by down-home singers like Patty Loveless and George Strait, that doesn't have strings on at least a couple of tracks.—bfw

455
Bully of the Town,
Gid Tanner & His Skillet Lickers
Produced by Frank Walker; Traditional
Columbia 15074-D   1926   Pre-chart

The Skillet Lickers, one of the standout string bands of country music's first decade, would likely never have existed if it weren't for the expanding possibilities of the recording studio. Or a record company A&R man's desire to sell more records.

That man was Columbia's Frank Walker. Recording in New York, he'd already done reasonably well with releases by fiddler Gid Tanner and guitarist Riley Puckett, and he'd cut a few less successful sides with fiddler Clayton McMichen. Finalizing the details for an upcoming recording session in Atlanta (where all three men were based), Walker already knew he wanted to work with larger ensembles, the better to take advantage of the superior sonic range available from the new electrical recording process. Why not get that bigger sound and potentially bigger sales too, he reasoned, by combining these musicians, who each had sizable followings thanks to extensive public and radio appearances in and around Atlanta.

The result was, as is often noted, country music's first super group—a unit designed to be, and that mostly remained, a studio-only team even after its records began selling in numbers that now and then rivaled Vernon Dalhart's. Tanner was the front man, a forty-something chicken farmer whose fiddling had long offered John Carson his stiffest competition at Atlanta fiddling contests. The much younger McMichen was a new breed fiddler, playing in a longbow style that clearly revealed his love for hot jazz. There was often a third fiddler present in the studio (on this first session, McMichen's brother-in-law Bert Layne) as well as banjoist Fate Norris. As Tanner shouted out encouraging asides on a dance party workout like, say, "Shortenin' Bread," all those fiddles would get to sawing away over, under, and around McMichen's swinging lines, and the Skillet Lickers sounded a bit like the Southeast's version of early Bob Wills.

The Skillet Lickers' first hit, a version of the late nineteenth-century standard "Bully Of The Town," eventually sold over 200,000 copies; in Charles Wolfe's estimation, it was "one of the best-selling, if not the absolute best-selling, fiddle band record of its age." On this particular stringband record, though, all those fiddles take a back seat to singer-guitarist Riley Puckett. At the start, providing the bottom needed to anchor all those crying fiddles, Puckett's plucking out a simple part for which the next generation of string bands would use a stand-up bass. The record is transformed, though, when he opens his mouth to sing. All he says, over and over, is that he's looking for, and can't find, the town bully. But his voice is such a delight it hardly matters *what* he's saying. Compared to most other singers of his era—country, pop, or otherwise—Puckett's tenor is full-bodied, expressive, intimate, modern. His voice has a lightness and fluidity with melody that at times even rivals Jimmie Rodgers's finest work, if not quite Bing Crosby's.

No wonder Riley was known as "the Ball Mountain Caruso."—dc

456

I Gotta Have My Baby Back, Floyd Tillman
Produced by Art Satherley; Written by Floyd Tillman
Columbia 20641   1949   #4 country

A faintly Hawaiian kickoff on the steel. An acoustic rhythm guitar part that sounds like a ukulele. A sweet pop melody and a lazy, swinging groove. A grand, jazzy piano solo. A crooner messing with meter and buh-buh-bingling his way through the last words of the title phrase.

Floyd Tillman's words say he just has to get his girl back. But the way he sings those words confesses another love altogether. This is what happens when a man with the vocal range of Ernest Tubb falls hard for Bing Crosby.—dc

457

Jimmie Rodgers' Last Blue Yodel, Jimmie Rodgers
Produced by Ralph Peer; Written by Jimmie Rodgers
Bluebird 5281   1933   Pre-chart

458

Honky Tonk Women, The Rolling Stones
Produced by Jimmy Miller;
Written by Mick Jagger and Keith Richards
London 910   1969   #1 pop (4 weeks)

"Women Make a Fool Out of Me," parts one and two.

In "Honky Tonk Women," Mick smirks at the thought of all those gin-soaked barroom queens and divorcees he's laid. In "Jimmie Rodgers' Last Blue Yodel" (originally "Women Make a Fool Out of Me"—the title was changed to capitalize on Rodgers's

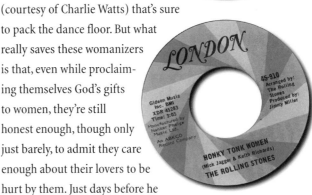

death), the Singing Brakeman brags about how he doesn't love any woman enough to marry her but that the ladies are lining up to pick up his tab all the same. The boasts of both these rakes go down easier because of the joyous musicality of their performances. In Rodgers's case, his playful phrasing and wistful yo-duh-lay-hee-ho; in Jagger's, a cowbell and bass-drum rhythm bed (courtesy of Charlie Watts) that's sure to pack the dance floor. But what really saves these womanizers is that, even while proclaiming themselves God's gifts to women, they're still honest enough, though only just barely, to admit they care enough about their lovers to be hurt by them. Just days before he succumbed to tuberculosis, Rodgers shakes his head and moans, "Women make a fool out of me." Nearly forty years later, Jagger does the same. "It's these haw-uh-ah-uh-awn-kee tonk women," he sings, practically yodeling, "that give me the honky-tonk blues."—dc

459

That Silver Haired Daddy of Mine,
Gene Autry and Jimmy Long
Produced by Art Satherley;
Written by Gene Autry and Jimmy Long
Banner 32349, Oriole 8109, Vocalion 02991, OKeh 02991, Conqueror 7908, Romeo 5109, Perfect 12775   1931
Pre-chart

Gene Autry got his start as a Jimmie Rodgers imitator but became a star as a singing cowboy. This record catches him in transition. One of country's biggest early hits, "That Silver Haired Daddy of Mine" features rich signifiers of country music's southeastern roots—keening Hawaiian steel guitar; high, wispy harmonies from partner Jimmy Long; and an opening line that places the title character not out on the prairie but in a mountain shack not unlike Fiddlin' John Carson's little old log cabin in the lane. The song's lilting melody and Autry's sweet, earnest delivery, on the other hand, point north to Tin Pan Alley, and out west to Hollywood.

"I wanted to be a dreamy-eyed singer of love songs like Rudy Vallee," Autry once said of his early days in show biz. Mix in the Singing Brakeman at his most sentimental, and that's pretty much what we've got here: a penitent, dreamy-eyed love song to dear old dad.—dc

460

The Golden Rocket, Hank Snow
Produced by Steve Sholes; Written by Hank Snow
RCA Victor 48-0400   1950   #1 country (2 weeks)

Hank Snow had been fiddling with Vernon Dalhart tunes on his guitar the day his mother brought home a copy of Jimmie Rodgers's "Moonlight and Skies." It was only after he heard Rodgers's record, though, that Hank knew he had to pursue a career as a singer. He wasn't the only one—Gene Autry, Jimmie Davis, Ernest Tubb, Lefty Frizzell, and dozens of others who came of age in the prewar era had the same idea, but none of them emulated Rodgers as assiduously as Snow did.

As a star in Canada during the thirties and forties, Hank didn't just sing and write like his hero, he billed himself as "Hank the Yodeling Ranger" (after Rodgers's moniker "America's Blue Yodeler"). Then, after his voice deepened and he couldn't copy his idol's trademark warble anymore, Snow dubbed himself "The Singing Ranger," a nod to Rodgers's other nickname, "The Singing Brakeman." Nevertheless, by the time he got to Nashville, Hank was his own man, and nothing demonstrates it better than "The Golden Rocket."

This isn't to say the record doesn't draw on Rodgers for inspiration. "The Golden Rocket" abounds with chugging rhythms and simulated train whistles, as well as Rodgers's patented railroad themes and imagery. But that's just it. Snow

means to invoke his hero; he's both ushering Rodgers's music into the postwar era and showing the world he's found his own voice. Hank's proto-rockabilly guitar solo on the break alone proves he's not just reviving music that straddles the nineteenth and twentieth centuries. And when he sings, "I was a good engine a-runnin' on time / But baby I've switched to another line," he's flat-out telling us he's jumped off Jimmie's old steam locomotive and hopped aboard a new streamlined train.—bfw

461

Miss the Mississippi and You, Jimmie Rodgers
Produced by Ralph Peer; Written by Bill Halley
Victor 23736   1932   Pre-chart

Sentimentality runs deep in the white southern psyche—deeper perhaps than in any other segment of the American population. Much of this excess emotion stems from feelings of nostalgia, the half-mythic memory of a time when things seemed simpler, people were closer to the land, and life moved at a slower pace. Yet there's also a more profound psychological dynamic at work: the longing for an idealized past to replace the legacy of poverty, seeming backwardness, and hatred from outsiders that each generation of southerners inherits. It's what W. J. Cash, writing in *The Mind of the South*, called "The South's perpetual need to justify its causes."

It's an understandable, if at times less than noble, impulse. It's receded some in the modern era where, among other things, advances in communications and the increased mobility afforded by interstate travel and mass transit have greatly homogenized American culture, rendering southern stigmas less conspicuous than before. Yet, during the Depression when Jimmie Rodgers recorded this paean to his home state, the southern hunger for a better past could hardly have been stronger. This was especially the case among white landowners who feared the arrival of industrialization. This class of people also lived with lingering shame about losing the Civil War, submitting to Reconstruction, and availing themselves of the de facto system of slavery that was Jim Crow.

This isn't to say that all picturesque portrayals of life in the south betray this anxiety and shame. Some, such as the Singing Brakeman's heartrending ode to life along the Mississippi, are touching declarations of a yearning for home that distance only seems to deepen. "Days are dark and dreary everywhere I roam . . . Nothing seems to cheer me under heaven's dome / Miss the

Mississippi and you," Jimmie moans, pining for his sweetheart and for the big river's "muddy water shore." Sweetened by strains of aching violins and a gently lowing clarinet, "Miss the Mississippi and You" is as heartfelt as any sentimental number in Rodgers's catalog. It also offers a striking contrast to "Mississippi Delta Blues," in which Rodgers embroiders his southern idyll with scenes of "darkies singing their melodies" as if the subsistence lives of those sharecroppers and domestic servants were crucial to his reverie.

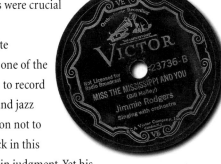

Some might cite Rodgers's rank as one of the first white singers to record with black blues and jazz musicians as reason not to put too much stock in this thoughtless lapse in judgment. Yet his caricature of black men and women blithely singing—one presumes, while indentured to the grandson of the master who owned their forebears—represents just the sort of whitewashing that was ingrained in the fabric of southern life when Rodgers was alive and, in some respects, still persists today. It's certainly the sort of tainted romanticism that Randy Newman, writing nearly forty years later, skewers in "Sail Away," the biting satire in which he makes slavery out to be a walk in the park. A southerner by birth, Newman certainly seemed to have the arrangement to "Miss the Mississippi and You" in mind when he steeped "Sail Away" in those gorgeous, but oh so astringent winds and strings.—bfw

462

The Battle of New Orleans, Johnny Horton

Produced by Don Law; Written by Jimmie Driftwood
Columbia 41339   1959
#1 country (10 weeks), #1 pop (6 weeks); #3 R&B

Ridiculous history, great record.

Arkansas folklorist, songwriter, and school teacher Jimmie Driftwood set his lyrics for "The Battle of New Orleans" to "The Eighth of January," an old fiddle tune commemorating the battle, in an attempt to get his sixth graders excited about American history. An admirable goal, but the result deserved its own chapter in historian James Loewen's *Lies My Teacher Told Me*.

The song delivers its who, what, and where in the opening lines: "In 1814, we took a little trip along with Colonel Jackson down the mighty Mississip' . . . and we fought the bloody British in the town of New Orleans." Unfortunately, the battle actually took place in 1815, two weeks after the war was over. And the rest of the song, even Driftwood's much longer original version, highlights cutesy punch lines ("We fired our cannon till the barrel melted down / So we grabbed an alligator and we fought another round") to the exclusion of the real teaching issue—why the war was fought in the first place. There's no mention here of the official pretense for the War of 1812 (a response to British impressments of American seamen), let alone of what Loewen and others maintain was its real purpose, further U.S. expansion into Indian territory. Forty years down the line, the lyrics serve less as a history lesson than an example of cold-war flag waving. And since "The Battle of New Orleans" arrived on the heels of the Battles of Montgomery and Little Rock, some listeners also used it, no doubt, as a reminder of an earlier instance of white southerners fighting back an invasion. The song begins, after all, with a snippet of "Dixie," even though that song wasn't composed until 1859.

But none of this had much to do with the lasting popularity of "The Battle of New Orleans." For one thing, when Johnny Horton recorded the song in 1959, it wasn't just popular with white southerners. In fact, it became for a time the most popular song in the country, topping the pop and country charts and even going Top Five R&B. While Horton's hit helped to create a brief demand for often patriotic "saga songs" (a mini-genre that Bill Malone has appropriately declared "pseudo-historical"), including Horton's own "Sink the Bismarck" and "Johnny Reb," none of these later songs approached its popularity.

The difference is in the groove. From Grady Martin's indelible electric-guitar lick up front through Harold Bradley's simple banjo part, Buddy Harman's martial drums, and the Jordanaires' sounding off in the background, the record is one big rhythmic hook in support of an unforgettable melody—if you've heard it once, you can hum it on demand. And when Horton cuts loose his near-rockabilly bark at the bridge, it's absolutely impossible not to sing along. Just don't believe a word of it.—dc

463

The Titanic, Ernest V. Stoneman
Produced by Ralph Peer; Written by Robert Brown
OKeh 40288   1925   Pre-chart

The 1927 Bristol sessions are considered the birth of country music, but if that's true, what do we make of Ernest Stoneman? By the time that Jimmie Rodgers showed up in Bristol for his first recording date, for example, Stoneman (who was at Bristol as well) had already cut some 100 sides. The first of them, "The Titanic," was a hit record, too, reportedly selling in the hundreds of thousands in 1925.

Stoneman was a carpenter from around Galax, Virginia (now known as the Old-Time Music Capital of the World), where he was an amateur banjoist, guitarist, and autoharp player until he heard a record by another local musician, Henry Whitter. Sure that he could do better himself, Ernest sought a chance to record. Over the next decade, alone or with his wife and other family members, he cut all kinds of country music—gospel songs, minstrel tunes, transplanted British folk songs, sentimental ballads, comedy and dance numbers—but he liked best the ones that told a story. "Any song with a story will go to people's hearts because they love stories," he said late in life.

For sheer drama, the story of the Titanic has it all, which no doubt accounts for why so many versions of the tale showed up in event songs in the decade following the 1912 accident. Accompanying himself on harmonica and autoharp in a combination that's reminiscent of a calliope, Stoneman's "The Titanic" provides tragedy on a grand scale ("1600 had to die") and the baldest form of class struggle ("the rich they decided they would not ride with the poor" who, forced below, were the "first who had to go"). It also places human hubris ("They were going to build a ship that water could not go through") face to face with a morally punitive universe ("But God with a mighty hand taught to the world that it could not stand"). Stoneman's rough-hewn voice, more eager than accomplished and betraying nary a blue note, sings "it was sad when that great ship went down." His delivery, though, sounds more "just the facts" than sad. Perhaps because that sadness *is* "just the facts."

The Depression effectively ended Stoneman's run as a "star" recording act; he was a casualty of the era's financial devastation but also of the thirties' musical revolutions. Jimmie Rodgers, with his affinities to pop, jazz, and the blues, his superior commercial success, and personal magnetism, presaged the country music

century and so remained a powerful presence even in death. Ironically, Stoneman actually lived to see much of the century that Rodgers anticipated. Yet even in the 1960s, when the Stoneman Family ("Pop," plus several of his children and assorted kin) had reestablished themselves via the festival circuit and a syndicated television program, Ernest always seemed like a throwback to a time and place apart from our own. A time when you could mail order autoharps from the Sears, Roebuck catalog; when faith in technological solutions still paled next to faith in God; and when event songs had yet to be supplanted by newsreels and radio reports, around the clock TV coverage, and blockbuster movies about doomed lovers and sinking ships.—dc

464

Blood Red and Goin' Down, Tanya Tucker
Produced by Bill Sherrill; Written by Curly Putman
Columbia 45892   1973   #1 country (1 week); #74 pop

Much is made of how, during her early career, Tanya Tucker's Lolita-like, fourteen-going-on-forty sexual persona lent her music a freakishly adult cast. But here, as with "Delta Dawn," it's not Tanya's libido that reveals a beyond-her-years maturity, but her ability to convey a genuine depth of perspective.

The plot that Tanya, playing the part of a wide-eyed ten year-old, unravels to Billy Sherrill's gloriously melodramatic arrangement is boilerplate Southern Gothic. Her mother runs off with another man while her daddy, out of his head with rage, goes after the couple and guns them down in a roadhouse in Georgia. What's unexpected, even shocking, about the story is how Tanya's father drags her along as he hunts down her mama. In the second verse, he even turns to the girl for advice as if *she's* the adult in the relationship. "At times like these a child of ten never knows exactly what to say," Tanya sings, confessing bewilderment, even as her drawling, not-so-little-girl contralto captures the tension between her confusion and her longing to find the words to stop the nightmare unfolding before her. Skittish cymbal-beats nervously tick away the minutes and Charlie McCoy's harmonica blows an ill wind until, on the final verse, we find Tanya trembling in the back of her daddy's car outside the beer joint where he's dispatching the souls of her mama and her paramour to hell. "That Georgia sun was blood red and goin' down," Tanya declares on the chorus, just as she, the Jordanaires, and the Nashville Edition have done throughout the record. The difference is that this time, more than just going down on the bodies of the ill-fated lovers, Tanya knows that big bloodstained ball is setting prematurely on her innocence as well.—bfw

465

Blue, LeAnn Rimes
Produced by Wilbur C. Rimes; Written by Bill Mack
Curb 76959   1996   #10 country; #26 pop

The easy route would be to compare LeAnn Rimes, a mere thirteen when "Blue" was released, to teen singers Brenda Lee and Tanya Tucker. On her debut, though, adolescence was about the only thing Rimes shared with those earlier acts. Whereas Lee and Tucker made their splashes with state-of-the-art country, Rimes began her career self-consciously out of date. "Blue" is the very definition of what gets called traditional: a pedal-steel-driven Texas shuffle combined with a vocal performance that sighs like Patsy Cline (Bill Mack wrote the song specifically for Patsy, though she never recorded it) and yodels like Eddy Arnold. This was on the radio in 1996? To pull off a similar feat, Lee would've needed to score her first hit mimicking Sara Carter.

   Which just means "Blue" wasn't traditional in any meaningful sense. It was retro. Big difference. On "Blue," rather than being a link in an ongoing chain of tradition, Rimes pretends that the past isn't really gone for good. Not that there's anything wrong with that. It's just that resurrecting the past isn't an option, even if it seems desirable. Still, when the music's this drop-dead gorgeous, you'd have to be buried already to avoid playing along for a couple of minutes.—dc

466

I Fall to Pieces, Patsy Cline
Produced by Owen Bradley;
Written by Hank Cochran and Harlan Howard
Decca 31205   1961   #1 country (2 weeks); #12 pop

The hit that set Cline down the path to stardom finds her falling apart every time she meets her old lover on the street or hears someone mention his name. With Hank Garland's chiming guitar serving as a nagging reminder of the wedding bells that could have been, Patsy sings in front of, behind, but hardly ever *on* the beat. This is more than just a saloon singer's trick she picked up from Kay Starr. It's as if the beats Patsy's avoiding are the facts she can't bear to face, most of all that she's going to have to settle for being friends with her ex. It's a stunning convergence of music and lyrics, and one that testifies to Cline and

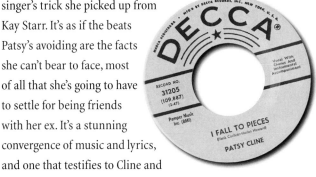

producer Owen Bradley's uncanny gift for making *records* as opposed to merely recording songs. Like "Crazy," "Sweet Dreams," "Walkin' after Midnight," or any number of the other hits they made together, "I Fall to Pieces" takes us to a place where sound and sense become one.—bfw

467

She Thinks I Still Care, George Jones
Produced by Harold "Pappy" Daily; Written by D. L. Lipscomb
United Artists 424   1962   #1 country (6 weeks)

If this record represents a classic case of denial, as its reputation says, then it's one of the least successful attempts in history. Not just because the evidence that Jones denies here is so damning— he's asking friends about his ex, talking about her, phoning her "by mistake," and falling to pieces when he sees her. He cares—and never more transparently than when he admits, "I'm not the happy guy I used to be" in a tortured gulp that sounds like he's spying a future as dark as his grave.

   What Jones's voice conveys here is more than sadness; it's despair. Which makes the title not ironic but deadly serious. He needs her; she doesn't need him; what's there to care about? He *doesn't* care, not about anything. Not anymore. Maybe not ever again.—dc

468

Hello Walls, Faron Young

Produced by Ken Nelson; Written by Willie Nelson

Capitol 4533   1961   #1 country (9 weeks); #12 pop

This one gives new meaning to the old adage "talking to the walls."

Turning to the plaster, Faron asks, "Hello walls, how'd things go for you today / Don't you miss her, since she upped and went away?" He's talking about the woman that's just walked out on him. No, make that *them*. Faron's got it so bad that every part of his room—the windows, the ceiling, you name it—personifies and shares his hurt. He even sees each raindrop streaming down his windowpane as a tear shed for his departed lover.

The mood and the music here—a brooding, tic-tac shuffle in Nashville Sound regalia—is a far cry from "Goin' Steady" and the other frisky romps the Young Sheriff was cranking out after he left the *Louisiana Hayride* during the early fifties. But more than just the arrangements have changed. Faron's drawling vocals have ripened some, and, along with lessons learned from the crooner-inspired honky-tonk of his pal Ray Price, *that's* what enables him to pull off something as deliriously bent as this. "We all must stick together or else I'll lose my mind," Faron confides to his taciturn companions; the chilling part, of course, is that he doesn't know he's already lost it.

"Hello Walls" was a huge record in every respect, becoming the biggest hit of Young's career and a crossover success to boot. It also established songwriter Willie Nelson as one of the premier country tunesmiths of his genera-tion. According to Willie, the song was inspired by the walls of the garage out back of his publishing company's offices. Sorta makes you wonder if walls can't talk after all.—bfw

469

Still, Bill Anderson

Produced by Owen Bradley; Written by Bill Anderson

Decca 31458   1963   #1 country (7 weeks); #8 pop

Bill Anderson's fans call him "Whispering Bill"—basically it's just an affectionate way of admitting the guy doesn't have much of a voice. So how does a man who can't really sing become one of the most successful recording artists in country music history? Well, first off, it helps if you're one of the best songwriters in country music history. It also helps a lot if you hook up early on with Ray Price. Price's 1958 recording of "City Lights" got Anderson his recording contract in the first place, and it was "That's What It's Like to Be Lonesome," Price's follow-up hit, that helped Anderson hang on to the deal until he began scoring his own Top Ten hits.

Oh yeah, and it also helps if you sing as little as possible. Anderson usually had the good sense to reserve his finest, most complex songs for better singers, leaving the more obviously sentimental and nostalgic numbers—often little more than cloying recitations interrupted every few lines by a catchy chorus—for his own sessions. His voice on these records, whether speaking or singing, is typically aspirated and unctu-ous—a high-school thespian's stage whisper. Even his strongest moments in the style ("Mama Sang a Song," for example) lack the power they would've had if, say, Jimmy Dickens or Porter Wagoner had recited them instead.

"Still" hews tightly to Anderson's vocal formula and so should have yielded similarly pedestrian results. Instead, it transcends its limitations and then some. The record is a kind of open letter, a lush long-distance dedication, that works because the sweetly romantic setting provided by producer Owen Bradley is consis-tently at odds with Whispering Bill's own demented testimony. "After all this time, you're still on my mind," he half talks, half sings. There's just something too much about it all, something pathetic and vaguely creepy about the way he both gulps and over-enunciates those lines; the way he seems to have a grin permanently fixed upon his face; the way he pledges to carry a torch, "like an eternal fire," for the woman who has disappeared from his life, even though his only hope is that she might hear this song. "I've lost count of the hours," he confesses, "I've lost track of the days." He's lost everything, really, except memories of this woman, and just as it dawns on you to declare the guy nuts, Anderson spares you the trouble. "My friends think I'm crazy," he gushes, "and maybe I am."

No wonder Bradley's background singers seem to be bouncing around in even more echo than normal; they're recording in a rubber room. —dc

470

The Most Beautiful Girl, Charlie Rich

Produced by Billy Sherrill;
Written by Billy Sherrill, Norro Wilson, and Rory Bourke
Epic 11040   1973   #1 country (3 weeks); #1 pop (2 weeks)

Many critics would have us believe that this single and its chart-topping predecessor, "Behind Closed Doors," are the apotheosis of countrypolitan schlock. Or at least that they're (wink, wink) guilty pleasures, pathetic indulgences that somehow transcend their excesses. Listen closely to either, though, and you'll be wondering what those writers are hearing. They're polished productions all right, but especially on "The Most Beautiful Girl," each burnished edge gleams like the blade stuck in Charlie's heart.

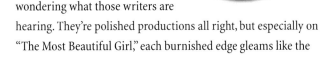

The record opens in a lean, down-home vein, with the restive strumming of a lone acoustic guitar followed by rolling piano and a lightly throbbing backbeat. "Hey," Charlie sings, trying to sound nonchalant, as if striking up a conversation with an old buddy, "did you happen to see the most beautiful girl in the world?" But Charlie *isn't* talking to someone he knows. If he were, he'd have mentioned the woman by name. No, as we soon learn, Charlie's girl has left him, and he's out of his head (on the streets perhaps?), beseeching what seems to be a parade of passersby for news of the nameless beauty that's slipped through his hands. The strings don't enter until he makes his second query, their heaving sigh (in tandem with Pete Drake's crying steel) echoing Charlie's regret as he proceeds to ask everyone he meets to tell his gal he's sorry. He also wants them to impress upon her how much

he loves and needs her; every time the Jordanaires lean into the word "need" it's like they're leaning on that knife.

"The Most Beautiful Girl" is a more refined production than the justly lionized sides Rich cut for Phillips, RCA, and Smash during the fifties and sixties. Its sophistication, however, doesn't mean it's compromised, less immediate or intense. Once you come under the spell of Charlie's smoky baritone and soulful phrasing, the record is undeniable. Granted, the years ahead would prove that he and Sherrill could churn out dreck with the worst of them, but that's hardly the case with "The Most Beautiful Girl." No less than "Lonely Weekends," "Mohair Sam," or "Life's Little Ups and Downs," it too is representative of the fabulous Charlie Rich. —bfw

471

Holding On to Nothin',
Porter Wagoner & Dolly Parton

Produced by Bob Ferguson; Written by Jerry Chesnut
RCA Victor 9490   1968   #7 country

Like Conway and Loretta's "After the Fire Is Gone," this is a great duet in which a couple languishes in a loveless marriage. Unlike Conway and Loretta, though, Porter and Dolly aren't slipping around on each other; they're just holding on, even though there's nothing left to cling to. They feel guilty about living a lie—Pete Drake's stabbing steel and Jerry Carrigan's nagging rimshots leave no doubt of that—yet they can't summon the nerve to call it quits. Maybe it's that Porter and Dolly look so good together; as they tell us, their friends envy what they seem to have. Maybe it's force of habit or that they fear being alone. But chances are it's that they sound so great together; they just can't deny how good it feels when Porter's Ozark drawl intertwines with Dolly's mountain tremolo.

This vocal chemistry was enough to keep Porter and Dolly working as a duo for the better part of a decade. While the results were always worth hearing, there were even better things in store when Dolly finally realized that holding on to what they had was just holding her down. That's when she stepped out on Porter and never looked back. —bfw

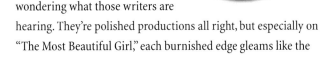

472
Girl on the Billboard, Del Reeves
Produced by Kelso Herston;
Written by Walter Haynes and Hank Mills
United Artists 824   1965   #1 country (2 weeks); #96 pop

First came Roger Miller with "Do-Wacka-Do," and then, just three months later, Del Reeves, sounding a lot like Miller, scatting "doodle-oo-doo-doo" to kick off this record. Something was going on, and, judging by their gonzo wordplay and speedball delivery, the two men had taken a shine to the "spontaneous bop prosody" of Jack Kerouac and the Beats (although the phrase "do-wacka-do" dates at least as far back as the Jazz Age.) Whatever the antecedent, Del and Roger sure didn't pick up stuff like this listening to the Grand Ole Opry. Witness the first of several tongue-twisting rambles that Del, playing the part of a love-starved over-the-road trucker, reels off here. "Who is the girl wearing nothing but a smile and a towel in the picture on the billboard in the field near the big old highway," he sings, ogling the hottie on the giant sign as that Tennessee Two–style locomotion and growling guitar fuel his libido.

At more than thirty syllables, Del's breathless rap has to be the longest opening line ever to appear on a country record. And yet for all its novelty, for all Del's clowning about the twenty wrecks that the picture of the scantily clad model has caused, the record has a serious side as well, much as there are sober undertones to many of Roger Miller's outwardly comic hits. The real reason Del's stuck on a woman who isn't real, he tells us, is that "a double-clutching weasel like me can hardly ever get a girl to look at him that a-way." So it's ultimately not the unattainable model on the billboard that explains why tiny pieces of his heart are scattered "every which a-way" along Route 66. Despite his insouciant "doodle-oo-doo-doos," it's that Del is on all-too-intimate terms with Roger Miller's not-so-silly one-liner "the last word in lonesome is me."—bfw

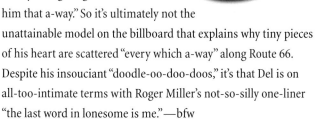

473
Rainin' in My Heart, Slim Harpo
Produced by Jay Miller;
Written by Jerry West
Excello 2194   1961   #17 R&B; #34 pop

Excello Records was born in 1952 when Ernie Young, a regional record distributor and proprietor of the world-renowned "Ernie's Record Mart," concluded that the Nashville competition was just too fierce for the hillbilly records he'd been releasing on the Nashboro label. Rhythm and blues, he figured, gave a local fellow a better shot at making a buck. Excello's initial releases were moderately successful, but they were also plagued by a tendency to chase after the hot R&B record of the moment. In 1955, though, Young finally landed a distinctive style when he met Jay Miller, an aspiring Louisiana producer best known for penning "It Wasn't God Who Made Honky Tonk Angels." The two men cut a deal where Miller recorded the R&B and Young released it. The artists Miller recorded became known collectively as purveyors of "swamp blues," an electric brand of down-home blues that was tremendously influential, inspiring later acts like Tony Joe White, Jerry Reed, and the Rolling Stones.

Excello's main claim to fame was Slim Harpo. His swamp blues masterpiece "Rainin' in My Heart" has a decidedly country feel, a partial result perhaps of Miller's prodding Harpo to sing more "like Hank Williams." Still, the most unmistakable connection here is to the Delmore Brothers' recordings of the late forties and early fifties. An easy, wistful melody, a crawling country boogie riff (courtesy longtime Harpo collaborator Lightnin' Slim), and the soft, lonesome squall of Harpo's own harmonica—the rain in Harpo's heart comes down in a musical language that's extremely close kin to the way the Delmores had begged the blues to stay away just a decade before. And from the weary sound of his voice, Harpo's plea isn't any more successful.—dc

474

Walk Softly on This Heart of Mine,
The Kentucky Headhunters
Produced by the Kentucky Headhunters;
Written by Bill Monroe and Jake Landers
Mercury 874744   1989   #25 country

In his original recording, Bill Monroe made this high-lonesome request humbly. But these latter-day sons of Kentucky romp and stomp more like drunken Georgia Satellites than Blue Grass Boys. Banging on arena-rock drums and brandishing blues-rock guitars, they have no intention of ever being walked on again. They say "walk softly," and to ensure your compliance, they brandish a really big stick.—dc

475

Walking to New Orleans, Fats Domino
Produced by Dave Bartholomew;
Written Antoine Domino, Dave Bartholomew, and Robert Guidry
Imperial 5675   1960   #6 pop; #2 R&B

Modern Sounds in Country and Western Music—and a good two years before Ray Charles released his album bearing the name. "Walking to New Orleans" isn't a country song like the couple dozen Brother Ray cut in 1962; it's a blues, and for the habitually rollicking Fats, a rare mournful one at that. But whereas Charles draped hillbilly tunes in lush or brassy pop orchestration, Domino's single crosses desire-drenched strings with a clip-clopping western beat, coming up with something closely akin to the shimmering Nashville Sound Owen Bradley was creating with Patsy Cline. Fats may claim he's headed back to the Crescent City, but the arrangement here suggests he's making tracks straight for Nashville.—bfw

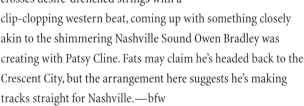

476

Who's Sorry Now? Milton Brown & His Brownies
Produced by Dave Kapp; Written by Ted Snyder, Bert Kalmer, and Harry Ruby
Decca 5158   1935   Pre-chart

Not the Brownies. Most recordings of this Tin Pan Alley standard, from the five charting versions in 1923 to the 1958 smash hit by Connie Francis, try to suggest that one of those who's sorry, still, is the singer. Milton Brown smokes the competition by playing it entirely straight. He's pleased, ecstatic even, that the one who hurt him is feeling the real pain, and right now. His band joins in the revelry—pianist Papa Calhoun

remakes the melody into his own private jig; fiddler Cecil Brower laughs through his solos; steel man Bob Dunn sounds like he's giving someone an amplified raspberry. Every note echoes their boss's glee. What goes around really does come around after all! When Milton takes the final verse himself ("I'm glad that you're sorry now," he concludes), he might as well be smirking: Na na nuh na na.—dc

477

Don't Let That Man Get You Down, Texas Ruby
with Curly Fox & His Fox Hunters
Produced by Art Satherley; Written by Fred Rose
Columbia 36901   1945   Pre-chart

Texas Ruby was the original honky-tonk angel, the prototype for the woman who broke Hank Thompson's heart in "The Wild Side of Life." A tough-talking, whiskey-drinking chain-smoker, Ruby, the kid sister of "Cattle Call" author Tex Owens, could hold her own with any man. At times she even sang like one, her deep, lusty voice sounding more at home in the lower registers than most tenors.

On this low-down blues Ruby passes herself off as an expert on men, advising a good-timing sister to steer clear of the rake who's just dumped her. "He can do the nicest things right before your eyes / He can say the sweetest words but most of them are lies," Ruby warns. "He's the kind of man who makes you lay that pistol down."

Belting out her lines over a jazzy trumpet figure, the devilish fiddling of her husband Curly Fox, and the juking guitars of Grady Martin and Jabbo Arrington, Ruby sounds a lot more like Bessie Smith here than country's answer to vaudeville star Sophie Tucker (which is how she was often billed). Her allusion to the gun-toting moll, though, is straight out of the honky-tonks—a nod to "Pistol Packin' Mama," a country and pop smash for both Al Dexter and Bing Crosby the previous year. Ruby's message: let down your guard the way I did, and "you're just as good as gone."

At least that's what she seems to be saying until the last verse when she finally shows her hand, revealing that all this sisterly wisdom was just a ploy to keep other honky-tonk women away from her guy. "So just remember that he's mine and that I'm somewhere around," she threatens. The alternative, obviously enough, is a trip to fist city.—bfw

478

Suspicious Minds, Elvis Presley
Produced by Chips Moman and Felton Jarvis;
Written by Mark James
RCA 47-9764   1969   #1 pop (1 week)

"Here we go again, asking where I been," Elvis protests, though of course that's hardly an unreasonable inquiry. He begs his wife (who he hints is paranoid but who has apparently heard this one before) to please just trust him if, say, an old girl friend should drop by for a visit. As he pleads, the American Studios house band, an irresistible rhythmic force if ever there was one, creates the anxious backdrop of a couple caught in a trap. Reggie Young's circular electric guitar rolls along, forever ending up right back where it started; Mike Leech's bass and Gene Chrisman's nervous drum taps seem to increase the momentum as they go; a female chorus dogs Presley's heels;

nagging strings and horns ratchet the tension. All of it snowballs to the moment where the record falls quiet, and Elvis swears, "But, honey, you know I'd never lie to you."

Well, that's the question, isn't it?—dc

479

She Still Comes Around (to Love What's Left of Me), Jerry Lee Lewis
Produced by Jerry Kennedy; Written by Glenn Sutton
Smash 2186   1968   #2 country

Yet another cheating man wondering how much more his woman can stand and still stand by him. The difference here is that Jerry Lee, doing his best George Jones imitation, actually sounds sorry for what he's done.

Yeah, right. That's just the booze talking.—bfw

480

Just Because, The Shelton Brothers
No producer credited; Written by Hubert Nelson and James Touchstone
Decca 5100   1935   Pre-chart

"But I'm telling you / Honey, I'm leaving you / Because, just because."

Well, not *just*. Sure, maybe that was the case a decade after Bob and Joe Shelton's recording, when Frankie Yankovic ("the King of the Polka") had a Top Ten hit, pop *and* country, with the same song. And it certainly was the case in 1954 when "Just Because" was done up rockabilly style by Elvis, who really did sound like he was breaking up with his baby for no more reason than that singing the song would be a hoot.

The Sheltons, however, have clearly been nursing some very specific grievances. Though hailing from east-central Texas, the Sheltons (born Bob and Joe Attlesey) play guitar and mandolin, and sing in a tight, close harmony style, as if they'd been raised a county over from the Delmores in northern Alabama. On "Just Because," the Sheltons' peevish, clipped enunciation curdles their every word—"You think you're so purr-tee . . . you think you're so

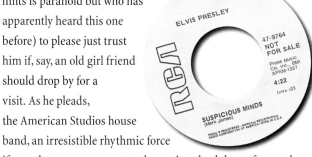

hot"—while Joe's mandolin is bickering and caustic. Why? Because the one and only reason this girl even wants her "Mr. Santy Claus" around is for his bank account. Well, Virginia, "there just ain't no Santy Clause," they tell her with a curled lip, and if she don't believe it, she can count the days he's gone.—dc

481

Queen of Hearts, Juice Newton
Produced by Richard Landis; Written by Hank DeVito
Capitol 4997   1981   #14 country; #2 pop

This jumpy little gem is the closest thing to new wave ever heard on country radio. Written by Hank DeVito, then the pedal steel player in Emmylou Harris's Hot Band, "Queen of Hearts" is a thinly veiled knockoff of Eddie Cochran's "Summertime Blues," right down to its fidgety guitar riff and its doubled hand claps. In fact, imagine Harris and Rockpile 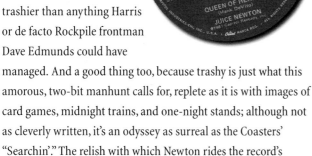 covering Cochran's hit, and you've pretty well got it. Pretty well, except that Newton's slightly raspy vocals and Richard Landis's cheesy production are trashier than anything Harris or de facto Rockpile frontman Dave Edmunds could have managed. And a good thing too, because trashy is just what this amorous, two-bit manhunt calls for, replete as it is with images of card games, midnight trains, and one-night stands; although not as cleverly written, it's an odyssey as surreal as the Coasters' "Searchin'." The relish with which Newton rides the record's thunderball bass leaves no doubt that, whoever she's lookin' for, she's gonna find him.—bfw

482

High-Falutin' Mama, Bill Nettles
Produced by Jim Bulleit; Written by Bill Nettles
Bullet 637   1947   (B side of "Too Many Blues")
Did not chart

Most histories of country music orbit around the biggest stars. It's an understandable and altogether fitting approach to telling the music's story. After all, country's perennial hit makers make the headlines, and their names come to define this or that moment,

style or trend. Yet for every Ernest Tubb, Dolly Parton, or Shania Twain that comes along, there are dozens of other more or less talented singers packing 'em in at honky-tonks and beer joints all over the country each weekend. Singers with fierce local followings who might never grab the brass ring (or even try), but who are as much a part of country's story as their more celebrated counterparts.

Bill Nettles could be the poster boy for this legion of coulda-been contenders. He and his brother Norman were stars on Shreveport's KWKH during the thirties and forties, and were among the cofounders of an early incarnation of the *Louisiana Hayride*, the radio barn dance that served as a stepping-stone to the Grand Ole Opry for everyone from Hank Williams to George Jones. Not only that, Bill was a prolific songwriter and the author, reputedly, of Jimmie Davis's 1934 hit "Nobody's Darling but Mine." (The story goes that, in exchange for getting him out of the drunk tank, Nettles sold Davis, who was then Shreveport's commissioner of public safety, the publishing rights to the song for twenty-five bucks.) Nettles also penned "God Bless My Darling, He's Somewhere," a wartime smash for pop singer Dick Haymes, and co-wrote "Have I Waited Too Long," which became the theme song of fellow Shreveport honky-tonker Faron Young.

Nettles himself recorded for more than a half-dozen labels from 1937 until his death in 1967. He and his band, the Dixie Blue Boys, even scored a Top Ten country hit in 1949 with "Hadacol Boogie," a honky-tonkin' paean to the nostrum patented by Louisiana politico Dudley LeBlanc. Yet despite his big-name cohorts (Davis apparently landed him his first record deal, with Vocalion, in 1937) and his own periodic brushes with fame, Nettles, who drank some and wasn't much of a businessman, never really broke through outside his native Louisiana. How he managed not to, with a roaring two-step like "High-Falutin' Mama," is anyone's guess.

Like many of Hank Thompson's hits, "High-Falutin' Mama" splits the difference between honky-tonk and western swing, with Bill, a fetching but hardly golden-throated singer, fusing the gravel-voiced delivery of Ernest Tubb with the jive banter of Bob Wills. Bill is shaking his head good-naturedly at his sweetheart, a material girl who's loaded but won't spend a dime of her own. "She's got this, she's got that / Three goldfish, a dog and cat / That shy, little high-falutin' mama," he beams while a puckish fiddle and bopping guitar, as foxy as the gal he's so smitten with, tiptoe all around him. There's nothing coy about that amplified, on-the-verge-of-distorting steel guitar that rips through the rest of the record, though. Or about Bill's intentions. He knows his mama will cost him a bundle, but he's only too ready to empty his pockets with a smile. It's no doubt just the sort of obliging attitude that kept Nettles content with his life as a local hero.—bfw

483

Honky Tonk Blues, Hank Williams
with His Drifting Cowboys
Produced by Fred Rose; Written by Hank Williams
MGM 11160   1952   #2 country

The downside of settin' the woods on fire.

Hank's leaving the old homestead for the bright lights of town and—judging by the sprightly rhythms of the record's first few bars and the giddy-up in Don Helms's opening steel lick—he's stepping out for good. But soon, after getting his fill of drinking, dancing, and carrying on, Hank changes his tune as his rambling fever gives way to a new disease. "Oh Lord, I've got 'em, I've got the honky-tonk blues," he moans, yodeling the first syllable of "honky" as if holding his head with a hangover that just won't quit. And, in life as in song, it never really did. Despite his vow to "tuck my worries underneath my arm and scat right back to my pappy's farm," Hank never made it back home; he never did shake the honky-tonk blues.

This was Williams's fourth recording of the song, but the first that producer Fred Rose deemed worthy enough to ship to the commercial market. It's no wonder—Hank's early versions of the song sound tentative, as if he's merely playing a part. This time—just a year before his death—he'd suffered the honky-tonk blues long enough to convey their ravages with chilling conviction.—bfw

484

Rock About My Saro Jane, Uncle Dave Macon
& His Fruit-Jar Drinkers
No producer credited; Traditional
Vocalion 5152   1927   Pre-chart

In which Uncle Dave goes the medieval philosopher Boethius one better and seeks consolation not in some parched philosophy, but in a steady stream of whiskey-soaked rhythms. Unlike the sixth-century Roman sophist, Macon isn't wasting away in a dank, dark cell; he's passing the jug with fiddlers Mazy Todd and Kirk McGee, and Kirk's brother Sam, and settin' the woods on fire.

Make that settin' the *ship* on fire. The woman's name invoked in the record's title could be someone's sweetheart, but more than likely it refers to a steamer. The song, one that Macon learned from black dock workers in Nashville, is a variant of "Cap'n Tom Ryman," a tribute to the noted riverboat man and builder of the Ryman Auditorium.

Things don't sound so good on board the Saro Jane either. Each verse after the first relates some dire turn of events—the ship's captain goes overboard, the boat suffers engine trouble— only to end, oddly enough, with a rousing chorus of "Oh, there's nothing to do but to sit down and sing / Oh, rock about, my Saro Jane." The ship's going down, but from those sawing fiddles to the way the flat-top picking of Sam McGee (who helped popularize the guitar as a solo instrument in country circles) dances to the tune of Uncle Dave's rollicking banjo, the four men seem bent on staying the course the best they know how. Drowning their cares and rocking away their blues.—bfw

485

I Ain't Never, Webb Pierce
Produced by Paul Cohen; Written by Mel Tillis and Webb Pierce
Decca 30923   1959   #2 country; #24 pop

"I ain't never" is right. Webb Pierce, the epitome of a country singer in the decade after Hank Williams's death, had never achieved this level of crossover success before and he never would again. In fact, since Elvis showed up, it has been rare for a country singer or single this unabashedly hillbilly to have made such inroads at pop radio. Much of Pierce's appeal is due to the work of Hank Garland, Buddy Harman, and the Jordanaires, some of the same musicians who within the year would be blurring still further the line between country, rock, and pop when they backed the King on *Elvis Is Back!* So in certain ways "I Ain't Never" isn't hillbilly at all. No way, though, can you miss the sawdust origins of that hard shuffle or of Garland's twangy electric lead. And even if you reinforced the Jordanaires' layered backing vocals with the Vienna Boys Choir, you still ain't never going to disguise the Louisiana yowl of Webb Pierce.—dc

486

One Hand Loose, Charlie Feathers,
with Jody and Jerry
Produced by Louis Innis; Written by Charlie Feathers,
Jody Chastain, and Jerry Huffman
King 4997   1956   Did not chart

Charlie Feathers was the man who might've been King, according to some folks—one of whom was Feathers himself. He claimed to his death that he invented rockabilly and shaped Elvis's sound during his concurrent mid-fifties stint at Sun Records, only to lose out when Sam Phillips chose to direct the label's energies elsewhere. There doesn't appear to be much evidence to support those claims, but Feathers most certainly did get a co-writer credit for Presley's early country hit "I Forgot to Remember to Forget." He also recorded some fine country sides for Phillips in a straight-up honky-tonk vein similar to the one mined by Carl Perkins's earliest sides. Frustrated, Feathers moved on to another Memphis outfit, Meteor Records, where he released a few fits of rockabilly madness. Still, even backed by the raucous new rhythms, Feathers's rockabilly sounded downright primitive next to the new-day-dawning work of Presley, Perkins, Jerry Lee Lewis, and the rest. Something in his slurred and loopy hillbilly exuberance made it seem as if Feathers would have been just as satisfied playing a banjo on some old number by Charlie Poole or Dave Macon.

Or covering a standard by Bill Monroe. Thanks to the Grand Ole Opry, Feathers had grown up a fan of Monroe and his Blue Grass Boys, but in Feathers's part of Mississippi there was no one around who could teach him to play that kind of music. Who was around was blues man Junior Kimbrough, who taught Feathers to pick guitar. "I was really singing bluegrass and rapping on the guitar like I heard those colored artists do it," Feathers said in 1991. "Bluegrass rock, that's what it really was . . . And drums don't really work with rockabilly."

That attitude accounts for why Feathers never thought much of the classic rockabilly sides he eventually made at King Records, where it's the drums that hold on to that skittering new beat, and it may also explain why the 45 uses such an old-time sounding credit: "Charlie Feathers, with string band." "Give me one hand loose, and I'll be satisfied," he shouts, warning that if he doesn't get what he wants he'll blow his top—right before his wired guitar does precisely that. He needs to be free to rock, by God, and he can do it one-handed, too, which is just as well since his other one's tied up holding on to his baby.—dc

487

Linda on My Mind, Conway Twitty
Produced by Owen Bradley; Written by Conway Twitty
MCA 40339   1975   #1 country (1 week); #61 pop

Conway Twitty was as intensely popular a figure with female fans as country music has ever seen, a connection he worked hard to cultivate. "Almost every song I've ever written," he once explained, "was created first of all with women in mind . . . Second, and very close to that, most men want to say these things to women but they just don't know how." Twitty's sensitive man image, however, was always a complicated one. Although he recorded his fair share of romantic love songs, particularly in the latter part of his career, his immense popularity with female fans always seemed partly dependent upon the low expectations many women have learned to have of men in the first place. After all, in the singles that made his reputation, the man Conway portrayed was not above hurting a woman if it suited his needs. The "sensitive" part was that he at least felt really, really bad about it when he did.

Case in point: "Linda on My Mind" is delivered from the point of view of a man who lies in bed with his wife while thinking of her friend Linda, with whom he plans to run away. "Now I'm lying here with Linda on my mind," he begins, which gets about a point and a half on the sensitivity scale. It's also not entirely accurate. He does think of Linda during the song, of course, and for a moment he even recalls the deep love he once felt for his wife. But mostly, and this is typical Conway, it's neither Linda nor his wife that's on his mind. His main concern is how bad he feels to be lying in the bed he's made. "And oh it's killing me to see her cry," he moans. That sounds about right, because as the song hits its final crescendo, you'd swear he's the one who's crying.—dc

488
I'm Not Lisa, Jessi Colter
Produced by Ken Mansfield and Waylon Jennings; Written by Jessi Colter
Capitol 4009   1975   #1 country (1 week); #4 pop

This string-laden, piano ballad sounded awfully pop coming from a woman with strong ties to the Outlaw crowd. Indeed, it's just the kind of crossover record that made Jessi's husband and co-producer Waylon Jennings brood, "Are you sure Hank done it this way?"

"I'm Not Lisa" opens with a forlorn piano figure and Jessi playing the part of a woman whose husband just called her by his ex's name. But instead of doing the proper Outlaw thing and giving her man what for, Jessi tenderly reaffirms her commitment to the guy. She's hurt, but she knows that *he* is hurting too. "My eyes are not blue, but mine won't leave you," she vows in an aching

Dolly-like soprano, underscoring the difference between herself and the woman who dumped him. Gauzy strings and pulsating bass enter on the following verse—Ralph Mooney's crying steel joins in later—as Jessi, fighting back tears, tells her man she understands as the record swells to its stirring climax.

Minus Johnny Gimble's fiddle and Mooney's steel guitar, "I'm Not Lisa" is just the sort of adult-pop record that either Barbra Streisand or Linda Ronstadt might have made at the time. It's hardly standard Outlaw fare. Or is it? The Outlaw movement wasn't so much about a particular sound as a sensibility, a determination on the part of the artists involved to record the songs they wanted to sing and to do it with the musicians they chose instead of with the material and session pros pressed upon them by the Nashville brass. Heard in this light, "I'm Not Lisa," a song written by Colter and cut with her husband's band the Waylors, is as Outlaw as they come. And that's to say nothing of Jessi's steel magnolia performance, a heartstopping show of strength that doubtless was much tougher to pull off than the macho posturing of Waylon and his running buddies.—bfw

489
You Never Even Called Me by My Name,
David Allan Coe
Produced by Ron Bledsoe; Written by Steve Goodman
Columbia 10159   1975   #8 country

No matter what Coe claims halfway, this is definitely *not* "the perfect country and western song." The first verse barely rises above generic, and the second and third mainly come off as excuses for David Allan to drop names, his own loudest of all. On the other hand, the hilarious final verse, which in just four lines references Mama, trains, trucks, prison, and gettin' drunk, at least makes the song one quarter of a

perfect country and western parody. And when Coe lays into that irresistible chorus—"And you don't have to call me darlin', darlin' / You never even called me by name"—you know that it just may be the perfect country and western sing-along.—dc

490

Guitars, Cadillacs, Dwight Yoakam
Produced by Pete Anderson; Written by Dwight Yoakam
Reprise 28688   1986   #4 country

Guitars, Cadillacs, hillbilly music, and "lonely, lonely streets that I call home" are what Dwight Yoakam focuses upon on his second charting single. As iconography goes, that list is about as received a collection of country signifiers as you could possibly imagine. Throughout his career, Yoakam has remained enthralled by the imagery of country music, from his western jackets and omnipresent cowboy hat to his teary lyrics—heavy on the wine and beer even though this teetotaler reportedly never touches the stuff. What makes Yoakam interest-

ing, though, is definitely *not* his retro chic (which usually comes off as little more than kitsch anyway). Rather, what makes his music work are all the twists that he and longtime producer-guitarist Pete Anderson bring to the party. For one thing, there's an unmistakably urban feel to even the pair's twangiest mo-ments—after all, those lonely, lonely streets mainly wind through L.A. (or "Babylon," as it's called here), not the Ohio River Valley where Yoakam grew up. For another, Anderson's country licks have a vicious rock & roll bite, and so does this record's drum-heavy rhythm section.

Yoakam headed to California in the first place, he claims, because Nashville found him "too country," an epithet that apparently followed him out west until he found refuge in the same punk-affiliated roots-rock scene that was then nurturing bands such as Lone Justice and Los Lobos. So it makes sense that "Guitars, Cadillacs" would have Yoakam succeeding on country radio not by looking back but by finding new ways to synthesize contemporary rock elements into his music. That's exactly the strategy that Yoakam and Anderson's heroes, Buck Owens and partner Don Rich, rode to success a quarter century before.—dc

491

Gone Country, Alan Jackson
Produced by Keith Stegall; Written by Bob McDill
Arista 12778   1994   #1 country (1 week)

492

The Prisoner's Song, Vernon Dalhart
Produced by Ralph Peer; Written by Guy Massey
Victor 19427   1925   Pre-chart

Nashville has long been a magnet for aspiring singers, pickers, and songwriters. So it comes as no surprise that in the late 1980s and 1990s, with country music moving more units than at any time in its history, a new throng of performers and industry wanna-bes de-scended upon "Nashvegas." Many of

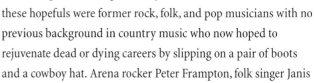

these hopefuls were former rock, folk, and pop musicians with no previous background in country music who now hoped to rejuvenate dead or dying careers by slipping on a pair of boots and a cowboy hat. Arena rocker Peter Frampton, folk singer Janis Ian, and pop rockers Nicolette Larson and Richard Marx, to cite just a few examples, all pulled stints in boomtown Nashville.

"Gone Country" responded to this migration by skewering three fictional opportunists. A Vegas lounge singer stares at her aging face in the mirror and rationalizes "I'm a simple girl myself, grew up on Long Island"; a folkie who has spent his career protesting "wealth and privilege" figures he can get rich quick by writing a few Dylanish country hits; an L.A. tunesmith decides moving to Nashville would be great for his kids, not to mention his bank account. Alan Jackson delivers these hilarious tales with hospitality, just the way southerners have responded to carpetbaggers for generations. "Here he come," Jackson drawls, just another good ol' boy greeting a friend. Only a stone idiot, or a carpetbagger, would miss the derision lurking beneath his smile.

Then again, if one of these newcomers made a great record,

who would really care where they came from? It's the music that matters in the end, not the resume—a distinction that "Gone Country" songwriter Bob McDill comprehended as well as anyone. Prior to a nearly three-decade-long hot streak that produced such country classics as "Just Like Real People," "Amanda," and "All the Good Ones Are Gone," he sang in a college folk group and authored hits for Perry Como and Sam the Sham & the Pharaohs.

So what else is new? "Going country" has been an important part of the music's commercial story virtually since its beginnings. Take Vernon Dalhart. Born Marion Slaughter in northeast Texas, he was first exposed to cowboy songs by listening to the ranch hands who worked his father's spread. Slaughter's musical passions, however, weren't quite so down-to-earth. In his mid-teens, he moved to Dallas where he received formal vocal training at the Dallas Conservatory of Music before heading to New York to sing operas and operettas. For the next decade and a half, Slaughter sang Puccini and Gilbert & Sullivan on stage, hired himself out as a singer for funerals and church services, and delivered whatever his many record companies needed in the studio: "coon" songs, WWI songs, Hawaiian songs, fox trots, nearly the entire spectrum of cylinder-era vaudeville and Tin Pan Alley pop. Just about everything but country.

In 1924, with his recording career on the skids and a family to feed, Slaughter noticed the budding market for "old time" songs and talked his label into letting him record a version of "The Wreck of the Old '97," an event song that had just been successfully recorded by Henry Whitter. Needing a B side, Dalhart produced "The Prisoner's Song," which he credited his cousin with writing but which was comprised of several older folk sources. Accompanied only by guitar and fiddle, Dalhart betrayed his stage background by over-enunciating every line of the song—he sounds like he's trying to show off for a diction coach. Even so, his croon is so sweetly poignant and the melody so irresistible, it doesn't much matter. When he sings "If I had wings like an angel, over these prison walls I would fly," it's clear yet again that lonesome is a concept unbound by biography.

Slaughter, now billing himself Vernon Dalhart (combining the names of two Texas towns), sold over a million copies of "The Prisoner's Song." The record made his career and, in large part, country music's. Attempting to capitalize on the runaway success of Dalhart's hit, Victor and other labels headed south to record rural folk musicians like never before. Down home was never the same again.—dc

493

Are You Sure Hank Done It This Way,
Waylon Jennings
Produced by Jack Clement and Waylon Jennings;
Written by Waylon Jennings
RCA Victor 10379   1975   #1 country (1 week); #60 pop

"Lord it's the same old tune, fiddle and guitar / Where do we take it from here," wonders Waylon on this history-conscious anthem from 1975. It was a good question at the time, yet questionable as music history, if only because the country music that followed in Hank's wake—the golden age of honky-tonk, the Nashville Sound of Chet Atkins and Owen Bradley, the countrypolitan of Billy Sherrill and Jim Malloy—was anything but monolithic. Indeed, more often than not those fiddles Waylon mentions were violins. Even so, with the watered-down pop of John Denver, Olivia Newton-John, Ronnie Milsap, and T. G. Sheppard making major inroads onto the country charts during the mid-seventies, Nashville's music industry certainly seemed to have lost its compass. Waylon's "we need a change" sounded like a cry from the wilderness.

True to Outlaw form, Waylon responds to his own challenge not by looking backwards for answers to Hank Williams or Bob Wills (the pioneer he salutes on the B side of this single) but by hoeing his own row. Dispensing with both fiddle and violins, Waylon and co-producer Jack Clement opt for a lean, hard-driving sound that's part big beat rock & roll akin to that which Jennings played with Buddy Holly and part twangy rock à la the Rolling Stones' *Sticky Fingers*. As evidence of the latter, witness Waylon's snaky lead guitar lines, which could easily pass for Keith Richards's playing on the Stones' "Dead Flowers."

All of which is to say that Waylon's idea of change resulted in music no more country-sounding than the latest singles by Denver or Milsap. But what it had that they lacked—and this *did* hark back to Hank—was soul. With Duke Goff's bass stubbornly hammering the point home, that was all the change that country music, circa 1975, really needed.—bfw

494
Walk a Mile in My Shoes, Joe South & the Believers
Produced by Joe South; Written by Joe South
Capitol 2704   1970   #56 country; #12 pop

In 1969, Joe South took Dixie nationwide with the smash hit "Games People Play," a pop-soul-country hybrid at the vanguard of what has since been termed the southernization of American popular culture—an era when Elvis ascended from rebel (to has-been) to icon, when Tammy Wynette could cross over, when TV images of the south shifted virtually overnight from Beverly-based hillbillies to hip Nashville-styled cats. By the mid-seventies, Roger Miller, Bobbie Gentry, Johnny Cash, Glen Campbell, Mac Davis, Jim Stafford, and Jerry Reed each had television variety series. Though he never attained that level of popularity, South was a major player in this trend, laying down guitar licks behind Aretha in Muscle Shoals and Dylan in Nashville, as well as having his songs recorded by everyone from Presley, Swamp Dogg, Billy Joe Royal, and Lynn Anderson to King Curtis, Dizzy Gillespie, and Mel Torme.

Like most of those artists, Joe South came up at a time when rock & roll, soul, gospel, and country intermingled quite naturally in the south. By the late sixties and early seventies, the result was a vibrant and increasingly integrated pop landscape—one where Elvis could introduce his live version of "Walk a Mile in My Shoes" by reciting a few lines from Luke The Drifter's "Men with Broken Hearts." South's song was pop in a more profound sense, too. Both musically and lyrically, it reached across demographic and musical lines not by condescending to any lowest common denominator but by pushing us to work for our highest ideals. Amid of-the-moment references to karma, long hair, ghettos, and reservations, "Walk a Mile" deploys a series of church-derived maxims: you reap what you sow; be careful of the stones you throw; there but for the grace of God go I. In the hands of Joe South & the Believers, these homilies transcend cliché and express a timeless human longing not merely for tolerance but also for understanding and connection.

"Well I may be common people, but I'm your brother," South testifies over a groove that invites the whole world to dance and sing along. "And when you strike out and try to hurt me, it's a-hurtin' you / Lord have mercy!" When South calls out "Walk a mile in my shoes," only someone lacking all trace of heart or soul could refuse to respond, "Amen."—dc

495
Blue Yodel No. 9 (Standin' on the Corner),
Jimmie Rodgers
Produced by Ralph Peer; Written by Jimmie Rodgers
Victor 23580   1930   Pre-chart

The blues in black and white.

"Blue Yodel No. 9" was the only time Louis Armstrong, the Father of Jazz, traded lines on record with Jimmie Rodgers, the Father of Country Music. It was a natural enough pairing, what with the music of both men so steeped in the blues. Not only that, Rodgers had recorded with jazz combos earlier in his career, and Armstrong had sung hillbilly music; late in life, Armstrong would even cut an entire album of country material.

Nevertheless, their one session, which took place in Holly-wood in July of 1930, was an anomaly for its day. Granted, black and white musicians often jammed together back then, but only informally, mostly at after-hours conclaves in locked jazz clubs and hotel rooms, or out in the sticks somewhere. But faced with the specter of segregation in the south and of racism throughout the U.S., blacks and whites seldom shared stages in public and rarely played on each other's records.

Which makes the fact that Armstrong isn't credited on this disc all the more galling. Neither was his wife Lillian, who lays down the black-bottomed rhythm on piano here. Not that all sidemen and sidewomen, black or white, received billing on records, then *or* now. But Louis Armstrong wasn't your average hired gun. In 1930 he was the single most important figure in the world of jazz, and Rodgers's manager Ralph Peer, the man who arranged the session and had helped launch Armstrong's career, knew it.

Whatever the reason for the slight, it certainly invests the opening lines of this blue yodel, a thinly veiled rewrite of "Frankie and Johnny," with added freight. "Standin' on the corner,

I didn't mean no harm / Along came a police, he took me by the arm," Rodgers complains from his vantage at the corner of Beale and Main. The name of the intersection is hardly trivial; with Beale signifying "black" and Main the "white" mainstream, it represents the crossroads where the two races meet. So it rings doubly ironic that Jimmie's getting badgered for standing there, and that Louis's contributions to this single were, as far as the public record goes, blotted out altogether.

Not that Rodgers and Armstrong negotiate the intersection all that smoothly, at least not on first listen. Jimmie's sense of rhythm is ragged, and Louis's blowing seems tentative, as if he can't quite lock into a groove. Then again, judging by the way the jazz man mimics the yodeler's lazy drawl, maybe he's just listening intently; maybe he's hanging onto Jimmie's every word so that he can complete their call-and-response. Just witness how Louis's solo after the second break echoes Jimmie's woozy vocals, his tone less imperious and more laid back than usual.

It all makes for a striking study in empathy, in one artist's ability, despite being saddled with the ficklest of rhythms, to enter into the heart and mind of another. Of course, it wasn't Pops playing "West End Blues" with Earl Hines, the man historians for years erroneously credited with playing the piano here. But it's about as close to that mythical exchange as country ever got.—bfw

496

Will the Wolf Survive? Los Lobos
Produced by T-Bone Burnett and Steve Berlin;
Written by David Hidalgo and Louie Perez
Slash 29093   1985   #78 pop

Twang-leaning rockers have looked to Bakersfield for inspiration at least since the Beatles cut "Act Naturally" in 1965. But never have the town's outsider ethos and hard-boiled aesthetic galvanized a rock scene the way they did in Los Angeles during the 1980s. Buck and Merle's influence first started creeping into the music of roots-punk bands like X, the Blasters, and Lone Justice. Before long it also became the driving force behind the neo-honky-tonk underground led by Dwight Yoakam and Pete Anderson, a like-minded cadre of pickers and singers that coalesced around North Hollywood's celebrated Palomino Club. By then people were calling L.A. "a town south of Bakersfield."

Los Lobos, a Chicano band from across the tracks in East

L.A., had more in common with the punks than the shit-kickers, and they would later broaden their sonic palette to include everything from junkyard noise to black and tan fantasies. Back in 1985, however, there was plenty of twang in their sound. Indeed, with "Will the Wolf Survive?" Los Lobos captured the ebullient spirit of Owens and his band better than any of their peers, even honorary Buckaroo, Yoakam.

Los Lobos attack the song, which Waylon Jennings took to the country Top Ten in 1986, like they're trying to play "Love's Gonna Live Here" in a hyperkinetic new key. Guitars chime and rhythms hurtle, while David Hidalgo's keening tenor rivals that of Buck himself. Not that there aren't shades of other things here as well: border music, big-beat rockabilly, R&B in search of soul. All things that Owens and his band once incorporated into their sound, right down to the lilting Mexican rhythms that Buck picked up as a kid in Texas and Arizona during the Depression. Contrary to Buck's famous bet-hedging proclamation that he'd never play anything but country, it is precisely this sort of musical ecumenism that lies at the heart of West Coast country's progressive impulse—the hunger to re-create and expand what the Blasters called "American Music."

"Sounds across the nation / Coming from young hearts and minds / Battered clubs and old guitars / Singing songs of passion / It's the truth that they all look for / Something they must keep alive / Will the wolf survive?" Hidalgo asks, contemplating the future of that American music in an anthem that goes a long way toward insuring that the answer will always be a resounding "Yes!"—bfw

497

Don't Fence Me In, Bing Crosby & the Andrews Sisters with Vic Shoen & His Orchestra
Produced by Jack Kapp;
Written by Cole Porter and Robert H. Fletcher
Decca 23364   1944   #1 pop (8 weeks); #9 R&B

It might seem ironic that Cole Porter bought "Don't Fence Me In" from Montana rancher Bob Fletcher, only to overhaul it according to Tin Pan Alley specs and transform it into one of the most enduring cowboy classics ever. Broadway, however, had been supplying country singers with material by way of traveling vaudeville shows for years, so why not a little quid pro quo? The give-and-take didn't end there either. After silver screen cowboy Roy Rogers recorded the song for the 1944 movie *Hollywood*

Canteen, Bing Crosby and the Andrews Sisters cut it for Decca and took it to the top of the pop charts. It stayed there for nearly two months, building on the success of their droll cover of honky-tonker Al Dexter's "Pistol Packin' Mama," and placing country and western music squarely within the pop mainstream.

Not that Crosby and company passed themselves off as real cowhands or anything. The first thing they did was chuck the song's opening passage, the part that introduces its protagonist, a rough and tumble buckaroo named Wildcat Kelly who's run afoul of the law and begs the sheriff to exile him to a stake of untamed ground (rather than putting him behind bars). The result is a dramatic shift in perspective. Instead of Kelly wanting to get *back* to the wide open spaces he calls home, we have Bing and the Andrews Sisters longing to get just far enough away from the city ("that place where the West commences") to be able to gaze up at a sky full of stars. That is, not so far away from town that they'll be cut off from the comforts and conveniences of home.

The arrangement evinces a similar shift, replacing the hop-along cadences of Rogers's recording with uptown rhythms, its rough-cut steel and accordion with big band horns and cabaret-style piano. And yet it's not a radical enough transformation to keep pop listeners from hearing the record as country. Indeed, more than just a series of moves that gave city folk something they could relate to, this is Bing fencing off a spot on the pop landscape for the country music he cherished.—bfw

498

If You Love Me (Let Me Know), Olivia Newton-John
Produced by John Farrar; Written by John Rostill
MCA 40209   1974   #2 country; #5 pop

In 1974, the Country Music Association awarded crossover pop singer Olivia Newton-John its Female Vocalist of the Year award. Outraged, some two dozen legends had soon convened at the home of Tammy Wynette and George Jones to discuss ways to protect the music from outside "agitators." As Jones later put it, "This middle of the road crap, this southern pop music for the dollar bill, just don't hook it." The result of such outrage was the Association of Country Entertainers (ACE). The group's complaint was initially couched in aesthetic terms, but it eventually came down to a group of established artists looking to protect their turf, which is to say their business interests. That, and a bad case of provincialism—Newton-John recorded in England, not Nashville, after all, and her accent was Australian, not southern. Certainly, "If You Love Me (Let Me Know)," her highest-charting country hit, was no less "country" sounding than contemporaneous hits by, say, Ronnie Milsap, the Statler Brothers, and Charlie Rich, to name three other CMA winners that year.

In truth, "If You Love Me" was even more "country" sounding. With an arrangement that sported pedal-steel guitar, an electric guitar part pulled straight from Roy Nichols's bag of riffs, and a back-up bass singer doing his southern gospel best, the wonder is that Newton-John's record ever managed to go *pop*, not country.—dc

499

Keep on the Sunny Side, The Carter Family
Produced by Ralph Peer; Written by Ada Blenkhorn and J. Howard Entwistle
Victor 21434   1928   Pre-chart

Cut at the Carter Family's first recording session following their legendary 1927 triumph in Bristol, Tennessee, "Keep on the Sunny Side" was a turn-of-the-century gospel number that the group discovered in an old shape-note hymnal. It was inspired by a wheelchair-bound relative of songwriter Ada Blenkhorn who would often request to be pushed down "the sunny side of the street." In the Carters' hands, the popular song became a resounding statement of human aspiration, and they adopted it as their theme: "There is a dark and a troubled side of life / There's a bright and a sunny side too."

It's a hopeful song, but not unrealistic. The close, overcast harmonies in which Sara, A. P., and Maybelle deliver their lines underscore that every human life will reckon with its share of light *and* darkness, guaranteed. Here they give the message an explicitly Christian spin, but it remains paramount even in many of country music's most secular moments—the understanding that time changes everything, the hope that tomorrow we'll dance.—dc

500

I Hope You Dance, Lee Ann Womack
(with Sons of the Desert)
Produced by Mark Wright;
Written by Mark D. Sanders and Tia Sillers
MCA Nashville 172158   2000   #1 country (6 weeks); #24 pop

In an era of Hot New Country when most Nashville acts sang about life and love in a single perky key, and in what sounded like the same arrangement, "I Hope You Dance" stood out from its first notes. A slurred, depressed bass introduces brushwork and brief, stabbing guitar licks before giving way to brooding cellos and violins. Then Lee Ann Womack begins to sing, sharing her hopes and dreams for someone she dearly loves. Her own daughters, most likely (a reading reinforced by the single's video), though on the record she could just as easily be singing to a departing lover or anyone willing to really listen. "I hope you never lose your sense of wonder," she sings in a voice suggestive of a young Dolly Parton: "May you never take one single breath for granted / God forbid love ever leave you empty handed / . . . and when you get the choice to sit it out or dance, I hope you dance."

Almost any other singer on country radio at the turn of the century would have turned this into a diva move, an unironic and preposterously sanguine proclamation of happiness guaranteed merely for the wishing—a musical Hallmark card, in other words. But Womack's record doesn't let us off so easy. Her guarded delivery, a rhythm track that feels held back even as it presses inexorably forward, the Sons of the Desert's baleful, contrapuntal vocals at the bridge—all betray her awareness that her daughters, her listeners, everyone will, at some point, fall short of these ideals. And not only that, but those dread-filled guitar licks keep returning to remind us that many risks will give way to losses and heartaches by the number. All along, those grim strings bode trouble, like dark clouds swirling ahead of a storm.

Still she wishes, passing along the few lessons, hard earned or handed down, she has to offer. The pickers, arrangements, and material push Womack to reach deep inside and sing her heart out, and what they have to tell is bleak, but not only that, not by a long shot. That bass up top isn't just depressed; it's rubbery and bounces back. That soft soulful beat isn't just restrained; it keeps circling around to begin anew, resilient, maybe even indomitable. The Sons' harmonies are there to help Womack through, even as she's there for her daughters. "When you come close to selling out, reconsider," she urges, and a pedal-steel guitar answers "Amen." "I Hope You Dance" abounds with complex, conflicting, and enduring adult emotions, feelings that Womack, inspired by her main man Conway Twitty, has said she very much wanted the record to convey.

A "Keep on the Sunny Side" for a new century, "I Hope You Dance" testifies that the scariest, most amazing parts of any ongoing story are unknown and always just around the bend.—bfw/dc

Once More with Feeling
An Alternate 100

All You Ever Do Is Bring Me Down, The Mavericks
Produced by Don Cook and Raul Malo;
Written by Raul Malo and Al Anderson
MCA 55154   1996   #13 country

Are You Lonesome Tonight? Elvis Presley
Produced by Steve Sholes; Written by Lou Harman and Roy Turk
RCA 47-7810   1960
#22 country; #1 pop (6 weeks); #3 R&B

A-Sleeping at the Foot of the Bed,
"Little" Jimmy Dickens
Produced by Don Law; Written by E. Wilson
Columbia 20644   1950   #6 country

Banjo Pickin' Girl, Coon Creek Girls
No producer credited; Traditional
Vocalion/OKeh 04413   1938   Pre-chart

Beneath Still Waters, Emmylou Harris
Produced by Brian Ahern; Written by Dallas Frazier
Warner 49164   1980   #1 country (1 week)

Birmingham Bounce, Red Foley
Produced by Paul Cohen; Written by Hard Rock Gunter
Decca 9-46234   1950   #1 country (4 weeks); #14 pop

Blood on the Saddle, Tex Ritter
Produced by Lee Gillette; Written by Everett Cheatham
Capitol 1958   1945   Did not chart

Can't Stop My Heart from Loving You, The O'Kanes
Produced by Jamie O'Hara and Kieran Kane;
Written by Kieran Kane and Jamie O'Hara
Columbia 06606   1987   #1 country (1 week)

Color Him Father, Linda Martell
Produced by Shelby Singleton; Written by Richard Spencer
Plantation 24   1969   #22 country

Defrost Your Heart, Charlie Feathers
Produced by Sam Phillips;
Written by Quinton Claunch and Bill Cantrell
Sun 231   1956   Did not chart

Dim Lights, Thick Smoke (and Loud, Loud Music),
Joe Maphis and Rose Lee
Produced by Don Law;
Written by Joe Maphis, M. Fidler, and Rose Lee
OKeh 18013   1953   Did not chart

Down by the O-H-I-O, Milton Brown
& His Musical Brownies
Produced by Dave Kapp; Traditional
Decca 5111   1935   Pre-chart

Down Yonder, Gid Tanner & the Skillet Lickers
Produced by Eli Oberstein; Traditional
Bluebird 5562   1934   Pre-chart

East Virginia, Buell Kazee
No producer credited; Traditional
Brunswick 154B   1929   Pre-chart

Flip Flop and Bop, Floyd Cramer
Produced by Chet Atkins; Written by Floyd Cramer
RCA Victor 7156   1958   #87 pop

Footprints in the Snow,
Bill Monroe & His Blue Grass Boys
Produced by Art Satherley; Written by Rupert Jones
Columbia 37151   1946   #5 country

Give Me Forty Acres to Turn this Rig Around,
The Willis Brothers
No producer credited; Written by Earl Green and Johnny W. Green
Starday 681   1964   #9 country

Gospel Ship, The Carter Family
Produced by Art Satherley; Traditional
Conqueror 8542   1935   Pre-chart

Guitar Boogie, Arthur Smith
No producer credited; Written by Arthur Smith
MGM 10293   1948   #8 country

Heartbroke, Ricky Skaggs
Produced by Ricky Skaggs; Written by Guy Clark
Epic 03212   1982   #1 country (1 week)

Hello Mary Lou, Ricky Nelson
Produced by Jimmie Haskell; Written by Gene Pitney
Imperial 5741   1961   #9 pop

Here in the Real World, Alan Jackson
Produced by Scott Hendricks and Keith Stegall;
Written by Alan Jackson and Mark Irwin
Arista 9922   1990   #3 country

Here's a Quarter (Call Someone Who Cares),
Travis Tritt
Produced by Gregg Brown; Written by Travis Tritt
Warner 19310   1991   #2 country

Hit Parade of Love, Jimmy Martin
Produced by Owen Bradley;
Written by Jimmy Martin and Wade Birchfield
Decca 30118   1956   Did not chart

Homegrown Tomatoes, Guy Clark
Produced by Rodney Crowell; Written by Guy Clark
Warner Brothers 29595   1983   #42 country

Honky Tonk Blues, Al Dexter & His Troopers
Produced by Art Satherley;
Written by James B. Paris and Albert Poindexter
Vocalion 3435   1937   Pre-chart

Honky Tonk Man, Johnny Horton
Produced by Don Law;
Written by Johnny Horton, Tillman Franks, and Howard Hausey
Columbia 21504   1956   #9 country

Humdinger, The Farmer Boys
Produced by Ken Nelson; Written by Tommy Collins
Capitol 3077   1953   Did not chart

I Don't Want to Spoil the Party, The Beatles
Produced by George Martin;
Written by John Lennon and Paul McCartney
Capitol 5371   1965   #39 pop

I Fought the Law, The Bobby Fuller Four
Produced by Bob Keane; Written by Bobby Fuller
Mustang 3014   1966   #9 pop

I Just Started Hating Cheating Songs Today,
Moe Bandy
Produced by Ray Baker; Written by A. L. Owens and S. D. Shafer
GRC 2006   1974   #17 country

I Let the Stars Get in My Eyes, Goldie Hill
Produced by Paul Cohen; Written by Slim Willet
Decca 28473   1953   #1 country (3 weeks)

I Still Believe in You, Vince Gill
Produced by Tony Brown; Written by Vince Gill and John Jarvis
MCA 54406   1992   #1 country (2 weeks)

I Still Miss Someone, Johnny Cash
Produced by Don Law; Written by Johnny Cash and R. Cash Jr.
Columbia 41313   1959   Did not chart

I Think I Know, Marion Worth
Produced by Don Law; Written by Curly Putman
Columbia 41799   1960   #7 country

I Wonder How the Old Folks Are, Mac Wiseman
No producer credited; Written by A. P. Carter
Dot 1115   1952   Did not chart

I'll Hold You in My Heart (Till I Can Hold You in My Arms), Eddy Arnold
Produced by Steve Sholes;
Written by Eddy Arnold, Hal Horton, and Tommy Dilbeck
RCA Victor 20-2332   1947   #1 country (21 weeks)

I'm a Man of Constant Sorrow, Stanley Brothers
Produced by Pearlman; Traditional
King 5269   1959   Did not chart

I'm a Truck, Red Simpson
Produced by Gene Breeden; Written by Bob Stanton
Capitol 3236   1971   #4 country

I'm an Old Cowhand (from the Rio Grande),
Bing Crosby
Produced by Jack Kapp; Written by Johnny Mercer
Decca 871   1936   Pre-chart

I'm No Stranger to the Rain, Keith Whitley
Produced by Garth Fundis and Keith Whitley;
Written by Sonny Curtis and Ron Hellard
RCA 8797   1989   #1 country (2 weeks)

I'm So Lonesome I Could Cry, B. J. Thomas
& the Triumphs
Produced by Charley Booth and Huey P. Meaux;
Written by Hank Williams
Scepter 12129   1966   #8 pop

I'm Using My Bible for a Road Map, Reno & Smiley
No producer credited;
Written by Don Reno and Charles Schroeder
King 1045   1952   Did not chart

If It Ain't Love (Let's Leave It Alone), Connie Smith
Produced by Bob Ferguson; Written by Dallas Frazier
RCA Victor 0752   1972   #7 country

If You're Not Back in Love By Monday, Millie Jackson
Produced by Brad Shapiro and Millie Jackson;
Written by Glenn Martin and Sonny Throckmorton
Spring 175   1977   #5 R&B; #43 pop

Jeannie's Afraid of the Dark,
Porter Wagoner and Dolly Parton
Produced by Bob Ferguson; Written by Dolly Parton
RCA Victor 9577   1968   #51 country

Kiss the Baby Goodnight, Charline Arthur
Produced by Steve Sholes; Written by Dan Welch
RCA Victor 20 47-6204B   1955   Did not chart

Let Me Go, Lover! Hank Snow
Produced by Steve Sholes;
Written by Jenny Lou Carson and Al Hill
RCA Victor 5960   1954   #1 country (2 weeks)

Let Old Mother Nature Have Her Way, Carl Smith
Produced by Don Law;
Written by Loys Sutherland (Wayne Raney)
Columbia 4-20862   1951   #1 country (8 weeks)

Little Maggie, Wade Mainer,
Zeke Morris, and Steve Ledford
No producer credited; Traditional
Bluebird B-7201   1937   Pre-chart

Lonesome 7-7203, Hawkshaw Hawkins
No producer credited; Written by Justin Tubb
King 5712   1963   #1 country (4 weeks); #108 pop

Lonesome, On'ry and Mean, Steve Young
Produced by Roy Dea; Written by Steve Young
RCA 10868   1977   Did not chart
(B side of "It's Not Supposed to Be That Way")

Lookin' for Love, Johnny Lee
Produced by John Boylan;
Written by Bob Morrison, Wanda Mallette, and Ralph Ryan
Full Moon 47004   1980   #1 country (3 weeks); #5 pop

**Lovin' Her Was Easier (Than Anything
I'll Ever Do Again),** Tompall & the Glaser Brothers
Produced by Tompall Glaser; Written by Kris Kristofferson
Elektra 47134   1981   #2 country

Luxury Liner, The International Submarine Band
Produced by Suzi Jane Hokum; Written by Gram Parsons
LHI 45-1205   1968   Did not chart

Maria Elina, Adolph Hofner & His Texans
No producer credited; Written by Lorenzo Barcelata
Bluebird B-8416   1940   Pre-chart

Match Box Blues, Blind Lemon Jefferson
No producer credited; Traditional
Paramount 12474   1927   Pre-chart

Mental Revenge, Mel Tillis & the Statesiders
Produced by Jim Vienneau; Written by Mel Tillis
MGM 14846   1976   #15 country

Mexicali Rose, Gene Autry
Produced by Art Satherley;
Written by Helen Stone and Jack Tenney
Vocalion 03097   1936   Pre-chart

Midnight Rider, Gregg Allman
Produced by Gregg Allman; Written by Gregg Allman
Capricorn 0035   1973   #19 pop

Midnight Train, Maddox Brothers and Rose
Producer and writer unknown
Four Star 1184   1947   Did not chart

My Rough and Rowdy Ways, Jimmie Rodgers
Produced by Ralph Peer;
Written by Jimmie Rodgers and Elsie McWilliams
Victor 22220   1929   Pre-chart

My Son Calls Another Man Daddy,
Hank Williams with His Drifting Cowboys
Produced by Fred Rose;
Written by Hank Williams and Jewell House
MGM K10645   1950   #9 country

A New Salty Dog, The Allen Brothers
No producer credited; Traditional
Bluebird B-4759/Victor 23514   1930   Pre-chart

New Steel Guitar Rag,
Bill Boyd & His Cowboy Ramblers
No producer credited; Written by Bill Boyd
RCA Victor 20 1907   1952 #5 country

Once More, The Osborne Brothers & Red Allen
Produced by Wesley Rose; Written by Dusty Owens
MGM 12583 1958   #13 country

Once More with Feeling, Jerry Lee Lewis
Produced by Jerry Kennedy;
Written by Kris Kristofferson and Shel Silverstein
Smash 2257   1970   #2 country

The Other Woman, Jean Shepard
Produced by Ken Nelson; Written by Beverly Small
Capitol F3727 1957 Did not chart

The Other Woman, Loretta Lynn
Produced by Owen Bradley; Written by Betty Sue Perry
Decca 31471 1963   #13 country

The Other Woman, Ray Price
Produced by Don Law and Frank Jones; Written by Don Rollins
Columbia 43264   1965   #2 country

Pancho and Lefty, Willie Nelson and Merle Haggard
Produced by Chips Moman, Merle Haggard, and Willie Nelson;
Written by Townes Van Zandt
Epic 03842   1983   #1 country (1 week)

Please Help Me, I'm Falling, Hank Locklin
Produced by Chet Atkins;
Written by Don Robertson and Hall Blair
RCA Victor 7692   1960   #1 country (14 weeks)

Polk Salad Annie, Tony Joe White
Produced by Billy Swan; Written by Tony Joe White
Monument 1104   1969   #8 pop

Pretty Polly, Dock Boggs
No producer credited; Traditional
Brunswick 132   1927   Pre-chart

Sadie Green (the Vamp of New Orleans),
Roy Newman & His Boys
Produced by Art Satherley;
Written by Wells, Dunn, and Hufner
Vocalion 03151   1935   Pre-chart

Satin Sheets, Jeanne Pruett
Produced by Walter Haynes; Written by John Volinkaty
MCA 40015   1973   # 1 country (3 weeks); #28 pop

Sea of Heartbreak, Don Gibson
Produced by Chet Atkins; Written by Don Gibson
RCA Victor 7890   1961   #2 country; #21 pop

Set 'Em Up Joe, Vern Gosdin
Produced by Bob Montgomery;
Written by Hank Cochran, Vern Gosdin, Dean Dillon,
and Buddy Cannon
Columbia 07762   1988   #1 country (1 week)

Seven Year Ache, Rosanne Cash
Produced by Rodney Crowell; Written by Rosanne Cash
Columbia 11426   1981   #1 country (1 week); #22 pop

Show Me, Joe Tex
Produced by Buddy Killen; Written by Joe Arrington Jr.
Dial 4055   1967   #24 R&B

Small Town, John Cougar Mellencamp
Produced by Little Bastard [John Mellencamp] and Don Gehman;
Written by John Mellencamp
Riva 884202   1985   #6 pop

Soldier's Last Letter, Ernest Tubb
Produced by Joe Perry;
Written by Ernest Tubb and Sgt. Henry Stewart
Decca 6098   1944   #1 country (4 weeks); #16 pop

Someone Is Looking for Someone Like You,
Gail Davies
Produced by Gail Davies; Written by Gail Davies
Lifesong 1784   1979   #11 country

Stay a Little Longer, Bob Wills & His Texas Playboys
Produced by Art Satherley;
Written by Bob Wills and Tommy Duncan
Columbia 37097   1947   #5 country

Summertime Blues, Eddie Cochran
Produced by Eddie Cochran and Jerry Capehart;
Written by Eddie Cochran and Jerry Capehart
Liberty 55144   1958   #8 pop

Take It Away, Leon, Leon McAuliffe
& His Western Swing Band
Produced by Steve Sholes;
Written by Marvis Billington, Washburn, and Johnson
Columbia 29782   1950   Did not chart

Teche Special, Iry LeJune
Producer and writer unknown
Folk-Star F-101   1950   Did not chart

Tennessee Waltz, Pee Wee King
& His Golden West Cowboys
Produced by Steve Sholes;
Written by Pee Wee King and Redd Stewart
RCA Victor 20-2680   1948   #3 country

There Goes My Everything, Jack Greene
Produced by Owen Bradley; Written by Dallas Frazier
Decca 32023   1966   #1 country (7 weeks); #65 pop

This Much a Man, Marty Robbins
Produced by Marty Robbins; Written by Marty Robbins
Decca 33006   1972   #11 country

The Three Bells, The Browns
Produced by Chet Atkins;
Written by Jean Villard and Bert Reisfeld
RCA Victor 7555   1959
#1 country (10 weeks); #1 pop (4 weeks)

A Tombstone Every Mile, Dick Curless
No producer credited; Written by Dan Fulkerson
Tower 124   1965   #5 country

Truck Driving Man, Terry Fell & the Fellers
No producer credited; Written by Terry Fell
X 0010   1954   Did not chart
(B side of "Don't Drop It")

(We're Not) The Jet Set,
George Jones & Tammy Wynette
Produced by Billy Sherrill; Written by Bobby Braddock
Epic 11083   1974   #15 country

When You Say Nothing at All, Allison Krauss
Produced by Randy Scruggs;
Written by Paul Overstreet and Don Schlitz
BNA 64277   1995   #3 country

Whoever's in New England, Reba McEntire
Produced by Jimmy Bowen and Reba McEntire;
Written by Kendal Franceschi and Quentin Powers
MCA 52767   1988   #1 country (1 week)

Why Don't You Haul Off and Love Me,
Wayne Raney
No producer credited; Written by Wayne Raney
King 791   1949   #1 country (3 weeks); #22 pop

Wine Me Up, Faron Young
Produced by Jerry Kennedy;
Written by Faron Young and E. Crandell
Mercury 72936   1969   #2 country

Wreck on the Southern Old '97, Henry Whitter
No producer credited; Traditional
OKeh   1924   Pre-chart

Wrong Side of Memphis, Trisha Yearwood
Produced by Garth Fundis;
Written by Matraca Berg and Gary Harrison
MCA 54414   1992   #5 country

You Better Not Do That, Tommy Collins
Produced by Ken Nelson; Written by Tommy Collins
Capitol 2701   1954   #2 country

List of Entries
Alphabetical by Title

List of Entries
Alphabetical by Artist

Selected Bibliography

Agee, James, and Walker Evans. *Let Us Now Praise Famous Men* (updated edition). Boston: Houghton Mifflin, 1980 (1939).

Allison, Dorothy. *Bastard Out of Carolina*. New York: Plume, 1993.

———. *Cavedweller*. New York: Dutton, 1998.

Amburn, Ellis. *Buddy Holly: A Biography*. New York: St. Martin's, 1995.

Ballinger, Lee. *Lynyrd Skynyrd: An Oral History*. New York: Avon, 1999.

Berry, Chuck. *Chuck Berry: The Autobiography*. New York: Harmony, 1987.

Booth, Stanley. *Rythm Oil: A Journey Through the Music of the American South*. New York: Vintage, 1993.

Bowman, Rob. "O. B. McClinton: Country Music, That's My Thing." *The Journal of Country Music* 14:2 (1992): 23–29.

———. *Soulsville, U.S.A.: The Story of Stax Records*. New York: Schirmer, 1997.

Boyd, Jean Ann. *The Jazz of the Southwest: An Oral History of Western Swing*. Austin: University of Texas Press, 1998.

Bufwack, Mary A., and Robert K. Oermann. *Finding Her Voice: The Illustrated History of Women in Country Music*. New York: Henry Holt and Company, 1993.

Cantwell, David. *George Strait: An Illustrated Musical History*. New York: Boulevard, 1996.

———. "The Voice: George Jones Runs up Against the Cold Hard Truth. Again." *No Depression* (September–October 1999): 76–88.

———. "Forging the Bridge from Hank to Bing: Ray Price Keeps Making Burning Memories." *No Depression* (May–June 2000): 78–93.

———. "Help Me Make It Through the Night: The Anatomy of a Record." *The Journal of Country Music* 21:3 (2000): 14–23.

———. "The Last Dance: Lee Ann Womack Gives Classic Country Hope." *Pitchweekly*, May 10, 2001.

———. "Grady Martin, 1929–2001." *Nashville Scene*, December 13, 2001.

———. "A Little Bit of Soul: Nashville's Essential Connection to Muscle Shoals." *No Depression* (January–February 2002).

Carr, Patrick, ed. *The Illustrated History of Country Music*. Garden City, N.Y.: Doubleday, 1979.

Cash, June Carter. *Among My Klediments*. Grand Rapids, Mich.: Zondervan, 1979.

———. *From the Heart*. New York: Prentice Hall, 1987.

Cash, W. J. *The Mind of the South*. New York: Vintage, 1991 (1941).

Christ, Carol, and Judith Plaskow, eds. *Womanspirit Rising: A Feminist Reader in Religion*. New York: Harper & Row, 1979.

Collins, Ace. *The Stories Behind Country Music's All-Time Greatest 100 Songs*. New York: Boulevard, 1996.

Cone, James H. *The Spirituals and the Blues*. New York: Seabury, 1972.

———. *God of the Oppressed*. New York: Seabury, 1975.

Cooper, Daniel. "Being Ray Price Means Never Having to Say You're Sorry." *The Journal of Country Music* 14:3 (1992): 22–31.

———. "Connie Smith: After the Ball." *The Journal of Country Music* 16:2 (1994): 35–44.

———. *Lefty Frizzell: The Honky-Tonk Life of Country Music's Greatest Singer*. Boston: Little, Brown, 1995.

Country Music Foundation. *Country: The Music and the Musicians*. New York: Abbeville, 1994.

Cusic, Don. *The Sound of Light: A History of Gospel Music*. Bowling Green, Ohio: Bowling Green University Press, 1990.

Dawidoff, Nicholas. *In the Country of Country: People and Places in American Music*. New York: Pantheon, 1997.

Day, Dorothy. *By Little and By Little: The Selected Writings of Dorothy Day*. New York: Knopf, 1988.

Dickinson, Chris. "Reba McEntire: Up Where She Belongs." *The Journal of Country Music* 19:2 (1997): 8–15.

———. "Stonewall Jackson." *The Journal of Country Music* 20:2 (1998): 26–27.

Ellison, Curtis W. *Country Music Culture: From Hard Times to Heaven*. Jackson: University Press of Mississippi, 1995.

Ellison, Ralph. *Shadow and Act*. New York: Random House, 1964.

Eng, Steve. *A Satisfied Mind: The Country Music Life of Porter Wagoner*. Nashville, Tenn.: Rutledge Hill, 1992.

Escott, Colin. *Good Rockin' Tonight: Sun Records and the Birth of Rock 'n' Roll*. New York: St. Martin's, 1991.

———. *Hank Williams: The Biography*. Boston: Little, Brown, 1994.

———. *Tattooed on Their Tongues: A Journey Through the Backrooms of American Music*. New York: Schirmer, 1996.

Floyd, John. *Sun Records: An Oral History*. New York: Avon, 1998.

Fong-Torres, Ben. *Hickory Wind: The Life and Times of Gram Parsons*. New York: Pocket, 1991.

Friskics-Warren, Bill. "The Scorch Will Rise Again: Jason & the Scorchers Reawaken Nashville to a Clear Impetuous Morning." *No Depression* (November–December 1996): 48–53.

———. "Kay Adams: Gear-swappin' Mama from Bakersfield." *The Journal of Country Music* 19:2 (1997): 3–7.

———. "That Ain't My Song on the Jukebox: Black Performers Struggle to Get Their Voices Heard in Country Music." *Nashville Scene*, August 28, 1997, 18–24.

———. "Setting the Record Straight: Six Years, Three Producers, and Two Record Labels Since Her Last Album, Lucinda Williams Finally Steered *Car Wheels* in the Right Direction." *No Depression* (July-August 1998): 58–67.

———. "How Ray Price Saved His Country." *The Washington Post*, August 9, 1998.

———. "Country's Grave Condition: Jon Langford Came to Nashville to Bury Country, Not to Praise It." *The Washington Post*, August 30, 1998.

———. "Dog Soldier: Swamp Dogg—A True Soul Survivor." *Nashville Scene*, September 24, 1998.

———. "Coal Miner's Sister." *No Depression* (March–April 1999): 72–88.

———. "Unbroken Circle: June Carter Cash Retraces Her Life's Work." *No Depression* (July–August 1999): 74–83.

———. "Kitty Wells: The Undisputed Queen." *Nashville Scene*, August 26, 1999, 19–30.

———. "Defying Gravity: Jimmie Dale Gilmore Stretches His Horizons from the Flat of the Land to the Curve of the Earth." *No Depression* (March–April 2000): 70–81.

———. "The Latest Conformist from Nashville West." *The New York Times*, May 7, 2000.

———. "Earl Scruggs: Still Pickin' up a Storm." *The Washington Post*, June 4, 2000.

———. "Second to None: Opry Veteran Jean Shepard Helped Pave the Way for Women in Country Music." *Nashville Scene*, June 8, 2000.

———. "Country Music Gets Back to an Old Standard: Music for Grown-ups." *The New York Times*, July 30, 2000.

———. "A Song of Her Own: With a Nod to Her Foremothers, Kim Richey Blazes a New Trail Through the Familiar Landscape of Heartbreak." *Oxford American* (July–August 2000): 70–72.

———. "Patsy Cline: Ours Truly." *The Washington Post*, August 27, 2000.

———. "A Survivor's Tale: Throughout a Life of Hit Songs and Hard Losses, Loretta Lynn Has Retained Her Distinctive Voice." *Nashville Scene*, October 19, 2000.

———. "Dolly Parton Reflects on Bluegrass Music, Her Public Image, and Her Proudest Achievement: Her Art." *Nashville Scene*, January 28, 2001.

———. "Rediscovering Nashville's Indie Heyday." *The New York Times*, March 11, 2001.

———. "Nobody's Darling: For Every Superstar Who Finds His or Her Way into the Country Music Spotlight, There Are Dozens of Singers Like Bill Nettles Who Dwell on the Margins." *Oxford American* (Fifth Annual Music Issue 2001): 138–41.

———. "A Soundtrack to the Heyday of the 18-Wheeler." *The New York Times*, January 13, 2002.

———. "Love and Theft: The Veiled But Tangled Toots of Jimmie Rodgers and Tommy Johnson." *No Depression* (January–February 2002):

Fromm, Erich. *Escape From Freedom*. New York: Avon, 1969.

George-Warren, Holly, and Patricia Romanowski, eds. *The Rolling Stone Encyclopedia of Rock & Roll: Revised and Updated for the 21st Century*. New York: Fireside/Rolling Stone Press, 2001.

Giddins, Gary. *Bing Crosby: A Pocketful of Dreams—the Early Years, 1903-1940*. Boston: Little, Brown, 2001.

Gillett, Charlie. *The Sound of the City: The Rise of Rock & Roll*. New York: Outerbridge and Dienstfrey, 1970.

Goodman, David. *Modern Twang: An Alternative Country Music Guide & Directory*. Nashville: Dowling Press, 1999.

Green, Douglas B. "The Singing Cowboy: An American Dream." *The Journal of Country Music* 7:2 (1978): 4–61.

Gregory, James N. *American Exodus: The Dust Bowl Migration and Okie Culture in California*. New York: Oxford University Press, 1989.

Guralnick, Peter. *Lost Highway: Journeys and Arrivals of American Musicians*. New York: Vintage, 1982.

———. *Sweet Soul Music: Rhythm and Blues and the American Dream of Freedom*. New York: Harper & Row, 1986.

———. *Feel Like Going Home*. Revised edition. New York: Harper & Row, 1989.

———. *Last Train to Memphis: The Rise of Elvis Presley*. Boston: Little, Brown, 1994.

———. *Careless Love: The Unmaking of Elvis Presley*. Boston: Little, Brown, 1999.

Guthrie, Woody. *Bound for Glory*. New York: Dutton, 1943.

Gutierrez, Gustavo. *A Theology of Liberation: History, Politics and Salvation*. New York: Orbis, 1973.

Haggard, Merle, with Peggy Russell. *Sing Me Back Home: My Story*. New York: Pocket, 1981.

Hazen, Cindy, and Mike Freeman. *Love Always: Patsy Cline's Letter to a Friend*. New York: Berkeley, 1999.

Heilbut, Tony. *The Gospel Sound: Good News and Bad Times*. Revised edition. New York: Limelight, 1985.

Hemphill, Paul. *The Nashville Sound: Bright Lights and Country Music*. New York: Simon and Schuster, 1970.

———. *The Good Old Boys*. New York: Simon and Schuster, 1974.

Horstman, Dorothy. *Sing Your Heart Out, Country Boy*. Nashville: Country Music Foundation Press, 1996.

Hoskyns, Barney. *Say It One Time for the Brokenhearted: Country Soul in the American South*. London: Bloomsbury, 1987.

Hurston, Zora Neale. *Their Eyes Were Watching God.* 1937; reprinted, Urbana: University of Illinois Press, 1978.

Johnson, James Weldon. *God's Trombones.* New York: Viking, 1927.

Jorgenson, Ernst. *Elvis Presley: A Life in Music—the Complete Recording Sessions*. New York: St. Martin's, 1998.

Kienzle, Rich. "The Forgotten Hank Garland." *The Journal of Country Music* 9:3 (1983): 28–32, 41–46.

———. "Grady Martin: Unsung and Unforgettable." *The Journal of Country Music* 10:2 (1985): 54–60.

Kingsbury, Paul, ed. *Country on Compact Disc: The Essential Guide to the Music*. New York: Grove, 1993.

———. *The Encyclopedia of Country Music*. New York: Oxford University Press, 1998.

———. *The Country Reader: Twenty-five Years of the Journal of Country Music*. Nashville, Tenn.: Vanderbilt University Press/Country Music Foundation Press, 1996.

Klein, Joe. *Woody Guthrie: A Life*. New York: Ballantine, 1980.

Lester, Julius. *Black Folk Tales.* New York: Grove, 1970.

Loewen, James W. *Lies My Teacher Told Me: Everything Your American History Textbook Got Wrong*. New York: Touchstone, 1995.

Lynn, Loretta, with George Vecsey. *Coal Miner's Daughter*. New York: Warner, 1976.

Malone, Bill C. *Southern Music, American Music*. Lexington: University Press of Kentucky, 1979.

———. *Country Music, U. S. A*. Austin: University of Texas Press, 1985.

———. *Singing Cowboys and Musical Mountaineers: Southern Culture and the Roots of Country Music*. Athens: University of Georgia Press, 1993.

Malone, Bill C., and Judith McCulloh, eds. *The Stars of Country Music: Uncle Dave Macon to Johnny Rodriguez*. Urbana: University of Illinois Press, 1975.

Marcus, Greil. *Mystery Train: Images of America in Rock & Roll Music*. New York: Dutton, 1982.

———. *Invisible Republic: Bob Dylan's Basement Tapes*. New York: Henry Holt and Company, 1997.

Marsh, Dave. *The Heart of Rock & Soul: The 1,001 Greatest Singles Ever Made*. New York: Da Capo Press, 1999.

Marsh, Dave, and Harold Leventhal, eds. *Pastures of Plenty: A Self Portrait—The Unpublished Writings of an American Folk Hero*. New York: Harper Collins, 1990.

McCloud, Barry. *Definitive Country: The Ultimate Encyclopedia of Country Music and Its Performers*. New York: Perigee, 1995.

Miller, Jim, ed. *The Rolling Stone Illustrated History of Rock & Roll*. New York: Random House/Rolling Stone Press, 1980.

Morley, Steve. "The Original Roy Orbison 'Oh Pretty Woman' Session: 1964." *Nashville Monitor*, April 15, 1990, 18–20.

Morrison, Craig. *Go Cat Go! Rockabilly Music and Its Makers*. Urbana: University of Illinois Press, 1999.

Morthland, John. *The Best of Country: A Critical and Historical Guide to the 750 Greatest Albums*. Garden City, N.Y.: Dolphin, 1984.

———. "Songwriter." *Texas Monthly* (December 1999). Reprinted in *Best Music Writing 2000*, edited by Peter Guralnick (New York: Da Capo, 2000), 273–277.

Morton, David C., with Charles K. Wolfe. "DeFord Bailey: They Turned Me Loose to Root Hog or Die." *The Journal of Country Music* 14:2 (1992): 13–17.

———. *DeFord Bailey: A Black Star in Early Country Music*. Knoxville: University of Tennessee Press, 1991.

Owens, William A. *This Stubborn Soil: A Frontier Boyhood*. New York: Vintage, 1986.

Palmer, Robert. *Deep Blues: A Musical and Cultural History of the Mississippi Delta.* New York: Viking, 1981.

Perkins, Carl, with David McGee. *Go, Cat, Go!: The Life and Times of Carl Perkins, the King of Rockabilly*. New York: Hyperion, 1997.

Peterson, Richard A. *Creating Country Music: Fabricating Authenticity*. Chicago: University of Chicago Press, 1997.

Porterfield, Nolan. *Jimmie Rodgers*. Urbana: University of Illinois Press, 1992.

Pugh, Ronnie. *Ernest Tubb: The Texas Troubadour*. Durham, N.C.: Duke University Press, 1996.

Reed, Ishmael. *Mumbo Jumbo.* New York: Doubleday, 1972.

Reed, John Shelton. *My Tears Spoiled My Aim: And Other Reflections on Southern Culture*. San Diego: Harvest, 1993.

Roland, Tom. *The Billboard Book of Number One Country Hits*. New York: Billboard, 1991.

Rosenberg, Neil V. *Bluegrass: A History*. Urbana: University of Illinois Press, 1993.

Rumble, John. "Roots of Rock & Roll: Henry Glover and King Records." *The Journal of Country Music* 14:2 (1992): 30–42.

Sample, Tex. *White Soul: Country Music, the Church, and Working Americans*. New York: Abingdon Press, 1996.

Shelton, Robert. *No Direction Home: The Life and Music of Bob Dylan*. New York: William and Morrow, 1986.

Shelton, Robert, and Burt Goldblatt. *The Country Music Story*. Indianapolis, Ind.: Bobbs-Merrill, 1966.

Singh, Rani. *Think of the Self Speaking: Harry Smith—Selected Interviews*. Seattle: Elbow/Citiful, 1999.

Smith, Lee. *The Devil's Dream*. New York: Ballantine, 1992.

Smith, Richard D. *Can't You Hear Me Callin': The Life of Bill Monroe, Father of Bluegrass*. Boston: Little, Brown, 2000.

Snow, Hank. *The Hank Snow Story*. Urbana: University of Illinois Press, 1994.

Stambler, Irwin, and Grelun Landon. *Encyclopedia of Folk, Country, and Western*. New York: St. Martin's, 1969.

Stepto, Robert B. *From Behind the Veil: A Study of Afro-American Narrative*. Urbana: University of Illinois Press, 1991.

Streissguth, Michael. *Eddy Arnold: Pioneer of the Nashville Sound*. New York: Schirmer, 1997.

———. *Like A Moth to a Flame: The Jim Reeves Story*. Nashville, Tenn.: Rutledge Hill, 1998.

Taylor, David L. *Happy Rhythm: A Biography of Hovie Lister & the Statesmen Quartet*. Lexington, Ky.: Taylormade Write, 1994.

Terrell, Bob. *The Music Men: The Story of Professional Gospel Quartet Singing*. Asheville, N.C.: Bob Terrell Publisher, 1990.

Tosches, Nick. *Country: The Twisted Roots of Rock 'n' Roll*. New York: Da Capo, 1996.

Vaughan, Diane. *Uncoupling: Turning Points in Intimate Relationships*. New York: Vintage, 1990.

Ward, Ed, Geoffrey Stokes, and Ken Tucker. *Rock of Ages: The Rolling Stone History of Rock & Roll*. New York: Rolling Stone Press/Summit Books, 1986.

Werner, Craig. *A Change Is Gonna Come: Music, Race & the Soul of America*. New York: Plume, 1998.

———. *Up Around the Bend: The Oral History of Creedence Clearwater Revival*. New York: Avon, 1998.

Whitburn, Joel. *Pop Memories, 1890-1954: The History of American Popular Music*. Menomonee Falls, Wisc.: Record Research, 1986.

———. *Top Country Singles, 1944 to 1997*. Menomonee Falls, Wisc.: Record Research, 1998.

———. *Top Pop Singles, 1955-1996*. Menomonee Falls, Wisc.: Record Research, 1997.

———. *Top R&B Singles, 1942-1995*. Menomonee Falls, Wisc.: Record Research, 1996.

Whiteside, Jonny. *Ramblin' Rose: The Life and Career of Rose Maddox*. Nashville, Tenn.: Vanderbilt University Press/Country Music Foundation Press, 1997.

Wiley, Dale. "Tender Tom Brumley: The Interview." *Maybelle* 4 (1995): 2–3, 25–26.

Williams, Roger M. *Sing a Sad Song: The Life of Hank Williams*. Urbana: University of Illinois Press, 1981.

Wilson, Charles Reagan, and William Ferris. *Encyclopedia of Southern Culture*. Chapel Hill: University of North Carolina Press, 1989.

Wolfe, Charles K. *Tennessee Strings: The Story of Country Music in Tennessee*. Knoxville: University of Tennessee Press, 1977.

———. "Presley and the Gospel Tradition." *The Elvis Reader: Texts and Sources on the King of Rock & Roll*. Edited by Kevin Quain. New York: St. Martin's, 1992.

———. *In Close Harmony: The Story of the Louvin Brothers*. Jackson: University Press of Mississippi, 1996.

———. *A Good Natured Riot: The Birth of the Grand Ole Opry*. Nashville, Tenn.: Vanderbilt University Press/Country Music Foundation Press, 1999.

Wolff, Kurt. *Country Music: The Rough Guide*. London: Rough Guides, 2000.

Woods, Jeff. "Color Me Country: Tales from the Frontlines." *The Journal of Country Music* 14:2 (1992): 9–12.

Wright, John. *Traveling the High Way Home: Ralph Stanley and the World of Traditional Bluegrass Music*. Urbana: University of Illinois Press, 1993.

Wynette, Tammy, with Joan Dew. *Stand By Your Man*. New York: Pocket, 1979.

Younger, Richard. *Get a Shot of Rhythm and Blues: The Arthur Alexander Story*. Tuscaloosa: University of Alabama Press, 2000.

Index

capitalism, 37, 64–65

Capitol Records, 11, 90, 97, 98, 99, 124, 147, 180, 196

Car Wheels on a Gravel Road, 131

Carlisle, Bill, 90, 179

Carlisle, Cliff, 179

Carlisle, Thumbs, 38

Carlisles, The, 179

Carlson, Ron, 81

Carnegie Hall, 191

Carolina Tar Heels, 18

"Carolyn," 11

Carpenter, Mary Chapin, 131, 205

Carr, J.H., 40

Carr, James, 144–45, 188

Carrigan, Jerry, 1, 2, 138, 143, 144, 156, 173, 190, 224

Carson, Fiddlin' John, 34–35, 217, 218

Carson, Johnny, 146

Carson, Ken, 50

Carson, Martha, 90

Carson, Wayne, 48, 213

Carter, A.A., 9

Carter, A.P., 3–4, 53, 59, 95–96, 141, 184–85, 236

Carter, Anita, 52, 100

Carter, Benny, 173

Carter, Brenda, 148, 149

Carter, Deana, 131, 203–4

Carter Family, x, xi, xvi, 3–4, 10, 37, 42, 53, 58, 75, 83, 95–96, 120, 142, 181, 184–85, 200, 205, 236

Carter, June (*see* Cash, June Carter)

Carter, Lonnie, 169

Carter, Mother Maybelle, 4, 53, 95, 120, 121, 184, 185, 200, 205, 236

Carter, Sara, 4, 10, 53, 96, 120, 185, 236

Carver, Cynthia May (*see* Cousin Emmy)

Cash, Johnny, xi, 3, 14, 26, 43, 52, 59, 99, 100, 112, 119, 125, 139, 140, 170, 171, 188, 234

Cash, June Carter, 52–53

"Cash on the Barrel Head," 100, 172–73

Cash, Rosanne, 206

Cash, W. J., 219

Cassell, Pete, 132

"Cattle Call, The," 49, 226

Cavedweller, 65

"CB Savage," 68

CCR (*see* Creedence Clearwater Revival)

"Ceremony, The," 111

Chalker, Curly, 29, 86–87, 183

Chance, Floyd Lightnin', 57

Chancey, Blake, 110

Chantels, 93

Chapel, Don, 110–11

Chapman, Beth Nielsen, 156

Charles, Ray, xi, 27, 76, 106, 144, 172, 173, 186, 216, 226

Charleton, Buddy, 179, 180

Charlie Daniels Band, 142

"Charlie's Shoes," 152–53

Chase, The, 169

Chastain, Jody, 230

Chatmon, Bo, 169

Chatmon, Lonnie, 169

"Chattanoogie Shoe Shine Boy," 62, 121, 122

cheating songs, 11–12, 51–52, 81–83, 114–16

Chekov, Anton, 78

"Cherokee Boogie," 176

Cherokee Cowboys, 6, 103, 172

Chesnut, Jerry, 114, 141, 224

Chesnutt, Mark, 150, 192

Chess, Leonard, 106

Chess Records, 22, 122, 144, 199

Cheyenne, 72

Chicanos, 128, 235

Choates, Harry, 117–18

"Chokin' Kind, The" 186

Chrisman, Gene, 89, 105, 177, 227

Christian, Charlie, 12, 121

Christmas Carol, A, 40

Christopher, Johnny, 213

Chuck Wagon Gang, 94, 184

"Chug-a-Lug," 78

"Circle Game, The," 200

"City Lights," 72, 93, 223

civil rights movement, 1, 24, 27, 30, 81, 197

Civil War, 30, 96

Clark, Guy, 16, 136

Clark, Royce, 50

Clash, The, 207

"Class of '55, The" 140

Claunch, Quentin, 144

Clement, Jack, 100, 106, 133, 150, 156, 157, 164, 165, 233

Clinch Mountain Boys, 186, 194

Clinch Mountain Clan, 94, 168

Cline, Charlie, 26

Cline, Cheryl, 59

Cline, Patsy, 3, 28, 45–46, 53, 57, 77, 91, 96, 113, 121, 162, 163, 164, 165, 166–67, 193, 195, 210, 222, 226

Clooney, Rosemary, 88

Coal Miner's Daughter, 20–21

"Coal Miner's Daughter," 45–46

coal mining songs, 45–46, 64–66

Coasters, 116, 157, 228

"Coat of Many Colors," 6–7

Cobb, George L., 134

Coben, Cy, 27–28

Cochran, Eddie, 228

Cochran, Hank, 32, 53, 77, 156, 179, 193, 222

Cody, Betty, 10

Coe, David Allan, 111, 171, 231–32

Coffey, Kevin, 85

Coffman, Wanna, 12

Cogbill, Tommy, 89–90, 104–5, 135, 145, 176, 177

Cohen, Paul, xvii, 9, 23, 26, 46, 51, 62, 82, 86, 88, 96, 121, 122, 126, 190, 230

"Cold, Cold Heart," 88–89

"Cold Hard Facts of Life, The," 93

Cold War, 220

Cole, Grady, 38

Cole, Hazel, 38

Collie, Biff, 29

Collins, Larry, 102

Collins, Tommy, 11, 156

"Color Song (I Lost My Love)," 97

Colter, Jesse, 138, 164, 231

Columbia Records, 55, 71, 88, 91, 94, 167, 181, 191, 193, 199, 214, 216, 217

Columbia Studios, 159, 160

"Columbus Stockade Blues," 181

Come on Over, 174

comedy records, 52–53, 69, 147

Como, Perry, 14, 23, 233

Compton, Harry, 11

Confederate Railroad, 142

conjunto, 128

Conlee, John, 17, 136, 210

"Convoy," 68

"Coo-Coo Bird, The," 115–16

Cooder, Ry, 157

Cook, Roger, 201

Cooke, Sam, 183

"Cool Drink of Water Blues," 22–23

"Cool Water," 99–100

Cooley, Ella Mae, 147

Cooley, Spade, 12, 147

Coon Creek Girls, 90, 95

Cooper, Gary, 71

Cooper, Stoney, 94

Cooper, Wilma Lee, 94, 97

Cooper, Wilma Lee and Stoney, 168

Copas, Cowboy, 77, 96, 121, 137, 146, 195

Copeland, Leon, 189

"Corinne, Corinna," 12

"Country Blues," 18

"Country Boy Rock 'N' Roll," 207–8

Country Boys, 122

Country Gentleman, 181, 186

Country Music Association (CMA), 2, 10, 27, 29, 46, 140, 213, 236

Country Music Hall of Fame, 29, 70

Country Music Television (CMT), 29

country rock, xvi, 33, 112, 129, 159, 160, 161, 166, 185, 209,

Country Shadows, 175

country soul, 1–2, 89–90, 143, 144–45, 186, 188, 189

"Country Sunshine," 164

countrypolitan, xii, 31–32, 34, 49, 53, 75, 107, 177, 216, 224, 233

Coursey, Farris, 62

Courtney, Freedy, 8

Cousin Emmy, 75, 95

Covered Wagon Jubilee, 132

cow punk, 159, 175, 185

cowboy songs, 19–20, 71–72, 110

Cox, Billy, 195

Cox, Patsi Bale, 14

Cozzens, Ellsworth, 181

Craddock, Billy Crash, 60

Cramer, Floyd, 3, 5, 6, 23, 45, 46, 77, 113

Crawford, Blackie, 86

Crawford, Homer, 18

"Crazy," 3, 77, 222

"Crazy Arms," 5–6

Crazy Tennesseans, 58

Crazy Water Crystals, 40

Creedence Clearwater Revival, xi, 34, 119, 120, 158, 209

Crickets, 166

Cropper, Steve, 73, 91

Crosby, Bing, xi, 12, 13, 19, 23–24, 30, 40–41, 55, 62, 76, 106, 110, 121, 122, 126, 132, 137, 145, 150, 187, 192, 211, 216, 218, 227, 235–36

Crowe, J. D. & the New South, xvi, 102, 186–87

Crowell, Rodney, 136, 157, 166, 206

Crudup, Arthur, 25

Crumpler, Denver, 59, 104

Crutchfield, Jan, 46

"Crying," 128–29

"Crying in the Chapel," 167

Cryner, Bobbie, 192

"Cuddle Buggin' Baby," 156–57

cultural miscegenation, xi, 12–13, 22–23, 23–24, 27, 29–30, 63–64, 70, 105, 118–19, 143–44, 169–70, 184, 234–35

Cumberland Mountain Folks, 38, 94–95

Curless, Dick, 68

Curtis, Hal, 179

Curtis, King, 101, 234

Cute 'n' Country, 27

Dacus, Smokey, 191

"Daddy Come and Get Me," 181

Daffan, Ted, 8, 67–68, 176

Dailey, Harold Pappy, 6, 51, 114, 124, 148, 222

Daily Worker, 37

Dalai Lama, 50

Dale, Dick, 32

Dalhart, Vernon, 22, 80, 217, 219

"Dallas," 50

Dalton, Lacy J., 192, 198, 199

Damone, Vic, 14

"Dance, The," 84–85, 169

"Dang Me," 78

Daniels, Charlie, 150

"Danny Boy," 39, 216–17

Darbone, Luderin, 108

Darby & Tarlton, 181–82

Darby, Tom, 181

"Dark as a Dungeon," 203

"Dark End of the Street, The," 92, 144–45

"Dark Was the Night, Cold the Ground," 7

"Darling Cory," 18

Darrell, Johnny, 160

Dave & Sugar, xii, 17

David Frost Show, The, 21

David, Hal, 71–72

David, Sonny (Roy Hall), 157

Davidoff, Nicholas, 123

Davis, Betty Jack, 193

Davis, Don, 2, 126

Davis, Jimmie, 42, 88, 133, 176, 219, 228

Davis, Lynn, 95

Davis, Mac, 234

Davis Sisters (Skeeter and Betty Jack), 10, 193, 215

Davis, Skeeter, 31, 93, 127, 193

Davis, Tex, 59

Day, Jimmy, ix, 6, 46, 153, 183

Dea, Roy, 48

"Dead Flowers," 233

"Dean, Dearest, 187

Dean, Eddie, 83, 187

"Dear John Letter, A," 97, 211

"Dear Uncle Sam," 34

DeArmon, Ramon, 158

death and bereavement, 26, 36–38, 39–40, 64–66, 92, 217

"Death of Country Music, The," 3–4

Decca Records, xvii, 10, 13, 42, 45, 50, 76, 96, 132, 153, 162, 166, 199, 236

Dee, Sylvia, 93

"Deep in the Heart of Texas," 110

Dees, Bill, 57

Def Leppard, 174

Del Lords, 36

DeLaughter, H.R., 92

"Delia's Gone," 139

Delmore, Alton, 147, 182

Delmore Brothers (Alton and Rabon), 40, 57, 63–64, 116, 120, 147–48, 170, 182, 194, 225, 227

Delmore, Lionel, 90

Delmore, Rabon, 147, 182

Georgia Crackers, 29–30

Georgia Satellites, 226

Georgia Wildcats, 203

Gerrard, Alice, 65

Gershwin, George, 125

Gibson, Don, 5, 27, 45, 56, 121, 192

Gibson, Susan, 110

Gilbert & Sullivan, 233

Gill, Vince, 174, 187

Gillespie, Haven, 12

Gillespie, Jerry, 187

Gillette, Lee, 64, 85, 98, 104, 122, 147, 187, 203

Gilley, Mickey, 166

Gilliland, Henry, 96

Gilmore, Jimmie Dale, 39, 50, 136

Gimble, Johnny, 37, 93, 231

"Gimme Shelter," 1

"Girl on the Billboard," 225

Girls of the Golden West, 95

"Give Me 40 Acres to Turn This Rig Around," 68

Glaser, Jim, 72

Glenn, Artie, 167

Glenn, Darrell, 167

Glover, Henry, 63–64, 176, 182

Gluck, Alma, 35

"God Bless America," 37

"God Bless America for What," 197

"God Bless My Darling, He's Somewhere," 228

"God Walks These Hills with Me," 113

"Gods Were Angry at Me, The," 85

Goff, Duke, 233

"Goin' Steady," 223

Golden Gate Quartet, 167

"Golden Ring," 110–11

"Golden Rocket," 219

Golden West Cowboys, 137, 146, 147, 195

Goldsboro, Bobby, xi

Goldwax Records, 145

"Gone," 5, 165–66

"Gone Country," 232–33

"Good Hearted Woman," 163

"Good Year for the Roses, A," 114

"Goodbye Earl," 41

Goodman, Steve, 231

Goodrum, Randy, 164

Goodwin, Joe, 85

Gordon, Howard, 184

Gordon, Kelly, 80–81

Gordy Jr., Emory, 15, 16, 157, 192

Gosdin, Vern, 17, 48, 192

Gospel Feast Party, 183

gospel music, 58–59, 132, 167, 168, 178, 183, 208

Graham, Billy, 132, 139

Grand Ole Opry, 3, 4, 21, 23–24, 27, 29, 30, 55, 58, 62, 63, 70, 73, 83, 90, 101, 102, 109, 112, 116, 118, 121, 122, 124, 148, 154, 159, 167, 176, 178, 179, 188, 194, 195, 196, 197, 198, 215, 225, 228, 230

"Grand Tour, The," 114

"Grandpa (Tell Me 'Bout the Good Old Days)," 201–2

Grant, Marshall, 100

Grapes of Wrath, The, 37

Graves, Uncle Josh, 100, 191

Gray, Billy, 124

Grayson, G.B., 18, 42

"Great Balls of Fire," 58, 106

Great Smoky Mountains, 70

"Great Speckle Bird," 10, 58

Green, Al, xi, 193

"Green, Green Grass of Home," 44, 75

Green, Lloyd, 18, 134, 149, 151, 152, 159, 183

Greene, Earl, 67, 68

Greene, Jack, 17, 18, 46, 60, 91, 92, 179

Greisham, Audrey, 46

Grievous Angel, 79

Griffin, Curly, 118

Griffin, Rex, 4, 17

Griffith, Andy, 120

Griffith, Nanci, 166, 206

Groove Records, 209, 216

Guidry, Robert, 226

"Guitars, Cadillacs," 232

Gunning, Sara Ogun, 65

Gunsmoke, 72

Guralnick, Peter, 22, 37, 90, 209

Guthrie, Jack, 98–99

Guthrie, Woody, 8, 36–37, 98–99, 119, 135, 200, 206

Hackberry Ramblers, 118–19, 153, 154

"Hadacol Boogie," 228

Haggard, Flossie, 36

Haggard, Merle, xi, 11, 14–15, 34, 36, 43, 44–45, 47, 60, 65, 67, 68, 79, 86, 109, 125, 127, 130, 156, 159, 170–71, 172, 175, 195, 196, 209, 216, 235

Hajacos, Rob, 174

"Half As Much," 88

Hall, Rick, 107, 143

Hall, Tom T., 74, 89, 91–92, 127

Hamblen, Stuart, 19–20, 58–59, 132

Hames, Dick, 228

Hammer, Jack, 58

Hammerstein, Oscar, 204

Hancock, Butch, 50

"Hanging Tree, The," 71

"Hank and Lefty Raised My Country Soul," 29

Happy Days, 166

Harbach, Otto, 204

"Hard Times in the Country," 112

Hardin, Glen D., 157

Harlan County U.S.A., 66

Harman, Murray Buddy, 3, 32, 45, 57, 77, 120, 121, 216, 220, 230

Harmonica Frank, 105

"Harper Valley P.T.A.," 89, 91, 92

Harpo, Slim, 170, 225

Harrell, Dickie, 60

Harris, Emmylou, 79–80, 157, 182, 187, 207, 228

Harris, Rebert, 23

Harris, Wynonie, 170, 176

Harrison, Gary, 203

Harrison, George, 189

Harrison, Lorenzo, 183

Hart, Bobby, 160

"Hart Brake Motel," 53

Hart, Dick, 125

Hart, Freddie, 199

Hart, Rhonda, 131

Hart, Rod, 68

Harte, Roy, 122

Hartford, John, 159, 213

Harvey, Alex, 102

Haskell, Jimmie, 80, 108

Have Gun Will Travel, 72

"Have I Got a Deal for You," 173–74

"Have I Waited Too Long," 228

Hawkins, Dale, 144

Hawkins, Erskine, 137

Hawkins, Hawkshaw, 77, 96, 195

Hay, George, 58, 155

Hayden Quartet, 126

Hayes, Billy, 126

Hayes, Ira, 99

Hayes, Isaac, 75

Hayes, Kendall, 82

Hayes, Red, 24

Hayes, William Shakespeare, 34–35

Haynes, Walter, 225

Hazel & Alice, 65

"He Set Me Free," 184

"He Stopped Loving Her Today," xiv, 44, 79

"He Touched Me," 168

"He'll Have to Go," 115

"He's Got the Whole World in His Hand," 194

"He's in a Hurry (to Get Home to My Wife)," 149

Heard, Dick, 145, 177

Heart of Rock and Soul, xiv

"Heartaches by the Number," ix, 126–27, 156

"Heartbreak Hotel," 60

"Heartbreak USA," 10

"Heaven Help the Working Girl," 202

"Heaven's Just a Sin Away," 187–88

"Heavy Traffic Ahead," 191

Hebb, Bobby, 197

Hee Haw, 19, 30, 47, 52, 173, 210

Heeney, Michael P., 173

"Hello Love," 204

"Hello, Mary Lou," 161

"Hello Walls," 61, 112, 223

Helm, Levon, 70

Helms, Don, 19, 68, 76, 103, 167, 175, 183, 229

"Help Me Make It through the Night," xii, 1–2, 165, 177, 208

Hendricks, Scott, 174

Hendrix, Jimi, xi

Henley, Larry, 162

Henry, John, 120, 151

Henson, Billy, 109

"Here Comes Santa Claus," 126

Hershey, June, 110

Herston, Kelso, 225

Hess, Jake, 18, 59, 104

"Hey, Good Lookin'," 61, 88–89, 156, 203

"Hey Joe!," 178–79

"Hey Porter," 142

Hi Records, 216

Hi Studios, 145

Hickory Records, 199

"Hickory Wind," 159

Hidalgo, David, 235

"High-Falutin' Mama," 228–29

High John the Conqueroo, 151

Hill and Range Songs, 5

Hill, Eddie, 116

Hill, Faith, 10, 156

Hill, Goldie, 10

Hill, Tommy, 86, 103

"Hillbilly Fever," 121, 122

Hilliard, Bob, 104–5, 145, 146

Hillman, Chris, 159

Hilltop Records, 77

Hines, Earl, 235

Hirshey, Geri, 144

"His Blood Now Covers My Sins," 168

"His Hand in Mine," 58–59

Hodges, Warner, 112

Hogin, Sam, 201

"Hold On, I'm Comin'," 108

"Holding On to Nothin'," 224

Holiday, Billie, 79

Holly, Buddy, 15, 106, 164, 166, 233

Hollywood Barn Dance, 99

Hollywood Canteen, 235

Holyfield, Wayland, 177

"Home on the Range," 49

"Homecoming," 74, 91

homelessness, 38, 102, 199

Homer & Jethro, 52–53

homesickness, 39–40, 73, 74, 134, 136, 190

"Hometown Reunion" radio show, 146

"Honey Bop," 124

"Honky Tonk Blues," 40, 74, 229

"Honky Tonk Man," 122

"Honky Tonk Song," 190

"Honky Tonk Women," 218

"Honky Tonkin'," 123

Hood, David, 212

Hoover, J. Edgar, 197

Hope, Dorothy Jo, 181

Hopkins, Jerry, 104

Hornsby, Bruce, 109

Horstman, Dorothy, 49, 139

Horton, Johnny, 60, 122, 190, 207, 220

Horton, Vaughan, 121

Hoskyns, Barney, 144

Hot Band, 187, 228

"Hot Burrito #1," 129–30

Hot New Country (radio format), xii, 4, 150, 237

"Hot Rod Lincoln," 212

"Hot Rod Race," 107

"Hound Dog," 5, 60, 190, 207

House of God (a.k.a. Church of the Living God), 183

"House of Secrets," xvi

House, Son, 23

Houston, David, 31, 214

Houston, Lew, 153

Houston, Whitney, 162

"How Can a Poor Man Stand Such Times and Live," 35–36

"How Far to Little Rock," 69

"How Long Will My Baby Be Gone'" 51

"How Many Biscuits Can You Eat," 95

"How Much More Can She Stand," 11–12

Howard, Harlan, ix, 48, 73, 77, 126, 126, 155, 156, 159, 172, 179, 180, 185, 186, 189, 191, 202, 215, 222

Howard, Jan, 185–86

Howard, Paul, 121, 122

"Howlin' at the Moon," 68

Howlin' Wolf, 22, 169

Hoyer, Mike, 141

Hubbard, Ray Wylie, 136

Huerta, Baldemar, 129

Huffman, Jerry, 230

Hughes, Jimmy, 143, 145

Hughes, Langston, 148

Hughes, Marvin, 115, 197

Hughes, Randy, 77, 96, 195

Hughey, John, 12, 48, 115, 189, 212

"Hula Rock," 207

Hull, Russ, 46

Humperdinck, Englebert, 75

"Hungry Eyes," 36, 125

Hunter, James, xiv

Hurley, John David, 89
Hurt, Mississippi John, 151
Huskey, Junior, 1, 2, 159
Husky, Ferlin, 5, 97, 165–66, 211
"Hustling Gamblers," 18
Huston, John, 44
Hutchison, Frank, 151
hymns, 183

"I Ain't Never," 230
"I Asked for Water (She Gave Me Gasoline)," 22
"I Been to Georgia on a Fast Train," 134–35
"I Believe in You," 201
"I Can Help," 177
"I Can't Stand Up Alone," 90
"I Can't Stop Loving You," 27, 56
"I Don't Believe You've Met My Baby," 87–88
"I Don't Hurt Anymore," 13–14
"I Don't Need Your Rocking Chair," 192
"I Don't Want to Spoil the Party," 33
"I Fall to Pieces," xiv, 77, 222
"I Forgot More Than You'll Ever Know," 193
"I Forgot to Remember to Forget," 230
"I Gotta Have My Baby Back," 218
"I Gotta Know," 124
"I Heard the Jukebox Playing," 180
"I Hope You Dance," 237
"I Know," 205–6
"I Love You a Thousand Ways," 30–31
"I Love You Because," 104
"I Love You So Much, It Hurts," 14
"I Met a Friend of Yours Today," 177
"I Never Go Around Mirrors," 182–83
"I Saw the Light," 94, 183, 184
"I Take a Lot of Pride in What I Am," 196
"I Take It on Home," 33
"I Walk Alone," 91
"I Walk the Line," 139
"I Wanna Be a Cowboy's Sweetheart," 10, 19–20, 110, 214
"I Want to Be with You Always," 31
"I Want to Live (So God Can Use Me)," 183
"I Want You, I Need You, I Love You," 6
"I Washed My Hands in Muddy Water," 184–85
"I Will Always Love You," 162

"I Wonder if They Ever Think of Me," 34
"(I Won't Go Huntin' Jake) But I'll Go Chasin' Women," 132
"I'll Fly Away," 184
"I'll Never Get Out of This World Alive," 18–19
"I'll Sail My Ship Alone," 176
"I'll Twine Midst the Ringlets," 96
"I'm a Lover, Not a Fighter," 170
"I'm a People," 124
"I'm a Truck," 68
"I'm an Old Cowhand," 41
"I'm an Old, Old Man (Tryin' to Live While I Can)," 182
"I'm Blue, I'm Lonesome," 21
"I'm Coming Home," 190
"I'm Moving On," 27
"I'm Not Lisa," 164, 231
"I'm Not Ready Yet," 91
"I'm Sitting on Top of the World," 170
"I'm So Lonesome I Could Cry," xiv, 28, 80, 167
"I'm Sorry," 108–9
"I'm the One Who Loves You, (Remember Me)," 132
"I'm Thinking Tonight of My Brown Eyes," 10, 58
"I'm Using My Bible for a Road Map," 207
"I've Been Everywhere," 38–39
"I've Got a Tiger by the Tail," 155, 189
"I've Got Someone to Kill, (Pardon Me)," 77, 149
Ian, Janis, 232
Ice-T, 151
"Ida Red," 107
"If I Lose, I Don't Care," 69–70
"If I Said You Had A Beautiful Body Would You Hold It against Me," 187–88
"If I'm Gonna Sink (I Might as Well Go to the Bottom)," 149
"If My Heart Had Windows," 192
"If the River Was Whiskey," 194
"If Tomorrow Never Comes," 85
"If We Make It through December," 125
"If You Ain't Lovin' (You Ain't Livin')," 156
"If You Love Me (Let Me Know)," 236
"If You've Got the Money, I've Got the Time," 155
"Illegal Smile," 193–94

"Image of Me, The," 153
Imperial Records, 144
Imperials Quartet, 168
"In Dreams," 128
"In My Life," 73
In My Own Way, 175
In Person, 134
In Spite of Ourselves, 194
"In the Chapel in the Moonlight," 61
"In the Ghetto," 41, 104
"In the Good Old Days (When Times Were Bad)," 173
"In the Pines," 21, 88
"Independence Day," 41
"Indian Love Call," 204
Ink Spots, 216
Inman, Autry, 87
Inmon, John, 136
Innis, Louis, 230
interracial romance, 145, 195
"Invitation to the Blues," 73, 78
Iovine, Jimmy, 185
Irby, Jerry, 211
Ireland, Mike, xvi
"Irma Jackson," 15, 195, 196
Isaacs, Bud, 86
"It Wasn't God Who Made Honky Tonk Angels," 9–11, 97, 225
"It's a Cheating Situation," 187
"It's a Sin," 132–33
"It's Mighty Dark to Travel," 62–63
"It's No Secret," 132
"It's Only Make Believe," 59–60
"It's Over," 128
Ives, Burl, 75, 113

Jackson, Al, Jr., 57, 91
Jackson, Alan, xi, xiii, 83, 174, 192, 206, 232–33
Jackson, Aunt Molly, 65
Jackson, Chuck, 105
Jackson, Shot, 10
Jackson, Stonewall, 43, 109, 184
Jackson, Tommy, ix, 6, 28, 94, 115
Jackson, Wanda, 11, 34, 123–24
Jacobs, Walker, 169
Jacobson, Erik, 138

KWKH (radio station, Shreveport, LA), 228

"L.A. Freeway," 136–37
"La Marseillaise," 118
Lady Chatterly's Lover, 161
LaFarge, Peter, 99
Lair, John, 95
Laird, Mrs. Elmer, 116
Lambert, Curley, 8
Lambert, Pee Wee, 167
Landers, Jake, 226
Landis, Richard, 228
Lane, Frankie, 88–89
Lane, Red, 162
Lang, Eddie, 12, 30
lang, k.d., 45
Lange, Daisy, 95
Lange, Dorothea, 36
Lange, Robert John Mutt, 174
Langford, Jon, 3–4
Larson, Nicolette, 232
"Last Letter, The," 17, 46
Last Real Texas Blues Band, 144
"Last Thing on My Mind, The," 114
"Last Train to Clarksville," 160
"Last Word in Lonesome is Me, The," 56
Lauderdale, Jim, 166, 192
Law, Don, 5, 13, 23, 30, 32, 43, 52, 54, 71, 72,
    81, 86, 98, 99, 102, 109, 113–14, 126, 140,
    152, 155, 159, 178, 184, 191, 192, 193, 195,
    199, 216, 220
Lawrence, D.H., 78
"Lay, Lady, Lay," 112
Layne, Bert, 217
Lazy Lester, 170
Lead Belly, 88, 119–20
"Lead Me On," 189
Leap, Jackson, 173
Leaves of Grass, 37
LeBlanc, Dudley, 228
Leblanc, Leo, 194
Ledbetter, Huddie (*see* Lead Belly)
Ledford, Lily May, 95
Ledford, Rosie, 95
Lee, Brenda, 45, 108–9, 222
Lee, Bud, 169
Leech, Mike, 227

Lehning, Kyle, 83
Leiber and Stoller, 128
Leiber, Jerry, 116
Leigh, Richard, 210
LeJune, Iry, 154
Lennon, John, 57, 73, 161
Leo Soileau's Three Aces, 117, 154
Leone, Sergio, 55
Lerner, Robin, 156
"Lesson in Leavin', A," 164
Lester, Julius, 151
"Let's Have a Party," 123–24
Leuzinger, Chris, 169
Leventhal, John, 205
Lewis, Curly, 125
Lewis Family, 168
Lewis, Jerry Lee, 4, 23, 58, 76, 81–82, 106, 112,
    144, 148, 149, 154, 157, 160, 166, 176, 190,
    227, 230
Lewis, Joe E., 12, 153
Lewis, Linda Gail, 81–82
Lewis, Little Roy, 168
Lewis, Pop, 168
Lewis, Talmadge, 168
Lewis, Tubby, 191
liberation theology, 38
Liberto, Vivian, 139
"Liberty Valance, (The Man Who Shot),"
    71–72
Liebert, Billy, 122
Lies My Teacher Told Me, 220
"Life to Go," 43
"Life's Little Ups and Downs," 16–17, 214, 224
Liggett, Walter, 155
Light Crust Doughboys, 12, 98, 158
Light, Ronnie, 163, 204
"Like a Rolling Stone," 112
"Like a Virgin," 108
Lilley, Joseph, J., 180
"Linda on My Mind," 230–31
Linde, Dennis, 150, 208
Lipscomb, D. L., 222
Lister, Hovie, 104
Lister, Mosie, 58–59
"Little Bessie," 181–82
Little Darlin' Records, 77, 78, 149
"Little Maggie," 18, 152

"Little Old Log Cabin in the Lane, The," 34–35
"Little Pink Mack," 66–67, 68
"Little Ramona (Gone Hillbilly Nuts)," 207
Little Richard, 124, 154, 176
"Little Sister," 120
"Live Fast, Love Hard, Die Young," 24, 60–61
"Living for the City," 41
Loesser, Frank, 52–53, 180
Loewen, James, 220
Log Cabin Dude Ranch, 214
Logan, Bud, 210
Loggins, Kenny, 85
Lomax, Alan, 119
Lomax, John, 119–20
London, Lauri, 194
"Londonderry Air," 216
Lone Justice, 185, 206, 232, 235
Lone Star Trail, 76
"Lonely Weekends," 16, 224
"Lonely Women Make Good Lovers," 177
"Long Black Limousine," 91, 92
"Long Black Veil, The," 113
"Long, Gone Lonesome Blues," 19
Long, Jimmy, 218
Long Ryders, 159
"Lookin' out My Back Door," 209
"Looking at the World through a Windshield,"
    141
"Lord Is That Me," 92
"Lord Knows I'm Drinking, The," 93, 168
Los Lobos, 128, 175, 176, 185, 232, 235
Lost Highway, 37
"Lost Highway," 2–3, 104, 112
Louisiana Hayride, 5, 61, 115, 223, 228
Louisiana State Farm at Angola, 120
Louvin Brothers (Ira and Charlie), 42–43, 57,
    80, 87–88, 100, 101, 128, 134, 141, 142, 159,
    172–73, 193
Louvin, Charlie, 141, 172–73
Louvin, Ira, 141, 172, 192
"Love Hurts," 79–80
"Love's Burning Ring of Fire," 52
"Love's Gonna Live Here," 33, 158, 235
Loveless, Patty with George Jones, 192
"Lovesick Blues," 29–30, 92, 121
Lovett, Lyle, 206
"Lovin' on Back Streets," 145

Miller, Frankie, 64–65

Miller, J. D., 170

Miller, J.D. Jay, 9

Miller, Jay, 225

Miller, Jimmy, 218

Miller, Mitch, 88

Miller, Roger, 38, 46, 48, 56, 73, 78–79, 131, 135, 156, 194, 225, 234

Miller, Treva, 166–67

"Miller's Cave," 150

Millinder, Lucky, 64

Mills, Hank, 225

Mills, Irving, 29

Milsap, Ronnie, 17, 60, 105, 233, 236

"Milwaukee, Here I Come," 148–49

Mind of the South, 219

"Misery Loves Company," 47–48

"Miss the Mississippi and You," 73, 219–20

"Mississippi Delta Blues," 220

Mississippi Sheiks, 22, 169–70

Mitchell, Charles, 133

Mitchell, Guy, 155–56

Mitchell, Joni, 200

Mize, Billy, 152

Mnich, Aileen, 204

Modern Mountaineers, 157–58

Modern Sounds in Country and Western Music, 27

Moeller, Dee, 194

"Mohair Sam," 16, 224

"Molly and Tenbrooks," 167

"Mom and Dad's Waltz," 31

Moman, Chips, 91, 104, 129, 144, 176, 177, 213, 227

"Mommy for a Day," 180–81

Monkees, 160

Monroe, Bill, xi, xii, 8, 21, 25–26, 29, 40, 45, 62–63, 75, 83, 86, 88, 96, 100, 101, 124, 137, 167, 169, 186, 191, 226, 230

Monroe Brothers (Bill and Charlie), 7, 40–41, 64, 87, 116, 181, 211

Monroe, Charlie, 40, 63

Montana, Patsy, xi, 10, 19–20, 180, 214

"Montana Plains," 19–20

Monterey Pop Festival, 73

Montgomery, Bob, 141

Montgomery, Carl, 67, 68

Montgomery Gentry, 142

Montgomery, Marvin, 158

Montgomery, Melba, 51–52, 72, 192

Mooney, Ralph, 5, 67, 127, 155, 172, 231

"Moonlight and Skies," 219

Moore, Bob, 3, 45, 89, 115, 120

Moore, Scotty, 5, 25, 57, 90, 120, 166, 170, 209

Moorer, Allison, 192

Morlix, Gurf, 130

Morthland, John, 8, 76, 138, 146

Moscheo, Joe, 168

Moss, Wayne, 57, 138

"Most Beautiful Girl, The," 224

"Motel Time Again," 149

Motown Records, xi, 70, 209

"Mountain Dew," 107, 194–95

Movin' On, 68

"Mr. Bojangles," 136

"Much Too Young (To Feel This Damn Old)," 85

Muhoberac, Larry, 11

"Mule Skinner Blues (Blue Yodel No. 8)," 84

Mullican, Moon, 67, 86, 117, 170, 176

Mullins, Cam, 54, 217

Mullins, Johnny, 131

murder ballads, 42–43, 113

Murphey, Joaquin, 147

Murphy, Jimmy, 100

Murrah, Roger, 174

Murray, Anne, xi, 210

Muscle Shoals, 90, 136, 138, 142, 143–44, 196, 212, 234

Music City News, 107

"Music City U.S.A.," 198–99

Musicor Records, 114

"My Adobe Hacienda," 214

"My Bucket's Got a Hole in It," 28

"My Darling, Nelly Gray," 145

"My Elusive Dreams," 214

"My Heart Skips a Beat," 33–34

"My Own Kind of Hat," 15

"My Tennessee Mountain Home," 73

"My Whole World Is Falling Down," 189

"My Wife Died Saturday Night," 154–55

"My Window Faces the South," 142

Myrick, Weldon, 27–28, 136, 138

"Mystery Train," 120

Nabor, Bob, 63

Nance, Jack, 59

Napier, Bill, 194–95

Nash, Bill, 1

"Nashville Cats," 138–39

Nashville Edition (vocal group), 18, 102, 222

Nashville Network, 47

Nashville Skyline, 111–12

Nashville Songwriter's Hall of Fame, 74

Nashville Sound, xi, xii, xiv, 1, 2, 4–5, 6, 27, 32–33, 39, 40, 47, 53, 56, 57, 60, 61, 72, 81, 82, 93, 109, 113, 115, 121, 124, 139, 150, 165–66, 166, 175, 193, 199, 215, 216, 223, 226, 233

Nathan, Sydney, 176, 194, 195, 207

National Barn Dance, 20, 95, 214

National Organization of Women (NOW), 21

Neil, Fred, 158

Nelson, Hubert, 227

Nelson, Ken, 5, 9–11, 14, 33, 36, 42, 44, 51, 59–60, 65, 87, 90, 96, 97, 101, 106, 107, 123, 125, 130, 155, 156, 165, 211, 223

Nelson, Rick, 139, 158, 161

Nelson, Steve, 145, 146

Nelson, Willie, xvi, 3, 15, 32, 55, 77, 103, 134, 135, 144, 156, 163, 170, 179, 189, 193, 194, 196, 204, 212, 213, 223

neo-traditionalists (new traditionalists), 16, 17, 83, 91, 151, 174, 187, 206

Nesmith, Michael, 160

Nettles, Bill, 228

Newman, Jimmy C., 118

Newman, Randy, 220

Newton, Ernie, 116

Newton, Juice, 228

Newton-John, Olivia, xi, 210, 233, 236

"Nice 'n' Easy," 209

Nicholas, Hayden, 109

Nichols, Roy, 15, 172, 236

"Night Life," 32–33

"Night Train to Memphis," 197

Nilsson, 158–59

Nirvana (rock band), 88, 119

Nite Owls, 198, 199

Nitty Gritty Dirt Band, 4, 136

Nixon, Richard, 65, 139

No Fences, 169

Pierce, Webb, 5, 47, 60, 61, 80, 82, 86, 153–54, 178, 190, 194, 207, 230
"Pig Got Up and Slowly Walked Away, The" 212
"Pill, The," 20–21
"Pine Grove Blues," 154
"Pipeliner's Blues," 176
"Pistol Packin' Mama," 41–42, 149–50, 227, 236
Pitney, Gene, 71–72, 161
Plantation Records, 50
Playboy, 66, 171
Playboy Trio, 162
Poco, 159
"Poison Love," 9, 116
Pomus, Doc, 120
Poole, Charlie, xi, 69–70, 71, 84
"Poor Ol' Koo-Liger," 53
"Pop a Top," 47
populism, 36, 37, 38
Porter, Bill, 120
Porter, Cole, 41, 235
Porter Wagoner Show, The, 47, 202
Porterfield, Nolan, 137
Possum Hunters, 154, 155
poverty, 6–7, 35–36
Presley, Elvis, xi, xii, xiv, 1, 4–5, 6, 18, 23, 24, 25–26, 39, 40, 56–57, 59, 60–61, 62, 75, 80, 83, 90, 91, 92, 103, 104–5, 106, 120, 121, 123–24, 126, 128, 135, 143, 144, 146, 157, 160, 161, 166, 167, 168, 169, 170, 176, 185, 186, 190, 193, 207, 208, 213, 216, 227, 230, 234
Preston, Terry, 166
Pretty Boy Floyd, 15, 37
"Pretty Boy Floyd," 37, 99
"Pretty Little Widow," 121
Price, Chilton, 146, 147
Price, Helen Peaches, 130
Price, Lloyd, 151
Price, Ray, ix, xi, 1, 5–6, 32–33, 39, 54–55, 57, 61, 72–73, 74, 75, 78, 91, 93, 102–3, 109, 122, 126–27, 135, 153, 156, 159, 166, 172, 178, 191–92, 193, 199, 216–17, 223
Pride, Charley, xi, 29, 62, 133–34, 143, 156, 188, 196
Prine, John, 193–94

prison songs, 14, 43–45
"Prisoner's Song," 232–33
Pruett, Jeanne, 122
Pruett, Sammy, 103
Pryor, Cactus, 210
"Psycho," 104
Puccini, 233
Puckett, Riley, 217–18
Pugh, Ronnie, 180
Pursell, Bill, 91, 217
"Pussy, Pussy, Pussy," 158
Putman, Curly, 44, 79, 180, 187, 214, 221
Putnam, Norbert, 143

"Queen of Hearts," 228

R, John (*see* Richbourg, John)
R.E.M., 207
Rabbitt, Eddie, 187
"Race is On, The," 124
racism, 27, 29–30, 62, 63, 65, 89, 195, 196–97, 201, 219–20, 234–35
"Raggedy Ann, (You've Been Quite a Doll)," 92–93
Railroad Bill, 15
"Rainin' in My Heart," 225
Rainwater, Cedric, 101
Rainwater, Jody, 191
Rakes, Ruby, 69
"Ramblin' Man" (Allman Brothers), 48
Ramones, 112
Rancheras, 128
Randall, Alice, 163
Randolph, Boots, 57, 121
Raney, Wayne, 64, 170, 182
"Rank Stranger," 7–8
Raphael, Mickey, 55, 194
Ray, Johnny, 23
RCA Records (*see also* Victor Talking Machine Company), xvii, 5, 9, 10, 21, 28, 60, 104, 106, 115, 116, 199, 208, 215, 224
Reagan, Ronald, 200
Reagan-Bush years, 201
recession, economic (1970s), 36, 125
recitations, 92–93, 199
Red Headed Stranger, 55
"Red Hot," 106

"Red Nightgown Blues," 133
Redding, Otis, 73, 188
Reddy, Helen, 102
Reed, Blind Alfred, 35–36
Reed, Jerry, xi, 40, 46, 47, 68, 69, 143, 178, 225, 234
Reed, Jimmy, 170
Reed, John Shelton, 39
Reeder, Russ, 17, 161
Reeves, Del, 141
Reeves, Jim, 5, 61, 78, 115, 121, 151, 162, 165
Reinhardt, Dick, 187
Reinhardt, Django, 121
"Release Me," 10, 102–3
Removing the Shadow, 175
Renfro Valley Barn Dance, 95
Reno & Smiley, 194, 207–8
Reno, Don, 71, 207
Replacements, The, 207
Republic Records, 198
Requiem for a Nun, 173
retro music, 222, 232
Revard, Jimmie, 158
Rey, Alvino, 110
Reynolds, Allen, 84, 165, 169, 210
Reynolds, Brownie, 94
Reynolds, Burt, 140
Rhodes, Dusty, 196
Rhodes, Jack, 24
Rhodes, Leon, 179, 180
"Rhumba Boogie," 116
Rice, Thomas Daddy, 29–30
Rich, Buddy, 32
Rich, Charlie, xi, 16–17, 33, 74, 91, 139–40, 144, 185, 186, 209, 216, 224, 236
Rich, Don, 34, 51, 155, 158, 189, 232
Rich, Fred, 168
Rich, Margaret Ann, 16–17, 209, 214
Rich Records, 197
Richards, Keith, 218, 233
Richardson, J.P., 124, 166
Richbourg, John, 186, 188, 197
Richey, George, 48, 143, 153
Richey, Kim, 205–6
Riddle, Nelson, 76
"Ridin' My Thumb to Mexico," 127
Rifleman, The, 72

Sprague, Carl, 19

Springfield, Dusty, 89–90

Springsteen, Bruce, 16, 40–41, 66, 109, 131, 166

St. Marie, Buffy, 139

Stackalee (a.k.a. Staggerlee), 22, 151

"Stackalee," 151

Stafford, Jim, 233, 234

Stafford, Jo, 76, 88–89, 146

Stafford, Terry, 50, 107

"Staggerlee," 151

Stampley, Joe, 143, 144

Stamps Quartet, 24, 184

Stamps-Baxter Publishing, 183

"Stand by Me," 143

Stand by Your Man, 110–11

"Stand by Your Man," 8–9, 11–12, 162, 163, 185, 205, 214

Stanley Brothers, & the Clinch Mountain Boys, 7–8, 25–26, 69, 75, 152, 167, 181, 186, 187, 194–95

Stanley, Carter, 7–8, 25, 69, 167, 194

Stanley, Ralph, 7–8, 69, 152, 167, 186, 194

Stanton, Harry Dean, 182

Stapp, Jack, 62

Star-lite Wranglers, 25

Starr, Edwin, 34

Starr, Kay, 146, 222

Starr, Ringo, 178, 189

"Star-Spangled Banner, The," 37, 118

Statesmen Quartet, 18, 58–59, 104, 167, 166

Statler Brothers, 140, 236

"Statue of a Fool," 46

Stax Records, 91, 188

"Steal Away," 145

steel guitar, 85–87, 179, 181, 183

Stegall, Keith, 83, 174, 232

Steinbeck, John, 37

Stepin Fetchit, 30

Stevens, Ray, 178

Stewart, Billy, 125

Stewart, Gary, 48, 196

Stewart, John, 206

Stewart, Redd, 137, 146, 147

Stewart, V.E., 113

Stewart, Wynn, 11, 127, 166, 172, 175

Sticky Fingers, 233

"Still," 223–24

Stinson, Harry, 163

Stoller, Mike, 116

Stone Canyon Band, 161

Stone, Cliffie, 66, 98, 106, 203, 210

Stone, Henry, 62

Stoneman, Ernest V. Pop, xvi, 221

Stoneman Family, 221

Stoneman, Ronnie, 221

"Stones in My Passway," 7

Stonewall Riot, 197

Storer, Lester Natchie the Indian, 195

"Story of My Life, The," 72

Strait, George, 17, 50–51, 85, 89, 151, 174, 213

"Stranger in My Own Home Town," 91

Strangers, 11, 14–15, 36, 44–45, 65, 141, 170

"Stratosphere Boogie," 106

Stratton, Dick, 198–99

"Strawberry Wine," 203–4

Street, Mel, 48, 145, 177, 192

"Streets of Bakersfield," 175–76

"Streets of Baltimore," 40

Streisand, Barbra, 231

Stricklin, Al, 98

Strong, Tommy, 188, 189

Stroud, James, 109

Stroud, Paul, 194

Strzelecki, Henry, 57

Stuart, Marty, 166

Stuckey, Nat, 47

"Success," 131–32

"Sugar Moon," 62

"Sugar Mountain," 200

"Sugarfoot Rag," 121

Sugarland Prison Farm, 119

suicide, 177

suicide songs, 17, 18–19

Sullivan, Gene, 211

"Summer of Love," 81, 82

"Summertime Blues," 228

Summey, Clell, 58

Sumner, J. D., 208

Sun Records, 5, 16, 23, 59–60, 104, 106, 120, 128, 138–39, 216

"Sunday Morning Coming Down," 177

"Sunny," 197

Sunny Mountain Boys, 21

Sunshine Boys, 176

Sunshine Boys Quartet, 23–24

"Superfly," 151

"Suspicious Minds," 104, 138, 213, 227

Sutee, Madge, 31

Sutton, Glenn, 31, 49, 148, 177, 227

Swaggart, Jimmy Lee, 58, 112

Swain, Charlie, 58

Swamp Dogg, 77, 196–97, 234

Swan, Billy, 178

Swander, Don, 110

"Sweet Dreams (of You)," 45–46, 56, 222

"Sweet Home Alabama," 142–43

Sweet Inspirations, 90

Sweetheart of the Rodeo, 130, 159, 160

"Swingin'," 90–91, 169

Sykes, Bobby, 72

"Take a Cold Tater and Wait," 92

"Take a Drink on Me," 69

"Take It Easy," 161, 213

"Take Me," 111

"Take Me Back to Tulsa," 62, 98, 150

"Take This Job and Shove It," 171–72

talking blues, 147

Talley, James, 36–37

Talley, Lewis, 211

Tally Records, 31

Tampa Red, 170

Tanner, Gid and the Skillet Lickers (*see also* Skillet Lickers), 4, 217

"Taps," 14

Tarlton, Jimmie, 181

Taylor, Chip, 176, 177

Taylor, Elizabeth, 66

Taylor, James, 85

Taylor, Red, 21, 96, 121

"Teddy Bear," 68, 199

"Teenage Boogie," 5

"Tejano," 128

Tennessee Cut-Ups, 207

Tennessee Mountain Boys, 116

Tennessee Plowboys, 132

Tennessee Records, 199

Tennessee Three, 52, 171

Tennessee Two, 14, 100, 139, 206, 225

"Tennessee Waltz, The," 88, 137, 146